FEMALE SS GUARDS AND WORKADAY VIOLENCE

FEMALE SS GUARDS AND WORKADAY VIOLENCE

The Majdanek Concentration Camp, 1942–1944

By Elissa Mailänder / Translated by Patricia Szobar

Michigan State University Press / East Lansing

The translation of this work was funded by Geisteswissenschaften International—Translation Funding for Humanities and Social Sciences from Germany, a joint initiative of the Fritz Thyssen Foundation, the German Federal Foreign Office, the collecting society VG WORT and the Börsenverein des Deutschen Buchhandels (German Publishers & Booksellers Association).

♾ The paper used in this publication meets the minimum requirements of ANSI/NISO Z39.48-1992 (R 1997) (Permanence of Paper).

Michigan State University Press
East Lansing, Michigan 48823-5245

Printed and bound in the United States of America.

21 20 19 18 17 16 15 1 2 3 4 5 6 7 8 9 10

Library of Congress Control Number: 2014954452
ISBN: 978-1-61186-170-9 (cloth)
ISBN: 978-1-60917-459-0 (ebook: PDF)
ISBN: 978-1-62895-231-5 (ebook: ePub)
ISBN: 978-1-62896-231-4 (ebook: Kindle)

Book design by Charlie Sharp, Sharp Des!gns, Lansing, Michigan
Cover design and map of the Majdanek camp by Travis Kimbel

Michigan State University Press is a member of the Green Press Initiative and is committed to developing and encouraging ecologically responsible publishing practices. For more information about the Green Press Initiative and the use of recycled paper in book publishing, please visit *www.greenpressinitiative.org*.

Visit Michigan State University Press at *www.msupress.org*

Contents

Illustrations

Acknowledgments

NO SCHOLARLY WORK IS EVER THE PRODUCT OF ONE SINGLE MIND. MANY INSTITUTIONS and people contributed to the publication of this study through their financial support, careful reading, critical suggestions, and friendship.

I gratefully acknowledge the financial support for my archival research that also gave me the opportunity to concentrate on writing: the Centre interdisciplinaire d'études et de recherches sur l'Allemagne (CIERA) in Paris, the Hamburger Stiftung zur Förderung von Wissenschaft und Kultur, and the Österreichische Akademie der Wissenschaften. Moreover, the Charles H. Revson Foundation Fellowship made it possible for me to spend three months in 2006 at the Center for Advanced Holocaust Studies in Washington, DC.

I would like to extend my sincere gratitude to Alf Lüdtke and Michael Werner for their scholarly and personal support and supervision; and to Birthe Kundrus, Christian Ingrao, and Michael Wildt for the stimulating conversations, constructive criticism, and helpful advice that they provided at various stages of the work. I would also like to express my deep appreciation for the valuable input I received from numerous colleagues at various times while researching and writing this book: Henriette Asséo, Susanne Beer, Falk Bretschneider, Patrick Bruneteaux, Michaela Christ, Paula Diehl, Marten Düring, Patrick Farges, Paola Ferruta, Winfried R. Garscha, Christian Gudehus, Karin Harrasser, Max Kramer, Tomasz Kranz, Françoise

Kreissler, Dan Magilow, Roland Müller, Alexandra Oeser, Véronique Padieu, Dieter Pohl, Else Rieger, Frédéric Saly-Giocanti, Veronika Springmann, Matthias Tronqual, Sigrid Weber, and Harald Welzer. To Anton Koslov goes my sincere gratitude for his emotional and intellectual support while I was researching and writing my German dissertation. I would also like to thank my colleagues at the doctoral seminars of CIERA, the research colloquium supervised by Alf Lüdtke, and the working group on "war and gender" created by Regina Mühlhäuser and Gaby Zipfel at the Institute for Sozialforschung in Hamburg, which since 2010 has become the international and interdisciplinary research network "Sexual Violence in Armed Conflict" (SVAC). These settings of constructive collaboration and criticism have provided, and continue to provide, support and sustenance to my work.

For this English edition, my special thanks go to Andrew Stuart Bergerson and Paul Steege, and to Elizabeth Harvey, Dagmar Herzog, Jennifer Rodgers, and Anne Ruderman. I am extremely lucky to have these inspiring people around me. Their sharp criticism considerably improved my thoughts as well as my English prose. I am also especially grateful to Sandra Mather and Ralph Gabriel who designed the maps for the English edition. Patricia Szobar's translation, as well as Paula Bradish's and Gabriel Dotto's editorial assistance were of great help in turning the German manuscript into an English book, and I greatly enjoyed our collaboration. My current workplace, the Centre d'Histoire de Sciences Po in Paris, provided outstanding personal and intellectual support during the revision of the translation. Among the many colleagues who have provided inspiration and support, I wish to particularly thank Claire Andrieu.

Throughout the long and often arduous process of producing this book, my family has shown immense interest and support, for which I am particularly grateful. I would also like to express my appreciation to Tom Streuber for his affection, support, and inspiration these past four years.

Last but not least, I would like to thank Dieter Ambach (1937–2011), who was one of the public prosecutors at the Düsseldorf Majdanek trial (1975–1981). When I contacted him in 2002, at the very beginning of my research, he and his wife, Dorothee, generously received me at their home. It was the beginning of a long and inspiring discussion as well as a friendship. As a young criminal prosecutor in his late thirties, Ambach took over the case in 1976, joining Wolfgang Weber from the Zentrale Stelle der Landesjustizverwaltungen zur Aufklärung von nationalsozialistischen Verbrechen. For more than five years, both prosecutors fought for a fair trial and to bring into light the crimes. Of course, Ambach was disappointed with the judgment and the light penalties. And yet, I have rarely met such a convinced democrat and fighter for justice. Moreover, it was the Majdanek trial that finally gave historians access to a variety of testimonies, which made this research project possible. Unfortunately, Ambach passed away in 2011. I would like to dedicate this book to him and his work.

Introduction

"In early October 1942, I set off for Lublin," Hermine Braunsteiner[1] recalled in a 1973 interrogation. "We took the train. There were nine of us guards and one chief guard."[2] On October 16, 1942, this first group of ten female guards (*SS-Aufseherinnen* in the terminology of the SS) arrived at the Majdanek Concentration and Extermination Camp[3] from the Ravensbrück women's concentration camp.[4] By the time Majdanek was evacuated in April 1944, a total of twenty-eight women had worked as guards at that camp, known for its particularly harsh conditions and the brutal behavior of its SS staff.[5] Prior to starting work as concentration camp guards, none of the women had a criminal record. Rather, they were unremarkable women, some with children or parents to support, motivated largely by the desire for a secure income. How, then, was it possible that such ordinary women[6] progressed to commit acts of such violence in Majdanek?

The voluminous research on Nazi concentration and extermination camps has largely neglected to address such acts of violence, focusing instead on the end result of killing.[7] This gap does not detract from the quality of these studies, which is undisputed, but illustrates the discrepancy between the mere mention of terms such as "violence" and "terror," and the lack of inquiry into this phenomenon as a subject in its own right. Indeed, many historical studies on concentration and extermination camps understand the perpetration of violence as a "logical" consequence of Nazi ideology and policies. Such studies scrutinize the historical, political, economic, and cultural background of the establishment and evolution of the camp system, posing structural and organizational questions. Though SS personnel in the camps perpetrated physical violence on a daily basis, its character, causes, consequences, and dynamics are generally not discussed as independent topics. This historical scholarship on the concentration camps has taken the view that the brutal and often murderous violence of the concentration camps (including the industrialized mass extermination within the camps) was a self-evident and self-explanatory consequence of Nazi ideology and its associated radical anti-Semitism. However, it is precisely the tremendous violence in the camps, both as perpetrated and as experienced, that demands additional exploration.

In the early 1990s, Wolfgang Kirstein offered a sociological and historical analysis of the Natzweiler concentration camp in Alsace.[8] By focusing on the sociology of power, Kirstein explained the violent behavior of the camp personnel as a product of conditioning and habituation. But it was another German sociologist, Wolfgang Sofsky, who first addressed specifically the question of violence—or terror—in the concentration camps and thereby exerted a major influence on the historiography of the camps.[9] Sofsky's macrostructural account of the "order of terror" analyzes the dynamic interplay between organizational structure and the social practices of the SS, which worked in tandem to transform the concentration camp into a site of absolute power.[10] Likewise, in *Maschinen des Terrors*, political scientist Wolfgang Armanski examines the National Socialist concentration camp and the Soviet gulag in terms of their relationship to modernity.[11] In their understanding, the violence perpetrated by the SS stemmed less from ideological beliefs than from the very structure of the camps. For instance, the flood of regulations and the camps' paramilitary framework did not only promote coercion, Sofsky asserts, but also provided room for maneuver (*Handlungsraum*). While the German sociologist recognizes the social foundations of violence, he rejects the possible impact of individual as well as cultural practices. Like Sofsky, Kirstein and Armanski also place primary emphasis on the institutional setting in an effort to understand this violence.

Too often, however, this focus on institutionalized and habituated terror in sociological investigations of power has obscured the microdynamics of power, reducing the Nazi concentration camp to an "institutional model"[12] and the camp staff to "machines."[13] Moreover, these descriptive and theoretical accounts often fail to address adequately questions of historical, political, geographic, institutional, and temporal contexts and connections. With the exception of Kirstein, who has carried out an empirical study of the Natzweiler camp, their work is concerned with ideal types and deals with "sample" or "model" camps that, historically speaking, never actually existed.

It is precisely in the specific historical situations of everyday life in actual camps, however, that violence exceeded expectations. In terms of both the quantity and quality of violence, historians are confronted with a significant gap between official guidelines and everyday practices in the Nazi camps. Orders and directives issued "from above"—that is, from Heinrich Himmler[14] and the central administration of concentration camps, the Inspectorate of Concentration Camps (IKL), and the Chief Economic and Administrative Office (WVHA)—were deciphered, implemented, and even expanded upon in a variety of ways by Majdanek's female guards and SS men "on the ground." Therefore, National Socialist policies of persecution and annihilation and the institutional framework of the concentration camp, as such, are not sufficient to explain the massive scale of this violence and annihilation. Rather, I would argue, this violence can only be fully comprehended by examining the everyday actions and perceptions of the female guards and SS men on the ground level. In the workaday context of the camp, material interests and personal subjectivities conjoined with National Socialist policies to lay the groundwork for persecution and murder.

This realization compels us to investigate more closely the agency of the perpetrators, framed within a microhistory of social and cultural dynamics in these particular settings. What were the social dynamics and cultural meanings associated with these violent practices? Which purposes did physical violence serve from the perpetrator's perspective? To what extent did the camp personnel on duty "create" concentrational violence? Though the concentration camp may seem to be a monolithic and static entity, when considered from a macroanalytic perspective, it is in fact extraordinarily dynamic. From a microsocial and microhistorical point of view, brutality and genocidal violence are not merely structural features of the concentration camp; rather, this violence is produced in a complex and multilayered interaction of individuals and groups, each pursuing their own motivations, needs, and agendas.[15] As the French historian and political scientist Jacques Sémelin points out, research on violence requires, above all, that one be interested in the moment of violence itself—in the "violent act."[16] Surprisingly, it is precisely this attention to historical acts of violence that, with some rare exceptions, remains absent from the scholarship of the camps.[17] While Marc Buggeln's Bourdieu-inspired praxological approach has made violence a focus of his study on slave labor in the Neuengamme camp complex,[18] nobody has to date studied in depth the violence of female camp personnel.

The total number of female guards who served in Nazi concentration camps from May 1939 to May 1945 can only be estimated. Nazi statistics for January 1945 show 3,508 female camp guards as opposed to 37,674 male SS.[19] The figures change over the course of the war and with the expansion of the concentration camp system. But the ratio of men to women working together in mixed camps remains constant throughout the entire period: a single camp might have a few dozen women, but hundreds of men. Following a strict gender separation in accordance with Heinrich Himmler's direct orders, female guards (*SS-Aufseherinnen*) were only employed in concentration camps for women. Female guards thus enjoyed a specific status in the hierarchy. On the one hand, like SS men, they benefited from their status as employees of the Reich, and came under the jurisdiction of the SS. On the other, and unlike their male equivalents, they were not formally members of the SS, and did not belong to the *SS-Sippschaft*, the "clan."[20] Their official designation—as "female auxiliaries [*weibliches Gefolge*] of the Armed SS"—denotes their special position: they were civil employees within a paramilitary organization. Yet to attribute to them a merely subordinate status fails to take into full account the historical reality. Responsible for roll calls, for organizing prisoners into *kommandos* (labor detachments), and for supervising women inmates in the barracks and at work, the guards exercised direct power over the prisoners.

This study examines one specific camp, the concentration and extermination camp Majdanek, where a total of twenty-eight female guards worked between the autumn of 1942 and the spring of 1944. What were the everyday experiences, practices, and interactions of these female SS personnel? What led them to a career in a concentration camp? How did they perform their guard duties? How did the female guards exercise power over the prisoners? What role did physical violence have in the interplay of actors? What made them remain in the camp, sometimes for up to six-and-a-half years?

Hence, we will frame individual acts of violence on the part of the female Majdanek camp guards in terms of the everyday culture and society of the concentration camp. Following Alf Lüdtke, the benefit of focusing on everyday life, as both an analytical concept and methodological approach, is that it allows the historian to reconstruct human experiences and social practices. By analyzing the actions of ordinary people, the history of everyday life allows the historian to observe the processes by which individuals appropriate norms, discourses, and practices in order to array themselves as subjects in wider sociopolitical landscapes.[21] *Alltagsgeschichte* (the history of everyday life) is thus ideally suited for the problem at hand; we will be able to make sense of concentrational violence only if we understand its situational function for its perpetrators: the ordinary camp guards.[22]

As an effort to integrate both cultural history and *Alltagsgeschichte*, this work will explore the daily experiences of female SS staff at Majdanek. The concept of *expérience concentrationnaire*[23]—the concentration camp experience—put forth by Austrian historian and sociologist Michael Pollak in his work on Auschwitz survivors, will serve as a framework for examining the experiences and motivations of the female guards and SS men in the camps. Likewise, this study will examine the concentration camp as a sociocultural environment, a set of living and working conditions perceived and interpreted by the actors in a variety of—at times contradictory—ways.

Following this introduction, the second chapter lays out the methodical and theoretical foundations of this work and introduces the sources on which the discussion is to be based. Chapter 3 provides an overview of the historical development of the Majdanek camp, taking into consideration its regional and political significance, particularly with respect to the duties of the SS staff assigned to the camp, and the living conditions of the prisoners detained there. Chapter 4 considers the different paths that led young German and Austrian women to their work as concentration camp guards.

In seeking to understand the actions and attitudes of female guards at Majdanek toward their work, it is of critical importance to consider their previous experiences—in particular, their earlier time as *Aufseherinnen* at the Ravensbrück women's concentration camp. Thus, chapter 5 takes a close look at the Ravensbrück camp in terms of its function as a "training camp" for the Majdanek guards. It was, after all, at Ravensbrück that many of these women first encountered the "concentration camp universe,"[24] and where the recruits first experienced certain key disciplinary techniques as part of their training. Moreover, it was at Ravensbrück that they first began to experiment with newfound opportunities for asserting power and violence.

For both the female guards and the SS men, the transfer to Majdanek required a great deal of adjustment, including to harsher climate conditions, but also—and more significantly—in terms of cultural and work practices, as chapters 6 and 7 illustrate.

Chapter 8 analyzes Majdanek in terms of its concurrent functions as both concentration and extermination camp, focusing especially on the ways in which the machinery of annihilation helped to shape the guards' workaday lives. It also explores how individual understandings of labor shaped the everyday work practices of the women, and their postwar rationale for their actions at the camp. To understand the violence perpetrated by the Majdanek camp staff, their experiences while off-duty are also of methodological importance. When considered alongside an examination of the guards' living and work conditions, it is precisely the perpetration of violence that constitutes the central topic of this work. This workaday violence will be analyzed as a social and cultural practice, and situated within its historical context.

Chapter 9 examines escape attempts by concentration camp prisoners, situating them within a complex web of meaning and significance. In chapter 10, the tensions and disjunctures between official regulations and actual workaday practices are addressed by examining the ways in which opportunities for agency and authority were exploited by camp staff. Finally, chapter 11 analyzes the microsocial and gender-specific dimensions of physical violence. The study closes with an exploration of the conceptual framework of "cruelty" as an explanation for the most extreme forms of violence carried out in the concentration camps.

Abbreviations

APMM	Archiwum Panstwowe Muzeum na Majdanku
BA	Bundesarchiv Berlin
BDC	Berlin Document Center
BDM	Bund Deutscher Mädel
CI	Civilian Internee
DAW	Deutsche Ausrüstungswerke
DÖW	Dokumentationsarchiv des österreichischen Widerstandes
FKL	Frauenkonzentrationslager (Women's Concentration Camp)
Ger. Rep.	Gerichte Republik
Gestapo	Geheime Staatspolizei
GG	Generalgouvernement (General Government)
GPO	Generalplan Ost (General Plan East)
HSSPF	Höherer SS- und Polizeiführer (Higher SS and Police Leader)
HStA	Hauptstaatsarchiv
IfZ	Institut für Zeitgeschichte, Munich
IG-Farben	Interessengemeinschaft Farbenindustrie AG
IKL	Inspektion der Konzentrationslager (Inspectorate of Concentration Camps)
KdF	Kraft durch Freude (Strength through Joy)

KL	Konzentrationslager (Concentration Camp)
KZ	Konzentrationslager (Concentration Camp)
LAV NRW	Landesarchiv Nordrhein-Westfalen
LG	Landesgericht (Regional Court)
MGR/SBG	Mahn- und Gedenkstätte Ravensbrück/Stiftung Brandenburgische Gedenkstätten
NARA	National Archives and Records Administration
NKVD	People's Commissariat for Internal Affairs (a Soviet authority)
NSDAP	Nationalsozialistische Deutsche Arbeiterpartei (National Socialist German Workers' Party)
OKW	Oberkommando der Wehrmacht
Oscha	Oberscharführer
Osti	Ostindustrie GmbH
PRO	Public Record Office
RFSS	Reichsführer-SS
RSHA	Reichssicherheitshauptamt (Reich Security Main Office)
RuSHA	Rasse- und Siedlungshauptamt (Race and Settlement Head Office)
SA	Sturmabteilung
SD	Sicherheitsdienst(Security Service)
SDG	Sanitätsdienstgrad (a medical orderly rank)
SS	Schutzstaffel
SSBF	SS-Brigadeführer
SSPF	SS-Polizeiführer
SS-T.-Reiterrgt	SS-Totenkopf-Reiterregiment (SS Death's Head Rider Regiment)
Stalag	Kriegsgefangenen-Stammlager der Wehrmacht (prisoner of war main camp of the Wehrmacht)
Tbc	Tuberculosis
Testa	Tesch und Stabenow, Internationale Gesellschaft zur Schädlingsbekämpfung (Tesch and Stabenow, International Pest Control Company)
USHMM	United States Holocaust Memorial Museum
VfZG	Vierteljahreshefte für Zeitgeschichte
WVHA	Wirtschaftsverwaltungshauptamt (Chief Economic and Administrative Office)
ZSL	Zentrale Stelle der Landesjustizverwaltungen zur Aufklärung von NS-Verbrechen in Ludwigsburg

1

Methodological and Theoretical Considerations

WHY DEVOTE A STUDY SOLELY TO FEMALE CONCENTRATION CAMP staff? Although Nazi concentration camps have been the subject of much historical study, the SS is still not a major subject in concentration camp research. The first study of concentration camp staff was undertaken by Karin Orth, who employed a sociohistorical perspective to examine the male administrative elite within the camp.[1] Orth has spurred new research into the history of perpetrators within the system of the concentration camp,[2] but apart from the excellent study of Marc Buggeln,[3] who combines structural history with a cultural historical perspective, this research continues to focus on structural causes rather than the violent behavior of the SS. Most of these recent studies concentrate on the SS elite who ran the camps.[4] Apart from one study exploring female SS guards, "ordinary" concentration camp staff have, to date, received little attention.[5] While there have been some biographical accounts of specific guards, and a rich historiography on postwar trials,[6] a collective biography has yet to be written. At the same time, it is noteworthy that ordinary SS men attract only scant historical attention, while female guards, not least because of their gender and the "exotic" subject of female violence, which in most cases is not problematized, continue to garner a certain public interest.[7] Except for Buggeln's work, lower-rank SS men remain invisible in scholarly literature. For this reason, the present study also seeks to pay particular attention to the male colleagues of the female Majdanek staff and the gender dynamics within the social framework of the camp.

Female Guards in Nazi Concentration Camps

The female SS guards entered the concentration camps relatively late, in 1938, joining a well-established and centralized administrative organization. The women's concentration camps were organized along similar lines as the men's camps.[8] As was the case for men, the practice of *Schutzhaft*—or protective custody—served as the legal basis for committing women to the concentration camp. Issued by President Paul von Hindenburg on the same day as the Reichstag Fire (27 February 1933), the "Decree of the Reich President for the Protection of the People and the State" legalized an indefinite term of detention that could be imposed by the executive authorities, entirely without judicial oversight.[9] Even though the term "protective custody" was not mentioned in this decree, this legal measure soon became referred to as *Schutzhaft*. Conceived as a preventive legal measure, *Schutzhaft* required no court order and followed no set criteria, and so granted the police and Gestapo wide latitude in its implementation.[10] The practice of protective custody, therefore, had nothing in common with the original meaning of the term "protective"—that is, detention for the protection of the individual in question.[11] Initially, protective custody was imposed directly by the police on a local level. Beginning in 1934, however, the Gestapo gradually assumed control over the practice of *Schutzhaft*.[12]

In the early 1930s, female detainees were held in existing prisons and concentration camps, in separate protective custody sections, which were not under the control of the SA (Sturmabteilung) or SS (Schutzstaffel).[13] In March 1934, the first autonomous women's camp, the Moringen provincial workhouse (*Provinzialwerkhaus*), was set up in Prussia.[14] Although Moringen also served as a detention center for women from other areas of the Reich, it was administered by the Hanover provincial government. At first, women there were guarded by the female staff of the workhouse, with auxiliary prison guards recruited from the local National Socialist Women's Organization (the NS Frauenschaft).[15]

In March 1938, Heinrich Himmler ordered the establishment of the first centralized concentration camp for female inmates, which was placed under the administration of the Inspectorate of Concentration Camps (Inspektion der Konzentrationslager). It was located in Lichtenburg Castle near Prettin, on the Elbe River.[16] In accordance with Himmler's orders, the daily guard duties at Lichtenburg were to be carried out only by women.[17] As at Moringen, the guards were recruited from among female prison wardens and members of the National Socialist Women's Organization. In May 1939, the establishment of the central women's camp at Ravensbrück (also ordered by Himmler) marked the inauguration of a new phase of incarceration[18] and also created a new type of female guard,[19] the *SS-Aufseherin*—literally, the

Women's *Stammlager* (1939–1945)

WOMEN'S CONCENTRATION CAMP	OPENING	CLOSURE/LIBERATION
Ravensbrück	15 May 1939	30 Apr. 1945
Stutthof	21 Jan. 1941	25 Apr. 1945
Auschwitz I	26 Mar. 1942	Aug. 1942
Birkenau	Aug. 1942	Jan. 1945
Lublin-Majdanek	15 Aug. 1942	Apr. 1944
Riga-Kaiserwald	15 Mar. 1943	Summer 1944
Herzogenbusch/Vught	12 Jun. 1943	5 Sep. 1944
Kaunas	15 May 1943	Summer 1945
Vaivara	15 Sep. 1943	29 Jun. 1944
Mauthausen	5 Oct. 1943	5 May 1945
Krakow-Płaszów	10 Jan. 1944	Summer 1944
Bergen-Belsen	7 Aug. 1944	15 Apr. 1945
Flossenbürg	14 Mar. 1945	23 Apr. 1945

Note: The table is compiled based on the information provided by Schwarz, *SS-Aufseherinnen*, 38. In one study, Gudrun Schwarz arrives at a figure of 350 satellite camps; Gudrun Schwarz, *Die nationalsozialistischen Lager* (Frankfurt, 1990). In collaboration with the various memorials, in 2005 Christl Wickert compiled an overview, counting at least 210 women's satellite camps. I thank Christl Wickert for this information.

"SS overseer"—as they were called in official documents. These women occupied an intermediate status within the SS hierarchy. Like the SS men, they were civil service employees of the Reich (*Reichsangestellte*) and therefore under the legal jurisdiction of the SS. However, they were not themselves members of the SS; the only women granted membership in the "SS clan" were the wives, daughters, and sisters of members of the Schwarzer Orden ("Black Order").[20] As we have seen, the female guards were civilian employees of the paramilitary Armed SS,[21] under the authority of the command staff headquarters, including the camp commandant and the higher SS leadership, all of which were positions staffed by men. On a day-to-day level, however, the *Aufseherinnen* had authority over the female inmates in the camp.

These guards were responsible for carrying out the daily roll call, assigning prisoners to labor detachments, and guarding women prisoners, both within the barracks area and at the prisoners' assigned place of work. As compared with the SS men, the female guards had only limited opportunities for advancement. "Upon demonstration of aptitude and ability,"[22] according to one official document, an *Aufseherin* might hope to be appointed head of a satellite camp (*Nebenlager*). The highest-ranking position for a woman in the concentration camp was the position of chief guard (*Oberaufseherin*), a rank equivalent to that of the camp compound leader (*Schutzhaftlagerführer*), the second-highest overall rank in the camp.[23] The chief guard supervised the regular *Aufseherinnen*. Again, following the model of the men's camps, Ravensbrück had official camp regulations, written especially for the women's camp and based, largely, on the "Dachau model."[24]

Until January 1941, Ravensbrück was the only concentration camp intended for female prisoners. Beginning with the occupation of Soviet territory in the fall of 1941, millions of Jewish and non-Jewish women deemed "racially inferior" or otherwise "undesirable" according to Nazi criteria came under German rule in the occupied East. The result was that, by the end of the war, thirteen women's *Stammlager* (main concentration camps) had been established, not including numerous satellite camps where female prisoners were also detained.

The Nazi administration distinguished between different types of concentration camps: the main camps, also called *Stammlager*, functioned as an independent entity and as the administration center (*Verwaltungsstelle*) for satellite camps (*Nebenlager*).[25] With the exception of Ravensbrück, the main camps listed here did not exclusively house women. Instead, separate units for female prisoners were typically set up within established men's camps.

It is only possible to estimate the number of female guards who worked in the concentration camps between May 1939 and May 1945. The archives of the Ravensbrück Memorial contain the names and identifying details of 3,950 *Aufseherinnen* who worked at the central women's camp between May 1939 and May 1945,[26] along with information on 2,639 salary accounts.[27] Ravensbrück was not only the primary women's camp—until September 1944, it also served as the training camp for female guards.[28] According to statistics maintained by the SS, as of January 1945 there were a total of 3,508 women working in concentration camps (as compared with 37,674 SS men).[29] But in the somewhat hurried and chaotic circumstances of 1945, the statistics available for Ravensbrück do not include those women recruited near the end of the war. For this reason, it is likely that the total number of *Aufseherinnen* was in fact much higher than official records suggest. Although the number of female guards employed in the camps varied over time (due, in part, to fluctuations in the number of prisoners in the concentration camps), these numbers suggest that, in most camps, several dozen women worked alongside a much larger number of male guards. The exception to this rule was Ravensbrück, where female staff predominated.

One reason for the comparatively small number of *Aufseherinnen* is that women were employed to supervise inmates in concentration camps, but not in extermination camps. Although female guards did work at Auschwitz and Majdanek, this resulted from the dual function of these two camps, which both served, concurrently, as concentration and extermination camps.

The question as to why female staff were recruited to guard female prisoners has received relatively little scholarly attention. As a rule, it is attributed to the division between the sexes, customary in Germany at the time, in prisons as well as in many schools. The introduction of female guards, as initially ordered by Heinrich Himmler, may also have been an attempt to prevent sexual contact between SS men and female prisoners. Although little is known about the conditions under which female prisoners were held in the early SA camps, a number of cases of sexual harassment and attacks on female political prisoners by SS men have been documented for the SA camp in Hohenstein.[30] It is likely that Heinrich Himmler, the *Reichsführer SS* (RFSS), wished to prevent excessive "contact" between SS men and imprisoned women, and that female guards were seen as less troublesome in this respect.

The concentration camp—a space dominated by men—offers a compelling setting in which to analyze questions of gender. In their function as female guards, these women moved into a militaristic sphere that was largely the province of men. Camps such as Majdanek, where female guards worked alongside a much larger contingent of male colleagues and superiors, offer a particularly useful context within which to consider questions of gender dynamics, including what role violence played in the interactions between male and female staff. For this reason, this study will incorporate a consideration of gender into its analysis of the relationship between power and violence at Majdanek, paying particular attention to questions of interaction, ambiguity, and change.[31]

Alltagsgeschichte as Methodology

As Geoff Eley rightly pointed out in his recent reflection on the historiography of the Third Reich, scholarly approaches have changed significantly since the 1980s, when practitioners of *Alltagsgeschichte* such as Alf Lüdtke, Lutz Niethammer, Dorothee Wierling, and Adelheid von Saldern began to scrutinize the penetration of Nazi politics into everyday life and to theorize the social efficiency of Nazi ideology.[32] This new approach to political history was empirically grounded, focused on local and concrete institutions (family, party organization, prison, workplace, and so forth) and on the people on the ground. Methodologically, it offered a new set of tools and a more nuanced understanding of the inner workings of the Third Reich, ultimately spurring a variety of new research. While macrohistorical studies on the Nazi economy and the Nazi state continue to attract the historian's attention,[33] the sociohistorical, local perspective has challenged the established historiography[34] and tapped into the energy of these forces from below.[35] *Alltagsgeschichte*, or the history of everyday life, was among the historiographical impulses that brought the agency of ordinary people—that is, "the capacity of historical actors to act creatively and efficaciously in and on their immediate social worlds"[36]—to the very center of discussions on the history of Nazism.

To explain the destruction wrought by the Third Reich, it was no longer sufficient to concentrate on Hitler's intentions, notorious ringleaders, and ideological fanatics (convinced Party members and blind followers). As Geoff Eley recently stated, "Once the compliance of wider social circles with Nazi policies was shown (civil servants, managers, businessmen, specialists and professionals of all kind), the responsibility of supposedly non-Nazi elites inevitably came on the agenda."[37] In the words of historian Alf Lüdtke, such questions of everyday reality and everyday practices offer the "provocative possibility that it is not only individuals at the 'level of command' who become visible as historical actors."[38] Within his focus on everyday practices, Lüdtke also linked modern warfare during the Second World War to industrial work, in effect putting the action of killing back in the center of the historical reflection. Indeed, allusions to work (division of labor, regularity of repetitious actions, professionalism, and so forth) allowed German Wehrmacht soldiers to normalize their actions and behavior. At the same time, however, a purely functionalist approach does not explain the massive violence. As Lüdtke explains, it was also "the intensity of terror and furor on the killing fields [that] enticed the soldiers to move beyond that very normalcy they longed for but also despised. It was this attraction of terror and furor that unsettled whatever claim soldiers (and bystanders) made that these actions were 'nothing but work.'"[39]

For the purposes of analytical scholarship, however, violence is only indirectly accessible, either through firsthand portrayals of the experience of violence, or as secondhand accounts of observed acts of violence. Only in rare cases do we have direct access to acts of violence in the form of photographic or cinematic documentation. Methodologically, *Alltagsgeschichte* aims to gain insight into the experience of everyday life by triangulation, as it were, using a close reading of the different types of sources available to us. The benefit of this approach to perpetrator history is its ability to embrace different shades of power under Nazism (as authority, domination, rule, consent, participation, self-empowerment), and to overcome the usual binary divides between the public sphere, politics and ideology, and the lived experience of the everyday.[40] *Alltagsgeschichte*, as practiced and developed by Alf Lüdtke, "turns the binary of coercion and consent into a dialectic."[41] As Lüdtke has emphasized, power exerted by the state or by a political party only becomes effective within the constellation of interests and needs of the various social actors; this assertion proves equally true when the state possesses overwhelming power or even simply lays claim to omnipotence. "In this approach, power is an element within a 'field of action' in which those who are supposedly 'ruled' are anything but passive."[42] Yet, as Eley has pointed out, this epistemological approach to Nazism has not become part of Holocaust historiography.[43] Despite the almost innumerable studies on Nazi concentration camps, few—if any—have addressed the "everyday life" of either victims or perpetrators in the camps.[44] As we will see, it is precisely in the everyday—or, more precisely, in everyday social practices—where ideological settings meet personal interests (private desires, professional identification with work, quotidian sociability, entertainment, family life) to enable historical agents not just to tolerate but to cooperate with the regime's demands.

Using the example of Majdanek and a group of twenty-eight guards, this study endeavors to examine how these women experienced their everyday work and life in a concentration and extermination camp, and more specifically, the role that violence played in that experience. Writing the everyday history of camp guards does not entail restoring missing historical subjects, but rather exploring the "subtleties and complexities of human agency."[45] Research into everyday historical realities explores an "inner perspective" on the acquisition and exercise of power by the ordinary SS guards. This book thus opens a window onto three different exemplary (though not exhaustive) forms of concentrational and genocidal violence: extermination, physical ill-treatment, and cruelty. A microanalytical approach complements a macroanalytical perspective precisely because it offers insights into the "underside" of this institution—its incoherent, fractured, and shifting side, where multiple discourses and practices intersect. Rather than treating these phenomena as preexisting norms that are passively internalized and enacted, this approach analyzes the making, remaking, and unmaking of conventions in social practices.[46] This microsocial and micropolitical perspective also compels scholars to recognize that institutions like concentration camps are also sites of labor: both in the metaphorical sense of places where we do work in the world, and in the literal sense of paid or unpaid employment in workplaces. Here, multiple agents encounter each other on a daily basis, acting and reacting with multiple intentions. But the microscopic and macroscopic perspectives are not actually distinct. By studying how the camp staff carry out their daily work and, in the process, contribute to building the institution of the concentration camp, we interrogate the rules, practices, objects, and spaces of everyday life that the agents themselves do not question. Consequently, as Paul Steege has emphasized, *Alltagsgeschichte* offers a way to integrate arguments about different layers of personal responsibility in and for Nazi rule.[47]

As an analytical category, everyday life encompasses more than daily routines. Rather, as defined by historians Klaus Bergmann and Susanne Thun, it is a "life world" in which "people confront their existing realities on a daily or regular basis through their actions, interactions, and responses."[48] Everyday life encompasses the sphere of work, leisure, living conditions, food, sexuality, and socialization, spheres that we might not immediately associate with concentration camps, violence, and genocide. In Lüdtke's definition, the everyday is the "overall context of production and reproduction, with all its reciprocal dependencies and contradictions."[49] Central to Lüdtke's conception of *Alltagsgeschichte* is the question of domination (*Herrschaft*) or, more precisely, the practices of domination. Daily life does not occur in an apolitical vacuum; rather, it takes place within a context where domination is a product of people's perceptions, interpretations, actions, and forms of expression. "It is the reciprocity of objective and subjective moments that allows and enables social reproduction and transformation."[50] In essence, then, *Alltagsgeschichte* is less about the distinction between the "ruler" and the "ruled." Instead, it entails an examination of the varied and ambivalent "relationships of power"[51] that transect the entirety of the social body.

With regard to concentration camps, *Alltagsgeschichte* turns our attention to the way institutions operate in everyday life. Its goal is to think more concretely about how ordinary people inhabit institutions in various ways: as the makers of policies (the camp commanders and high-ranking SS officers), as the workers who implement them (the SS men and female camp guards), and the people who become their objects (the camp inmates who themselves occupy different categories). To quote Paul Steege: "While acknowledging how structures of power, and the people who inhabit them, can limit the room for maneuver available to individual actors, it [*Alltagsgeschichte*] also leaves room for their mutual complicity in producing those same structures of power."[52] By examining the various spheres of power within the "concentration camp universe," this study also aims to grasp the dissonances and differences that existed among the female guards, SS men, and higher SS leadership: In what ways and under what circumstances did the various actors attempt to assert themselves vis-à-vis their colleagues? How did they situate themselves within the daily realities of life in the concentration camp? How did everyday practices influence the participation and independent initiative of camp staff? To what extent did what I refer to as "concentrational" and exterminatory violence become the everyday norm of life and work in the concentration camp? The Majdanek concentration camp thus emerges as an "arena"[53] in which a variety of agents engage and interact with one another. The ethical aspects of power, force, politics, and violence are central to this study.[54] The key question is: How did the actions of ordinary people within these institutions influence the manner in which these institutions functioned?

The question of the political is indeed central to an investigation of daily life. From the perspective of *Alltagsgeschichte*, the political encompasses not only the formulation, organization, and implementation of collective interests, but also the articulation and assertion of individual interests and needs.[55] My analysis focuses on the ways in which the female guards and SS men appropriated what was now "their" world, that is, the Majdanek Concentration and Extermination Camp.[56] Drawing inspiration from the works of Karl Marx, Alf Lüdtke developed this concept of "appropriation" or *Aneignung* to signify a diverse, formative, and "sensual" interpretation of social norms, discourses, practices, and compulsions by the actors. "During appropriation, agents that 'function' [or don't function] become actors who interpret and demonstrate, insist or refuse."[57] In this context, social norms are not understood as a given, but as something that individual actors must first imbue with meaning and then put into action. Through these attributions of meaning, individuals make inferences about their world and respond to the mechanisms of power within which they are embedded in ways that are not always consistent or coherent.

Scholars such as Erving Goffman and Michel Foucault have underlined the *totalizing* character of institutions such as prisons, mental hospitals, military camps, and the like.[58] Others, including Wolfgang Kirstein and Zygmunt Baumann, have observed similar patterns in the concentration camp system.[59] In Baumann's work, the Nazi regime's institutions of bureaucratic murder serve as an archetype of modernity.[60] Works focusing on *Alltag*, however, have challenged the totalizing character of the institution by asking *how* institutions operate "on the ground."[61]

Institutions are designed to shape the lived environment and mold human behavior according to desired outcomes. But we can discover the actual relationship between policy and practice, ideology and implementation, only in everyday life. Understanding the everyday operations of institutions is relevant for understanding the very functioning of politics, especially in a dictatorship such as the Third Reich. These everyday operations raise ethical questions about responsibility for the violence, whether intentional or not, that is inherent to various degrees in many of our modern institutions. Here the concentration camps are instructive precisely because institutional violence took on such extreme forms of terror and genocide.

From an everyday historical perspective, the acting out and the experience of physical violence serve to constitute the institution; yet when analyzing this violence within concentration and extermination camps, care must be taken to distinguish between different practices of violence, and therefore to draw a conceptual framework that can serve as a point of orientation for our analysis.

Theories of Power, Violence, and Cruelty

In the early 1970s, Michel Foucault developed a theory of power as a foundational social phenomenon. He worked from the assumption that there is no such thing as a single, homogeneous mode of power. Society is not a "unitary body in which one power and one power only exercises itself," but rather is a "juxtaposition, a liaising, a coordination, a hierarchy, too, of different powers which nonetheless regain their specificity."[62]

Using the examples of psychiatry and the prison system, Foucault undertook a microsocial investigation of the mechanisms and relations of power.[63] Power as such is not centralized, but is instead something inherent in the relationships between individuals and groups. Power is thus an action exercised upon another, or, in Foucault's description, an "ensemble of actions that induce others and follow from one another."[64] From a Foucauldian perspective, power exists only when it is exercised. Foucault posits that it acts directly and immediately, and also influences the actions of individuals. He sees power as a mode of action that reacts to other forces. "It incites, induces, and seduces"; power can simplify or obstruct an individual's action. Furthermore, it is constantly negotiated—or, more precisely, exerted—among individuals or groups within a broad range of possibilities.[65] Therefore, power relations are necessarily communicative—they are an assertion of influence of one over another. While there are differences and asymmetries between the individual social actors, there can be no action outside of or beyond these complex relations of power. According to this concept of power, all people are "affected" by power;[66] all individuals exercise power just as, at all times, power is being exerted upon them. By the same token, the exercise of power on other social actors is neither static nor constant; instead, it is constantly renegotiated and renewed.

This view of power relations—which situates the female guards and SS men as both the objects and subjects of power—is extremely useful for an investigation of the everyday actions of the camp staff and particularly for analyzing the dynamic interactions within the SS hierarchy. Within the context of Majdanek, this concept of power allows us to scrutinize how female guards and SS men in the camp reproduced, expanded upon, and appropriated the rules and regulations that had been communicated to them. At this microsocial level of analysis, my study will examine how vigorously the SS employees executed orders given to them, and examine how the local and central camp administration (such as the Inspectorate of Concentration Camps or the Chief Economic and Administrative Office) dealt with possible violations of camp regulations. When scrutinized from an everyday historical perspective, we can see that the camp regulations did not function only as commands and prohibitions. Rather, for the camp guards, the regulations also functioned as "appeals to act" that left open various possibilities for interpretation and action. In a Foucauldian conception of power, power is always "productive, creative, and generative."[67] Within our context of the concentration camps, this suggests two questions. What implicit latitude for interpretation did such orders and prohibitions contain? And to what extent did the concrete execution of commands, prohibitions and guidelines provoke a "creative" backlash that made even greater violence appear acceptable? By analyzing the relationships between and among the female guards and SS men at Majdanek, a layer of social relationships, interactions, and conflicts comes into view that Holocaust studies otherwise tend to overlook. Within the camp, physical violence was a distinct social and cultural practice within a multivalent, inherently contradictory, and ambiguous "field of force"[68] by which female guards and SS men structured their everyday lives and negotiated relationships of power within the group.

By contrast, Foucault's conception of power does not lend itself well to the analysis of the complex relationship between SS staff and prisoners. The Foucauldian concept of power always implies a degree of consent among social actors, a notion that clearly fails to reflect the absolute subjugation experienced by the prisoners in the camps. Following Elias Canetti's concept of power, I prefer the term "overwhelming dominance" (*Übermacht*)[69] when it comes to situations characterized by a total dissymmetry between the torturer (the SS) on one side, and the target of their extreme violence (the inmate) on the other. As this study will show, in these situations of overwhelming domination, we can no longer refer to *relations* of power. When power is inescapable, prisoners can only react or endure in response. In this context, the question instead becomes how the SS women and men produced this overwhelming power and placed it on display.

VIOLENCE AND CRUELTY

As historians such as Thomas Lindenberger and Alf Lüdtke have noted, physical violence is experienced on the body. Exercised on the human body, physical violence encompasses a broad spectrum of actions and experiences, beginning with actions as minimal as a threatening word or gesture, extending to physical injury and, finally, to killing. For those who endured it in the Nazi concentration camps, violence brought pain and fear. For those who exercised and performed it, violence brought a feeling of power and, in many cases, pleasure.[70] Violence is both a mode of experience and a form of action, an interplay of social practice, symbolic attribution, and the production of meaning.

The German scholar Jan Philipp Reemtsma recently emphasized the physicality of violence: "Violence is first and foremost physical violence, the nonconsensual assault on another's body. 'First and foremost' means that physical violence is the point of reference for other, nonphysical forms of violence."[71] In this sense, then, physical violence is our frame of reference even for nonphysical forms of violence. According to Reemtsma, the reduction of the person to the body postulated by the violent act is the reason why violence is primarily understood as physical or bodily. "Violence has two components: the inflicting of it and the suffering of it. What unites the two is the reduction of the person who suffers violence to his or her body."[72] Violence, to adopt one of Foucault's formulations, is exercised directly on human bodies or objects: violence forces, bends, breaks, and destroys.[73]

French historian and political scientist Jacques Sémelin has defined "extreme" violence as an act of violence that in some way resides beyond ordinary violence (*au-delà de la violence*), or that exceeds ordinary violence qualitatively (due to the extent of the act's brutality, described by some scholars as "cruelty") and quantitatively (through its immensity, as when it descends into massacre).[74] The adjective "extreme" thus describes a twofold transgression of a boundary. According to Sémelin, such an extreme act of violence also strips its victim of all humanity, often reducing the victim to the status of an animal or object prior to killing.[75] For the scholar, therefore, the phenomenon of extreme violence requires that we attend to the relationship and interrelationship between rationality and irrationality.

In this investigation, cruelty is defined as a specific, conceptually distinct form of violence. Cruelty has a semantic affinity to blood: the Latin word *cruor* describes blood and raw flesh, or by extension, a bloodbath or slaughter. As an adjective and adverb, *crudus* describes a ruthless act of violence. In German, the term *Grausamkeit* or its adjectival form *grausam* derives from the Middle High German term *gruwe* or *gruwesam*, meaning "horror" or "shudder."[76] Cruelty is a specific form of violence distinguished by its intensity and motivation. While violence is an assault that causes different levels of pain, cruelty is always committed with the explicit intent of inflicting pain on its victim. According to French anthropologist Véronique Nahoum-Grappe, the quantitative and qualitative "excess" of cruelty aims not just to achieve physical pain but also to confer degradation and humiliation on the victim.[77] For this reason, cruelty—unlike violence—can *never* be acknowledged as "justified" by its victims.[78]

Cruelty is thus not only a more extreme form of violence; it distinguishes itself from violence by the semantics of its gesture: as Nahoum-Grappe points out, to inflict pain and degradation always demands a higher degree of "clear-sightedness." "The violent gesture is less precise, it approaches the object or the enemy as an obstacle and destroys it. On the other hand, the transgressive quality of cruelty [*surenchère*] requires that the victim can be defiled and vilified before the eyes of the perpetrator."[79] To comprehend the semantics of the cruel gesture, the action must be deconstructed and reconstructed within its social and cultural context. This study does not endeavor to diagnose cruelty in terms of its psychology or as a supposed expression of sexual or sadistic pathology. Instead, this investigation will focus on the praxis of violence, its microsocial context, and the semantic meanings and attributions accorded to cruelty in the Majdanek camp.

ANNIHILATION

As Jacques Sémelin has noted, the concept of genocide developed by Raphaël Lemkin in 1944 and enshrined by the UN Convention of 1948 is more misleading than helpful for scholarly research, particularly because there is no generally accepted definition as to which acts constitute genocide and which do not.[80] The UN convention defined genocide as the deliberate partial or complete destruction of a national, ethnic, racial, or religious group.[81] According to Sémelin, this juridical concept of genocide retains too many moral, political, and legal implications to be truly useful as a social-scientific category of analysis.[82] For the social sciences, therefore, Sémelin instead proposes the concept of "destruction."[83] As a semantic category, "destruction" encompasses the annihilation and extermination (*extirpation*), uprooting, elimination, and eradication (*éradication*) of human beings, as well as the destruction, razing, laying waste to, and devastation of material goods (*déstruction*).

The concept of destruction, then, is broader in scope than the juridical concept of murder. The concept of destruction encompasses the processes by which victims are dehumanized before their elimination. It does not specify any particular method of annihilation, which can include fire, water, gas, starvation, cold, or any other method of killing, whether quick and direct, or slow and indirect.[84] As Sémelin points out, mass destruction necessarily requires a certain degree of organization, although this does not preclude improvisation, acceleration, pauses, and radicalization by implementers at ground level. When exercised against noncombatant civilians or disabled combatants, collective violence and killing always entails a considerable or total asymmetry between aggressor and victim, to become what Sémelin has described as a "one-sided destruction."

Sémelin's concept of destruction is useful for analyzing the mass killing at

Majdanek because it allows for an analysis of not only the extermination of European Jews but also the mass killing of prisoners of other nationalities. This analysis will entail situating specific practices or acts of violence, as they were carried out at Majdanek, within their historical, political, and social context.

Source Materials

This study draws upon a very heterogeneous body of sources that will—wherever possible—be placed in counterpoint to one another.

INTERROGATIONS AND COURT TESTIMONY

Immediately following Germany's surrender (in both the East and the West), speaking publicly about work in the concentration camps became taboo in both Germany and Austria, a taboo that continues to this day. At least in part because of this taboo, scholars have largely been unable to obtain first-hand accounts from former female (and male) camp guards about their experiences. As Insa Eschebach, religious studies scholar and director of the Ravensbrück Memorial, has noted,[85] "Where we do succeed in obtaining such testimony, it soon becomes clear how difficult it must have been to articulate experiences for which there is no accepted language [*Sprechmuster*]."[86] One of the few moments in which the female guards spoke—or were forced to speak—was before the courts.

To form the basis of my study, I endeavored to find a group of guards who, while comparatively well-documented, have until now received only scant scholarly attention. In addition, I searched for a body of sources that would allow me to compare the female guards with their male counterparts, the SS men. In the end, I elected to focus on Majdanek, in large part due to the sources made available as a result of the Majdanek Trial—the last major postwar trial, which took place between November 26, 1975, and June 30, 1981. In the Majdanek Trial, charges were brought against a group of six former guards (Hermine Böttcher, Hildegard Lächert, Charlotte Mayer née Wöllert, Alice Orlowski, Hermine Ryan Braunsteiner, Rosa Süss née Reischl), and eleven SS men (Thomas Ellwanger, Heinrich Groffmann, Hermann Hackmann, Günther Konietzny, Emil Laurich, Fritz Petrick, August Wilhelm Reinartz, Ernst Schmidt, Robert Seitz, Arnold Strippel, Heinz Villain). Alongside the defendants, an additional 340 witnesses testified, among them 215 Majdanek survivors.

The Majdanek trial was an extraordinarily complex proceeding; unfortunately, space constraints preclude me from offering a detailed examination of the trial.[87] It is important to note, however, that the source materials obtained from the trial are also problematic, not least because verbatim transcripts of witness testimony had been abolished for Regional Courts and Higher Regional Courts (*Landgerichte* and *Oberlandesgerichte*) by a reform of criminal procedure passed on December 9, 1974.[88]

Initially, the Majdanek courtroom proceedings were recorded, but this practice was abandoned after some of the defense lawyers objected. While the investigation launched by the Cologne public prosecutor in 1960 is amply documented, there are no official, verbatim transcripts for the main hearings, held over a period of nearly six years. Instead, we must rely on the written notes kept by public prosecutors, investigative judges, and police authorities. A selection of these documents was published in 2003 by former public prosecutor Dieter Ambach.[89]

This study also draws on interrogations carried out for the Krakow Auschwitz Trial (1946–1947), in which a number of Majdanek staff were charged, including the head of the crematorium, Erich Muhsfeldt, and the guards Else Ehrich, Luise Danz, Hildegard Lächert, and Alice Orlowski. These transcripts are held in the Düsseldorf Main State Archive. In addition, Hermine Braunsteiner was tried before an Austrian denazification tribunal called the *Volksgericht* in her home city of Vienna between 1946 and 1949.[90] I consulted the records from this trial, now held at the Documentation Centre of Austrian Resistance. Hertha Ehlert was charged in the first Bergen-Belsen Trial, which took place from September 17, 1945, to November 17, 1945, in Lüneburg; Gertrud Heise was a defendant in the second Bergen-Belsen Trial, held in May 1946 before a British military court in Celle.[91] Also, the Regional Criminal Court in Graz conducted a murder investigation against Alois K., an Austrian citizen who was head of the 3rd Guard Company at Majdanek. During the course of these proceedings, a number of other Austrian citizens were investigated, among them several members of the guard unit (Alois K., Johann G., Johann F., Karl R., Eduard R., Georg W.), two female guards (Edith W., Erna Wallisch née Pfannstiel), and one former prisoner-functionary (Karl Johann G.). On January 12, 1973, however, the court issued a determination of insufficient evidence and discontinued the investigation.[92] At the Documentation Centre of Austrian Resistance, however, I did have the opportunity to examine these investigative records.[93] Regarding the names of the former male and female camp guards, the sources often contain a variety of different spellings (for example, Muhsfeldt vs. Mussfeldt, or Herta vs. Hertha Ehlert). In addition, many of the women married, divorced and/or remarried after the war. For this reason, many of the individuals reappear in the source documents under new names (Frau Ehlert became Frau Naumann, and Hermine Braunsteiner became Mrs. Ryan). To avoid confusion, I have chosen to use the maiden names for the women throughout, and to spell the names of all SS members in the body of the text in uniform fashion.

Virtually no written documentation has survived to document the mass killings carried out at the Majdanek Concentration and Extermination Camp or the daily acts of violence carried out there. As in other trials involving National Socialist criminality, witness testimony proved all the more important at the Majdanek Trial. Of the survivors who testified, most were Polish men and women, including Jewish men and women born in Poland. Generally, non-Jewish Polish prisoners spent more time in the camp than did Jewish prisoners. Many of these Polish former prisoners had carried out functions in the camp that provided them with a broader overview of events, sometimes including the opportunity to witness the actions of the SS at close hand. By contrast, Jewish inmates who survived Majdanek generally spent only a few months there, after which they were transferred to other camps, including Auschwitz. Barbara Briks, Maria Kaufmann-Krasowska, and Maryla Reich are exceptions to this rule, having all been interned in February 1942 with false identity documents, which classified them as Polish. Maria Kaufmann-Krasowska was released from Majdanek in September of that year, while Barbara Briks and Maryla Reich remained there until the camp was evacuated in late April 1944. Very few Jewish prisoners from the Soviet Union and Slovakia survived Majdanek. For this reason, the primary group of witnesses at the Majdanek Trial consisted of Polish former inmates who had been classified as political prisoners.

However, the retrospective accounts offered by witnesses and defendants during the postwar investigations and trials are highly problematic sources that must be approached with caution.

LEGAL EVIDENCE AS SOURCES

As historical sources, courtroom and legal records pose inherent problems. Pierre Bourdieu considers police or judicial interrogations liminal spaces, thus representing a biography told in institutionalized form.[94] Michael Pollak has similarly argued that statements made before the court are an "extreme case," because of both the circumstances surrounding their creation, and the public attention they attract.[95] Moreover, it is not only defendants and suspects who are affected by the circumstances under which legal and courtroom testimony takes place; the same holds true for witnesses. Police and legal testimony is a rigidly hierarchical, formalized, and ritualized form of speech.[96] The questioners and the questioned are not on an equal footing; only the police or the court determines who is permitted to speak. In contrast to autobiographical accounts presented in oral histories, speech in police and legal proceedings is often recorded only in partial form. Many interview transcripts record only responses to questions asked by the prosecutors or investigative judges, but not the questions themselves. While historians must be content with the material at hand, we must remember that police and judicial interrogations always seek to investigate a criminal act. Any testimony must be read with the knowledge that it was offered as a form of self-justification and self-defense.[97] Despite these limitations, the product of these testimonies can be read as a "life story" of sorts.

The question of memory must also be kept in mind. Memories are not objective reproductions of past realities. Instead, they are forms of narrative self-representation, shaped and filtered through the retrospective lens of autobiography and the process of forgetting, repression, and rationalization.[98] The time factor is another issue; many of the statements at the Majdanek Trial were made forty years after the event. As Harald Welzer, a social psychologist who is an expert on memory, has emphasized, it is important to take into account the "filter of memory" that is at work, particularly when it comes to an individual's recounting of perceptions and experiences.[99] Finally, in the analysis of statements made by contemporary witnesses (including interviews and interrogations), we must also take into account the circumstances under which the retelling took place.[100]

In the police and legal sources that form the basis of much of this study, the former camp staff obviously attempted to present themselves in the best possible light. Survivors who testified in court may have also remained silent about certain events that in their perception might have placed them in a compromising light. In other instances, they may have cast certain events in a more positive light. For their part, the former SS staff generally attempted to deny participation in violent and criminal acts, in hopes of deflecting additional probing questions from the prosecutors and judges. Nonetheless, as I will show, there are a few instances of astonishingly frank testimony, including testimony about violent acts. For obvious reasons, former camp staff members were generally more willing to speak about more trivial camp experiences, including topics such as work conditions, leisure activities, uniforms, and so forth. This testimony, some of which is extremely detailed, also speaks to a desire, even a compulsion, to tell their stories and to remember and to "normalize" their work.

As is true for all autobiographic accounts, we must critically examine the manner in which the account attempts to retrospectively construct and shape events. This study thus aims to decipher the narratives of victims and perpetrators and make visible the perceptions and constructions of the "self" and the "other" inherent in these narratives. Although the testimonies offered by former SS staff are problematic in numerous respects (most particularly with respect to their self-exculpatory character and their silence about questions of violence), they are still rich sources for a history that takes an *Alltagsgeschichte* approach. I return here to Insa Eschebach's point, and see the lack of a "coherent historical account" not as a shortcoming but as an opportunity to include the retrospective interpretations, and even the distortions, contained in the interrogation records as an integral aspect of the history that is being told.[101]

Despite its limitations, the verbatim testimony that forms the basis of this work can be usefully analyzed from a discursive point of view. For example, how did former camp staff present and justify their own actions, and what arguments did they draw upon? By placing these statements in their cultural and historical context, we can often obtain glimpses of how the events being related were perceived at the time. A discursive analysis also offers the possibility of reconstructing the internal logic and code of values of the female guards and SS men. On occasions where statements by several different people describe a particular action or event, we can also analyze its social dimension.[102] This study will thus combine historical and ethnographic methodologies to gain insight into the daily lives and the practice of violence by the SS staff at the Majdanek camp. By counterposing the everyday lives of the camp staff with the experiences of the former prisoners, I will draw out and highlight the contrasts. For the prisoners, the concentration camp was a place of suffering, hunger, constant fear, the threat of violence, and an inhumane struggle to survive. For the camp staff, it was first and foremost a place to live and work.

CONTEMPORARY WRITTEN SOURCES

Although a great deal of written source material has survived from the Nazi era, in many ways it remains fragmented and incomplete. Still, the Nazi concentration camp system was administered by a large and complex bureaucratic apparatus. Every day, the concentration camps produced reams of documents that went into the administrative files; telexes were exchanged between the central administration in Oranienburg and the concentration camps. However, as the SS began to evacuate the camps, they worked systematically to destroy all written records held in the camps. Due to time pressure and the sheer volume of material, they did not manage to destroy it all. On July 23, 1944, when the Red Army liberated Majdanek, a large number of official documents were discovered (including camp correspondence, reports, SS personnel files, some prisoner logs, and more) and brought to Moscow.

It is not only the fragmented survival of documents that challenges the historians. An even more fundamental problem for researchers studying the concentration camps is that there were no written orders or even administrative documents regarding the mass murder of prisoners. Indeed, it is unlikely that such documents ever existed, as the entire camp system was designed to erase all traces of the killing that had taken place. For example, when selections were carried out on incoming transports, new arrivals were not registered in the camp log before they were killed. For those who were already registered in the camp, their killing was either undocumented or covered up. According to Majdanek survivors who had worked in the camp's record office, prisoners who had been killed were generally recorded as transfers. "When prisoners were transferred to another camp, we wrote down: 'Transferred to Ravensbrück,' or something like that," Maria Kaufmann-Krasowska recalled in her 1978 testimony before the Düsseldorf court. "But when the records said only 'transferred,' that meant that the women had died in the gas chamber."[103] In other cases, for example when a prisoner was killed in the infirmary, the "death book" indicated that the prisoner had died of "natural" causes. These falsified death notices were sometimes also sent to family members. As Julian Gregorowicz, a prisoner assigned to work as a scribe in the records office, later recalled, "As a death scribe, I received reports from the blocks when a patient had died. I had a collection of pre-approved medical histories. . . . I wrote my fictitious reports in the office, and then they were forwarded to the camp administration."[104] As these two statements also show, the administrative language was highly euphemistic and misleading for anyone not versed in the language of the camps.

By contrast, documents pertaining to the SS staff at Majdanek are relatively well preserved. These include guard regulations, directives issued by the commandant, reports, duty rosters, and so forth. These items were probably considered harmless or at least not particularly compromising when the SS carried out its mass destruction of camp records in 1944. Because these documents are also written in euphemistic language and appear to reveal little about the camp inmates and the killing operations, they have received only limited scholarly attention. In the large historiography of the camp, these records often serve only as footnote materials, or to provide illustrative examples. On closer scrutiny, though, these administrative documents offer important albeit fragmentary glimpses into the institutional framework of camp life, including everyday existence in the camp, day-to-day administration, and the relationships among the camp staff. Indeed, it is precisely because of the coded nature of the language that these documents are so interesting: they offer a different perspective on Nazi ideology and the self-representation of the SS.

Although the camp files originally came from the Archives of the Majdanek Memorial (Archiwum Panstwowe Muzeum na Majdanku), I consulted these materials at the State Archive Nordrhein-Westfalen (Main State Archive division) in Düsseldorf. Documents relating to the Ravensbrück Women's Concentration Camp are held in the Ravensbrück Memorial archive and in the German Federal Archives.

AUTOBIOGRAPHICAL ACCOUNTS

Verbal and written autobiographical testimony forms another important basis for my work. My research draws on memoirs and other testimony written in (or translated into) German, English, and French. However, since the vast majority of the Majdanek prisoners came from Eastern Europe, comparatively little testimony on Majdanek has been written in these three languages.[105]

Because it was written while the war was still in progress, the report by Dionys Lenard, "Flucht aus Majdanek," is particularly relevant to this study.[106] Lenard, a Slovak escapee, was deported to Majdanek in April 1942. After three months in the camp, he managed to escape without being recaptured; it was during that same year that he wrote his report in Slovak. Lenard later turned up in Hungary, after which all traces of him vanish. In all likelihood, he perished in the war.

A large number of memoirs and firsthand accounts pertaining to the Ravensbrück women's concentration camp have been preserved. The observations of female prisoner-functionaries, who were in daily contact with the female guards, are particularly valuable in this respect, all the more so because there are no written accounts by former guards. The accounts by German and Austrian prisoners, who shared a common language and cultural background with their guards, are often particularly insightful in their observations.[107] The account by French ethnologist Germaine Tillion, which is extremely precise and detailed in its observations, is also central to this study.[108] However, in drawing on these firsthand sources, it is important to keep in mind the context and the forms in which they were written.

As Michael Pollak has shown, after the war only a small number of concentration camp survivors felt empowered to speak and bear witness. To this day, the majority of memoir accounts were written by former political prisoners (whose ranks also include Germaine Tillion). Due to their strong and largely positive sense of group identity, the political prisoners were most likely to set down their memories for a broader audience.[109] Other prisoner groups, by contrast, including homosexuals and prisoners classified as "asocials," have largely preferred to remain silent in the face of what even today might be perceived as a public stigma attached to their persecution.[110]

Concentration camp functionaries have composed only a few postwar accounts of their experiences. One is by former Auschwitz commandant, Rudolf Höss, which he wrote while awaiting trial for war crimes.[111] Originally published by Martin Broszat in 1958, Höss's account was intended as self-exculpation and so must be read with a critical eye. Nonetheless, it is a rich source, which also offers the perspective of a male officer in charge of the female guards. Other personal accounts include private letters by concentration camp physicians, written to wives, family members, and colleagues.[112]

By contrast, the female guards and low-level SS men, whether due to the nature of the duties they carried out in the camp, or due to their educational and social background, were less likely to record their experiences in writing. In postwar West Germany, concentration camp physicians were only rarely called to account for their actions, either morally or legally. Most continued to practice medicine, whereas the former female and male guards found themselves socially marginalized and, beginning in the late 1950s, were increasingly called before the police and the courts. Nonetheless, apart from a few journalists who reported on the trials, this low-level staff proved of little interest to either scholars or the public at large.

Between 1975 and 1981, Eberhard Fechner filmed what later became a documentary on the Majdanek Trial in Düsseldorf. The film is an exceptional source of information because defendants who were largely reticent at the trial itself spoke relatively freely before the camera. Also, its visual form perhaps better suited the Majdanek guards, who were less inclined to provide a written account of their experiences.[113] Alongside numerous witnesses, Fechner featured five defendants—Hermann Hackmann, the first camp compound leader (*Schutzhaftlagerführer*), Rottenführer Heinz Villain, Unterscharführer Emil Laurich, and the guards Hildegard Lächert and Rosa Süss née Reischl. A number of SS staff also offered testimony, including former guards Luzie H. and Erna Wallisch née Pfannstiel, and Otto Z. Former camp staff were surprisingly willing to offer testimony, in part because Fechner had negotiated a deal with the court that he would not release the documentary until after the verdicts had been issued, and that none of the interviews for his documentary could be used as legal evidence.[114] The film centers on the statements made by various individuals involved in the trial. The visual aspect plays a relatively insignificant role: the camera is static and shows only the faces of the interviewees, a film technique media scholar

Simone Emmelius has called "filmed dialogue."[115] Similar to the police and court interrogators, however, Fechner filmed only the replies, and not the questions that he posed. Since these questions would likely have shed light on the interactions between Fechner and his interview subjects and their mutual expectations of one another, their absence represents an important shortcoming of the documentary as a source.

In the case of Erna Pfannstiel (married name Wallisch), I was also able to consult a transcript of her interview with Eberhard Fechner.[116] In the fall of 2007, Pfannstiel was tracked down in Vienna by a British journalist; her case made headlines in the Austrian press until her death in the spring of 2008.[117]

PHOTOGRAPHS

All of the concentration camps had a special photographic identification unit, called the Erkennungsdienst. This department was responsible for all photographic processing in the camp. Duties included taking ID photos of prisoners, and passport and portrait photos of SS staff; documenting the progress of construction projects; and capturing a visual record of high-level visits and various official festivities. As was posted on signs located both within the camp and along its perimeter, outsiders were strictly prohibited from taking photographs in the camp. A regulation first issued in 1937 also forbade SS staff to take photographs in the camp.[118] Unofficially, however, the practice appears to have been tolerated, as many personal snapshots exist. Even though the SS attempted to systematically destroy all photographic evidence during the evacuation, unofficial photographs have survived from most of the concentration camps.

Official photographs in the camps were taken at important events, celebrations, visits by high SS officials, and all visits by Heinrich Himmler. Personal photographs and snapshots taken by the SS reveal the pride they took in their membership in the group as well as a desire to portray an image of camaraderie. These photographs document the living conditions of camp staff, their lodgings, and the uniforms they wore, and offer brief—albeit "sanitized"—glimpses of their work and leisure activities. For the guards, the concentration camp was also a place of residence and leisure; after work, the women sought recreation in nearby towns and cities. In this sense, the photographic evidence offers important insights for understanding how these women could spend years working in the concentration camps.

In both official and personal photographs taken in the camps, little is seen of the everyday lives of the prisoners, the terrible hygienic conditions, the daily violence they faced, or the myriad forms of mass annihilation. The only exceptions are photographs depicting the arrival of prisoner transports, which the SS evidently deemed unusual and thus extraordinary enough to warrant recording, and a small number of photographs that, for bureaucratic reasons, were taken to document some prisoner deaths.[119] Despite the fact that they aim to depict the prisoners, both types of photographs tell us more about the SS and its values than the life of the inmates.

In this sense, they could be understood as photographic "self-representations." A collection of concentration camp photographs, all taken at Mauthausen and its satellite camps, were displayed at a Mauthausen exhibition in 2005. In the first major exhibition of its kind, the photographs had been retrieved from locations as far afield as France, Austria, Spain, the Czech Republic, and the United States. As the exhibition curators—photographic historian Ilsen About and Stephan Matyus, staff member of the Mauthausen Memorial—have emphasized, however, these images likewise must be decoded with care.

At first glance, SS photographs taken at official occasions and those meant for personal use appear easy to interpret, even unambiguous. But the details contained in the images and the context in which they were taken suggest that they "disguise more than they reveal."[120] The sanitized scenes in the official photographs sought to present the men and women who worked in the camp as a comradely group, a unified entity[121]—which was anything but the truth, as far as their workaday lives were concerned. The photographs of the camp architecture portray a level of efficiency and discipline which, as other sources reveal, never existed. They also depict Heinrich Himmler as a "hands-on" administrator, who inspected the concentration camps, bestowing smiles and handshakes upon the SS staff in recognition of their service in the camps.[122] In these images, two radically different experiences collide: that of the SS, and that of the prisoners. Both experiences are staged, but it is the world of the prisoners that remains entirely invisible to the viewer, since the daily violence suffered by the prisoners is almost wholly absent from the photographs. Even though the experiences are diametrically opposed, they are deeply intertwined.

While these photographs are invaluable resources to historians, accessing them for analysis can present some serious difficulties—and ironies—for scholars. The Landesarchiv Nordrhein-Westfalen granted me the right to use their photographs in the German edition of this book in 2009. In 2014, however, the archive initially refused to extend permission to publish the three images of female SS guards in supposedly private settings (figures 14, 15, and 16). After protracted negotiations, the archive's legal division finally acceded and allowed the reproduction of the three photographs, but only if the faces of the women were obscured. There has been no amendment to the legal statutes pertaining to the use of these images since 2009. Nevertheless, the archive now interprets the pursuant law more strictly and literally, by arguing that these images were private photographs under German law §22 of the Kunsturheberrechtsgesetz (German Art Copyright Act).[123] To the archive, these women now have the legal right to their own images

While I accepted these conditions because these photographs are critical resources for my argument, it is important to note that I do not agree with the archive's amended interpretation of the law. My opinion is based on several considerations. The group images were certainly private photographs, with figures 15 and 16 representing almost the entire staff of female SS guards at a birthday party in Lublin at the German House (Deutsches Haus) and figure 14 showing a three guards standing in front of their barracks during their leisure time. Yet these snapshots were taken in the very specific professional and political contexts of concentration camps in Nazi-occupied Poland. Furthermore, the images represent what is referred to as "*Personen der Zeitgeschichte*" or contemporary historical figures. From an everyday historical perspective, it is important to acknowledge the facial expressions of happiness and wellbeing of the guards enjoying their free time because it juxtaposes the violent nature of their work and the surrounding misery of the prisoners. More generally, the refusal to reproduce and thus show these pictures to a larger audience is a great concern and handicap for historians employing images in their studies. Obscuring the faces of individuals represents a logical fallacy in my opinion. These images are, first and foremost, already publicly available in my work. I would thus invite the reader to refer to the German edition of this book with the unedited versions of the photos.

In this study, I drew primarily on photographs from the Ravensbrück Memorial and photographs given to the Düsseldorf regional court by former guards. These materials are not intended to illustrate or serve as "proof" for a historical reconstruction. Instead, they will be closely analyzed for what they can reveal about their cultural and historical context. In so doing, I do not strive for coherence, but rather aim to uncover the many layers of meaning, and even the contradictions, they reveal.

These contradictions are central to the analysis, and serve as an expression of the manifold histories that underpin the broader narrative accounts. For all my sources, I do not strive primarily for coherence. Instead, I seek to uncover the many layers of meaning, and even the contradictions, the different types of sources reveal. These ambivalences are central to the analysis, and serve as an expression of the manifold histories that underpin the broader narrative accounts.

2

The Majdanek Concentration and Death Camp

An Overview

On June 22, 1941, Germany invaded the Soviet Union. Only two days before Operation Barbarossa—the German code name for the invasion—began, Heinrich Himmler paid a visit to Lublin. On June 20, 1941, Himmler ordered the establishment of a new concentration camp in Lublin. With respect to both its genesis and function, the Lublin camp would be something of an oddity within the concentration camp system. The camp, nicknamed "Majdanek" or "Little Majdan" by its inmates (after the district of Majdan Tatarski in the city of Lublin), fulfilled a variety of functions during its operation. Between 1941 and 1944, it served as a prisoner of war camp for Soviet soldiers; as a labor camp mainly for Jewish, but also for Polish prisoners; as a hostage and internment camp for the Polish and Soviet civilian population (primarily the rural population); and, finally, as a concentration camp for political prisoners, most of whom were Polish. In fall 1942, a separate women's camp was established within the men's camp. At times, Jewish children were also held in Majdanek. Most of these children were systematically murdered in the camp, as from the summer of 1942 through the fall of 1943 Majdanek served as an extermination camp for Jews from all of Europe. As this chapter will briefly outline, the camp's history is also closely linked with the policy of occupation and annihilation in occupied Poland, as well as with the course of the war on the Eastern Front.

The Lublin District: A Racial-Political Testing Ground

The campaign against Poland began with the German invasion on September 1, 1939, and ended when the last Polish troops capitulated just over a month later, on October 5. In accordance with the German-Soviet pact signed on August 28, 1939, the territory of Poland was partitioned, with the western portions assigned to Germany, and the eastern ones to the Soviet Union. The western provinces of German-occupied Poland were subsequently incorporated directly into the Reich.[1] On September 25, 1939, the former Polish voivodeships of Lublin, Kielce, and Warsaw were, by order of the Führer, placed under German military authority and became the Generalgouvernement (General Government). The Generalgouvernement initially encompassed a territory of approximately 95,000 square kilometers. It was divided into four districts: Warsaw, Radom, Lublin, and Krakow—with Krakow serving as the seat of the Generalgouvernement's administrative headquarters. In July 1941, after the addition of Galicia as the fifth district, the Generalgouvernement encompassed approximately 145,000 square kilometers. By 1942, it had a population of approximately 17.7 million.[2]

As the Polish historian Bogdan Musial has outlined in his study, the German occupation in the Generalgouvernement consisted of the Wehrmacht, a civilian authority, as well as the SS and police apparatus. The Generalgouvernement administration was strictly German in composition, and was responsible for the cultural subjugation of Poland as enacted through educational and cultural policies, as well as the economic exploitation and plundering of Jews and Poles; from 1939 to late 1941, it also administered the anti-Jewish policies, largely on its own authority.[3] In the scholarly literature, the Generalgouvernement administration is generally called the "civilian administration," a term that I have adopted for the purpose of this study. Strictly speaking, however, it was a civilian occupation authority. All four organizations carried out the German occupation policy, with the SS and police as the main executive agents.

Hans Frank, whom Hitler had appointed governor-general (Generalgouverneur) of occupied Poland, headed the civilian administration.[4] Within the Generalgouvernement, each district was managed by a civilian district governor, who presided over a series of municipal and rural subdistricts (Kreis- and Stadthauptmannschaften).[5] Capitalizing on the war and the occupation of Poland, Reichsführer SS Heinrich Himmler continued to assert his administrative independence by expanding the SS and police apparatus. Under the leadership of SS Obergruppenführer Friedrich Wilhelm Krüger,[6] who had been appointed by Himmler, the SS and police apparatus assumed a central, terrorizing role in the administration of the Generalgouvernement.[7]

From the beginning of the occupation, the Lublin district was accorded a leading role, both administratively and symbolically, in the implementation of anti-Jewish and racial policies within the Generalgouvernement.[8] For the German occupation

FIGURE 1. Nazi-annexed territories and the General Government, late 1941

authorities, who found themselves presiding over a territory in which the percentage of Jews within the population was fifty times higher than in the Reich, the "Jewish question" took on an entirely new dimension. The total number of Jews in the borders of the German Reich in 1933 was less than 500,000. Due to Nazi persecution, suicide and forced emigration, by late 1939 this figure had dropped to approximately 190,000 Jews within the Reich. In 1933, therefore, the Jewish population represented less than 1 percent of Germany's total population. By late 1939, Jews made up no more than 0.28 percent of an estimated population of 68 million Reich citizens.[9]

At various points in time, the Nazi leadership espoused a variety of different plans and ideas as to how to "handle" this "problem."[10] In the early weeks of the occupation, the SS leadership was already envisioning that a "Jewish reservation" holding five million people would be established in the Lublin district. From fall 1939 to summer 1940, the occupation authorities pursued a "Jewish policy" governed largely by ideological—that is, "racial-political"—objectives. In practice, this entailed the "removal" of the Jewish population from the territory of the German Reich, and its "resettlement" in the Lublin district. From the very start of the occupation, therefore, the Lublin district was something of a racial-political testing ground.[11] Furthermore, the district served as an "intake area" for Poles and Jews who had been deported from "annexed" territories.[12] Between summer 1940 and winter 1941, isolation, ghettoization, expropriation, and forced labor were the central elements within a systematic policy of exploitation and plunder.[13] Until 1941, however, the ghettoization of the Jewish population in the Generalgouvernement was viewed as only a temporary solution, after which the Jews would be deported to a reservation in the swamps of Soviet Belarus.[14]

The war against the Soviet Union, then, had a decisive impact—in terms of both military strategy and racial policy—on the status of the Generalgouvernement within the areas under National Socialist control. Until June 22, 1941, the General Government was situated on the eastern periphery of the Reich. By summer 1941, this region, which had previously been accorded little economic or political significance, was suddenly located in a military corridor, central to the transport of reinforcements and supplies to the front.[15] Immediately upon relocation of the border, the Generalgouvernement became of decisive relevance to Himmler's German resettlement plans.

The invasion of the Soviet Union, which was an initial success, spurred the Nazi leadership to launch a comprehensive and radical Volkstumspolitik: a racial settlement and population policy for Eastern Europe. Dubbed the General Plan East, this policy called for an "authentic" German population to settle Poland, the Baltic region, the Crimea, and parts of the occupied Soviet Union as a buffer zone against the Soviet Union itself.[16] The plan called for 20 million Poles to be removed from the Generalgouvernement and replaced by ethnic Germans from throughout Eastern Europe.[17] From the very beginning, Hitler's policy aimed to incorporate ethnic Germans (Volksdeutsche) living outside German borders into the German Reich. This goal was ideologically paired with the acquisition of a vast new empire of "living space" (Lebensraum) in eastern Europe. With the initial success of Operation Barbarossa, the district of Lublin and, most especially the capital city of Lublin itself, took on a new strategic significance within Hitler's plan for a "Lebensraum Ost." Henceforth, this region was regarded not only as a new German settlement area, but also as a "racial barrier" between the Reich and the additional Lebensraum that that would result from forthcoming conquests to the east.[18] These German resettlement plans contributed to the radicalization of anti-Jewish policies and also affected German policies on Poland, and thus had far-reaching consequences for the Generalgouvernement and especially the Lublin district.[19] The reorganization of Poland along *völkisch* or national and ethnic lines went hand in hand with ethnic cleansing policies. Historian Dieter Pohl was the first to note the link between policies affecting the Jewish and non-Jewish Polish population, both of which were targeted by the Nazi resettlement measures: "The continuity of murder in the Generalgouvernement affected Poles as well as Jews. Shootings, ill-treatment, and abuse were a constant under German rule."[20]

In 1941, a number of developments converged, including a catastrophic deterioration in housing, food, and hygiene conditions in the ghettos and forced-labor camps. In addition, the faltering, though not yet abandoned German military offensive on the Eastern Front resulted in a scaling back of the ambitious German resettlement plans. Despite military setbacks that had already become apparent by fall 1941, Himmler instructed SS and Police Leader Odilo Globocnik to proceed with plans for German settlement of the Lublin district. Under his command, the Lublin and Zamość regions were to be Germanized by the end of the war. In order to create Lebensraum for ethnic Germans, the plan called for Poles and Jews to be "removed" from the region. Meanwhile, local conditions were further exacerbated by poor harvests in 1941 and 1942, and by the needs of the Wehrmacht, which now had to feed not only its own soldiers but also hundreds of thousands of Soviet prisoners of war. It was at this same time that the plan to relocate the local Jewish population to Belarus was deemed impossible by Himmler and the SS administration, as well as by military authorities on the Eastern Front. Taken together, these conditions contributed to a dynamic that culminated in the systematic murder of Jews within the district, undertaken with the support of German military and civilian occupation authorities.[21]

The Evolution of the Camp (1941–1944)

On July 17, 1941, Heinrich Himmler appointed Odilo Globocnik, leader of the SS Brigade and SS and Police Leader of Lublin, to the post of "plenipotentiary for the establishment of SS and police bases in the new eastern territories."[22] Just three days later, Himmler paid a visit to the district capital of Lublin, the city for which he had such ambitious plans. During this visit, he instructed Globocnik to establish a concentration camp for "25,000–50,000 prisoners who are to be used in workshops and on construction projects for the SS and police in Lublin."[23] This project, which came to be known as the Heinrich Program, got underway in summer 1941. It called for the construction of a veritable SS city, with barracks for three Armed SS regiments, housing for their families, technical facilities, a military depot, and a large number of industrial work sites.[24] Both the location and timing of the operation were carefully thought out: between 1939 and 1941, the district of Lublin constituted the "borderland" to the Soviet Union. As such, it was well situated to take advantage of the presence of both Soviet prisoners of war and the Jewish civilian population, which would eventually fall under German authority as the Wehrmacht continued its advance onto Soviet soil.

Thus, Majdanek was established to create a reservoir of labor for the planned reconfiguration of the Generalgouvernement,[25] and also as part of Himmler's strategy to expand the police and SS apparatus (as well as his own influence within occupied Poland). Majdanek was officially designated a "prisoner of war camp (KGL) of the Armed SS in Lublin," with the stated intention that it would house captured Soviet soldiers. Majdanek was, however, a prisoner of war camp in name only. This fact is supported by the 1942 recollection of Karl Naumann, head of the central construction office in Lublin.[26] According to Naumann, Majdanek was under the authority of the Inspectorate of Concentration Camps (IKL) and was built and operated along the model of a concentration camp from the very start.[27] For the SS, the advantages of designating Majdanek as a prisoner of war camp were twofold. First, as a "prisoner of war camp" it was more likely the project would be approved by Governor-General Frank.[28] At the same time, the designation would help deflect any future attempt by the civilian authorities to assert exclusive control over the camp's administration vis-à-vis the SS.[29] Finally, questions of funding and the procurement of construction material (in short supply due to the war) also played a role. Because the war against the Soviet Union was so central to the regime's racial ideology, such an endeavor would be accorded a higher priority than other construction projects, making it easier to obtain funding for a prisoner of war camp than a concentration camp.

In the following, I will briefly elaborate on the evolution of the Majdanek concentration camp, which the Polish historian and director of the research center at the State Museum at Majdanek, Tomasz Kranz, divided into five different phases.[30]

First Phase: Construction (October 1941 to mid-1942)

For the Lublin concentration camp, Globocnik chose a site on the eastern edge of the district capital, situated in an open field five kilometers from the center of town, directly adjacent to the road leading from Lublin to Chełm. It is worth noting that this was a rather unusual spot for a concentration camp; while Majdanek was favorably located adjacent to transportation routes, it was (unlike other concentration camps) not "protected" by any natural barriers, such as a forest. On September 1, 1941, the Inspectorate of Concentration Camps (IKL) transferred the first SS men from the Buchenwald Concentration Camp to Majdanek.[31] Although the exact beginning of the construction work is unknown, it is likely that it began in October. Approximately at that same time, the first 2,000 Soviet prisoners of war arrived from the Wehrmacht's Stalag 319 POW camp in Chełm.[32] One month later, the first prisoners who were Reichsdeutsch—or citizens of the German Reich—arrived. The majority of these were political prisoners from Sachsenhausen.

Not long after construction got underway, problems began to arise. Within just a few weeks of their arrival, Soviet POWs were suffering from exhaustion, exacerbated by constant hunger. While Hermann Hackmann, camp compound leader at Majdanek, later recalled a total of 10,000 Soviet POWs,[33] the precise number of Soviet prisoners of war who arrived in Majdanek during the winter of 1941–1942 is unknown. In any event, the SS had made no provisions to house these prisoners. At the start of construction, the camp grounds had just nine barracks. A further twenty-five barracks were planned, but the material to build them had not yet been delivered. Majdanek had housing for just 4,500 people—less than half the number of prisoners of war held in the camp. This situation became even more desperate with arrival of winter, which comes early to this region. The POWs had no protection from the snow and freezing temperatures, and the frozen ground made their construction work more arduous. Malnutrition, a catastrophic lack of sanitation, and outbreaks of epidemics resulted in an extremely high mortality rate.[34]

From that point on, Polish civilian workers and Jewish forced laborers were increasingly put to work on construction projects. Initially, Jewish forced laborers were not housed at the camp, living instead (under desperate conditions) in ghettos and forced-labor camps. Even this influx, however, failed to meet the increased labor requirements. Hence, in mid-December 1941, the SS began to carry out raids in the ghetto and on the streets of Lublin.[35] According to the historian Barbara Schwindt, from fall 1941 to summer 1942, Majdanek served as a labor camp for 5,000 Jews from Lublin and the surrounding area, along with 7,000 Jews from Slovakia, 2,000 Jews from the Protectorate of Bohemia and Moravia, 2,000 Jews from Reich territories, and another 800 Jews from Austria.[36]

In the fall of 1941, the first significant transition in terms of the camp's function took place. Increasingly, it was mainly the labor of Jews, rather than that of Soviet prisoners of war, that was exploited. Schwindt argues that Majdanek was not primarily conceived as a Soviet POW camp, but rather was expressly planned as a work camp for Jews from the very start. According to the 1941 plan, Jewish forced laborers who survived Majdanek were to be deported to occupied areas of the Soviet Union.[37] It is unknown whether the extremely high death rate among Soviet POWs was responsible for this shift, or whether the deployment of Jewish forced laborers at Majdanek was planned from the very start. What is certain is that, as of the summer and fall of 1941, IKL concentration camps had not yet assumed the primary function of a site for the persecution of Jews.[38] As Schwindt emphasizes, Majdanek was, in a sense, without precedent, as it was the first concentration camp in which Jews would eventually be incarcerated en masse.[39]

In addition to building the barracks at the Majdanek main camp, Jewish laborers helped build the subcamp known as the Old Airfield Camp (Alter Flugplatz), located in the vicinity of the camp on Chelmska Street, which included the SS Clothing Works (SS-Bekleidungswerke) as well as a railway connection that led directly to the site. After 1942, this railway connection also served as the incoming station for prisoner transports.[40] Beginning in late 1941 and early 1942, Majdanek also served as a penal camp for the local Polish population. The first transports of Polish civilians—mainly farmers who had been arrested for not delivering the mandatory quota of food and supplies to the occupation forces—arrived in early January 1942. As Tomasz Kranz notes, this group of prisoners represented a large segment of the inmate population, approximately 20 percent of Majdanek's total inmate population between 1941 and 1944. In all, approximately 57,000 farmers from Poland and the Soviet Union were incarcerated at the camp.

Thus, as early as the first half of 1942, Majdanek had several functions: it was a POW camp for Soviet soldiers, a work camp for Jews, and a penal or concentration camp for Polish civilians. By summer 1942, mass detentions of both Jewish and Polish residents of the Lublin district, undertaken as part of a comprehensive program of resettlement and reprisal, had increased the number of inmates to over 10,000.[41] At that same time, as confirmed by many survivors and former SS members, the camp remained very much in a state of construction.[42]

Second Phase: Work and Annihilation Camp (Mid- to Late 1942)

The period from summer 1942 to spring 1943 marked the transition of Majdanek from being primarily a forced-labor camp to being a place of mass annihilation. Ever since the euthanasia programs began in the camps in spring 1941, the concentration camps had been a site of systematic killing.[43] And Majdanek was no exception; sick prisoners and those deemed unable to work had been shot from the start of the camp's existence. However, by spring 1942, it had become apparent that the Heinrich Program—the plan to make Lublin an "SS city" and headquarters for a future colonization of the East—was destined to fail, not least due to the military reversals on the eastern front and the resulting transportation difficulties and shortages of building materials.[44] This realization had a profound impact on the regime's Jewish policies. As already noted above, with the failure of Operation Barbarossa, the Lublin district became the new epicenter of the Final Solution.[45]

According to historical research, in summer 1942 Himmler issued a verbal order for construction of a separate women's camp within the men's camp at Majdanek. At the same time, the munitions and armaments factories went into operation there.[46] Construction of the women's camp coincided with the initial implementation of the Final Solution in the Generalgouvernement. On October 1, 1942, the first group of 136 women, who had been arrested during a "resettlement action" in the Wieniawa district of Lublin, arrived at Majdanek.[47] The first *Aufseherinnen* arrived about two weeks later. Between mid-October 1942 and mid-April 1944, when the women's camp was closed during the evacuation of Majdanek, a total of twenty-eight female guards worked at the camp. To remedy a labor shortage, Odilo Globocnik reached an agreement with Camp Commandant Max Koegel that the female prisoners would work at the clothing factory, located within the Airfield camp, which belonged to the German Equipment Works (Deutsche Ausrüstungswerke; DAW). The female prisoners were under the authority of the Majdanek camp administration, and were supervised during their work by female SS guards.

As Schwindt notes, the relocation of the German Equipment Works facility to the Majdanek concentration camp, and the plan to establish the new women's camp at the Airfield camp illustrate the close connection between Majdanek and Globocnik's forced-labor camps.[48] However, this forced labor was also closely linked to the murder of Jewish inmates. Beginning in March 1942, the factory at the Old Airfield Camp shifted from production to processing—namely, the sorting, disinfecting, and preparing for shipping of the clothing that had belonged to Jewish men, women, and children killed at the Operation Reinhardt extermination centers.[49] Until spring 1943, the majority of *Aufseherinnen* were charged with overseeing female inmates at the SS Clothing Works.[50] After establishment of the women's camp at Field V in Majdanek, the female guards worked mainly within the concentration camp itself.

Third Phase: Mass Extermination (1943)

The third phase of the camp was characterized by the systematic mass murder of Jewish inmates. By fall 1941, the annihilation of Jews in the Generalgouvernement was already in the planning stages. This was a "special program" that was initiated prior to, and independently of, the decision to kill all European Jews (a decision that was later reached in Berlin).[51] However, historians disagree on whether the initial policy applied to the Lublin district alone, or to the Generalgouvernement as a whole.[52] In any case, while it is certain that the transition from locally organized to state-sponsored mass murder was implemented at the Wannsee Conference on January 20, 1942,[53] the precise timing and sequence of decisions is a matter of heated historical and political debate and exceeds the scope of this study.[54] After the Wannsee Conference, however, the German occupation in the Generalgouvernement shifted its focus to laying the organizational groundwork necessary for implementing the Final Solution.

SS and Police Leader Odilo Globocnik was assigned to oversee the industrial organization designed to facilitate the mass murder of the Jews. The Bełzec extermination camp went into operation in the Lublin district on March 16, 1942—the date that is generally recognized as the beginning of the genocide of European Jews in the Generalgouvernement.[55] The deportation from Galicia to Bełzec also began on that date, and within just a matter of days, nearly 18,000 Jews had already been killed.[56] Less than two months later, Sobibor—the second extermination camp—went into operation. In summer 1942, the construction of concrete gas chambers began at Majdanek; they were completed in October 1942.[57] It is likely that the first gassings at Majdanek took place in summer 1942. The Lublin district, then, which was home to two death camps—Bełzec and Sobibor[58]—as well as the Majdanek Concentration and Extermination Camp, played a central role in the murder of the European Jews. From his base in the district capital, Globocnik coordinated the "Final Solution," which was given the name "Operation Reinhardt" in the Generalgouvernement.[59]

From spring to fall 1943, Majdanek was used both as an extermination camp and a labor camp for Polish prisoners. On March 12, 1943, Oswald Pohl instructed the SS Chief Economic and Administrative Office (WVHA) to found the "Ostindustrie GmbH"—or "Osti"—corporation, which was responsible for converting the existing Jewish forced-labor camps in the Lublin district into concentration camps. These concentration camps would later be used for the processing and exploitation of Jewish property.[60] In summer 1943, about 10,000 people from the Zamość area arrived at Majdanek, the majority of them from "resettled" rural populations. At this time, Jews constituted the largest group of prisoners. Some 45,000 Jews were sent to Majdanek, including 16,000 from the Warsaw ghetto, 5,000 from ghettos in the Lublin district, 1,000 from the Netherlands and Auschwitz, 11,000 from the Białystok ghetto, and 12,000 prisoners from forced-labor camps in Lublin. Most of these prisoners were either killed in the gas chambers or shot elsewhere.[61] In light of the reversals at the front, Pohl hoped to make greater use of the Jewish prisoners of Majdanek as a source of labor, but these efforts were to no avail. In fall 1943, after the revolts in Treblinka on August 2 and Sobibor on October 14, 1943, the Nazi leadership made the decision to kill all the Jews in Majdanek.[62] On November 3–4, the remaining Jewish forced laborers in the Lublin district were killed in a massacre called "Operation Harvest Festival" (Aktion Erntefest) at Majdanek; after that date, very few Jewish prisoners remained in the camp.[63]

The extent to which the Majdanek camp was included in Operation Reinhardt is also a matter of dispute among researchers. Dieter Pohl argues that Majdanek served as a "runoff camp" for the overburdened camps of Operation Reinhardt.[64] By contrast, Kranz argues that there is no evidence that Majdanek was systematically incorporated at all into Operation Reinhardt during its early phase.[65] Schwindt, in turn, says that Globocnik played a decisive role in increasing Majdanek's level of involvement in the Final Solution.[66] Finally, Pohl views Lublin as a "hub" of the genocide and argues that by 1943, at least a million Jews had been killed in the Lublin district.[67]

This question cannot be resolved in this study, but it is nevertheless crucial to underline the multifunctional character of Majdanek. In addition to its role as an extermination camp, Majdanek continued to function as a prisoner of war camp for Soviet soldiers and a detention camp for the rural Polish population. Beginning in January 1943, Majdanek also began to detain Poles active in the resistance, who arrived at the camp from Gestapo prisons in the Lublin district, as well as from prisons in Warsaw and Radom. From then on, Majdanek increasingly served as a concentration camp for political prisoners. By December 1943, more than 40,000 political prisoners had been transferred to Majdanek.[68] As part of the battle against the partisan resistance, Himmler ordered the Einsatzgruppen in Belarus, Russia, and the Ukraine to detain civilians, including women and children, and deport them to Auschwitz and Majdanek. Between February 1943 and March 1944, approximately 20,000 people—mainly women and children—were deported from occupied areas of the Soviet Union and sent to Majdanek.

Fourth Phase: Camp for the Sick and Dying, and Site of Execution (Winter 1943–44 to March 1944)

Beginning in December 1943, Majdanek started to serve as a camp for the dying and as a place for killing sick prisoners brought there from other concentration camps. That same month, the Reich Security Main Office (RSHA) decided to establish an infirmary there for seriously ill prisoners from other camps. About 8,000 prisoners—the majority of whom were exhausted and emaciated forced laborers from the munitions factories of the Dachau, Dora, Flossenbürg, Gross-Rosen, and Neuengamme camps—were sent to Majdanek to make room for prisoners deemed fit to work.[69] It was only at this point that Western Europeans first constituted a substantial portion of the camp's prisoners. Majdanek additionally served as an execution site for Polish civilians in what were called "reprisal operations" for "partisan attacks." Although gassings and the systematic murder of Jews had by then been discontinued in Majdanek, seriously ill prisoners and those classified as unable to work continued to be killed there at irregular intervals.[70]

Fifth Phase: Evacuation (April to July 1944)

As the Red Army continued its advance and the frontline moved ever closer—by mid-March 1944 the front was just 150 kilometers east of Lublin—evacuations began in the Lublin district. According to a figure provided by the Polish resistance movement, Majdanek by this time housed 12,327 prisoners.[71] The evacuation began on April 1 with the dissolution of the women's camp.[72] Jewish women were sent to Auschwitz and Płaszów, while Polish women were sent to Ravensbrück. The eighteen female guards active at Majdanek at that time were transferred to Auschwitz and Płaszów. Despite the evacuation, the plan of the WVHA was to resume operations in Majdanek as soon as the situation on the Eastern Front improved. As Richard Glücks, Inspector of Concentration Camps, wrote to the commandants of Auschwitz and Majdanek:

> The guards will remain at the Auschwitz II concentration camp only for the duration of the evacuation of the Lublin concentration camp. After the Lublin camp is reestablished, they will return there.[73]

The male prisoners were evacuated to Auschwitz, Bergen-Belsen, Gross Rosen, Natzweiler, and Płaszów.

Due to the subsequent interruption of the Soviet advance, however, the liquidation of Majdanek was not complete until the summer of 1944.[74] In early May of that year, there were still 1,700 prisoners at the camp. The majority of these remaining prisoners were the sick and weak, or they were Soviet POWs. On July 22, the final evacuation transport, carrying more than 1,000 prisoners, left the camp. Just one day later, on July 23, 1944, the Red Army liberated Majdanek.[75]

The Inner Organization of Majdanek

Although Majdanek was not officially renamed Concentration Camp Lublin until February 16, 1943, it was operated as a concentration camp from the beginning, and was first under the overall direction of the Inspectorate of Concentration Camps (IFK) and later, the WVHA's Office Group D. In accordance with the system devised by Theodor Eicke, which remained broadly in effect until 1945, Majdanek was structured into five administrative departments: the Headquarters (Department I), the Political Department (Department II), the Camp Compound (Department III), the Administration (Department IV), and the Chief Camp Physician (Department V). The following discussion will offer a brief description of the camp departments.

In 1933, in his capacity as *Reichsführer SS*, Heinrich Himmler had named Obergruppenführer Theodor Eicke commandant of Dachau, and had charged him with the task of reorganizing the camp. Immediately following the Nazi seizure of power, the Sturmabteilung, or SA—the paramilitary wing of the Nazi party—launched a wave of public violence against political opponents. Beginning in February 1933, the SA also established provisional detention and torture centers throughout Germany, some of which were subordinated to the SA, others to the Schutzstaffel, or SS.[76] Eicke separated the camp administration (the headquarters) from the guard unit. The former was responsible for guarding prisoners within the camp compound, while the latter was responsible for external security of the camp complex. Eicke also established the individual camp departments and drafted new camp regulations (the *Lagerordnung*) that went into effect on October 1, 1933.[77] This reorganization of Dachau would have far-reaching effects for the entire Nazi concentration camp system. In May 1934, Himmler directed Eicke to apply the organizational system he had established at Dachau to all of the concentration camps within Germany. Consequently, the SA camps were either dissolved or reorganized according to Eicke's model.

Beginning in summer 1934, the Dachau camp structure was introduced in all concentration camps and remained in effect, with only minor changes, until the war's end. The proliferation of what Martin Broszat has called the "Dachau model"[78] began with the SS takeover and regularization of the concentration camps. For Himmler, this model brought with it a systematization of terror, a standardization of force and

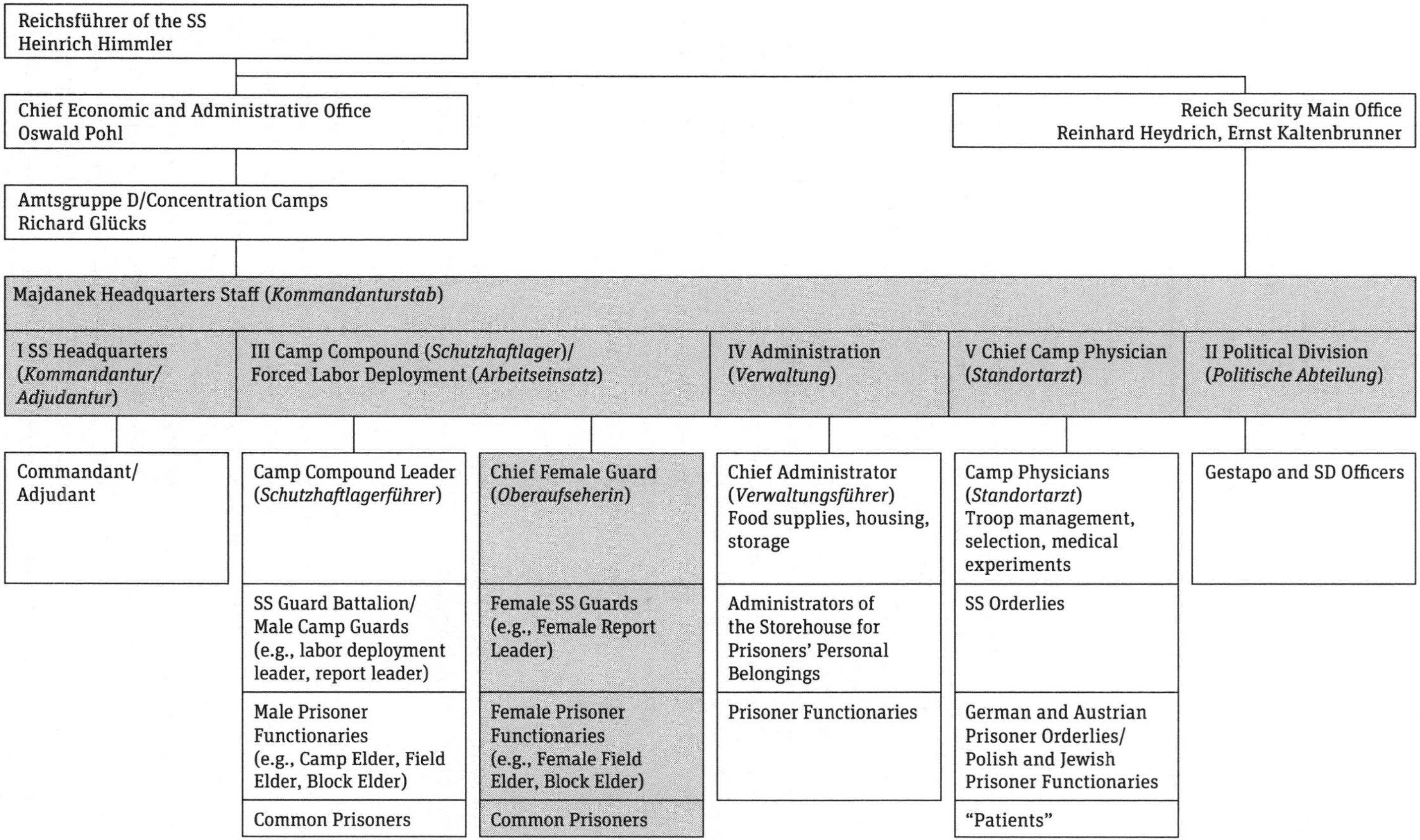

Reichsführer of the SS
Heinrich Himmler

Chief Economic and Administrative Office
Oswald Pohl

Reich Security Main Office
Reinhard Heydrich, Ernst Kaltenbrunner

Amtsgruppe D/Concentration Camps
Richard Glücks

Majdanek Headquarters Staff (*Kommandanturstab*)

I SS Headquarters (*Kommandantur/ Adjudantur*)

III Camp Compound (*Schutzhaftlager*)/
Forced Labor Deployment (*Arbeitseinsatz*)

IV Administration (*Verwaltung*)

V Chief Camp Physician (*Standortarzt*)

II Political Division (*Politische Abteilung*)

Commandant/
Adjudant

Camp Compound Leader (*Schutzhaftlagerführer*)

SS Guard Battalion/
Male Camp Guards
(e.g., labor deployment leader, report leader)

Male Prisoner Functionaries
(e.g., Camp Elder, Field Elder, Block Elder)

Common Prisoners

Chief Female Guard (*Oberaufseherin*)

Female SS Guards
(e.g., Female Report Leader)

Female Prisoner Functionaries
(e.g., Female Field Elder, Block Elder)

Common Prisoners

Chief Administrator (*Verwaltungsführer*)
Food supplies, housing, storage

Administrators of the Storehouse for Prisoners' Personal Belongings

Prisoner Functionaries

Camp Physicians (*Standortarzt*)
Troop management, selection, medical experiments

SS Orderlies

German and Austrian Prisoner Orderlies/
Polish and Jewish Prisoner Functionaries

"Patients"

Gestapo and SD Officers

Elissa Mailänder, drawn by Ralph Gabriel

FIGURE 2. Organizational chart of SS personnel for Concentration and Extermination Camp Majdanek

violence that made it both more predictable and less amenable to outside influence and interference.[79] After SA head Ernst Röhm was killed on July 1, 1934, Eicke was named Inspector of Concentration Camps and Leader of the SS Guard Units on July 4. As a result, all of the detention centers that were operated as concentration camps were subordinated to the Inspectorate of Concentration Camps, which was headquartered in Oranienburg.[80] In 1942, the IKL was incorporated into the newly established SS Chief Economic and Administrative Office (WVHA) as Office Group D (*Amtsgruppe D*).[81]

Headquarters (Department I)

As was the case at all concentration camps, a commandant, a higher-level SS officer, headed Majdanek. Over the course of its operation, Majdanek had five commandants.[82] The first was the former commandant of Buchenwald, Karl Otto Koch, who was appointed by Himmler in summer 1941 and finally took office in January 1942.[83] Koch, however, was dismissed on August 1, 1942, amid embezzlement charges. His replacement, the commandant of Ravensbrück, SS-Obersturmbannführer Max Koegel, was appointed on August 20. It was Koegel who established the women's camp at Majdanek; once the mission was accomplished, he was recalled in November 1942. The third commandant, SS-Hauptsturmführer Hermann Florstedt, arrived at Majdanek from Buchenwald; after nine months he, too, was replaced following an accusation of corruption.[84] His replacement was Martin Weiss, former commandant of Neuengamme, Arbeitsdorf, and Dachau, who headed Majdanek from November 1943 to mid-April 1944.[85] The last commandant of Majdanek, Arthur Liebehenschel, headed the camp until the SS abandoned it on July 22, 1944, the day before its liberation by the Red Army.[86]

The Commandant's office, run by the camp commandant and his adjutant, served as the camp's headquarters. It oversaw the administration of the entire camp, including bookkeeping, maintenance of the camp registry, and official correspondence. The office also served as personnel department and was responsible for the SS troops. As head of the camp, the commandant was charged with acting as "ultimate authority in all official matters, including both personnel and substantive matters."[87] The commandant had disciplinary authority over the entire camp, including not only the inmates of the camp compound but also all SS personnel. He could order transfers and had the authority to award promotions up to the rank of *SS-Scharführer.* The commandant was also responsible for ensuring that all directives and regulations of the IKL (and, from 1942 on, the WVHA) were carried out in the camp. To aid in executing this duty, concentration camp commandants were required to attend "Führer conferences" in Oranienburg at regular intervals.[88] Within the camp itself, the commandant and his adjutant supervised the overall operations, coordinated personnel, and issued orders. Some of these orders—including personnel and administrative orders, which had to do with daily camp operations as well as staff and disciplinary matters—were issued in writing. Orders to kill, on the other hand, were issued verbally.[89]

Political Department (Department II)

The political department was the first encountered by newly arrived prisoners.[90] Its main function was to register all new arrivals and maintain and update prisoner records. SS officers of the identification service (Erkennungsdienst), usually members of the Gestapo or the Criminal Police, took scrupulous care to assign prisoner categories to the new arrivals and to establish a file on each prisoner, containing items such as identification photographs, transcripts of interrogations, medical records, and so forth. This section of the camp was responsible for maintaining records on prisoners, from their arrival at the camp to their transfer to another camp or their death. The political department had its own registry office, responsible for informing families of a prisoner's death—although this was generally done only in the case of inmates who had been Reich citizens. Charged with camp security, the SS officers of the political department conducted criminal interrogations, at times at the behest of outside police and administrative entities. In certain matters, the political department operated independently of the camp headquarters and its directives, since the department was under the direct authority of the Gestapo and (from September 1939) the Reich Security Main Office (RSHA) in Berlin.[91]

Camp Compound (Department III)

The first camp compound leader (*Erster Schutzhaftlagerführer*) was responsible for the organization of the actual prisoners' camp, and also stood in for the commandant in his absence. SS-Hauptsturmführer Herrmann Hackmann, formerly Koch's adjutant at Buchenwald, held this post in Majdanek from fall 1941 to September 1942. Between September 1942 and February 1943, SS-Hauptscharführer Westel Wimmer held the position. Wimmer's successor was SS-Obersturmführer Anton Thumann, who served at Majdanek until May 1944. SS-Oberscharführer Ernst Kostial was the last to hold the position, from April to July 1944.[92]

Several SS officers, who were designated as camp compound leaders or "acting camp leaders,"[93] supported the first camp compound leader in his work. The latter was responsible for coordinating all SS troops that guarded prisoners in the camp compound, which was a major responsibility as the prisoner camp was Majdanek's largest department. The first camp compound leader was also in charge of all report leaders (*Rapportführer*), squad leaders (*Kommandoführer)* and block leaders (*Block-führer*), who regulated and dictated the day-to-day lives of the prisoners. Another of the central duties of the first camp compound leader and, by association, the SS troops under his command, was to monitor the camp's statistics. For this purpose, all prisoners were counted at least twice a day in a prisoner roll call. The figures were then sent by telex from the camp headquarters to the central administration in Oranienburg.

Chief Guard Else Ehrich, for instance, was in charge of the female guard staff and the female prisoners.[94] She reported the roll-call numbers to the camp headquarters, and was responsible for ensuring that the *Aufseherinnen* carried out their duties. In that sense, the chief guard (*Oberaufseherin*) acted as a liaison between headquarters and the female guards. In postwar interrogations, some of the guards referred to her as the *Schutzhaftlagerführerin*—the "[female] leader of the camp compound."[95] As laid down in the Ravensbrück Service Regulations, which applied to all women's camps, the *Oberaufseherin* reported to the camp compound leader. As his "deputy," she was to act in a "supportive capacity" and serve "in an advisory capacity in all matters involving women."[96] Ehrich and the next-highest ranking guard, Report Leader Hermine Braunsteiner, coordinated daily and work schedules from an office within the women's camp.[97] It was also at this office where Ehrich and Braunsteiner received reports from their colleagues regarding any incidents, accidents, illnesses, and deaths.

Prisoner-Functionaries

The SS delegated an immense variety of guarding, monitoring, and administrative tasks to prisoner-functionaries.[98] These prisoner-functionaries were necessary because there were far too few SS troops at Majdanek to sufficiently monitor the tens of thousands of prisoners held in the men's camp. In the women's camp, this situation was even more acute. Prisoner-functionaries were appointed and assigned duties by the SS. They worked in nearly every section of the camp, including the infirmary, the laundry, the clerk's office, the warehouse where the personal effects of incoming prisoners were stored, and other areas. Unlike at other concentration camps, where block leaders were generally SS guards, at Majdanek, German political prisoners acted as block leaders in the women's camp.[99] While the use of prisoner-functionaries did help limit costs and meet staffing requirements, it was also part of a deliberate strategy of domination and control, carried out along the principle of "divide and conquer."

The prisoner-functionaries constituted both the lowest level of a multitiered system of surveillance and control, and the pinnacle of the prisoner hierarchy (see figure 2). Though the SS referred to this system of control as a form of "self-governance," this was clearly a misnomer, as the prisoner-functionaries were required to act as deputies of the SS within the ranks of prisoners.[100]

In Majdanek the SS installed "Reich German" prisoners in the highest functionary posts, which generally meant they led detachments or guarded a block. Poles and Jews were also employed in certain administrative tasks, as prisoner-orderlies, and as prisoner-physicians. To be appointed to these latter posts required that the prisoner-functionary have a particular skill—knowledge of German and Eastern European languages, knowledge of an important manual craft, or bureaucratic, organizational, medical, or administrative skills. Finally, personal factors ranging from friendships and sympathies to favoritism and cronyism also played a role in the assignment of these posts.[101]

Among the German and Austrian prisoner-functionaries, "racial affiliation" alone determined the supremacy of each within the *Häftlingszwangsgesellschaft*—the community of prisoners that was, in reality, a society held together by force. Settling on a term that adequately depicts this prisoners' community, marked as it was by tensions both among and within the various inmate categories, is no simple task. Historians have offered different terms to describe this community. Klaus Drobisch and Günther Wieland employ the term "camp community" (*Lagergemeinschaft*),[102] while Eugen Kogon—himself a survivor of the Nazi concentration camp system—refers to the "prisoner community" (*Häftlingsgemeinschaft*).[103] H. G. Adler employs the term "forced community" (*Zwangsgemeinschaft*).[104] Meanwhile, Falk Pingel chose the term "prisoner collectivity" (*Häftlingsgesamtheit*).[105] This book's use of the term *Häftlingszwangsgesellschaft*[106]—or "forced prisoner society"—seeks to underscore the coercive nature of the community that existed among the prisoners, while at the same time emphasizing that social relationships and bonds did exist between and among the inmates, even under conditions of extremity.[107]

To date, there has been no study specific to the German and Austrian inmates at Majdanek as a separate prisoner category, particularly vis-à-vis the categories of inmates situated beneath them in the prisoner hierarchy.

Administration (Department IV)

The fourth department was responsible for housing, food, and clothing for both prisoners and SS personnel. All of the camp's workshops and production sites were also under its authority, including mechanical and equipment facilities, the food storehouse, and the *Effektenkammer*—the storehouse for clothes, valuables, and personal belongings that had been taken from the prisoners. At Majdanek, the *Effektenkammer* was particularly large, both because Majdanek was as an extermination camp, and because it was used as a temporary storage site for the shoes and clothing of persons who had been killed in other Operation Reinhardt death camps.[108] In summer 1941, Himmler ordered the establishment of the SS Clothing Works (*SS-Bekleidungswerke*) on the premises of the former Lublin aircraft factory. In this facility, prisoners sorted and disinfected the property that had belonged to the Jews who had been killed—property which was then shipped to the Reich.

Chief Physician (Department V)

The fifth department called Chief Camp Physician (*Standortarzt)* encompassed all medical personnel—SS doctors and SS orderlies, as well as nurses and pharmacists. A number of physicians were employed at Majdanek, among them Heinrich Schmidt (April 1942–fall 1943), Franz von Bodmann (February–April 1943), Heinrich Rindfleisch (March 1943–July 1944), and Max Blanke (April–July 1944).[109] Medical care for SS troops was handled separately from that of the prisoners. However, the term "medical care" cannot in good faith be used in the case of the prisoners. Rather, SS physicians in Nazi concentration camps often exploited conditions at the camps to carry out their own medical research, which involved conducting experiments on prisoners without regard for ethical or moral considerations.[110]

Guards

In his new camp regulations issued in 1934, Theodor Eicke had separated the camp administration (the camp commandant's office) from the guard battalion, which was known as the SS Totenkopfsturmbann—the SS Death's Head Battalion.[111] This SS unit was responsible for guarding the perimeter of the concentration camps, but had no official permission to enter the prisoners' camps (the camp compound). There were between 900 and 1,200 of these SS troops stationed at Majdanek, most of whom were "ethnic Germans" from Lithuania, the Ukraine, Romania, and Croatia.[112] This guard unit was not formally attached to the camp headquarters. Rather, it reported to its own superior officer, an *SS-Standartenführer*, or colonel. As the senior SS officer on site, however, the camp commandant had final disciplinary authority over all SS guards, as well as authority over all service-related issues that concerned the camp. As the historian Günter Morsch has noted, this dual structure of subordination was characteristic of the Third Reich. The leaders of these guard units took part in the commandants' staff meetings, while some military exercises and ideological training sessions were also conducted jointly.[113] Officially, however, the SS Death's Head unit was not permitted to enter the camp compound. Rather, the unit was responsible for guarding the camp's perimeter and accompanying prisoner detachments while on labor assignments outside the camp. Guard towers; a tall, high-voltage barbed-wire fence; and guard patrols secured the site.

Prisoners' Living Conditions

When they arrived at Majdanek, prisoners received colored, triangular pieces of cloth called "chevrons" (*Winkel*) that could be worn in combination to indicate the prisoner's category as designated by the political department. This system of inmate classification was a technique developed by the SS to aid in prisoner surveillance and control. This classification system was also at least nominally successful in achieving an additional objective—that is, to prevent the formation of alliances among prisoners. In April 1942, a system of prisoner numbering was also introduced in Majdanek. A total of 20,000 numbers were assigned in sequence, with new arrivals receiving the numbers previously assigned to their deceased predecessors. The women's camp had a similar numbering system.[114]

The camp consisted of a total of five rectangular fields (*Felder*), each about six hectares in size.[115] Twenty-two barracks stood on each field in two opposite rows. The open space in between was used as a roll-call ground. Here, prisoners assembled twice a day to be counted. It was also here that public punishments were meted out. In addition to the routine daily brutality of the SS troops, the chaotic administration of the camp also had a devastating impact on the day-to-day lives of the prisoners held there. Living conditions in Majdanek were extremely harsh. To borrow the words of a Jewish survivor who described conditions at Majdanek in Eberhard Fechner's documentary:

> There is no one on this earth whose language is adequate to describe what Majdanek was. It was—it is—impossible. Just imagine, one day we heard that some SS troops were at Majdanek looking for people—women—to go to Auschwitz. And we knew that Auschwitz was no bed and breakfast. We knew Auschwitz was a bad place. But we didn't care; we just wanted to get out of where we were.[116]

From its earliest weeks, Majdanek suffered from a water shortage, which contributed to frequent epidemics and outbreaks of disease among the prisoners. According to Wolfgang Scheffler, while the original plan had called for connecting Majdanek to Lublin's municipal water supply, the civilian administration of Lublin had rejected the proposal, arguing that the city could not afford to surrender such a large share of its water supply.[117] Consequently, the camp at Majdanek relied on a single well for all of its drinking water. Further compounding this issue was the well's position immediately adjacent to the latrines and the kitchen. In its initial phase, the women's camp had no latrines. Instead, the female prisoners were forced to relieve themselves in trenches that had been dug behind the barracks.[118] It was not until summer 1943 that a barrack at the end of each field was set up to serve as a washing facility and latrine. Depending on the camp's occupancy, anywhere between 1,000 and 6,000 women shared the use of these facilities at any given time.

In the evenings after curfew, the women were not allowed to leave their barracks. Each barrack had only a single bucket, in which hundreds of inmates were forced to relieve themselves. Given that the meals consisted largely of water (at midday and in the evening, the women typically received turnip or nettle soup, while the morning's meager rations consisted of dandelion coffee), sanitary conditions within the barracks were beyond deplorable. Many of the women, even those not suffering from typhoid, were so weak that it was virtually impossible for them to climb down from the triple-deck bunks and make it to the bucket in time.

Thus, it was not long before the prisoners' barracks became filthy, lice-infested breeding grounds for disease and epidemics. Not surprisingly, the constant fear of disease had the effect of discouraging interaction among the prisoners. Poorly constructed barracks along with a lack of furnishings and other amenities added to the risk of disease.[119] Because each barrack was equipped with only one stove, the women subsisted in near-freezing winter temperatures. By contrast, the wooden frame barracks trapped the summer heat, leaving the women to swelter.

Within just a few months of the camp's establishment, it was clear the high death rate was interfering with the goal of exploiting the prisoners' labor. In March 1942, the WVHA launched its first attempt to improve the disastrous conditions in the concentration camp. In August 1942, the Chief Economic and Administrative Office issued a directive to decrease the mortality.[120] However, because the SS camp administration still retained responsibility for obtaining and distributing food and medications to the inmates, there was essentially no change at Majdanek after this edict. The Majdanek administration made little to no effort to improve food and living conditions for the prisoners, nor did it attempt to interfere with the brutal treatment meted out by the SS guards. Instead, the camp administration employed various ruses to conceal the high mortality rate. For example, in camp log books, the names of deceased inmates would be replaced with those of incoming prisoners whose names had not yet been officially registered. These and other loopholes for manipulating prisoner statistics were common throughout the concentration camp system.

In fall 1942, the WVHA again emphasized its intention to exploit Jewish prisoners for labor. By that time, however, the Jewish prisoners in Majdanek had either died from starvation and disease, or had been shot. Between April and October 1943, various German companies and the WVHA in Oranienburg again attempted to exert influence over camp personnel, and strengthen ties between Majdanek's forced-labor resources and the German armaments industry by expanding the "Osti" factory.[121] However, it was not long before this effort to build an SS economic empire on a foundation of Jewish forced labor faltered.

Catastrophic living conditions and a resultant high mortality rate, however, were not only a result of poor facilities, misadministration on the part of the WVHA, and negligence on the part of the camp commandant and camp compound leader.[122] In reality, the camp guards held sway over much of the day-to-day lives of prisoners within the various camps that made up Majdanek, as well as the various labor detachments in which prisoners worked. By way of their brutality, the female guards and the male SS troops greatly exacerbated the prisoners' already precarious circumstances. For example, the *Aufseherin* Hildegard Lächert distributed ballroom dresses, children's sweaters, and high-heeled shoes to new arrivals, even though the camp was well-supplied with the practical clothing, shoes, and other items necessary for daily camp life (all of which came from the camp's storehouses, stacked high with possessions taken from new arrivals).[123] In other words, this unsuitable clothing was distributed not out of necessity, but rather with the intention of making life even more difficult for the prisoners. As it was, given the living and work conditions at Majdanek, being forced to wear inadequate clothing was very much a life-threatening ordeal.

In the Nazi racial hierarchy, the various categories of prisoners were not equal. Within this system, "Aryan" German and Austrian inmates occupied the top of the hierarchy, followed by Northern and Western Europeans. Next came Czechs, Poles, Russians, and Soviet prisoners of war, all deemed "racially inferior." At the bottom of the hierarchy were the Jewish prisoners and the Sinti and Roma. However, even within a particular category, the inmates were not all equal. As a rule, prisoner-functionaries (*Funktionshäftlinge*) were granted a slightly larger food ration, enjoyed better sanitary conditions, and were exempted from the most grueling manual labor. The prisoner-functionaries, therefore, occupied a visible position, symbolized by a special armband that identified them within the forced prisoner community. A functionary position also entailed working in direct cooperation with the SS, whether on the camp grounds, in administrative offices, or on labor detachments. Functionary posts offered a position of comparative prominence within the forced society of prisoners, including a better chance at survival and a degree of decision-making authority over fellow inmates. However, these advantages came with the burden of helping to enforce the will of the SS. The rights and privileges accorded to prisoner-functionaries, including their power over other prisoners, could take a variety of forms. This special status, in turn, could spell the difference between survival and death for their fellow inmates.[124]

Majdanek: A Product of Nazi Occupation and Extermination Policies

Majdanek served, variously, as a POW and transit camp, a penal and labor camp, a concentration camp, a women's concentration camp, and an extermination camp.[125] Tomasz Kranz coined the term "multifunctional makeshift solution" (*multifunktionales Provisorium*)[126] to describe this state of affairs, underscoring not only the variety of functions fulfilled by the camp, but also its improvisational nature, its resistance to categorization, and the ambiguity of its meaning. Last but not least, this multifunctionality was among the factors that, from the camp's inception, had an extremely detrimental impact on the internal administration of the camp, the conduct of the SS troops, and the day-to-day existence of prisoners in the camp.

In terms of its genesis and function as a concentration camp, Majdanek does not easily lend itself to categorization. Majdanek was, in essence, a product of Nazi wartime policies of occupation and extermination. As a combined concentration and extermination camp, it is most readily comparable to Auschwitz. From the very start, in both camps, Soviet prisoners of war and inmates who were sick, old, frail, or otherwise deemed unable to work were killed. Indeed, by summer and fall of 1942, both camps became centers for the annihilation of European Jews. At Majdanek, however, this mass extermination was carried out at the main camp, whereas in the Auschwitz complex the killing operations took place mainly at Birkenau (Auschwitz II).

However, despite its function as a site of mass extermination, Majdanek must be regarded in the early stage foremost as a labor camp, as Barbara Schwindt has argued in her study. The very fact that the commandant of Ravensbrück, Max Koegel, was sent to Majdanek for a short time in fall 1942, in order to help establish the women's camp, underlines this theory. Koegel was the only commandant within the Nazi camp system with several years' experience at the women's camps. After having run the Lichtenburg concentration camp, Koegel was sent to Ravensbrück in 1939. Had Majdanek been solely an extermination camp, his expertise—and the presence of female guards—would have been immaterial. Indeed, Bełzec, Sobibor, and Treblinka had no *Aufseherinnen*. Thus, Koegel's presence in October 1942, and the presence of female SS staff, is evidence that despite the progression of Operation Reinhardt, Majdanek's function went beyond that of extermination. Rather, Majdanek also—and perhaps primarily—served as a labor camp.

Scholars have estimated the number of prisoners who died at Majdanek at between 170,000 and 250,000 people, among them 90,000 Jews.[127] By contrast, Barbara Schwindt calculated that approximately 80,000 Jews were deported to Majdanek, of whom more than 90 percent were either killed immediately or died of disease.[128] In 2005, Tomasz Kranz calculated that 74,000 Jews were deported to Majdanek.[129] According to his most recent findings, a total of 78,000 prisoners, among them 59,000 Jews, died in Majdanek.[130]

Due to the paucity of evidence and source material, Kranz argues that the number of people killed in the gas chambers of Majdanek cannot be determined with any precision. However, an analysis of the records has demonstrated that, as compared with Auschwitz, Majdanek held a relatively higher percentage of Jewish prisoners—and allowed a relatively larger percentage of Jews to survive selections. According to Kranz, 60 percent of the camp's victims did not die in the gas chambers. Instead, he calculates that two-thirds of Majdanek's victims succumbed to the horrific conditions that prevailed at the camp, including starvation, forced labor, epidemics, and brutal physical abuse at the hands of camp personnel.[131] Hence, it was not only the camp leadership who bore responsibility for the deadly conditions that prevailed at Majdanek. Rather, it was also the female guards and SS troops who, in carrying out their day-to-day duties, ruled over life and death in the camp.

3

Women Looking for Work

Paths to Careers in the Concentration Camps

When the Ravensbrück women's concentration camp commenced operation in May 1939, the SS began searching for female guards to staff the new facility. At that time, it continued to be mainly political opponents and individuals persecuted on "social-racial" grounds who were held in the concentration camps. This category included individuals associated with groups that had been classified as "asocial." From 1939 until 1941, Ravensbrück was the only location where female concentration camp prisoners were held. Even after that, it remained the only major camp for women in the Third Reich. As such, Ravensbrück was a key factor in the National Socialist persecution of women. Furthermore, Ravensbrück also served as a training camp for all female concentration camp guards, including the women who later were transferred to Majdanek.[1]

The female concentration camp guards (*Aufseherinnen*) who began arriving at Ravensbrück in May 1939 had been recruited in a variety of ways. Gudrun Schwarz has identified three different recruitment sources, apart from women filing applications on their own initiative: recruitment directly by the employment office (Arbeitsamt); recruitment by armaments companies that employed female concentration camp inmates; and direct recruitment of female factory workers by the SS.[2] Former inmates who had worked as clerks in the concentration camp, and who had access to the SS personnel files there, later spoke of newspaper announcements that advertised for "guards for a camp for delinquent [*verwahrloste*] women."[3] In postwar interrogations, some of these women confirmed they had replied to help-wanted ads in newspapers.[4] Unfortunately, only a few such ads have been located. The historian Irmtraud Heike discovered one such announcement in the *Hannoversche Kurier* dated August 1944, which reads as follows:

> Female workers between 20–40 years of age sought for work at a military installation. Remuneration will be made in accordance with the salary agreement for civil service employees (TO.A). Also supplied are: free housing, meals, and clothing (uniform).[5]

To date, no advertising posters or forms issued by the employment office have been found. Also, since virtually no source materials on these topics have survived, little is known about SS recruitment procedures and advertising efforts.

One of the few documents that have been found is an undated, preprinted form from Ravensbrück, which bears the heading "Re: Application for position as camp guard [*Aufseherin*]."[6] Since the document refers to satellite camps, the historian Bernhard Strebel has suggested that it must date from some time after late 1942 or early 1943.[7] According to Strebel, the document could possibly be an updated copy of an earlier text. It should be noted, however, that the application form reads more like an internal information sheet that might have been used during job interviews, than it does an employment advertisement. It's also possible that it was distributed to employment offices, factories, and other types of companies. In any case, the document provides important information regarding SS recruitment practices and criteria, the salary paid to female guards, and the official status of these women within the SS.

> To follow up on your application for a position as a guard, we provide you with a brief outline of the task to which you would be entrusted.
>
> Age: 21–45 years
>
> The women who are being held at Ravensbrück Concentration Camp have committed an offense against the Volk community [*Volksgemeinschaft*] and now must be isolated to prevent them from doing further harm. These women must be supervised during their work duties within and outside the camp. As a camp guard, you do not need any special qualifications, since the position entails only the guarding of these inmates.
>
> The *Aufseherinnen* are employees of the Reich and will be paid in accordance with the wage agreement for employees (TO.A). The initial salary grade is Group IX; after completion of a three-month probationary period, you will be classified as Group VIII. An unmarried *Aufseherin* aged 25 would receive RM 185.68 gross per month; following the deduction of social insurance contributions, taxes, and other statutory deductions and costs, as well as the cost of food and lodging, the net salary would be RM 105.10 per month. Within the camp, you will receive common meals (the same meals served to troops), which is equivalent to RM 1.20 per day.

> Work clothing, such as the cloth and canvas uniform, as well as some underclothing, is provided free of charge. As lodging, you will be provided with staff housing, which is well-appointed.
>
> Upon demonstration of aptitude and ability, you would have the opportunity to be assigned as head of one of the subcamps of the Ravensbrück Concentration Camp, which would entail a promotion to salary category VI.
>
> Your service would be recognized as a form of wartime service. You would also be a member of the Armed SS. Thus, prerequisites for the position require that you have no criminal record and be in good physical health. You are therefore requested to submit the following documentation:
>
> Police certificate of good conduct
> Resume
> Photograph
> Physician's health certificate
> Your employment office assignment.
>
> The attached staff questionnaire should be filled out with care and returned. You will then receive further notification. However, any final hiring decision will depend on the results of a medical examination conducted by the on-site physician. Once all criteria for application have been met, employment may commence on the 1st or 15th of the following month.

As this description shows, the applicants were informed only that their duties at Ravensbrück would entail guarding women who had "in some manner" committed an offense against the "Volk community." This decidedly vague statement served to identify the incarcerated women as criminals, while suggesting that they constituted a danger to the larger population. The phrasing thus served to legitimize the persecution and incarceration of these women, without offering any evidence in support of the accusations being made against them.

The criminalization and social exclusion of specific individuals and groups always serves the additional function of legitimizing their persecution. According to Michel Foucault, this strategy is a particularly effective form of circular reasoning. While prisons and police intervention stoke the public's fear of criminals, this fear, in turn, encourages popular acceptance of the practices of incarceration and police control:

> The more offenders there are . . . the more fear there will be within the population. And the more fear there is in the population, the more acceptable, even desirable, the system of police control will become. The existence of this small permanent internal danger is one of the conditions of acceptability of this system of control.[8]

Applicants for a position as a camp guard in a concentration camp were also required to submit a certificate of health, a resume with a photograph, and a police certificate of good conduct, all of which were typical requirements for a civil service employment application. The women were also required to confirm their "Aryan" background, and to attest that they met the requirements for inclusion in the National Socialist "Volk community":

> I certify that, despite careful research, no circumstances are known to me that could contradict the assumption that I am of Aryan descent, or that could suggest that one of my parents or grandparents was a member of the Jewish religion at any point in time. The same applies to my wife/husband.
>
> I am aware that I will be dismissed without notice if this declaration is found to be false.[9]

As a rule, most of the *Aufseherinnen* were in fact unmarried at the time of their hiring. However, as this document demonstrates, being unmarried was not a requirement for employment as a concentration camp guard.

Female guards sent to work in camps in occupied Poland were required to sign an additional form confirming that they were not related by blood or marriage to "former citizens of the former Polish state who did not obtain German citizenship."[10] The prerequisite for employment as an *Aufseherin*, therefore, was meeting specific racial, eugenic, and national security criteria. It seems character and political attitudes were given only cursory scrutiny, an issue that was raised in a June 1943 letter from the Chief Economic and Administrative Office (WVHA) to all concentration camp commandants who employed female guards:

> In some cases, female guards have been hired without a proper background investigation pertaining to any criminal records and to their political reliability.
>
> As a matter of course, every applicant's background should be carefully scrutinized prior to hiring (including police and political certificate of good conduct, and an extract from the judicial record of any criminal convictions).
>
> It has been decided by *Obergruppenführer* Pohl that, for all future prospective hires, he is to be presented with the application and corresponding documents (questionnaire, resume, police certificate of good conduct, and extract from the judicial record), after which he will make a decision.
>
> These above materials should be submitted to Department D—Administration, which will obtain the approval.
>
> The same guidelines should be followed for the hiring of all other employees under ordinary contract (switchboard operators, stenographers, and so forth).[11]

The female guards were not required to have any form of vocational training. The SS was looking to hire women between twenty-one and forty-five years of age who possessed no specific vocational background or skills. By implication, then, the target group was limited to women from the lower social classes, who either had to earn their own living, or who needed to help support their families.[12]

Furthermore, the *Aufseherinnen* were women auxiliaries (*weibliches Gefolge*) of the Waffen-SS, rather than full members of the SS.[13] As employees of the Inspectorate of Concentration Camps (IKL) and later (after March 1942) of the WVHA's Office Group D, they were subject to the salary agreement for civil service employees, where they were classified as Group VIII or IX on the pay scale. As they were not official members of the military, the *Aufseherinnen* had no soldier's pay book (*Soldbuch*). However, in January 1944, special "duty books" were introduced for the female camp guards, which were also used by women working as auxiliaries for the Wehrmacht and SS.[14]

In accordance with the civil-service salary agreement A, the regular salary of a female camp guard over age twenty-one was RM 115 during the probationary period, and RM 135 thereafter. The highest salary grade that a woman could attain was RM 155 per month. At age twenty-seven, salaries increased by RM 30 per month in each salary category. In case the camp guard had children to support, the net salary increased by RM 20 per month for each child.[15] According to the Ravensbrück application form, an unmarried guard who was twenty-five years of age would have a gross monthly income of RM 185.68 after deductions for social insurance, taxes, and the cost of food and lodging (the *Aufseherinnen* were housed in staff housing in the SS section of the camp, and also received their meals there), yielding a net monthly income of RM 105.10.[16] According to a letter dated 1944, this base salary was eligible for an overtime supplement of RM 35 per month.[17] However, this letter also implies that the regular work week encompassed 68 hours, and that the overtime supplement was only paid when the female guards worked more than 300 hours per month.[18]

The historian Götz Aly has said that a good rule of thumb when attempting to gain a sense of the present value of reichsmarks in today's euros is to multiply the reichsmark by a factor of ten; this would suggest "a net monthly salary of 200 Reichsmark in 1939 was an above-average salary."[19] Therefore, particularly for young women with no career training, this was, indeed, good pay.

The First Recruitment Wave (1939–1941): Women Applicants

The best-documented female guard at Majdanek is Hermine Braunsteiner, born in Vienna in 1919. Much of what is known about Braunsteiner is derived from the records of numerous interrogations carried out by German and Austrian judicial authorities in the aftermath of the war. From 1946 to 1949, the Vienna People's Court (Volksgericht) investigated Braunsteiner for acts of violence and other abuses carried out during her tenure at the Ravensbrück concentration camp (from 1939 to 1942). The only female Majdanek guard ever brought before a court for offenses in Ravensbrück, Braunsteiner was also later tried for murder during the Majdanek Trial, which took place in Düsseldorf from 1975 to 1981.

Braunsteiner grew up in what she later described as a "poor" family in Nussdorf, a district on the edge of Vienna.[20]

> My father was a driver for a brewery. He held the same job for 33 years. My mother worked, too. She did laundry, some of which she took in at home, and some of which she did elsewhere. We lived in a 3-room apartment provided by the brewery. In all, there were seven children, and I am the youngest. . . . My mother was 45 when I was born. . . . The owner of the brewery where my father worked was Baron von B. My father worked for him first as a coachman and, later, as a private chauffeur. Eventually, he became a truck driver for the brewery."[21]

In her testimony, Braunsteiner noted that she completed her schooling with satisfactory results, a fact in which she appeared to take pride.

> I attended primary school for four years, and then secondary school for four years. I never had to repeat a grade. I was an average student. I left school with good qualifications. . . .
>
> My plan was to train as a nurse, but the training cost money. My parents couldn't afford that. After I left school, my mother kept me home for six months to help her in the household.[22]

Her father's sudden death in 1934 forced Hermine, who was fifteen at the time, to find work to help support her family.

> At the time, Baron von B. was looking to replace a chambermaid who was sick. . . . From about May 1934 to July 1936, I worked in the Baron's household as a chambermaid. . . . I earned just one schilling a day, even though the standard monthly salary was 80 schillings. I worked there because I wanted to help support my mother, after my father's death. She and one of my sisters still lived in the apartment. My sister was an apprentice. I didn't earn much, but I was also able to bring my mother some food from the Baron's household.[23]

At the time, girls who had no job qualifications often worked as housemaids.[24] Unemployment was high in Austria as a result of the global economic crisis, and well-paying jobs were especially scarce. Braunsteiner's entry into the work world also happened to coincide with the peak of a political crisis. In February 1934, in response to Austria's 1933 ban on all political parties, including the Social Democratic Party, widespread revolts broke out in Vienna, Upper Austria, Tyrol, and Styria. At the same time, the Austro-fascist regime, which had been bolstered by the corporatist constitution of May 1934, was unsuccessful in reversing the economic downswing.[25]

To escape these difficult circumstances, Braunsteiner began searching for employment abroad:[26]

> Since I earned so little working for the Baron, I tried to find a new job. I went to Holland, where one of my married sisters lived.... But I couldn't find a job, because foreigners weren't allowed to get work permits in Holland at the time.... After about three months, in October 1936, I returned home to live with my mother in Vienna.[27]

After her unsuccessful bid to find employment in Holland, Braunsteiner took a job at the brewery and continued to live with her mother.

> I had a job as an unskilled worker. I worked at the machine that filled the beer bottles. I also worked at other machines, including the washing machine, the labeling machine, and so forth. It was very hard work. That's why I wanted to find another job.[28]

When a chance to leave the brewery presented itself, Braunsteiner seized the opportunity:

> A girl who lived on our street came home from England for a visit. I asked her if she would be able to find a job for me there. About 6 weeks later, she helped me find a job with an American family who lived in London. Because I was still a minor, my mother had to give her written permission.
>
> The head of the American family was an engineer who worked for a large company and traveled from one country to the next; he had just arrived in London from Japan. In London, they lived in a furnished ten-room apartment. The parents lived there with their daughter, who was about 14. I had to take care of the household. I did the cooking and cleaning.
>
> I left Vienna for England on 17 Dec. 1937, and stayed there until late May 1938. When I arrived in England, I couldn't speak much English. In Vienna, though, the *Krone* newspaper had always had a small feature called "How to Learn English." I'd managed to learn a few words from that.[29]

Just eighteen years old, Braunsteiner moved to a foreign country, with next to no knowledge of English, which is itself a testament to her courage and sense of adventure. After the Austrian "Anschluss"—the annexation of Austria into Nazi Germany on March 13, 1938—Braunsteiner was faced with the possibility that she might be interned in England in the event of war.

> It was a time of political turmoil in England, and everyone was talking about whether there would be a war. My friend told me that she found out that, if there was a war, all Germans in England might face internment. That worried us, so we

> both returned to Vienna in late May 1938. The American family I was working for didn't want me to leave. They wanted me to stay. In Vienna, I moved back in with my mother.[30]

In later testimony, Braunsteiner took care to emphasize her success in England, depicting herself as someone who had performed very capably in a traditionally female job. In that respect, leaving this position and returning to Vienna could only have meant a step down for her. At the same time, however, Braunsteiner had hopes that under the new government there might be the possibility that she could train as a nurse, free of charge.

> I hoped that the so-called assumption of power would also provide me with a career opportunity, and the chance to train for a profession free of charge. That's why I sent my documents to Berlin, to the main office of the so-called "Blaue Schwesternschaft,"[31] in the hopes that I would be able to get a trainee position there.[32]

Braunsteiner's hopes coincided with political developments. By 1936, preparations for war were underway in Germany, with Austria following in Germany's footsteps by 1938. These preparations also led to an increased need for professional nurses and the establishment of new nursing schools. For many young women who been affected by high unemployment rates during the economic crisis, this offered an attractive opportunity to train for a profession. As a result, there were many more applications than there were training spots.

In her Düsseldorf testimony, Braunsteiner said that she waited for many months for a reply from Berlin. When no such reply arrived, she began looking for another position, eventually ending up back at the brewery.

> To bridge the gap, while I was waiting for word of my acceptance, I went back to my old job at the brewery. I also went back to my *Turnverein* [gymnastics association]. But months later, I still hadn't received an answer from Berlin, and I wanted to get away from the hard work at the brewery, so I started looking for other work. One evening, a girl at the *Turnverein* told me she was leaving for Berlin. The employment office was arranging for a transport to a munitions factory. I thought, well I have nothing to lose, so the next day I went to the employment office and put in an application.[33]

In August 1938, just three months after returning home to Vienna, Braunsteiner had herself placed on the employment office's list for work in Germany. In this respect, she benefited from the Nazi regime's new policies on women's employment. In 1938, in response to economic and political considerations, the regime shifted from restrictive and discriminatory labor market policies vis-à-vis women to a greater utilization of women's labor capacity.[34]

According to her testimony, one week after Braunsteiner went to the employment office in Vienna, she joined a group of one hundred young Austrian women sent to the village of Grüneberg, near Berlin. There, the young women were met by the head of a factory, and were assigned living quarters.[35] Braunsteiner and another young woman whom she knew from the gymnastics association were sent to Fürstenberg, a town in Mecklenburg, where they lived with the family of the local chief of police. The village was located an hour's train ride from the munitions factory in Grüneberg:

> We had to take the train to and from Grüneberg every day. Back at the employment office in Vienna, I had had to agree to spend a year at the munitions factory. The first six months in the factory, I worked at a machine that might have been producing fuses, but I can't remember it all that well anymore. After that, I volunteered, because I wanted to get the special ration of milk. I wore protective gloves, and used tongs to fill small metal tips with phosphorus. . . . I earned 18 reichsmarks and a few pfennigs per week. I had to pay five marks a week for rent, four marks sixty for my train tickets, and live off the rest. The rest of my earnings were just enough to buy enough milk and pieces of cake to survive.[36]

For Braunsteiner, the work on the assembly line at the munitions factory was no less arduous and frustrating than her work at the brewery had been. The two-hour daily commute, irregular work hours, and, especially, working night shifts added to the burden.

> The police chief's family was nice to us. As far as I can remember, we didn't talk about politics. But they did say that money was tight. That's why the police chief told us that . . . the commandant of the Ravensbrück re-education camp [*sic*] had asked him if he knew any girls who would be suited to supervising the prisoners.[37]

For Braunsteiner, the opportunity to escape the factory assembly line and earn a higher salary was a welcome one. Moreover, the workplace would be closer, not far from Fürstenberg.

> I knew that a camp was being built in Ravensbrück, the village next to Fürstenberg. The police chief told us only that we would have to supervise prisoners. I didn't ask at the time what kind of prisoners they were, or exactly what our work would entail. But the police chief told us that we would receive lodging and a warm meal, in other words, room and board, along with about 60 to 70 reichsmarks. This was a good salary . . . so I sent an application for employment to the commandant of the camp.

> . . . We received a reply from the camp commandant that we were to start work on August 15, 1939. That didn't cause any problems for us with the munitions factory, because the year that we had promised to work was just up.[38]

Braunsteiner's testimony here is interesting, as she implies that she would not have taken the position at Ravensbrück had she known more about the camp. Whether details about the Ravensbrück concentration camp and its prisoners would have been known to the surrounding community in Fürstenberg at this early stage is uncertain.[39] However, it is equally likely that Braunsteiner's depiction is a rhetorical strategy intended to disavow responsibility. In any case, on August 15, 1939, she began work as Guard No. 28 in Ravensbrück.[40]

◆ ◆ ◆

Another *Aufseherin* at Majdanek was Erna Pfannstiel, born in Benshausen in the state of Thuringia, in 1922. In a judicial inquiry conducted in Austria in 1965, Pfannstiel also said that she had applied to work as an *Aufseherin* at Ravensbrück on her own initiative:

> After attending school in Benshausen, I completed my year of obligatory service,[41] and then attended a two-year vocational program in home economics. After that, I volunteered for the Reich Labor Service, where I stayed for one year. Then I took a position as a maid in Berlin. In May 1941, I applied to work as a guard at the Ravensbrück Concentration Camp. I worked there until October 1942, and then was transferred to the Majdanek Concentration Camp.[42]

As Erna Pfannstiel recounted in her testimony, she left secondary school before obtaining a diploma, and then took part in a number of state-sponsored services and institutions. First she did the *Pflichtjahr*, or year of compulsory service, which in 1938 had already been expanded to include single women under age twenty-five.[43] Afterwards, Pfannstiel took part in the Reichsarbeitsdienst (RAD or Reich Labor Service), another major organization initially established by the regime to help alleviate male unemployment. With the beginning of the war, the compulsory labor service was expanded to unmarried women and consistently extended to an indefinite term by November of 1944.[44]

In 1980, Pfannstiel described her social and work background more fully in Eberhard Fechner's documentary film about the Majdanek trial.

EBERHARD FECHNER: Did you have a happy childhood?

ERNA WALLISCH: No, I didn't. Well, actually, it was fine until I turned 13. But after that . . . Well, my father's marriage wasn't very good. Then he got involved with a younger woman, and my mother threatened to commit suicide. She wanted to jump out of the window. But my sister stopped her, at the last moment. And then he sent her to Hadamar, near Limburg.[45] Later I found out that they also killed people there. . . . My mother was there, yes. She was, I think, there until about 1941, and then a notice of her death arrived in the mail. They wrote that she'd died of a thrombosis.

EBERHARD FECHNER: Hmm. But it's still possible that she was killed.

ERNA WALLISCH: Yes, I assume she was, sure. But back then, I didn't know about that yet. . . . I visited her there once, and she behaved normally. She just told me that I should tell my father, tell him that he should also come and visit her. . . . After that, I moved out. The situation at home wasn't good any more, and he was only interested in his young woman. We had a big apartment at the time, but he got rid of all of the children. There were four of us, and God, well, I was the youngest one, you know? The rest of them had left already. So I just wandered back and forth, basically. I joined the labor service when I was seventeen. I joined voluntarily.[46]

According to her testimony, Pfannstiel took the first opportunity to leave home after her father had her mother committed to Hadamar, a psychiatric hospital and euthanasia center. Again, a state-sponsored youth organization became decisive for her future profession. Pfannstiel volunteered with the labor service even though she originally had hoped to pursue a different career:

ERNA WALLISCH: Yes, I wanted to become a saleswoman. But that would have . . . I did do a year of labor service beforehand. But my father never wanted to spend any money on me, you know? He didn't have much interest in me, so I didn't have much of a choice. So I spent some time working in a factory, and then went into the labor service. But to be a labor-service leader, I would have needed more school. And I didn't have that. So I . . .

EBERHARD FECHNER: Oh, so your *Volksschule*[47] diploma wasn't enough?

ERNA WALLISCH: No, that wasn't enough. As a labor-service leader, I would have needed a diploma from an academic secondary school [*Höhere Schule*]. And I didn't have that. At the time, what I went to wasn't even a *Hauptschule*, it was eight years of a *Volksschule*.

EBERHARD FECHNER: And when you were done with the labor service, what did you do then?

ERNA WALLISCH: Well, then I went home, but my father didn't have a room for me. It was very depressing there for me, back then. So I applied for a position as a housemaid. That was in Berlin. In the Zehlendorf district of Berlin. I went there as a maid, and that's where I met the person who told me about Ravensbrück.[48]

In much the same way as Braunsteiner, Wallisch's education and vocational training limited her career opportunities. She seems to have been dissatisfied with both her position as housemaid and her job in the factory. The chance to work as a camp guard, which—at least as she remembers it—was described by her acquaintance in positive terms, most likely seemed a welcome opportunity to make a fresh start. Indeed, according to Wallisch, the acquaintance indicated that she, herself, would have applied to work as a concentration camp guard, had she not been too old to meet the stated guidelines for the position.

EBERHARD FECHNER: And what was that? What did she say?

ERNA WALLISCH: She said she knew people at Ravensbrück. They lived there. Those were the people I also met later. And she also would have liked to work at Ravensbrück, but I believe she was already too old at the time. They wouldn't take her. That's what she told me.

EBERHARD FECHNER: And what did she say? Do you still remember that?

ERNA WALLISCH: Well, that there was a camp, and that they had guards, and that the guards watched over the prisoners. So I applied for the job and they took me. . . .

EBERHARD FECHNER: But you didn't know exactly what it was, right? Or did you?

ERNA WALLISCH: I didn't, no. She just told me it wasn't that bad, and it was easy work, and things like that.[49]

In this description, again, the job of an *Aufseherin* was described as easy work.

The War Years (1941–1942): Recruitment by the Labor Office

Beginning in the summer of 1941, the war on the Eastern Front led to a rapid expansion of the concentration camp system. This, in turn, led to an increase in the need for female concentration camp guards. The winter of 1942–1943, however, brought a turning point in Germany's war against its neighbors. By then, Allied forces had begun to gain an upper hand in the air battle, and the German Wehrmacht had lost the battle for Stalingrad. At that same time, the armaments industry was operating in high gear, and the wartime economy, under the leadership of Albert Speer, was being reconfigured according to Fordist principles of mass production. In December 1942, in response to Germany's military predicament, efforts to mobilize women as a national resource were again stepped up; all women between the ages of seventeen and forty-five were required to register for labor service.[50] Based on interviews of both former female concentration camp guards and former camp prisoners, we know that many of the recruits who arrived at Ravensbrück had been sent there by the labor office.

Margarete Buber-Neumann, a political prisoner who arrived in Ravensbrück in August 1940 and who was assigned to work in the office of Chief Guard Johanna Langefeld, described the process of recruitment by the labor office as follows:

> There were also cases in which women were sent by one of the labor offices to work as guards at Ravensbrück. This happened most often to women who had refused once

> or even twice to take the job that had been assigned to them, which meant they were likely to be arrested the next time they refused to take the work assigned to them.[51]

Rosa Reischl, a former Majdanek *Aufseherin* who was born in the Bavarian town of Gänswies in 1920, described her hiring in the following terms:

> My father was an official with the railway company. I have six brothers and sisters. I was the second-oldest child. After attending *Volksschule* [primary school], I went to Tennisberg in the Oberpfalz, where I was trained as an infant care nurse at an NSV [National Socialist People's Welfare Organization] Home. That's where I received my training. After about a year, I started working as an infant care nurse, where I was assigned to work short-term at various locations. I went back home in August 1942. The labor office was planning to send me to work at a sawmill. Until that point, I'd only been wearing a nursing uniform, so I told them they would have to provide me with civilian attire. They told me I was being impertinent. A few days later, I was told to report to the health authorities. Then, on October 1 or 15, 1942, I was conscripted to work at Ravensbrück.[52]

Reischl was not the only trained nurse who was sent by the employment office to work in a concentration camp. Charlotte W. (born in 1901), who was a trained nurse from Gute Herberge, in the district of Danziger Höhe, also reported that she had been "conscripted" by the labor office:

> I worked for the tax authorities until 1942, even though I was a trained nanny and nurse. Because of my special skills and education, I was transferred from my post at the tax office and sent to the concentration camp at Ravensbrück.[53]

Labor offices across the entire Reich territory participated in recruiting women as concentration camp guards.[54] The establishment of additional concentration camps for women at Auschwitz and Majdanek in the spring and fall of 1942 resulted in a shortage of female concentration camp guards. It appears that women who had trained as nurses were specifically sought out during the hiring process. Another *Aufseherin*, Charlotte Wöllert (born in 1918), also trained as a nurse, arrived at the concentration camp from the small town of Friedenland, in the northeastern state of Mecklenburg.

> After attending *Volksschule* [primary school], I spent about 3½ years working as household help. Then I was sent to work as a nurse at the Domjüch psychiatric hospital and sanatorium. In 1942, I was conscripted into the labor service and sent to Ravensbrück to work as an SS *Aufseherin*.[55]

Wöllert described the process of her recruitment by the labor office somewhat differently than her colleagues. Like the other women, she said she had been "conscripted" (*dienstverpflichtet*). When she was confronted in 1973 with a resume she had submitted in 1943, she then stated that she accepted the job after it had been offered to her:

> The resume dated 25 February 1943, which is contained in my DC[56] documents, is accurate. However, my statement that I had volunteered for work at the concentration camp is incorrect. What actually happened is that, after working at the Domjoch [Domjüch] psychiatric hospital and sanatorium from 1936 to 1942, I contacted the labor office, because I didn't want to work at the sanatorium any longer. They offered me the job at Ravensbrück and I accepted it, because I didn't know what it was all about.[57]

At Domjüch, the patients were assessed under the T4 "euthanasia program," administered from Berlin, and were subsequently transferred to the "appropriate" facility.[58] According to the historian Christiane Witzke, many patients were transferred to Sachsenberg in Schwerin. Some were later transferred to Bernburg, where they were gassed. In 1942, the psychiatric and nursing facility at Domjüch—which had been operating at a loss since 1933—was closed; a year later, the facility was converted to a tuberculosis sanatorium. In all likelihood, the plan to close Domjüch played a role in Wöllert's decision to request a new posting at the labor office.[59]

Another guard, Hildegard Lächert, born in Berlin in 1920, also stated that she had been conscripted into service at the concentration camp. After finishing *Volksschule* (primary school) in 1934, she began an apprenticeship as a tailor. After she broke off her training, in 1937, she was conscripted into the labor service. During her time in the service, she worked as a laborer in several factories, including an aircraft manufacturing facility, and, according to a later statement, completed an eighteen-month nurse-training program with the Red Cross.[60] On August 23, 1939, she bore a son out of wedlock. By September 1939, she had already been assigned to take up work in a munitions factory. Lächert had a second child, a daughter, on April 3, 1941. For some time after the birth, she was unemployed. Later that year, however, she began working as a Red Cross nurse in a Luftwaffe hospital in the Tegel district of Berlin. In March 1942, she was sent to the Ravensbrück concentration camp:[61] "While I was there [at the Luftwaffe hospital], we were taken over by the Ministry—I was taken over by the Ministry of the Interior—and in '42, I was assigned to the SS as an *Aufseherin* in Ravensbrück."[62]

In April 1942, despite being a single mother with two children, Lächert began working at the Ravensbrück concentration camp:

> My children and the other guards' children were to go into the so-called nursery. . . . I was at Ravensbrück from April 1942 to late October 1942. I had my daughter there with me, and my son stayed with my mother. But it didn't work out with my daughter at the concentration camp. She got sick after three months, and was sent

> to a hospital in Berlin, where she stayed for about nine months. After that, she went to my mother, who didn't want her to return to the concentration camp.[63]

The *Aufseherinnen* at Ravensbrück were permitted to bring their young children with them. Ravensbrück was built according to modern specifications, with a nursery for children of the camp staff.[64] At Majdanek, however, where Lächert was transferred in October 1942, there were no childcare facilities.

In Eberhard Fechner's documentary, Lächert described her work in the concentration camp as a duty that had been assigned to her:

> There was a war, you know. In wartime, everyone has to . . . do something for the Fatherland—even the youngest ones, and even the generals' wives, who had to go into the munitions factories, and everywhere else. And we had to, too. The young people and the old ones, the old ones just like the young ones, too.[65]

In this respect, Lächert echoed the theme of "wartime service and service to the Fatherland," which was also one of the strategies employed by Nazi propaganda in its recruitment of women. In the later Majdanek trial, this argument was used within a discourse of justification and mitigation. Nonetheless, it is apparent that work in the concentration camp was an important source of income for the recruited women. A letter written by the chief guard at Majdanek in 1943 confirms that Lächert supported her family with the salary she earned as a guard. In that letter, the chief guard notes: "*Aufseherin* Lächert sends all that she can spare from her earnings to her family back at home."[66]

According to an SS document, Luzie H. (born in Breslau in 1910) began work at the Ravensbrück concentration camp on November 16, 1942.[67] In her interrogations, she too described her work at the concentration camp as a form of labor conscription:

> I was working for an accountant, and I started having stomach problems from sitting constantly while hunched over. I had stomach surgery. Then, during the war, I was called to the labor office and told they wanted to put me to work digging trenches. I reminded them of my stomach surgery. Some time later, they called me in again, and told me that they had found work for me that wouldn't require physical labor. And if I turned it down, they would send me to a concentration camp for refusing to work.[68]

In Fechner's documentary, Luzie H. described her recruitment as follows:

> The third time they called me in, they told me, 'Today we have a job for you where you won't have to perform physical labor, and if you don't accept this job, then you'll be sent to a concentration camp yourself for refusing to work. And there you'll join the other work-shy riff-raff [*arbeitsscheuer Gesindel*].[69]

As in earlier descriptions, Luzie H. also recalls being told she was being assigned "easy work," and says she was threatened with being branded as "work shy" if she were to turn the job down. However, it is neither possible to confirm whether this was indeed the phrasing used by the employment official, nor to be certain what consequences Luzie H. would have faced had she refused the position.

During the second phase of recruitment, some women volunteered to work as concentration camp guards. One was Anna M., a single mother from Lower Bavaria born in 1921, who was the only *Aufseherin* at Majdanek who was a Nazi Party member[70] and a member of the Bund Deutscher Mädel (BDM):[71]

> In mid-November 1941 [October 1942], I received notification from the commandant of the Ravensbrück concentration camp for women to report there as a guard. By way of additional explanation, I should note that in about July or August 1941, there was a BDM camp in Tiefenbach, near Marktredwitz, which lasted for several weeks. During the camp, one of the leaders, someone higher up, told us we should all register for wartime service on a farm or volunteer as a guard at the Ravensbrück women's concentration camp. We were especially encouraged to go to Ravensbrück, because they didn't have enough guards. They told us it would be a pleasant job and we would be able to leave again after three months. So I went ahead and reported for duty at the Ravensbrück women's concentration camp. We had no idea what to expect there.[72]

According to Anna M.'s contract, she began work on October 23, 1942. In Anna M.'s case, we also know that she had responded to a recruitment drive carried out through the Bund Deutscher Mädel, which appears to have aggressively pursued the recruitment of young women for work as concentration camp guards at that time. Whether Anna M. truly believed that her work at Ravensbrück would last only three months remains an open question.

Total War (1943–1945): Direct Recruitment by the SS

After 1942, concentration camp inmates were increasingly put to work in industrial facilities; as a result, armaments companies opened production sites near many of the camps.[73] At the same time, the number of female inmates continued to increase; this, in turn, led to an increased need for female guards.[74] Beginning in January 1943, an increase in the number of satellite camps meant a greater need for female guard staff. Recruitment policies, in turn, became increasingly rigorous following the proclamation of "total war" and the "Decree on the Registration of Men and Women for the Defense of the Reich," issued on January 27, 1943.[75] In 1944, an additional decree extended the age of women required to report for labor service to fifty. Only pregnant women, women with a child younger than school age, and women with more than two children under age fourteen were exempt. In reality, women from the working and middle classes were compelled to work, even those who were pregnant or who had young children.[76]

According to the historian Stefanie Oppel, the "registration decree" of January 1943 met with only limited success in its recruitment of female concentration camp guards. Moreover, the employment offices had already begun "conscripting" women as early as 1940, several years before the 1943 decree.[77] The recruitment effort launched by the SS later that spring would prove more efficient and direct. As part of this initiative, the Ravensbrück concentration camp began recruiting women from among workers at nearby factories in the spring of 1943—in other words, women were being recruited by the SS straight from the assembly lines. As part of this effort, camp compound leader Edmund Bräuning paid visits to a number of facilities, among them the Heinkel factory in Oranienburg. Margarete Buber-Neumann, a survivor of the Ravensbrück concentration camp, recalled these new recruitment methods as follows:

> With tens of thousands of inmates in the camps, the SS kept having to hire more female guards. The head of the camp compound, Bräuning, went on what can only be called recruitment drives. They gathered all the female workers together, and he gave an eloquent speech designed to convince the women that a re-education camp was looking to hire suitable staff whose jobs would entail only supervisory duties. He described the delightful housing in the most glowing terms,[78] the exemplary meals, the varied opportunities for conviviality, and, especially, the high salaries they could expect. The word "concentration camp," of course, was entirely absent from his speech. His efforts met with some success. After all, what woman working in wartime factory production wouldn't choose to give up her physically grueling work in favor of such an enticing supervisory position?!—Whenever the camp compound leader went on a recruitment drive, another 20 or more young female factory workers came to us to begin their new careers.[79]

Even though Buber-Neumann described this method of recruitment as a success, the number of recruits still failed to meet the rising need. As a result, the employment offices stepped up their efforts to enlist unemployed women, and women who were looking for work. At the same time, more and more companies began to rely on the labor of concentration camp inmates. Due to the chronic shortage of concentration camp guards, some of these companies were forced to assign their own regular staff to supervise the forced laborers or, alternatively, to allocate some of their own female staff directly to the concentration camp guard units.[80] As the former commandant of Auschwitz, Rudolf Höss, later explained in his postwar account:

> Even with diligent recruitment efforts on the part of the Nazi women's organization, very few women volunteered for service as concentration camp guards. As the need

> for *Aufseherinnen* was increasing daily, we had to resort to other measures. Every armaments firm that was assigned female concentration camp inmates was required to delegate a certain percentage of its female workers, who would be employed as female guards.[81]

Many former *Aufseherinnen* also described these recruitment measures as a form of forced recruitment, including Gertrud Heise, who worked from September 1939 to October 1942 on the assembly line of a Berlin aircraft manufacturer:[82]

> In November 1939, I had to give up my job as a seamstress at the Otte company in Berlin. As part of the labor service program, I was sent to the Heinkel aircraft manufacturing company in the Reinickendorf district of Berlin and, in October 1942, I was sent to the Ravensbrück women's concentration camp.[83]

In fall 1942, Hermine Brückner (born in 1918), from Wustung in the Friedland district of the Sudetenland, was sent directly from the Heinkel factory to Ravensbrück:

> In April 1942, I was sent as part of the labor service program to the Heinkel factory in Oranienburg. I stayed there until fall 1942, when I was sent to work as an *Aufseherin* in the Ravensbrück women's concentration camp. I can't remember anymore exactly how this labor assignment was carried out. I believe I was transferred to the concentration camp without anyone asking my permission beforehand. But it's possible that I signed an agreement beforehand.[84]

Brückner was recruited in fall 1942, at a time when the newly established women's camps at Auschwitz and Majdanek were critically understaffed. According to Brückner, she remained at Ravensbrück for the obligatory three-month training period, after which she was immediately transferred to Majdanek.

Herta B., who came from Greppin in the Bitterfeld district (born in 1921), described her recruitment, in early summer 1943, as follows:

> I attended *Volksschule* [primary school] for 8 years. After that, I worked as domestic help for two years, and then I took a job at the factory where my father worked. I did that from 1938 until 1943. In 1943, a recruiter from the Armed SS showed up at the factory where I worked. To my surprise, my supervisor told me that he put my name on the list, and I would soon be working for the SS. He said that if I refused, he would have my son, who was born in 1939, sent to an orphanage. Under those conditions, I felt I had no choice other than to work for the SS. . . . Some time later, the social worker, Fraulein S., accompanied me to Berlin. She brought me to a place where there were other women who were supposed to start working for the SS. We then went as a group to Ravensbrück. As far as I can remember, this was in June 1943.[85]

According to Herta B., her supervisor pressured her by threatening to have custody of her son revoked, which left her no choice but to agree to the transfer. Whether this claim is a form of self-justification or whether she genuinely had no alternative but to comply remains unknown. In any case, in June 1943, Herta B. was sent to Ravensbrück for four weeks' training. On July 21, 1943, she was transferred to Majdanek as part of a group of five *Aufseherinnen*.[86] Herta B.'s interrogation record makes no mention of where her four-year-old son lived during that period.

Elisabeth H., née Radojewski (born in 1921), also came from Greppin. She was a coworker of Herta B.'s and was recruited under like circumstances, although her description differs somewhat from that of her coworker:

> In early 1943, I worked at the IG Farben factory in Wolfen, in the Bitterfeld district. One day, my supervisor told us we could volunteer to work as female guards, supervising foreign laborers. My colleague Herta B. and I decided to accept this offer. At the time, I didn't know that this meant I would be working as a guard in a concentration camp. In summer 1943—it might have been as early as June 1, 1943—I was sent to the Ravensbrück concentration camp.[87]

Unlike her colleague, who claimed to have been compelled by their supervisor to comply, Elisabeth H. said that she accepted, of her own accord, the offer to work as a concentration camp guard. Also of note, she was one of the few married women recruited to the position of *Aufseherin*.

Even though she had a job at the post office at the time, Luise Danz (born in 1917) from Walldorf, in Thuringia, was sent by the local employment office to work as a guard at Ravensbrück:

> From 1937 to late January 1940, I worked as an assistant at a bakery in Brandenburg. After that, I returned to live with my parents in Schmalkalden, because my parents were old already and my sisters had all married. That's when I got a job at the post office. In late February 1943, the local employment office informed me that I would be sent to work at Ravensbrück. I tried to turn down that assignment, but didn't succeed in that.[88]

In 1943, Alice Orlowski (born in 1903 in Berlin) was also recruited through the employment office. According to her later testimony, she was sent to Ravensbrück after being "conscripted for labor":[89]

> In 1943, I was living with my parents in Himmelspfort, near Templin. That's where I was when the local employment office in Prenzlau found me. I was conscripted for labor as a guard at the Ravensbrück concentration camp. I spent only a week there.[90]

After seven days of training, Orlowski was transferred from Ravensbrück to

Majdanek.[91] She was the only Majdanek *Aufseherin* who came from a middle-class background; her father was a head tax inspector, while she herself had completed secondary education and studied medicine for four semesters.[92]

> I attended a secondary school for girls [*Lyzeum*] in Berlin, and then studied medicine for four semesters. After that, I worked as a freelance model at fashion shows. I had left university because of financial problems. I met my husband, who comes from a noble family from Belorussia. We married around 1930. He owned a leather-goods shop. I ran the store largely on my own, because my husband was sick a lot. We divorced around 1936. The store was nearly bankrupt. I went to Aachen, and took over a bar.[93]

After the bar was destroyed in a bombing raid in 1943, Orlowski was forced to look for another job:

> The labor office where I had to register sent me to work in a factory, even though I had asked them to take my training and experience into account. Finally I started working as a guard in the Ravensbrück concentration camp.[94]

The interrogation records make no mention as to whether Orlowski herself requested this transfer. However, it is clear that by 1943, the original three-month training period had been abandoned in favor of a much briefer training period. This was most likely due to the acute labor shortage in women's concentration camps in occupied Poland.

SS Men and Their Career Paths to Concentration Camps

By way of brief contrast, the following discussion examines the backgrounds of male guards who were employed at Majdanek, and their superiors within the camp hierarchy. The discussion will distinguish between the higher-ranked SS officers, those in the lower ranks of the SS headquarters staff, and members of the SS Death's Head Battalion.

Hermann Hackmann, camp compound leader at Majdanek, was born in Osnabrück in 1913. After completing secondary school (*Mittlere Reife*), he apprenticed as a bricklayer between 1930 and 1933. After the apprenticeship ended, he had hoped to become an architect, but was forced to abandon that plan due to economic conditions.[95] In Eberhard Fechner's documentary filmed during the Düsseldorf Majdanek trial (1975–1981), Hackmann explained that he had joined the SS in 1933, during the period marked by "national revival": "I was a member of a gymnastics club, and some of the other like-minded members convinced me that this was the best course of action for a young man."[96] Years later, in 1967, Hackmann described his political evolution as follows:

> Before 1933, I was a member of the gymnastics association in Osnabrück. I wasn't a member of a political party. I was put in touch with the SS through some other members of the gymnastics association, and the constant exposure to their slogans and goals led me to join the General SS [*Allgemeine SS*].[97] In addition, the political conditions prior to 1933 didn't appeal to me. My father was a member of the SPD. But none of the political parties gave us young people anything like a clear goal to strive for. For these reasons, I volunteered to join the SS. On November 1, 1933, I was taken on as an *Anwärter* in the General SS.[98] I had originally hoped to attend a school for architecture in Höxter in 1934. In early 1934, though, the members of the General SS were told that an Active SS was under development.[99] For us young people, we were told, this would be a unique opportunity to do something for Germany. They were describing our future in glowing terms. That was also part of why I joined the Active SS in August 1934. Along with about 15 or 16 comrades, I was sent to the "Freisland" SS guard troop. After a very thorough examination, only about 50 percent of us were accepted. The rest were classified as unfit. That's how I joined the Active SS. My number was 164,705.[100]

From August 1934 to January 1935, Hackmann was a member of the SS guard unit at Ostfriesland. He was trained at the Esterwegen concentration camp, after which he was promoted to *SS Sturmmann*. As Hackmann described, "I was fairly ambitious, and as a result I was selected to undergo formal training at Esterwegen, with the special prisoners [*Ehrenhäftlinge*] there.[101] At the time, I considered that a mark of distinction."[102] When the Esterwegen camp was closed as part of Himmler's restructuring of the concentration camp system, Hackmann was sent to the SS Death's Head Guard Battalion Brandenburg in Berlin, where he worked for the administrative department. In winter 1935–36, he was promoted to *SS Unterscharführer* and sent to the Oranienburg concentration camp to serve as report leader. In 1937, he was sent to the Buchenwald concentration camp, which was under construction at the time. In Hackmann's words: "I was trained as a report leader there [at Oranienburg] and served in that same capacity in Buchenwald."[103] In 1939, he was promoted to *SS Scharführer*, but continued to serve as report leader, a supervisory function that put him into direct contact with the male guards. That November, he was promoted to *SS Untersturmführer* and was appointed as second camp compound leader at Buchenwald. Two years later, he was promoted to *SS Hauptsturmführer* and began serving as adjutant to the commandant of Buchenwald, Karl Otto Koch. By fall 1941, when the then twenty-eight-year-old Hackmann was transferred to Majdanek to begin serving as first camp compound leader, a key position within the camp, he already had eight years' experience as an SS officer in the concentration camps.

Heinz Villain, who served as field commandant at Majdanek, described his background to Fechner as follows: "From 1927 to 1935, I attended *Volksschule* [primary school] in Rheinsberg [in Brandenburg, note by author]. Back then, it was difficult—in terms of careers. So I trained as a blacksmith."[104] In 1938, Villain completed his apprenticeship and took his journeyman's examination. In April 1938, he joined the Armed SS. Several months later, on November 1, 1938, he was sent to the SS Death's Head Regiment Brandenburg in Oranienburg. In Villain's description: "In other words, I had agreed to serve for twelve years, so that I could then join the civil service, meaning the police. That was my plan."[105] After the war broke out, Villain and his unit were deployed on the Westerplatte peninsula and in France; on May 27, 1940, Villain was wounded in battle. After his recovery, he was deemed unfit for the front, and was instead posted to the headquarters of the Majdanek Concentration and Extermination Camp, where he remained until his transfer in May 1944. However, as he described in Fechner's documentary in the 1970s, his hoped-for police career never came to fruition:

> What angers me the most: back then, we volunteered in order to secure our future. We didn't know back then how long the Hitler dictatorship would last, after all. And my goal was to join the police when my twelve years were up.[106]

By contrast, the example of Wilhelm Reinarz, who was born in 1910 and went on to become an *SS Unterscharführer* in the medical corps, demonstrates that male concentration camp staff were also recruited from health-care professions:

> Sometime around 1935, my brother opened a gas station in Cologne, where I worked for a time. When my brother died six months later, I had to find different work. Later . . . I started working as a nurse orderly at the state hospital in Langenfelt. I worked as a nurse orderly until I was drafted in September 1939.
>
> In 1934, I joined the General SS. In September 1939, I was drafted into the SS-Leibstandarte Adolf Hitler in Lichterfelde. I was immediately transferred to an SS Death's Head Division, established in Adlershof. . . . In Adlershof, I went through basic training. Then I was sent along with my SS division, which, as far as I can remember, was attached to an army unit, to France and then to the northern section of Russia. I was a medical orderly and was a member of the medical division of this SS unit. Toward the end of 1941, after I had been in Russia for about six months, I was wounded. I was sent to the military hospital at Halberstadt. After I had recovered, which was around spring 1942, I was posted first to Oranienburg and then to Lublin.[107]

Because of his experience as a nurse orderly, Reinartz was posted to an SS unit as a medical orderly. After being wounded, he was assigned to duty in the concentration camps, and was posted to Majdanek.

Eduard R., born in 1922 in Vienna, was just sixteen years old when he volunteered in May 1938, shortly after the Anschluss, to join the SS Death's Head Regiment Brandenburg.[108] As a member of this unit, he participated in the invasion of the Sudetenland and the campaign in Poland. Like Reinartz, he was transferred to serve at a concentration camp after he was wounded at the front:

> On May 25, 1940, I was wounded at Chalais. I spent time in various military hospitals in France and Germany, and then was sent to Prague as part of the 2nd Conv. Reserve Company. . . . I spent about six months in Prague with the convalescent unit, and then was transferred to the guard unit at Buchenwald concentration camp. After that, I was sent to the Flossenbürg concentration camp, where I also was posted to the SS guard unit. On June 21, 1942, I was transferred to the Lublin concentration camp.[109]

In Majdanek, Eduard R. was assigned to the guard company of the 3rd SS Death's Head Division.

Like Eduard R., Georg W., born in 1922, was Austrian. In May 1938, he volunteered for duty with the Armed SS.

> I was sent to Oranienburg near Berlin, where I was assigned to the 7th Training Unit of the SS Death's Head Division. After about nine months of training, I was sent to the 2nd Company of the Death's Head Division stationed in Oranienburg. I accompanied that unit in the occupation of the Sudetenland and Bohemia. After duty in the Sudetenland, I was detailed to the Flossenbürg concentration camp for about four weeks, after which I returned to Oranienburg. I was named SS Section Leader at Oranienburg in 1940. Around 1941—I can't remember the precise date—I was transferred to the Majdanek-Lublin concentration camp.[110]

The interrogation report offers no information as to why the two Austrian men volunteered with the SS. Both were barely twenty years old when they were assigned as training leaders to the 3rd Company of the SS Death's Head Division.

However, most of the men serving in the guard unit at Majdanek were not from Germany or Austria, but came from Romania, Hungary, and the Baltic states. As *Volksdeutsche* or "ethnic Germans," some had been conscripted into the Armed SS, but many had also joined voluntarily. While at Oranienburg, the men received an accelerated course of training that lasted between two and three full weeks, after which they were transferred directly to Majdanek. As one of the guards, Otto Z., born in 1925 in Latvia, described: "The Ukrainian guard company, which included Ukrainians, Latvians, and a few Lithuanians, all recruited from Russian prisoner of war camps [*sic*], had all made the choice to serve as guards, rather than be guarded themselves."[111] In a later interrogation, Otto Z. described his own path to Majdanek as follows:

> On October 21, 1941, I was drafted from the Heilbronn am Neckar resettlement camp to the Armed SS. I was first sent to a training company of the SS T.Stuba. Buchenwald. After finishing my term as a recruit I was sent in January 1942 to the SS guard company of the Hinzert special camp [*Sonderlager*] in the Hunsrück region. In April 1942, I was transferred to the guard battalion of the Arbeitsdorf concentration camp near Fallersleben. After the camp was dissolved in October 1942, I was transferred to the SS guard battalion at the Debica special camp in Poland. In November 1942, I was transferred to the SS guard battalion at the Lublin concentration camp, where I stayed until late June 1944.[112]

For these SS men, joining the SS also meant financial and social advancement. In contrast to the female guards, however, SS men had military training and several years of experience. Many of the men joined the SS at a very young age, sometimes well before the age of majority. Like the women, the young men took advantage of opportunities provided by the Nazi state that afforded them greater independence and the ability to strike out on their own. Moreover, a number of the male SS guards at Majdanek had been sent there after having been wounded at the front. Although this appears to have been a common practice at the time, existing documents offer little insight as to why, or according to which criteria, it was decided that these SS men would be transferred for service in a concentration camp.[113]

Concentration Camp Service: The Professional and Social Dimension

Of the twenty-eight *Aufseherinnen* who worked at Majdanek, testimony and other source materials are available for thirteen of them. As these sources show, the women ranged from nineteen to forty-two years old—twenty-six years old, on average—when they entered service at the concentration camp. Most of the women were working class or lower-middle class, and the majority came from large families. All of these young women had completed at least eight years of compulsory education. Only a few of the women had been able to train for a career. This group included four trained nurses, one woman who had worked in a service industry, and one who had been employed at the post office. Most of the women had no specialized vocational training and had been previously employed as unskilled factory workers or as household help.[114] Alice Orlowski was the only member of this group who had completed upper-level secondary school; she had also completed four semesters at university and later operated her own business. Orlowski was also one of the oldest women in this group. At the time of their recruitment, most of the women were unmarried. As single, widowed, or divorced women, they were dependent on their work as a source of regular income. This group of recruits also included two single mothers. Prior to 1942, many of the women had either volunteered for work as concentration camp guards on their own initiative, or had been encouraged to apply by friends, acquaintances, or family members.[115]

Even though many of these women applied for work as camp guards on their own initiative, little is known about ideological or political factors that might have played a role. This also holds true for Hermine Braunsteiner, who was among the first women to volunteer for work at a concentration camp. Political motivations appear to have played a role for just one of the women, who had been an active member of the Bund Deutscher Mädel for a number of years. For the remaining recruits, the decision to apply for work as a camp guard appears to have been motivated most often by a desire for financial security and social advancement. Most of these women appear to have been motivated by either unemployment, or a desire to find different, more appealing work. At the time of their recruitment, most of the women were either unemployed, or employed in physically demanding and monotonous factory work. These young women most likely viewed guard work at Ravensbrück as a well-paid and secure job that brought enhanced social status and the benefits of civil service employment (including, in this case, cheap room and board and the provision of uniforms).[116]

In later testimony, most of the guards at Majdanek said the local labor office had assigned them to work at the concentration camp between 1942 and 1943.[117] Of the thirteen women in this group, four had worked in nearby armaments factories from which they had been recruited for work at the concentration camp. The majority of the women claimed to have been conscripted to serve as guards, either by the labor office or by pressure from recruitment efforts carried out at the factories where they worked. Whether these claims of conscription are credible, or whether the women were simply trying to evade punishment by the courts, remains unknown. In a few instances, at least, women appear to have succeeded in refusing employment at a concentration camp, including Ravensbrück, without experiencing reprisals or ill effects.[118] Whether this was a common occurrence or an exception to the rule is unknown.

According to the historian Gudrun Schwarz, the labor-conscription process these former guards described before the courts was indeed a common form of wartime recruitment, but it was not always compulsory in nature.[119] Stephanie Oppel also argues that even women who were threatened with fines or jail sentences had some room for maneuver when it came to labor assignments.[120] According to Oppel, the women could have made their employment preferences clear at the labor office. Alternatively, they could have elected to perform poorly during training, in an effort to have been classified as "unsuited" to the work.[121] By contrast, Irmtraud Heike and Bernhard Strebel argue that, especially after January 1943, the women who were subjected to compulsory recruitment by labor offices and factories did face real penalties for refusing assigned work.[122] It is likely that, over the course of the war, expanded armaments production (and the corresponding expansion of the concentration camp system) made it increasingly difficult for women to refuse labor assignments.

Also worth mention is that four of the women—Hildegard Lächert, Rosa Reischl, Charlotte W., and Charlotte Wöllert—had worked as nurses. Whether the labor offices might have had instructions to recruit women with specific career experience for work in concentration camps is uncertain. However, this cluster of women suggests that the recruitment process may have favored women with particular social and work backgrounds.

Leaving aside the question of voluntary recruitment or conscription, all of the recruited women had in common that they belonged to the SS's target group, which included unemployed women and women in low-level jobs from the lower-middle and working classes.[123] For unskilled factory workers and housemaids, employment as a concentration camp guard represented both financial security and social advancement. In this sense, the wartime economy also offered these women new social mobility. For many of these women, the decision to seek work with the SS or to apply for a position as a concentration camp guard was made in order to escape difficult family circumstances or simply to attain greater independence.[124]

In contrast to the female guards, the male SS officers—Hermann Hackmann and Heinz Villain, in particular—made it clear they were motivated by the perceived opportunity for career advancement. In his interview, for example, Hackmann said that his ambition led him to seek a career in the SS, while Villain saw his voluntary service with the Armed SS as part of a broader plan to eventually enter the civil service and work for the police. Although their career paths were no doubt shaped by outside circumstances and the progression of the war, the men (unlike most of the women) reported in postwar testimony that they had entered concentration camp service motivated by a clear vision and future career goals.

Exactly what these young SS men and female recruits knew about conditions within the National Socialist concentration camps remains unknown. Although rumors abounded in Germany and Austria, it is likely that most of the young female recruits had little idea what was in store for them at their new workplace. Likewise, whether some of the potential recruits might have been able to reject work in the concentration camps in favor of "civilian" employment also remains unknown. What is certain, however, is that social background, political conviction, and ideological indoctrination are of only limited value in explaining the brutality later displayed by these young women in their work in the concentration camps. Far more enlightening are the workplace routines and daily structures that characterized their work in the camp.

4

Ravensbrück Training Camp

The Concentration Camp as Disciplinary Space

"AT RAVENSBRÜCK, I RECEIVED TRAINING IN HOW TO GUARD PRISONERS,"[1] Alice Orlowski remembered in her 1973 testimony. Like all *Aufseherinnen* who worked at the Majdanek Concentration and Extermination Camp between 1942 and 1944, Orlowski passed through the women's camp at Ravensbrück, which had been established in May 1939. At Ravensbrück, recruits were trained and received their first contact with the "concentration camp universe."[2] As stated on the application form, the new guards were subject to a three-month probationary period.[3] The following discussion explores Ravensbrück's function as a training camp for newly hired *Aufseherinnen*.

> When they first arrived at the camp, the female guards were usually appalled and took some time before they approached the same level of cruelty and debauchery.[4] For some of us, it was a small and rather bitter game we played, measuring the amount of time it took a new *Aufseherin* to catch up with the brutality of her more experienced colleagues. For one young, 20-year-old guard, who on the day of her arrival knew so little about what constituted good manners in the camp that she said "excuse me" when she passed by a prisoner, and who was visibly distressed at the first acts of violence she witnessed, it took exactly four days[5] until she herself had acquired the same tone and behavior that were quite obviously new to her. This

> young woman was obviously quite talented in the repertoire under examination here. As for the others, it generally took them between eight and fifteen days, at most a month, to acclimate themselves. But once I did hear of a very young *Aufseherin*, who could not get used to the debaucheries and brutalities of her colleagues. . . . That was the only such case I heard of.[6]

As one of the "Night and Fog" prisoners, Germaine Tillion arrived at Ravensbrück from France in late October 1943.[7] A professional ethnologist, Tillion had, by 1946, already published a comprehensive study of the history of the women's concentration camps.[8] Like Tillion, Margarete Buber-Neumann, a political prisoner at Ravensbrück from 1940 to 1945, also had ample occasion to observe how recent recruits adapted to their new environment. Buber-Neumann, who worked in the office of Chief Guard Johanna Langefeld, recalled the "shocked" look of new recruits, dismayed as they discovered what awaited them at the camp:

> I saw it happen over and over, half of these women, at some point in the first few days of their life as an *Aufseherin*: they came to the chief guard's office, weeping, and demanded to be discharged from service immediately. They were informed that only the camp compound leader or the camp commandant could release them from their work. But only a few dared take that step. Their fear of approaching an officer who then might berate them held them back. And, of course, many of them were also reluctant to disgrace themselves by returning to the factory. Obviously, too, there was the temptation posed by this work, which, though unpleasant, was not terribly strenuous and was exceptionally well-paid. . . . And very few *Aufseherinnen*, possessed of both the courage and moral will to resist, were able to convince the camp leadership to release them from their "conscription" before the end of their three-month probationary term. As for the rest, we were again subjected to the sad spectacle of these former factory workers who, after fourteen days, would begin issuing commands as though born into the barrack yard—and who, very soon, just like the old ones, would threaten to report prisoners and start beating them with their bare hands.[9]

As Buber-Neumann thus notes, it was not just the social and financial benefits of work as a concentration camp guard that convinced new recruits to acclimate themselves to a situation many initially found repugnant; it was also a fear of the SS leadership. As a rule, the only grounds for an *Aufseherin* to obtain dismissal from service were either pregnancy, psychological difficulties, or an illness of a serious or chronic nature.[10] Outside of pregnancy, however, it was the *Aufseherin* who generally had to take the initiative to obtain a dismissal. It appears that, at least for some of the young women, fear of their superior SS officers was too great to risk seeking dismissal from the guard unit.

According to both Tillion and Buber-Neumann, most recruits overcame their initial reluctance rather quickly, acclimating themselves to their guard duties and the daily realities of the camp. Still, this contrast between the initial reactions of shock and dismay, followed by quick adaptation to the daily realities of life in the camp, raises a number of questions. What, exactly, happened during the first weeks at the camp? How were they trained to carry out their duties? What effect did living in a concentration camp and wearing a uniform have on these women? And, what aspects of their work did they view as positive? To answer these questions, I will examine the orientation process for female recruits, beginning with barracks assignments and receipt of uniforms.

For the hierarchically organized SS staff, efficiency and coordination were of paramount importance. In Ravensbrück, as in all other concentration camps, disciplinary techniques aimed at optimizing the guards' efficiency were employed from the very start. In an effort to increase efficiency and control the activities and behavior of the staff, time, space, and clothing were recorded, coordinated, and monitored. In his analysis of schools, the military, and the workshop, Michel Foucault has described such "individualizing technologies of power" as a disciplinary strategy aimed at both the body and the behavior of the individual.[11] Because Ravensbrück recruits were subjected to similar disciplinary technologies, Foucault's analysis offers an enlightening perspective from which to analyze their training and assimilation.

Such disciplinary methods, however, should not be understood solely in the negative, as the set of laws, prohibitions, and rules drew the boundary between actions that were prohibited and those that were deemed acceptable.[12] As Foucault always insisted, this disciplinary structure should not be reduced to its basic repressive function—that is, the power to say "you must not." Rather, understanding power also requires that we examine its positive and productive mechanisms:

> If we admit that power only has the function of forbidding, we must invent some types of mechanisms . . . to be able to say: we self-identify with power; or otherwise we say that there is a masochistic relation of power that is established, which makes us love the one who prohibits. But, then again, once you admit that the function of power is not essentially to prohibit, but to produce, to produce pleasure, at that moment you can perfectly understand how we are able to obey power and find pleasure in this obedience, which isn't necessarily masochistic.[13]

For the concentration camp staff, then, regulation of their work and free time, their living quarters, and their clothing constituted not only a form of compulsion and constraint, but also offered rights and privileges, a sense of belonging and identification, and the opportunity to exercise power and authority in their work. To date, scholars have paid little attention to the different forms of power that were exercised within the camp, each of which involved unique modes of operation, processes, and techniques.[14] The concentration camp was not a unified entity, governed by a single mode of power. Rather, Foucault's apt description of power as a "juxtaposition, a liaising, a coordination, a hierarchy, too, of different powers which nonetheless regain their specificity" also applies to disciplinary power in the concentration camp.[15] Nonetheless, there was a fundamental divide between the camp guards and the prisoners they oversaw: in the case of the prisoners, any rights and privileges they were accorded were provisional and temporary, entirely dependent on the whims of the SS. However, while the female camp staff was most certainly subject to SS authority, which was organized along paramilitary lines, they also possessed considerable personal agency and decision-making authority.[16]

Training and Orientation

Because so many records were systematically destroyed shortly before liberation and during evacuation of the concentration camps, we have only fragmented information regarding the training and orientation of *Aufseherinnen* recruits. After the war, the legal authorities focused most of their attention on the guards' time in Majdanek. Nonetheless, several postwar interrogations of the women who worked at Majdanek do shed some light on their early days at Ravensbrück. For example, Herta B., a factory worker who arrived at Ravensbrück in June 1943 for a four-week training period, described the very large number of documents she was required to sign upon arrival: "At the Ravensbrück concentration camp, we were first given a huge stack of documents, though I can't remember exactly what they were any more. We had to sign them, and then we were brought to our lodgings."[17]

Of the documents presented to Ravensbrück recruits (as well as to new transfers at other concentration camps), a number have been preserved. These remaining documents include copies of the employment contract and a description of pay.

Employment Contract

Mr. (Mrs., Miss)
.... is entering into regular salaried employment beginning on .... —for an indefinite period—for the period of .... in accordance with the General Wage Scale (ATO) and Wage Scale A for Auxiliary Members in the Civil Service (TO.A), the General Service Regulations for these salary scales (ADO.), the General Service Regulations for Administrative Offices and Businesses of the Reich, and the special Service Regulations for Salaried Employees of the Reichsführer SS and Chief of Police in the Reich Ministry of the Interior with classification into the salary category ....
Ravensbrück Concentration Camp, Postal Address Fürstenberg i. Meckl. at the Uckermark Youth Camp Compound, Ravensbrück, Post Fürstenberg i. Meckl.

Any future amendments to the ATO. and TO.A or the Service Regulations or any salary scale replacing those contained herein shall be valid from the date in which the amendment takes effect and shall also apply to the contractual relationship described herein.

The salaried employee will be insured with the ....
.... in accordance with the General Service Regulations for Administrative Offices and Businesses of the Reich through the additional retirement and surviving dependent's pension program for non–civil service auxiliary members.

Ravensbrück, dated .... 19 ....
....

The Camp Commandant[18]

In addition, the *Aufseherinnen* were informed that as "Auxiliary Members of the Armed SS," they were subject to the jurisdiction of the SS and police.

I, the undersigned, hereby declare and confirm through my signature that at my hiring I was instructed that I am subject to the jurisdiction of the SS special courts for any crime which I may commit while I am an auxiliary member of a unit of the Armed SS, and thus am subject to the regulations of the Military Penal Code, the Wartime Special Penal Code, and the Wartime Regulations for Criminal Procedures. This shall in particular apply to the penal provisions regarding military offenses, including treason, espionage, aiding and abetting the escape of a prisoner, absences without leave, knowingly submitting a false report, bribery, damage to official property, etc.

I am also aware that legal decisions issued in wartime proceedings are not subject to appeal.

Lublin, dated

signed[19]

The women were further required to sign a declaration of confidentiality.

Declaration of Confidentiality

The undersigned hereby agrees to maintain strict confidentiality, both verbally and in writing, regarding all confidential material and all actions undertaken on the basis of this material, including after dismissal from service with the SS. I am aware that I will be guilty of a violation of a service command if I disclose any confidential material and fail to uphold this order. I am also aware that a violation of this order will be deemed treason.

> I also agree to immediately report any violations of confidentiality of which I may become aware.
>
> I am aware that, if I fail to report such a violation of confidentiality, my criminal liability will be equal to that of the criminal himself.
>
> read, approved and signed
>
> First and last name
>
> The Leader of the Auxiliary Members[20]

Finally, female recruits were also instructed on their "dealings with prisoners":

> Lublin, dated
>
> **Declaration on Dealings with Prisoners**
>
> I, ... born on . . . . was instructed today regarding the following 6 points and agree to observe and obey them in every detail.
>
> 1.) I will not disclose any confidential information which I may see or hear within the buildings of the SS Chief Economic and Administrative Office—Office Group D—to any third party.
> 2.) Any personal conversation with prisoners is strictly prohibited.
> 3.) I may not accept gifts or other objects from prisoners, or distribute or sell such items to prisoners.
> 4.) Accepting any letters or notes from prisoners and removing such letters and notes from the premises is high treason. Any such requests on the part of prisoners must be reported immediately.
> 5.) Conveying any verbal request or request for a meeting to a third party on behalf of a prisoner is liable to criminal sanctions.
> 6.) I am aware that any violations of these regulations are punishable by law.
>
> First and last name[21]

At the same time, the new *Aufseherinnen* were instructed on numerous occasions that they were permitted neither to impose punishments on their own authority, nor to physically assault prisoners. In her postwar testimony, Rosa Reischl, who began working at Ravensbrück in October 1942, said: "I had to fill out forms that told me I had to maintain the proper distance from prisoners, and that hitting or yelling at prisoners was not allowed."[22] In her postwar testimony, Elisabeth R. said that during her orientation at Ravensbrück in 1943, she was expressly instructed that she was not permitted to hit or beat the inmates.[23] Herta B. recalled receiving similar instructions:

When I was hired at Ravensbrück concentration camp in June 1943, I had to sign a lot of papers. I can't remember if any of them instructed me on the treatment of prisoners. We were told, verbally, that we were not permitted to injure the prisoners.[24]

The female guards and the SS men were required to sign a declaration to that effect:

Declaration of Honor

It is the Führer who makes decisions on the life or death of an enemy of the state.

No National Socialist has the right to strike an enemy of the state or to subject him to physical abuse.

I hereby declare on my honor that I will follow the Führer's instructions in all camps, which I confirm with my signature.

Ravensbrück, dated ______________________

____

Signature

____

Rank[25]

Finally, the women had to swear loyalty to their superiors and to Adolf Hitler.

Oath

The auxiliary member .... born on ...., who is employed by the headquarters of the prisoner of war camp of the Armed SS of Lublin, has today made a pledge of loyalty before the leader of auxiliary members or his representative, and confirmed this pledge with a handshake.

I pledge my loyalty and obedience to the Führer of the German Reich and people, Adolf Hitler, and I pledge to carry out my duties selflessly and with diligence.

Read, approved and signed

First and last name

Lublin, the leader of the auxiliary members[26]

TRAINING

In March 1942, the first documented six-week training session for female guards took place.[27] Buber-Neumann, who observed several of these sessions, later described them as follows:

> The commandant and the camp compound leader instructed the new *Aufseherinnen* on their duties. The prisoners were described as women who were degenerate and of inferior value, who were to be handled with the utmost strictness. Of course, the importance of their new office was duly underscored, and they were warned repeatedly to observe all official regulations. They were threatened with punishment if they had any personal interactions with the concentration camp inmates, who were the dregs of humanity. Every few days, there was yet another roll call for the female guards, where they were exhorted to be strict, as strict as possible.[28]

As Buber-Neumann's description shows, the new *Aufseherinnen* were instructed that they would be supervising the outcasts of the Nazi *Volksgemeinschaft.* The prisoners under their authority and control were women who were "minderwertig," literally of inferior value, a racial hygiene category that had its origins in the welfare policies of Imperial and Weimar Germany. Under National Socialism, however, the category of the "minderwertig" was more than simply a social stigma, since individuals who had been deemed "asocial" by the authorities could be subject to a variety of repressive measures, including sterilization and incarceration in a concentration camp.[29] In Nazi Germany, the distinction between women who were racially and socially "valuable" and women who were racially and socially "inferior" served to further distinguish between respectable single women and "asocial" women, such as prostitutes.[30] For the newly arrived *Aufseherinnen,* the reams of documents that they were required to read and sign would have served to powerfully affirm their own status as full and valued members of the *Volksgemeinschaft,* a superior caste to whom the state could properly entrust the responsibility of exerting surveillance and control over politically and socially "dangerous" women.

No documents have survived that describe the actual training program for *Aufseherinnen.* However, in contrast to the SS men in Majdanek's SS Death's Head Battalion (for whom training documents still exist), it is unlikely that the women were required to perform military drill exercises, or that they received instruction in military site regulations and ranks, or in the proper behavior toward their superior officers.[31] Most likely, the training received by female guards was entirely less military in nature. Anna David recalls taking part in a course in Ravensbrück in June 1942:

> At the very beginning, we were issued a uniform and had to give an oath. They instructed us on methods for dealing with prisoners. We were told that escape attempts must be prevented at any cost, and that we were to report even the smallest violation on the part of the prisoners. . . . During the training course, every graduate had to take part in various duties, and learn how to carry them out in accordance with camp regulations. . . . Each graduate was observed very closely, and we were constantly reminded to carry out our orders with the utmost attention to duty.[32]

One thing known for certain is that the *Aufseherinnen* at Majdanek received firearms instruction. Hermine Braunsteiner, who came to Ravensbrück on August 15, 1939, confirmed in her 1946 testimony that all female guards received instruction on how to handle, shoot, and clean their service weapon.[33] Another existing document that serves as proof of such weapons training is an internal memo in which the camp commandant ordered a target-practice session for the *Aufseherinnen*, at 10 A.M. on April 11, 1943—a Sunday morning.[34]

At least as recalled by the female recruits, the training program for new female guards at Ravensbrück seems to have been based on the principle of "learning by doing," a marked contrast with the training male guards received. Additionally, each female recruit was assigned an experienced *Aufseherin* as mentor.[35] For example, Braunsteiner was instructed in her duties by a more experienced colleague during the summer of 1939:

> I received training as a guard from Maria Mandel. She showed me how to supervise the prisoners, to ensure that they carried out their work. Maria Mandel was very strict. My training with her wasn't very good, and what I saw was also unfavorable. What I mean by that is that she often hit the prisoners. We didn't have any whips or sticks. I spent two months with her in this unit, which had about 100 to 120 prisoners.[36]

Braunsteiner was assigned to the penal barrack for nine months, and remained at Ravensbrück for over three years, until October 1942 (when she was transferred to Majdanek).[37]

The women who were recruited at Ravensbrück after 1939 also reported having been assigned to "older *Aufseherinnen*," and being immediately introduced to the day-to-day realities of their work.[38] For example, Charlotte Wöllert testified that when she arrived in 1942, an experienced *Aufseherin* supervised her during a three-month probationary period, after which she gradually "settled" into her new position.[39] Likewise, Erika W., who arrived in Ravensbrück in summer 1942, reported:

> In Ravensbrück, I received no training and was immediately assigned to supervise a prisoner unit. In other words, together with more experienced colleagues, I supervised prisoner details during their work on the camp grounds or while they stacked coal in the underground shelters.[40]

In 1943, when the number of female guards began to rise sharply, the training period at Ravensbrück was again cut, to just a few weeks. In summer 1943, Herta B. received only four weeks' training before she was transferred.[41] Just a few months earlier, in March 1943, Alice Orlowski had received only one week of training.[42]

IDEOLOGICAL INSTRUCTION

According to the Commandant's Order No. 3 of July 24, 1942—the only commandant's order from Ravensbrück to have survived the war[43]—the *Aufseherinnen* received instruction from the camp's head of ideological training every Saturday from 5 to 6 P.M.[44] However, there is no documentation regarding exactly what the female guards at Ravensbrück—or at the other women's concentration camps—were taught. According to Bernhard Strebel, the women were instructed regarding the "proper dealings of the guard units with the prisoners,"[45] the "guard troop's duties and obligations,"[46] "discipline among the *Aufseherinnen*,"[47] and the "supervision of prisoners at work by their assigned guard troops."[48] We know that SS men at Sachsenhausen attended lectures on politics, as well as Strength through Joy leisure-time events.[49] Within the Nazi regime, the Nazi leisure organization Kraft durch Freude (KdF) was responsible for arranging leisure activities for Germans, especially workers. Its various branches covered the sectors of tourism, after-work entertainment, education, folklore, and the beautification of work sites.[50] In terms of policy, the goal was to reach Germans in their everyday work routine as well as in their private sphere, and thereby to strengthen the *Volksgemeinschaft* and broaden popular support.[51] However, there are no attendance records for these training sessions, which generally took place during the SS men's free time; in fact, due to poor attendance, the department in charge of ideological training at the Gross-Rosen concentration camp was disbanded after just one year.[52]

Likewise, at the women's concentration camp at Majdanek, an August 1943 letter of complaint submitted by the chief guard unit to the camp commandant suggests that some of the *Aufseherinnen* were less than diligent in attending training sessions. The letter states that, notwithstanding guards either sick or on leave, eight of nineteen available *Aufseherinnen* had missed the training session in question:

> On Wednesday, August 25, 1943, the camp commandant issued an order that all SS staff, including female guards, were required to take part in the lecture to be held on August 25. Even though all the women were aware of the lecture, the *Aufseherinnen*
>
> Danz — Mayer
> Pfannstiel — Radojewski
> Zimmermann — Lächert
> Brückener — David
>
> failed to attend. I would also like to note that this is not the first time that orders by the camp commandant have been ignored.
>
> I request that the above-listed *Aufseherinnen* be disciplined.[53]

In his study of the Armed SS, Bernd Wegner argues that, over time, the SS de-emphasized regularly scheduled training sessions in favor of ad hoc ideological instruction. Such ideological training, it was claimed, could not and should not be imposed in the form of weekly lectures. As one regimental order admonished, "It must take place always and everywhere."[54] The Ravensbrück camp regulations adopted a similar stance:

> At certain intervals, he [the camp commandant] or his representative will hold in-depth training sessions for the SS staff and the entire female guard unit regarding their duties in the concentration camp. This training will offer instruction on camp rules and regulations by way of clear, practical examples, which will emphasize the magnitude of the guard duties and the heavy responsibility borne by the guard units here at the concentration camp. Punishments which have already been carried out for negligence and other violations [*sic*] in the female guards' handling of prisoners will be a repeated topic of discussion. The training will also place special emphasis on the severe punishments that are issued for documented mistreatment of prisoners.[55]

In addition to this ideological training, the Ravensbrück camp held daily one-hour roll-call sessions for *Aufseherinnen*, and a weekly training session that addressed the guards' daily duties and practical issues related to their work. Eventually, all the women's concentration camps instituted similar sessions for their female guard staff.[56]

During postwar restoration work at the Ravensbrück Memorial, carried out in 1995, a screening room was discovered, which was situated across from the headquarters building in the basement of the garage tract.[57] In all likelihood, it was in this room that concentration camp staff were shown films of an ideological nature. In a 2001 interview carried out by the ethnologist Jeanette Toussaint, Anna G., a former guard, reported that obligatory film screenings were held in the Ravensbrück camp screening room. *Jud Süss* was one of the films shown, as the former *Aufseherin* Anna G. remembered.[58] According to Berndt Wegner, this kind of informal instruction was popular within the SS as early as the late 1930s.[59] The emphasis on visual material in part reflected a belief that many people were "more likely to be influenced by the image rather than the word." Moreover, as noted in documents from the period, the films offered a "significant advantage" in that they could not be "arbitrarily adapted," presumably by the training staff.[60]

Finally, the reading habits of the *Aufseherinnen* were also monitored and steered in what was deemed an appropriate direction. For the Majdanek concentration camp, a number of "routing slips" related to such activity have survived.[61] Four such routing slips included books that female guards had checked out of the camp's library, which was called the Alfred Rosenberg Donation Library.[62] The books included three romances and one novel set in a historical village—in other words, popular literature intended for a female audience.[63] Although it is impossible to say whether this enterprise was successful, it certainly demonstrates that the SS administration took the political use of popular entertainment very seriously as an elegant way to root propaganda in the camp staff's everyday lives and their leisure time.

• • •

Due to the scarcity of source materials, little is known about the content of ideological training conducted at the concentration camps, or about the methods used for this instruction. Instead, recent studies of the SS and police tend to focus primarily on the "Jewish question" and emphasize that the intent of the training was to legitimize the activities of these organizations and their members.[64] Bernd Wegner, however, argues that many postwar studies have tended to put too heavy an emphasis on the importance of ideological instruction within the SS. According to Wegner, even in the early years of the SS's existence, ideological instruction never exceeded the compulsory two hours per week, and even at that, these sessions frequently failed to take place.[65] It is likely that the concentration camps were similarly lax in carrying out such training. Surviving source materials for Majdanek suggest that recreational activities often merged the personal with the political, and that the camp leader deliberately took advantage of such activities to exert influence over the staff.

The question posed by Margarete Buber-Neumann and Germaine Tillion regarding the process of acclimation for new *Aufseherinnen* in the camp is key in this respect. For the recruits, the principle of "learning by doing" meant an abrupt immersion into life in the camp. In all likelihood, the orientation system, in which each recruit was assigned to a more experienced staff member, explains the rapid acclimation of the new arrivals. Learning through the example of these more experienced colleagues, the new arrivals were constantly reminded that the very conditions they found so shocking were, in fact, an ordinary aspect of their duties and life at the camp. At the same time, the many documents and forms the new *Aufseherinnen* had been required to sign had a legitimizing effect. Thus, the countless regulations did more than simply impose limits on the female guards' actions—they served to validate the power accorded to them as they began their duties at the camp.

Finally, the initial process of assigning uniforms and housing to the newly hired *Aufseherinnen* may well have helped the women assimilate to their new identity as concentration camp guards, allowing them to more quickly overcome any sense of shock and hesitation they may have experienced at the outset.

The Concentration Camp as Residence: Architecture and Its Effects

In her postwar account, Isa Vermehren, a survivor of the concentration camps, described her impressions on arrival at the Ravensbrück camp in February 1944:[66]

> Just past Fürstenberg, the truck turned off the main street onto a smaller street, which seemed like it was still under construction in parts. A short time after that, we drove by a work detail—women in blue and white striped clothing, with shaved heads, guarded by SS men, who stood there with their carbines hanging. . . . The

> paved path turned into an asphalt roadway, and to the right and left there were attractive housing settlements, with groomed gardens. A bit further away was a peaceful lake, with the silhouette of the town of Fürstenberg on the other side, with the red tile rooftops nestled beneath the church tower like chicks under a hen. The truck stopped in front of the wide gateway to the commandant's headquarters, which was about five or six years old. Just like everything else I could see, it looked quite new and not lived-in. . . . The inside of the headquarters building was empty, clean, and restrained, without much color; it had tile floors, smooth doors, smooth walls, a lot of wood, and some wrought iron. It was all covered in an oppressive silence, which contrasted greatly to the bright sunlight outside, and to the bright light that filled the entire facility.[67]

The Ravensbrück concentration camp was located on the eastern bank of Lake Schwedt, overlooking the town of Fürstenberg an der Havel, which had made a name for itself earlier in the century as a spa resort. Fürstenberg was situated on what then was the highway between Berlin and Stralsund, and also had good railway connections to the capital. Construction of the women's concentration camp began in November 1938. By the end of the war, the camp complex was as large as the town itself.[68] Like all concentration camps, Ravensbrück had a prisoners' camp, a camp jail, various utility buildings (including farm buildings and workshops), administrative buildings, the camp headquarters, and a residential section for the SS staff.

The concentration camps were all planned as self-contained entities, complete with the facilities and infrastructure necessary to function much as a small town would. The facilities and infrastructure were also adapted, as necessary, for changing uses, needs, and political priorities.[69] According to the architect Reinhard Plewe and the art historian Jan Thomas Köhler, Ravensbrück was a "small SS settlement" that had been "carefully planned to remain in ongoing operation," with modern sanitary facilities, its own waste treatment plant, a high-security camp compound for the prisoners, its own facilities for industrial production, and a railway connection.[70]

BARRACKS LIFE AS A FORM OF DISCIPLINE

When they joined the SS, the concentration camp guard staff—both male and female—joined an organization in which their living environment and their daily schedules were regimented along military lines. In order to create an "orderly" unit out of the assemblage of German and Austrian women recruited to work as *Aufseherinnen*, the female guards' housing barracks were situated in various locations around the camp grounds, in accordance with military principles. As in all military institutions, monastic principles were also employed in the concentration camp. Similar to a cloister, these disciplinary techniques governed the administration of time and space in the workshops, the industrial production sites, and in the staff barracks.[71]

The system of zones used at Sachsenhausen was also implemented during the construction of Ravensbrück. The camp complex was divided into a number of separate and self-contained sections, each with a specific function delineated by a very simple set of signifiers. Though he was writing about Sachsenhausen, the architect and historian Ralph Gabriel's comments are equally applicable to Ravensbrück:

> Division of the camp into zones resulted in a spatial separation of the different functions. The camp jail was cordoned off from the rest of the camp by a high wall. The infirmary, the garden nursery, the isolation and quarantine zones were all separated from the rest of the camp by a fence. Over the years, the boundaries of the zones shifted, and the function of the zones underwent reorganization as well.[72]

The SS personnel were not permitted to move about freely within the camp. Only authorized staff could enter the various zones. Staff identification cards were color coded as follows: green, for members of the headquarters' staff; gray, for camp guards; red, for members of the political division. In addition, specially issued passes were utilized to control access to various areas of the camp.[73]

According to Reinhard Plewe and Hans Jürgen Köhler, within the architecture of the entire camp grounds, priority was clearly accorded to the SS housing estate, which faced the town of Ravensbrück.[74] The SS housing estate was comprised of four single-family homes in a random arrangement, ten duplex houses, and eight buildings that housed *Aufseherinnen*.

All staff was housed according to rank, with the commandant and higher SS leadership and their families residing in the "Führer House." Twenty lower-ranking SS men and their families were assigned to the "Lower Führer House." Finally, the female guards, most of whom were young and unmarried, were housed in apartments within eight designated buildings, located at an intentional distance from facilities in which their male counterparts were housed. Most of the women who were later reassigned to Majdanek had lived in these units. Married women and women with children might also be housed in private lodgings outside the camp.[75] The barracks belonging to the male guard troops, the members of the SS Death's Head Battalion, were located at the other end of the camp, on the southeastern side near the men's prisoner camp.[76] Almost certainly, it was by design that the residences for the male and female guards were located in separate sections of the camp.

Daily camp routines were subject to strict military regimentation. For camp guards, the workday was divided into reveille, rising, the morning muster, daytime and nighttime work routines, roll call for the prisoners and staff, and finally, the end of the workday. In addition to work, mealtimes, recreation, and permission to leave the camp grounds were also subject to strict protocol. For example, concentration camp staff took their meals together at set times and locations. The regular guard staff—meaning the *Aufseherinnen*, the male guard detail, and the lower-ranking SS men from the men's camp—ate together in a common canteen.

The male leadership—meaning the higher-ranking SS officers—ate in a separate canteen.[77] Although no longer standing, the canteen for the *Aufseherinnen* and the SS guard detail was located within the camp compound, somewhat to the side and to the north of the camp gate (see figure 3).[78] It was separated from the adjacent prisoners' camp by a barbed-wire fence, and because the male guard detail was not permitted access to the prisoners' camp, it was accessible only via the camp gate.[79]

As Foucault explained, the "art of distributions" is a technique frequently employed to establish discipline over a heterogeneous group of individuals.[80] At the same time, the technique aims to preemptively neutralize potential disruptions to the established order. Within the concentration camp, this meant that the staff were divided into smaller groups according to defined functional criteria, and placed within a clearly defined hierarchy that was more amenable to coordination and control. The spatial distribution of the camp staff served both as an expression of this internal hierarchy and as a disciplinary technique. For example, housing for the highest-ranking officers was located at the highest point on the camp grounds, across from and overlooking the buildings that housed the female guards. Thus, the concentration camp was a sophisticated disciplinary space, in which the behavior of the guard staff could be readily monitored, disciplined, and sanctioned. In Foucault's words, it "was a question of organizing the multiple, of providing oneself with an instrument to cover it and master it; it was a question of imposing upon it 'an order.'"[81]

Due to the scarcity of sources, the exact staffing of Ravensbrück cannot be reconstructed today. According to Bernhard Strebel, by late 1940, about 110 female guards had passed through Ravensbrück, along with five SS leaders (higher-ranking officers who worked for the camp headquarters, and also physicians), and fifty lower-ranking SS men who worked for the headquarters staff.[82] The number of men in the guard detail is unknown.

HOUSING THE *AUFSEHERINNEN*

The SS housing estate, which included the buildings that housed the female guards, is one of the few groups of buildings still standing at Ravensbrück today. The SS estate was part of the "civilian world" of the camp, as Insa Eschebach has termed it.[83] Ravensbrück was the only concentration camp that had purpose-built housing for its female staff. In all the other women's concentration camps, the *Aufseherinnen* were housed either in barracks or other existing buildings. However, when Ravensbrück opened, in May 1939, construction of the housing units for the female guards was not yet complete. For this reason, in the first eighteen months of the camp's operation, some of the women were housed within the camp compound—first, in a barracks next to the infirmary, and later, in lodgings next to the prisoners' bath.[84] According to Reinhard Plewe and Jan Thomas Köhler, by late 1940, one single-family home, two duplex houses, and five buildings for the *Aufseherinnen* were ready for occupancy.[85] By the time the photographs from the SS photo album were taken—most likely in

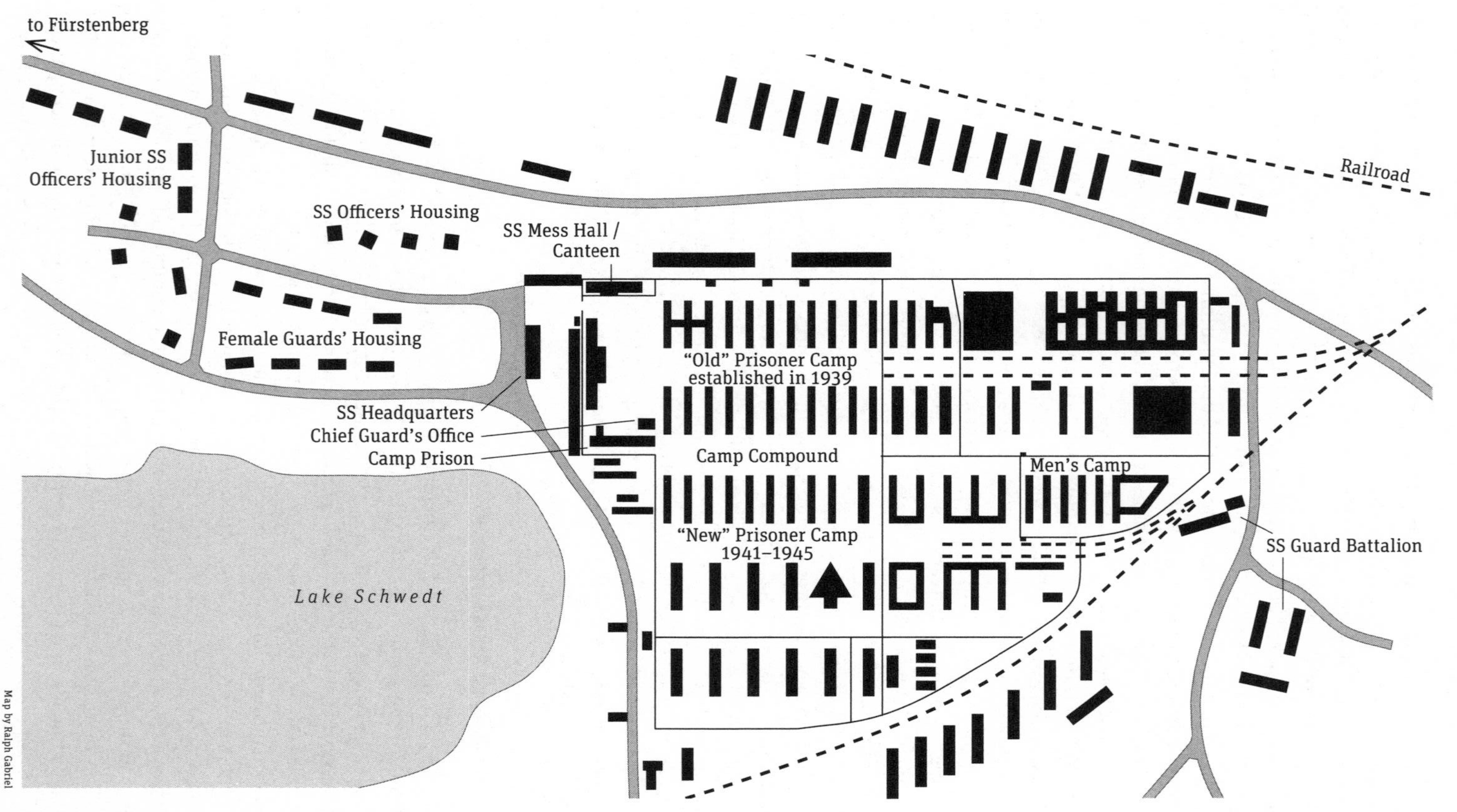

FIGURE 3. Map of Ravensbrück Women's Concentration Camp

1941—most of the estate was complete (see figures 4 and 5).[86] The eight buildings that housed the female SS staff were built in two rows that adjoined an open square.[87] Each building was two stories high and contained ten one-room apartments and four attic rooms, each of which housed either one or two women. Each building could thus house a minimum of fourteen women; altogether, the buildings had room for at least 112 *Aufseherinnen*.

In an effort to reconstruct how many women served as guards at Ravensbrück, Bernhard Strebel has used payroll records from the Fürstenberg branch of the Neustrelitz district and savings bank. According to his count, by late 1942 a total of 313 *Aufseherinnen* had served at Ravensbrück.[88] With continued expansion of the concentration camp system, the intensive recruitment of new staff in 1943, and the evacuations of the "eastern" camps that began in spring 1944, the number of female guards at Ravensbrück continued to rise, as did the number of inmates. At that point, the SS estate could no longer accommodate all the staff, and some of the *Aufseherinnen* had to be housed in barracks outside the settlement. In postwar testimony, the women said that it was mainly the "volunteers" who were housed in the SS estate, while the "labor conscripts" and the women who had received only brief training at Ravensbrück were more likely to be assigned to the barracks.[89]

The estate apartments, which were probably about 25 or 30 square meters in area, encompassed a sleeping and living area furnished with a built-in wardrobe and a sink.[90] For most of the women, who came from humble backgrounds, this would have represented a good standard of comfort. Each floor on the building had a toilet, a bathroom, and a tea kitchen, shared by the five women on that floor. Given the backgrounds of the *Aufseherinnen* and the housing standards of the era, these facilities would have been considered quite modern and advanced. The basement of each building had a laundry room for common use, while the second floor had a loggia overlooking Lake Schwedt. According to Insa Eschebach, in other concentration camps such "comparatively luxurious buildings" would have been intended for use by the higher-ranking SS leadership, which implies that their assignment to the female guards had a certain gendered dimension:

> In other SS estates located within concentration camps, such as the one at Buchenwald, the female staff were either quartered in large, two-story communal buildings, very similar to barracks and with a quasi-military character, or they lived in plain, barrack-like buildings. For the *Aufseherinnen* at Ravensbrück, however, generously sized buildings in a country-house style were erected. . . . These generously sized residential buildings with their park-like surroundings were presumably intended to make the women's work environment at Ravensbrück as pleasant as possible.[91]

In his postwar testimony, Rudolf Höss, who was assigned the task of establishing a women's camp at Auschwitz in spring 1942, claimed that the *Aufseherinnen* who had arrived there from Ravensbrück had been "spoiled" by their time at that camp:

Mahn-und Gedenkstätte Ravensbrück/Stiftung Brandenburgische Gedenkstätten Fo II/D10-1639

FIGURE 4. View of the female guards' housing from the headquarters building

Mahn-und Gedenkstätte Ravensbrück/Stiftung Brandenburgische Gedenkstätten Fo II/D10-1704

FIGURE 5. Construction by female prisoners in the female guards' housing estate

> The female guards at Ravensbrück were very spoiled. Everything had been done for them in order to keep them at the FKL [the women's concentration camp], and the advantageous living conditions there were used to recruit new female staff. The women had excellent housing, and received salaries they would never have achieved elsewhere. Their duties weren't overly strenuous, either. In short, the RFSS [Reich SS Leader] and especially Pohl [Oswald Pohl of the WVHA] wanted the *Aufseherinnen* to be shown the greatest consideration. Conditions at Ravensbrück at that time were still normal, and the camp wasn't overcrowded yet.[92]

As Insa Eschebach has noted, the architecture of the SS estate buildings also reflected the image of women propagated by the SS.[93] In this sense, the estate's architecture reinforced the ideological and experiential world in which the female SS staff lived and worked. Eschebach has compared these residential buildings with housing that was built in the 1920s and 1930s specifically for women who worked at nearby industrial plants.[94] According to her findings, the National Socialists drew upon this architecture in the camp's purpose-built "residences for working women," as they were called at the time. Eschebach cites from the 1943 dissertation by Elisabeth Portmann on the topic of "Protection and Oversight of Working Women during the War":

> Women are unusually dependent on the manner in which they live and work. For this reason, even the factories take care to ensure that women who have been removed from their familiar surroundings and brought to an unfamiliar area among strangers in order to carry out what is generally strenuous work are housed in a healthy and appropriate manner.[95]

Both a sense of ambivalence and allusions to contemporary discourses of social hygiene are typical of National Socialist attitudes toward working women. On the one hand, women's work was essential to the wartime economy; on the other hand, the lives of employed women—and especially of female factory workers—did not correspond with National Socialist ideals of the female sphere, in which women would ideally embrace their reproductive duty, become mothers, and remain in their "familiar surroundings." Portmann's arguments evoke both paternalistic tendencies and a desire to ensure the welfare of working women. It was intended that both of these goals could be achieved through architectural design. The young and generally single women were to be housed in residences attached to their workplace, rather than in "lonely and unfriendly rooms." There, the women would enjoy "companionship provided by their female comrades" rather than "spending their evenings at nightclubs and the like."[96] The housing facilities for the *Aufseherinnen* were a case in point: employed women who lived apart from their families were not to be left to their own devices, but were to be housed in "lodgings that will encourage a sense of community."[97]

Both Toussaint's interviews with former guards and an examination of the women's personal photographs offer evidence that the women took advantage of the many recreational opportunities available in the area. In warmer months, they swam and went rowing on Lake Schwedt, went on walks, and took part in festivals put on by local marksmen's associations. In the winter, they went ice skating on the lake, and made outings to the pub, café, and cinema in Fürstenberg.[98] When they had a weekend off, the women sometimes went on excursions to Berlin. Because the women were only allowed to leave the camp premises on certain days, and were required to be back at the camp by 11 P.M., evenings after work were most often spent in the common rooms at their residences. There was also a hair salon on the camp premises, staffed by prisoners, that was intended for the *Aufseherinnen* and wives of SS officers.[99] At the residences, each floor also had a sewing room, apparently a feature typical in women's residences at the time.[100] Since concentration camp inmates took care of the day-to-day laundry, ironing, and sewing tasks for the entire camp, it is likely that these sewing rooms were intended as a place for the women to sew, crochet, and knit during their leisure time.

Of course, the *Aufseherinnen* could also spend their free time and evenings in their own rooms, each of which had a wooden door that led to a communal hallway.[101] All the doors had an opaque glass window, through which the interior of the apartment was visible in shadowy form. In a Foucauldian sense, these windows could be understood as offering a view of the women's private sphere, which was almost certainly intended to enable a form of social control over their private as well as their sexual lives. Beginning no later than 1942, each residence also had an assigned house elder, a post that rotated among the residents on a weekly basis. During her assigned week, this woman was responsible for ensuring that all residents followed house rules, and for reporting any infractions to the camp commandant.[102] In a social sense, this policy encouraged a form of mutual surveillance among the residents that entailed a subtle and reciprocal disciplining of both the self and the other.

The architecture of the buildings used to house female guards thus embodies the inherent tensions between its disciplinary function and the desire to create a familiar, safe haven for the working women. The residences aimed to evoke the feel of a country house, with all the modern comforts. At the same time, however, the architecture took on distinct disciplinary and social-welfare characteristics. For example, as part of its disciplinary function, the architecture encouraged the women to spend their free time on needlework and other handicrafts, activities that contrasted sharply with the brutality and violence of their workaday life—work that, moreover, offered the women opportunities for agency that contrasted sharply with contemporary models of femininity and the female sphere. Thus, at the end of each work day, the residences offered the *Aufseherinnen* a respite from the daily realities of their work in the prisoners' camp. However, as Eschebach has rightly emphasized, even in their residences, the women could not entirely ignore their surroundings, as the prisoners' camp was just five minutes away on foot, with the daily operations of the concentration camp remaining "always in view":[103]

> There was a tension between the desire to create an idyllic world—of which the paradigm was the nature- and animal-loving Rudolf Höss—and a disciplinary perfection that extended all the way to the point of annihilation, that might be said to constitute the defining characteristic of the Nazi concentration camp.[104]

The architecture of the Ravensbrück camp in general, and the SS housing estate in particular, is reflective of the desire to organize and divide space so as to monitor and discipline the concentration camp staff. As one might expect in a school, hospital, or workshop, time and space, as well as the movements and activities of the female guards, were encoded, made visible, controlled, and—when possible—corrected. Using these disciplinary techniques, the SS attempted to transform the female recruits into "disciplined" auxiliary members of the Armed SS who, as such, were both "subjects and agents of military authority."[105]

As a place of both residence and work, the concentration camp was imbued with a complex set of meanings for the female SS staff. On the one hand, it offered a comparatively modern and comfortable living and work environment for women of their social background at that time. As Eschebach has noted, the estate bore some similarity to an industrial residential estate, with the camp compound taking the place of the factory.[106] The camp gate marked the division between the two worlds, dividing the prisoners' camp from the civilian part of the concentration camp. Though residential buildings in the SS estate were to some extent part of the private sphere, they still belonged to the camp grounds, which were organized along (para) military lines. The female guards who were housed in the SS estate were, in a sense, living in barracks housing, where "barracks" is understood to mean a fenced-in space containing residential and technical buildings, with access controlled by guards.[107] The *Aufseherinnen* could only leave the camp grounds with permission. Moreover, even within the SS estate, camp regulations remained in force, with wearing of the proper uniform and the proper form of greetings to superior officers required at all times. Furthermore, practices of containment, surveillance, and control were still in effect within the estate. The physical and mental interventions experienced by the female guards were enacted on the smallest of scales, and appeared harmless enough as compared with the disciplinary tactics employed in the men's barracks. However, this was precisely what constituted the "elegance"[108] of this disciplinary control, which aims to regulate the body with a pervasive, unnoticeable, and internalized form of surveillance and policing of the self.[109]

Nonetheless, for the female (and for the male) SS staff, life in the concentration camp was not limited to rules and regimentation; it also offered modern comforts, along with a comparatively high standard of living. The women sat down each day to meals that had been made for them, and did not have to handle their own laundry, or clean their own living quarters. Cooking, doing dishes, laundry, ironing, mending, and cleaning were chores carried out by camp inmates, under supervision of the SS. Few, if any, of the *Aufseherinnen* would have had access to this level of comfort in their civilian lives. For women of their standing, such comforts would have been particularly appealing, since housework within the family was largely the duty of wives or unmarried daughters, with working single women generally looking after themselves. Finally, the comingling of work, living space, and recreation within the confines of Ravensbrück also had some positive elements: among them, an element of expediency.

In a postwar cross-examination, Hertha Ehlert described her circumstances as a camp guard at Ravensbrück as follows: "Well, I want to be quite honest, I had never such a good life as in the beginning at Ravensbrück when I arrived."[110] Particularly during the early phase of the camp's operation, life at the camp offered the women a heretofore unknown standard of "luxury," with a room of her own for each *Aufseherin*, regular leisure time, and a decent salary.

Clothes Make the Woman: The Uniform as a Source of Power

In the early phase of Ravensbrück's existence, the *Aufseherinnen* did not wear uniforms. "We had only blue smocks," Hermine Braunsteiner recalled.[111] "Six months later, or maybe a year later—I can't remember exactly—we received uniforms. The jacket and culottes were made out of loden material, in light gray. We also had light blue blouses, boots, and a light gray side cap."[112]

According to Erika W., the uniforms included a plain skirt, a gray blouse worn with a black necktie, a pair of culottes, high boots, and a cap.[113] In her postwar testimony, Charlotte Wöllert also recalled that the guards who arrived at Ravensbrück in 1942 were issued a gray skirt, a jacket, and a gray-green colored blouse. Also issued were a pair of both high boots and regular shoes. In Wöllert's recollection, however, the women did not wear neckties.[114]

Following Himmler's visit to Ravensbrück, a standardized uniform for the female SS staff was introduced in spring 1940.[115] After this time, newly arrived guards were assigned two uniforms (winter and summer) in military gray, two pairs of boots, one pair of regular shoes, socks, uniform blouses, a cap, and some sports apparel.[116] The Ravensbrück regulations contain the following note about the uniforms to be worn by the *Aufseherinnen*:

> Uniform: gray service uniform, hat (when very hot, a straw hat). Female guards for the external details without a dog with pistol (t) m 24. Service uniform without jewelry.[117]

At this point in time, uniforms were still a relatively new form of work wear for women. Uniforms for women were first seen during World War I, when women were mobilized on a large scale to fill "male" civil service jobs, as letter carriers, railway conductors, and the like. However, as cultural historian Gundula Wolter emphasizes, it is important not to overestimate the gender equality denoted by the uniforms. That is, this "equality" existed in name only, with women not yet even permitted to wear trousers, which were deemed too masculine.[118] In this respect, too, the culottes assigned to the *Aufseherinnen* presented a good compromise: culottes were functional and plain, yet by no means seen as unfeminine. The uniforms worn by the female SS guards must also be understood as a functional and protective form of work wear. The wind and weather–resistant herringbone twill (made out of a heavy linen or cotton material) and the sturdy shoes were practical and functional, while accessories such as caps and hats offered additional protection from the elements. However, the uniforms were also functional in terms of style, with the severe and gender-neutral shape of the uniform offering the women a degree of invisibility against advances or attention from their male counterparts.[119]

Finally, the uniforms issued to the *Aufseherinnen* were most definitely intended as a uniform, in the (para)military sense of the word, as discussed below.

THE HOMOGENIZING EFFECT OF THE UNIFORM

Later, former Ravensbrück inmates often recalled the female guards as depersonalized entities, "as a homogeneous force of fate that had no personally identifiable traits."[120] According to Insa Eschebach, this is also a result of the fact that prisoners did not know the names of the guards and were required to address the women by title, as "Frau Aufseherin." In reference to the black capes they wore, Polish inmates often referred to the female guards as "the black crows."[121] In the Majdanek trials, too, many former inmates said they tended to perceive concentration camp staff, frequently there only a short period before being transferred, more as "uniforms" than as individuals.

By sheathing their bodies in identical clothing, the uniforms effectively homogenized the appearance of their wearers (see figures 6 and 7). They directed the attention of observers away from individual physical characteristics, and toward the standardized appearance of the wearer, so that individual members of the staff were essentially "absorbed" within the group. The standardized, uniformed body thus created for both the wearer and the observer the sense of a closed group. As sociologist and political scientist Paula Diehl noted in her study on body ideals of SS men:

> Uniforms are distinguished from civilian attire by the necessity to present a unified group image. . . . They identify membership via appearance and so serve to separate insiders from outsiders. An imaginary line is drawn between the interior and the exterior whenever a uniformed group or individual is confronted with someone of a different appearance, regardless of whether this confrontation takes place in a real or an imaginary context.[122]

Mahn-und Gedenkstätte Ravensbrück/Stiftung Brandenburgische Gedenkstätten, Fo II/D, 10-1622, taken from the SS album compiled in 1941

FIGURE 6. Female guards of the Ravensbrück Women's Concentration Camp in formation for the visit of Reichsführer-SS Heinrich Himmler

Mahn-und Gedenkstätte Ravensbrück/Stiftung Brandenburgische Gedenkstätten, Fo II/D, 10-1624, taken from the SS album compiled in 1941

FIGURE 7. Reichsführer-SS Heinrich Himmler inspecting the female SS guards

Every form of clothing is coded; that is, it provides information about the social milieu of its wearer and, together with body language and comportment, also serves as a marker for social affiliations. Thus, in the case of SS uniforms, the standardization made possible by the uniforms helped disguise differences in social origin among SS members and, as such, served to instill solidarity within the group. As an example, the camp dress code made particular note that uniforms were to be worn "without jewelry."[123] While on duty, the female guards were forbidden to wear any personal accessories at all, including jewelry, handbags, or the like. This was intended to eliminate social distinctions and to generate a unified and collective image. In practice, however, this objective was not entirely achieved since, in addition to clothing, gestures and speech also served as clues to differences in social background.

In addition, as is the case with all military uniforms, the uniforms worn by the female guards made certain "fine distinctions." For example, rank was denoted by aluminum braiding on the shoulders and sleeves. These distinguishing markers were not decodable by outsiders, but rather served as signals to SS members and others who were familiar with the SS hierarchy. A regulation issued by the Chief Economic and Administrative Office (WVHA) in March 1944 describes the various insignias:

> Effective immediately, the head of the Chief Office—SS Obergruppenführer Pohl—has approved the following insignias for the female guards in the concentration camps.

Chief guard	3 aluminum stripes (Art. No.:1302 Collar braid-alu. 9mm) <u>also: the upper edge of the hat</u> <u>has a silver-gray braid.</u> (Art. No. 1327 Braid. Silver-gray)	Comp. Group[124]
a) Leader of a detail of a work camp	<u>1 Alu stripe</u>	Comp. Group VII
b) Report leader, work leader, penal block leader, block leader, dog leader, tech. leader	<u>1 bar with star</u> (previous insignia) (Art. No. 60168)	
Deputy block leader Guard	<u>1 bar</u> (previous insignia) (Art. No. 60167)	Comp. Group VIII

> Method of wearing:
> The stripes and badges are worn on the lower left arm. The lower edge of the strip or the tip of the badge should be 12 cm. from the bottom edge of the sleeve. Each additional stripe should be positioned 5 mm. above the last.
>
> The female guards are to affix the new insignia immediately.
>
> Sign. Glücks
> SS Gruppenführer and General of the Armed SS[125]

The aluminum stripes signaled the rank of the wearer, identified her within the internal SS hierarchy, and assigned her a fixed position within the chain of command. At the same time, the insignia served to distinguish the guards among themselves and made visible any gradations among the women. Depending on the female guard's "behavior" and "performance," the hierarchical order could shift—for example, due to promotions, demotions, or staff departures. As Luzie H. explained in an interrogation: "I was addressed as 'Frau Aufseherin' and had the rank of Feldwebel. We wore badges signifying the rank we had been promoted to on our sleeves."[126] Even though the female guards were civilian employees and had no military rank, this statement implies that they nonetheless understood themselves as military staff. In Luzie H.'s unusually introspective statement, military rank was described as a positive factor.

In addition to insignias denoting rank, other badges and medals that indicated various honors served as further marks of differentiation. Several *Aufseherinnen* were awarded the War Merit Medal 2nd Class, introduced in August 1940 as the lowest-ranking war service medal.[127] In her postwar testimony, Hermine Braunstein recalled the honor as follows:

> I received the medal. But it was the commandant of the Ravensbrück camp—Kögel—who nominated me for the medal. It's possible that I was finally given the medal by Commandant Florstedt in Lublin. . . . I wore the war merit medal in the buttonhole of my uniform jacket. Next to it, on the left side of my uniform jacket, I wore the sports badge.[128]

However, Braunsteiner could no longer remember why she was awarded the medal of merit. In her recollection, it was awarded to all female guards who had three years of service.[129] The fact that it was a frequently awarded medal, and was entirely civilian in nature, appears to have made little difference to her. Braunsteiner wore the war service medal on her uniform jacket during her day-to-day duties at Majdanek. Ultimately, it was one of the distinguishing characteristics that made it possible for the majority of witnesses to identify Braunsteiner at the Majdanek trial.[130]

UNIFORMS AS SYMBOLS OF POWER AND VIOLENCE

The uniforms established a symbolic border that divided insiders and outsiders and served as a daily and tangible reminder of Nazi authority and might:

> With military and police uniforms, the symbolic character is expressed through badges and other markers that are associated with violence. Their wearers are distinguished from other people in uniform largely due to the carrying of weapons. Military staff and police officers are not just representatives of state power, but embody and exercise violence in the name of the state.[131]

The death's head insignia and the deliberate use of the color black on the SS uniforms effectively symbolized power and death[132] (see figures 8 and 9). In contrast to the male SS members, who wore black uniforms, the *Aufseherinnen* were clothed in gray. The death's head emblem, which was the Schutzstaffel or SS insignia, was only permitted to be worn by SS members who had an SS number and identity card—in other words, men only. They were worn on the collar patch, and attached to the black hat. The female guards, classified as "civilian employees of the SS" or "auxiliaries of the Armed SS," were also not permitted to wear the *sigrune*, or "victory runes," which SS men wore on their collar patches. As Erika W. recounted in a postwar interview: "We wore the Reich eagle on our sleeves and on our caps."[133] The Reich eagle was considered a national emblem; since 1871, it had been the German national symbol, used to indicate that the wearer or the object bearing it was a representative of the state. In the Third Reich, the Nazi Party symbol—a depiction of a Roman legionary eagle with a swastika in its claws—became the new symbol of the state.

One photograph depicting Herta (last name unknown), an *Aufseherin* from Grüneberg, along with her service dog, contains an interesting detail (see figure 10). It was a personal photograph, which had, in a manner typical of the time, been printed as a postcard. In it, the dog was wearing a bib adorned with SS runes, which indicated membership in the Armed SS. This photo is the only known image in which a dog is wearing anything adorned with an SS rune. On the reverse of the photo is the inscription: "In memory of my pleasant service in Grüneberg, to my dear parents, your Herta, 24 March 1944. This is my dear and loyal dog Greif." Here, it is apparent that the symbolically charged quality of the uniform was part of its appeal for young women. The fact that the young woman posed in full uniform, for a photograph that was perhaps taken by a colleague, and later sent the photograph home to her parents suggests that she was proud of her work uniform and that it represented something meaningful to her.[134] For both the concentration camp inmates and the wearers themselves, the uniform symbolized power. The fact that nearly all the women remembered their uniforms and were able to describe them in detail, with some sense of nostalgia, suggests that the uniforms held some appeal.

FIGURE 8. Portrait of Hermann Hackmann, the first protective custody camp leader, presumably from camp records, probably taken between November 1941 and September 1942

Landesarchiv Nordrhein-Westfalen, Rheinland Division, RWB 28560

Date unknown. Research Centre Postwar Justice

FIGURE 9. Portraits of guard Alois Kurz from camp records

Collection Vaclav Nemec, Muzeum Sokolov Czech Republic

FIGURE 10. Private photo of dog handler Herta with "Greif" at Ravensbrück

Conversely, in postwar testimony, none of the female guards reflected upon the image conveyed by their uniform. To explore that question, then, we must turn to the accounts of former prisoners, in whose lives the uniformed female guards played a critical role. For example, in Ravensbrück, Margarete Buber-Neumann observed a group of about twenty young female factory workers, who had been conscripted by Edmund Bräuning directly from their workplace in a munitions factory:[135]

> Even before they received their field-gray *Aufseherin* uniform, they were sent in a group to the chief guard. Most of them were dressed very simply, even somewhat shabbily. They stood there shyly, ill at ease, with a bashful look on their faces; many of them didn't know what to do with their hands. The [chief guard] Langefeld told them what house they would be living in, where they would receive their uniforms, and when their duties would begin.—Then I would often watch through the window as they walked across the camp square, nudging each other, and staring with shocked looks at the prisoners who were marching by.—In some cases, the transformation happened as soon as they were "outfitted." Once in their high boots, they strode in quite differently; then all it took was a cap perched on their heads, and suddenly they acquired a bit of self-assurance along with it.[136]

In Buber-Neumann's description, clothes did truly "make the woman," and the uniforms were a crucial step on the path to turning the young factory workers, who were initially shocked at the prisoners' appearance, into concentration camp guards. For the young women, the uniforms represented more than just clothing—they became a symbol of the "protection of the institution itself." At the same time, the uniforms embodied the women's subordination to the Armed SS, an authority to which the wearers had sworn their obedience. By donning their uniforms, the *Aufseherinnen* could share in this experience of the collective and partake of its might.

One of the more important elements of the uniform, which potently symbolized the power accorded to the wearer, were the black leather knee-high boots.[137] The boots featured prominently in the guards' postwar testimony. As Hermine Böttcher later recalled: "Our shoes were ordinary military boots, much like 'jack boots.'"[138] Here Böttcher's use of the term "jack boots" explicitly recalls the military context.[139] Likewise, in her testimony before the court, Rosa Reischl also referred to the "jack boots" worn by the female guards.[140]

Well into the twentieth century, high leather boots were regarded as very masculine footwear, with a distinctly military connotation. As Paula Diehl has noted, these high black boots, also worn by SS men, were one of the key symbolic elements in the Nazi aesthetic of power.[141] At the same time, as Diehl emphasizes, the boots were an eminently practical article of clothing, especially for the female and male camp guards. As Hildegard Lächert reported in Eberhard Fechner's film documentary on Majdanek: "it was so dirty there, especially when it rained, because of the clay soil."[142] The Ravensbrück camp grounds were also largely covered in hard dirt. The leather boots offered protection from puddles, mud, and sharp objects, making it possible for the *Aufseherinnen* to stride with confidence through the camp. With their military presence, the "jack boots" were both a practical and symbolic element in the women's daily exercise of authority. Within the context of the concentration camp, the boots were also a weapon, which could be used to injure the inmates or even kick them to death, all the while offering protection from blood.[143] This form of brutality would have been far less likely had the female guards been wearing long skirts and ladies' shoes.

From her cell on the north side of the prison section, Isa Vermehren had a view of the office of the chief guard, located about eight meters away (see figure 3). From that vantage point, she was able to observe the *Aufseherinnen* at work around the clock. Immediately after the war, Vermehren recorded her impressions:

> I believe that the uniforms played the decisive role. For women in uniform, the strongest effect is felt in the boots which, as though with magnetic force, forced the adoption of a masculine manner of walking. All the *Aufseherinnen* walked in the same way, because all of them were making a clumsy attempt to live up to the ideal—the ideal that had over the previous twelve years been pushed on us through propaganda in word and image. . . . It's nearly impossible to imagine the grotesque

hermaphroditic quality of these uniformed beings: bodies entirely female—and with it, the forced masculine movements; stiff manes of curls and thick earrings—paired with culottes and high boots; sad child-like eyes—paired with hard, loud voices; the entire appearance that of a caricature of a cook clothed in the attitude of a general.[144]

As Vermehren explains, the *Aufseherinnen*, with their physical bearing and their uniforms, were not always genuinely intimidating in appearance—at times they could appear clumsy, even grotesque. In this sense, the symbolism of the uniforms operated on more than one level, and could take on a variety of implications. Signs and symbols are inherently ambiguous and overlaid with a variety of signifiers, which depending on context can be interpreted in different ways. As Alf Lüdtke has noted, symbols take on meaning within specific situations, but those meanings are never fully constrained by the situation at hand. When it comes to symbols, "the curious attraction they exert, and their effectiveness, lies in their ability to allow seemingly incompatible meanings to coexist, and even to 'tease out' or intensify these meanings."[145] Vermehren's imagery, with its elements of caricature, mirrors the social chasm that separated the female guards from Vermehren's own understanding of femininity, instilled in her by her educated, middle-class background. The seemingly clumsy, awkward, and "masculine" gestures and comportment of the *Aufseherinnen*, in other words, did not correlate with Vermehren's own sense of the proper feminine ideal.

The uniforms served to mold the women's bodies and confer upon them the symbols and aura of power and might, with the aim of enhancing the guard's status, both physically and psychologically.[146] The uniforms thus served as a tool for intimidating the inmates, and identifying the wearer as a representative of the state. In that sense, the uniforms offered both practical protection and the symbolic protection of the state, while at the same time conveying social authority and prestige. Wearing their uniforms, the female guards served as representatives of the state and could partake of its authority and might.

At the same time, the uniform also embedded the wearer within a "rhetoric of honour,"[147] signifying the wearer's subordination to the Armed SS, to which the *Aufseherinnen* had pledged their loyalty. As Margarete Buber-Neumann and Isa Vermehren noted, the uniform helped create and convey the women's identity as SS staff, shaping their self-perception and the image they wished to project, all while serving as a source of empowerment. The uniforms were a decisive element in the transformation of shy recruits into self-assured concentration camp guards. The effectiveness of the uniforms is evident in the prominence they later assumed in the memories of the survivors. This is demonstrated by the following comment from Fechner's Majdanek documentary:

After 33 years, we are different people. When we saw them, they were young, strong, well-dressed—in uniforms with a large hat—we were small, and they were big and

> powerful. . . . And now, after 33 years, we saw their bent backs, the gray hair . . . how is that possible . . . ?![148]

The words of Jan Novak, a former inmate at Majdanek, suggest surprise and, perhaps, even a mild disappointment at the appearance of the defendants thirty years after the end of the war.

Discipline and Self-Discipline: The Commandant's Order No. 3

The commandant's order of July 24, 1942, offers insight into the tension between camp regulations and their practical application:

> Ravensbrück Concentration Camp, Ravensbrück, 24 July 1942
>
> Headquarters
>
> Commandant Order No. 3
>
> Distribution:
>
> | | |
> |---|---|
> | 1 | Head of Department D—Concentration Camp |
> | 2 | Dept. I |
> | 1 | II |
> | 2 | III |
> | 1 | IV |
> | 1 | V |
> | 1 | VI |
> | 1 | Mail Censorship Department |
> | 1 | Motor Pool |
> | 1 | Technical Department |
> | 1 | Guard Women's Concentration Camp |
> | 1 | SS-T.Stuba.Rav. |
> | 1 | Jug.Sch.L.U. |
> | 1 | Comthurey |
> | 2 | Chief guard |
> | 1 | Textile and Leathers. M. b. K. |
> | 3 | Reserve |
>
> 1. On 1 Aug. 1942, a curfew was established for the female SS auxiliary members who live on-site. It has been determined that the female guards often do not return home until it is time to resume duty in the morning, and are consequently too tired to properly carry out their duties. They either sleep on duty, or call in sick. For this reason, beginning on 1 Aug. 1942, all *Aufseherinnen* who live in the camp must be home by 12 midnight. Requests for extensions must be submitted to the chief guard. The curfew is suspended on Saturdays for female guards who are not on

duty on Sunday. The house elder on duty that week must report to me any women who violate this order.

2. Recently, *Aufseherinnen* have been leaving for holidays in Berlin wearing unacceptable attire. Outfits such as a silk dress with duty boots, half-civilian, or civilian attire, with a bread bag and so forth are not uncommon. In the future, uniforms may no longer be worn when on leave outside the camp. Either the woman must wear civilian attire, or she must wear the entire dress uniform as required, with a skirt, regular shoes, and a cap, never a hat. Any violations should be reported to me by the chief guard.

. . .

4. I have repeatedly issued instructions regarding what the female guards must do and what they are not permitted to do. The following is a summary of recent complaints:

No gifts may be accepted from prisoners. The *Aufseherinnen* may not post mail for prisoners.

Whistling and singing is not permitted on duty, nor are conversations with prisoners or private individuals.

Aufseherinnen must remain close enough to their assigned detail so that they can keep the prisoners entrusted to them within view.

No prisoner may leave the detail, or be sent away. The prisoner lavatory is located directly next to the detail; the female guards must be at a distance of at least 20 meters from the detail.

When work details arrive and leave [the prisoners' camp], they must remain at a distance of at least 10 meters from one another. Guards should be approximately 5 meters behind the columns. When arriving at the gate, no work detail may pass another one, as that makes the count more difficult for the guard detail. The *Aufseherin* shall remain behind the column until the count is complete.

Personal handbags may not be taken along during duty outside the camp. A sandwich bag and bottle is sufficient.

Flowers [*sic*] and berries may not be picked while on duty.

Dog handlers are responsible for their dogs. They must feed the dogs and keep them groomed. Dogs must be treated with strictness, but may not be mistreated.

Whether on- or off-duty, all female guards must greet and salute their direct superiors.

The pistol and cap shall be worn while on duty.

No *Aufseherin* has the right to punish a prisoner. However, she is required to report any violations of camp regulations on the part of a prisoner.

Female guards are not permitted to converse with male guard details [*sic*], and any conversation with male prisoners will be strictly punished.

Aufseherinnen are not permitted to exchange prisoners with another work detail. Any exchange of prisoners in the clothing factory will be handled by the head of the protective custody camp upon request of the factory head.

> *Aufseherinnen* who assume supervision of a work detail must inform themselves where that work will be performed and what tasks are to be carried out. Female guards are responsible for ensuring that all work is done quickly and competently.
>
> I stress once again that *Aufseherinnen* and employees of the camp are subject to the legal authority of the SS. Any violations of duty, theft from camp staff, dishonesty, etc., will be brought before the SS court.
>
> Currently, the comradeship among the civil employees leaves much to be desired.
>
> . . .
>
> The Camp Commandant
> SS Obersturmbannführer[149]

This document suggests that the women did not always find it easy to follow the military regulations, and also that they sometimes did not return to camp until after curfew. In their postwar testimony, many *Aufseherinnen* said that when they were off-duty, they often ate just a quick sandwich in the canteen for dinner, and then left for the cinema or headed to pubs in Fürstenberg.[150] The commandant's directive also implies that the women sometimes strayed into areas of the camp that were off-limits to them. In his directive, the camp commandant emphasizes to the women that they are not permitted to go to the industrial area, the new building, or the male guard troops' residences, and that any violations would result in arrest. In addition, personal conversations between female guards and SS men were prohibited while on duty. While in uniform, it was essential for the "behavior" and "comportment" of the *Aufseherinnen* to conform to regulations, whether on camp premises, or outside the camp. Appearing in public in "unacceptable attire" was deemed harmful to the image of the SS.

However, the commandant's directive does more than signal that some women struggled to follow the military dress code. Instead, wearing a silk dress with work boots might also be seen as signaling a positive identification with one's duties, or even an act of self-affirmation—especially because, as Rosa Reischl remembered, the female guards were also in possession of a dress uniform and brown shoes.[151] As the regulation implies, some women wore articles of personal clothing in combination with parts of their uniform, such as their leather boots or lunch bag. On duty, some *Aufseherinnen* accessorized their uniforms, even wearing jewelry or earrings, as in Isa Vermehren's description. This could be understood as a gendered behavior, expressing a desire on the part of the women to feminize or embellish their uniforms. At the same time, combining military garb with civilian attire could indicate a desire to flout convention and assert a sense of individual identity, along the lines of what Alf Lüdtke has described as "Eigen-Sinn." In this sense, the combination of military and civilian attire could be understood as a form of "willfulness" or a refusal to conform.[152] Such "Eigen-Sinn," in Lüdtke's definition, represents a particular moment within the interaction of domination and freedom; it is a moment of dissent or nonconformity towards the demands of one's superiors, which does not fundamentally call into question that subservience.[153]

In the case of the *Aufseherinnen*, their flouting of the military dress code should not be understood as a rebellion against their superior officers or the institution of the concentration camp, but rather as signaling a rejection "of limitations placed on their own desires and needs."[154] As Alf Lüdtke has described, "Eigen-Sinn" during work hours can take on a variety of forms, ranging from wandering about, to daydreaming, to chatting and joking with colleagues.[155] "Eigen-Sinn" thus represents a concept more ambiguous and elusive than simple "resistance": it represents a moment in which the individual engages in willful behavior, briefly distancing him- or herself from the constraints of superiors and the demands of the workplace. "Eigen-Sinn" is an individualistic stance, a momentary affirmation of one's own interests and needs (at times at the expense of one's coworkers), with the aim of making the work day incrementally more agreeable.[156] In this sense, the female guards' unconventional attire can be seen as a brief escape from the military order to which they were subjected. It was a moment in which these women were acting in accordance with their own desires and agendas, without taking possible repercussions into account.

As the commandant's directive also implies, the *Aufseherinnen* were also known to exceed their authority by issuing punishments to prisoners. As we have seen, the female guards were not permitted to mete out punishments at will. Instead they were required to report any "violations" on the part of the prisoners.[157] Actions such as picking flowers and berries while on duty were part of various strategies the women employed to make their workday more pleasant—a workday in which brutality and leisure coexisted. Indeed, on other occasions the very same flower-picking *Aufseherin* might have carried out physical punishments. This coexistence of brutality and leisure, in turn, can be understood as a demonstration of how the female guards assimilated and came to terms with the work conditions in which they found themselves.

Nonetheless, once these accommodations had been made, work as a female camp guard did offer numerous benefits. Indeed, women who left the camp to take up other work could find it difficult to reacclimatize to "civilian" existence, as this 1942 application sent to the commandant of Majdanek demonstrates:

Munich, 10 October 1942

Herr Sturmbannführer Max Koegel, Lublin.

You will be surprised to get this note from me today, I'm sure.

After three years of duty, I left the Ravensbrück Women's Concentration Camp on January 1 of this year, and am now in Munich working as an entry level clerk for the Reich Leadership. Since this office position doesn't really suit me, I would like to inquire whether you might have a position for me, possibly in the office. I would be happy to

> return there. I am not enclosing my resume, since you will remember my work. But if you do require it, I would be happy to still submit it. I would be able to begin work on 1 December. If a suitable position is available for me, please let me know as soon as possible, because I would have to give notice for my current position.
>
> Hoping for a positive response. Heil Hitler,
> Hildegard B.![158]

5

Going East

Transfer to the Majdanek Concentration and Extermination Camp, 1942–1944

Asked in 1980 by Eberhard Fechner how long she had worked at the Ravensbrück camp, Erna Pfannstiel answered:

> I guess about a year, and then we were transferred. . . . The other ten were moved too. We paid a visit to the camp commandant at the time. I don't even know what his name was anymore. I think it was Kögel. Well, we were transferred. Though we didn't want to go, I tell you. First of all it was too far away. . . . No, no, we even went up there, but it was no use.[1]

Pfannstiel was part of the first group of guards sent from Ravensbrück to Lublin in October 1942. By her account, she was transferred against her will, in spite of having "visited" Commandant Max Koegel "up there" at headquarters. Pfannstiel's account of this turning point in her career is echoed by the testimony of the other *Aufseherinnen* who were transferred along with her.

Promotion or Disciplinary Transfer?

In their testimony, the women were generally quite specific in reporting the reasons for their transfers from Ravensbrück to Majdanek. Only Luise Danz said she could no longer remember the reasons for her transfer.[2] Her colleague Rosa Reischl, on the other hand, recalled the events as follows:

> I was transferred from Ravensbrück to Lublin [on January 27, 1943] for disciplinary reasons, along with five other women. Toward the end of my time at Ravensbrück, I supervised a small detachment of about three women who mowed the lawn. One of the women was crying and told me she had been separated from her three small children because of some trivial offense. I sent a letter to her husband for her. He must have written back, because I was then accused of having forwarded a letter. Another *Aufseherin* was given a disciplinary transfer along with me, because she'd had her hair done by another woman prisoner who was a hairdresser.[3]

During their testimony, most of the former guards said they had been transferred to Poland for disciplinary reasons. For example, Gertrud Heise said she had been "transferred for disciplinary reasons, upon orders from the Ravensbrück commandant, to the Lublin-Majdanek Concentration Camp" in March 1943.[4] Alice Orlowski testified that she had been sent to Majdanek only days after her arrival at Ravensbrück because she had had "a run-in"[5] with Fritz Suhren, who was the commandant of Ravensbrück at the time. In one interview, she described the circumstances in greater detail:

> It happened because I did not greet a superior on the street. When they asked me why, I told him I was used to ladies being greeted first on the street. I was transferred to Lublin for disciplinary reasons along with two other female guards, also new arrivals who were out in the world for the first time.[6]

According to Orlowski, her transfer was a punishment for her refusal to acknowledge the military code of salutation and her insistence on conventional gender roles (the man greets the woman). Likewise, Hermine Braunsteiner left no doubt about why she was moved. At both the Vienna trial and in her testimony for the Majdanek trial, she stated that, in 1942, the administrative director of the Ravensbrück camp[7] wanted to, in her words, "get fresh"[8] with her. He had attempted to approach her intimately, after which the relationship became "intolerable."

For her part, Hertha Ehlert indicated that she had been denounced by a Gestapo officer for her "humane attitude toward the prisoners"[9] and was transferred to Majdanek as punishment.

> I believe it was in January 1943 that I received a disciplinary transfer from Ravensbrück to the Lublin camp, but I can't remember the exact date anymore. I had a hard

time watching the prisoners in my labor detail go hungry. I often gave my bread bag to the prisoners and instructed them to throw the contents into the wastebasket. There were still sandwiches inside. I knew the prisoners would take them out. One day, some asocial[10] prisoners told a Gestapo officer. I was given house arrest. There was talk of putting me in front of an SS court. Then, I was supposed to get a disciplinary transfer to Auschwitz. Since I had heard how awful conditions there were, I objected and asked to be discharged. The commandant of the Ravensbrück camp then shouted at me during questioning, saying, wouldn't being discharged suit me just fine. "Off to Lublin!" I seem to remember that other *Aufseherininnen* from Ravensbrück came with me to Lublin. But I don't remember anymore who it was or how many we were.[11]

In a later account, Margarete Buber-Neumann confirmed Hertha Ehlert's description of her treatment of the prisoners in her detachment:

She was a big blonde Valkyrie who enjoyed laughing loudly, eating well and amply, and she was horrified by the idea that others had to starve. She was kind and often gave food to the prisoners in her detail. "Go back there to the office cabinet and throw that packet into the waste basket! But look inside first!" And then they found several sandwiches inside.[12]

In contrast to the female guards' recountings, former Ravensbrück prisoner Nanda Herbermann later offered testimony on the spring 1942 transfers of *Aufseherinnen* to Auschwitz, and to Majdanek the following fall. "It was clear that only the most brutal of the women were promoted," she said.[13]

Suddenly there were all kinds of transfers among the *Aufseherinnen*. The "most proven," that is, generally the most brutal of them, were ordered to the Lublin camp and to Auschwitz, together with Commandant Kögel and Chief Guard Mandel and Ehrich. . . . Those poor, poor people they were let loose upon![14]

While it is no longer possible to determine the exact grounds for the transfers, the alleged or actual sexual harassment Braunsteiner referred to suggests that the female SS staff, most of whom were just over the age of majority, were subject to sexual and other pressure by SS officers. Rebuffing a superior's advances could easily result in a female employee's transfer. However, it is important to bear in mind that the women offered these allegations in courtroom testimony, almost certainly with the purpose of exonerating themselves.

As we have seen, Alice Orlowski—who allegedly failed to greet a superior—remained at Ravensbrück for only seven more days after the incident. Whether the brevity of her training and her subsequent transfer were indeed disciplinary in nature, or whether an acute staff shortage also played a role, is unknown. Nonetheless, her testimony would seem to contradict survivors' assertions that a transfer to Majdanek was, in fact, tantamount to a promotion.

Recent research on SS personnel policy has demonstrated that within the SS, transfers to the "East" were a common way of getting rid of disagreeable or undisciplined staff members. This policy extended even to transfers of commandants. For example, after a corruption scandal in fall 1941, Karl Otto Koch was transferred from Buchenwald to Majdanek, with the personal approval of Heinrich Himmler. The transfer was at once a punishment and a test.[15] Another noteworthy transfer was that of Arthur Liebehenschel. Liebehenschel was, initially, a long-serving member of the Inspectorate of Concentration Camps (IKL); later, from spring 1942, he served as chief of Office Group D I in the SS Chief Economic and Administration Office (WVHA). A married man, Liebehenschel divorced his wife of sixteen years shortly before the birth of his fourth child, due to an intimate relationship with a WVHA secretary fifteen years his junior. This lapse in personal conduct resulted in his transfer and appointment as commandant of Auschwitz in fall 1943. However, his superiors, Oswald Pohl and Heinrich Himmler, later decreed that he was not up to the task, after which he was sent still further east, to Majdanek.[16] As Karin Orth has noted, from the time Liebehenschel arrived in Lublin on May 16, 1944, until July 23, 1944 (when Majdanek was liberated by the Red Army), the camp was virtually empty, with nearly all of the prisoners having previously been evacuated. This, too, points to the likelihood that Liebehenschel's transfer was a punitive measure.[17]

Through research into the personnel policies of the civil administration in the Generalgouvernement, historian Bogdan Musial has been able to establish that Reich authorities tended to punish staff who were deemed incompetent or who had fallen into disfavor by sending them to the Generalgouvernement. According to Musial, complaints from staff who had been banished in this way were common through the end of the war. Within the Reich, the Generalgouvernement was increasingly regarded as a "repository for elements that had become, for whatever reason, unpopular with the authorities at home."[18] In many circles, the Generalgouvernement was referred to derisively as the "gangster district."[19] In spring 1942, Propaganda Minister Joseph Goebbels even referred to the "East" as a "dumping ground for civil servants and officers who have failed in the Reich" and a place for "short-sighted authorities" to transfer unwanted staff, in accordance with the principle that "those who have proven themselves useless within the Fatherland are nonetheless acceptable for the East, indeed, perhaps even too good for the East."[20]

Transfers to the "East" thus became an expedient means of getting rid of unpopular personnel, including those who had committed criminal offenses. Still, staff transferred for disciplinary reasons constituted a minority among administrative civil servants in the East; most had been, in fact, recently recruited. For this reason, it is difficult to say with certainty whether the female guards who arrived at Majdanek from other camps had, in reality, been transferred because they had fallen out of favor with their superiors. Whatever the case, the former

Aufseherinnen themselves regarded these transfers—in retrospect—as having been punitive in nature.

Grandiose Plans and Chaotic Reality

Within a few weeks of Himmler's visit to Lublin in summer 1941, plans were drawn up for a camp of enormous proportions to be constructed at the site. In October of 1941, then, with victory seemingly within reach, and mindful of economic, security, and resettlement considerations, SS officials at the Chief Office for Budget and Buildings in Berlin projected that the camp would need to be able to accommodate a minimum of 100,000 prisoners. In September, Himmler and Pohl had reached agreements with the Wehrmacht Supreme Command (OKW) calling for Majdanek to be built using unpaid Soviet prisoners of war as laborers. On November 1, a construction order was issued for Majdanek, as well as Auschwitz (which was to be expanded as a POW camp).[21] According to the construction order, Majdanek was, by then, intended to have a capacity of 125,000 Soviet POWs.[22] Within a month, the head of Office II (Buildings), SS Oberführer Hans Kammler, had further revised the order, expanding the capacity to 150,000.

A master blueprint dated March 23, 1942, illustrates how the SS envisioned the future camp complex.[23] According to the plan, Majdanek was to cover a surface area of 516 hectares, and include three separate divisions with a total projected capacity of 250,000 inmates.[24] Coming at a time when a 10,000 inmate capacity was considered enormous,[25] such a plan would have made Majdanek the largest camp of its kind. As historian Wolfgang Scheffler has underscored, the grandiosity of this plan is indicative of the regime's "megalomania"[26] and its assumption that victory was a forgone conclusion.

By April 1942, however, Himmler had scaled back the planned construction, which had been deemed unfeasible given the wartime conditions. The revised blueprint called for a total capacity of 50,000 prisoners, to be interned in eight "fields." In the end, the camp that was built was a fraction of the size envisioned in the original plan. In summer 1943, when the Majdanek complex was functioning at its highest capacity, it encompassed a total area of 270 hectares, divided into three zones: the camp compound; an SS area with buildings for accommodation and meals; and an extensive industrial complex.

The SS tract was comprised of administrative buildings, a canteen, residences for higher officers, a barracks for the men of the SS Death's Head regiment, and a barrack-style residence for the female guards. The industrial complex included a farm called Felin, a nursery, a warehouse, and various workshops (including a blacksmith, a shoemaker, a carpentry shop, and a tailor).

By 1944, however, only five prisoner fields, consisting of accommodation barracks and two strips of land referred to as "intermediate fields," had been completed.[27]

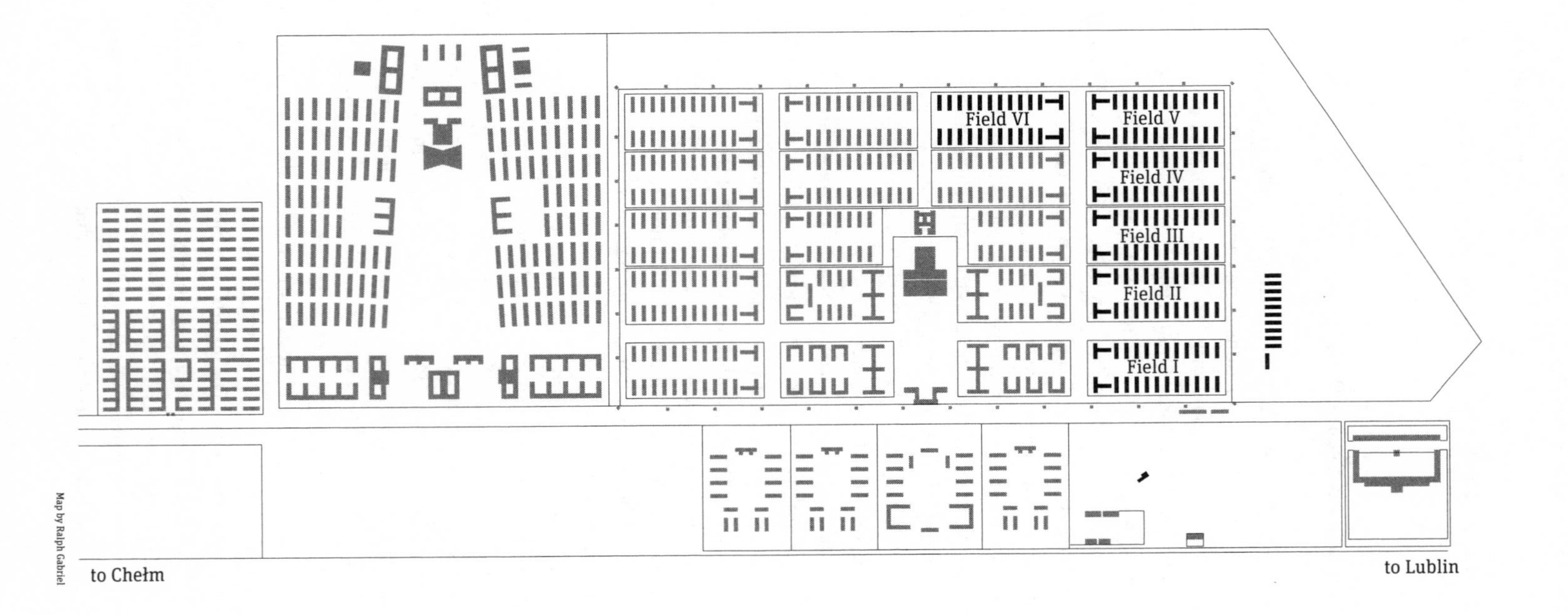

FIGURE 11. Draft plan for Majdanek, dated March 1942 (only partially realized)

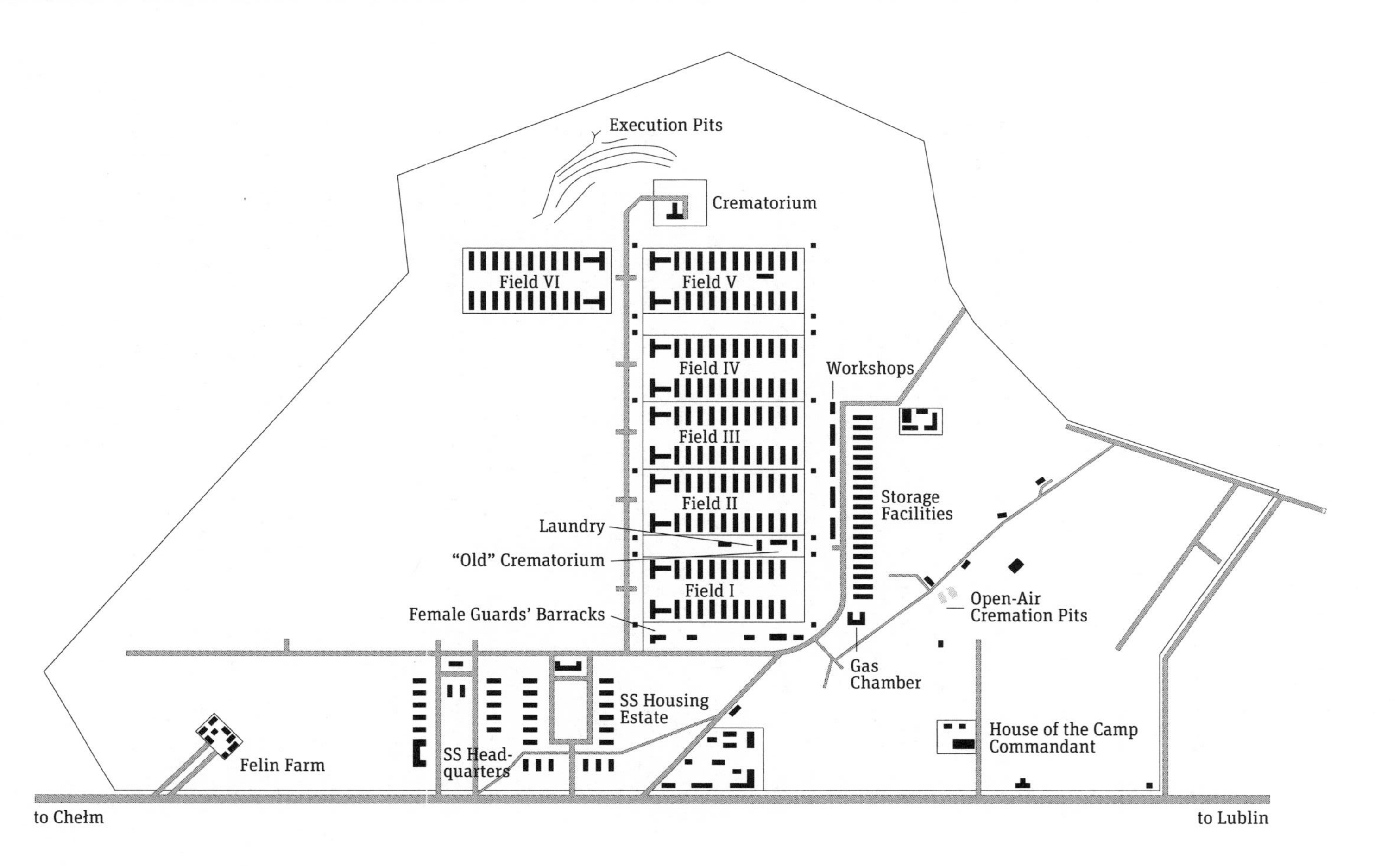

FIGURE 12. Map of the Majdanek camp area (completed construction)

At any given time, the camp typically held between 10,000 and 15,000 inmates, with the total prisoner count never exceeding 25,000.[28]

The Shock of Arrival

On January 29, 1943, former Ravensbrück guard Rosa Reischl arrived at Majdanek along with four colleagues. In later testimony, she describes the horrific scene that awaited the women upon their arrival:[29]

> We five *Aufseherinnen* . . . arrived at the camp at night. SS guards took us to our barracks. . . . The SS men offered us alcohol. Miss Ehlert and I did not drink. When I went outside, an SS officer came over and told me, be careful, they want to get you. The other three female guards were already drunk. I went with Ehlert out into the dark night. We were looking for our quarters, but there were so many barracks that we couldn't find our way in the dark. After a while we arrived at a barracks. I opened the door. Inside there was a dog and a 16- or 17-year-old Jewish boy. He said to us, "What are you doing? You're not allowed in here." I was confused but I went inside the dark vestibule. Then I saw a light, opened the door, and saw three SS men lying in beds. There was a radio in the room. There was a skull on it. One of the SS men, who was still in uniform, immediately grabbed Herta and wanted to pull her toward him. Another one said I should sit down on his bed. Herta and I pulled up some chairs. I showed Herta the skull. We both started trembling and held onto each other. Herta said we should get out of there. I ran to a door, thinking it was the exit, but instead ended up inside a large room. In the light from the door I could see a big oven. Oil was dripping from it. An SS man ran after me. I was faster, and he didn't catch me. There was a door at the other end of the room, and in my fear I ran toward it. The room was pitch dark. When I ran in, I fell straight onto a pile of corpses. I screamed but at that point I must have fainted. Once I came to, I ran back.[30]

Whether this description is a collage of impressions or whether Rosa Reischl did, in her confusion, run into the crematorium that first night, is impossible to answer.[31] However, even if these memories are a retrospective product of Reischl's shock and fear upon her arrival, there can be no doubt that she remembered Majdanek as a menacing place—rife with threatening SS men,[32] excess, and death.

For the new arrivals at Majdanek, the living and work conditions at the camp, and as I shall discuss further below, the local climate, most certainly called for a great deal of adjustment; for many, it must have been a source of great personal turmoil.

LIVING CONDITIONS FOR FEMALE GUARDS IN MAJDANEK

According to Charlotte Wöllert, when she arrived on October 16, 1942, there were no accommodations for *Aufseherinnen*: "An SS man picked us up in Lublin, and brought us to a building in the central district."[33] Because the camp was unprepared for their arrival, the women spent the first night in the city. The women, who had not agreed to be transferred to Majdanek, were "extremely annoyed about the whole situation."[34]

The SS administration had long recognized that the lack of housing for incoming female guards at Majdanek would be an issue. Even before construction began on the women's camp, Odilo Globocnik, the SS Police Leader of Lublin, wrote to WVHA chief Oswald Pohl in July 1942, noting, "It will not be easy to acquire *Aufseherinnen* and build halfway decent quarters for them."[35] According to an agreement between Globocnik and the Majdanek administration, the women would be assigned to the SS Clothing Works at the Old Airfield Camp rather than to labor detachments within the camp proper. A December 17, 1943, letter sent to the commandant of Majdanek confirms that all fourteen female guards stationed at the camp between October 1942 and March 1943 were, in fact, housed at the clothing works.[36] In a later interrogation, Charlotte Wöllert recalled these lodgings: "A few days later we—I believe all of us—were sent to the camp's SS clothing works. There, an SS man first explained our assignments to us and then lectured us on our rights and duties."[37] Hermine Braunsteiner confirmed this account: "We wound up in a small camp called the Old Airfield camp. All of the *Aufseherinnen* lived there in several rooms of an old stone building."[38] The building was located, according to Ruth E., in an open field between the camp and the clothing works.[39] According to Charlotte W., "The house was about three- to four hundred meters from the actual concentration camp. . . . If you were on the road to Lublin, you had to cross a field to reach the house."[40] And, in Hertha Ehlert's words:

> Our quarters were not within the camp itself. If you took the road out of the camp toward Lublin, we were on the left. The camp itself was on the right. As far as I can remember, there were one or more houses there. . . . It was about a twenty-minute walk from our lodgings to the camp.[41]

Instead of having private rooms, the women had to share accommodations. By Wöllert's account, some SS officers also lived in the building,[42] including the camp compound leader, Anton Thumann,[43] and, most likely for a time, his predecessor Hermann Hackmann.[44] During the trial, Wöllert recalled that the dining room for the senior SS officers was located on the ground floor. However, the house did not meet the standards of the officers, who felt it was "too primitive."[45] In any case, most of the higher SS leaders did not live inside the camp, but instead lived with their families in the city or on the SS estate.[46]

For her part, however, Charlotte Wöllert indicated that the guards also found the quarters too spartan for their tastes. According to Wöllert, the woman staffers who worked in the clothing works stayed in this "white house" for approximately six to seven weeks, after which they moved into a shared apartment located within the garment works proper. There, two to three *Aufseherinnen* were again forced to share a room.[47] Anna M. recalled what happened after this latter move:

> As long as I was working in the garment shop, I lived together with the other guards in that building. But after I returned to the main camp, I was put up in a barracks right next to the headquarters, where all the *Aufseherinnen* were placed.[48]

In March 1943, the female guards were assigned to their own L-shaped barracks in the main camp, immediately adjacent to the first field of the prisoners' area (see figure 12). They remained at that location until the camp's evacuation in May 1944.[49] "In this barracks every *Aufseherin* had a room to herself," said Hermine Böttcher in her testimony. "We were 15 to 20 *Aufseherinnen* in all."[50]

This building still exists today. Unlike the female guards' lodgings in Ravensbrück, it was a simple wood barracks without any special amenities. In an interview with Eberhard Fechner, Erna Pfannstiel said Majdanek was "more primitive"[51] than Ravensbrück. Also at Majdanek, the sanitation arrangements were inferior, both in the prisoners' area, where there were constant problems with the sewage system,[52] and in the *Aufseherinnen* barracks, which were outfitted with latrines rather than indoor plumbing.[53]

The "women's barracks,"[54] as the female guards' quarters were known, were positioned diagonally from the barracks that housed the SS guard battalion. In the guards' lodgings, according to Otto Z., the men slept seven to a room.[55]

In postwar interrogations, nearly all the female guards recalled the presence of the men in great detail.[56] In Charlotte Runge's statement, she mentioned: "I recall four barracks one behind the other. They were meant for the SS men, the guards, the *Aufseherinnen*, and the administration."[57] Likewise, Alice Orlowski remembered, "SS officers and men were quartered in the neighboring barracks."[58] "First of all in front, as I said, were the SS barracks," Elisabeth H. stated. "There were an awful lot of them, the guard troops."[59]

As this testimony shows, the female guards from Ravensbrück were unaccustomed to such close physical proximity between men and women. Unlike at Ravensbrück, where the SS men, higher SS officers, and male SS guards had constituted a clear minority, Majdanek was staffed almost entirely by men, with just twenty *Aufseherinnen* serving alongside 1,200 SS troops.

CLIMATE AND WEATHER

"I remember it was very cold back then,"[60] testified former guard Hertha Ehlert, who came to Majdanek in January 1943. Indeed, weather reports of the Wehrmacht's

Elissa Mailänder

FIGURE 13. The former guards' housing barracks, 2004

Central Meteorological Service indicate that at least during the first winter of the war, in 1939–40, it was particularly cold and snowy.[61] The climate in the Lublin District is generally continental in nature, marked by strong seasonal temperature fluctuations, and occasionally extreme conditions in both summer and winter. In those years, the Baedeker travel guide described the climate of the Generalgouvernement as follows:

> The region's *climate*[62] is determined by altitude and location on the continent. Altitude largely determines the climate in the south, and in the Carpathian mountain region. In the largely flat lowlands of the north and the vast, nearly unforested plains of Lublin and Podolia, the far-reaching influence of its continental location is more strongly felt. . . .
>
> In general, as one heads east the summers and winters become longer and more intense, at the expense of the transitional seasons. The often-sudden spring thaw and especially the greater frequency of torrential rains, combined with poor water absorption in large areas and unbalanced gradients [*sic*] in major rivers contribute to what is often catastrophic flooding.[63]

The meteorological evaluation for the Wehrmacht put it in these terms:

> The extreme cold of the winters poses immense physical hardship. This is particularly true when accompanied by high winds, which cause nearly unbearable loss of heat for anyone exposed to it, even at temperatures of just –10 to –15°C. In addition, the winds carry ice crystals aloft, rendering outdoor activities impossible.[64]

The Reich Office for Meteorological Service also commented on the rainy transitional seasons, when flooding, ice, and mud could be particularly problematic. In its September 1943 brochure titled "Mud Accumulation in European Russia," the introduction states, "Substantial mud accumulation is endemic to this area of Russia in spring and fall. It creates difficulties for vehicle and air traffic of a nature rarely encountered in Germany."[65]

Assuming that roughly the same climatic conditions prevailed in Poland as in western Ukraine, Belarus, and the western part of Russia, it is easy to imagine the difficult adjustment a transfer to Majdanek posed for the *Aufseherinnen*. Although outfitted for all weather eventualities, with both summer and winter uniforms, hats, and leather boots, and with access to sufficient food, adequate housing, and good medical care, a number of the women in later testimony recalled the climate as an annoyance or hardship. For example, in later testimony Erika W., who stayed at Majdanek only two months before being transferred, had virtually no memories of the camp itself, except to recall the camp's "muddy paths."[66]

COMPOSITION OF THE PRISONER POPULATION

Erna Pfannstiel mentioned in an interview with Eberhard Fechner that she had been astonished at the composition of the prisoners at Majdanek. "Well, we were told that it would be the same as at Ravensbrück. That the prisoners were the same. We didn't know that it would be only Jews there."[67] Asked by Fechner whether there weren't also Polish Christians among the prisoners at Majdanek, Pfannstiel's reply makes clear that she remembered all the prisoners as "Jews" and recalled the camp exclusively as a "Jews' camp." Anna M., who came to Majdanek on October 16, 1942, with the first group of *Aufseherinnen*, recounted the composition of the women's camp as follows:

> As far as I remember at the beginning, meaning when I showed up there, about 1,500 women, including Jews, Poles, Lithuanians, and Russians, were held at the camp. Most were Jews and Poles. For short periods, the population increased to between three and five thousand women. I can't give a precise number, though, because those of us who weren't involved with the roll call didn't have a good overview. So, the numbers I give you are estimates. . . . Most of the camp was occupied by men, of course. One of the fields was for Russian prisoners of war, some of whom were wounded. . . . The prisoners included Jews, Poles, Ukrainians, and Germans. The German inmates included political prisoners, criminals, and asocials who were used in the camp as capos and foremen. It's possible that the Lublin camp also included prisoners of other ethnicities.[68]

Alice Orlowski, who came to Majdanek in July 1943, testified as follows:

> On average, there were about 5,000 prisoners in the women's camp. There were Polish, Russian, Jewish, as well as German women. The German women were a definite minority. There were still about 5,000 women in the camp when it was evacuated in March 1944.[69]

The differences between Majdanek and Ravensbrück went beyond numbers, though. Not only did each female guard have more prisoners to monitor; the composition of the prisoner population was also radically different. Until 1942, the *Aufseherinnen* in Ravensbrück guarded mainly women from Germany and Austria, with whom they shared a common language and cultural framework. In Majdanek, on the other hand, they encountered mostly Eastern European women, few of whom spoke German.

One former guard, Gertrud Heise, stated explicitly that the differing conditions between the two camps resulted in differences in behavior among the *Aufseherinnen*. In October 1942, Heise began working at the Ravensbrück women's camp, where she was assigned to the "furrier workshop" labor detail. Shortly after the war, she testified regarding her work at Ravensbrück:

> The conditions under which the prisoners lived and worked at Ravensbrück were not so bad. The food was adequate. The prisoners worked well and to my full satisfaction. I didn't have any trouble with my troop. I never struck or otherwise mistreated a prisoner in that camp, and never saw or heard that anyone else did either.[70]

Without a doubt, beatings did indeed take place at Ravensbrück, and Heise's failure to disclose this violence was most certainly an attempt to shield herself from legal scrutiny. However, the contrasting nonchalance with which Heise admitted to later slapping prisoners at Majdanek is remarkable. At Majdanek, violence toward prisoners was clearly a matter of course:

> I myself didn't have much aggravation with the prisoners and I only rarely had to get involved with them that way. I didn't have to slap a prisoner very often, just every now and then, and when I did slap someone, I only used my hands and never seriously hurt anyone.[71]

These statements strongly suggest that violence was employed to a greater extent at Majdanek than in Ravensbrück.[72]

EPIDEMICS

Barbara Schwindt has calculated that in 1942 alone, a total of 2,211 kilograms of Zyklon B were delivered to Majdanek.[73] As she concludes, the quantity of the poison gas, which was used in small amounts to kill inmates and large amounts to disinfect textiles and fumigate buildings, speaks volumes about the hygienic conditions in the camp. Because of its poor water supply and disastrous sanitary conditions, epidemic disease was rampant at Majdanek.[74] With little or no opportunity to maintain basic hygiene, inmates were virtually defenseless against the spread of disease. Inadequate clothing and nutrition among prisoners further contributed to the rapid spread of disease. The typhoid epidemics that broke out in summer and fall 1942, and early

1943, were especially severe. Countless inmates died in the epidemics, while many more who had not yet succumbed to the disease itself were shot by SS guards.[75] Despite widespread use of Zyklon B as a disinfectant, the SS was unable to stem the spread of epidemic disease, as the true cause of the epidemics—the conditions under which the prisoners were forced to live—remained unchanged.

Conditions in the camp were so poor that many camp staff also fell ill.[76] As Hermine Braunsteiner recalled in her postwar testimony:

> I was on Christmas leave. I came back afterwards with a fever. I had dysentery and was sick about four weeks. During this time I still lived at the Old Airfield Camp. On February 11, 1943, I came down with typhus and was sent to the infirmary in Lublin, where I stayed until April. . . . Afterwards, I was sent for a month to an SS convalescent home in the town of Miesbach in Bavaria. Elsa [Else] Ehrich was with me there; she had come down with typhus three days before me. In late 1943, I returned from the convalescent home. . . . On October 13, 1943, I fell sick again, from enteric fever, jaundice, and Wolhynia fever. That time, I stayed in the infirmary in Lublin until late December 1943. While I was in the hospital, I applied for a transfer back to Ravensbrück. The doctors supported my application. I submitted the application because I was sick, constantly. I had a good reason to want to get away from the camp.[77]

According to Braunsteiner, she spent more than five months sick in 1943, and her case was no exception. In her 1973 testimony, Hildegard Lächert also remembered falling ill soon after her arrival at Majdanek:

> I had typhus and enteric fever while I was at the Airfield camp [from October 1942 to April 1943]. I spent eight weeks in a Polish hospital, where Polish doctors treated me. After my arrival in Lublin, I was first at the clothing works in the Old Airfield Camp. Then, I fell sick and was granted home leave. I spent Christmas in Berlin. I returned from leave in mid- or late January. . . . About two or three weeks later I returned to the Old Airfield Camp. I was the only *Aufseherin* there at the time. I stayed there until mid- or late April. . . . After I returned to the main camp, I got a severe sore throat and wound up back in the infirmary. I don't remember how long I was there.[78]

Both Herta B. and Ruth W.[79] fell sick with paratyphoid fever within weeks of their arrival at Majdanek. In Herta B.'s description:

> I was in the military hospital in Lublin. Afterwards, I was put in an isolation ward. Then I was granted leave. After I had been in the hospital for some time, "Rosl" was brought into my room for a short while. The priest came and gave her the last rites.[80]

According to her fellow guards, it was Rosa Reischl who was worst affected; Reischl contracted paratyphoid B, canefield fever, and swamp fever. As Elisabeth H. reported in her postwar testimony: "Herta B. and Anna S. got sick with her, and I believe also Anna M. . . . But those three weren't as sick as Reichel [Reischl]."[81] In Reischl's own account, she stated, "I was unconscious. Then I was brought to the military hospital in Lublin for six weeks. After I recovered, I had four weeks of home leave and then four weeks of convalescence."[82] Reischl's father was also questioned during the 1975 investigation, and recalled the incident as follows:

> In about the middle of August 1943 I received a telegram saying she was gravely ill and dying. . . . I took time off work and took the military train to Lublin. I spent two days traveling and was then allowed to stay in Lublin for five days. Toward the end of my visit, my daughter's condition improved. Around late-September 1943, she was released from the hospital and came to us in Neureichenau to recuperate. She stayed with us until roughly late October 1943. Afterwards, she spent another four weeks of convalescence leave at Lake Tegernsee, and then returned to Lublin.[83]

Nor were the male guards spared from disease. According to Hermann Hackmann, superior officer of Arnold Strippel (the second camp compound leader), Strippel also contracted typhus.[84] According to his later testimony, SS medic Wilhelm Reinartz was hospitalized in Lublin with typhus from fall 1942 to early 1943.[85] Records also show that the deputy director of the crematorium, Robert Seitz, was treated at the Robert Koch Hospital in Lublin in December 1943.[86]

Leave certificates and sanatorium visits recorded in camp correspondence also document the various illnesses suffered by camp staff. For Reischl, for example, there is a receipt for her stay at the Lublin Reserve Infirmary, which puts her admission on August 26, 1943, and her release on October 5, 1943.[87] Afterwards, records confirm that she was admitted to the SS convalescent home in Gmunden at Lake Tegernsee.[88] It is also documented that both Ehrich and Braunsteiner stayed at the Armed SS "Stadelberghaus" rest home in Miesbach, Upper Bavaria, from April 14 to May 12, 1943, with expenses paid for by the Majdanek concentration camp.[89]

The epidemics were a result of the prisoners' deplorable living conditions, and thus were a catastrophe of the SS's own creation. In Majdanek, the constant threat of disease served to further amplify the chasm between the SS personnel and prisoners, one that was already mandated politically, socially, and racially by the organization of Nazi concentration camps. Quarantines were imposed during typhoid epidemics, during which inmates were forbidden to leave their barracks. Some of the camp staff began to refuse to enter the prisoner tracts.

Among the camp staff, a feeling of disgust and revulsion emerged toward the physically weakened and sick inmates.[90] For the SS, the prisoners were feared as potential transmitters of disease. As Elias Canetti pointed out in his study *Crowds and Power*, fear of contagion leads people to shield themselves from one another.[91] Unlike a direct confrontation with an opponent, during an epidemic the enemy is unseen; its presence cannot be discerned with certainty, except when it is too late and illness has set in. The danger, therefore, is omnipresent. Those who are still healthy share a common feeling of fear and suspicion, both of which result in increased physical and emotional separation between people. Fear of infection, combined with revulsion at the prisoners' condition, were key factors in the indifference of camp staff toward the prisoners' suffering—and served as an underlying motivation for the physical violence directed toward the inmates.[92]

In addition to the danger posed to personal health, epidemics brought with them other "inconveniences" for the SS camp staff. Due to the risk of contagion, for example, they could no longer send their clothing to be washed in the camp laundry. A letter from the leader of the SS Death's Head unit on February 22, 1943, requisitioning laundry detergent indicates that because of the camp quarantine, unit members had to wash their own clothing that month.[93] According to a letter by Commandant Hermann Florstedt to the chief guard, however, the *Aufseherinnen* were permitted to take their clothes to a laundry in the town of Lublin.[94] Although today, it may seem a bizarre triviality or a sign of the camp staff's cynicism, these circumstances may well have been sufficient, at the time, to affect the SS unit's morale and sense of well-being.

◆ ◆ ◆

For female guards who had previously served in Ravensbrück, life at Majdanek was in many ways far more "primitive" and offered comparatively less comfort. Upon their arrival at Majdanek, the women—most of whom had had single rooms at Ravensbrück—now had to share a room in provisional lodgings. The lodgings (see figures 13 and 14) into which the *Aufseherinnen* moved in spring 1943 also offered fewer comforts than the women's quarters back at Ravensbrück. Still, compared with men of the guard battalion, who lived seven to a room and had to wash their own clothes during camp quarantines, the female guards enjoyed a variety of privileges accorded them as a result of their status as women and civilians. Nonetheless, the physical proximity to the SS troops, who greatly outnumbered them, was something to which the new guards had to grow accustomed. The ever-present threat of disease was yet another significant burden of life at Majdanek. This was only compounded by the fact that Lublin was located on the fringes of the Reich, rather than at its center, as Ravensbrück had been.

In fact, travel to the Generalgouvernement from Germany was no simple matter at the time. According to the Baedeker guide, entering the Generalgouvernement required a transit permit in addition to a photo ID or passport.[95] This meant that any visits by friends and relatives had to be planned months in advance. Depending on any number of variables, including transportation connections and the location of the front at any given moment, not to mention the stated purpose and urgency of the visit, the train journey from Berlin to Lublin, via Warsaw, could take anywhere between one and several days. Also, unlike at Ravensbrück, weekends on leave could not be taken advantage of as a time for visiting friends or family within Reich territory, or for getaways to Berlin. Despite these perceived hardships, however, the female guards' stay in the Generalgouvernement was not a wholly negative experience.

The Eastern Experience: Hegemony in the "Wild East"

In December 1939, just a few months after Poland fell to German occupation, the German city governor of Lublin, Dr. Fritz Cuhorst, described his impressions in a letter home:

> Eight days ago today the mayor was here with Mr. Könekamp. In the last four weeks, they have been our only visitors from the old Reich who did not have a specific agenda. The gentlemen were in luck. It was Jew Monday.
>
> On Saturday, December 2, the Jews had been informed that all men between 15 and 55 were to assemble on a sports field between 7 and 8 o'clock. Then, at 8 o'clock the ghetto was combed for slackers and merchandise. What a sight!! The Jews who'd been caught out were beaten miserably and then made to line up with their heads against the wall on Lubartowka [Street]. In the ghetto pistols were cracking and women were screaming. I went along for two hours, and grabbed a Torah scroll for myself. Apart from that, I kept my hands clean, of course. By then, Standartenführer Gunst had sorted the Jews on the sports field according to profession. All the tradesmen were taken to the racetrack and have since been building an assembly camp. The Jewish religious community has been feeding them. The rest of the Jews stood all day long in groups of 100, monitored by 10 SS men with sticks but no pistols, until evening. Unfortunately, our project went askew because the nighttime march, which was supposed to rid us of 3,000 Jews, could not be carried out. Most were released again. In Chełm, on December 3 it worked better: There, 1,000 Jews were forced to march, guarded by SS mounted troops. At dusk, there was a small revolt when the Jews tried to give their 30 escorts the slip. By the time the shooting ended more than 600 were killed. At our Jew Monday not even 20 bit the dust.
>
> The mayor was surprised that we worked without guards and mingled so freely with the pack of swine, but what else could we do? The police force in Lublin has only 30 men!! So we just had to do our duty and trust in God. Recently, the electric lights went out for an hour and a half. The whole city was dark. So we practiced defense exercises: at three windows, one pistol apiece with magazines. The carbine with 120 rounds sat next to me on the sofa. . . . During the night, a policeman was shot; he's at death's door. In response, five Poles and eight Jews have been eliminated in each of 12 precincts of the district. The life of a German must be completely inviolable. Reich German standards aren't enough to survive here.

> The people [the Poles] here enjoy nothing better than to swarm into the public offices. No matter how clear our signs and notices are, they still keep coming. They enjoy standing in line in front of shops just as much. It's a kind of entertainment for people like them. At an official meeting last Saturday we decided to behave exactly opposite to how we would as civil servants back home, i.e., like pigs. One doesn't greet Poles anyway. It's a matter of course that I go through the door first, even if a Polish woman is there. . . .
>
> We don't notice it's Christmastime at all. Everything that isn't Lublin feels so terribly far away! We lose all sense of time and barely even realize that it's Sunday. My apartment is getting cozier, it's the one and only place one can feel safe, at least as far as the people here are concerned. We [Germans] always stick together well and help one other with small matters, the kinds of things that are barely noticed back home but are very important here. I'll be home at Christmas and tell you more about it.[96]

Apart from the astonishing master-race mentality exhibited in this letter, it also displays what might best be termed a "Wild West" attitude. In a sense, the Generalgouvernement and Lublin were frontier territory, where different rules applied than at home. In the view of the occupiers, their supposed "racial" superiority conferred upon them wide-ranging power over the local Polish and Jewish population. In the Generalgouvernement, the authorities could act with impunity, without any obligation to take the needs of the local population into account. At the same time, however, Cuhorst's letter reveals a sense of isolation, of having been marooned at the periphery.

This sense of abandonment persisted despite efforts by the Nazi leadership, and especially Governor-General Hans Frank, to make the Generalgouvernement more attractive to Germans from the Reich. Indeed, Frank wrote the opening words to the Baedeker travel guide to the region, published in 1943:

> For those traveling to the Reich from the east, upon arriving at the Generalgouvernement you will feel you were born and raised here; for those traveling east from the Reich, however, it will be their first welcome from the Eastern world.
>
> Governor-General and Reich Minister Dr. Frank[97]

Frank was both paraphrasing a quote from Goethe's *Italian Journey*[98] and evoking the theme of a border region that draws its charm from its unique blend of cultures.[99] This flight of fancy is all the more jarring in light of Frank's actual policies toward the occupied territory. In October 1939, for example, Frank had requisitioned from Himmler "suitable men with a willingness to fight."[100] Indeed, Frank made it clear that he intended to respond to the "welcome" extended by the "East" by turning the Generalgouvernement into a "model of true efficiency" filled with "warriors absolutely determined to liquidate the Poles."[101] Eradicating the Polish population would, in turn, render the Generalgouvernement even more strongly "reminiscent of home."

Unlike the Protectorate of Bohemia and Moravia, the Generalgouvernement was not incorporated into the "Greater German Reich," but instead maintained its own currency, import and export customs, and administrative policies. "All in all, the Generalgouvernement is a singular kind of creation," as the Baedeker travel guide put it. "The Führer himself designated it the 'forecourt' of the Reich, while the Governor-General referred to it as the 'country neighboring the Reich.'"[102] Unlike occupied Western Europe, including France, the Netherlands, and Norway, in the Generalgouvernement Hitler rejected the idea of retaining a local administration that would be placed under German supervision. Instead, Poland was to be administered directly and solely by Germans. Banned from holding positions of leadership, Poles were relegated to menial administrative roles. At the same time, the local Polish population was subject entirely to German control. Bogdan Musial characterized this form of governance as a mixture of a "governance administration" (*Regierungsverwaltung*) and "colonial administration" (*Kolonialverwaltung*).[103]

In his autobiography, Rudolf Höss prefaced his reflections by introducing Auschwitz as that place "far away, back there in Poland."[104] Although Auschwitz was not in the Generalgouvernement but, rather, was situated in a part of Polish Silesia that had been annexed by Germany, Höss's phrasing suggests how distant and remote Poland was considered at the time—a perception that was also reflected in the Western European notion of the "East" as foreign and inferior. This discursive construction of an inferior and "alien" region later helped lend a sense of legitimacy to Germany's hegemonic claims to domination and its aggressive and radical appropriation of the "Other."[105]

Historian Vejas Gabriel Liulevicius was the first to analyze the German perceptions of the "East" that prevailed during the First World War.[106] In the first half of the twentieth century, Eastern and East-Central Europe were the regions upon which Germany projected its fantasies of a "German East."[107] These images of the "East" that had their origins in the First World War and the interwar period were later repeated in the National Socialist slogan that the Germans were a "people without space," and used to justify the conquest of neighboring nations, which were to become German "living space" (*Lebensraum*).[108] Germany's belief in its cultural superiority over the "Slavs" (the Russians, in particular), already characterized by racist overtones, existed prior to and during the First World War.[109] For the camp staff, then, Nazi ideology and particularly its "racial theories" provided a matrix for their actions.

THE "SLAVIC" ENEMY

In his testimony, Polish survivor and former prisoner-physician Jan Novak shared his vivid memories of how Hermann Hackmann, the first camp compound leader at Majdanek, treated Soviet prisoners of war:

> Hackmann was a repulsive figure in the concentration camp. At the time, he was a young man in his thirties, elegant, and he often wore white gloves. I remember

> that he held the morning roll call in front of block one in Field 1. Only about 35 men remained of what had once been a large group of Russian POWs, and they stood in rags, Russian caps, and long uniform coats before him, the elegant one. The contrast was at once devastating and depressing. That was in late February 1942. . . . During roll call he went to the prisoners of war and struck them on their caps with a whip, some sort of dog whip or riding whip. This wasn't meant as a beating or a form of abuse; it was a gesture of contempt.[110]

In a military context, lashing at the Soviet soldiers with a whip that was meant for animals—and, especially, lashing them in the face—was doubly humiliating. The visual contrast of the SS officer's impeccable dress with the tattered condition of the Soviet soldiers' uniforms symbolized SS superiority over its racial enemy. At the same time, Hackmann's gestures illustrate the pleasure he took in his position of superiority and the opportunity it presented for humiliating the Soviet POWs.

Hermann Hackmann, otherwise always circumspect and reserved in court testimony, was less guarded in his interview for Eberhard Fechner's documentary:

> I came, then, in 1941—in July—I came to Lublin. The camp was under construction, it was being built by civilians, Polish civilian workers and Germans who oversaw them. That continued about from July to late fall. Late that fall was when the first *Unter-* . . . [Hackmann paused for a moment], I mean Russian prisoners of war were brought in. At the time they lived in burrows, which they had dug underground. It had already snowed when they arrived. There wasn't a soul to be seen, and then at a whistle they'd all come crawling out of their holes.[111]

It is remarkable that almost thirty-five years later, in front of a running camera, Hackmann still dared speak of the Soviet POWs using Nazi slang, beginning to call them "subhumans" (*Untermenschen*) before he caught his indiscretion and corrected himself. Hackmann's portrayal of the Soviet prisoners of war bears resemblance to the image expressed by his colleague Rudolf Höss, commandant of Auschwitz, in his postwar account.[112] Clearly, Hackmann gave no thought to the fact that when the first convoys of Soviet POWs arrived at Majdanek, only four barracks had as yet been built in which to house them, with the result that the men were forced to seek shelter from the cold in underground burrows. As late as the 1970s, the main focus of Hermann Hackmann's memories was the labor shortage that was exacerbated by a high mortality rate among Soviet POWs. "Because most of the Russian POWs were sick and unsuitable for work,"[113] Hackmann stated, "we had to bring in others [other prisoners, mainly Jews] to finish building the camp."[114]

In National Socialist ideology and propaganda related to the "East," two figures played a prominent role: first, the "Judeo-Bolsheviks," and secondly, the Slavs, who were to become slaves once Germany had completed its conquest of the "East."[115] The ideology joined together derogatory stereotypes of Russia and Russians with a belief in the racial and eugenic superiority of the German people. To this mix was added a geopolitical fear of the "Asiatic" Soviet superpower. Taken together, these ideologies constituted the "semantic matrix"[116] that, for the camp staff, became conflated with real or imagined experiences and anxieties—such as the fear of "partisan attacks" Hertha Ehlert mentioned in her later testimony.[117] Such fears and anxieties directly influenced the violence carried out at and near the Eastern Front.[118]

However, the "new" and "dangerous" could also exert a certain appeal. In Fechner's documentary, for example, Elisabeth H. mentioned that her mother objected to her transfer to Majdanek. "Yes, well, I wasn't supposed to go. But I told her, why not? Why not get away from here for a while?"[119] As her statement makes clear, the transfer also offered an opportunity for adventure. The "East" was not just foreign and dangerous; it also represented a chance to "get away for a while." By the same token, the purported danger posed by partisan attacks on occupation forces was exploited for propaganda purposes and used as a tool for mobilization. In Hertha Ehlert's case, her supposed fear of partisan attacks probably also represented an attempt to portray herself as a victim rather than a perpetrator.

"EASTERN JEWS"

For many of the female guards then, apart from the Berlin and Vienna natives among them, the "Jewish question" was probably a rather abstract issue—that is, until they set foot in Majdanek. In Ravensbrück, most of the female prisoners were ideological opponents of the Nazi regime, meaning they were political prisoners, Jehovah's Witnesses, or women who had been classified as "criminal" or "asocial." In Majdanek, however, the inmates were mainly Polish and Jewish. In eastern Poland, moreover, only a fairly small percentage of the Jewish population were assimilated. Whereas in Western Europe, the Jewish population was set apart from the mainstream mainly in terms of religion, at Majdanek, the Polish Jews also differed from their Christian counterparts in language, culture, and clothing.

The so-called "Eastern Jews" had figured prominently in anti-Semitic propaganda even before 1939. Hostility toward Eastern European Jews had escalated after the First World War, becoming more belligerent and more widespread in Germany and Austria than the "traditional" form of anti-Semitism directed toward assimilated Jews.[120] Indeed, Hitler claimed that it was the Galician Jews who arrived in Vienna during the First World War who had opened his eyes to the "Jewish Question."[121] After the Nazi seizure of power, it was the easily identifiable "Eastern Jews" who became the preferred targets of violence and discrimination.[122]

According to Bogdan Musial, German civil servants who came to the Generalgouvernement to work for the occupation experienced a form of "culture shock."[123] For these functionaries, the Jews of the Generalgouvernement embodied what they had come to see as the "typical Eastern Jew." Veit Harlan, who directed the anti-Semitic propaganda film *Jud Süss*, traveled to Lublin in early 1940 to negotiate an agreement with the district chief to use two hundred Jews from Lublin as extras for his film. The plan failed because the Jews could not obtain documents for travel to Berlin.[124] According to Musial, for Germans in the Generalgouvernement, negative stereotypes of Jews promoted within Nazi propaganda were generally confirmed and reinforced.[125] Historian Elizabeth Harvey has explored how letters and other documents of the time from soldiers, police, teachers, and settlement aides reveal an ambivalence that ranged from fascination and curiosity to contempt and disgust regarding their encounters with Jews from the ghettos.[126] The *Aufseherinnen* and male SS guards at Majdanek may well have felt a similar range of responses.

That the postwar testimonies of the female guards include few derogatory comments about Jewish prisoners is likely because the murder of the Jews was the primary focus of the Majdanek investigation and trial; as a result, the former guards were probably particularly cautious in this respect. However, language employed in their testimonies does offer some hint at their objectification of the inmates, as well as a glimpse of their sense of alienation and their desire to distance themselves from the prisoners. Glimpses of this depersonalizing language can be seen in Charlotte Wöllert's descriptions of her work as a guard in the tailor's workshop when she stated: "The Jewish laborers were delivered from the clothing works."[127] In their testimony, Wöllert and her counterparts also tended to refer to Jewish and Polish prisoners as though they were objects, saying, for example, that the prisoners had been "handed out," and referring to the workers as having been "delivered" to them. In the female guards' testimonies, the female prisoners rarely appear as subjects of the narrative, instead appearing mainly in object form. At the same time, the frequent use of possessive pronouns when referring to the prisoners demonstrates a sense of paternalism, even ownership, on the part of the *Aufseherinnen* toward the inmates.

ENHANCED STATUS IN AN "APARTHEID SOCIETY"

Just as the job of camp guard meant social advancement for most of the young women who worked as camp guards, assignment to Majdanek involved another step up the social ladder. This is because the Generalgouvernement was, essentially, an "apartheid" society in which Germans, simply by virtue of being German, enjoyed many privileges. The General Government required that all "non-Germans" in the territory carry an identification card that also indicated whether they were an ethnic Pole, a "Volksdeutscher," or another nationality.[128] In everyday life, Poles were strictly segregated from the "Reich German" occupiers, including on railway trains and in hotels. The Baedeker travel guide described this situation as follows:

> The managers of large and mid-sized train stations are German civil servants, while elsewhere mainly Polish and Ukrainian personnel are used, though they mostly speak

> a bit of German. For German passengers, special ticket windows, waiting rooms, gates, and railway cars are available.[129]

In this context, the social dynamics were different than within the Reich.[130] In the Generalgouvernement, even "Reich Germans" from very modest social backgrounds advanced to the highest level of the social hierarchy due to their "racial" and cultural status, which in turn served to further enhance their sense of German superiority.[131] For the German occupiers in wartime Poland, the cultural superiority to which they laid claim was an everyday fact of life, as evidenced by this description in the Baedeker guide:

> Larger *hotels* under German management are currently found in the Generalgouvernement almost exclusively in the district capitals and the important spas and health resorts. . . . However, German hotels have also been established in a series of secondary towns (often under the name Deutsches Haus), many of which offer a high standard of quality. In smaller towns, non-German hotels sometimes reserve a number of beds for Germans. In emergencies, travelers may consult the German authorities (governor's office, municipal commissioner, NSDAP). . . .
>
> German restaurants and cafés are available in all significant towns and cities, many of them newly built and furnished to a high standard, often in northern German style. Many establishments are under construction or in the planning stages, as there is urgent need for German restaurants to replace the domesticity that is lacking in the Generalgouvernement. For this reason, all district capitals, most secondary cities, and many smaller towns have established German clubs (cafeterias), which serve as the Deutsches Haus and social center for the local German community. Many train station restaurants also have German managers now and some also offer good cuisine.[132]

This colonial political context also had the effect of altering the nature of gender relations in occupied Poland. Simply by virtue of their "racial" affiliation, "Reich German" women wielded power and authority over Polish men.[133] In this context, Elizabeth Harvey has referred to the "consciousness of their own mastery" (*Herrenbewusstsein*) that was encouraged among the German women who worked as settlement and village instructors.[134] This self-assurance is also evident during the female guards' after-work visits to the Deutsches Haus (German House) in Lublin. In Fechner's documentary, Erna Pfannstiel reminisced about the women's outings to Lublin, accompanied by SS men stationed at the camp:

ERNA WALLISCH: Many evenings, we went to Lublin. The Deutsches Haus was there. We went there quite a bit. . . .
EBERHARD FECHNER: Hmm, you weren't allowed to go elsewhere?
ERNA WALLISCH: Well, let's just say that the other places were Polish.[135]

The Deutsches Haus, located centrally on Krakauer Strasse 56, was a café, restaurant, dance hall, and concert house all in one. On the second floor, there was a district club open only to "members of the district authorities and their guests."[136] Only *Aufseherinnen* invited by SS officers or senior district civil servants would have had access to the club. The female SS staff did, however, frequent the dance hall on the ground floor. During the 1975 Majdanek trial, Elisabeth H. presented the court with two group snapshots taken at a March 1944 birthday party for chief guard Else Ehrich, who was born on March 3, 1914.[137]

The photographs, which show the *Aufseherinnen* seated at a festively set table, provide a view of the interior décor of one of the many rooms in the Deutsches Haus. Although in the background, one wall holds a landscape painting, apart from that lone decorative element the room and its furnishings appear rather austere and functional.

In Eberhard Fechner's documentary, Luzie H. recalled the Deutsches Haus as her "favorite spot":

> When we entered the café, where we used to spend our time, and the band saw me, they always played "Alte Kameraden," because they knew it was my favorite song. So then I bought them a round, of course. Once, my husband's cousin [was visiting], and he was astonished when they played my song and the band raised their glasses to us. And I said, yes, this is our favorite place and that's my favorite song.[138]

This description is remarkable in the way that Luzie H. portrays herself—at least in retrospect—as behaving in an almost patronizing manner toward her male relative, assuming what (in a different social context) would have been a masculine role. Her self-confident and even "masterful" demeanor in the dance hall is reflective of her status as a "Reich German" in wartime Poland, as well as her day-to-day experiences of superiority within the camp and occupation hierarchy.[139]

The Scrutinized Masters

Based on the postwar statements, it is evident that intimate relationships often developed at Majdanek between the female guards and the SS men stationed there. However, when an *Aufseherin* and her partner decided to marry, they faced numerous hurdles. Most significantly, the marriage authorization directive issued in 1943 applied not only to SS men, but also to female civilian employees of the police and SS. On September 10, 1943, Himmler issued a separate directive for these female civilian employees. Beginning in mid-October of that year, the female guards at Majdanek were obligated to provide a signature acknowledging that this directive had been presented to them.[140]

The procedures for obtaining a marriage license help put in focus the work and living situation of female guards at Majdanek. In practical terms, the directives demonstrate disciplinary strategies and reflect how the women were viewed by the senior Nazi administration, particularly the Chief Economic and Administrative Office and the Race and Settlement Head Office. The Race and Settlement Head Office (RuSHA) was the oldest head office at the SS, and was responsible for carrying out racial background checks on SS applicants and their intended wives.[141] Once the RuSHA had carried out this detailed investigation, it was Himmler himself who then issued the authorization to join the SS, or to marry an SS man. For the female guards at Majdanek, submitting to this review process would have represented a significant investment of time and energy.[142] Moreover, the process of obtaining the necessary documentation to prove racial purity and hereditary health always bore the risk that information might be uncovered that would result in the applicant being stripped of full membership in the *Volksgemeinschaft*.

The following is the verbatim text of Himmler's marriage order:

> The Chief of the Race and
> Settlement Head Office—SS
> Staff leadership/Div. Ia
> Az.: B/i Lö./Fa. Berlin, Sep. 29, 1943
>
> In what follows I provide you with the Reichsführer directive dated Sep. 10, 1943, which states that female employees of the SS and police must obtain permission of the Reichsführer-SS to wed.
>
> Applications are to be submitted to the Marriage Office in the Race and Settlement Head Office-SS for personal decision.
>
> All female employees belonging to these and subordinate units must be informed of this order!
>
> The order takes effect immediately.
>
> The Reichsführer Field Command Post, Sep. 10, 1943.
>
> Marriages of female employees in offices of the SS and the police require authorization.
>
> The genealogical chart extending back to the grandparents as well as the health and hereditary health forms of the [illegible] must be submitted.
>
> Submission [of the marriage proposal] is not required when a female employee marries a member of the SS. Here the regular [stricter] provisions apply.
>
> Married female employees need submit only their husband's genealogical chart.
>
> H. Himmler
> The Chief of the Race and Settlement Head Office-SS
> Hildebrandt
> SS-Obergruppenführer and General of Police[143]

This order by Himmler applied to female concentration camp guards as well as female police and Wehrmacht auxiliaries. It is not documented whether, by October 17, 1943, all already-married *Aufseherinnen* had actually submitted their husband's genealogical chart, or whether women who had already been engaged (at the time of the directive) submitted their health and hereditary health certificates. To date, no evidence has been uncovered regarding how the marriage authorization procedure was handled for *Aufseherinnen*. In any case, the directive was in force for just over one year before it was suspended on December 30, 1944, for the remainder of the war. What is certain, however, is that the bureaucratic hurdle the female guards faced was significantly lower than that faced by a woman engaged to an SS man, for whom marriage would have conferred membership in the "SS clan." As Gudrun Schwarz has shown in her study of SS wives, an SS officer and his fiancée had to obtain 186 documents just to complete the required "SS genealogical chart."[144]

Documentation has, however, survived for the process *Aufseherinnen* needed to follow to obtain permission to marry an SS man while at Majdanek. Such marriages required a genealogical chart for all ancestors born after January 1, 1800. In addition, the prospective bride and groom had to document the following information, as far back as their great-great-great-grandparents: (1) name, (2) date and place of birth, (3) date and place of death, (4) religion, (5) profession, and (6) date and place of marriage. The application also had to include a superior's assessment. The RuSHA also painstakingly examined the career and "economic circumstances" of both the SS man and his intended wife. In addition, both partners had to fill out a "race and settlement form" that included its own SS hereditary health questionnaire. This form required that all illnesses, disabilities, and surgeries for all known family members and ancestors be listed, along with the results of the applicants' own medical examination. The prospective groom also had to appoint two guarantors, ideally SS men, to answer the following questions about his future wife:

> Fond or not fond of children?
> Comradely or domineering?
> Thrifty or wasteful?
> Domestic or flighty, obsessively clean?
> Is the family thrifty or are they spendthrifts?
> Are you aware of mental illness, nervous disorders, tuberculosis, or other serious illnesses in the family and among her ancestors?
> Have there been instances of suicide or suicide attempts?
> Did the future bride and her family take part in the National Socialist revival or are they reliable defenders of the National Socialist worldview today?
> In your opinion, is the future bride a suitable wife for a member of the SS?
> Are you aware of any other notably positive or conspicuously negative characteristics of the bride?[145]

The questionnaire leaves no doubt regarding the ideal qualities of a future SS wife: she must be of sound health, child-loving, domestic, thrifty, and politically reliable. Special attention was directed towards her role as a mother-to-be. Within two years of being granted permission to marry, the bride was required to enroll in a maternal training course and provide documentation of instruction in cooking, sewing, infant care, home nursing, child-rearing, and home design.[146]

In many cases, the application process required weeks, even months, of back-and-forth communication. If the application was approved, the RuSHA marriage office issued permission to marry, or what in Nazi jargon was known as the "Certificate of Unobjectionability to Marry" (*Eheunbedenklichkeitsbescheinigung*), which verified the physical and mental fitness of the applicants and confirmed that nothing "adverse" was known in terms of the applicants' "health and hereditary biology." One such documented procedure was the marriage application of Ferdinand K. (born 1916), *Oberscharführer* of the SS Death's Head Division, and the *Aufseherin* Elisabeth E. (born 1919).[147] In late February 1943, Ferdinand K. applied for permission to marry on April 1 of that same year. The authorization arrived so promptly that Ferdinand K. and Elisabeth E. instead married on March 18, 1943. However, Ferdinand K.'s application had a rather unusual history. Ferdinand K. was a "Sudeten German"—meaning he had been born in the Sudetenland and was of "ethnic German" descent. In September 1942 he had sought permission to marry Maria W., a young woman from his hometown of Klein Mohrau in the Freudenthal district. This marriage did not come to fruition, however, because the RuSHA recommended that he marry a "Reich German" woman. In his second application, Ferdinand K. stated that he met Elisabeth E. on November 15, 1942.[148] Thus, in his second attempt at finding a wife, it appears Ferdinand K. sought to make certain his prospective bride was of "Reich German" descent.

Another application to marry was submitted by SS-Unterscharführer Robert M. (born 1917), of the SS Death's Head Division. Robert M. wished to marry the *Aufseherin* Charlotte Wöllert (born 1918), whom he had met while working in the SS Clothing Works.[149] Their application did not go quite as smoothly, as the RuSHA in Berlin wrote with multiple demands for additional medical documentation. On March 8, 1943, the head of the marriage office again wrote to demand additional information regarding the health and medical histories of both bride and groom. The groom was required to submit a report by an ear, nose, and throat specialist regarding the onset and progression of his father's hearing loss.[150] The bride was required to submit her high school diploma, as well as information about her sister, including documentation as to how often the sister had been forced to repeat a grade and "why she had failed to graduate from *Volksschule* [primary school]."[151]

In response, Robert M. sent a telegram to Berlin with the following text: "Am total bombing victim cannot send required documents also I can expect posting to the front any day now if authorization not possible then will forego marriage."[152] Robert M.'s obvious resentment of the demands being made by the RuSHA, which he clearly regarded as unreasonable, may be taken as an example of "Eigen-Sinn." Just ten days later, the RuSHA marriage office sent a detailed reply that was implicitly both a bureaucratic self-justification and a reprimand:

> Enclosed the Race and Settlement Head Office-SS forwards to you the registry office certification.
>
> It must be remarked that your telegram of March 13, 1943, to the Race and Settlement Head Office-SS was composed in a peculiar manner. You write, e.g., that you will forego the marriage should marriage authorization not be possible.
>
> In clarification it must be said that only you, and not the Race and Settlement Head Office-SS, intends to enter into a marriage with Miss Charlotte Wöllert. It would appear that your fondness for Miss Wöllert is quite weak; otherwise, it seems you would not have made such a statement. The SS Race and Settlement Department is doing its utmost; rest assured that this office is not a marriage prevention institute. The SS Race and Settlement Department must ensure that, in accordance with the Reichsführer order, only those marriages are authorized that are suitable in terms of genealogy, hereditary, and general health, and which will result in a marriage from which only genetically and physically healthy children will issue.
>
> In conclusion, you are advised to conduct yourself in an appropriate tone in future communications with SS offices.[153]

According to Charlotte Wöllert, the wedding finally took place in April 1943.[154]

In October 1943, SS-Rottenführer Georg W. (born 1922), member of the 3rd SS Death's Head Division and a Vienna native, requested forms for an application to marry.[155] According to his November 1943 application, his prospective bride, Erna Pfannstiel (born 1922), was in her fourth month of pregnancy.[156] As Pfannstiel testified after the war: "I met my former spouse Georg W. in Majdanek, and he got me pregnant."[157] Due to her pregnancy, Pfannstiel was transferred to Ravensbrück on January 15, 1944, under an evacuation order for women and children in the Lublin area.[158] Once at Ravensbrück, and by then in an advanced state of pregnancy, Pfannstiel submitted her own request for permission to marry. She also sent several telegrams to the camp headquarters in Lublin, asking whether the wedding should take place in the Reich or in the Generalgouvernement.[159] At the time of her inquiry, Commandant Martin Weiss was already preparing for the camp's impending evacuation. The Majdanek headquarters suggested a wedding by proxy through both the Fürstenberg (Ravensbrück) and Lublin (Majdanek) registry offices.[160] However, Pfannstiel later reported to Majdanek that the Fürstenberg registry office refused to perform a proxy wedding.[161] Since Georg W. had been in detention since June 1943 on suspicion of theft and was not permitted to enter Reich territory, Weiss finally authorized a wedding in Lublin.[162] After a protracted bureaucratic exchange, the authorities issued papers for Pfannstiel to travel to the Generalgouvernement on March 20, 1944.[163] As Pfannstiel recalled: "On March 24, 1944, I was married in Lublin. At the time, I was living with my sister in Suhl-Linsenhof in Thuringia and traveled to Lublin for the wedding."[164] Erna Pfannstiel's daughter was born shortly after the wedding, on April 9, 1944.

Anton W. (born 1902), an *SS-Sturmmann*, and *Aufseherin* Ruth E. (born 1922) had met while both were serving at Ravensbrück. Ruth E. later recounted:

> While I was in the labor service, I had been recruited for a position in the youth protection camp at Ravensbrück. I went there as a guard. One day I was caught allowing my future husband to stay in my room overnight. After that I was transferred to Auschwitz for disciplinary reasons. At my own request I was then—that would have been about October 1942—transferred to Lublin.[165]

According to SS documents, Ruth E. was transferred from Auschwitz to Majdanek on November 12, 1942.[166] Anton W., who was still at Ravensbrück, submitted an application for permission to marry in March 1943.[167] Ruth E., who at this point was in her fifth month of pregnancy, was classified by the RuSHA as "ideologically sound" (*weltanschaulich gefestigt*). However, the marriage office expressed concerns related to her father, whose identity was unknown, as well as regarding some missing hereditary health data.[168] A marginal note dated March 26, 1943, by the *SS-Hauptsturmführer* and case officer at the marriage office read:

> The prospective bride was born out of wedlock. According to statements from her mother, the father has never been identified. Because of the incompleteness of the genealogical chart, the case worker in charge must raise an objection to the granting of an engagement and marriage authorization.[169]

Above all, however, it was the twenty-one-year age difference between Ruth E. and Anton W. that appears to have been the greatest cause for concern. Nonetheless, on April 1, 1943, the RuSHA issued a marriage authorization, albeit with some reservations, and with the pointed notation that the marriage would be taking place at the couple's own discretion:

> Due to the status of the war, your application for engagement and marriage cannot be finalized. . . . With reference to the documents presented in the application, we have reached the following determinations:
>
> 1. An evaluation of Miss Ruth E.'s hereditary health is not possible, as her father's identity is unknown;
> 2. You have had a venereal disease (gonorrhea);
> 3. You are nearsighted in the right eye;
> 4. An unfavorable age difference exists between you and Miss Ruth E.

> For these reasons, the final decision reached on your application for engagement and permission to marry is that the marriage will be permitted to take place at the sole discretion of both parties.[170]

As these marriage files illustrate, the RuSHA delved deeply into the SS members' private and family lives. The marriage authorizations also demonstrate that even members of the SS could never be entirely certain that "hereditary defects" might not call into question their "racial superiority." While the occupation forces and the camp staff could be sure of their superiority vis-à-vis the prisoners and the local Polish population, as potential German fathers and mothers they were required to submit to intense scrutiny. For SS men, this entailed having to prove their "fitness for duty" all over again, years after having joined the SS. Even these members of the "master race" could never be entirely certain of their privileged status, particularly when it came to matters of "hereditary health."

Based on her study of the 1937 film *Victims of the Past*, political scientist Paula Diehl has analyzed the concepts of illness and of the enemy as exemplified by Nazi racial and eugenic policy and propaganda. In the film, a couple—a man and his bride-to-be—is sitting in a doctor's waiting room, in anticipation of a routine pre-wedding checkup. Another patient engages the two in conversation, asking what the groom would do if his fiancée did not pass the hereditary health examination:

PATIENT: Enough said about the hereditary health examination. It could happen to you, too.
GROOM: Aren't you a pleasant one. It can't happen to me.
PATIENT: And what if your bride isn't healthy?
GROOM: She is healthy.
PATIENT: Well, it's always possible that she isn't actually healthy.
GROOM: You've heard it, she is healthy.
PATIENT: Well, maybe she isn't healthy.
GROOM: That's up to the doctor to decide and not you.[171]

The question of possible "hereditary defects" weighed on every couple. It determined whether one belonged to the "Aryan race" and was a full member of the *Volksgemeinschaft*. According to Paula Diehl, this ever-present tension, the promise of privilege coupled with the threat of its loss, played an important role in the regime's policies of control—a control the marriage-minded *Aufseherinnen* and SS men would have experienced in a very direct form.[172] On the one hand, the camp staff at Majdanek could revel in their authority over the Slavic and Jewish prisoners in the concentration camp, and even over the local Polish population during their leisure hours. On the other hand, the marriage application process and other forms of control exerted by the SS leadership made it eminently clear to camp staff that their status as *Übermensch* was anything but a sure thing. As psychologist Gudrun

Brockhaus has noted, "Behind the overbearing, martial quality of many a Nazi's pronouncements lurks the fear that one might oneself belong to the category of those marginalized by one's professed ideals."[173] For the Majdanek camp staff, this fear and uncertainty—of loss of status, of no longer belonging—must certainly have provided an additional impetus for the violence that was directed at prisoners. In the daily violence they meted out so casually, the *Aufseherinnen* and SS men found a reassuring confirmation of their own dominance and superiority.[174]

Between the "Thrill of the East" and the Sober Reality

In Eberhard Fechner's documentary, Heinz Villain, a former field officer and *SS-Unterscharführer*, offered a laconic summary of his impressions upon arrival at Majdanek in fall 1941: "Conditions were lousy."[175] The surviving source materials suggest that the arrival at Majdanek was a shock to both the female staff and the SS men transferred there. Asked by Fechner to describe Majdanek, Erna Pfannstiel responded:

ERNA WALLISCH: It was very different from Ravensbrück. I mean, the barracks at Ravensbrück were all fenced in. And all around there were the guards. But in Lublin, it was more of an open field. And Ravensbrück was practically in the town of Fürstenberg. Just a bit outside the town, near the lake.

EBERHARD FECHNER: Hm.

ERNA WALLISCH: But, well, Ravensbrück was more of a place. Lublin was a little creepy. Compared to Ravensbrück.[176]

Contrary to the initial perception, however, a transfer to the Generalgouvernement brought with it more than disadvantages. As Hildegard Lächert confirmed in court: "We received goods from private dealers,[177] lots of vodka, for example, which I could then go to the Poles in exchange for eggs and bacon, that's how we traded with the Poles there."[178] In addition to this kind of barter with foodstuffs—which played an important role during wartime—service in the Generalgouvernement also offered the camp staff an occasion for personal gain in the form of personal effects left behind by Jews murdered in Operation Reinhardt. Otto Z., a former member of the guard battalion, testified the following:

> There were SS men, including myself, who had Polish civilians place sausage and bread on top of rocks along the guard cordon. Then a prisoner would come and put money or valuables there and take the food. The SS man then took the money for himself.[179]

"Trading went on with and for everything,"[180] said the former guard Otto Z. in Fechner's documentary. Likewise, Georg W., a member of the guard unit, described how he acquired valuables while on duty at the gate post, as the camp entrance was called, which was in immediate proximity to the gas chambers:

> As far as appropriation of the prisoners' belongings is concerned I would like to state here that the Jews in question threw the jewelry to the ground about 20 meters away from me while being escorted into the camp by SS members. This took place without them having been asked to do so or demanding any kind of favor from me beforehand. The reason was probably that they expected the SS to take away their valuables upon arrival anyway. Afterwards, I went to where the valuables were lying and took possession of them.[181]

Georg W. admitted in his 1965 testimony that, despite official bans and strict punishment imposed by the SS authorities,[182] the SS men working in the protective custody camp often kept valuables taken from the prisoners.[183]

In addition to theft or directly accepting valuables, the *Aufseherinnen* and SS men could secretly "supply" themselves with clothing, shoes, and all kinds of commodities from the camp's well-stocked storerooms. These kinds of illicit practices were not as prevalent in camps within the Reich. In remote Majdanek, however, the rules were more easily skirted, presenting greater opportunity for personal enrichment, corruption, and trade. There were also other benefits that came along with "colonial rule." Under the occupation, "Reich Germans" occupied the highest rung on the ladder—higher, obviously, than the Poles, but also higher than "ethnic Germans." In this way, the female guards became beneficiaries of the policies of occupation and annihilation, in much the same way as the women in historian Elizabeth Harvey's research. This may well have been one of the reasons why, in their postwar testimony, some of the *Aufseherinnen* implied that, despite all its negative aspects, they left the "East" only reluctantly.

What, then, was behind the unease expressed by Erna Pfannstiel? The cross-examination of former guard Hertha Ehlert during the British Bergen-Belsen trial provides some insight. Although Ehlert stressed that conditions in Majdanek were "horrible" for the prisoners, she also said that conditions at Majdanek posed such an unreasonable imposition on the female guards that their transfer to the camp was tantamount to punishment. When queried as to why service at Majdanek constituted punishment despite the better pay—staffers received a bonus for service abroad—Ehlert replied:

EHLERT: Because the camps in Poland were nowhere near as cultivated as the camps in the German Reich.

COLONEL BACKHOUSE: I think the translation is wrong.

THE PRESIDENT: I think she meant "civilized."

COLONEL BACKHOUSE: Yes.

THE JUDGE ADVOCATE: Do you mean the living conditions for the S.S. were better in Ravensbrück than they were in Lublin?

EHLERT: No, they were better in the East, in Lublin.

Q: I do not want to waste time, so I will just put it to you once again, and then I will leave it. I gather you performed the same sort of duties as an *Aufseherin*, you got the same pay and a bonus, and the conditions were no worse for you. Why do you say it was a punishment?

EHLERT: It is a punishment because you do not feel very well in such a camp.[184]

Despite the material advantages, therefore, Hertha Ehlert felt that a Lublin posting was subjectively less appealing than a posting at Ravensbrück. Despite the attractive "advantages" service in Lublin brought with it, even years later it was the emotional experience that remained foremost in her mind. The strong emotions attached to service in "the East" decisively shaped the actions of the female guards and SS men stationed in Majdanek.

6 Work Conditions at Majdanek

For the *Aufseherinnen* at Majdanek, the work day began with the prisoners' roll call at 8 A.M. on the central grounds of the women's camp, the final count from which was typically reported to Hermine Braunsteiner:[1] "The chief guard took our count and went over the day's schedule with us. She assigned us to the different work details."[2] Afterwards, the female guards proceeded to their work assignments, where it was their job to supervise the prisoners.[3] As was the case in other concentration camps, the majority of the female guards did not have a permanent work assignment; rather, they were sent to different labor detachments on a rotating basis. The purpose of this strategy was to prevent the formation of personal relationships between the prisoners and the *Aufseherinnen*, as Erna Pfannstiel also noted:

> We were swapped around from time to time between the work details, which was to make sure that the female guards wouldn't have too much contact with the prisoners, so that they wouldn't get too close to them, somehow. So that we wouldn't get too involved with them. . . . Because if you always have the same work detail, then you get to know the people, right, and then something usually develops out of that, right?[4]

This time-tested SS principle was not, however, as easy to implement at Majdanek, where the guard units were chronically short-staffed. This staff shortage, which had been an issue since the women's camp first came into operation, had been the subject of numerous complaints made to the Chief Economic and Administrative Office (WVHA), by the Chief Guard unit, as well as successive camp commandants.

Staff Shortages

The first group of ten *Aufseherinnen* arrived in Lublin on October 16, 1942, from Ravensbrück.[5] The initial group included Hermine Braunsteiner, Else Ehrich, Elisabeth E., Hildegard Lächert, Anna M., Erna Pfannstiel, Charlotte W., Erika W., Edith W., and Charlotte Wöllert.[6] Within just a few weeks, however, Erika W. was exchanged with Ruth E., a guard from Auschwitz.[7] As Erika W. recalled in later testimony: "We received instructions that the women who had not yet reached the age of majority could not be deployed outside Reich territory. . . . I was then sent to Auschwitz-Birkenau, where I remained in service as an *Aufseherin* until December 1944."[8]

An internal memo written by Chief Guard Else Ehrich to Commandant Florstedt on December 1, 1942, suggests that, at that time, there were just ten *Aufseherinnen* for 2,000 female inmates. According to Ehrich, this was not sufficient to ensure orderly operations within the camp:

> In the clothing works belonging to the Armed SS, there are currently 2,097 female prisoners. Approximately 1,350 of these prisoners are working at any given moment, alternating between day and night shifts.
>
> Just 1 chief guard and 9 *Aufseherinnen*, 2 or 3 of whom are generally off sick, are assigned to supervise these inmates. In other words, we have only 6 female guards to supervise the prisoners at any one time.
>
> Additional female guards are urgently required to maintain order, prevent theft, and prevent possible escape attempts.[9]

A few days later, the commandant sent an appeal to the inspector of concentration camps in Oranienburg, SS Brigadeführer Richard Glücks:

> The headquarters of KGL [concentration camp] Lublin has asked that we supply 30 *Aufseherinnen* for the women's camp. Only ten women have been transferred there thus far, which is why the department is now requesting an additional 20 female guards.[10]

Glücks responded to the appeal on January 23, 1943, promising Odilo Globocnik, the SS and Police Leader of the district of Lublin, that within five days he would "pull out" some "suitable guards" from Ravensbrück and send them to Lublin.[11] On January 29,

1943, five additional *Aufseherinnen*—Hermine Brückner, Anna David, Hertha Ehlert, Irmgard K., and Rosa Reischl—arrived at Majdanek from Ravensbrück.

Despite these reinforcements, Majdanek suffered continued staff shortages. "There was something new every day," Charlotte Wöllert remembered. "Half of the *Aufseherinnen* were constantly sick, lying in the infirmary."[12] The many sick days, as well as vacation time, only exacerbated the staff shortage.[13] For example, due to enteric and typhoid fever, Hildegard Lächert was out sick from November 1942 to February 1943.[14] Anna M. was sick and unable to work from February to mid-August 1943.[15] That same June, Charlotte W. was sent to an SS infirmary for a suspected case of tuberculosis; she remained there for three months.[16] In addition, a number of female guards were transferred back to Ravensbrück. Still others left to marry, or because they had become pregnant.[17]

At that same time, another guard, Irmgard K., was still a minor and as such was transferred back to Auschwitz on February 16, 1943.[18] Her replacement, Gertrud Heise, arrived at Majdanek on March 1, 1943.[19] On March 25, 1943, another four *Aufseherinnen* (Helene D., Luzie H., Emilie Macha, and Anna S.) were transferred from Ravensbrück to Majdanek.[20] Another guard, Luise Danz, also from Ravensbrück, arrived in late March 1943.[21]

Presumably in response to an inquiry sent by the WVHA on behalf of Majdanek, the commandant of Ravensbrück, Fritz Suhren, justified the transfer of these *Aufseherinnen* as follows:[22]

> As can be seen from the personnel files of Helene D. and Macha, the likely reason for the transfer was the unreliable work performance of these two female guards. Since such elements are in no way suited to the Ravensbrück concentration camp, we request that the commandant of the Auschwitz concentration camp be informed that Ravensbrück is not a repository for impure elements. In the case of Luzie H. and Anna S., who, according to the report of the SS physician at Ravensbrück concentration camp, are completely fit for service, the supposed reason for their transfer is that they were also involved in the theft affair.[23]

It appears that Ravensbrück made an effort to retain *Aufseherinnen* who were deemed suitable, while guards who had attracted negative attention were transferred to Auschwitz and Majdanek.[24] This led to a series of contentious letters discussing these transfers, which were exchanged between Auschwitz, Majdanek, Ravensbrück, and Oranienburg. It would appear that the camps all attempted to transfer the female staff deemed "unsuited" to the work.

As the number of inmates at the women's camp continued to rise, the shortage of *Aufseherinnen* grew ever more acute. On June 28, 1943, during the "height" of the killing of Jewish inmates at Majdanek, Commandant Florstedt sent an appeal to the WVHA:

> We expect a large number of new female inmates to arrive shortly. I have 17 *Aufseherinnen* for a female inmate population of 7,141. To ensure orderly camp operations, I request that we receive at least 15 additional female guards.[25]

By July 5, Oranienburg had already agreed to send Florstedt five guards from Ravensbrück.[26] According to that letter, the number of transfers was limited to five because Ravensbrück was also short-staffed, largely due to the expanded role of concentration camp inmates in the wartime economy, including as forced labor on work details outside the camp (which necessitated even more intense supervision).[27] In the end, however, only four guards were transferred from Ravensbrück to Lublin. Herta B., Alice Orlowski, Elisabeth H., and Elfriede Zimmermann arrived at Majdanek on July 21, 1943.[28] Florstedt quickly sent a letter of complaint to the WVHA: "In the order of 5 July 1943, I was promised five *Aufseherinnen*. Of these five, only four have arrived. I request that the fifth guard be dispatched immediately and also request the secondment of five additional ones."[29] Two days later, the following reply arrived:

> Due to the formation of new work details with female inmates, there is currently such a scarcity of *Aufseherinnen* at Ravensbrück that not even the most important work details are being guarded. The fifth guard promised to the concentration camp will report to Ravensbrück shortly and then will be transferred.[30]

As the letter notes, in fall and winter 1943, there were nineteen *Aufseherinnen* for more than 7,000 female inmates at Majdanek.[31] In December 1942, the chief guard had already complained about a ratio of ten female guards to 2,000 inmates, which suggests that by late 1943, the staff shortage at Majdanek had become even more acute.

In late November 1943, the commandant of Majdanek, Martin Weiss, asked the WVHA to approve an exchange of staff members Hertha Ehlert, Luzie H., Emilie Macha, and Charlotte W. with guards from the Ravensbrück camp. The following letter was written by the Majdanek commandant:

> The Lublin concentration camp headquarters [at Majdanek] reports that the main reason for the transfer of the four above-cited *Aufseherinnen* is that they do not get along with their co-workers, and could be described as oppositional. In some cases, they have engaged in minor infractions of service regulations due to intimate relationships with SS men. For this reason, we urgently advise their transfer.[32]

However, Ravensbrück refused to accept their transfer, and the women remained at Majdanek until the camp's evacuation in April 1944.

In November 1943, *Aufseherin* Elisabeth H. resigned from her position as a result of her marriage, which had taken place two months earlier, in September.[33] However, her actual discharge from duty took some time, because no replacement could be found for her.[34] Hermine Braunsteiner's request for a transfer was granted on January 15, 1944.[35] A new guard, Frieda T., was sent as her replacement.[36] However, because Frieda T. was under twenty-one, she was sent back to Ravensbrück on February 8, 1944.[37] At the same time, due to her pregnancy, Erna Pfannstiel was transferred to Ravensbrück to work in a more "congenial" setting before her final dismissal from service.[38] Erna Bodem arrived from Ravensbrück as her replacement on February 8, 1944.[39] Bodem was the last female guard sent to Majdanek. During the evacuation of the women's camp in spring 1944, the remaining eighteen *Aufseherinnen* (including the chief guard, Else Ehrich) were transferred to Auschwitz and Płaszów.[40]

Conflicts among the SS

The collaboration among the guards at Majdanek was not always cohesive, which was certainly due, in part, to the close quarters in which the women lived and worked.[41] In postwar testimony, many of the former *Aufseherinnen* confirmed there wasn't a great deal of solidarity within the group. Rather, there was a "clique,"[42] with the chief guard, Else Ehrich, and her friend Hermine Braunsteiner at its center.[43] In her 1980 interview with Eberhard Fechner, Erna Pfannstiel described Ehrich in what can at best be described as neutral terms:

EBERHARD FECHNER: And, what kind of a person was she, how would you describe Frau Ehrich?
ERNA WALLISCH: She was a chief guard.
EBERHARD FECHNER: Yes. Was she a nice person? Or what?
ERNA WALLISCH: Well, what should I say? She was very conscious of her position.[44]

Describing Hermine Braunsteiner, Pfannstiel continued:

> Braunsteiner was very aware of the fact that she was deputy. In general, Braunsteiner was a rather unapproachable sort. Well, she always seemed to feel like she was a bit better than me.[45]

Charlotte Wöllert also reported feeling somewhat isolated within the group because she did not get along with Ehrich and Braunsteiner:[46] "There wasn't a lot of contact among us guards."[47] Elfriede Z. and Herta B. also said they were somewhat on the fringes of the group, and they became friends in part for that reason.[48] Hermine Brückner's testimony was quite similar:

> It's true that there was a group who clustered around the chief guard and another group who kept more to themselves. I was part of that second group. You couldn't

> tell anyone anything without taking the risk of being reported and punished. I mean, if you did something that wasn't allowed, like if you often didn't enforce the rules. There were no real friendships among us *Aufseherinnen*. We all kept to ourselves.[49]

According to Luzie H., even guards assigned to the same labor detachment tended not to socialize with each other:

> I didn't have any real contact with the *Aufseherin* who supervised the other shift in the tailor's workshop. I never saw her when I went on or off duty. I always had my own work detail. I didn't have any real contact with the other guard in the clothing works.[50]

Rosa Reischl, who was from Bavaria, described herself as an absolute outsider:

> I felt distant from the other *Aufseherinnen*, in part due to my dialect. I only had a bit of contact with Mayer [Wöllert], who was an earlier defendant, because we had similar opinions about certain things.[51]

In their reminiscences, Reischl's former colleagues corroborated, however unintentionally, that she was the target of some mockery. For example, Herta B. described Reischl as the "plump Bavarian,"[52] and Hertha Ehlert described her as "the fat one."[53] Likewise, in her interrogation before the court, Erika W. stated that she, herself, was constantly teased about her "skinny legs," while she, in turn, had envied Braunsteiner for her attractive figure.[54]

As these statements make clear, the relationship among the female guards was not as harmonious as surviving photographs might suggest (see figures 14, 15, and 16). Among other things, standards of female beauty, place of origin, and dialect served to create boundaries between the "in group" and the outsiders.

With reference to the context of colonial policies, I will, in closing, shift my focus from the smaller group of female guards to the male guard troops of Majdanek, and the chasm that existed within the SS: the distinction between the "Reich German" and the *volksdeutsche* ("ethnic German") members of the SS Death's Head Battalion.[55]

Within the SS hierarchy, the non-German members of the Armed SS occupied a distinctly inferior position. Although the "Reich Germans" were numerically in the minority, they generally held the leadership positions.[56] Most of the guard battalion, which numbered around 1,200 members, was made up of men from Croatia, Latvia, Lithuania, Romania, Ukraine, and Hungary. As Untersturmführer Arnold Brendler, former leader of a guard company, recalled: "The guard battalion was made up of three companies, largely comprised of *Volksdeutsche*."[57] In addition, there was a fourth company, called the "Ukrainian guard company."[58] This was comprised mainly of Ukrainians, along with some Latvians and Lithuanians. The 3rd company of the guard unit was made up "primarily of Hungarians and Romanians," as Georg W., an Austrian who helped train the guards, remembered. "Only the Unterführer were

Photographer unknown. Landesarchiv Nordrhein-Westfalen, Rheinland Division, RWB 28561

FIGURE 14. Three female SS guards—Hildegard Lächert is on the right—taken between October 1942 and April 1944 in Majdanek

of German descent. The 3rd company was made up of about 100 men, on average, along with about 15–20 Unterführer."[59] A January 1943 internal memo of a leader of the battalion illustrated the relationship between the "Reich Germans" and the Ukrainians in the guard troops:

> The leader of the SS D-Battalion of the Lublin concentration camp of the Armed SS Lublin reports to the commandant that Ukr. troops smoke while on duty. Matter has been discussed.
>
> Due to language barriers, he most likely understood only the overall meaning, and that only due to the loudness of the reprimand. The next morning, the Ukr. guard had vanished, without taking his gun.[60]

There was also frequent tension between the *volksdeutsche* guards, the "Ukrainians," and the roughly two hundred SS men of the headquarters staff who worked in the camp compound (the prisoners' camp). These SS men, who generally came from Germany and Austria, tended to feel superior to the *volksdeutche*, and did not accept

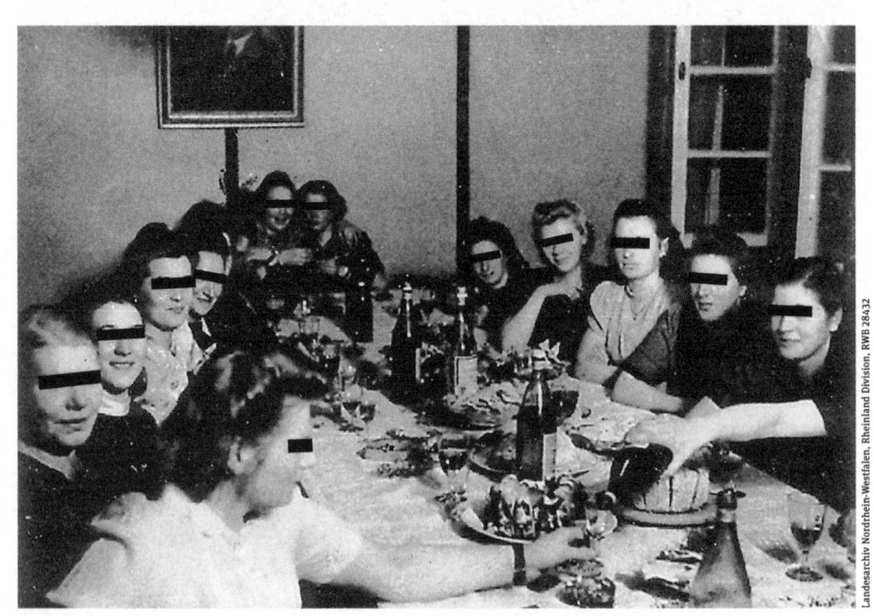

Landesarchiv Nordrhein-Westfalen, Rheinland Division, RWB 28432

FIGURES 15 AND 16. A birthday party at the “Deutsches Haus” in Lublin

them as "equal" members of the SS community, as Anton K., a former guard from Croatia, recalled in his postwar testimony:

> We had very little contact with the headquarters' staff, because they didn't really accept us as equals. They were Reich Germans and we were the *Beutegermanen* [Trophy Germans]. When we greeted them, they often barely replied, or didn't reply at all. But God forbid if one of us ever failed to greet one of them![61]

On January 31, 1944, the next-to-last commandant of Majdanek, Martin Weiss, issued a directive to his troops that included an order from Himmler on how to address the *volksdeutsche* troops:

> All members of the SS should be informed of the following directive by the Reichsführer-SS.
>
> I request that the expression "Reich Germans and *volksdeutscher*," and, in particular, the expression *volksdeutscher*, generally used in a disparaging manner by Germans within the Reich borders, be avoided whenever possible. When it is necessary to make a distinction between persons who are "Reich Germans" and *volksdeutsche*, the proper phrasing is "Germans inside and outside the Reich borders," or "Germans from within the Reich" and Germans "of ethnic extraction." Whenever possible, however, we should say only, "He is a German."[62]

Despite this directive, tensions remained. As described by Otto Z., who was from Latvia:

> In the case of the block leaders [members of the headquarters' staff], we noticed that they were much wealthier than we were, in the guard troops, and that they had the freedom to do as they wished. There was tension between us and all those headquarters' folks, who thought they were better than we were.[63]

However, national and ethnic differences were not the only cause for disputes between the members of the headquarters' staff and the guard battalions. Another factor was that the headquarters staff also had more opportunity to confiscate the prisoners' belongings for their own personal gain.

Also of interest in this respect is the WVHA's directive, issued on February 15, 1943, that wives of SS guard troops be drawn into service to help alleviate the shortage of female guards. On March 1, 1943, Commandant Florstedt sent an internal memo to the SS Death's Head divisions stationed at Majdanek:

> Re: Work deployment of wives of SS members with no children
>
> Re: Directive of the SS-WVHA
>
> To the SS D-Battalion Concentration Camp Lublin

> Following a request by the head of the SS-WVHA, the wives of SS members who do not have children should be deployed as female guards in a women's concentration camp.
>
> For this reason, we must immediately determine which SS members in the battalion are married. These men are to be instructed by the leader of their battalion that they are to instruct their wives to enter service as *Aufseherinnen*.
>
> A report with names and the results of this initiative should be submitted to headquarters by 4 March 1943.[64]

Two days later, the leader of the battalion responded with the following inquiry:

> A report with names and other details regarding the labor deployment of wives of SS men who do not have children as guards in women's concentration camps cannot yet be delivered, as the deadline given by the battalion is too short. The wives of many battalion members live in the Reich, or in Croatia, Hungary, and so forth. Just notifying these wives would normally take about 10 to 14 days.
>
> Within the companies, the men are being instructed in accordance with the directive. We will report with results as soon as these are received.
>
> In addition, we ask for clarification regarding the extent to which the directive applies to wives of *volksdeutsche* members from Croatia, Hungary, and Romania.[65]

However, as soon as it became clear that the majority of the wives affected by this directive were *volksdeutsche*, the commandant revised his original instructions. In a reply to the leader of the battalion, Florstedt stated that "the labor deployment will affect only those SS officers whose wives are Reich Germans."[66]

In contrast to the SS men, then, the female guards were required to be "Reich Germans." Although the reason for this remains unknown, this was presumably not Florstedt's own decision. Moreover, whether the initiative was based on an order from Himmler or whether the entire initiative was based solely on the order issued by the WVHA is also unknown.

Gender Relations

While at work, the *Aufseherinnen* at Majdanek were supervised by a male SS staff. At all times, two SS men monitored the number of prisoners in each labor detachment as they departed and returned to the camp.[67] Also, the commandant and the camp compound leader often patrolled the camp to inspect the work of the female guards.[68] It was also men who assumed the leadership roles at the prisoners' workplaces. As Charlotte Wöllert recalled, an SS man supervised the *Aufseherinnen* in the clothing works.[69] An SS man, SS-Unterscharführer P., also headed the laundry,[70] while SS-Unterscharführer Fritz D., who was a gardener by profession, headed the garden. For both the SS men and the female guards, this collaboration was not always easy.

Rudolf Höss, who after spring 1942 was also in charge of a women's camp at Auschwitz, vigorously disagreed with Himmler's demand that female prisoners be supervised by female guards. If we follow Karin Orth in her argument that the SS officers assigned to concentration camps all received similar training and workplace indoctrination, it is likely that Höss's views of female guards, as described in his postwar account, were shared by most of his colleagues.[71] According to Höss, the *Aufseherinnen* who were transferred from Ravensbrück to Auschwitz were confronted with a difficult transition:

> These women came to Auschwitz—but none of them did so voluntarily—and were supposed to adapt to the difficult circumstances there. From the time they arrived, most wanted to just run away, back to the quiet, comfortable, and peaceful life they had at Ravensbrück. . . . These experienced *Aufseherinnen*, however, still towered over those who followed afterwards. Despite diligent recruitment efforts by Nazi women's organizations, very few women volunteered for duty as concentration camp guards. As a result, the need for *Aufseherinnen*, which was growing more acute by the day, had to be met via forcible measures. Every munitions company scheduled to be assigned female prisoners had to commit a certain percentage of female employees who were then deployed as guards. Given the overall wartime lack of good female laborers, it is understandable that the companies did not contribute their best workers. At best, the female guards received several weeks' "training" at Ravensbrück, and then were let loose on the prisoners.[72]

The image of the *Aufseherinnen* that Höss portrayed in his postwar account was extremely pejorative. According to Höss, the women received inadequate training, and the ones who were transferred to Auschwitz were the worst of the lot. He was convinced that Ravensbrück deliberately placed Auschwitz at a disadvantage in the assignment of female guards:

> Because the selection and assignments were made by Ravensbrück, Auschwitz was at the bottom of the list. And of course, Ravensbrück kept the workers who seemed most promising for their own soon-to-be-established women's labor camp. That is the sort of female guard we ended up with at the Auschwitz women's concentration camp. They were all of very, very low moral character. Many *Aufseherinnen* were tried before the SS courts because of thefts carried out during Operation Reinhardt. But only a few were ever caught. Even though severe punishments were meted out as deterrence, theft continued to be commonplace, and prisoners continued to be used as middlemen in the thefts.[73]

It is also true that Höss complained about the male staff assigned to Auschwitz, saying that the majority of the men were examples of "human inadequacy and obduracy."[74] However, even though a number of his male staff were also later charged before the SS courts, it still angered Höss more that there were women who had helped themselves to "Jewish inventory" and "Reich property."

In his postwar account, Höss also described the horrific conditions in the women's camp:

> Conditions in the women's camp were much worse in every respect. . . . To create some semblance of order in this swarming, teeming nest of ants, we would have needed an entirely different category of female guards. . . . The *Aufseherinnen* ran around in this chaos like confused and overwrought hens. The three or four good ones were driven mad by the rest.[75]

Höss's criticisms also imply that he believed the women had no sense of discipline or order, and that they were less emotionally resilient than their male colleagues. In this sense, his own ideals of femininity collided with his view of the women who had been assigned to work as guards under his command:

> I always had a great deal of respect for women, on the whole. But at Auschwitz, I learned that I needed to dial down my view of them, and that it was important to take a good look at a woman before according her such deep respect.[76]

As commandant of Auschwitz, Höss had an extremely negative opinion of the chief guard, Johanna Langefeld (born in 1900), who he said was utterly lacking in leadership qualities:

> The chief guard at the time, Frau Langefeldt, was completely unable to cope with the situation, but she stubbornly ignored all instructions given to her by the camp compound leader. Eventually, I realized the sloppiness couldn't be allowed to continue, and I took it upon myself to reassign responsibility for the women's concentration camp to the head of the camp compound leader. Almost every single day, there were discrepancies in the prisoners' count.[77]

Before her transfer to Auschwitz, Langefeld had already come into conflict with Commandant Koegel at Ravensbrück as a result of the practice of floggings.[78] Disputes over jurisdiction and problems with the exclusively male headquarters staff continued to escalate after she took over as chief guard at the Auschwitz women's camp in fall 1942. During a visit by Himmler in July 1942, Langefeld had lodged a complaint with the Reichsführer-SS, which is confirmed by a note Himmler wrote in his duty calendar on July 18.[79] Langefeld's conversation with Himmler had consequences for the camp system as a whole—on October 24 of that year, Himmler issued a directive that the camp compound leaders were to be removed from oversight of the existing women's concentration camps at Ravensbrück, Auschwitz, and Majdanek, and that the chief guards were to resume their duties effective immediately.[80]

Höss described these events in the following terms:

> Because the chief guard saw herself as the independent leader of the camp, she complained about her subordination to an officer of her own rank. And then I was actually forced to revoke my decision. During the Reichsführer-SS's visit to the camp in July 1942, I described to him the administrative shortcomings, in the presence of the chief guard. I informed him that Frau Langefeldt [Langefeld] was not now and would never be in a position to effectively manage and develop the Auschwitz women's concentration camp, and I asked that she remain subordinate to the first camp compound leader. Although he was given clear evidence of the shortcomings of the chief guard and the other *Aufseherinnen*, he rejected this suggestion. He wanted women's camps to be headed by women, and I was supposed to assign an SS leader to assist her. But what leader would allow himself to be subordinated to such a woman? Everyone I was forced to assign this task to soon returned to me and asked to be removed from the position.[81]

Given the paramilitary context in which they worked, it was a stretch, in the first place, for the men to accept women as colleagues; to further accept the notion, then, that a woman could potentially be the superior of a man was even more vexing. In that sense, as Bernhard Strebel notes, it comes as little surprise that there is no evidence this order was implemented in any of the concentration camps named in the directive.[82] Displeased with the outcome of her complaint, Langefeld took her grievance to yet another, higher SS official, Oswald Pohl of the WVHA. This time, however, her persistence led to her dismissal, in spring 1943.[83]

The question becomes, then, how did the female guards at Majdanek experience their relationship to the SS men at the camp? Both in their work and during their leisure time, the women were routinely confronted with the presence of the male SS staff, who far outnumbered the female staff in the camp. The men and women lived in close proximity and encountered each other on the camp grounds during their work, as well as in the shared canteen. The incompatibility of traditional standards of femininity with the workaday world of the female guards, coupled with the sorts of stereotypes rampant in Rudolf Höss's postwar account, would suggest that their collaboration with the male SS officers was often fraught with tension.

Indeed, the Majdanek files on Erna Pfannstiel and Charlotte Wöllert document a clash with SS officers in the camp. On April 17, 1943, the report leader, Oberscharführer Heinz Petrick, issued the following report:

> On 16 April 1943, the first camp compound leader, SS Untersturmf. Thumann, ordered me to supervise the female prisoners in the bath. For that reason, I supervised the bathing today—that is, I spoke early in the day with Report Leader Knoblich [nee Wöllert] about how the bathing could be executed smoothly. . . . By 15:00, only 400 prisoners had bathed. SS U-Sturmf. Thumann was quite indignant about this situation. By 14:00, I

> had already investigated why the bathing was proceeding so slowly, only to discover that the prisoners' clothing was not being bundled properly before it was sent to the gassing room, which created a great deal of confusion. The person responsible for this issue was O.-Scha. Perschon. Then, between 15:00 and 17:00, the bathing was interrupted, because a company was using the bath.
>
> When I carried out another inspection at 18:30, I told *Aufseherin* Pfannstiel in the bath that another 200 prisoners would still need to bathe today, and that the gardening work detail would need to head out for duty in the morning. SS U-Sturmf. Thumann had issued that order. She [Pfannstiel] was extremely annoyed to hear this, and said that she knew nothing of the gardening work detail being scheduled for duty in the morning. She knew only that the tailoring work detail was scheduled for duty. She said all kinds of things, such as, "We're not at an idiot's school here," and, "They can all just kiss our a—. We're just women, right. First they order one thing, and then they tell us to do something else." SS-U.Stuf. Thumann was standing nearby and heard it all. *Aufseherin* Wöllert was also enraged, and said that they had never experienced such chaos at Ravensbrück, and that she had been on duty since 4:30 that morning. I tried to calm her down, but she was extremely agitated. When I came back out of the bath, SS-U.Stuf. Thumann ordered me to report this matter.[84]

A day later, the first camp compound leader, SS-Untersturmführer Anton Thumann, issued a report on Wöllert and Pfannstiel's "behavior" to the commandant of the camp:

> After she was informed that the gardening work detail was to head out in the morning, *Aufseherin* Pfannstiel spoke in such a harsh tone of voice that I was forced to take her to task. She seemed to believe it was not necessary to allow me to speak, so I ordered her to leave the bathing area and to return to her lodgings.
>
> I should mention that there had been an earlier occasion when *Aufseherin* Pfannstiel had spoken to me in an extremely untoward tone of voice and seemed to believe she could do whatever she pleased. On that occasion, *Aufseherin* Wöllert was standing right next to her, inside the door, and must certainly have heard *Aufseherin* Pfannstiel's remarks. I asked Wöllert what Pfannstiel's name was, because I didn't know it. At that time, I also told her that she would probably be asked to make a report on the remarks that had been made to me. *Aufseherin* Wöllert told me that would be out of the question, and that she would rather have herself locked up. . . .
>
> I was outraged, and I said to *Aufseherin* Pfannstiel that her mouth was nothing but a snout. I should mention that *Aufseherin* Pfannstiel was also extremely rude in her behavior, a fact SS-Oberscharführer Petrick will be able to confirm, which is the reason I felt compelled to respond in kind.[85]

As this episode demonstrates, neither the female guards nor the SS men were accustomed to working together. Particularly at Ravensbrück, the *Aufseherinnen* were used to working independently. This conflict points to some of the gender dynamics that later developed among the staff at Majdanek. In a demonstration of what Alf Lüdtke might have termed "Eigen-Sinn," Pfannstiel took the offensive against her fellow SS colleague and even her superior, refusing the demand that she work longer hours and give up some of her leisure time.

In response, Anton Thumann, camp compound leader, ordered Pfannstiel to leave her post and "return to her quarters." It would appear, then, that Thumann was either unable or unwilling to defuse the situation and negotiate a solution on the spot. For her part, Wöllert sided with her fellow *Aufseherin*, and cited her experiences at Ravensbrück to justify her indignation, emphasize her qualifications as a female guard, and express her disdain for Thumann and "his" camp. In so doing, Wöllert helped to escalate the situation and made it abundantly clear to Thumann that he would not be able to count on her support. Her statement that she would rather allow herself to be "locked up" than issue a statement against her fellow comrade demonstrates her willingness to take a strong stand—at least verbally—in a direct confrontation with male SS staff.

This dispute in the bathing barracks is just one example of the tensions encountered during daily operations at Majdanek. Coupled with the fundamental issues surrounding the employment of women in the concentration camps, it is likely that many of these daily conflicts between male SS officers and female guards played out along gendered lines.[86]

At the same time, as an analysis of postwar testimony shows, a number of female guards appear to have been romantically involved with SS men.[87] For example, in her court interrogation, Reischl at first refused to reply when she was asked who Braunsteiner had been involved with at Majdanek. However, Braunsteiner called over to Reischl from her spot in the defendant's corner, telling her to "tell them!" At that point, Reischl responded, "Braunsteiner was involved with Officer F. I also went out with him twice when she was sick."[88] Another former *Aufseherin*, Charlotte W., stated that she had been involved with an SS officer, Jan M.: "M. and I had an affair. I knew that he was married. So that his marriage wouldn't end, I helped him get an apartment in Lublin, so that he could have his wife move out, too."[89] Jan M. confirmed her account: "I was involved with Charlotte W. until my wife came to Lublin, which would have been about mid-1943. My wife stayed in Lublin until around March 20, 1944, and then went back to Berlin."[90] Jan M. and his wife had married in 1938, and had three children between 1938 and 1940; all three children accompanied his wife to Lublin.

The Kapo in charge of the bathing facilities, Georg Gröner, reported that the SS medic in charge of the gas chamber, SS Oberscharführer Hans Perschon, "had a relationship with the *Aufseherin* Anni David, and one day he was so broken-hearted that he even wanted to take his own life in the gas chamber."[91] In April 1944, Hildegard Lächert bore her third child, who died shortly after birth. During her interrogations, she refused to name the father of her child, saying only that he was an SS man at an air base: "In Lublin, I was friendly with Untersturmführer D., and after he left, I was involved with another man. The second one was an Unterscharführer. Both worked in the administration."[92] In one of her interrogations, Rosa Reischl admitted that the SS men often "used naughty words to try to have their way with me."[93] Otto Z. recalled that the medic for the gas chamber, SS-Oberscharführer Karl Endress, "was involved with a female SS guard, who was also involved with the SS Schtz. B., from the canine unit, at the same time."[94]

In light of this testimony, it is clear that the strict separation between the sexes, to which both administrators in Oranienburg and camp commandants attached great importance, was, in practice, impossible to enforce:

Lublin, 22 February 1943

Special Directive

To the Divisions I, II, III, IV, V, VI, Labor Assignment, W. u. G. Camp Engineer, Car Pool, Operator, Chief Guard, Women's Concentration Camp, Construction Administration KOL., SS Court Leader, Mail Station, SS D.H.-Division. . . .[95]

To eliminate any further confusion, I order that only female guards will oversee and supervise the entire area inside the women's concentration camp. This applies also to when the women are changing their clothes, bathing, and washing. During the women's bathing hours, no SS man or male prisoner is to have access to the area. The only exception is the camp physician, if he deems his participation necessary. The chief guard is responsible for enforcing this directive.

During all work carried out by female prisoners where any men are present (whether they be SS men, civilian workers, or others), an *Aufseherin* must also be present nearby. The latter is especially important during renovation of the laundry, where a close eye must be kept on the Polish civilian workers.

SS members are not permitted to enter the Block Leader Room Field V.

In the event that any *Aufseherin* should violate this directive in any way, I again draw your attention to the fact that the female guards are subject to the SS and police courts, and that I, myself, will punish all violations to the fullest extent of my authority.[96]

Signed, The Camp Commandant (H. Florstedt)

In his decree, Florstedt—who was himself rumored to have been involved with Else Ehrich, the chief guard[97]—directs particular attention to "SS members," that is, the men who worked for the camp administration or in the prisoner camp. For Florstedt, the inability to enforce the separation between the sexes was a vexing problem and a major point of conflict. These interactions between male and female staff interfered with the ability to divide the camp into separate entities, which, as discussed above, was intended as a disciplinary measure, meant to help maintain control among the guard troops. In his directive 1/44 dated January 31, 1944, Commandant Weiss also reprimanded his troops:

> Entering in the Women's Barracks
>
> I hereby repeat the order I have issued on numerous occasions regarding entering the barracks where the female guards are housed. Except when carrying out official duties, entering the *Aufseherin* barracks is prohibited for all officers, noncommissioned officers, and SS men. I will personally patrol and supervise enforcement of this order, and any SS member who violates this order, as well as any *Aufseherin* who permits unauthorized access to the barracks, will be severely punished.[98]

The significance of this prohibition is further underscored by the fact that this directive also makes mention of sexually transmitted diseases and extramarital sexual relations:

> Prevention of Sexually Transmitted Diseases
>
> We once again draw your attention to the sanitation order issued by the Reichsführer SS on 9 September 1943. This order instructs all members of the SS to carry out sanitary measures after any extramarital sexual relations.[99]

For the female guards, the work at Majdanek came with daily challenges, tension, and conflict with both male and female coworkers. They were routinely confronted with disgruntled and dissatisfied superiors, as well as petty rivalries from both male and female colleagues. The *Aufseherinnen* held a tenuous position within the male-dominated ranks at Majdanek. On the one hand, they were outnumbered by the regular SS staff, who often took it upon themselves to exert various forms of pressure on them. At the same time, they faced frequent disapproval and skepticism from higher-ranking SS officers. Nonetheless, they displayed moments of "Eigen-Sinn" and self-assertion vis-à-vis their male superiors.

An additional factor was that the female guards lived on-site in a "foreign" and militarized environment in the Generalgouvernement. At times, the women became intimately involved with married SS men, who found it easy to conceal these illicit relationships from their wives back home. For those women who were inclined to become romantically entangled with SS (or non-SS) men, the large numbers of available men and a relative scarcity of women might well have held an appeal. In this sense, the young women who worked at Majdanek enjoyed an unaccustomed level of opportunity and choice.[100] Pregnancies known to have resulted among the female guards provide further substantiation that the orders for strict separation between the sexes were frequently disregarded.

For some of the female guards, their posting at Majdanek also offered the opportunity to find a husband. Two *Aufseherinnen* married noncommissioned SS men (an *Unterscharführer* and an *Oberscharführer*), one married a *Sturmmann*, while another married a *Rottenführer*. There were, however, no marriages between the female guards and higher-ranking SS officers. This would perhaps suggest that, despite the relative shortage of women and the exceptional circumstances in which they lived and worked at Majdanek (living in a barracks, coupled with working at an extermination camp), social barriers continued to hold sway.

7 Annihilation as Work

The Daily Work of Killing in the Camp

As an institution, the concentration and extermination camp produced death on a mass scale. For this reason, killing was a central work duty for most camp staff. In what follows, I will examine the daily work duties of the female guards and the SS men who served at the Majdanek camp. This analysis will primarily entail exploration of how the mass killing of prisoners shaped day-to-day work routines.

A central element of this process of annihilation is that it was carried out within a highly structured work process that involved numerous steps, in which many individuals in different functions played an active or supervisory role. The process involved selections among the prisoners, bathing of some of the prisoners, the actual "work" of killing, and the confiscation and plundering of belongings. After the fact, the bodies of the dead were removed from the gas chambers. Any gold teeth were pulled, and their hair was cut. Finally, the bodies of the dead were carted away and then disposed of—again, in a process that involved multiple steps.

Most of these final tasks were the responsibility of prisoners who served on special work details (*Sonderkommando*) at both the gas chamber and the crematorium. These detachments were made up primarily of Jewish and Russian prisoners, working under the direction of "Reich German" prisoners, all of whom were, in turn, supervised by SS staff. These workers helped the victims remove their clothing, and sorted the clothing and other possessions after they had been removed. Afterward, the members of the *Sonderkommando* removed the bodies of the dead from the gas chamber, including any bodies that were stuck and thus difficult to extract. They aired out the gas chambers, and cleaned the bodies of excrement, blood, and vomit. Other prisoners cut the hair of the victims, and pulled their gold teeth. Finally, the corpses were loaded onto wooden carts and brought to the location where they would be buried or burned. There, other prisoners dug mass graves or burned the corpses in ovens.[1]

In what follows, the focus will be on the steps within this process of annihilation—or what Jacques Sémelin has described more aptly as destruction—that were carried out by the camp SS. I will consider a number of representative examples of the process of selection, killing, and disposal of the bodies.

Selection

The first step in the killing process was the selection of the prisoners who would be killed. The criteria used to determine who would live and who would die were the inmate's (apparent) health, and his or her capacity for work.

SELECTIONS IN THE INFIRMARY

One place where selections took place on a regular basis was the infirmary (*Krankenbau*), as it was called. In spring 1942, a provisional, poorly equipped infirmary for sick, wounded, or exhausted prisoners was established on Field I. In the words of Hermann Hackmann, physicians were "removed" from the inmate population to staff the infirmary: "The prisoner-physicians took care of the sick, under the direction of a physician who held the rank of Sturmbannführer, within the limits of what was possible at the time."[2] However, these possibilities were, in reality, extremely limited. The prisoner-physicians had little food or medication to give the prisoners, and no surgical facilities. For this reason, Jan Novak, a prisoner-physician from Poland, called the infirmary a "terminal ward"—a place where inmates were sent to die:

> The infirmary barracks were equipped with wood pallets and with two ovens—coal ovens made of iron—a table for the doctor, and drains for the planned toilets. The infirmary had room for about 200 people, including the spots for the nurse-orderlies. . . . Our job was helping maintain their blood pressure and fighting diarrhea and pneumonia. There was only enough medication for a few people.[3]

Officially, the SS orderlies were responsible for making all decisions as to how long prisoners remained in the infirmary and when they were released. SS orderlies also determined which prisoners were to be killed. German and Austrian prisoner-functionaries were then responsible for carrying out the orders of the SS. They had authority over the prisoner-physicians and the prisoner-orderlies, most of whom were Polish (see figure 2). Despite this racial hierarchy, the prisoner-physicians did have authority over the SS orderlies when it came to medical decisions; according to Novak, the SS orderlies were permitted to give administrative but not medical orders to the prisoner-physicians.[4] This gave the prisoner-physicians some scope for independent decision-making, which they could exploit for the benefit of the inmates. For example, a prisoner-physician might enter influenza rather than typhoid or other serious illness as the diagnosis in the patient records, a deception that saved many inmates' lives.

> As physicians . . . we employed various strategies to try to argue that they could be cured in order to reduce the number of inmates who were classified as unable to work. The German physician [on duty] would speak with me about sick inmates in my block. . . . The German physician spoke with me only about general medical matters.[5]

Given the overcrowding in the infirmary and the constant pressure to refer patients for extermination, there was relatively little the physician-prisoners could do to help. At all times, it was the SS physicians who had the final say when it came to judging a patient's health and capacity to work. For that reason, the majority of inmates in the infirmary were at risk of being deemed incapable of work by the SS and, ultimately, being killed.

Until fall 1943, the infirmary capacity increased in conjunction with the rising inmate population, and a corresponding increase in cases of typhus, paratyphoid, and dysentery. Between late April and mid-May 1943, when many transports from Białystok and the Warsaw ghetto arrived at Majdanek, the camp reached its highest number of prisoners. As Novak described to the court, as the camp grew ever more crowded and epidemics continued to spread, the selection of sick inmates in the infirmary became increasingly radical:

> Those who could no longer rise out of bed were taken away. Each time, the prisoner-physician was asked if the patient could be cured or not. . . . Over time, the process grew even more brutal. Anyone who couldn't walk was assigned to the group that would be gassed. Decisions were made on the fly by the Kapo and the SDG [*Sanitätsdienstgrad*, an SS rank for nurse-orderlies]. The SS physicians were always there in the infirmary at the beginning and then they left, leaving the work for the Kapo or SDG.[6]

In Novak's memory, by September 1943, the entire left side of Field I had been turned into an infirmary. The Russian POWs had their own infirmary on Field II.[7] There were also additional infirmaries on Fields III and IV. The women's camp on Field V had its own separate infirmary, staffed by female physicians.

According to Novak's testimony, regular selections took place in the infirmary "whenever the number of new patients led to overcrowding, and there was no more room for new patients. In that case, a group of SS members would appear unannounced. The group included an SS physician, some SS orderlies and an infirmary Kapo."[8] Novak further explained to the Düsseldorf court that Heinrich Schmidt, an SS physician who held the rank of *Hauptsturmführer*, was the ranking physician at Majdanek and also the physician for the troops. In addition, he was the official responsible for the overall coordination of selections, and for subsequent killings. Within the individual infirmaries, selections were carried out by SS orderlies, particularly Unterscharführer Günther Konietzny and Unterscharführer Wilhelm Reinartz, who were assisted by Ludwig Benden, a German prisoner-orderly. According to Novak, the SS physicians did not take an active part in the selections but, rather, were a passive presence. For the SS physicians, the presence of the prisoner-physicians was a source of shame that forced them to confront a professional and ethical dilemma:

> They were ashamed there in the presence of a prisoner who was also doctor and someone with whom they otherwise discussed issues related to medical care in the camp, and whose (negative) opinion on the topic of selections was something of which they were, of course, well aware. I would say, however, that these physicians also took note of those individuals who attempted to defend the honor of the medical profession, especially in such situations where a physician was urgently needed.[9]

For their part, the lower-ranking SS orderlies also varied in the rigor with which they carried out their duties, as Josef Ochlewski, a prisoner-scribe, later described:

> Reinartz and Konietzny did not carry out selections in the same way. Konietzny was "cold" and carried out the selections with a great degree of cynicism, but Reinartz—in my opinion—had a much harder time with his role. He was often hesitant when carrying out the selections and he was often drunk, so I felt and I believe that he was acting against his will. He took the opinions of Dr. Wieliczanski [a prisoner-physician] into account, when the physician said that he thought the prisoner in question might still "recover."[10]

In the infirmary, Ochlewski had the opportunity to observe the SS staff more closely:

> One evening on Christmas Eve or sometime during the Christmas holidays, Reinartz came to us in the infirmary and asked me and Dr. Wieliczanski to join him at the table. Then he got out a bottle of wine, loosened the cap with his revolver, threw it in the corner, and said to us, "I want to drink with you as a colleague and as a person." Then he spent an hour telling us about his family and his life.[11]

While prisoner-orderly Ludwig Benden and SS orderly Günther Konietzny were universally remembered as brutal individuals[12] whom the prisoners feared, Reinartz was described by Polish survivors who worked in the infirmary as a person who struggled with remorse and seemed to have a troubled conscience. Novak recalled Reinartz as having a somewhat "humane attitude,"[13] and said that Reinartz sometimes smuggled small packages and other items into the camp for the prisoners:[14]

> Reinartz took part in a few selections, but he always tried to hang behind his colleagues from the SS infirmary. . . . I remember that he once used words like "this is all shit," that he seemed to feel he had blood on his hands. That was probably after one of the executions that had been ordered.[15]

Novak, who apparently was on good terms with Reinartz, also said that he was willing to ask Reinartz questions about specific incidents in the camp, which he wouldn't have dared to ask any of the other SS orderlies.[16]

SELECTIONS IN THE PRISONERS' CAMP

More and more often, as overcrowding increased and epidemics became frequent, selections were also carried out in the prisoners' camp. SS physicians, assisted by field and block leaders in the men's camp and the female guards in the women's camp, selected for killing prisoners who were sick or deemed unfit for work. According to Hermann Hackmann, the former first camp compound leader, the commandant would assemble the SS physicians "at preset times" and issue his "directives,"[17] meaning he would instruct them as to how many prisoners deemed sick or unfit for work were to be selected from each field. In the women's camp, the *Aufseherinnen* carried out the selections under the direction of Chief Guard Else Ehrich during the daily roll call.

The survivors vividly recall the selections carried out by Field Leader Hermine Braunsteiner:

> She could even select during roll call. If she didn't like the look of someone, if they were too weak, or too thin—then she was liable to say [survivor imitates a gesture, and a wave of the hand]: "Away."[18]

Dora Abend described to the court how *Aufseherin* Hildegard Lächert, called "Brigida" by the prisoners, carried out this task:

> In the women's field, selections took place almost every day—even on Sunday. At roll call, "Brigida" would appear with several SS men, who would point their fingers at certain women. "Brigida" would fetch them from the rows, yanking by the shoulders, or by their hair or ears. About ten to twenty women were pulled out

> from each block. "Brigida" always had a smile on her face as she did her work. She used to always have a dog with her, and she struck our heads and faces in a dreadful manner with her thick, long whip.[19]

For their part, the female guards varied widely in their testimony. For example, Erna Pfannstiel recalled in a postwar interrogation:

> I believe it was twice that I saw the chief guard [Else Ehrich] and *Aufseherin* Braunsteiner walk through the rows of assembled prisoners on the roll-call grounds of Field V. They pointed at the prisoners, the women, with their finger or with a stick they were carrying, to pick them out from the rest. The women then had to stand over to the side. . . . Then I saw Ehrich and Braunsteiner bring the women they had chosen away. They said they were bringing them to the bath. . . . But I knew the women would not be returning from the bath, because they were being taken next door to the gas chamber. Then we had to calm them down. We had to talk to them, and with hand gestures calm them down. Some of the women spoke German.[20]

Pfannstiel did not describe in any greater detail what she meant by "hand gestures." However, based on Dora Abend's description, it is likely these "hand gestures" were, in fact, slaps, blows, and other like gestures.[21]

SELECTIONS DURING INCOMING TRANSPORTS

Between fall 1942 and spring 1944, when transports of Jews including women and children arrived at Majdanek, the female guards also took part in the "incoming selections." These selections generally took place outside the camp, in front of the prisoners' bath and the disinfection chamber (the latter of which doubled as the gas chamber) (see figure 12). "On arrival at the camp, they selected the younger women, the older ones, and the women with children." The SS women included the *Aufseherin* "Brigida" (Hildegard Lächert) and "Mutti" (Emilie Macha),[22] as survivor Chela Apelbaum described in her testimony before the court. "During the arrival selection, 'Brigida' tore the struggling children away from their mothers, threw them to the floor, and kicked them. When a mother came over, 'Brigida' would kick her in the back of the head."[23] Although selections always involved violence toward prisoners on the part of the female guards and SS men, some *Aufseherinnen* and male guards were remembered for their particular zeal.[24]

In their interrogations, the former *Aufseherinnen* generally denied taking part in selections, and assigned all responsibility to the higher SS leadership, SS physicians and orderlies, and prisoner-functionaries.[25] The testimony of survivors, however, clearly documents the participation of the female guards. Because they had a duty rotation, it is likely that all the *Aufseherinnen* who served as block, field, and roll-call leaders took part, at times, in selections.

The selections in the camp affected all inmate groups, but to varying degrees. For example, from summer 1942 to spring 1943, Jewish prisoners were particularly affected. Because they were at the bottom rung of the prisoner hierarchy, they had the most grueling labor assignments, the poorest quality food, and were most vulnerable to disease; they were also most likely to suffer violence at the hands of the SS.[26] Selections among Polish and Soviet prisoners, and prisoners of other nationalities, were carried out on a more irregular basis, and typically targeted the elderly, children, and inmates who were ill and weak. For Jewish inmates, however, selections were a near-daily event, and the Final Solution meant that all Jewish inmates were affected. Beginning in spring 1943, Jewish prisoners at Majdanek were systematically killed.[27]

Killing

The following is a description of the methods used to kill men, women, and children at Majdanek.

DEATH BY LETHAL INJECTION

Inmates in the infirmary were killed by lethal injection, using phenol, gasoline, or evipan. SS physicians generally delegated the actual injections to the SS orderlies. Prisoners were told that the injections were part of a "vaccine program,"[28] probably as a means to maintain calm.

In August or September 1942, Georg Gröner, a German prisoner-functionary, witnessed such a killing by lethal injection when he spent several weeks as a patient in the infirmary:

> Another prisoner, a fairly burly man whose name I didn't know, was in the same room as me. SS orderly Reinartz gave him an injection. It was in his left arm, if I'm not mistaken. I didn't attach much importance to it at the time. But I remember that, a few hours later, he was carried out of the room dead. I don't know whether he might have been injected with "evipan." But I do remember that I was very surprised at his sudden death. As far as I could tell, he wasn't that sick—I thought he would recover and leave the infirmary, much as I expected to.[29]

However, lethal injections were not a suitable method of killing during epidemics, when inmates were killed in larger numbers.

DEATH BY SHOOTING

Until the gas chambers went into operation in October 1942,[30] when larger groups of inmates were to be killed they were shot at the edge of the camp grounds, or in the Krepiecki forest, located twelve kilometers outside Lublin, toward Chełm. In his testimony, the former first camp compound leader Hermann Hackmann stated that Odilo Globocnik, the SS and police leader of Lublin, had ordered the killing of sick inmates during the first typhoid epidemic of winter 1941:

> Through Koch, I found out that Globocnik had issued a general directive that prisoners who were suffering from typhoid, and actually all prisoners suffering from contagious diseases, were to be liquidated. The reason given for the directive was that civilian laborers in the camp no longer wanted to work because they were afraid they would be infected. We were also told that there was a risk that the epidemic would spread to Lublin, which could place new troops arriving to serve at the front at risk. We had typhoid as early as 1941.[31]

In the Krakow Auschwitz trial, Erich Muhsfeldt, former head of the crematorium, stated that, in the winter of 1941–1942, prisoners with typhoid were, on Globocnik's order, shot behind Field IV, with the aim of "liquidating" the epidemic. "The only thing that was done to combat the epidemic was to shoot sick inmates."[32] "Liquidating the epidemic," for the SS, meant "liquidating" the prisoners who might spread disease to the camp staff. Other measures to halt the spread of the epidemic, such as improving hygiene conditions in the camp, were unthinkable. Describing the epidemics and shootings in Fechner's 1980 documentary, Emil Laurich said, "You can think it over and twist it this way and that, but we had to move, we had to take action against it."[33] In other words, almost four decades later in West Germany, Laurich still regarded the murder of the inmates as an appropriate response. For the inmates at Majdanek, the rampant epidemics and shootings of sick prisoners existed alongside the mass killing by shooting and poison gas as one of the myriad ways in which they were brutalized and killed in the camp.

Between March and June 1942, Jews from Austria, Slovakia, the Protectorate, and the "Old Reich" had been deported to Majdanek. A second typhoid epidemic broke out in late June of that year, again due to acute overcrowding and disastrous conditions in the camp. "There were so many typhoid patients that we didn't have enough room for them in the infirmary," Novak recalled. "So they had to stay in their barracks."[34] In early July 1943, the prisoner-physicians were ordered to take all seriously ill patients from the infirmary and the other blocks and bring them outside. Camp compound leader Hermann Hackmann described what followed:

> I was told two or three times that typhoid patients were to be selected, brought outside the camp in trucks, and then shot. . . . Around spring 1942, I heard at Koch's canteen that prisoners with typhoid were to be shot. All the SS leaders in the camp were there when we were told this. We weren't told who was to carry out these shootings.[35]

Before the mass shootings, Russian POWs were ordered to dig pits in the Krepiecki Forest. Former Field Leader (*Feldführer*) Heinz Petrick described the location: "It was at a spot near the road that headed from the camp to Chełm. From the road, you had to go to the right to get to the forest. There was a clearing in the forest."[36] According to Novak, in early July 1942, 1,500 prisoners who had typhoid were executed there, and then buried in the forest.[37]

Otto Z., a member of the guard battalion that arrived at Majdanek in late fall 1942, was once ordered to accompany a labor detachment sent to dig pits in the forest where the bodies were to be buried. This was done, he said, "because the crematorium did not have sufficient capacity."[38] On that occasion, he also witnessed the fate of the prisoners who dug the pits:

> It was cold and the guards were drinking vodka. Then a few prisoners were chased down a path in the forest, and they shot at them. I think two of them died. I was terribly afraid. I allowed it to happen without saying anything. . . . The forest labor detail included an entire truck full of people. I was the only German. I was armed with a Karabiner 98K, and the Ukrainians had an old gun. The prisoners had a Kapo along, who was drunk.[39]

"The forest labor detail was the least popular one, because there were always problems,"[40] according to Otto Z. For that reason, all the camp staff "tried to avoid it."[41] As an inducement, or to make the task more tolerable, "participants in these special operations usually received alcohol and cigarettes."[42] In part because the labor detail was so "unpopular," the assigned guards were usually *volksdeutsche* (ethnic German) SS men and Ukrainian auxiliaries.[43] However, as Josef B., block leader and later head of the mailroom testified, some "Reich German" headquarters staff also volunteered to take part in the executions.[44]

In summer 1944, residents of the village of Prepiece testified that, beginning in April 1942, unidentified SS men began to shoot Jewish men, women, and children in the Krepiecki Forest.[45] According to their testimony, the SS men usually did not bother to aim directly at their victims, who instead died a slow death as a result of their injuries. After the executions, Soviet prisoners of war were made to cover the pit with a layer of lime in the belief that this would prevent the spread of disease. We can only speculate on the identity of the victims. In a later interrogation, the former first camp compound leader, Hermann Hackmann, confirmed that in spring 1942, civilians had been sent to Majdanek on Globocnik's orders:

> The members of this transport, as L. told me, were to be shot in the forest. Most of them were men, although there were a few women. They were Polish Jews from the Lublin area. They weren't registered in our camp. They were sent by SD and Police Leader Globocnik.[46]

Most of the people shot in the forest were of Jewish origin. However, as part of the Germanization measures and forced resettlements in the Generalgouvernement, some non-Jewish Poles were also shot in the Krepiecki Forest.[47]

OPERATION HARVEST FESTIVAL

The largest mass shooting of Jews during the war within the concentration camp system took place in Majdanek on November 3, 1943.[48] Available source materials allow us to document just how the female guards perceived this "operation." The massacre, which was given the code name Operation Harvest Festival ("Erntefest"), was primarily a response to the August 2 revolt in the Treblinka concentration camp, and the October 14 uprising in Sobibor. On November 3, 1943, in less than twenty-four hours, a total of 42,000 Jews were killed in the Lublin district, including 18,000 at the Majdanek concentration camp.

On the morning of November 3, field leaders and female guards separated the remaining 8,000 Jewish inmates from the other prisoners in the Majdanek camp. Early that same morning, another 10,000 Jews from the Poniatowa and Trawniki labor camps, situated in the vicinity of Lublin, were forced to march to Majdanek on foot.[49] Henryka Ostrowska later recalled that roll call was held in the women's camp earlier than usual that day. The camp runners (*Lagerläufer*), who served as messengers inside the camp compound and who thus were permitted to move between various sections of the camp, arrived at the women's field and called, "All Jewish women, roll call! All Jewish women, roll call!"[50] This caused major turmoil in the camp, as prisoners began running in various directions, or tried to hide. The SS brought in dogs to help in the search, and the prisoners were assembled in one spot. Danuta Medryk, a Polish survivor, later described the events:

> It was still dark when they called roll call on that foggy morning. We could see the uniformed staff standing along the camp street. They were facing each other in two rows, to create a kind of alley. The guards were carrying machine pistols. Then the camp was put on lockdown. Afterwards we heard Viennese waltzes and similar music coming through the loudspeakers. Suddenly women came out of the functionary block and called out that a progrom [*sic*] was taking place. That's when we remembered the graves behind Field V. Then female guards arrived, and got the sick Jewish prisoners out of the infirmary. I believe that all the *Aufseherinnen* took part in this operation. They killed several thousand women that day, after all.[51]

To drown out the noise of the shooting, loudspeakers were set up in the camp. The propaganda department in Lublin had provided vehicles equipped with a radio transmitter system especially for the occasion. As Erich Muhsfeldt, head of the crematorium, recalled during the Krakow Auschwitz trial, "They played marches,

German songs, and dance music."[52] However, as survivor Henryka Ostrowska later recalled, the waltzes and tango melodies could not drown out the sound of machine gun fire.[53]

One of the few Jewish women to survive these events was Maryla Reich, who had arrived at the camp with false identity documents and had been incarcerated as a Pole. She later recalled what she had witnessed that day:

> On the morning of November 3, 1943, they held a very long roll call. We heard loud music begin to play as the roll call began. Two *Aufseherinnen* came from the office and I heard one of them say to the other one, "What? Today of all days?" Afterwards we had to return to the barracks. From our position in the barracks, we saw groups of Jews—including children—pass along Lagerstrasse, past our field, heading for Field V. But we didn't suspect anything bad yet.[54]

The Jewish inmates were forced to walk along Camp Street to the graves behind the new crematorium (see figure 12). There, they were made to disrobe and then line up along the pits, with their arms raised and hands folded behind their necks.[55] Next, the Security Service (SD) staff and the police battalions, who had come from Lublin especially for the operation, opened fire. As the head of the crematorium later told the Krakow court, he witnessed the executions at close range:

> There [at the pit], they had to lie down, and the SS men of the Sonderkommando, who were standing at the side of the pit, shot at them. Then, the next group was forced to the edge of the pit. They had to lie down on the bodies of the ones who were already shot, and then they were shot too. The graves slowly filled up, almost to the very top. The men were shot separately, meaning in separate groups. The women were also shot in their own groups. . . . The SS men who were part of the execution detail took turns, and drove to the SS canteen in town for meals, but the operation continued, without a pause.[56]

In this mass execution, as in the killings in Krepiecki Forest, the killers did not bother to take aim, with the result that many of the victims were still alive when they were buried under the bodies of the next group shot. Johann B., a former member of a police battalion, described the massacre in Eberhard Fechner's documentary:

> There were young ones, too. Many young women came up to us and said, "Why? What have we ever done to you?" I said, "I'm sorry. There's nothing I can do." There were men, women and children. They were separated, the men and the women. And they did curse us. They cursed us, and some came at us with raised fists. And they yelled, "Nazi pigs." You can hardly blame them. We might have done the same thing, if we'd been the ones feeling the heat.[57]

According to Otto Z., the headquarters staff and members of the guard battalions had been asked if they wanted to volunteer to take part in the execution:

> On the early morning of November 3, 1943, we were told that anyone who wanted could take part. We would get 2 liters of vodka and 400 cigarettes for the special operation. At the time, we all knew that "special operation" meant shooting. That was the standard term that was used.[58]

The female guards also had clear memories of November 3, 1943. In postwar interrogations, all of them claimed not to have left their residences that day. They said their barracks had been locked, and guards had been posted in front.[59] Alice Orlowski was one of the *Aufseherinnen* who offered a description of that day:

> I can remember the date November 3, 1943, very well. On that day, without warning, the camp was placed on lockdown. None of the members of the camp staff were allowed to leave their lodgings. I was staying in the female guards' block. . . .
>
> Soon afterwards, a large number of trucks drove onto the grounds of the prisoners' camp. I caught a quick glimpse and saw that some of the vehicles had a camouflage paint job. One truck stopped just 10 meters or so from my lodgings. . . . A short time later, after the lockdown was lifted, one of the SS men told me the trucks were from Auschwitz. . . . After the operation was over, we saw that there were no more Jews in the camp.[60]

As former *Aufseherin* Erna Pfannstiel testified, she had a hard time dealing with constant questions from the "extremely frightened" Jewish women and with the "terrible shooting."[61] "I was so upset that I had a nervous breakdown. I was four months' pregnant at the time."[62] Luzie H. also remembered the day well:

> Very early that morning, we *Aufseherinnen* gathered in our office, which was just to the left of the entrance. The chief guard came and said we were to spend the entire day in the office because something was going on. When we asked what was happening, she said it was sad, and she would come back and tell us.[63]

In a later interrogation, Luzie H. recalled, "From the window, we could see the line of Jews. Many of them had to be carried, because they had been shot at along the way."[64] In Eberhard Fechner's documentary, she recalled the chief guard's words to the assembled *Aufseherinnen* that morning: "Then she said, 'Well, today is a hard day for us. It might go well, but it might go badly. You need to stay on your toes, and no alcohol is allowed today.'"[65]

Although the former female guards claimed that they had been locked in their office all day, survivors Danuta Medryk and Maryla Reich said that at least a few *Aufseherinnen* were carrying out selections in the women's camp and in the infirmary that day:

> In the afternoon, around 3 P.M.—it was still light outside—an *Aufseherin* entered every barrack, and called, "All Jews step forward and line up." The mood in the barracks changed suddenly. It got chaotic. After all the Jewish women lined up, they did an inspection. The Jewish women were brought out onto the field, while we had to line up for a roll call, which took hours. Toward evening, a drunken SS man who otherwise worked in the infirmary [this SS man was not identified, but may have been Wilhelm Reinartz] came to the infirmary [within the female camp section] and said to the patients who were eating dinner, "What, you can eat, with everything that's happening out back?" Then he told us about the shooting of Jews in the graves behind Field V. Apparently it was all too much for him.[66]

"It was evening before we were allowed to eat in the canteen," Hertha Ehlert said. "Of course I asked my acquaintance Gregorek what was going on. He said something like, 'It's better that you don't know.'"[67]

Nonetheless, the mass execution must have been the topic of much conversation within the camp, because even female guards who were on leave or for other reasons not at Majdanek at the time remembered it during the Düsseldorf trial.[68] Of the evening after the massacre, Otto Z. later recalled, "We were very worked up about what happened that day and we spoke to each other from one room to the next."[69] Some of the camp staff were drinking and celebrating in the room next to his:

> I went into his room once because of all the drinking, and found Lausberg and Gehr bragging about having taken part in the executions voluntarily, and about having shot the "bums" (Jews). They each got 2 liters of vodka and 200 cigarettes for it. I remember that Lausberg's boots were bloody.[70]

DEATH BY HANGING IN THE OLD CREMATORIUM

The first crematorium, which was built in 1942, was another place where prisoners were killed. Josef M. was a "Reich German" political prisoner who arrived at Majdanek in June 1942. He worked as a *Kapo* distributing food at mealtimes, and was occasionally also assigned to the "corpse detachment" (*Leichenkommando*). On those occasions, he spent the time between meals gathering up bodies that were lying in front of the barracks and bringing them to the crematorium.

> Several times, I saw that several prisoners had been hanged, in groups, on several hooks in one of the crematorium rooms. . . . When Muhsfeldt asked me if I wanted to be his Kapo, he told me that I wouldn't need to do any of that myself; that was

> done by people in the prisoner detachments. They were Russians and also Jews, it depended. The prisoners were replaced from time to time. I wouldn't see them one day, and then there would be new faces there. I assume that they had been gassed.[71]

This was confirmed by the deputy head of the crematorium, Robert Seitz:

> About once a week, two, three, or sometimes more prisoners were sent to us from the prisoners' infirmary. They were then hanged by Kapo Fischer and his prisoner detachment in the mortuary of the crematorium, and subsequently burned. . . . The prisoners had to stand on a small set of steps, and then Fischer and his men put the rope around their neck. Then the small steps were pulled out from under them. When there were more prisoners than hooks, the remaining prisoners had to wait in the crematorium vestibule until it was their turn.[72]

Aufseherin Luzie H. once witnessed a hanging in the crematorium when she went there to get some eggs from Muhsfeldt:

> The SS man Mussfeldt came toward me and said, "Don't look." I had to go through the vestibule to reach his room, and there was a big area, with nooses up top, where all the partisans had been hanged. The bodies had been taken down already, yes; they were all lying on the floor.[73]

According to Seitz, these hangings were only carried out in the "small first crematorium." After the "large crematorium" was completed, in January 1944, no more hangings were carried out within the crematoria.

DEATH BY GASSING

The historian Barbara Schwindt dates the decision to build gas chambers at Majdanek to July 1, 1942.[74] According to a report by Karl Naumann, head of the central construction office in Lublin, the gas chamber complex, which consisted of several rooms, was completed on October 22, 1942.[75] However, the killing installations went into operation before that, probably in summer 1942. The victims of the first gassings were Slovakian Jews, who had arrived in Majdanek in spring of that year.[76]

The gassing complex consisted of two buildings designated as "bathing barracks," which bore the numbers 41 and 42. They were just to the right of the main entrance to the prisoner camp, parallel to Field I (see figure 12). This barracks complex was next to the *Effektenkammer*, the storehouse where the personal property taken from inmates was kept. By the time the Red Army liberated Majdanek on July 23, 1944, the SS had destroyed much of the camp, but the area described above remained intact. To the rear of barrack 41, there was a separate building with three intact gas chambers.

A Polish-Soviet commission of engineers, chemists, and architects immediately undertook an investigation. The result of this investigation showed that the three gas chambers behind barrack 41 were installations designed to kill using Zyklon B[77] and carbon monoxide gas.[78] Chambers I and II were 17.1 m^2 each, while chamber III was 36.6 m^2. Chambers I and II could kill between 125 and 175 people at one time, while in chamber III between 250 and 300 people could be gassed at once. The floors of the three chambers were made of concrete. The walls were constructed of brick, and the airtight doors were fabricated from cast iron. Chambers I and II had a hermetically sealable hatch in the ceiling through which the Zyklon B was poured. In addition, chamber I had a gas line with many small openings that extended horizontally 30 centimeters above the floor. It ran the length of the room and led to a chamber in which bottles filled with carbon monoxide were stored. The largest chamber, chamber III, had only one gas line which, as in Chamber II, led to a storage room. Two round openings on the long side walls went to the outside, and could be used to pipe hot air into the room.

According to the commission, barrack 41 also held a gas chamber, in addition to those in Chambers I and II. This barrack, designated as "Bath and Disinfection I," also contained a shower room, with showerheads on the ceiling. Directly behind it was a large fourth chamber, 72.2 square meters in size, which was soundproofed, as were the three other gas chambers. Judging by the blue stains on the wall, it is likely that Zyklon B was also employed there. Whether chamber IV was used solely for disinfection purposes, or whether it was also a killing installation, can no longer be determined with certainty.[79] However, according to a calculation by French historian Jean-Claude Pressac, it was possible for as many as 700 people to be killed at Majdanek within a 24-hour period.[80]

In order to help keep the killings hidden from the remaining prisoners, the gas chambers at Majdanek were used mainly at night. Nonetheless, it was widely known among prisoners that people were being gassed to death there.[81] The guard Georg W. later said it was an "open secret" that Jewish prisoners were gassed there.[82] Indeed, according to Georg W., "the entire city of Lublin"[83] was aware of the "purpose" for which the gas chambers were being used.

SS-Oberscharführer Anton Endress was responsible for overseeing the gassing.[84] The SS orderlies Wilhelm Reinartz and Hans Perschon, both *SS Oberscharführer*, also worked in the gas chambers. As the wife of SS orderly Herbert H. recalled, orderlies from the infirmary staff were also sometimes called in.[85] In interrogations carried out by the Soviet People's Commissariat for Internal Affairs (NKVD) in fall 1945, SS orderly Wilhelm Reinartz gave an extremely detailed description of the gassing process.[86] According to Reinartz, the camp commandant would issue the order to "clear" a barracks. The block and field leaders then told the prisoners they were being brought to the bathing barracks next to the gas chamber. They were told to undress for bathing, under the supervision of the prisoners assigned to the gas chamber detachment. Once naked, they were ordered into the gas chambers by the SS. The SS physicians and orderlies were responsible for ensuring that the gas chambers operated properly, and also monitored the process. The SS man in charge could observe the gassing through a window set into the door that led to the gas storage room. On the inside of the gas chamber, bars protected this window so the people being gassed could not break it. Once the SS orderlies had verified that all victims were dead, the bodies were removed from the gas chambers by the prisoner detachment, loaded onto carts, and then taken for burial or brought to the crematorium where they were burned.

Ernst Fischer, who was transferred from the Dachau concentration camp to Majdanek in June 1942, worked as a "bath Kapo" from June to October 1942. In a later interrogation, he provided additional details about the gassings: "I was assigned a prisoner detachment of about 22 or 23 Jewish men. This detachment spent the day in a special room by the bath, where we deloused the clothing."[87] Between March and June 1942, the Jews who arrived at Majdanek came mainly from the "old Reich," the Protectorate, Slovakia, and Austria. Beginning in August of that year, the arriving Jews came mainly from the Lublin region: "As the number of transports arriving at Lublin-Majdanek began to increase, the first gassings of people were carried out," Fisher reported. He and his labor detail were also made to clean the gas chambers, during which they observed the procedure at close range:

> When people refused, SS members hit them with truncheons and forced them into the bath or the gas chamber. The gas chamber ceiling had a hatch in it, which was used to gas people. An SS member used a ladder to climb to the roof, opened the hatch, and threw the gas [the Zyklon B crystals] through the hatch and into the gas chamber.[88]

Georg Gröner, a prisoner-functionary, described the gassing process in the "new" and larger gas chambers, completed in late 1942:

> When new prisoner transports arrived at the camp . . . the entire transport was usually brought to a fenced-in area behind the bathing facility. I used to call the area the "rose garden." . . . Afterwards, the camp physician, camp commandant, and the camp compound leader sorted the inmates into groups. Sometimes two physicians were present.
>
> During the sorting (selection), the prisoners had to walk past the physician, who either sent them from the "rose garden" to the bathing facility, or sent them over to an empty area on the other side of the rose garden.[89]

According to Gröner, the first camp physician, Dr. Franz von Bodmann, was particularly meticulous in the selections. In March 1943, when Dr. Heinrich Rindfleisch[90] was transferred from Ravensbrück to Majdanek to take on the post of second camp physician, Bodmann instructed him on how to carry out his duties.[91] According to

Gröner, when a new transport arrived, the people classified as healthy and able to work were sent to the bath first. Meanwhile, new arrivals who had failed the selection were made to wait in front of the gas chambers:

> SS members stood in a cordon between the rose garden and the bathing facility so that no one could escape. In the bathing facility, the prisoners first showered and then were given their prisoner's uniforms. Afterwards, they were distributed to the various fields. For a larger incoming transport, the process of bathing and dressing the prisoners usually took until past midnight. Afterwards, the Jewish people who had remained behind in the rose garden were gassed.[92]

What role did the female guards at Majdanek play in the killing of prisoners? Since they had no assigned duties in the gas chambers or the crematorium, *Aufseherinnen* were not directly involved in the killing process. However, they were present at selections carried out in front of the gas chamber. Whether they guarded inmates in front of the gas chambers is not known, but a statement made by Erna Pfannstiel suggests this might be the case:

> There were old and young women and also children, who I saw being led into the gas chamber. . . . I never brought the women who Ehrich and Braunsteiner had selected from Field V to the bath. . . . I didn't see the women's hair being cut off. I always went right back out. . . .
>
> Usually it was Braunsteiner and Ehrich who were present in delicate situations. By "delicate situations" I mean situations like at the bath. . . . I also never took part in selections.[93]

Hertha Ehlert was one of the few *Aufseherinnen* willing to speak about the proximity of the showering and the gassing facilities. In her testimony, she related that during one incoming transport, Erna Pfannstiel told her that a gas chamber was located on the other side of the bathing barrack: "Erna Pfannstiel took me over there and showed it to me."[94] For her part, Luzie H. reported that she often witnessed gassings when she went out at night to fetch water for the prisoners who worked in the tailor's workshop adjacent to the gas chamber. On several occasions, including once in Eberhard Fechner's documentary, she described seeing the bodies:

> When we went to fetch water, there was a tractor with a trailer. The door was open and there were Russian men there. Prisoners. And when they opened the door, the bodies fell out. They were shoved in there very tightly. They couldn't fall over inside [the gas chamber]. They grabbed them under their arms and legs and swung them [imitates the hand motion] onto the truck.[95]

In her testimony, Luzie H. described having been profoundly affected by what she had seen. "There were arms and legs hanging down from the trailer. For years after that, I couldn't bear to hear the sound of tractor engines."[96]

Removal of the Bodies

One of the key tasks in the killing process was "disposal" of the bodies. The bodies had to be removed as efficiently as possible, both to prevent the spread of disease, and to minimize evidence of the mass killings. At Majdanek, this task was carried out by special prisoner details, which employed a number of different methods over the course of time. The two SS men who headed these detachments were Oberscharführer Erich Muhsfeldt, head of the crematorium, and deputy head Unterscharführer Robert Seitz. According to his own statement, Muhsfeldt arrived at Majdanek on November 15, 1941, while Seitz arrived in very late 1941 or the beginning of 1942.

By Muhsfeldt's estimate, he and his labor detachment buried or burned the bodies of over 33,000 victims over the course of 2.5 years. These large numbers could only be managed using the *Sonderkommandos*, a group of prisoners who had been specially trained for the task. According to Muhsfeldt, the first such detachment, consisting of Polish Jews, was assembled in fall 1941. In March 1942, Muhsfeldt was assigned a new detachment, this time made up of Russian prisoners. The third detachment, assigned to him by the camp compound leader, was made up of French and German Jews. The last detachment assigned to him, after the November 3, 1943, massacre until the time of his transfer to Auschwitz in May 1944, was again made up of Russian prisoners.[97] This testimony is further proof that the prisoners who worked in the gas chamber and crematorium detachments were themselves killed at regular intervals. Ernst Fischer, the "bath Kapo," testified that prisoners were also sometimes forced to serve as temporary assistants to the "permanent" labor detachments. According to Fisher, "after they carried out their duties, they did not return to the prisoner camp, but were instead gassed."[98]

BURIAL OF THE BODIES NEAR THE CAMP: NOVEMBER 1941 TO JUNE 1942

As soon as Erich Muhsfeldt arrived at Majdanek, the commandant assigned him responsibility for the burial detachment, a duty Muhsfeldt said he assumed unwillingly.[99] Between November 1941 and June 1942, according to Muhsfeldt, the bodies of dead inmates were buried in mass graves behind the area that later became Field V. As the death rate continued to rise, the size of the mass graves grew proportionately.[100] In his testimony, Seitz also said that, at least during the initial period, the bodies were "buried."[101] "The transport and burial of the corpses was carried out by a special detachment, made up of Polish and Jewish prisoners of war,"[102] Muhsfeldt stated in the 1947 Auschwitz trial in Krakow.

BURNING THE BODIES IN THE "OLD" CREMATORIUM: JUNE TO OCTOBER 1942

In June 1942, the first crematorium was built between Fields I and II, situated diagonally across from the bathing barracks and, later, the gas chambers. This facility was later renamed the "old" crematorium. At that time, the burial detail had only recently been formed, as Seitz later explained:

> My boss was the Oscha [Oberscharführer] Mussfeld [*sic*]. Apart from us two SS men, the crematorium also had a labor detachment made up of about six Russian prisoners of war, who were under the command of the Reich German prisoner Fischer. . . . The crematorium detachment was responsible for burning the prisoners who had died in the camp. There were two ovens in the crematorium.[103]

According to Seitz, dead prisoners were brought to the crematorium on small carts.[104] Directly across from the crematorium was the laundry, where prisoners worked around the clock (see figure 12). Survivor Wanda Bialas, who was assigned to the laundry from January 1943 until the evacuation of the women's camp in April 1944, recalls watching bodies being unloaded from the laundry window:

> In the beginning, we could see through the window when they loaded up carts with the frozen bodies of the dead. Later, the windows on that side of the laundry were painted over with white paint, so that we could only see the bodies when we left the barracks to go to the latrines.[105]

In 1961, Seitz was no longer able to estimate how many bodies had been burned in the "old" crematorium. He also could no longer remember with certainty "whether there were two or three ovens in our crematorium. They were very large ovens, in any case."[106] In the Krakow Auschwitz trial, however, Muhsfeldt provided a detailed description of the crematorium's operations:

> The crematorium was built by Kori, a Berlin-based company. It contained two iron ovens, lined on the inside with firebricks. The two ovens operated independently. They each had a chimney and were heated with oil. . . . The ovens were brought to Majdanek from the Sachsenhausen concentration camp. . . . Before the ovens were assembled, I was sent to Sachsenhausen for training. I spent a week there, and the leader of the crematorium detachment, Hauptscharführer Klein, taught me how to operate the ovens. . . . Each crematorium oven had only one incineration chamber. The chamber could hold between 2 and 5 bodies. With round-the-clock operation, each oven could incinerate about 100 bodies per day. . . . The first crematorium was in operation until late October 1942. . . . Between June and October 1942, I was in charge of the work at the crematorium, so I can report that about 5,000 bodies were incinerated in that crematorium during that period.[107]

The Kori Company, a competitor of Topf & Söhne, specialized in heating systems, delousing installations, and incineration ovens for cremation and waste incineration.[108] As in all concentration and extermination camps, however, the cremations that took place at Majdanek were not done in the "proper" manner, as more than one body at a time was incinerated in each chamber.[109] The ashes of the incinerated bodies fell into metal containers located beneath the grates. As the former Polish inmate and "scribe for the dead" (*Totenschreiber*) Julian Gregorowicz told the Düsseldorf regional court, "When a Reich German family asked us to provide the ashes of their dead relatives, they were just given something from that large pile."[110]

BURYING THE BODIES IN THE KREPIECKI FOREST: NOVEMBER 1942 TO JANUARY 1943

According to Muhsfeldt, the crematorium ovens were taken out of service in November 1942 when the camp started running out of oil to operate them.[111] Instead, the crematorium detachment began to again bury the bodies.[112] If Muhsfeldt's estimates are accurate, his detachment buried about 2,000 bodies in the Krepiecki Forest between November 1942 and January 1943. SS men brought the bodies by truck to the forest. "My detachment had 20 French and German Jews," Muhsfeldt told the Krakow court. "Apart from those 20 Jews, the detachment also had three Russian POWs and a German Kapo."[113] But this was only an interim solution. On February 19 of that year, Muhsfeldt was sent to another training course, this time at Auschwitz-Birkenau, where he was taught how to burn bodies in open pits.

BURNING BODIES IN OPEN PITS: FEBRUARY TO LATE OCTOBER, 1943

After Muhsfeldt returned from Auschwitz, Hermann Florstedt ordered him and his team to begin exhuming the bodies that had been buried in mass graves in the forest and at the edge of Field V, and burn them in open pits,[114] presumably with the intention of destroying evidence of the killings. Henceforth, prisoners who were gassed or died of other causes were to be "disposed" of in this same manner. In 1961, Seitz offered the following description of this work:

> I accompanied the detachment to the forest about two times. The detachment included about 20 Jewish workers. By my estimate, the forest area was about eight kilometers from the Majdanek concentration camp. The site where the bodies were burned was in the middle of the forest. A grate had been prepared using railway tracks, and a space had been hollowed out underneath them. The oil I mentioned before was used as fuel. Four or five members of the SS guard troops accompanied me to help guard the prisoners.[115]

At the Krakow Auschwitz trail, Muhsfeldt provided a more detailed description of the burning technique:

> First, I excavated the pit. But burning the bodies in the pit didn't work, so I constructed a set-up to handle the burning of the bodies. I placed an old truck chassis on top of some tall stones. Then I put the bodies on top of that and poured methanol over them. There was a layer of wood underneath the truck chassis, and these were set on fire. About 100 corpses were burned at a time. The bodies included those excavated from the pits and fresh bodies from the camp. After one load was burned, the ashes were ground into meal and poured into the same pits that the bodies had been removed from before burning. To grind the bones, we used an iron plate and an iron rammer. . . . Using this method, by late October 1943 I had burned all the bodies in the forest, as well as the bodies from the pits behind Field V in the camp.[116]

By Muhsfeldt's estimate, using this technique, he burned approximately 6,000 bodies in the forest and about 3,000 bodies from behind Field V.

BURNING BODIES IN OPEN PITS: NOVEMBER 5–24, 1943

The day after the massacre of November 3, 1943, the departing Commandant Florstedt and his successor, Commandant Martin Weiss, ordered Muhsfeldt's detachment to burn the 18,000 bodies located behind the crematorium. To do so, Muhsfeldt used the technique he had learned at Auschwitz:

> On the 4th, I gathered some wood and boards, and on November 4, 1943, I began burning the bodies. The part of the pit where the victims had approached the pit was not filled with bodies, so I filled that area with some soil to make the pit a bit shallower, which made for better traction. Then I set up a kind of grate made of wood on the ground. On top of that, the prisoners layered the bodies they had removed from the graves. When they had layered enough bodies to create a pile, methanol was poured on top of them, and set on fire. The next layers of bodies were then piled up in the section of the pit that had just been cleared of bodies, which were now burning. Once the ashes had cooled off, prisoners in my detachment brought them up to the surface, where they were ground to bone meal using a special mill powered by gasoline. Then the meal was poured into paper sacks and loaded onto trucks, which hauled them to the SS property located near the camp.[117]

According to Muhsfeldt, an official from the Security Service (SD) in Lublin monitored the work and checked to make sure that all the corpses were being burned, which offers further support to the assertion that the main purpose of the operation was to destroy evidence of the killings. At the Krakow trial, Muhsfeldt emphasized the efficiency of the process: "The burning of the 17,000 Jews [according to scholarly estimates, the number of people killed was closer to 18,000] murdered on November 3, 1943, was completed before Christmas 1943."[118] The open graves were then filled with soil and the surface was leveled.

The former *Aufseherinnen*, including Luzie H., recalled the smell that accompanied the burning of the bodies:

> After the shootings they always shoveled them over, right, and then burned the corpses, a body at a time. That smelled terrible. It really stunk! The smoke drifted across Lagerstrasse, where we walked to go to work. Then we walked through the smoke to work like this [covers her nose and mouth with her left hand], holding a handkerchief.[119]

Anna M. also recalled the unpleasant odor: "It continued night and day, and it smelled awful."[120]

CREMATION: JANUARY TO MAY/JUNE 1944

In September 1943, construction on the new crematorium was already underway, although it was not completed until January 1944. Like the others, this new crematorium was built by the Berlin-based Kori Company; however, this one had five incineration chambers, which substantially increased its capacity. It also burned coke as fuel,[121] which made it cheaper to operate.[122] Muhsfeldt recalled the crematorium's operation as follows:

> We didn't start burning bodies in the new crematorium until January 1944. As I already mentioned, it was just a few bodies, so I wasn't able to see how many bodies this crematorium could have handled each day while I was still at Majdanek. . . . Only one body was put in each incineration chamber. The incineration took about one hour. I burned bodies in every oven, one after the next, to test them all. The bodies took a long time to burn, because the chimney draft in the ovens was quite weak. Because one chimney had to handle all the incinerators, it didn't create a very good draft, and the incineration process took a long time.[123]

The lack of proper ventilation was also partly responsible for the unpleasant odor that permeated the camp. The odor later featured prominently in the staff's description of their daily work at the camp. As Luzie H. recalled, "The smell was terrible."[124]

After Work: Leisure and Family

In one of her interrogations, Charlotte Wöllert clearly distinguished between the time she spent on duty and her leisure time: "After work, I went to my quarters and had nothing more to do with the prisoners."[125] Like Charlotte Wöllert, the female guards generally returned to their residences after work—residences that had been cleaned and tidied by prisoners. Instead of eating in the canteen, the *Aufseherinnen* prepared meals together in the common kitchen, and did their hand washing and mending, as Luzie H. and Hildegard Lächert later recalled in Eberhard Fechner's documentary.

Despite the women's descriptions, however, it is worth asking whether work and leisure time could in fact be kept separate within the context of daily life in the camp. For the *Aufseherinnen*, their leisure and personal life took place largely on camp grounds and with their colleagues. The odor of the burning bodies, for example, would also have stayed with the female guards even during their leisure time. How, then, did the camp staff experience the contradiction between private life and their daily duties in the extermination camp?

Luzie H.'s later testimony shows that prisoners could also have an impact on the guard's leisure time:

> A Polish officer's wife cleaned my room in Lublin. I gave her five cigarettes a day, and a piece of sausage that was like this [indicates a length of 10 centimeters]. Every day. But you know, I had a box full of briquettes. I had a wonderful fire in my oven, and when I came home, there were grated potatoes waiting for me, left in a pile for me, because she knew I was going to make Polish dumplings [smiles at the thought].[126]

Luzie H., who was born in Breslau, shared a common culinary tradition with the Polish prisoner. In some ways, the interaction between Luzie H. and the prisoner who cleaned her room is not unlike the relationship between the SS physicians and the prisoner-physicians. In both instances, a certain "recognition"—founded on shared experience—was accorded to the prisoners (whether in the medical or the culinary sphere). Acknowledged by both parties, this connection allowed a level of interaction that would not have otherwise occurred.

During her leisure time, Hildegard Lächert enjoyed horseback riding—a pastime that would have otherwise been a luxury for someone of her social background. As Lächert recalled in Fechner's documentary:

> When we went home, to our barracks. Later, we all had our own rooms. Well, we were tired, we were wrecked, sometimes we had a letter to write, or we had to take care of our clothes. . . .
>
> Yes, by then we'd really all had enough. We were happy that we were finally getting ten minutes to ourselves, where we could read a book. And thank God, I was sometimes able to pay a visit to the Felin farm. That's where we went horseback riding, through the forest and everything. They had Arabian thoroughbreds; they're a bit smaller than other thoroughbreds. They needed to be exercised daily, and they were very grateful whenever I took one and went riding.[127]

Hildegard Lächert, Alice Orlowski and, chief guard Else Ehrich were among the few *Aufseherinnen* who went horseback riding at Majdanek.[128] Whether they had already known how to ride, or whether they learned to do so at the camp, is not known.

The female guards went into town to shop, to pass time at one of the many cafés in Lublin, to pay a visit to the Deutsches Haus, to mail letters, and to have their hair done. "We spent more time together when we were off duty," Lächert recalled.[129] There were also occasional celebrations among the camp staff, as well as other opportunities for socializing. One such occasion is depicted in two photographs from Else Ehlert's March 1944 birthday celebration, given in 1975 to the Cologne public prosecutor's office by Elisabeth H. (see figures 15 and 16). The *Aufseherinnen* sometimes accompanied SS men to Lublin to visit the Deutsches Haus, where there was dancing in the evenings. Sometimes it was not until very late at night that they returned to the camp, as recalled by Erna Pfannstiel in a 1980 conversation with Eberhard Fechner:

> Well, we usually took a carriage there, the kind that they used to have; the ones with horses, which brought us back home in the evening. . . . Yes, it was quite the distance from Lublin to [Majdanek]. . . . It was pretty far. . . . Well, when you're young, going to bed late once in a while isn't such a big deal, even when you have to get up early in the morning.[130]

Unlike the *Aufseherinnen*, married SS men had the option of living with their spouse, either in an apartment in Lublin or in the SS estate not far from the camp. This implies that, for the female guards at least, the basic assumption was that their work duties were deemed incompatible with the responsibilities of having a family on-site. The "self-caterers," as they were called in SS documents, included SS orderly Herbert H. and his wife Luzie, Commandant Hermann Florstedt and his wife Charlotte, and Erich Muhsfeldt, who lived with his wife and son in Lublin. The SS men who lived with their families in Lublin could leave the camp after their work was done for the day, and spend their evenings at home with their wives.

"You know, it was like this: in the morning we had to go on duty, in the evening we went off duty, and then we left,"[131] former field leader Heinz Villain explained in Fechner's documentary. Lilli Laurich, the wife of Emil Laurich, who had been employed in the political division of Majdanek since April 1942, also joined her husband in the Generalgouvernement and took a position as manager of the department in charge of women's wartime employment at the political division of Majdanek. Lilli Laurich recalled the situation as follows:

> As far as I can remember, my husband worked from 8 A.M. to 5 P.M. . . . My husband was always home at 5 P.M.; sometimes he was even home before me. I can't remember him ever coming home after me. . . . He was never late coming home. . . . My husband often put out dinner for us, because I got home later than he did.[132]

The Laurichs lived in an apartment in Lublin and, according to Lilli Laurich, they enjoyed the time they spent there: "We had our apartment and we made it nice and comfortable, and in the evenings we sometimes went to the theater or the cinema, or for a walk, things like that."[133]

The manner in which the former concentration camp staff spoke after the war, of their time at Majdanek, illustrates the importance they attached to their leisure time while there. Their leisure time, and time spent with family and friends, was important in terms of enabling the female guards and SS men to adjust to and "perform" their work.

A statement by former *Aufseherin* Luzie H., however, demonstrates how deeply the daily work of annihilation at the extermination camp penetrated into their off-duty existence as well. After work, Luzie H. sometimes paid a visit to an SS man with whom she was friendly. He worked as a so-called "dentist" along with the gas chamber detachment, removing gold teeth from the bodies of the dead:

> I had an acquaintance there, a dentist. When he did his work up there. Well, I don't know where that was, but when he came back, he knocked on my door. And the first time—I didn't know what he'd been doing—I said to him, "Aren't you going to shake my hand?" And he replied, "Luzie, we'll talk about that later. But I can't shake your hand right now."[134]

As this example shows, despite efforts on the part of the concentration camp staff to keep their work lives separate from their personal lives, work necessarily encroached on the private sphere (for example, the women's fear of the crematorium, the jokes made by their colleagues, the unpleasant odor of the burning bodies, the sound of gunfire, and so forth). Although the camp staff likely grew accustomed to these aspects of life at the camp, a certain level of unease must have remained a constant presence during their time there.

In all likelihood, camp staff said little of their work to outsiders, and offered even spouses and girlfriends only vague or guarded details. As we know from the example of the November 3, 1943, massacre, however, there was plenty of conversation about events among the camp staff themselves—including the killing of inmates—whether in the canteen, or in the evenings "among friends."[135]

Work and Its Meaning in the Context of the Concentration Camp

In the daily carrying out of their duties and decisions in the camp, the men and women who worked at Majdanek were instrumental in ensuring continued operation of the camp and, by extension, the larger concentration camp system. In considering how camp staff internalized and understood their work, a key factor is that the work process was segmented into separate and discrete steps, so that (as a rule) staff who took part in selections or brought the prisoners to the place where they were to be killed, or who guarded them while at those places, were not the ones who carried out the killing. Moreover, staff members were typically assigned a range of duties; further, it is likely that assignment to detachments responsible for carrying out mass shootings rotated among the SS men.

This "method" of killing had originally been developed by mobile killing units of the Security Police (SD) in Galicia in 1941. The division of labor, developed on-site by the Security Service, made it possible to kill quickly, effectively, and without resistance on the part of the victims. However, as French historian Christian Ingrao emphasizes, it also aimed to reduce the psychological impact on the men who carried out the killing.[136] For example, the leadership attached great importance to ensuring that each member of the unit took part in the mass shootings at least once. A similar logic appears to have been at work in Majdanek, as well. It appears that most of the male camp staff there did, in fact, take an active role in the systematic mass annihilation.

Moreover, the "productive" work carried out at the camp (in the tailor's workshop and the laundry, for example) and the systematic killing of prisoners (in the gas chamber and old crematorium) happened in close proximity to one another. Even if the female guards did not themselves take part in the killing, they were nonetheless accessories, taking part in selections, and guarding prisoners as they waited to be sent into the gas chambers. During their daily duties in conjunction with the work detachments, the mass killing—that is, its sounds, sights, and odors—was an inescapable reality.

The female guards assigned to the laundry and tailor's workshop worked directly across from the gassing installation and the crematorium. From their canteen, the SS staff had a view of the gas chamber complex (see figure 12). From their barrack quarters, the *Aufseherinnen* overlooked Field I of the prisoners' camp. For this reason, participation in the violence and killing cannot be considered solely in terms of whether an individual took part, directly, in acts of violence and killing. Rather, participation also included seeing and looking away, taking indirect part through one's daily duties, and giving tacit consent.

This awareness of what was happening around them is particularly evident in the testimony of Hertha Ehlert, who recalled as disturbing her occasional assignments in the prisoner's bath, which was part of the gas chamber complex at Majdanek. In one interrogation, she described the "screams and wails"[137] of the Polish women and children who were sent there to shower and dress before being sent to the prisoner's camp: "After working there for a few hours, I was such a nervous wreck that I had to go out. Once outside, I was so overcome I suffered a nervous attack."[138] By contrast, according to Ehlert, she rather enjoyed her work in the laundry, from which she could see and hear little of what was going on elsewhere in the camp: "It was pleasant there, to the extent that anything can be pleasant in a concentration camp."[139] For camp staff, looking away and averting their eyes was a form of accommodation. More significantly, it would appear that even as the day-to-day horrors of the camp could not be banished entirely, work at Majdanek could otherwise be quite "pleasant" in many respects.

For the SS at Majdanek, fear—for example, the fear of contagion during the many epidemics that raged through the camp—also featured prominently in their day-to-day experience of the camp. In postwar testimony of camp staff, fear of "partisans" and "commissars" also received frequent mention as a rationale for the hangings in the crematorium and even the mass shootings. These fears regarding health and security voiced by former camp staff cannot be entirely dismissed as attempts to deflect responsibility for their acts. Rather, these attempts at self-justification were also vestiges of a discourse in which actual experiences of fear and threat at the camp comingled with ideologically charged images of the "enemy."[140] Anxieties surrounding a real or imagined threat posed by the prisoners allowed the staff to rationalize the killing of defenseless prisoners of war and civilians, including men, women, and children, as an act of "self-defense." In their testimony, none of the former camp staff mentioned motives such as taking pleasure in killing or an enjoyment of the power they held over the prisoners. Still, this by no means proves such motives were nonexistent, as will be demonstrated in chapter 11, in which the actions and social interactions of the camp staff will be analyzed.[141]

Any attempt to grapple with the scope and extent of the annihilation of human life in the Nazi extermination camps presupposes an understanding of the organization of this "work"—and an understanding of what the individuals and groups who carried out this "work" understood to be the nature of their task. Murder on such a mass scale was only possible because camp staff drew upon industrial work processes and perfected them in a step-by-step manner with the purpose of annihilating human life.[142] The process of selection, murder, and disposal of the bodies was a "specialized skill," as the example of Muhsfeldt demonstrates—a skill that was carefully developed and painstakingly implemented by the SS. Thus, for example, on the morning of November 3, 1943, the chief guard made sure to inform her staff that they had "difficult work" to perform that day and it would be important to "stay on task." However, the mechanization, streamlining, and standardization of death in the concentration and extermination camps did not mean that killing could be accomplished without "hands-on" work; nor was the process of killing and annihilation always a "smoothly functioning" operation—indeed, quite often, it was anything but.

Dieter Pohl has described this process of industrialized annihilation as a blend of organization and chaos.[143] For the camp staff, the mass murder of the Jews, in particular, posed significant "logistical problems" that they had to surmount.[144] The camp staff had a quota to fill, which, in turn, meant they had to "process" an increasing number of bodies, rectify technical breakdowns (such as defective machinery or scarcity of raw materials), and much more. These daily challenges required the staff to exhibit a modicum of "professionalism," a "problem-solving attitude,"[145] and mental "toughness." For the camp staff, what Alf Lüdtke has referred to as the "appeal to professionalism"—a self-reinforcing mindset of "professional expertise"—linked the process of murder with an ethic of professional work.[146] At the same time, this professional ethic served as both impetus and justification for demanding the utmost from others—and, by association, from oneself.[147] In a sense, then, performing "high quality" work was its own reward, "even when destruction, not production, was the goal or the result."[148]

This concept of "work" was promoted by Heinrich Himmler himself. The genocide of the European Jews in the regime's concentration and extermination camps was not a matter of official record, but rather a "state secret" (*geheime Reichssache*). The destruction of European Jewry was decided upon at the Wannsee Conference, but, apart from the Wannsee Protocols, there is no evidence that a written order by Hitler regarding the Final Solution (or euthanasia, for that matter) ever existed. An excerpt from Himmler's speech to a group of *SS Gruppenführer* at a conference in Posen (now the Polish city of Poznań) on October 4, 1943, illustrates how these appeals to professionalism and to the weighty necessity of "state secrets" were joined together and reinforced:

> I want to also mention a very difficult subject before you, with complete candor. It should be discussed amongst us, yet nevertheless, we will never speak about it in public. Just as we did not hesitate on June 30, 1934 to carry out our duty as ordered, standing comrades who had failed against the wall, and shooting them—about which we have never spoken, and never will speak. That was, thank God, a kind of tact natural to us, a foregone conclusion of that tact, that we have never conversed about it amongst ourselves, never spoken about it. Everyone shuddered, and everyone was clear that the next time, he would do the same thing again, if it were commanded and necessary.
>
> I am talking about the evacuation of the Jews, the extermination of the Jewish people. It is one of those things that is easily said. "The Jewish people is being exterminated," every Party member will tell you, "perfectly clear, it's part of our plans, we're eliminating the Jews, exterminating them, a small matter." And then along they all come, all the 80 million upright Germans, and each one has his decent Jew. They say: "All the others are swine, but here is a first-class Jew." And none of them has seen it, has endured it. Most of you will know what it means when 100 bodies lie together, when 500 are there, or when there are 1000. And to have seen this through and—with the exception of human weakness—to have remained decent, has made us hard and is a page of glory never mentioned and never to be mentioned. Because we know how difficult things would be, if today in every city during the bomb attacks, with the burdens of war and the privations, we still had Jews as secret saboteurs, agitators and instigators. We would probably be at the same stage as in 1916–1917, if the Jews still resided in the body of the German people.
>
> We have taken away the riches that they had, and I have given a strict order, which Obergruppenführer Pohl has carried out. We have delivered these riches to the Reich, to the State. We have taken nothing from them for ourselves. A few, who have offended

> against this, will be judged in accordance with an order, that I gave at the beginning: he who takes even one Mark of this is a dead man. A number of SS men have offended against this order. They are very few, and they will be dead men without mercy! We have the moral right; we had the duty to our people to do it, to kill this people who would kill us. We however do not have the right to enrich ourselves with even one fur, with one Mark, with one cigarette, with one watch, with anything. That we do not have. Because we don't want, at the end of all this, to get sick and die from the same bacillus that we have exterminated. I will never see it happen that even one bit of putrefaction comes in contact with us, or takes root in us. On the contrary, where it might try to take root, we will burn it out together. But altogether we can say: We have carried out this most difficult task for the love of our people. And we have suffered no defect within us, in our soul, or in our character.[149]

Himmler's speech sent an ambiguous message: we are proud of what we are doing, but no one must know about it—in a sense, we must even deny it to ourselves. Fundamental to Himmler's vision was the professionalism and "hardness" with which the "task" was carried out. The men who were taking part in killing operations should see their work as an honorable duty and service. As Karin Orth has demonstrated, for the SS and to Himmler, honor and decency meant, above all, that the participants not benefit by plundering the property of the Jews they were planning to kill; their duty involved more important matters than mundane material enrichment. Nor was cruelty befitting of an SS man.[150] Sociologist Harald Welzer has also underscored the importance of Himmler's speech for the "ordinary" perpetrator in the killing process. For individuals, then, their role in the killing could be understood as part of their ordinary and everyday duties, rather than as part of an "eruption of chaos." As Welzer has argued, "This precisely is the basis of the ethos of decency as defined by Heinrich Himmler in his 1943 speech in Posen when he made explicit reference to instances of 'human weakness,' which he insisted were nothing more than 'unfortunate exceptions.'"[151] As we have seen, however, this was belied by the day-to-day practice of killing in the camps.

Nonetheless, Himmler's speech made it possible for the perpetrators to perceive themselves as victims who suffered under the duties assigned to them. According to Harald Welzer, this was an important element in the Nazi regime's success at instilling a readiness to kill in ordinary people.[152] Likewise, psychologist Gudrun Brockhaus emphasizes the importance of this "rhetoric of duty and victimhood,"[153] which allowed the perpetrators to derive a sense of moral superiority from their supposed struggle and sacrifice.

> The SS members demonstrate their exemplary character through murder. . . . They derived self-esteem and a sense of superiority from the fact that they were capable of such monstrosities. A true SS officer assumes such duties and carries them out even when he finds them repulsive. . . . The constant emphasis on secondary virtues

> [*Sekundärtugenden*] legitimizes aggression, exclusion, war, and the extermination of Jews. Precisely because they go to such effort and extremes, they are permitted to violate basic ethical precepts. The difficulty and the ongoing nature of the battle against one's weaker inner self [*innere Schweinehund*] is the currency that buys one the right to violate our civilization's taboos.[154]

The "hard work" carried out by staff in the concentration and extermination camps was also revered. At Majdanek, for example, Heinz Villain and Robert Seitz were nominated in December 1943 by the higher SS and Police Leader in the Generalgouvernement to receive the War Merit Cross 2nd Class with Swords. In Villain's case, the nomination stated, "He carries out the difficult duties gladly and selflessly. Villain fell ill with typhus but still regularly took part in special operations."[155] In Seitz's case, the nomination stated, "He undertakes his hazardous duties with full commitment and has done much to help secure the camp. Seitz regularly takes part in special operations."[156] The two men were given their medals on April 20, 1944. The awards were not only a sign of appreciation for their "service," but also intended as a means of spurring motivation among other staff—both male and female—in the camp.[157] Ultimately, therefore, Himmler's reference to "difficult work" was part of a larger effort to normalize the "work" that was being carried out at the camp as a demanding but honorable duty.

But awards and accolades alone were not sufficient motivation even for the SS man. As we have seen, what Himmler euphemistically described as "work assignments" were also compensated with material rewards. Camp staff who took part in the killing were routinely rewarded with extra cigarettes and rations of alcohol—with the alcohol serving both as an incentive and as a means of decompressing in the killing's aftermath. The violence was enhanced by alcohol's ability to lower inhibitions and its numbing effect. As the former guard Otto Z. described his troops: "We didn't cut a dashing figure, our group—we were more of a lost and forlorn bunch."[158]

In Eberhard Fechner's documentary, former guard Rosa Reischl also offered a description of the SS men that was not in keeping with their official image: "Well, in the end, the poor sods were drunk all the time anyhow. Right, so that they could [stops for a moment]—they knew what was coming, after all—and they were all plastered. You couldn't even talk to them anymore; it was like they'd all just checked out."[159] The fact that the chief guard instructed the *Aufseherinnen* on the day of the massacre of November 3, 1943, that they were not to drink is an indication that alcohol consumption was also common among the female SS staff.

8 Escapes and Their Meaning within the Structure of Power and Violence in the Camp

THE GUARDS WERE TO PREVENT ESCAPES AT ALL COSTS AND, WHEN escapes did occur, they resulted in severe punishments and reprisals. As already described in chapter 4, the very architecture of the camp served as an instrument of domination and control. No one was permitted to leave the camp without authorization. Control over space, then, was a defining aspect of the camp as an institution.[1] However, although the camp was a closed space, its borders were not as impermeable as one might assume. Two incidents at Majdanek—the overnight escape of eighty-six Soviet prisoners on June 14–15, 1942, and the hanging of a young woman captured during an escape attempt in the summer of 1943—illustrate the significance accorded by the SS to escape attempts, their response to such attempts, and the impact of such attempts on other prisoners in the camp.

The Concentration Camps and Escape Attempts

In his postwar account, Rudolf Höss, commandant of Auschwitz, recalled a visit by Himmler to Auschwitz in summer 1942. During that visit, the *Reichsführer SS* reprimanded him for the large and "unprecedented" number of escapes from Auschwitz, and said to him, "I encourage you to employ *every means*—and he repeated that—every means to prevent escapes. The epidemic of escapes from Auschwitz must end."[2]

As was the case in other concentration camps, any suspected escape attempt on the part of a prisoner resulted in a large-scale search. As Höss explained, the SS called on a "formidable apparatus" to aid in such searches. Höss described escape attempts that occurred during his time at Sachsenhausen, from 1938 to 1940:

> Although an escape was an exceptional situation at Dachau, at Sachsenhausen, Eicke's nearby presence [Theodor Eicke, the Inspector of Concentration Camps] meant it was an even bigger event. If Eicke was present at Oranienburg, he would come to the camp as soon as the sirens sounded. He wanted to know every single detail of the escape, and was tenacious in tracking down the individuals who, through inattention or negligence, had allowed the escape to occur. The cordon of guards often remained in place for three or four days if there was any indication that the prisoner might still be within the cordoned area. Everything was searched, combed through, night and day. Every SS man on the site was drawn into the search. The camp leaders, especially the camp commandant, the camp compound leader, and the duty officer, didn't have a quiet moment, since Eicke constantly asked for progress reports on the search. He believed that no escape must be allowed to succeed. . . . Any available SS or police officer would be drawn into the search. The railway and roads were monitored. Following instructions radioed to them, the motorized gendarmerie scoured the streets and roadways. All bridges, across the many waterways that passed through Oranienburg, were monitored.[3]

At camps situated within the "old Reich"—or Germany proper—the SS relied on the cooperation of the surrounding civilian population:[4] "The residents of the nearby houses were notified and warned. Most of them already knew what the sirens meant. With assistance from the local population, we were able to recapture a few prisoners. . . . They immediately reported anything they observed to the camp or to the search troops."[5] The SS also received a "finder's fee" as an added incentive for capturing an escaped prisoner:

> An SS man who found or recaptured an escapee not only received praise during daily orders, but was also given special leave. Outsiders, police officers or civilians, received a cash award. When an SS man prevented an escape through his prudence and vigilance, Eicke would reward him with leave and a promotion.[6]

As Höss's postwar account demonstrates, the concentration camp administration, and Theodor Eicke, in particular, attached enormous significance to the capture of escaped inmates. Moreover, the concentration camps devoted substantial technical and personnel resources to preventing escape attempts. For example, guards monitored the barriers at every camp entryway around the clock. Three guards armed with machine guns, grenades, and spotlights manned the towers that flanked the prisoners' areas in most of the camps. Between the perimeter towers, additional towers were erected at irregular intervals on the open ground. A cordon of guards secured all camp buildings, including workshops, depots, and warehouses. According to Dionys Lenard, a Jewish inmate from Slovakia who arrived at Majdanek in April 1942, Majdanek also had a "two-meter-wide strip between the sections of the prisoners' camp, which served as a kind of corridor where guards were stationed. At night, spotlights illuminated the prisoners' camp. There were also four additional guard towers, equipped with machine guns."[7] Several months after his arrival, in late June or early July 1942, Lenard managed to escape. He recorded his recollection of the surveillance system at Majdanek later that same year, making it a unique document in this regard.

To prevent escapes, the camp administration ordered severe punishments of prisoners, enjoined the SS to maintain strict surveillance, recruited additional guards to the camps, introduced technical enhancements such as electrified fences and mine fields, and employed dog patrols. Nonetheless, prisoners occasionally succeeded in escaping from Majdanek and from the other concentration camps.[8] Although state-of-the art for its time, the surveillance system at Majdanek was by no means foolproof—every successful escape, every electric fence circumvented, and every guard outwitted served as proof of its shortcomings. In a successful escape, the seemingly implacable power of the SS was subverted, and the purported impenetrability of the concentration camp system was undermined.

Whereas violence is a physical phenomenon, exerted by an individual or group directly upon the body of a person or object, Michel Foucault defines the exercise of power as control enacted over another individual or object. In a relationship of power, "the other" is acknowledged as a subject with his or her own agency, and an attempt is made to exert control over this agency. By contrast, in relationships of violence, "the other" is not acknowledged as a subject; rather, the goal is to break or to destroy the individual in question:

> A relationship of violence acts upon a body or upon things; it forces, it bends, it breaks the wheel, it destroys, or it closes the door on all possibilities. Its opposite pole can only be passivity, and if it comes up against any resistance, it has no other option but to try to minimize it. On the other hand, a power relationship can only be articulated on the basis of two elements which are each indispensable if it is to be a power relationship: that "the other" (the one over whom power is exercised) be thoroughly recognized and maintained to the very end as a person who acts; and that, faced with a relationship of power, a whole field of responses, reactions, results and possible interventions may open up.[9]

This relationship of violence was an undeniable feature of concentration camp life, with uniformed and armed male guard troops and *Aufseherinnen* embodying an ever-present threat of violence and death. In addition to the threat of physical violence located in the electrified barbed-wire fence and the armed guards on the towers, the concentration camp as a site and space, and the SS as the agents of that space, also had a symbolic and real power and deterrent effect. Through such tactics, a comparatively small number of staff were able to maintain control over a much larger inmate population. Whether due to fear of the consequences of an escape attempt or because of the overwhelming power of the SS, the majority of concentration camp inmates made no attempt to escape. As Dionys Lenard wrote after his own successful escape, "Each section was surrounded with two barbed-wire fences, which at that time [spring/summer 1942] were not yet electrified, as some mistakenly believed."[10] Even though the interior fences at Majdanek were not electrified until 1943, Lenard's account illustrates that the SS had largely succeeded in deceiving the prisoners.

For the SS, escapes from the camp represented an obvious and immense threat to their authority. At the same time, a successful escape forced the SS to acknowledge the prisoners as active agents who, however briefly, were capable of undermining the fundamental power structure within the camp. This fact explains the enormous effort and manpower accorded to preventing escapes and recapturing escaped prisoners.

The Escape of the Soviet Prisoners of War

The most famous escape from Majdanek was the escape of eighty-six Soviet prisoners of war during the night of June 14–15, 1942. According to members of the guard battalion interrogated during the Majdanek trial, the escapees used blankets and boards to climb the "electrified barbed-wire fence" at the front of the second section of the prisoners' camp, which faced in the direction of Chełm.[11] An SS guard on duty that night described the events as follows:

> I had just been relieved from duty at the tower near Field I or II. It was still quite dark. I noticed there was a lot of activity over in the Russian section. There was a latrine not far from the back of that field, and a large number of prisoners were headed in that direction. I assume, now, that it was the Russians who broke out of the camp some time afterwards. We were then sent in every possible direction. I was told to go to the spot where they had broken out. You could still see items of clothing and blankets lying on top of the fence.[12]

Hermann Hackmann, the first camp compound leader, was notified immediately by telephone:

> The block leader on duty was on the phone. He told me an escape was in progress. I think it was before midnight. I rang the commandant immediately. He was at

> Gartenstasse [the commandant and his wife lived in town, not at the camp]. He came to the telephone right away. . . . During our conversation, Koch told me to go to the camp right away and see what was happening. He would follow immediately. I got dressed. I left the house about three minutes after receiving the call.[13]

On the night of the escape, Commandant Karl Otto Koch had just returned from an official trip to Berlin.[14] Koch was still en route from his home in Lublin when the camp compound leader, who lived nearby, arrived at the camp. Meanwhile, a group of SS men arrived at the entrance to Field II. Among them was the leader of Field II, Fritz Petrick; the deputy camp compound leader, Arnold Strippel; and Hermann Hackmann, first camp compound leader. Hackmann ordered Petrick to convene a roll call in order to obtain an estimate of how many prisoners had fled. It was then they realized that of approximately 150 Soviet prisoners of war incarcerated in that section, about 86 had managed to escape into the surrounding forest.[15]

Once the number of escaped prisoners had been determined, a siren was sounded in the camp. However, as the headquarters staff officer Heinz Villain later explained in Eberhard Fechner's documentary, the search met with little success: "There was an alarm, we arrived, and were given our assignments. We went to the surrounding villages and areas to carry out a search. We did that for a while and searched everywhere, but we didn't find anyone and then we went back."[16] Hackmann described the events as follows: "It was very dark, and we could barely see. The lights from the camp extended only about 40 to 50 meters past the fence of the camp. We searched several hundred meters around the area of the breakout. We had lights with us."[17] Despite the search, the camp SS did not recapture any of the escaped inmates. In his interview for Fechner's documentary, Hackmann blamed the guard troops for the escape: "Of about 90 Russians who had to climb a barbed-wire fence to escape, the guards shot just two. In other words, the guards on duty were an utter failure. Those weren't guards, they were jumping jacks."[18]

To distract Oranienburg's attention from the disgrace of this large-scale escape and the fruitless search attempts, that same night Commandant Koch ordered that the Soviet prisoners who had remained behind be shot on the roll-call grounds of Field II. Field Leader Fritz Petrick described the events:[19]

> I no longer remember who gave the order to shoot the prisoners. It might have been Commandant Koch, but it could also have been Hackmann, camp compound leader, who ordered the Russian prisoners of war to be shot. But I think it is more likely that Koch gave the order for the shootings, because I remember that Hackmann said to us, "It's good that the old guy [Koch] is already back from Berlin, so I'm not the one who will have to pay for this."[20]

In one of his interrogations, Petrick described how the prisoners of war were made to lie down, face to the ground, and then were shot in the back of the head. After the war, no one was willing to admit to carrying out the shootings, so the exact identity of the shooters remains unknown. In his postwar interrogation, Otto Peer, a prisoner-functionary from Austria assigned to Field II, described the events as follows:

> It was night and there was an alarm. I heard shooting. I went outside the barracks and stood next to the entrance. As I stood in front of the barracks, I saw the Russian prisoners of war being gathered together on the roll-call grounds, near the water basin. . . . From my position, I saw SS officer Hackmann coming from the direction of the first barracks near the entrance to the field, pushing five or six Russians forward. He was carrying a submachine gun. The Russians were walking next to each other, in front of him. They were a few meters away from him. . . . Still some distance away from the barracks next to our Kapo barracks, he told the Russians to stop at the roll-call grounds. They had to turn around and look at him. He then shot the Russians at stomach height, sweeping from left to right with his machine pistol. . . . I saw the Russians all collapse. We Kapos then returned quickly to our barracks, because we were afraid of all the shooting.
>
> Once Hackmann was done shooting and it had grown quiet again, we left the barracks and went toward the roll-call grounds. That's when I saw that the remaining Russian prisoners of war had been herded together at the roll-call grounds. I can't remember how many there were. I saw how they were forced to lie down, face to the ground. They had to put their hands underneath their faces. Then the SS men shot them from behind with their submachine guns.[21]

That very night, Koch ordered Hackmann to write a report about the "Russian escape." On the morning of June 15, the report was sent by telex to the Chief Economic and Administrative Office (WVHA). Oranienburg was told that the Soviets who had been executed were "shot while attempting to escape." As Hermann Hackmann explained in Fechner's film: "In other words, we were saying that the prisoners had been shot while attempting to escape as a way of claiming, 'Look, we did manage to get forty of them.'"[22] According to Hackmann, Koch had also failed to inform Odilo Globocnik, the SS and Police Leader of Lublin, of the escape until the following morning. Globocnik, who had wanted to be informed of all events at the camp, was displeased with the delay, and accused Commandant Koch of being uncooperative.[23] "Koch told me that Globocnik had rebuked him, and he said Globocnik was a big asshole," Hackmann later testified.[24]

This incident demonstrates the issues such a large-scale escape created for the administrators at Majdanek. Hence, in a hasty ploy to make it appear that at least some of the escaping prisoners had been captured, the commandant and his first camp compound leader came up with a plan to carry out a mass reprisal. Their reasons for doing so were driven primarily by a desire to save face before their superiors at the WVHA, rather than out of a sense of duty or principle.

Hangings as Punishment and as Instrument of Terror

When the SS did succeed in capturing prisoners who had escaped from the concentration camps, they meted out draconian punishments as a deterrent, usually putting the prisoners to death. The degradations to which the captured fugitive was subjected were directed at the entire prisoner population. Sociologist Wolfgang Sofsky has termed these the "terror punishments," demonstrative penalties intended to have a deterrent effect.[25] These public punishments could also be understood as an attempt to restore authority. "The brutality of the punishment and the mockery of the victim restored power's sway."[26] Even within the context of the concentration camp, therefore, the physical violence and penal sanctions were intended to have a demonstrative quality; it is this performative aspect that requires further analysis.[27]

At Sachsenhausen, according to Höss, captured prisoners were dragged back into camp, made to wear mocking signs around their necks, and "paraded" in front of their fellow prisoners:

> When an escaped prisoner was found, he was paraded in front of the assembled inmates, wearing a large sign around his neck that said, "I've returned"—preferably with Eicke there as well.[28] Then he had to beat a large drum, which had also been hung around his neck. After this procession, he was punished with 25 blows of the stick, and then sent to the penal brigade. . . . The SS men who allowed an escape to take place were also punished severely, even if they bore very little blame. The prisoners who aided an escape were punished more severely still.[29]

At Majdanek, hanging signs around the necks of prisoners who spoke mainly Polish or Russian would have made little sense. But at Majdanek, too, the SS made it clear that no mercy would be shown to any prisoner who attempted an escape. The mere suggestion that a prisoner might be planning an escape was sufficient grounds for him to be shot or hanged. Immediately upon arrival at the concentration camp, all prisoners were subject to the "disciplinary regulations," a detailed catalog of twenty-one items describing acts that constituted a "violation" of camp regulations.[30] The disciplinary and penal regulations, originally established by Eicke himself, envisioned a multitude of punishments, ranging from work in a penal brigade, to internment in a prison barrack, to flogging.[31] However, nowhere does the term "death penalty" appear on this list of regulations, because to have made any such specific reference would have implied an assumption of the powers of state and the law. There was, however, one exception: the draft regulations of 1933 stated that saboteurs and mutineers should, under the law of the revolution, be "shot on the spot or hanged afterwards."[32] In this SS document, the death penalty was described as a measure for restoring the order that had been threatened by saboteurs and mutineers—with escaped prisoners being included in this category.

According to survivors, in all the concentration camps, whether in the "East" or within the territories of the "old German Reich," the punishment for an escape attempt was the same—execution by hanging.[33] Hermann Hackmann, the first camp compound leader at Majdanek from July 1941 to summer 1942, gave the following explanation:

> A prisoner was hanged while I was at Lublin. . . . I believe it was toward the end of my time at Lublin, when we discovered that a prisoner was missing at the evening roll call. This was reported to the commandant. The commandant ordered all the labor details to head back out again and, together with the SS, carry out a search for the prisoner. [At the time, Majdanek was still under construction and there was a severe staff shortage. EM]. The prisoner was then found somewhere, some distance away from the Field, and returned to the camp. I believe it was a prisoner from Field II. The other prisoners of that field had to return to the roll-call grounds. The commandant was informed. . . . In the meantime, a gallows had been set up on the square. I can't remember if the prisoner was asked to explain why he fled. Apart from the commandant and myself, the other SS men who worked in the prisoner camp were also there. Commandant Koch instructed me to inform the assembled prisoners that the hanging they were about to witness would await any prisoner who attempted to flee. The prisoner was then hanged.[34]

Hanging as a punishment was carried out in much the same way in all the concentration camps. An SS man led the condemned person to the gallows, in front of the assembled male or female prisoners. According to postwar statements made by former SS staff and prisoners, the rank of these SS escorts and their gender varied, but the hanging itself always followed a similar pattern. According to Fritz Petrick (who also witnessed the hanging described above):

> The hangings always took place after roll call, either in the morning or in the evening. Generally, the camp compound leader was present, and read a directive to the assembled prisoners that explained why the person was being hanged. I no longer recall who carried out the actual hanging, but I believe it was also prisoners, maybe the block elders. I can't remember whether members of the SS also had a direct hand in the hangings.[35]

According to Hermann Hackmann, by summer 1942, the RSHA had already issued an order that any recaptured escapees were to be hanged:

> I can't remember such an order existing during the time I worked in Buchenwald. I would even say that it didn't yet exist at that time. But I remember that in a meeting, Koch told us about a directive of this nature issued by the Reich Security Main Office.

> He read it aloud to us. . . . It is possible that this order only referred to camps in the Generalgouvernement.[36]

A similar memo issued by the Reich Security Main Office (RSHA) in January 1943 outlined the procedure to be followed when carrying out the death penalty in a concentration camp. This document declared that all inmates subject to this punishment—whether "Reich Germans" or *Volksdeutsche*—would be put to death by hanging. The memo further stipulated that these executions would be carried out by prisoners, and not by the SS.[37]

For the prisoners, it was an additional humiliation that "Reich German" prisoner-functionaries, or occasionally Polish or Jewish prisoners, were forced to carry out the hangings. As Andrzej Stanislawski, a survivor from Poland, described:

> When I was a runner in Field II, I was one of many thousands who were forced to stand at the square and witness executions, which were carried out at the light pole there, in the middle of the Field. At every execution, the victim was hanged at the gallows. . . . There were also many SS men present from the camp staff, both higher as well as lower ranking ones. . . . The victim had to stand on a footstool, which had been specially brought out from the block. Then it was generally Wyderko, but sometimes also a German Kapo, like Galka, who put the rope around the victim's neck, and kicked the stool out from underneath the victim. The executions generally took place after the evening roll call, between 6 and 7 pm. Usually Wyderko told the assembled prisoners, in his broken Polish, that the person was being hanged because he had attempted to escape. In reality, though, there were very few actual escape attempts. But if a prisoner had fallen asleep somewhere on the very large camp grounds and failed to hear the order to assemble, that was enough to justify an accusation that he had attempted to escape.[38]

This form of killing was chosen intentionally, as death by hanging had long been considered among the most humiliating forms of the death penalty. First, death by hanging implied that the criminal, whether due to social status or because of the crime committed, was not worthy of execution in a manner that required use of a weapon. Moreover, the condemned individual was generally shackled or bound with ropes when led to the gallows, which denied all freedom of movement.[39] In the 1930s, hanging as a form of the death penalty was still employed in Britain and Austria, as it was considered relatively "humane" since it resulted in a fairly quick death.

After the eighteenth century in Germany, however, hanging was an uncommon penalty, and it was not included in any penal code.[40] In fact, it was not adopted again until after the National Socialists came to power.[41] On March 29, 1933, the government of President Paul von Hindenburg passed a law that called for death by hanging for Marinus van der Lubbe, the man who (allegedly) carried out the arson attack on the Reichstag, as well as any other person found guilty of arson, treason, conspiracy, armed resistance, hostage-taking for political purposes, or similar crimes. Called the "Lex van der Lubbe," the law was made retroactive to January 31, 1933, Hitler's first day in power. When van der Lubbe was hanged in 1933, there were numerous protests, and many newspaper readers wrote letters of complaint. The German public believed hanging was an unacceptable form of the death penalty.[42] Twelve years later, however, public hanging of alleged traitors was a commonly employed form of terror across Germany.[43]

In the concentration camps, therefore, the SS deliberately employed a form of capital punishment that was regarded as dishonorable. It also had the advantage of being "quick, cheap and relatively clean," as British historian Richard J. Evans has noted.[44] In actual practice, however, the person condemned to death was likely to suffer for more than just a few moments. The sociologist Wolfgang Sofsky pointed out that death by hanging can often take "several excruciating minutes," and depending on the length of the rope and the height of the gallows, death often results from slow suffocation rather than a broken neck.[45] Moreover, as the survivor Jerzy Kwiatowski recalls, the SS men or prisoner functionaries at Majdanek often deliberately drew out the process of death:

> I witnessed death by hanging a number of times. This happened when a prisoner fell asleep during roll call, or when a prisoner failed to appear for the midday roll call, which the SS men interpreted as an escape attempt. I should note that the prisoners were not hanged in such a manner that their necks were broken. Rather, to heighten the agony, the rope was placed around their neck while they were still standing on the ground, and then they were pulled up. Death occurred by suffocation, which extended the prisoner's agony. These executions were public, and carried out in the presence of the Majdanek leadership. The executions were also photographed.[46]

The concentration camp inmates served as the audience for this ritualized degradation. As described by former guard Luzie H., "If we had a case where someone tried to do a bunker and was caught, then he was hanged. We had a roll call with a count of the prisoners, and the commandos [the prisoners] had to stand there for a long time."[47] However, this "audience" was anything but voluntary. The survivor Maryla Reich recalled how, in summer 1943, the inmates were herded into the central square of the women's camp to watch the hanging of a young woman: "Some time later, we had to assemble for roll call. With blows, they forced us to go toward the middle of the field, where the gallows had been set up."[48]

According to Chela Apelbaum and many other witnesses, the bodies of the dead were often left to hang at the gallows for hours:

> They built a gallows, and we were told to assemble for roll call. An SS man and "Brigida" [Hildegard Lächert] were standing at the gallows. They told us this would

happen to anyone who attempted to escape. Then they put the loop around the girl's neck. She screamed and tried to turn away, because the loop was so tight. We all started sobbing, loudly, which almost drove "Brigida" mad. Laughing, she kicked the stool out from under the girl. The girl hung from the gallows for quite a long time. . . . We had to remain standing and look toward the gallows. By the time we were finally led away, it was already growing dark. The next morning, the girl's body was blue, and she was still hanging on the gallows. Then she was finally removed.[49]

As Luzie H., the former *Aufseherin*, explained in her later testimony, the prisoners who had been hanged were left at the gallows until the next roll call "so that they could be included in the count."[50] Leaving the bodies of the dead hanging after their execution also served as a form of public display, intended as an additional degradation and as a warning for the prisoners who were forced to watch.[51]

Hanging as a form of execution thus bore some similarity to the pillory, which had humiliation as one of its main objectives, and in which public display was a central element of the punishment. "In the ceremonies of public execution, the main character was the people, whose real and immediate presence was required for the performance," as Michel Foucault wrote.[52] There was, however, some variation in the punishments of prisoners who attempted to escape from Majdanek. Anna Biel, who arrived at Majdanek in February 1943, when Hermann Florstedt was commandant of the camp, soon became witness to the following punishment:

A few days after our arrival at Majdanek, three men who had arrived with me in a transport from Lemberg escaped from Field 3. They were caught the next night, and in the next days, I saw two of them. They had been bound with barbed wire, naked, to the posts in Field 3. These posts stood about 20 meters away from the gate to Field 3. They had been put there on purpose, so that we would see how the camp administration dealt with fugitives. It was a terrible sight. The men looked like two bloodied washcloths, scraps of humanity bound to the post with a wire. One of them died of exhaustion and exposure around 3 pm. The other lived, so the remaining prisoners told me, until evening.[53]

This form of punishment is also highly reminiscent of the public punishment of the pillory.[54] As a form of public punishment, the pillory aimed to make the punishment visible to fellow prisoners, in order to humiliate and intimidate them, while having a deterrent effect.[55] The SS intended the punishments as a visible demonstration of the imbalance of power, and as evidence of their absolute authority over the inmates.

Thus, the spectacle of punishment and violence was an important means of communicating the relationship of power.[56] In enacting this spectacle, the SS was addressing its actions to all of the onlookers who, by association, were forced to take part in the ritual of punishment. First, the person being punished was degraded and executed. At the same time, the prisoners who were forced to witness the execution were reminded of their own powerlessness. Finally, the spectacle was also directed at the SS, to whom the punishment gave affirmation of their own power. At these executions, the prisoners vastly outnumbered the guard staff. This imbalance, coupled with the prisoners' helplessness, certainly contributed to a sense of triumph on the part of the SS. For the SS, participation as a group in this ritual of punishment also served to create a sense of "community,"[57] one from which they derived pleasure. As Henrika Mitron recalled, the SS men and women often joked with each other during the hangings: "For them, it was a moment of entertainment."[58]

Escape in the Discursive Retellings of Survivors

After the war, the Majdanek trial at the Dusseldorf regional court devoted a great deal of attention to the hanging, in summer 1943, of a young woman at the women's camp. The prosecution had charged former *Aufseherinnen* Hildegard Lächert and Hermine Braunsteiner as accessories to murder for their part in this incident.[59] During the trial, however, it became apparent that the court was approaching the limits of what the law could accomplish in avenging Nazi crimes. The testimony of witnesses was particularly problematic for the prosecution. Under German law, it was not sufficient for the witnesses to have a clear memory of the crime. Rather, the crime had to meet the legal criteria for murder, which required the court to establish the precise course of events and the specific actions of the people involved. As a result, the judges and prosecutors were obligated to carefully question the witnesses to determine the precise actions of the defendants, as well as the specifics as to time, location, and circumstance of the crime.

Even though the entire women's camp had witnessed the execution, the accounts by survivors varied substantially in their descriptions. The sole point of agreement among the survivors was that the hanging had taken place in either May or June 1943, and that the victim was a young woman between fifteen and twenty-two years of age. Nechama Frenkel remembered a well-dressed, neatly coiffed woman being led to the gallows.[60] According to Maryla Reich, the woman was not clothed in prisoner's garb. She recalled that the woman's long braid had been cut off, and that she was led barefoot, hands bound, to the gallows.[61] Hela Rosenbaum confirmed this version, saying that she remembered the young woman's clothing: "The girl wasn't wearing shoes when she was led to the gate. She was forced to carry the stool. . . . The girl was barefoot, and even today I can still see her red sweater and brown skirt before my eyes."[62] According to Janina Rawska-Bot, a red lamp was burning during the hanging, and music was playing over the loudspeakers.[63] Riwka Landau also testified that the young woman was forced to carry the stool that was later kicked out from under her.[64]

However, there were a number of key points on which the witnesses did not agree, including whether the hanging took place at a morning or an evening roll call, which SS men and female guards were present, whether the young woman was Jewish or Polish, and the content of her final words. The witnesses also offered varying descriptions of the details of the hanging, which made it difficult to identify the men and women responsible with the degree of certainty required in a court of law. With the deliberate aim of dragging out the evidentiary hearings, the defense took advantage of these discrepancies to call ever more witnesses to the stand.[65] Although 150 witnesses eventually testified at the Düsseldorf trial regarding this hanging, the charges were ultimately dropped.

As Christopher Browning demonstrated in his study of Hamburg's Reserve Battalion 101, such evidentiary difficulties were characteristic of postwar prosecutions of National Socialist crimes. When the men of Police Battalion 101 described their experiences in wartime Poland twenty-five years later, they had nearly all "repressed or forgotten certain aspects of the battalion's experiences, or reshaped [their] memory of them in a different way," Browning noted.[66] Paradoxically, a single detailed account might well have shed greater clarity—however illusory—than did the multitude of contradictory details offered in 125 separate accounts. In the end, the various accounts given by witnesses to the hanging at Majdanek's women's camp also offered a "confusing array of perspectives and memories."[67] The differences in the various witness accounts can be readily explained by the process that memories undergo over time.[68] Memories are not simple reconstructions of events witnessed and experienced, but subjective interpretations that are shaped and influenced by the experiences of intervening years. So, too, each witness in the trial had formed her own subjective recollection of the events that surrounded the hanging that had taken place more than thirty years earlier.[69]

In the case of the hanging, however, it was also its "performative quality" that further prevented the formation of a coherent narrative of the event. As the historian Jürgen Martschukat has noted, any performance entails an interaction between the performers and the audience:

> It is this interaction that allows the performance to generate meaning. For the individual observer, his or her position in the room determines the manner in which he or she experiences the "performance" as part of the audience. For this reason, the audience . . . must be analyzed in a nuanced and differentiated manner.[70]

Material and situational factors also help shape what is perceived and, therefore, what is later remembered. What the concentration camp inmates were able to see and comprehend of events was even more limited by the fact that they were always at constant risk of becoming victims of violence themselves. For the Jewish prisoners at Majdanek, in particular, direct eye contact with a member of the SS staff was liable to result in a beating, so they tended to avoid eye contact and instead fix their gaze on the uniform.[71] A prisoner's physical location also determined how much he or she was able to see of any particular event. Individual factors could also influence what was seen: while one prisoner might observe an execution closely, another might feel compelled to look away at the moment of killing. Fear, exhaustion, and being lost in one's own thoughts and emotions could all influence what was actually seen, as well as how closely it was observed. In addition, the prisoner population, itself, was in constant flux. Many survivors had spent only a few weeks at Majdanek, and many were transferred from camp to camp, with the result that memories of experiences could easily become confused or conflated.

However, it was not only these institutional factors that shaped and limited prisoners' awareness of what was happening around them. Theater-studies scholar Erika Fischer-Lichte has described the factors that help shape perceptions of cultural performances; these factors apply, in heightened form, to the prisoners' awareness of the violence that took place within the concentration camp.[72] Violent situations engage several modes of sensory perception simultaneously, including visual perception, hearing, and smell. For the prisoners, it was virtually impossible to apprehend every detail—every movement, gesture, sound, and odor—surrounding the young woman's execution as an event. Finally, other individual factors, including age, nationality, religious affiliation, personal characteristics, and prisoner category, could also affect which specific details each observer would notice and remember.

Nearly all of the surviving witnesses reported that both the SS and the young woman gave a speech to the assembled prisoners before the hanging. The survivors all remembered the SS speech as an explicit threat and warning. However, their memories of the young woman's final words, and the language in which she spoke, varied. Krystina Tarasiewicz, a survivor from Poland, recalled, "[She said] 'I wanted to live. Don't forget me.' . . . Our barracks began singing a hymn in Polish."[73] Barbara Steiner, a Jewish woman who had been interned at Majdanek, gave a different description: "The girl stood on a chair, with the rope around her neck, and told us that we must try to survive."[74] Another former Jewish prisoner, Mira Awronski, recalled that the woman said, "Stay strong, then you will be free again one day."[75] Wanda Bialas, from Poland, recalled the events somewhat differently:

> A higher-ranking SS man, Dr. Blanke, a tall and good-looking officer who also took part in all of the selections, asked her before the hanging if she would try to escape again. When the girl answered "Yes," he kicked the stool she had been standing on out from under her.[76]

Maryla Reich, the Jewish survivor from Poland, described the scene as follows: "I heard the crematorist ask the girl something. She replied that she would run away again, to die in freedom. Then she called out something like, 'Long live freedom!' Then they removed her stool, and she was dead."[77] Dora Abend's memory was again somewhat different: "The SS staff asked the girl if she regretted her actions. The girl just spat at them and called out, 'I will greet my death with a smile!'"[78]

Most of the Polish witnesses remembered that the young woman spoke her final words in Polish, and some ascribed a patriotic or religious meaning to her statement. Many Jewish survivors, however, interpreted her final words differently. Maria Kaufmann-Krasowska recalled hearing an SS man ask the young woman if she was afraid yet:

> She replied, "No, I would rather die than be captive." As she stood underneath the gallows, she said in a loud voice to the people standing around her, "Today I will die, but you will survive. Then our homeland will be free again." They pulled the rope tight right in the middle of her final word. . . . It is possible that she said "Poland isn't lost yet" as she stood beneath the gallows, and that I have misremembered her words as, "Our fatherland must be free again."[79]

By contrast, Rachel Nurman told the court that the young woman had called out in Hebrew: "Take revenge. Death to the Germans, the SS!" When the prosecutor told Nurman that other witnesses had reported that the young woman had said something like, "Long live Poland!" or "Poland is not yet lost!" Nurman replied, "As a Jewish woman, she wouldn't have said that. The Poles helped destroy us, after all. In any case, hundreds of young female prisoners were hanged after attempting to escape."[80]

Even though the survivors had all witnessed the same event, each remembered it differently, typically along national, religious, and social lines. Despite the differences and contradictions in their recollections, however, the memories contain one common element: the witnesses all described the young woman in positive terms and praised her as a symbol of self-determination. As their testimony suggests, the shared experience of violence and humiliation helped create a sense of community—or, perhaps more aptly stated, *communities*—among the prisoners. Though the hanging was staged as a ritual of shunning and exclusion, this aspect met with little success. Nor did the SS succeed in convincing the assembled prisoners to identify with the perpetrators rather than the victim. Instead, the testimony of the witnesses suggests that the Jewish and Polish prisoners each claimed the young woman as one of their own.

This positive connotation, however, is called into question by Dionys Lenard's account, written after his escape. According to Lenard, the power the SS wielded over the prisoners was effective, in part, because it encouraged surveillance among the prisoners: "Because of the terrible living conditions and the constant abuse, people were so afraid, I ended up regretting having told some of them that I was planning an escape."[81] Although Lenard didn't explain himself further here, he implies that there were conflicts among the prisoners and that he was afraid that some of his fellow prisoners might betray him, possibly out of fear of reprisal. Lenard had originally planned to escape with two fellow prisoners. In the end, though, the two other men elected to remain. Regarding the day of the escape, Lenard wrote:

> I asked them if they had prepared everything for the evening. They evaded my question. I concluded that meant they no longer wanted to escape, or that they had been seized with fear, now that the moment was approaching. I thought it might just be a momentary thing, a mood that would soon pass. . . . I told them that the right moment would happen soon. They replied that they hadn't decided yet. They also tried to persuade me to give up my plan. They tried to convince me that it was too dangerous. I was furious, and in my agitation I had some harsh words for them. . . . I told them that they were acquiescing to slavery.[82]

Once it had become clear that his friends would not attempt to escape with him, Lenard began to mistrust them, fearing they might betray him. This phenomenon, in itself, demonstrates the perfidy of the camp system. Lenard's final sentence suggests a very important point, one rarely mentioned in survivor testimony. To the prisoners, electing to remain in the camp rather than attempting an escape constituted an act of resignation. Those left behind after an escape, however, often felt abandoned to their fate, left to confront even more degradation and violence.

Not every prisoner had the courage or stamina to attempt an escape, and the fear of reprisal was entirely valid. While Lenard did succeed, most who attempted an escape were in fact recaptured. What Lenard does not describe—could not describe—was the fate that awaited his fellow prisoners, left behind in the camp: hours of standing at roll call while the search continued, missed meals, and the likelihood of being forced to assemble for his hanging had he been recaptured. While this extended, forced assembly was extremely grueling for those who were sick and weak, it was arduous even for the relatively healthy, and some prisoners were likely to die as a result. Given these circumstances, for the remaining prisoners, the capture or execution of an escaped inmate might even represent a "respite" from their ordeal; they would finally be able to leave the roll-call grounds, return to their barracks, and rest after a long and strenuous day of forced labor. For prisoners in the camp, life was a constant struggle for survival, which required a careful hoarding of every ounce of remaining strength. Even after the war, such escape attempts, whether successful or not, could easily have "burdened" survivors with conflicting emotions. Where the escapee had "taken a stand," the survivor might feel she had merely "endured"—and might even be burdened with the memory of hoping for a swift recapture, as an end to her own ordeal.

In any case, the memories of the hanging as recounted by Majdanek survivors make it clear that they refused to conform to the SS version of events. Rather, they laid claim to the young woman as a martyr or even a symbol of resistance. Nonetheless, despite these expressions of solidarity and the desire to lay claim to the young woman as one of their own, it is important to recognize that their postwar testimony bears witness to a fundamental problem—namely, that every escape confronted the prisoners with a profound dilemma, both on a symbolic level as a reminder of their own imprisonment, and in terms of their immediate, day-to-day survival.

At the same time, personal reflections offered by survivors demonstrate that the interpretations and meaning ascribed to this ritualized punishment were not entirely within the control of those who enacted it. Despite the overwhelming power of the SS, they could not dictate how events were perceived and understood by the prisoners. So, too, the interpretations ascribed to the hanging of the young woman resisted all attempts on the part of the SS to dictate, co-opt, and control its meaning. Even while still in the camp, inmates ascribed their own meaning and interpretation to the symbolic degradation, violence, and executions they witnessed. Often, the meaning that prisoners ascribed to the ritualized spectacles of punishment was in direct conflict with the message the SS wished to communicate. At the Majdanek trial, the former prisoners were granted a role never envisioned by the SS, who had clearly intended the elimination of any possible witnesses. As witnesses before the court, the survivors were granted a position of authority over their former captors. Their testimony was crucial to establishing what actions had been carried out by the SS, and what would, in the future, be remembered. Through their testimony, a measure of definitional authority was restored to the witnesses. In this sense, their testimony before the court is itself an illustration of the shifts that occur, over time, in configurations of power.

9

License to Kill?

Unauthorized Actions by the Camp Guards

THE DISCIPLINARY AND PENAL CODE FOR THE CONCENTRATION CAMPS spelled out the treatment of prisoners in precise detail. However, the daily violence and punishments meted out by the SS often bore little relation to these official guidelines, a discrepancy that has received comparatively little attention in the scholarship on Nazi concentration camps. In this chapter, I will examine this contradiction and explore the opportunities for independent action afforded to the female guards and SS men during their daily duties. To what extent were their actions guided by the regulations, and how were these regulations implemented in their daily duties in the camp?

At the postwar Majdanek trial, former *Aufseherinnen* and SS men alike invoked the familiar claim that they had only been carrying out their duties and had no choice but to follow orders. For example, Erna Pfannstiel, who had also carried out selections while at Majdanek, stated the following in her testimony: "If I am told that my statements mean that I was an accessory to murder, then I have to ask, why is that? We had no other choice. We had to follow orders. Had I refused, I might have been locked up myself."[1] In Eberhard Fechner's documentary, Hildegard Lächert described the situation as follows:

> We weren't actually human any more. And then there were the constant orders. We had no chance to develop our own point of view. We weren't permitted to speak with the prisoners, the inmates. That was forbidden.[2]

The deputy head of the crematorium, Robert Seitz, described the hangings at the crematorium in similar terms: "When I was the one who took the call from the infirmary and then told Kapo Fischer that a prisoner was to be hanged, I was acting on orders. Refusing to carry out those orders would certainly have led to serious punishment."[3] The issuance and following of orders was a constitutive element of work at a concentration camp, which was organized along military lines. Within this hierarchical structure, the female guards and SS men were indeed subject to the orders of their superiors. Upon closer analysis, however, it is clear there were differences in how the *Aufseherinnen* carried out their duties in daily practice. Here the concept of appropriation or "Aneignung," as discussed by Alf Lütdke, can be a useful model for understanding these individual and group dynamics. Even within the context of this supposedly all-powerful institutional compulsion, the camp guards nonetheless managed to find ways to appropriate those institutional constraints, contributing to the social dynamics of camp life.[4]

Corporal Punishment at Ravensbrück and Majdanek

Within the Nazi concentration camps, the regulations governing floggings were outlined in precise bureaucratic detail. For example, a 1942 letter from the Chief Economic and Administrative Office (WVHA) to all camp commandants decreed that floggings were to be employed "only as a last resort."

> [This punishment] shall be undertaken only under the following circumstances:
>
> a) When all other penalties outlined in the camp regulations, including confinement to a cell, confinement to a dark cell, withholding of meals, and hard labor have been of no avail.
>
> b) In individual cases, such as escape attempts or actual attacks, which must be inflicted as a deterrent, and when an example must be made.
>
> Further, the Reichsführer-SS has stated floggings are not a tool to be employed by commandants, supervising custodians, and female guards who are too lazy or incompetent to reeducate prisoners. In a case where a prisoner has stolen food from another prisoner, the guilty party is to be punished by the withholding of food or, if this is not possible for health reasons, with bread and water rations for 3 to 5 days on a first offense. The flogging penalty is to be inflicted only upon a repeated offense.
>
> Applications for penal rulings that have been submitted to date have clearly demonstrated that the purpose of the most serious camp penalty (the flogging penalty) has been misunderstood in most instances.

> The camp commandants are instructed to pay special attention to implementation of the Reichsführer's directive and are to submit requests for the imposition of flogging penalties only under justifiable circumstances.
>
> The Head of the Central Office[5]

This document confirms that the WVHA was displeased with the administration of floggings as punishment within the camps. A few weeks later, Himmler reaffirmed that floggings were to be administered as punishments only under "exceptional circumstances."[6]

The implementation of corporal punishment in the camps can be best understood by way of the example set at the Ravensbrück women's concentration camp. (Because Majdanek was both a concentration and an extermination camp, and also had an extremely high death rate, other forms of violence and killing were accorded greater attention in postwar legal testimony and memoir accounts.) Moreover, Ravensbrück is also where the *Aufseherinnen* from Majdanek were trained and, as such, where they first encountered the penal system of the concentration camps.

Following the example of the men's camps, Ravensbrück was governed by a set of official camp regulations,[7] written expressly for the women's camp, that closely followed the "Dachau model."[8] The Ravensbrück camp regulations contained three separate sections: first, the duty regulations, which governed the duties of the concentration camp staff; second, the "general camp regulations," which addressed the prisoners' living and work conditions—or, as it was termed, their "rights" and duties; and finally, the "disciplinary and penal regulations."[9] All prisoners at the camp were subject to the "disciplinary regulations," which included a detailed catalog of prohibited acts, summarized in 21 separate points. Individuals committing the following infractions were to be punished:

> 1.) Anyone who does not immediately follow an order issued by an SS superior, an *Aufseherin*, or a staff member,
> 2.) Anyone who fails to report a contagious disease or infestation with pests,
> 3.) Anyone who fails to pay the required respect or who is guilty of some other breach of respect,
> 4.) Anyone who refuses to follow the orders, or who reluctantly follows the orders, of the block or room elder,
> 5.) Anyone who enters areas of the camp other than those expressly assigned to the prisoner. Prior permission from the block leader is required to enter the canteen for purchases [sic] or for brief visits,
> 6.) Anyone who smokes or who encourages another prisoner to smoke or who obtains tobacco products,
> 7.) Anyone who obtains alcohol in a prohibited matter and who consumes alcohol. Alcohol consumption is forbidden.
> 8.) Anyone who fails to rise immediately when awakened, or who leaves their bed after

curfew. Leaving lodgings (the barracks) is prohibited between the hours of curfew and waking, and entails a risk to life,

9.) Anyone who remains in bed without a note from a doctor and who is determined not to be sufficiently ill to require bed rest, or who lies down in bed during the daytime,

10.) Anyone who avoids work, is lazy, or who is negligent in carrying out her work,

11.) Anyone who claims to be sick in order to avoid work, or who registers as sick for the same reason, and who is later deemed by the physician to be healthy and capable of work,

12.) Anyone who undertakes prohibited contact or relationships (verbally or in writing) with other prisoners, particularly prisoners from other blocks,

13.) Anyone who deliberately damages, removes, or unlawfully acquires property of the state or other objects belonging to the camp,

14.) Anyone who violates the mail regulations, which were explained to every prisoner on arrival at the camp, or whose letters include any defamatory criticisms or impudent remarks in either word or form,

15.) Anyone who interferes with the wire fence or throws an object over it,

16.) Anyone who, when the alarm is sounded, does not immediately return to her quarters and close the windows and doors, unless specifically ordered not to do so. In the event of a fire alarm, the prisoners whose accommodations are burning shall assemble in front of the burning barracks; all other prisoners should remain in their barracks,

17.) Anyone who makes unnecessary noise or who is loud or who is noisy during the night hours, or who approaches other prisoners in a lesbian manner or who engages in lesbian obscenities, or who fails to report such activities,

18.) Anyone who lies to, steals from, or abuses a fellow prisoner,

19.) Anyone who engages in preparations for an escape attempt or encourages fellow prisoners to do so or who fails to report such activities. An escape attempt will be suspected when a prisoner leaves the camp compound without a female guard's presence, or enters the neutral zone, or interferes with the wire fence,

20.) Anyone who disobeys camp discipline or regulations, or who in any way violates the security of the camp,

21.) Any inmate who attacks an SS guard, an *Aufseherin*, or other superior, threatens them with an object, or who is intending such an attack, will be immediately shot.[10]

Generally speaking, however, prisoners in Nazi concentration camps were not informed of the camp regulations. Instead, they were left on their own to discern the rules of the concentration camp, both written and unwritten. Such lessons often came by way of painful experience. In his account, Dionys Lenard described his "apprenticeship" to life at Majdanek as follows:

> One day, the work leader, the carpenter, told me to get a wrench from the camp. I went there and reported to the SS man on duty. I told him that the work leader had

> told me to get the wrench from the warehouse. The SS man lunged at me for my poorly issued report and hit me over the head with a metal bar. I was sure that he had shattered my skull. I told him that I didn't know how to issue a report properly. "You bastard swine" [*Schweinehund*], and "you pig, son of a Jew," this is how you're supposed to report: "Prisoner No. 2828 is temporarily entering the camp." I thanked him for the "friendly" suggestion and went to the infirmary to bandage my head, which was bleeding heavily. Then I went to fetch the wrench and returned. That time, I reported correctly: "Prisoner No. 2828 is returning from the camp."[11]

New arrivals to the camp were told the rules by experienced inmates, friends, relatives, or inmates from the same religious, national, or political "network." Those inmates who did not belong to any group learned these rules by way of brutality and force suffered at the hands of the guards, or even their fellow inmates. Whether this was the practice during the early phase of the camp's operation, or whether it was a practice that developed over time, is unclear. What is certain is that the guards' deliberate failure to inform the prisoners of camp rules had the effect of heightening the guards' arbitrary authority. In this way, the prisoners' utter vulnerability and their subjection to the whims of the guards and *Aufseherinnen* was underscored.

Even when the prisoners were aware of the penal code, it was nearly impossible for them to follow it in its entirety. Furthermore, the punishments meted out by the female guards and SS men did not always follow the 21-point list to the letter. The majority of survivors later described the behavior of the guards as arbitrary and high-handed. For example, Paul Martin Neurath, a prisoner from Vienna who was incarcerated from April 1938 to May 1939 in the Dachau and Buchenwald concentration camps, described the punishments meted out by the guards as random and indiscriminate:

> Given the absurdity of the rules and the terrible punishments that were meted out for breaking them, it seems obvious that the rules were designed to be broken. . . . Under such conditions, rules and punishments no longer have the same connotation they do in ordinary existence: guidelines upon which one can reflect, and then choose to either uphold or violate, along with corresponding stipulated punishments, meted out in the event one chooses to break the rules. In the concentration camp, most of the rules consisted of little more than loosely strung-together arbitrariness, and the punishments were nothing less than organized abuse. . . . When arbitrariness is itself the intention, the rules that govern the process of punishment are themselves superfluous.[12]

According to Neurath, therefore, the regulations were little more than a sham. The regulations did not serve as guidelines for behavior, but rather as a means of sowing confusion and ensuring the prisoners' complete subjugation. As Ravensbrück survivor Lucia Schmidt-Fels later recalled, "In reality, everything was forbidden. . . .

Since it was impossible to completely avoid doing something that was forbidden, we lived under the constant threat of punishment."[13]

The camp regulations described countless potential offenses. Such "excessive overregulation"[14] provided the guard staff with an endless pretext for sanctions and abuse. Wolfgang Sofsky has pointed out that the bureaucratic structure generated a "matrix for punitive action," creating on the ground a "gray zone of unofficial and spontaneous punitive measures."[15] Given this context, it is no surprise that French Ravensbrück survivors later referred to the "laws of the jungle" or the "jungle of punishments" when they spoke of the camps.[16] "There were no camp regulations. Nothing was forbidden because everything was forbidden, without question. A gesture that was permitted one day could the following day result in hours of brutality meted out by the SS."[17]

Officially, however, the duty regulations that applied to all concentration camps expressly forbade the female guards from carrying out corporal punishments, or from exacting punishments on their own initiative, even when the prisoner had violated stated camp regulations. Under official duty regulations, concentration camp staff were only authorized to "reprimand slatternly inmates from their own block or their own area of supervision, issue verbal warnings, or impose special duties (barracks orderly duties)."[18] According to these duty regulations, the primary duty of the *Aufseherinnen* was to ensure that daily and work routines were carried out in an orderly manner.[19] "SS supervisors and female guards" were permitted to "make use of their weapons" only in the event that they were attacked.[20] *Aufseherinnen* were also permitted to shoot in the event of an escape attempt, using the pistol that, according to duty regulations, they had been assigned for the sole purpose of self-defense. Here, it is worth remembering the "Declaration of Honor" that every SS *Aufseherin* and SS man was required to sign upon entering service at a concentration camp. This declaration stipulated that only the Führer had the right to make decisions on the "life or death of an enemy of the state," and that no National Socialist "has the right to strike an enemy of the state or to subject him to physical abuse."[21] Officially, then, only the camp commandants, who held the final say in all service-related matters within the camps, had the right to issue punishments.

As the ranking SS officer, the commandant had authority over all SS staff and all camp prisoners, including responsibility for all labor detail and disciplinary matters. The commandant also acted as the local representative of the WVHA and reported to that office.[22] The commandant's official description of duties also required him to instruct all male and female concentration camp staff that they would be "subject to severe penalties if proven to have abused any prisoners."[23] Any *Aufseherin* who accused an inmate of a violation of camp regulations was required to submit a written "report" to the chief guard, following official channels. (SS men were required to submit a similar report to the camp compound leader.)[24] At Ravensbrück, the chief guard herself convened a "penal report" once a week, during which she questioned the accused prisoner and decided whether the "report" would be submitted.[25] This process gave the chief guard significant decision-making authority in her own right,[26] although only the camp commandant had the authority to issue punishments and decide what type of penalty would be imposed.

The list of punishments handed down ranged from administrative sanctions, to detention, to floggings.

> The following penalties may be imposed:
>
> 1.) Administrative sanctions, including:
>
> a) Warnings, including warning of penalty on repeated offense,
>
> b) Penal labor during leisure time under supervision of an *Aufseherin*,
>
> c) Prohibition on writing or receiving personal letters,
>
> d) Withholding of midday meal or evening meal, while still on full labor duties,
>
> e) Transfer to punishment block,
>
> f) Hard labor in a cell after daily labor detail work is finished for the day.
>
> 2. Detention:
>
> a) Detention, medium, Level I, up to three days.
> Implementation: wood pallet, light cell;
> Meals are bread and water.
>
> b) Detention, heightened, Level II, up to 42 days.
> Implementation: wood pallet, dark cell;
> Meals are bread and water with full rations every fourth day.
>
> c) Detention, strict, Level III, up to 3 days.
> Implementation: No ability to sit or lie down, dark cell;
> Meals are bread and water.
>
> Level III may be imposed as a stand-alone penalty or to exacerbate Level II on a day-by-day basis.
>
> 3.) Corporal punishment:
>
> Between 5 and 25 blows may be administered on the buttocks and thighs. The number of blows is at the discretion of the camp director, and will be entered on the corresponding line in the penal order.[27]

The penal regulations also described the official and proper method for imposing and carrying out penalties in great detail. The designated punishments, along with a precise description of the "penal offense," were recorded onto multiple copies of the "penal order" forms.[28] The white original was to be placed in the prisoner's file, while a yellow carbon copy was archived in a "punishments" dossier at headquarters. In cases of corporal punishment, the red carbon copy was sent to the Inspector of Concentration Camps or to Himmler himself, in Oranienburg, for approval. The process of imposing and recording penalties was thus subject to a strict and time-consuming bureaucratic procedure.

The same is true for the execution of floggings. After approval was obtained from the relevant authorities, floggings were carried out in the presence of the camp

Direktion
des Fr.-Konz.-Lagers
Ravensbrück

Ravensbrück, den .... 19......

Personalien der Täterin:

(Zu- und Vorname): ....

geb. am .... in ....

Tatbestand: (wann, wo, was, wie?)

hat am .... Uhr ....

Grund der Schutzhaft:	
politisch	....
pol. rückfällig	....
Bibelforscher	....
Rasseschänder	....
Emigrant	....
Ausweisung	....
Berufsverbrecher	....
Asozial	....
....	....
....	....

Strafverfügung!

Gemäß Straffordnung für die Konzentrationslager und Kraft der mir als Lagerdirektor übertragenen Disziplinarstrafgewalt verhänge ich nach reiflicher Prüfung über die Täterin folgende Strafe:

Ordnungsstrafen:

.... Verwarnung unter Androhung einer Bestrafung.

.... Stunden Strafarbeit in der Freizeit unter Aufsicht der Aufseherin ....

Verbot, Privatbriefe zu schreiben oder zu empfangen auf die Dauer von .... Tagen.

Entzug der Mittagskost bei voller Beschäftigung am .... / .... / ....

Entzug sämtlicher Vergünstigungen auf .... Tage, bis auf Weiteres.

Arrest:

Stufe I mittel	Stufe II verschärft
bis zu 3 Tagen	bis zu 42 Tagen
Holzpritsche	
helle Zelle	dunkle Zelle
Verpflegung: Wasser und Brot; jeden 4. Tag volle Verpflegung	
Tage	

Vollzug!

Stufe I
verbüßt vom .... mit ....

Stufe II
verbüßt vom .... mit ....

Ravensbrück, den .... 19......

Der Lagerdirektor

SS-Standartenführer

E/0101

FIGURE 17. Penal order request form from Ravensbrück Women's Concentration Camp

commandant, the chief guard, and a camp physician. There was also an additional form to be filled out.

A flogging entailed between 5 and 25 blows from a stick. Himmler himself had issued instructions on how floggings were to be carried out in the women's camp, and who was authorized to carry them out. Beginning in April 1942, Himmler's instructions specified that, as was the case with male prisoners, floggings of female prisoners were to be administered to naked buttocks.[29] Until 1943, corporal punishment was administered by *Aufseherinnen* assigned to the "cell block building" (as the SS termed it) or the "bunker" (as it was called in prisoner parlance). On July 14, 1943, this process was amended so that henceforth it would no longer be the female guards who administered the floggings; instead, after that point, the prisoners themselves were to carry out the punishment. Polish prisoners were to carry out floggings on Russian prisoners, while Russians were to carry out floggings on Ukrainian and Polish prisoners. The written directive also stated, "Under no circumstances may German inmates be used to administer these punishments. . . . The prisoners who carry out these punishments may be given several cigarettes as a reward."[30] These instructions were part of a deliberate strategy on the part of the SS to solidify its domination by fomenting national, religious, political, social, and "racial" tensions among the prisoners. By pitting the various prisoner factions against one another in a deliberate strategy of "divide and conquer," the SS was more readily able to maintain control over the camp.

There was also a set pattern according to which floggings were to be carried out:

> First, the camp physician examines the prisoner. The physician signs the penal order, indicating whether there are any medical concerns regarding the use of corporal punishment. The penal order (in triplicate) is sent to the Inspector of Concentration Camps, the Reichsführer-SS, and the Head of German Police for approval. After approval is obtained from the Inspector of Concentration Camps, the Reichsführer-SS, and the Head of German Police, the punishment is carried out in the presence of the camp director, the chief guard, and the camp physician. All sign the penal order to confirm the punishment has been carried out in accordance with regulations. The camp director decides whether a limited number of additional witnesses should be present as an audience.[31]

This standardized procedure was intended to ensure that the imposition of punishments was controlled by Berlin and, personally, by Himmler. The procedure served as a form of monitoring by which concentration camp staff could be scrutinized, disciplined, and, where necessary, reprimanded or sanctioned. For the central Oranienburg administration, this was considered a way of ensuring the "productivity" and "efficiency" within the concentration camp system. However, as Dorothea Binz, former head of the Ravensbrück jail, testified during the first Ravensbrück trial in Hamburg in 1946, the official procedure was not always followed. According to Dorothea Binz, Commandant Koegel in the summer of 1940 verbally instructed

Körperliche Züchtigung:

Anzahl der Schläge*)	
5	
10	
15	
20	
25	

*) Anzahl einsetzen

Vorschriften:

Zuvor Untersuchung durch den Arzt! Schläge mit einer einrutigen Lederpeitsche kurz hintereinander verabfolgen, dabei Schläge zählen; Entkleiden und Entblößung gewisser Körperteile streng untersagt. Der zu Bestrafende darf nicht angeschnallt werden, sondern hat frei auf einer Bank zu liegen. Es darf nur auf das Gesäß und die Oberschenkel geschlagen werden.

Der Täter ist bereits körperlich gezüchtigt worden:	
am	Schläge

Ärztliches Gutachten:

Der umseits bezeichnete Häftling wurde vor dem Vollzug der körperlichen Züchtigung von mir ärztlich untersucht; vom ärztlichen Standpunkt aus erhebe ich keine Bedenken gegen die Anwendung der körperlichen Züchtigung.

Gegen die Anwendung der körperlichen Züchtigung erhebe ich als Arzt Bedenken, weil ....

....

Der Lagerarzt:

....

Der Lagerkommandant:

....

Dienstaufsicht:

Der Vollzug der körperlichen Züchtigung wird im Hinblick auf die Tat und gestützt auf das vorliegende ärztliche Gutachten genehmigt – nicht genehmigt.

SS-Wirtschafts-Verwaltungshauptamt
Amtsgruppenchef D
Konzentrationslager

Oranienburg, den .... 194....

Ausführende:

Die Strafe der körperlichen Züchtigung haben folgende Häftlinge am ...., ... Uhr vollzogen.

Name: .... H.-Nr.: ....

" .... " ....

Zeugen und Aufsicht:

Als verantwortliche SS-Führer und Zeugen waren bei dem Strafvollzug zugegen:

eigenhändige Unterschrift

.... Lagerkommandant

.... Schutzhaftlagerführer

.... Lagerarzt

1. Originalverfügung zu den Schutzhaftakten.
2. Abschrift zum Sammelakt: Strafen.
3. Abschrift an Amtsgruppenchef D.

FIGURE 18. Execution of sentence form

Institut für Zeitgeschichte, Fa 183, p. 26

her and the *Aufseherinnen* working in the camp prison to flog unofficially those inmates scheduled for disciplinary action. Only after the punishment was carried out did Koegel obtain official permission from Himmler. This meant that in "several instances," floggings were carried out "before permission was received from the higher level."[32]

However, according to official camp regulations, floggings only happened twice a week, behind closed doors in the camp jail or "cell block building," with the camp commandant, a camp physician, and the chief guard present. Charlotte Müller, Ravensbrück survivor, described the room as follows:

> When our work detail was assigned to do something in the cell block building, we sometimes took a look inside the flogging room. The flogging bench was in the middle of the room. On the right wall, there was a rail with hooks, with a bullwhip and towels hanging on it. The bullwhip was made out of woven leather, and had a strap at the grip. The person administering the whipping would wrap it around her hand, so that she could strike with greater force. There was a pail over at the basin on the other side. The pail was used to pour water on the prisoner if she was whipped into unconsciousness. The water flowed into a drain next to the flogging bench. There was also a bench, with several blankets on it.[33]

Based on Müller's description, it appears the floggings were carried out in a room that had been specially equipped for the purpose. The room was functional, with the equipment lending an air of modernity and professionalism. At the center of the room was the flogging bench, to which the prisoner was trestled at hip height. The prisoner's legs were held in a wood frame, and the upper body was secured with leather straps. There was a drain nearby so that the prisoner's blood, the water that was poured over them, as well as the water used to clean the bench, could all be washed away. The whips had loops on the handles so that the person administering the punishment could get a better grip. Blankets were kept nearby to help muffle the prisoner's screams. According to Jürgen Martschukat, the furnishings and equipment in the room, the construction of the flogging bench, the instruments used for inflicting the flogging, and the arrangements made for the removal of blood all served to communicate the brutality of the punishments and to make visible the physical suffering of the victim.[34] As "professional" work equipment, the flogging bench also had a legitimizing function.

The formalization and attempt at professionalization of the punishment was not intended to reduce physical pain and suffering; rather, it was intended as a means of heightening the agony. The presence of a doctor, as the medical authority who oversaw administration of the flogging, was not meant to preserve the prisoner's health. As physicians virtually never objected to an intended flogging, their assessment was a mere formality that served to legitimize the punishment. According to Germaine Tillion, the official maximum of 25 lashes was often exceeded: "In

Stiftung Brandenburgische Gedenkstätten/Sachsenhausen Archive (Photo: F. Hoffmann)

FIGURE 19. Flogging trestle

Ravensbrück, the standard punishment was 25 lashes, but sometimes it could be 50 or even 70, although not always. When 50 lashes were administered all at once, the victim often died; 75 lashes meant certain death."[35]

All of the concentration camps had a flogging bench, including Majdanek. As Hermann Hackmann, the first camp compound leader, explained in a postwar interrogation:

> In summer 1942, it was discovered during inspections (carried out when prisoners returned to the barracks after work) that letters and so forth were being smuggled into camp by prisoners. That resulted in floggings. In the meantime, a flogging bench had arrived. The commandant applied to Berlin, and the floggings were approved.[36]

According to Hackmann, a block leader used a leather whip to carry out the floggings at Majdanek.[37] Hackmann could no longer remember whether the floggings took place in a special room, or perhaps occurred during roll call before SS or the assembled prisoners. According to the *Aufseherin* Luzie H., by 1943 every field had its own flogging bench: "At the entrance to each gate was the block leader's room, where the prisoners had to lie across the stool, and receive 25 on the ass. They even had to help count the blows."[38] The fact that Luzie H. called the flogging bench a "stool" in Eberhard Fechner's documentary is characteristic of her trivialization and her acceptance of these punishments.

Many Majdanek survivors described the brutality of the floggings. Eugenia Lipinska later recalled having been subjected to a flogging:

> I received 25 blows on my buttocks from the *Aufseherin* Rosa [Reischl]. . . . When all the blocks had assembled, Rosa came into the barracks with a whip. She told us to come out and lift our skirts. Then she administered 25 blows on our buttocks, along with a 26th blow, to our head, using the metal grip of the whip.[39]

Danuta Medryk also reported that the female guards administered the whippings with great force:

> Often the women took turns administering the whippings at the bench. *Aufseherin* Braunsteiner and *Aufseherin* Lächert administered the most punishments. There were major differences in how hard they hit. We preferred to have *Aufseherin* Anni David carry out the punishments. But *Aufseherinnen* Braunsteiner, Lächert, and Orlowski administered the sharpest blows.[40]

At her interrogations before the British military tribunal, the former *Aufseherin* Hertha Ehlert described the practice of punishments in Ravensbrück, and indirectly contrasted it with how they were carried out at Majdanek, Płaszów, and Bergen-Belsen, where she also had been employed:

A[NSWER]: In Ravensbrück, I never witnessed certain things that I saw in other camps. In Ravensbrück, for instance, you could never beat a prisoner publicly; for the slightest offense you had to take a report to the commandant of the camp. . . . I want to add that there were beatings at Ravensbrück, but they were done on orders of Himmler.[41]

In her testimony, Ehlert (who had arrived at Majdanek in January 1943) thus implied that the punishments were administered with greater harshness at Majdanek than at Ravensbrück, and also that, in contrast to Ravensbrück, the female guards and SS men at Majdanek no longer bothered to maintain even a semblance of following the regulations. It is certainly still true, though, that severe punishments were carried out at Ravensbrück, and that a number of "incidents" occurred in the "bunker" there.[42] Space constraints, however, prohibit going into further detail regarding these events.

What distinguishes Majdanek in Ehlert's testimony, though, is the public nature and the apparent routine quality of the violence there.

"Shot While Attempting to Escape"

As in all concentration camps, the guard troops of the SS Death's Head Battalion were responsible for guarding the perimeter of the camp and for accompanying prisoner details assigned to work outside the prisoner camp.[43] As in the case of the *Aufseherinnen* and the male guards, members of the guard battalion were permitted neither to discipline the prisoners on their own authority, nor to abuse or kill them. The Majdanek guard battalions were also required to observe the camp's strict regulations regarding the use of their service weapons, which stated:

> After calling "halt" three times while drawing his weapon, the guard is permitted to shoot under the following circumstances:
>
> During an escape attempt on the part of a prisoner.
>
> A prisoner will be suspected of attempting to escape if he or she leaves the prisoner camp or the workplace without an escort, enters the neutral zone, passes/breaks through the chain of guard posts, or tampers with the camp compound fence.[44]
>
> If a section of prisoners is mutinous or revolting, all supervising guards are ordered to shoot. When the order "everyone lie down" is issued, all prisoners must immediately lie down, facing the ground. Anyone who raises his or her head, thus demonstrating intent to flee, will be immediately shot.
>
> Guards are authorized to shoot without warning: When, unless otherwise ordered, prisoners do not immediately on the sounding of an alarm return to their lodgings and shut the windows and doors. . . .
>
> When any inmate attacks an SS guard, a supervising guard, or other SS superior, threatens them with an object, or intends such an attack. Any attack by a prisoner shall not be subdued with physical force, but with the firearm (self-defense).[45]

Officially, therefore, the female and male guards had only a very limited "license" to kill. Both the guard regulations and training sessions repeatedly emphasized that guards were under order by the WVHA to avoid physical violence.

> All escape attempts must be prevented. Every guard must remain at least 6 steps away from the prisoners. . . . The escort is responsible for guarding the inmates. They also keep an eye on the prisoners' behavior while at work. Only the foreman is permitted to admonish inmates who are sluggish in their work. If the work output is still insufficient, the SS guard should issue a report to the camp compound leader at the end of work, upon return to the camp. Any abuse or threats are strictly forbidden; forcing the inmates to lie down is also considered abuse.[46]

Another training document stated: "Corporal punishment of a prisoner is forbidden," and "When a prisoner is escaping, the guard must call 'halt' three times while drawing his weapon."[47] According to official regulations, the SS Death's Head Battalion guards were only permitted to shoot or resort to physical violence when a guard was being attacked by a prisoner, or when a prisoner was attempting to flee. The requirement that guards remain at a distance of at least six steps from inmates was apparently intended to ensure that they would have enough time to draw their weapon and shoot in an emergency. In any case, this was what the guards were told during training,[48] although it was presumably also intended to prevent the guards from having any direct physical contact with the prisoners. However, the training documents (which also included question and answer sections) also instructed the new recruits as follows:

Q[UESTION]: What must you keep in mind regarding your weapon?
A[NSWER]: That it is our proud right to be permitted to carry a weapon.
Q[UESTION]: And what obligation does this right entail?
A[NSWER]: It obligates us to handle our weapons prudently and with care, but to use them with cold-blooded efficiency if so required.[49]

Although this passage is cautionary in tone, it also confers substantial decision-making authority upon the guards. And, as it was left to each SS man to decide when "prudence" was warranted and when "cold-blooded efficiency" was required, the instructions also confer substantial scope for independent action—and, indeed, an implied duty to act.

According to court testimony provided by Otto Z., a former member of the guard battalion, the guards at Majdanek were not formally trained on their arrival at the camp. Instead, they received "a brief set of instructions from the group leader":[50]

> I don't remember receiving any training when I arrived at Majdanek. It was clear that we were intended to shoot without warning in the event of an escape attempt. . . . Well, we were to shoot first, and call out a warning afterwards. In the Reich, we were supposed to call "halt" three times before shooting. That must have been the rule at Majdanek, too. But on the outside work details at Majdanek, as far as I remember, we shot first.[51]

Although there was a staff member who was charged with training activities, severe personnel shortages meant that no regular evening sessions were held for the guard troops.[52] When he arrived at Majdanek in late fall 1942, Otto Z. was assigned to the "forest detachment":[53]

> There were about 5 or 6 Ukrainians in my guard unit. The Unterführer was also Ukrainian. The Ukrainians always had alcohol with them and they were quite drunk.

> I can no longer remember whether they used sticks or the butts of their guns, but they hit a Jew who was standing next to a pit and told him to run away. The Jew ran away from the pit. About three Ukrainians then shot the Jew from behind as he ran, at a distance of about 10 or 15 meters. . . . The Ukrainian Unterführer told other Jews to retrieve him. . . . I saw that he was still alive. The Ukrainian Unterführer took a gun and shot the Jew in the head, I think from behind, and then he was dead. . . . They unloaded the body in the camp. I don't know what happened to it afterwards. I went to the records barracks and submitted a report on a pre-printed form. The report was called "Report of a Death or Escape." Naturally, the report also contained an entry for: "Prisoners shot while attempting to escape." You just recorded the number, in writing, and signed the form. The forms were available in the records office.[54]

As the testimony by Otto Z. suggests, in daily practice, the designation "shot while attempting to escape" served as a means of disguising killings that had been ordered and carried out without official sanction.

According to Hermann Hackmann, the former first camp compound leader, informal rules of confidentiality in shootings ensured that "only persons who were directly involved were aware of them."[55] It is unknown whether the murder described by Otto Z. was carried out by the Ukrainian guards on their own initiative, or whether it might have been carried out at the behest of a secret order by the commandant. In any case, his description shows how easy it was to cover up the shooting of a Jewish prisoner. "The actual course of events wasn't part of the written report. The form just had an entry for 'shot while attempting to escape' and a space for the prisoner's number,"[56] as Otto Z. recalled in his testimony. In other words, the official documentation of a shooting served the same purpose as the documentation given to female guards at the Ravensbrück training camp, and the administrative documentation of corporal punishments: it served to cast a veneer of lawfulness and legitimacy over the guards' actions; indeed, that may have been its main purpose.

In Majdanek, as in other concentration camps, arbitrary killings of inmates were classified, after the fact, as escape attempts in order to avoid investigations into the deaths, or what the camp staff referred to as "hassle." This widespread practice made it relatively simple for the camp SS to conceal the murder of inmates. However, this presumed that colleagues would also play along. In order for the cover-up to succeed, no other staff could make a report, and the camp commandant had to be willing to ignore the matter. At times, SS men deliberately provoked escape attempts for entertainment and to relieve boredom, or—as the survivor Jerzy Kwiatowski later recalled—to obtain the five extra vacation days that were awarded for preventing an escape attempt. Kwiatowski also recounted a detail that the former SS guards failed to mention in their later interrogations:

> Inmates who wanted to commit suicide to escape the terrible conditions in the camp but who lacked the courage to throw themselves against the fence did this by

> walking slowly toward the fence until one of the SS men, the guards in the towers, shot and killed them. For every inmate shot in this way, the SS men received up to 5 days' holiday.[57]

In Eberhard Fechner's documentary, the former *Aufseherin* Luzie H. described what she saw one morning on her way to work: "Early in the morning, the dead bodies of the escaped prisoners who tried to climb over the fence were lying on the path, or hanging from the electric fence."[58]

Disciplinary Proceedings against Female Guards and SS Men at Majdanek

It was the commandant who punished violations of camp regulations on the part of camp staff. Here, it is important to keep in mind that violations only made their way into the official record when they were reported or addressed. The commandant was supported by the so-called "court officers" (*Gerichtsführer*). One of the court officers at Majdanek, who served from spring to fall 1943, was SS Hauptsturmführer Ernst F. He was responsible for conducting investigations into accusations of embezzlement, theft, bribery, and similar offenses. His second official function was to investigate unnatural deaths. It was his responsibility to order autopsies and open official investigations.[59] However, as Ernst F. explained in his 1973 testimony, his main task was to investigate misdoings by guards. Lesser offenses, such as failing to observe the curfew, were handled by the guard's immediate superior.[60] In more serious violations, Ernst F. led the investigation, interrogating both the accused and any witnesses. In order for this to happen, though, an official "case" had to be opened, which meant that a report had been filed. The results of the investigation were then sent to the commandant, who reported the findings to Berlin and decided what sanctions to impose:

> I remember three important cases that I worked on. In one case, an SS Unterführer was accused of having broken into the home of a Polish family while drunk, where he was said to have harassed the women, among other things. In another case, an SS Oberscharführer was accused of having stolen gold or some other valuable. The man committed suicide during the investigation. The third case involved my clerk. As sometimes happened, he had been assigned to guard one of the larger prisoner transports. Sometimes we didn't have enough guards and then the clerks were called in as reinforcements. In one such instance, my clerk took valuables the prisoners had hidden on their persons. I can't remember any further details of the case. The man was dismissed from his position as clerk and punished. As far as I can remember, I was never assigned any investigations that had to do with any actions taken by the SS within the actual prisoners' camp. . . . I also can't remember ever interrogating a prisoner.[61]

During the investigation, the presiding judge asked Ernst F. whether the court leader was also responsible for investigating inmate killings, including hangings, shootings, fatal beatings, drownings, and gassings, all of which were commonplace at Majdanek. Ernst F. stated, in reply: "I have to say, this question is absurd. Anyone with any understanding of how things worked at the time would know that it's completely unthinkable that actions of that nature would have resulted in court or disciplinary proceedings."[62] Although Ernst F. certainly intended his statement as a form of self-defense, it does highlight the fact that SS staff never for a moment considered the possibility that inmate killings would be investigated and punished.

The following list of female guards who had been sanctioned illustrates the manner in which penalties at Majdanek were imposed. On December 28, 1943, Himmler sent a telex to all concentration camps that included women's sections, ordering them to send a report to Oranienburg describing "how many *Aufseherinnen* have been punished in the concentration camps, and for which offenses."[63] Majdanek returned the following report:

Aufseherinnen who have been punished at the Lublin FKL (Women's Concentration Camp)

Last Name	First Name	Date of birth	Date of Hiring
D.	Helene	6 Nov. 11	15 Apr. 1940 (dismissed)
Theft of Reich Property.		3 months' jail.	
Heise	Gertrud	23 Jul. 21	16 Oct. 1942
Guard violation.		5 days' heightened detention.	
Lächert	Hildegard	19 Mar. 20	1 Apr. 1942 (dismissed)
Curfew violation exceeded by 15 hours.		5 days' heightened detention.	
Loss of service weapon.		8 days' heightened detention.	
H.	Elisabeth	19 Jul. 21	1 Jun. 43
Danz	Luise	11 Dec. 17	1 Mar. 43
Mayer Nee Wöllert	Charlotte	7 Feb. 18	15 Sep. 41
Z.	Elfriede	20 Jan. 22	1 Jun. 43
Brückner	Hermine	26 Apr. 18	16 Oct. 42
Pfannstiel	Erna	10 Feb. 22	1 May 41
Failure to follow an order.		Stern reprimand.	
David	Anna	1 Aug. 21	16 Oct. 42
Failure to follow an order.		Stern reprimand.	
Injury of an inmate resulting in death due to negligent use of service weapon.[64]		5 days light detention.	

As this document shows, the penalty for "theft of Reich property" was three months' jail, while a female guard's "negligent killing" of a prisoner with her service revolver merited only five days' "light detention."[65] Failure to follow an order resulted only in a stern reprimand.

At Majdanek, as in other camps, thefts were severely punished.[66] A number of SS men at Majdanek were arrested for receiving stolen goods. In early 1943, Field Leader Fritz Petrick was arrested for the first time and sentenced to one month's detention. In summer 1943, he was again accused of embezzlement and misappropriation of property:[67]

> In June 1943, I was arrested for misappropriation of property. . . . I was held at the jail in Lublin Castle until February 1944. . . . Then I was sent to Buchenwald for a court proceeding. In March 1944, I was sent to the SS penal camp at Dachau. I remained there until late 1944 and was then sent to an SS and Police probation unit.[68]

The SS and police court adjudicated "serious" offenses, which included "theft of Reich property."[69] For example, on March 23, 1944, the SS and police court of Kassel convicted Fritz Petrick of "repeated military theft, repeated professional and habitual receiving of stolen goods, and repeated currency violations." He was fined and sentenced to 3.5 years in the penitentiary.[70]

A guard in the battalion met a similar fate. As already mentioned, at the time of their wedding in March 1944, Erna Pfannstiel's fiancé was being held in investigative custody in Lublin on theft charges.[71] In a 1965 interrogation, Pfannstiel confirmed that her husband Georg had been transferred to Weimar in 1944, where an SS court sentenced him to three years in jail.[72] The severity of his punishment clearly demonstrates where the disciplinary priorities lay. Even the highest ranks of the camp SS were subject to disciplinary proceedings. For example, both Karl Koch and Hermann Hackmann were brought before SS courts in response to their actions in conjunction with the mass escape of Soviet prisoners of war, described earlier.[73]

The investigation of Commandant Karl Koch and Hermann Hackmann, the first camp compound leader, for "negligent release of prisoners" was launched in summer 1942.[74] The accusation rested on the many errors made during the search for the escaped prisoners, as well as the behavior of the SS men, who had violated numerous regulations during the incident. However, the subsequent execution of the prisoners of war who had remained in the camp was not part of the investigation. It was determined by the investigative commission that the guard troops had been inadequately trained, and also, because they had not been issued machine pistols, that they were poorly equipped.[75] According to the final report issued by the SS and Police Court IV of Krakow, the guard unit initially believed that just fifteen prisoners of war had escaped, rather than the actual eighty-six, and as a result failed to undertake the necessary actions in their response. In fact, it was not until 3 A.M. the following morning that it became clear that eighty-six prisoners had escaped.[76] According to the court and the administrative division, the higher SS leaders—meaning the commandant and the first camp compound leader—had failed in their duties. In the end, only Koch and Hackmann were disciplined.[77] Koch was relieved of his post as commandant in late July 1942. In late September 1942, Hackmann was transferred to the SS "Prince Eugen" volunteer division in occupied Yugoslavia.[78]

Just two years later, both men were again under investigation by an SS and police court. However, as the charge of "negligent release of prisoners" had been dropped for lack of evidence in February 1943, this second investigation had nothing to do with the escape of Soviet POWs from Majdanek. Rather, Karl Koch and Hermann Hackmann were convicted on several counts of theft committed while at the Buchenwald and Majdanek concentration camps. For these charges, each was sentenced to death.[79] The SS court in Kassel sentenced Karl Koch to death in December 1944; he was executed in April 1945.[80] In June 1944, in Kassel, Hermann Hackmann was sentenced to death; his sentence, however, was later commuted to a prison sentence. He was sent to the SS penal camp at Dachau on July 1, 1944, and in early 1945 was sent to a combat unit in the vicinity of Munich; that April, he was captured by the U.S. military.[81] Hermann Florstedt, who served as Koch's adjutant at Buchenwald and who was appointed commandant of Majdanek in November 1942, was also tried for embezzlement and misappropriation of property before an SS court and sentenced to death. Whether the verdict against Florstedt was carried out is unknown.[82]

Individual Agency, Superior Orders, and Obedience

For the WVHA in Oranienburg—as well as for Himmler himself—the priority was to ensure that the concentration camps were operated in an "efficient" and "orderly manner" by reliable and obedient staff. Arbitrary and unauthorized acts of violence toward the inmates were seen as "disruptive" to this orderly operation. In reality, however, official regulations were often disregarded during the day-to-day supervision and discipline of camp inmates.

Though not always implemented in practice, the many official regulations and admonishments issued by the WVHA must be understood as more than a mere "bureaucratic sham," as Wolfgang Sofsky has called them.[83] Rather, they indicate a conflict of interest between the concentration camp staff, on the one hand, and the central administration in Oranienburg, on the other—a conflict that itself demonstrates the existence of a certain scope for agency among concentration camp staff "on the ground." In his study of the mentality of the SS, Hans Buchheim distinguished between the commandants of the concentration camps, and the "professional ideologues" of the central SS administration.[84] With its regular inspections and letters of admonishment, the WVHA sought to assert its authority and prevent undue autonomy at the concentration camps. To maintain discipline over camp staff and to ensure that the violence carried out was conducted according to prescribed methods, Himmler and the central administration in Oranienburg retained decision-making authority over every corporal punishment carried out at the concentration camps. Ensuring the smooth operation of the camps and enforcing discipline among the staff took on an ever-greater importance following the expansion of the camp system in the East (1939), the systematic murder of European Jews (1942–1944), and the expansion of SS economic activities (which peaked in 1943–1945). However, the WVHA's "managerial" efforts to enforce discipline by establishing a militarized setting, and by issuing detailed service regulations that governed work and leisure in the camps, could not always be enforced as intended.

As we have seen, there was substantial room for maneuver between the meticulously spelled-out camp and penal regulations and the daily practice of work and punishment at the camps. As analysis of the day-to-day work practices at Majdanek has demonstrated, camp staff were subject to a detailed set of policies and rules that outlined exactly how the inmates were to be treated. Despite these social and institutional constraints, however, camp staff had substantial leeway to interpret and apply the rules and regulations as each saw fit. In their day-to-day duties, the camp staff had ample opportunity to exercise their own authority and to subvert regulations, in further demonstration of what Alf Lüdtke has described as "Eigen-Sinn." The *Aufseherinnen* and SS men varied in the extent to which they took advantage of the leeway available to them. As we have seen, rather than simply administer the prescribed 25 lashes, a female guard might add an extra one for good measure; nor was one whipping exactly like the next, since *Aufseherinnen* were free to choose how vigorously to administer the blows. At the same time, the highly bureaucratic and strictly regulated administration of corporal punishment created a formal framework that in a sense protected the perpetrators by providing a veneer of legality and legitimacy. In this sense, the camp staff's obedience, and belief in the legitimacy of their actions, was more than simply the product of orders issued "from above." Rather, it was produced and reinforced through the exercise of their day-to-day duties in the camp.[85]

However, highly regulated and standardized penalties, such as floggings, were by no means the most prevalent form of violence in the camps. Rather, violence and abuse ranged from the carrying out of "official" penalties, to routine brutal treatment of inmates that was without penal intent, to random "spontaneous" acts of abuse.[86] An examination of the concrete practices of violence and discipline in the camps demonstrates that the boundary between arbitrary brutality and officially sanctioned and controlled violence cannot be neatly drawn. Rather, in daily practice the various forms of violence tended to merge, shifting between sanctioned violence and arbitrary brutality. When viewed in this light, then, the "controlled" violence prescribed in the service and penal regulations and the "routine" violence meted out by the guards on their own initiative are not contradictions, but, rather, indicative of a dynamic in which normative and arbitrary authority coexisted. It is important to keep in mind, too, that any prohibition and any rule always bears within it the possibility and the pleasure of its own transgression. In this sense, then, the threat of disciplinary action could potentially heighten the pleasure accorded by any such transgression. Despite strict regulations and a prohibition against killing and abuse, the majority of *Aufseherinnen* and SS guards wielded their authority with great arbitrariness and cruelty.

As an analysis of actual and alleged escape attempts by Majdanek prisoners demonstrates, arbitrary enforcement—and even subversion of camp regulations—was a daily reality of the guards' work in the camps. Indeed, it is likely that these practices had their roots in the earliest days of the Nazi concentration camps, beginning with the SS men trained under Eicke at the "Dachau school" and spreading to the entire network of concentration camps.[87] The commandants and higher SS leadership, many of whom had first met at Dachau, embraced an atmosphere that promoted violence with impunity in the camps. For example, the designation "shot while attempting to escape" served as carte blanche for legitimizing and, essentially, "legalizing" arbitrary killings by SS staff. Given that the punishment of prisoners even at Ravensbrück, located just a few kilometers from WVHA headquarters, was not always carried out in accordance with regulations, it comes as little surprise that penal practices at Majdanek, located at a distance of several days' travel from Berlin, were even more "relaxed." As the former guard Otto Z. noted in a later interrogation, at Majdanek no one bothered to notice "when a block leader killed a prisoner by shooting him or beating him to death. The death rate in the camp was very high."[88]

Here, again, it is worth revisiting the occasion of the mass escape of Soviet prisoners of war from Majdanek.[89] In that incident, described in an earlier chapter, Commandant Karl Koch acted on his own initiative when he ordered the killing of those Soviet POWs who had remained in the camp. This action was not required by any existing regulation for guarding prisoners, or any administrative order. Hermann Hackmann, the first camp compound leader, conveyed the order to unspecified SS men from the guard battalion and headquarters staff. Actions later claimed by Hermann Hackmann, Fritz Petrick, and other participants to have been carried out under their "duty to follow orders" were, in reality, undertaken with far less duress than they claimed in their interrogations.

Of course, the camp staff did not have completely free rein to act on its own authority. As Hans Buchheim noted in his report about the 1964 Auschwitz trial, superior officers issued orders with absolute authority and required absolute obedience. This structure prohibited any critical reflection on the part of the camp staff.[90] Despite the conditions of duress, for the SS staff, obedience was not a life-or-death matter. To date, no instance has been found in which an SS man or an *Aufseherin* was punished with death for failing to carry out an order. Rather, as the disciplinary report compiled for the Majdanek female guards illustrates, *Aufseherinnen* who failed to follow orders were subject only to verbal reprimand. Moreover, the duty to obey, as described in the military penal code, applied only to orders of a military nature—not to orders that violated the German penal code; even at that time, murder was a violation of the German penal code.[91]

Moreover, military structures are not synonymous with total obedience. Although camp staff were subject to the orders of their superiors, they in fact possessed considerable scope for independent action. Their military role and their position within the camp hierarchy not only served as a constraint to action, but also offered opportunities for independent action. As was true for soldiers in the Wehrmacht, when it came to the concentration camps, the officials issuing the orders were located far from where the orders were ultimately received.[92] Thus, in many cases, it was left to the recipients of the orders to decide when and how to implement any instructions. For this reason, the orders received by camp staff did not merely serve to dictate or to limit their actions; rather, they also served as an impetus and an empowerment to act. As Alf Lüdtke has emphasized, expectations of obedience on the part of superiors are not always "seamlessly internalized" by subordinates.[93] For example, orders by a superior can also be anticipated or expanded upon. Thus, the concept of obedience has many faces; among other things, it may entail a zealous and preemptive anticipation of superior orders.

The autonomous actions by the recipients of these orders, and their "Eigen-Sinn" in adapting those orders to their own wants and needs, point to the unstable boundaries of authoritarian organizations and institutions, and also illustrate the influence of group dynamics. When the criminal chamber of the Düsseldorf regional courts later asked Hertha Ehlert whether female guards could refuse to take part in a selection or a flogging, she replied that an *Aufseherin* always had the option of "avoiding a task she could not reconcile with her conscience." Ehlert added, however: "That could lead to a bit of aggravation, which is also what happened to me."[94] Here, Ehlert was referring to the mocking remarks she endured from the camp SS. In a later testimony, Ehlert confirmed to the court that the female guards did have some leeway in refusing to follow orders, but added, "I'm not aware of any cases in which someone refused to follow an order."[95] Nonconformist behavior could mean exclusion from the group, or draw teasing and mockery from fellow camp staff or superiors. Thus, the extent to which the *Aufseherinnen* took advantage of the leeway available to them depended on their willingness to risk rejection by their colleagues and peers.

10

Violence as Social Practice

According to sociologist Albert Scherr, physical violence is an act whereby the perpetrator "communicates something about himself or herself, about his or her relationship to the victim and, finally, may also be addressing a third party."[1] Although the female guards and SS men who worked at the concentration camps were clearly in a position of superiority over the prisoners, they were themselves embedded within a system of complex relationships alternating between power and dependency. The *Aufseherinnen* and SS men exerted violence over the prisoners and power over their coworkers, rendering them not only the agents, but also the recipients of power. Even when they were able to evade or ignore such behaviors, or to remain passive in the face of them, they had no choice but to interact with one another.

To explain the massive use of physical violence at Majdanek, then, we must also address the relationships at work between the SS staff at the camp. The "vulnerable" (*verletzungsoffene*) bodies of the prisoners occupy the center of a "field of force" that encompasses the complex and multivalent links between the female guards, their male colleagues and superiors, and the prisoners, both within and between each group.[2] As historian of everyday life Alf Lüdtke points out, such a "field of force" is not a static entity. Rather, it serves both to enable and to place limits upon the actions of the individual, while at the same time regulating the behavior of those who do not act.[3] In this sense, the "field of force" fluctuates, based on the actions of those who operate within it.

On the Practice and Function of Slaps, Kicks, and Verbal Invective

According to prisoner reports and courtroom testimony, the most frequent forms of violence employed by guards at Majdanek were slaps and verbal insults, followed by kicks. In the testimony of survivors, slaps rained down upon them constantly, meted out by both the SS men and the *Aufseherinnen*. To examine this phenomenon, I will first consider the actions of Hermine Braunsteiner in her day-to-day work, initially at the Ravensbrück concentration camp and, later, at the Majdanek women's camp.

From May 1941 to October 1942, Hermine Braunsteiner was in charge of the clothing room at Ravensbrück, where she supervised a labor detachment with twenty prisoners, the majority of whom were political prisoners from Austria. The detachment was responsible for distributing clothing and shoes to their fellow prisoners, under the supervision and direction of the *Aufseherin*. In 1949, a survivor of Ravensbrück recalled procedures followed in the clothing room to the Vienna regional court:

> Because of my painful feet, I wasn't able to walk with the wood slippers they gave us, so I went to the room to ask if I could get a pair of shoes instead of the wood slippers. A lot of prisoners were lined up there already and of course it wasn't a perfectly straight line. When the defendant came out, she wasn't able to pass by us. So she fished an old Polish woman out of the line for herself, and hit her until she fell over, and then she kicked her, too. . . . I had to go there twice to exchange clothing from the infirmary, and several times I saw her hit women who were old enough to be her mother, slap them until the blood flowed from their nose and mouth. . . . All that needed to happen was for someone to block her way, or for her to be in a bad mood.[4]

For the prisoners, the availability of clothing and shoes was a matter of life or death. As survivor Viktoria Filler later recalled for the Vienna court, there was always a crowd in front of the clothing room:

> When I arrived at the clothing room, the defendant suddenly came out, and kicked me so hard that I fell over. She needed more room, and because I was standing there, she took the opportunity to give me a kick. . . . The defendant was quite nervous most of the time, and whenever she came out, she needed a lot of space.[5]

For her part, Braunsteiner justified her use of violence as a disciplinary measure and as a legitimate means of maintaining order. She described the distribution of clothing as a "frenzied" affair, in which the prisoners bickered amongst themselves over the clothing, saying that "getting rough" and "stepping in" were often necessary in order to maintain control:[6]

> When the prisoners came in for new shoes that was the worst. . . . Then, some of the people made such a fuss that there was nothing else I could do but give them a swat on the head, just to break up the arguments between the prisoners. . . . I never imagined I would be called into account for a few swats on the head, because I was much too young for the job I was doing.[7]

The *Aufseherinnen*, who occupied the bottom rung in the SS hierarchy, were at all times subject to the orders of their superiors. However, while guarding the labor detachments, overseeing roll calls, inspecting the blocks, and carrying out other daily duties, they themselves were in command of the prisoners. It is clear that, as far as Braunsteiner was concerned, slaps were a legitimate and comparatively harmless form of punishment.

As Alf Lüdtke has shown, slaps are a "conventional" and socially acceptable means of reprimand—a "minor" form of violence that is, in reality, far more harmful than it might at first appear.[8] A slap, first of all, is an expression of a difference in status between the person who issues the slap and the person who receives it. Slaps are generally issued from a position of "superiority" to a position of "inferiority"—an adult, therefore, might slap a child. In addition, a slap always has a symbolic quality, even when it takes place outside the view of others, or when it purports to be a "knee jerk" response of an unpremeditated nature. When directed at an adult woman, a slap is both a form of infantilization and humiliation. From a social point of view, slaps to the face must be seen as a tool of domination, an effort on the part of the aggressor to claim power and dominance.

Often, the female guards were supervising the prisoners as they carried out tasks in which the prisoners had greater expertise than did the *Aufseherinnen* themselves. This implies that physical violence toward the prisoners may also have represented an attempt to compensate for their own lack of knowledge and competence—an effort to assert authority over the prisoners. With physical violence, the *Aufseherinnen* demonstrated their ability to infantilize and subjugate "their" prisoners every day anew, as when Braunsteiner hit and kicked her way through the crowd. The female guards' use of violence was a demonstration of their own superiority, made manifest. This demonstration, however, was not directed solely at the victim; it was also directed at the other prisoners, who were meant to be intimidated by the show of violence. Here, it is important to remember that in the labor detachments it was typically just one *Aufseherin* (usually armed with a weapon) who was charged with supervising a large number of prisoners. As Edith W. recalled in a later interrogation:

> My detachment in the clothing works was made up of about 100 prisoners. I can't remember if any male guards were there too. I didn't have a gun, nor did I have a

> truncheon or anything like that. . . . If the prisoners had banded together, I would have been defenseless against them.[9]

From the point of view of the female guards, the use of beatings and other forms of physical violence served as an instrument to establish order and prevent insubordination. In reality, however, it was the combined effect of the disastrous living conditions, the inner workings of the concentration camp, and the guards' arbitrary violent outbursts that together served to subjugate the prisoners and suppress even the smallest attempt at resistance.[10]

Social factors and social distinctions also played a significant role in the expression and escalation of violence within the camp. This was also true within the inmate community, where political prisoners and members of the European middle and upper classes were forced into a proximity with so-called "career criminals" and "asocials" that would have been unthinkable under previous circumstances. In any case, daily interactions between the *Aufseherinnen* and the inmates were rife with social conflicts and distinctions. Until the evacuation of the concentration camps in the East, the female guards in Ravensbrück mainly oversaw prisoners from Western Europe. Of these, a majority were women from Germany and Austria, as well as some from the Netherlands (many of whom also spoke German). At Majdanek, by contrast, the inmates were mainly from Eastern Europe. The German and Austrian political prisoners in Ravensbrück, and the German-speaking Jewish and Polish prisoners at Majdanek were often better educated than the *Aufseherinnen* who guarded them, another fact that also led to tension. At Ravensbrück, political prisoners often tried to take advantage of their social status to intimidate the female guards and subvert the relationships of dominance that defined the camp hierarchy.[11] Some *Aufseherinnen* could be manipulated through these means, while others refused to respond to these tactics. Often, disparities in social and educational status between the prisoners and the female guards, most of whom came from modest backgrounds, served to heighten the potential for conflict and increased the likelihood that the *Aufseherinnen* would resort to violence.

Personal accounts and court testimony by former political prisoners also make evident the pervasive sense of cultural and political superiority they felt vis-à-vis the *Aufseherinnen*. For example, Charlotte Müller, a political inmate and communist, offered the following description of the Ravensbrück guards:

> As fanatical Nazi supporters, they didn't see the concentration camp prisoners as human, and as women with very primitive thought processes and a low educational level, they sensed the moral and intellectual superiority of the political prisoners, and so they took special care to persecute them with extreme rage—to prove their mastery over them.[12]

The political prisoners and other prisoners from the educated middle and upper classes tended to view slapping a grown woman in the face as a "primitive" behavior that was a sign of weakness. The former political prisoners who testified at the Vienna regional court also regarded Hermine Braunsteiner's tendency toward violence less as an expression of power and authority than as an expression of moodiness or "nerves."[13] Given that these interpretations were being offered at a criminal trial, such attempts to psychologize Braunsteiner's behavior have the effect of minimizing, somewhat, her responsibility for her own actions. Indeed, ascribing a lack of self-control to one's former tormenters is a common topos for both men and women. But this ascription can also be seen in a different light—that is, as a survival strategy that enables the victimized to live with the humiliation they experienced. By disparaging the perpetrators of the violence, and discrediting them on an intellectual and social level, the victim can redeem the past experience of physical inferiority through a present-day social and intellectual superiority. For the victims, the slaps and blows experienced at the hands of the *Aufseherinnen* were anything but trivial. Indeed, a slap to the face had a painful and terrorizing effect.

In his essay on torture, Jean Améry described the effect of blows to the face as follows:

> Even a sudden joyful surprise is felt; for the physical pain is not at all unbearable. The blows that descend upon us have, above all, an objective spatial and acoustical quality: spatial insofar as the prisoner who is being struck in the face and on the head has the impression that the room and all the visible objects in it are shifting position; acoustical, because he believes to hear a dull thundering, which finally submerges in a general roaring. The blow acts as its own anesthetic. A feeling of pain that would be comparable to a violent toothache or the pulsating burning of a festering wound does not emerge.[14]

For Jean Améry, the meaning of the first blow at the hands of the police official in his interrogation was less the immediate sensation of pain than it was a warning of everything that was to follow.

In Ravensbrück and Majdanek as well, every slap to the face represented a similar threat. In most cases, the first blow was not the last of it, and any slap had the potential to end in a deadly rain of physical abuse. In that sense, then, even a single slap brought with it the risk of death.

Within the context of the concentration camp, violence as basic as a slap in the face was laden with import and semantic meaning. According to the witnesses at the Vienna trial, at Ravensbrück Hermine Braunsteiner was particularly violent toward Polish and Jewish women—that is, the women who, because they occupied the bottom rung of the Nazi prisoner hierarchy, had the least power. Braunsteiner's penchant for abusing older women also signaled to the prisoners that she would show no mercy toward even the elderly or the infirm. With a single blow, Braunsteiner demonstrated that all social and cultural boundaries and restraints had been crossed.

In addition, a slap to the face made the humiliation and powerlessness of the victim visible and tangible—not just to the victim but also to other prisoners who witnessed it. The slaps meted out by Braunsteiner were perceived by the prisoners as a shameful humiliation, whether experienced on their own bodies, or merely as bystanders.

Like Lucia Schmidt-Fels, many survivors later reported that they were more traumatized by the violence they witnessed than by that they experienced directly.

> But—as I often experienced later in the camp [Ravensbrück]: one generally suffers more in empathy than due to one's own suffering. That is why they [the Gestapo, in interrogations] preferred to torture a loved one right before your eyes, for example a son before the eyes of his mother. . . . In the camp, I was also beaten and abused, but I suffered more deeply when I had to witness this happening to others. You experience the helplessness of the other person, and at the same time you feel shame on behalf of the abuser, that he is demeaning his own humanity with kicks in that way. . . . As the abuses continued, the pain was blunted a bit, a pain that was felt even more strongly emotionally than physically, but whenever I saw one of my comrades being abused, the tears came to my eyes immediately.[15]

In Eberhard Fechner's documentary, a Majdanek survivor recalled a similar feeling, but in even more acute detail:

> For the prisoners, daily life was so dreadful that sometimes death was preferable to living. And here before the court, we testify about selections and the specific cases of murder, but we don't testify that every prisoner experienced his own death many times over.[16]

At Majdanek, Braunsteiner not only beat the prisoners more frequently than she had at Ravensbrück; she also hit them harder: "On two occasions, she hit me so hard that my eyebrow and, later, my cheek, were ripped open," survivor Janina Rawska-Bot later reported.[17]

Likewise, Eugenia Lipinska recalled: "Braunsteiner once hit me in the face. As she did that, she asked me, 'You pig, why are you [*Du*] laughing?' She hit me with her hand, hard, on my cheek."[18] This episode illustrates how verbal and physical violence comingled. Setting aside the larger question of the reciprocal relationship between verbal and physical violence, there is one further point that bears mention. Under ordinary circumstances, the use of "Du" toward an adult—that is, use of the informal mode of address in German—signals a familial, friendly, or collegial relationship, and is an expression of a mutual appreciation of the closeness of this relationship, indicating a certain agreed-upon familiarity.[19] By contrast, however, Braunsteiner's use of the informal "Du" signals her sense of superiority and her disdain for the prisoners. Austrian survivors who had been political prisoners at Ravensbrück recalled Braunsteiner's exceptional penchant for verbal abuse, mentioning her use of phrases they connoted as particularly "Reich German," including "stupid" (*blöd*), "you pruned eel" (*Du bestutzter Aal*), "slag" (*Schlampe*), and "dirty pig" (*Drecksau*),[20] though the latter term was also described as equally Viennese in origin. At Majdanek, insulting and abusive language toward the prisoners by all of the *Aufseherinnen* was the order of the day.[21]

Many of the female guards at Majdanek used whips and sticks to hit prisoners, in part to reduce the risk of contagion that might result from physical contact:[22] "The *Aufseherinnen* were afraid to touch prisoners. They always spoke of the 'mangy Jewesses.'"[23] The use of implements made the blows harder, and represented an added humiliation. "They beat the prisoners just like animals,"[24] Stanislaw Chwiejczak later recalled before the court. Lola Givner, who arrived at Majdanek in May 1943, recalled the following encounter with Hermine Braunsteiner:

> "Kobyla" [Braunsteiner] was tall, she kicked prisoners, and she practically ran over them. "Kobyla" kicked me and I still have the scars to prove it. That happened to me more than once. She walked through the barracks or the field. Whenever someone was standing in her way, she would raise her foot and kick her. What happened to me was this: I encountered her in the field and I couldn't get out of her way quickly enough. She kicked me so hard that I fell over. As I was lying there on the ground, she kept kicking me. First, when I was standing, she kicked me on my back, so I fell on my stomach. Then she kept kicking me, until she went away and left me lying there.[25]

For the victim, kicks constituted an even greater degradation than slaps. A kick is a gesture of contempt. For example, a dog might perhaps be kicked, but never a person. Even more than a slap to the face, a kick signals the lack of symmetry between the agent of violence and her victim. In the incident just described, the victim is lying on the floor, while the *Aufseherin* is standing over her. Essentially, Braunsteiner uses her leather boots as weapons. The boots protect her from injury while at the same time helping her to avoid direct physical contact with the victim.[26] For the victim, the increased force of the impact heightens the risk of severe injury. Braunsteiner's kicks were carefully aimed, targeted at particularly sensitive parts of the body such as the stomach, the lower abdomen, and the back. During her tenure at Majdanek, kicks became Braunsteiner's "trademark," earning her the nickname "Kobyla" (the mare).[27]

Not all the *Aufseherinnen* struck the prisoners as frequently, or as hard, as did Braunsteiner. Emilie Macha was given the nickname "Mutti" (mama). According to Bronislawa Ulasowa, "She used vulgar expressions, but she had a good heart."[28] In the Majdanek trial, a number of survivors described Hermine Brückner as a "good" or a "humane" *Aufseherin*. She was given the nickname "Perelka" (Polish for "little pearl"). As Nechama Frenkel recalled, "When she was in charge of roll call, we knew that no blood would flow that day."[29] In Maria Kaufmann-Krasowska's description, "Perelka was one of the better ones; she may have been the most decent of them. Those last two [Macha and Brückner] were still somewhat human, even though they did hit us now and again."[30] Another survivor, Barbara Steiner, recalled Brückner as follows:

> She was a good person. In the case of Perelka, I remember the following event: She brought us to some place where we had to work. It was terribly cold and we weren't wearing much in the way of clothes. Also, most of the girls were sick and hungry. So Perelka told us we should stand close to each other to stay warm. She put three women in each corner to keep watch and warn us if any other SS member was headed our way.[31]

Many of the prisoners also described Charlotte Wöllert as comparatively good-natured: "We always tried to walk on the same side as *Aufseherin* Mayer [Wöllert], because she didn't hit as hard as the other female guards.[32] However, these descriptions must be understood within the context of the immense daily violence and brutality meted out by the *Aufseherinnen.* As Danuta Medryk explained to the Düsseldorf regional court, "What I describe as 'ordinary' behavior for the women means that they walked through our ranks and hit us, just not in a particularly targeted or sadistic way."[33] In other words, when it came to the female guards, the prisoners set the bar extremely low in terms of their expectations for humane treatment.

Interestingly enough, in postwar testimony the *Aufseherinnen* recalled circumstances in which they had *not* felt called upon to kill or mete out physical abuse as having been comparatively privileged situations. Hertha Ehlert, for example, described the laundry detachment as "one of the quietest and nicest detachments. The others envied me because of it. In our detachment, there were no beatings, nor were other cruelties meted out."[34] As a statement made to the court, this was most certainly intended as a form of self-defense; by extension, however, it demonstrates the ubiquity of violence, and illustrates how violence was accepted as a matter of course. The laundry at Majdanek was located near the old crematorium, which Ehlert said was in constant operation.[35] The laundry was also located across from the gas chambers, where laundry was taken for delousing (see figure 12).[36] As Alice Orlowski confirmed in her testimony, the laundry was a "highly sought-after post."[37] "It was quiet there; I didn't see or hear anything," Ehlert said. "It was pleasant there, to the extent that anything can be pleasant in a concentration camp."[38] For Ehlert, an *Aufseherin* who was described as a "nice one," her motto was to "look away"—the less she saw and knew, the better.

For the malnourished and sick inmates, simply not being hit on any given day would certainly have made their work day easier. Even so, this comparative lenience should not be overrated. As Luzie H. explained in Eberhard Fechner's documentary: "I was lucky that I was assigned to the tailor detachment. You know, in a way, the prisoners were, in a way [extends her arms] my baby chicks."[39] To prove her exceptionally good relationship to the inmates, she showed Fechner a gift that the women in her detachment had given her:

> I still have a handkerchief that the prisoners embroidered with my name [shows it to the camera]. They asked me, meaning the Kapo asked me when my birthday was, because they wanted to do something nice for me. Some of my workers were skilled and able to do very delicate work.[40]

The prisoners' positive feelings were likely also related to the fact that Luzie H. was in charge of what was comparatively agreeable work, not least because it was conducted indoors—a situation that gave the *Aufseherinnen* a good deal of latitude to run things as they saw fit. However, neither the laundry nor the tailor's workshop were without violence, as illustrated by one survivor in Fechner's documentary: "We were making dolls, sewing, and she [Luzie H.] wanted us to finish a certain number of them. I don't remember how many it was, maybe one hundred, or two hundred. If you don't do this, you will be shot. If you don't manage that, you will be shot."[41] Nonetheless, despite the ever-present threat of violence, for the prisoners, work in the laundry and the tailor's workshop brought with it important, even life-saving, benefits. As Jewish survivor Henrika Mitron explained to the court, "This work was privileged; normally, we weren't required to be present during selections."[42]

As these fragmented glimpses reveal, though, the day-to-day work in the camp laundry and tailor's workshop was at all times shaped by an overwhelming disparity of power, along with an ever-present threat of violence. Every day, even on these coveted work details, the *Aufseherinnen* wielded power and dominance over the prisoners, whether by issuing death threats that could be carried out at any moment, or by allowing their benevolence to be "purchased" with small gifts and the taking of personal gain from the prisoners' labor. On closer analysis, this dynamic again represents a form of dominance and subjection. In much the same way as Insa Eschebach described the Ravensbrück *Aufseherinnen*, there were survivors who called some of Majdanek's female guards "good," "humane," or decent" simply because they had made minor exceptions here and there, or even because they simply didn't hit quite as hard as their colleagues. By comparison, then, certain *Aufseherinnen* were described in what appeared almost to be a positive light. As Eschebach noted, "It almost sounds like gratitude."[43] However, these narratives replicate with stark clarity the infantilization and domination that female prisoners were forced to accept in the camp. At the same time, such expressions of gratitude reinforce that there were, indeed, differences in behavior among the female guards, and that the *Aufseherinnen* differed in how they wielded the power accorded them.

Group and Gender Dynamics in the Use of Violence

> I didn't go to Field III very often, at most a few times a month. I did that on purpose, because whenever the Kapos Wyderko, Schmuck, and Lipinski saw one of us doctors, they escalated their terror toward the prisoners in their charge. I believe they were

> trying to intimidate us doctors with macabre scenes of murder, because the Kapos didn't have direct authority over us. Any time I returned from Field III back to Field I, I had a hard time calming down enough to work, because the scenes I'd seen in Field I and Field III were so dreadful that just witnessing these incidents was enough to make my hands tremble and leave me utterly shaken. . . . To this day, the memory is still vivid before me how the edge of the spade slid down from the back of the prisoner's head and onto his neck and entered the nape of his neck. The prisoner fell dead to the ground. . . . Every time I was witness to such a crime, there were always at least two Kapos taking part. I believe that was because they wanted to provide protection to one another, just in case the prisoners tried, in desperation, in self-defense, to resist.[44]

On several occasions, Jan Novak, the Polish prisoner-physician, witnessed German and Austrian prisoner-functionaries killing other inmates. Novak believed these killings were directed at him, as an audience, with the intent to intimidate him. As described earlier, the same factors that theater-studies scholar Erika Fischer-Lichte has identified with respect to cultural performances apply to the exercise of physical violence: the others who are present are not just impartial observers, but are implicated in various ways in the events that they observe.[45] Such performances of violence necessarily entail a three-way negotiation of the power relationship inherent between perpetrators, victims, and onlookers.

In keeping with Foucault's concept of power, every female guard and SS man at Majdanek was embedded within a complex web of power relations; they were, at once, both the objects of disciplinary measures and the agents of domination and violence. As previously discussed, within power relationships, the agent, in attempting to influence the actions of the other, implicitly acknowledges the other as a subject capable of action. Relationships of violence, by contrast, do not acknowledge the other as an active subject but as an object; they aim to break or destroy the other.[46] Relationships of power, however, do not preclude the use of violence; rather, at the microsocial level, physical violence is a means (or what Foucault would term "an instrument") by which to lay claim to power within a social context.[47] "Power exists only as an exercise by some on others, only when it is put into action."[48] Power is always exercised within a "field of possibilities" by the subject upon the other. As such, it serves to articulate the relationship between the various agents.

As we have seen, the female guards and SS men exerted direct and frequent physical violence on the prisoners. Although the relationship between the all-powerful *Aufseherinnen* and the powerless prisoners was by definition asymmetric, the guards felt compelled to constantly reassert their authority vis-à-vis the prisoners, their colleagues, and their superiors. In overpowering and dominating the prisoners, the female and male guard staff not only directed an implicit threat of violence toward prisoners who were forced to watch; they also staked out a claim to power, demonstrating to their colleagues and superiors a willingness to act, however violently, as called upon. The abuse and violence directed at the prisoners, therefore, was also a means for the *Aufseherinnen* to assert their own position of power within the SS hierarchy.

On a social level, however, power is not exercised and affirmed solely through physical violence; rather, power is also performatively produced and communicated through implicit threats of violence, gestures, and glances. Illustrative in this respect is the scene described by Jan Novak, in which Hermann Hackmann faced the starving Soviet POWs standing before him in their tattered clothing.[49] Dressed in full uniform and white gloves, with a riding crop in hand, Hackmann strode through the rows of prisoners, striking them on their caps with his whip. As Novak explained, "This wasn't meant as a beating or a form of abuse; it was intended as a gesture of contempt."[50]

This scene contrasts with Hackmann's actions at the Buchenwald concentration camp, when he was still meting out blows by his own hand:

> In a few instances, I also hit people with my fists or hands, when I wasn't an officer. I hit when there was a violation of camp regulations, in those cases where I had decided not to report it. But as an officer, I didn't feel that hitting, myself, was appropriate.[51]

As the first camp compound leader and the second highest-ranking SS officer at Majdanek, Hackmann clearly thought it no longer befitted his status to abuse or strike prisoners directly. Rather, by way of his demeanor and appearance, and the casual scorn of his gestures, he communicated his position of dominance and authority to both the prisoners and the SS men he commanded. The fact that Hackmann most often wore gloves on duty was, in part, intended to avoid physical contact with the prisoners. As he later explained, the fear of contagion played into his avoidance of such contact.[52] However, the gloves also served to underscore his status as an officer. Beginning in the middle ages, gloves were part of clerical and seigniorial regalia and, thus, were a symbol of power and dignity; as such, they signified the status and power of the wearer. At the same time, gloves were considered standard work attire, worn to protect the hands during work in the factory or on the fields.[53] In a sense, Hackmann's gloves served as a visible sign of his power, illustrative of his self-image as the leader of the prisoner camp.

In the recollections of both the prisoners and her colleagues, Chief Guard Else Ehrich was remembered as one of the few female staff members who, by her demeanor, managed to affect a genuinely militaristic and masterful appearance. As survivor Henryka Ostrowska recalled, "Chief Guard Ehrich always carried a switch with her, which she liked to stick in her boot."[54] However, it was not just her appearance, but also the manner in which she struck the prisoners, as well as her general comportment, that accorded her a militaristic presence. As survivor Hanna Narkiewicz-Jodko recalled:

> Commandant Ehrich was cruel, strict, very careful in her dress, very militaristic in her movements. It seemed to us that she hit us with complete intentionality, short and hard, and employed particularly humiliating and denigrating language. She usually kicked and hit us with her riding crop, which I saw over and over again. The other *Aufseherinnen* also carried crops.[55]

Hermann Hackmann and Else Ehrich—both of whom were remembered by prisoners and female guards, alike, as having exercised violence in a very "exacting" manner—distinguished themselves from their colleagues—that is, the SS men and *Aufseherinnen* who were less discriminate in their abuse. In so doing, they signaled their power and status both to the prisoners and to their colleagues and subordinates. Within the context of the camp, self-control was thus also a mark of distinction and dominance.

According to the prisoners, Else Ehrich's "trusted associate,"[56] Report Leader Hermine Braunsteiner, adopted a similar demeanor: "She also carried a whip with her all the time; she used to hold it under the prisoner's chins," as Maryla Reich recalled.[57] But survivors' descriptions also emphasize a difference between the two women:

> I remember now that we also called the defendant, Braunsteiner, "Kobyla" [mare]. She was tall and she had a very masculine way about her. Comparing Commandant [Chief Guard] Ehrich, *Aufseherin* Braunsteiner, and "bloody Brigida" [Hildegard Lächert], I can say the following: Chief Guard Ehrich strode and struck us as elegantly as an officer. *Aufseherin* Hermine Braunsteiner did this, like the other female guards, with brutality and an evident sadistic satisfaction. "Bloody Brigida" behaved with peasant-like crudeness.[58]

A photograph of a beating that took place in the Cieszanow labor camp is illustrative in this respect. The photograph is one of the few surviving snapshots that capture a scene of violence at a Nazi concentration camp. In it, three guards, presumably Trawniki guards,[59] are kicking and using sticks to beat a man who is lying on the ground. Next to them is a group of prisoners, who are being forced to watch. Two more guards are observing the event. One of the guards, hands clasped, is visible only from behind; he is kicking the prisoner with what can only be described as a sort of casual contempt. The violence depicted in this scene illustrates the many different forms that kicks and blows can take—forms that, while demonstrating cruelty and brutality, can also be seen as an attempt on the part of the guards to emphasize their superiority, perhaps even to display a certain "elegance," as they saw it.

The SS guards' actions not only took place under the watchful eyes of the inmates; they were also under scrutiny by their colleagues. At Majdanek, Hildegard Lächert was later remembered, by both the prisoners and her fellow colleagues, as having had an exceptional propensity toward violence. Lächert's readiness to resort

United States Holocaust Memorial Museum, courtesy of Jerzy Tomaszewski, USHMM Photo Archives, #200.7019, W/S #5063

FIGURE 20. Camp guards beat a prisoner at the Cieszanow labor camp, date and photographer unknown (ca. 1941–1944)

to violence appears to have been frowned upon by her superiors, a fact supported in a certificate of conduct issued by Chief Guard Else Ehrich in July 1943:

> With her unusually tense and nervous manner, *Aufseherin* Lächert doesn't make a good impression on the prisoners. As soon as she assumes control over the detachment, she starts running riot with the prisoners.
>
> *Aufseherin* Lächert has received numerous official reprimands on the matter.
>
> By contrast, while off-duty, *Aufseherin* Lächert is on very good terms with the remaining female guards. She is very good-natured and has never been the cause of any ill will.[60]

And yet, in their postwar interrogations, Lächert's former colleagues all described her as an outsider, in part because she did not "belong to the group around Ehrich, like most of the *Aufseherinnen* did,"[61] as Charlotte Wöllert recalled. "Ehrich didn't like Lächert and always gave her assignments that were a bit out of the way, as far as possible from the camp itself."[62] However, Lächert's outsider status was also due to her aggressively violent behavior[63] and her low social status. Lächert was the mother of two out-of-wedlock children, both of whom lived with her mother while she worked at the camp. While at Majdanek, Lächert had become pregnant a third time; the father was an SS officer at Majdanek. As a single mother of three children by three different men, had she been within "Reich" territory, Lächert might well have found herself classified as "asocial."[64]

In contrast to the survivors, in their postwar testimony, Lächert's colleagues described her as anything but a fearsome or imposing figure: "Frau Lächert was always a bit of a 'poor little rabbit,' because Ehrich always pushed her aside," Charlotte Wöllert told the Düsseldorf court. "This might have also had something to do with her appearance; she wore a very ill-fitting uniform, and she was never successful in asserting herself with Ehrich."[65] According to Elisabeth H., the antipathy between Hildegard Lächert, Chief Guard Ehrich, and Hermine Braunsteiner, her deputy, was mutual: "She always behaved in a very provocative way.... Braunsteiner and Ehrich couldn't stand Lächert, because she was constantly back-talking them."[66] Although Lächert's crude and violent behavior did not meet with approval, most of her colleagues respected her for her confrontational stance toward the chief guard, and her good-natured way with her fellow *Aufseherinnen*. "Personally, I didn't like Ehrich, but I did like Lächert," Erika W. recalled.[67] In her 1980 testimony, Erna Pfannstiel also recalled Lächert favorably: "She was a cheerful person. She was always very cheerful and all that."[68]

As this testimony also shows, in spite of the authority she wielded in the camp, Else Ehrich was not universally popular among her fellow *Aufseherinnen*. Among the staff, Ehrich was generally regarded as a strict guard and superior who was not necessarily popular, but who nonetheless garnered their respect.[69] "She was very hard and heartless and showed no mercy. She wasn't just strict and uncompromising toward the prisoners—she was also like that toward us," Erna Pfannstiel recalled.[70] Elisabeth H. called her "very arrogant,"[71] while Hertha Ehlert described her as "cynical and cold"[72] and "extremely harsh":[73]

> The chief guard was brutal and she struck the female prisoners with leather straps. When Frau Mayer [Charlotte Wöllert, married name Mayer] and I would pass by the women's field in the morning, we sometimes heard the beatings. It was the chief guard, who had put a prisoner on the whipping block and was thrashing away. She also whipped old women. I always looked away, because I couldn't stand the sight of it.[74]

Ehlert also described how she and Charlotte Wöllert once saw the chief guard beat a female prisoner:

> The reason why I had a good opinion of Mayer [Charlotte Wöllert, married name Mayer] is as follows: Once I accompanied Mayer through the camp. As we were walking, we saw Ehrich, who was beating an older woman for some reason. Mayer spit on the ground in a pointed way and said, "What a pig she is, hitting an old woman."[75]

As this testimony demonstrates, at least in Ehlert's recollection, Mayer [Charlotte Wöllert] had expressed her misgivings about the violent punishment to her colleague, albeit privately, rather than in public. Thus, it would appear that even though the

Aufseherinnen were aware of such violent behavior among their colleagues, they went out of their way to avoid any direct confrontation.

The female guards differed in their assessments of Hermine Braunsteiner, Ehlert's deputy and also, as it happened, her close friend. Elisabeth H., for example, described her as "arrogant" and "unappealing."[76] Ruth E., by contrast, remembered Braunsteiner in favorable terms—as a very "comradely"[77] person who had taken Ruth E. under her wing.

Generally speaking, the former *Aufseherinnen* tended to defend one another in their postwar testimony, as this statement by Charlotte W. illustrates:

> The girls who worked for me often gave me small hints about how they had been treated in other labor detachments. But they were very reserved and I imagine they were also afraid to go into detail, or to put a name to the people they were talking about. But I do remember that some of them told me prisoners in their labor detachments had been struck with spades or whips, quite badly. And I heard that Anna M. had once ordered a dog to attack someone, and used her whip. But I don't think she would have killed anyone.[78]

While obviously part of an attempt to help exonerate their colleagues in court, these positive assessments also resulted from friendship, camaraderie, and other forms of social affinity that existed between the former *Aufseherinnen*. In the end, however, the former guards' efforts to protect their old colleagues and to play down their "out of control" behavior also serve to demonstrate just how socially acceptable violent behavior had become at the camp.

These three *Aufseherinnen*—Else Ehrich, Hildegard Lächert, and Hermine Braunsteiner—thus each differed in their use of violence. Else Ehrich often employed physical violence in a targeted manner as a penal and disciplinary instrument, while Braunsteiner and Lächert tended to resort to kicks and blows as a day-to-day means of managing the work at hand. It appears that Lächert's extreme displays of violence may also have been an attempt to assert or distinguish herself amongst her fellow guards. Although the violence employed by these three guards did not always meet with the approval of their colleagues, a certain level of respect is nonetheless evident in their postwar testimony.

Even in retrospect, none of the women called into fundamental question Ehlert's leadership and authority. Likewise, even though postwar testimony made frequent mention of Braunsteiner's arrogance, it is likely that some of the *Aufseherinnen* were, at the same time, intimidated by her—perhaps even more so because she was known to be the chief guard's close friend and confidant. For her part, in her postwar testimony, Lächert emphasized her resistance to the chief guard, which was also demonstrated through her own displays of physical violence. Here, it is important to remember that violence, whether enacted or experienced, is characterized by ambiguity and contradiction. Violence may be condemned even as it is admired, perhaps even envied. In the postwar testimony, such expressions of admiration and fascination surfaced only indirectly, however, and presumably were also associated with feelings of shame. That does not mean, however, that this admiration and fascination did not exist.

GENDER AND VIOLENCE

> Within the group of SS women, there were also those who beat the prisoners like crazy, especially when a man was watching. I still remember it quite clearly: the way they first would fawn over the SS man, and then, when the labor detail headed out, go after the prisoners, berating and beating them, showing how brutal they could be, in order to please him. [In Ravensbrück] there were fewer SS men than women in the camp, so all the men had flattery heaped upon them. The *Aufseherinnen* flirted by showing the men they could behave in an equally masculine fashion, beating the prisoners half to death; they wanted to show what kind of a "fellow" they were, so to speak.[79]

As survivor Hilde Zimmerman reported, the female guards at Ravensbrück also used violence as a means of impressing their male colleagues. This description also illustrates a tension that underlies the postwar accounts of the women's behavior: their routine use of extreme violence is described, but there is a clear sense of unease and discomfort at the fact that it was women who were carrying it out. In this sense, Zimmerman's suggestion that the *Aufseherinnen* also used brutality in order to appeal to the male staff can be read as an attempt to make sense of the disconcerting violence employed by female guard staff in the camp.

As we have seen, while kicks and blows served as a form of humiliation and abuse, such acts were not meant only for the victims themselves. In the concentration camp, acts of violence were also an instrument of humiliation and intimidation directed toward other prisoners as witnesses. At the same time, displays of violence were equally directed toward the other *Aufseherinnen* and male camp staff, as a form of intimidation or to garner their admiration. Moreover, as Zimmermann noted in her discussion of Ravensbrück, the problem of violence on the part of female staff took on a gendered dimension. This can be seen, for example, in the "demonstrative" use of violence by the female guards intent on impressing their male colleagues and superiors. This phenomenon was referenced in numerous accounts by Ravensbrück survivors, among them Charlotte Müller, who recalled the actions of the *Aufseherinnen* in the penal block:

> The most brutal *Aufseherinnen* maintained a reign of terror. Boundless egotism, together with other deplorable personal qualities such as vindictiveness and violence,

> were the trademarks of the female guards, who did whatever they could to match the sadism of the SS men.[80]

Margarete Buber-Neumann offered a similar account:

> During their leisure hours, the new *Aufseherinnen* enjoyed socializing with the SS men from the guard troops. They soon noticed that the brutal ones enjoyed particular success with the men, and bragged to them about their acts of heroism.[81]

According to survivors, therefore, the *Aufseherinnen* performed acts of violence for the SS men, both to assert their own equality and to attract male attention. Similar accounts came from survivors of Majdanek, where the female guards made up just a small minority of the camp staff (as opposed to Ravensbrück, where they enjoyed a majority status).

In the testimony of Majdanek survivors, Hildegard Lächert's behavior was particularly striking in this respect. "She was a good-looking woman, who always held her head high as she strode through the camp," Judith Gelbard, a former inmate, recalled. "She acted like a woman who wanted to be noticed by the SS men."[82] This description contrasts starkly with that of her colleagues, who thought of her as a "poor little rabbit" in an ill-fitting uniform. Hanna Narkiewicz-Jodko, another Majdanek survivor, offered the following testimony to the court:

> A 25-year-old female prisoner was caught with turnips. She was to be punished with 25 blows while lying on a footstool at roll call. An SS man began carrying out the punishment. After he had struck the prisoner six or seven times, Lächert jumped forward, grabbed the whip out of his hand, and began whipping with all the strength she could muster. Apparently, the SS man wasn't whipping hard enough to suit Frau Lächert.[83]

In this way, Lächert demonstrated not only that she could match the SS man blow for blow, but also that she would show no deference when it came to the gender of her victim. Lächert's violent attacks on male inmates served to further set her apart from the other *Aufseherinnen* at Majdanek. In her court testimony, Irena Marzalek described one such attack on a male prisoner who was slow, and kept stumbling and falling to the ground:

> "Brigida" came up to him and began thrashing him with a whip, or something similar to that.[84] . . . Some SS men were also there. From the sewing barracks, which was almost directly adjacent to Field II, I saw the male prisoner being beaten. The entire incident took place on a path. The victim was carried away by other prisoners. From where I was standing, I couldn't tell how badly he was injured. I don't think he would

> have survived that abuse, but sometimes it did happen that someone who had been beaten terribly would miraculously manage to survive.[85]

On this occasion, too, the events took place before an audience of SS men, making it seem likely that Lächert's act of violence was also directed at—perhaps even intended for—her male colleagues. Barbara Steiner's testimony before the Düsseldorf court suggests that such circumstances could have a reciprocal and escalating effect:

> We didn't have toilets at Majdanek. We had a kind of barrel, which was covered with boards. They were in a spot outside the women's field. We used to have to go there with five or six other women to empty the barrels. We used sticks to carry the barrel on our shoulders. It was my job to give notice of the detachment's departure. I said, in German, "Beg leave to report, six women are going to work." Hermenda [*sic*] replied, "You are not a woman, you are shit." The man who was standing next to her was holding a cigarette, which he used to burn me. She was holding a whip, which she used to strike me, several times.[86]

Hermine Braunsteiner's verbal invective led to a painful and humiliating act of abuse on the part of the SS man, whereupon Braunsteiner reciprocated with lashes of the whip. As this episode demonstrates, violence could take the form of mutual escalation. This self-fulfilling dynamic of violence and the desire to vie with and outdo one's colleague also occurred during the women's interactions with one another. Gender is also at stake in so-called homosocial spaces;[87] as Germaine Tillion recalled of her time at Ravensbrück, the presence of female colleagues also caused the *Aufseherinnen* to escalate their brutality and aggression.[88]

By the same token, the SS men at Majdanek also made a show of violence to impress their female colleagues. For example, a number of *Aufseherinnen* later recalled that Erich Muhsfeldt, the head of the crematorium detachment at Majdanek, enjoyed playing jokes, often at the women's expense. "He was always crude toward us *Aufseherinnen*, in a joking kind of way,"[89] as Anna M. recalled. Even years later, most of the women had vivid recollections of Muhsfeldt, who was known for provoking the female staff with his "gallows humor." In one postwar interrogation, for example, Hertha Ehlert recalled, "The man in charge of the crematorium, Mussfeld [*sic*], knew that I found the place repulsive. That's why he often called out 'crematorium' to me when I walked by, or waved a dead body part at me."[90] Based on this account, it appears that Muhsfeldt was deliberately playing into the gendered stereotype of the nervous and fearful woman, and that he deliberately adopted the role of the man who would stop at nothing, not even touching a corpse, to get her attention. By her own account, Ehlert was disgusted by Muhsfeldt's humor:

> Once I said to him that he would probably stick me in an oven, too. He told me that if he was ordered to do so, and he could, he would do it immediately. Then he spoke badly of me to the commandant. I told Commandant Florstedt that I

> despised Musfeld [*sic*] and had no intention of acting kindly toward him. He said to me, just between the two of us, that he understood that, because his wife also despised Musfeld [*sic*].[91]

Within the camp hierarchy, the entire crematorium staff were considered outsiders. Although it was not stated explicitly, postwar testimony of SS staff shows that the burning of bodies was considered "dirty" work. By contrast, similar negative sentiments did not seem to apply to the infirmary orderlies who killed infirm inmates by lethal injection, nor to those who poured the Zyklon B into the gas chambers, nor to the men who took part in shooting detachments. While other SS men limited themselves to the killing and mistreatment of inmates, Muhsfeldt was in direct and constant contact with the dead. Also worth noting is that while the commandant expressed an understanding of Ehlert's complaint, he did so only indirectly, referencing his wife's distaste for the man.

Alf Lüdtke has studied the banter and "horseplay" among factory workers, both verbal and nonverbal, as indicators of social interaction and mutual respect. As he has shown, these occasionally brutal forms of workplace teasing are an expression of group dynamics and, also, of the esteem—or the lack thereof—workers feel toward their colleagues.[92] Banter and "horseplay," according to Lüdtke, can also be read as an affirmation of shared experience—the experience of being "bound, and bound to a specific location, marked and identified, and soiled."[93] Muhsfeldt's macabre jokes were a drastic means of making it clear to the *Aufseherinnen* exactly what kind of a place and location Majdanek was.

Of course, Erich Muhsfeldt's "teasing" may also have been an attempt to establish or even force a sense of familiarity. In this sense, his "horseplay" may be seen as a distraction, a momentary subversion of the pressure he was under, and even as a "product" of that pressure. Finally, his "teasing" may be taken as yet one more example of how the SS staff attempted to secure their position and status within their workplace—the concentration camp.

If Women Start to Shoot, We'll Have to Evacuate the Camp

According to the accounts of survivors, all of the female guards and SS men were armed with pistols.[94] "Most *Aufseherinnen* carried a whip. Every guard also had a holster with a pistol in it. I remember that very well,"[95] Natalia Grzybek, a Majdanek survivor, recalled. At the Majdanek trial, however, many of the former *Aufseherinnen* vehemently denied having carried a weapon while on duty, an assertion that was almost certainly meant to deflect responsibility before the court.[96] However, others, including Hildegard Lächert, admitted to having been armed:

> I carried a pistol on duty at Majdanek. I didn't have it straight away, but later. We practiced shooting, but I don't remember how often. I never shot at a person. We

> were under orders to shoot any prisoner who was attempting to escape, after calling to them. . . . As far as I know, all the *Aufseherinnen* had a pistol, but I'm not 100 percent sure.[97]

"When I was assigned to an outside detachment, I took my pistol along,"[98] Hermine Brückner recalled. Elisabeth H. gave a similar account: "Many of the *Aufseherinnen* had a pistol. . . . We were instructed to shoot if any prisoner tried to escape[99] from an outside detachment."[100] Luzie H. offered the following testimony: "The *Aufseherinnen* were armed with pistols. They wore waist holsters with a pouch for a pistol. . . . I kept my pistol in my briefcase in my office. I trusted my prisoners."[101]

Hertha Ehlert recalled that the female guards wore pistols while guarding inmates.[102] Ehlert also claimed they were required to wear their pistols when socializing after hours in Lublin, as a precaution against the possibility of partisan attacks. According to Ehlert, however, she never carried anything like a whip, stick, or rubber truncheon.[103] And, though she never personally experienced a partisan attack, she recalled being repeatedly warned of the risk.[104]

In her 1946 testimony before the Vienna court, Hermine Braunsteiner confirmed that each *Aufseherin* was issued a service pistol and received training in the shooting, handling, and care of their weapon.[105] On April 10, 1943, Commandant Florstedt wrote to her and to Else Ehrich, who were both on sick leave at the time, instructing them to send their wardrobe keys to Lublin because their pistols were urgently needed (presumably for target practice), only to discover that both had taken their weapons to Bavaria.[106] Finally, the Majdanek archival records include "routing slips," which confirmed that the *Aufseherinnen* returned their service weapons upon termination of their employment at the camp.[107]

Even among the SS men, shooting was not the most common form of violence or killing within the prisoner camp; rather, beatings and kicks, followed by drowning or strangulation were the more frequently employed forms of abuse. Leo Miller, a Jewish survivor, recalled often hearing the saying, "For Jews, even a bullet is too expensive."[108] However, by all accounts, the *Aufseherinnen* made far less use of their weapons than did the male staff. Survivors who testified at the Majdanek trial recall only a single incident in which a prisoner was shot by a female guard, although the interrogation records show that no direct eyewitnesses to the incident were interviewed. In her testimony, Boleslawa Janiszek described the incident as follows:

> In late September [1943] I was assigned to a detachment that worked the fields on the Felin farm. I was assigned to the detachment after an incident in which the German *Aufseherin* Anna David shot and killed a Polish woman by the name of Radke. I saw Radke being brought to the infirmary; she was completely blue. Then I heard that she had been shot by Anna David at the Felin farm. According to the reports, Anna David aimed her pistol at Radke and said, "I'm going to shoot you."

> Supposedly she said that several times. Then she actually did shoot, and Radke was mortally wounded. David supposedly wept afterwards, and another German *Aufseherin* slapped her in the face and told her not to cry.[109]

Krystyna Suchanska gave the following statement:

> In late summer, the other female prisoners told me that the *Aufseherin* we called "Myszka" (little mouse) had shot a prisoner, a woman called Radke, who was the Kapo in the Felin farm detachment. They told me that "Myszka" claimed afterwards that she had shot Radek [*sic*] by accident when she was cleaning her weapon. But eyewitnesses told me that "Myszka" shot Radek [*sic*] on purpose.[110]

A number of female guards who, like Charlotte W., had heard about the incident secondhand also recalled the event:

> I still remember exactly how a prisoner who had been shot around that time was brought back. The prisoner was a member of the peat-digging detachment, which was supervised by *Aufseherin* David. At the time, David told me that the female prisoner had attempted to escape. As far as I can remember, she told me something to the effect that the woman tried to run away, and so she shot her. I explained to her that she wasn't allowed to shoot the prisoners right away, but first had to fire a warning shot into the air. Then she said that she had no intention of being locked up because a prisoner had escaped. She didn't give me any details about the escape attempt. I saw the dead female prisoner myself.[111]

Luzie H. offered the following testimony:

> She [David] was supposedly fiddling around with her pistol. Then she fired a shot, by accident. The Kapo was sitting next to her. She hit the woman in the arm. By coincidence, a horse-drawn cart came by. The injured woman was loaded onto it, but she bled to death on the way to the camp. That's what the female guards were saying. The SS *Aufseherin* was sent to the bunker in punishment. I can't remember the name of the guard. It might have been David, but I can't say for sure.[112]

Hermine Brückner described the incident as follows:

> When *Aufseherin* David took over my detachment on the farm one time, she shot and killed a female prisoner "due to some foolishness." As far as I know, she hadn't intended to shoot. But afterwards, she was a nervous wreck.[113]

Elisabeth H. offered the most succinct explanation for the incident: "David was hysterical."[114] Rosa Reischl recalled: "I heard from others that SS *Aufseherin* David was drunk, and shot and killed a female inmate while on an outside detachment. But it was prisoners who told me that."[115]

The fact that nearly all the female guards remembered this incident, including those who had only heard about it secondhand, shows how unusual it must have been. Even at Majdanek, where violence was commonplace, a women shooting at a prisoner was an "atypical" occurrence. It is no longer possible to reconstruct exactly how this killing took place. In any case, it is worth noting that four *Aufseherinnen* said David's carelessness was to blame for what happened, with specific mention of drunkenness, hysteria, foolishness, and "fiddling around with" her pistol. In particular, the reference to "hysteria" is highly gendered and sexualized.[116] Indeed, even the prisoners remembered David as being comparatively amiable.

When she returned to the camp, David had to make a report to *Aufseherin* Charlotte W. In that report, David claimed there had been an "escape attempt." Ultimately, however, the incident was officially recorded as the "fatal injury of a prisoner through negligent handling of the service pistol," and not as an attempted escape.[117] As we have seen, similar incidents at the hands of SS men were "given a pass,"[118] but this does not appear to have been the case when it was a female guard at fault in the incident.

Why did the *Aufseherinnen* make such infrequent use of their weapons, given that they did not shy away from other forms of brutal abuse, beatings and blows, and even killing? The reason, I suggest, can be found in the gendered significance attached to firearms. In this respect, two statements by former *Aufseherinnen* are particularly insightful. In one of her interrogations, Hildegard Lächert described the following incident:[119]

> Once, when I was hanging out at the airfield in Swidnik, among the officers who were stationed there, who were all acquaintances of my fiancé, one of the officers, Major D., took my duty weapon away from me. Every *Aufseherin* on duty had a pistol. Major D. said to me at the time that, in his opinion, women shouldn't be carrying a pistol.[120]

Alice Orlowski offered a similar description: "The SS men said, if women start to shoot, we'll have to evacuate the camp entirely. I never used my weapon."[121]

Why, though, was such a powerful taboo attached to the notion of a weapon in the hands of an *Aufseherin*? In fact, the gendered taboo surrounding weapons or specific types of weapons is a very old one. French ethnologist Alain Testart has investigated the division of labor in hunter-and-gatherer societies.[122] Although women participated in many forms of fishing as well as in the hunt, they were given access to only a limited range of weapons (such as fire, ropes, sticks, and dogs). Women were strictly prohibited from using weapons that penetrated the flesh of the animal, including knives, arrows, and spears. As Testart explained it, the taboo surrounding certain types of weapons for women resulted from a cultural ideology in which blood was considered to have a social significance. These cultural and social mores meant, essentially, that these modes of killing were the domain of men, and men only.

In all of the above-cited cases—Major D., Rudolf Höss, and the SS men cited by Alice Orlowski—the veto on firearms for women was justified with references to their supposedly innate biology. According to this argument, women lacked the physical and mental capacity necessary to handle a pistol. As we have seen, however, this was not a formal or written prohibition; rather, it emerged within the day-to-day context of work in the camp.[123] Outfitted with firearms and uniformed dress, as they were, the female guards had succeeded in penetrating a professional and paramilitary domain that had previously been the sole province of men. Through their presence, the women constituted a threat to the prevailing gender order, as Insa Eschebach has emphasized:[124]

> Unlike the male commanding officer, an armed or even a uniformed woman represented a breach of social convention since, in Western European civilization, the military sphere was solely the domain of men. The very notion of a "female commandant" [*Kommandeuse*] is unsettling because it disrupts the patriarchal gender order. She is a "gunwoman" [*Flintenweib*], an "SS shrew" [*SS-Megäre*], a woman who kills rather than gives birth.[125]

The accounts by former *Aufseherinnen* show that they accepted both the unspoken ban on their use of firearms and the gendered meanings ascribed to that prohibition. The patronizing judgments of the SS men coincide with testimony offered by Hermine Brückner, Luzie H., Elisabeth H., and Rosa Reischl regarding the incident involving Anna David in that they, too, ascribed the shooting to women's apparently innate ineptness when it came to the use of firearms. Uniformed and violent, the *Aufseherinnen* had breached a professional domain that was formerly an exclusively male province. Nonetheless, the use of firearms remained a particularly masculine form of violence. The use of firearms was, in this sense, the final male-only domain. Even in a paramilitary sphere in which women wore uniforms and carried weapons, shooting a gun was a uniquely masculine and soldierly privilege. While officially the female guards were permitted to shoot—Hermine Braunsteiner even took her service weapon with her to Lake Tegernsee—there was, in reality, an informal yet powerful taboo attached to their use of weapons. In this respect, group and gender dynamics played a powerful role in the specific meanings and practices of violence that emerged within the concentration camps.

11

Cruelty

An Anthropological Perspective

In her postwar account, French ethnologist Germaine Tillion described the aftermath of a flogging that took place in the Ravensbrück bunker. While Tillion did not witness the scene herself, a friend who was imprisoned in the bunker for an extended period told her of it. Describing her friend as a woman with "excellent powers of judgment," Tillion later relayed her friend's account of the actions of *Aufseherin* Dorothea Binz:[1]

> After one such flogging, my friend ventured a look through a gap in the floorboards; by then, the punishment was over, and the prisoner was lying half-naked with her face to the floor, obviously unconscious and covered in blood from her ankles to her waist. Binz looked at the woman, and without saying anything, stood on top of her blood-covered calves, her heel on one calf, and the tips of her toes on the other, and began rocking back and forth by shifting her body weight from her toes to her heels. It's possible the woman was already dead; in any case, she was not conscious, because she displayed no reaction. After a while, Binz left; her boots were covered in blood.[2]

What is noteworthy about this incident is that the "official" punishment had already been carried out, and Deputy Chief Guard Binz believed she was alone and unobserved in the bunker. In other words, her additional mistreatment of the prisoner was carried out solely for her own benefit, and not for the benefit of any observer. In Tillion's description, this act of violence was "gratuitous"—qualitatively different from the ordinary, day-to-day violence meted out by the female guards.[3]

Sociologist Wolfgang Sofsky has developed the concept of "excess" as a means of distinguishing between "regulated" violence and "excessive" violence, which is characterized by its lack of purpose or meaning. Here Sofsky is following Primo Levi's distinction between "useful" violence and "useless" (*violenza gratuita*), by which Levi means violent acts undertaken solely for the sake of the violence itself, and in which the sole aim is to cause the victim severe pain and bodily harm:[4]

> Excess bursts the framework of regulated violence. It is not a punishment, or a torture, or an execution. Punishment follows an infraction; its severity depends on the crime. Torture is an operation of calculation and comparison; it seeks to extort a statement from its victim. Execution is a public ritual of deadly power. Excess has nothing in common with these. At best, it takes punishment and torture as a welcome occasion for its own devices. Yet it usually comes to pass without any motivating occasion, without any command or purpose. In excess, power runs riot, letting off steam through the outlet of the defenseless. It is rooted in a situation of omnipotence. In excess, the perpetrators demonstrate their triumph over the other. They show just how free they are. Excess is a violent force for its own sake: terror per se. It has no goal; it is not a means to an end. Cruelty wills nothing but itself, the absolute freedom of arbitrary action, which it realizes by countless new ideas and variations.[5]

Sofsky's analysis here highlights the omnipotence the perpetrators experience as they revel in their triumph over the other, which demonstrates just how "free" they are. But Sofsky's analysis largely elides the agent by, in essence, "personifying" cruelty and power, which now emerge as active agents. If we follow Sofsky's argument, excess now comes to pass "without any motivating occasion, without any command or purpose."[6] In this sense, Sofsky is following a legal taxonomy that describes violent acts that go beyond orders, or that are committed by perpetrators entirely on their own initiative, as "excesses."[7]

In the end, however, this analysis raises more questions than it answers. What does the category of "excessive" acts actually illuminate, and how does defining certain acts of violence as "gratuitous" help to advance our understanding? Is it even possible, in this context, to distinguish so clearly between "justifiable" and "purposeful" violence, and violence that is "gratuitous"? And finally, even if we assume that violence need not always be instrumental in the Weberian sense, is there such a thing as violence that is entirely "gratuitous" or without purpose? Perhaps we should rather insist that every act of violence, even acts of great cruelty, be isolated and analyzed within a specific and identifiable configuration of actors, incitements and stimuli, and contexts. According to French anthropologist Véronique Nahoum-Grappe, in order to analyze the violence and cruelty of specific acts, we must first "perceive" this violence as a sequence of physical and material actions. For this reason, we must not only describe such practices of violence and cruelty, but problematize the actions as such.[8]

Domination and Power

On numerous occasions, Polish prisoner-physician Jan Novak witnessed prisoners being abused at the hands of Heinz Villain, the leader of Field III (who at times was also assigned to the Political Division). "On three occasions, I saw Villain with his bent knee up against the throat of a prisoner who was lying on the ground. And then I saw that the prisoner didn't get back up again."[9] This particular act of violence is reminiscent of the opening scene to this chapter involving *Aufseherin* Binz at Ravensbrück, as described by Germaine Tillion. Lying helpless in the middle of the men's Field III, which primarily held Jewish prisoners, the prisoner was being subdued by Villain in a particularly savage manner. However, in the case of Villain's abuse, the events took place in public, in front of witnesses, none of whom offered help, protested, or attempted to intercede as the SS man choked the prisoner to death.

One key precondition for any act of cruelty is that it requires an imbalance of power. Cruelty is only possible when the perpetrator, whether acting as an individual or as part of a group, is in a position of overwhelming power and dominance over the "object of the abuse." The agent of cruelty is always in a position of political or physical dominance; this contrasts with violence, where the agent of violence may be less powerful than its object.[10] The larger the power differential, the more likely it is that the perpetrators will take pleasure in their power and in the transgression of accepted moral limits. Cruelty can only be imagined or enacted within this configuration of power; once such dominance no longer exists, cruelty becomes increasingly less likely.[11]

Unfortunately, it is all too likely that Novak was correct in his assumption that the prisoner died after the attack. This raises a further question: what purpose is served by the degradation or killing of a completely defenseless victim? In *Crowds and Power*, Elias Canetti reflects upon killing and connects it to survival, in which fear plays a decisive role.[12] At all times, the human body is vulnerable to attack from without and from within. In the act of overpowering or killing, however, the perpetrator achieves a sense of superiority.[13] According to Canetti, the act of killing is more than simply the taking of a life: in taking a life, the killer becomes a survivor; this survival—the outliving of others—is one of the rare moments in which a person can *discover* his own aliveness. The "moment of *survival* is the moment of power," Canetti asserts.[14] The moment of survival, then, is the "most elementary and most obvious form of success."[15] For the survivor, the violent overpowering of another human being yields an incomparable satisfaction and vital affirmation of the self.

Cruelty always entails a moment of total overpowering, which is why the inability of the victim to offer resistance does not reduce the cruelty that is administered. The point, then, is not to measure one's strength against someone of similar or perhaps even greater strength. To the contrary, the victims are often targeted precisely due to their appearance of vulnerability and weakness. It is for this reason, then, that women (as the physically weaker sex), the old and infirm, defenseless and innocent children, and even pregnant (and thus particularly vulnerable) women, are more likely to be the victims of extreme cruelty.[16] According to Nahoum-Grappe, it is this instrumentalization of weakness and pain that conveys to the perpetrator of violence a powerful affirmation of the self.

However, this experience of being overpowered is only rarely described in the accounts offered by survivors of the Majdanek and Ravensbrück concentration camps. For this reason, I will once again turn to Jean Améry's essay in which he describes and reflects upon the torture he experienced at the hands of the Gestapo:

> The first blow brings home to the prisoner that he is *helpless*, and thus it already contains in the bud everything that is to come. One may have known about torture and death in the cell . . . but upon the first blow they are anticipated as real possibilities, yes, as certainties. They are permitted to punch me in the face, the victim feels in numb surprise and concludes in just as numb certainty: they will do with me what they want. Whoever would rush to the prisoner's aid—a wife, a mother, a brother, a friend—he won't get this far.[17]

This first blow, according to Améry, calls forth an "existential fright" that in part results from a realization that resistance is impossible. Even worse, though, is the realization that the basic expectation of help does not apply in this context—that is, the Gestapo bunker, the interrogation that is taking place—and that no outside assistance is forthcoming:

> In almost all situations in life where there is bodily injury there is also the expectation of help; the former is compensated by the latter. But with the first blow from a policeman's fist, against which there can be no defense and which no helping hand will ward off, a part of our life ends and it can never again be revived.[18]

The first blow is not an injury to the body alone; rather, it penetrates far more deeply into one's very being:

> The boundaries of my body are also the boundaries of my self. My skin surface shields me against the external world. If I am to trust, I must feel on it only what I *want* to feel. At the first blow, however, this trust in the world breaks down. The

> other person, *opposite* whom I exist physically in the world, and with whom I can exist only as long as he does not touch my skin surface as border, forces his own corporeality on me with the first blow. He is on me and thereby destroys me. It is like a rape, a sexual act without the consent of one of the two partners.[19]

For Améry, bodily injury is experienced as physical trespass, a wrongful invasion akin to rape. Here Améry makes reference to a long-standing trope, which "ever since antiquity has produced alternative or subversive narratives, that depict the extent of injury in a rape as a 'breach' or 'rupture' not only of the of the victim's psyche, but also of the trust upon which the social contract is founded."[20] According to literary theorist Christine Künzel, the metaphor of rape Améry draws conveys the difficulty of communicating the victim's suffering and the injury that has been inflicted. As Améry emphasizes, the traumatic experience of physical violation is not exclusively physical; rather, it breaks down one's trust in the world and in one's corporeal integrity. If no help can be expected, and no opportunity for resistance exists, "this physical overwhelming by the other then becomes an existential consummation of destruction altogether."[21] The experience of complete helplessness is an experience that defies communication:[22]

> The pain was what it was. Beyond that there is nothing to say. Qualities of feeling are as incomparable as they are indescribable. They mark the limit of the capacity of language to communicate. If someone wanted to impart his physical pain, he would be forced to inflict it and thereby become a torturer himself. Since the *how* of pain defies communication through language, perhaps I can at least approximately state *what* it was. It contained everything that was already ascertained earlier in regard to a beating by the police: the border violation of my self by the other, which can be neither neutralized by the expectation of help nor rectified through resistance. Torture is all that, but in addition very much more. Whoever is overcome with pain by torture experiences his body as never before. In self-negation, his flesh becomes a total reality.[23]

Under these conditions, the "tortured person becomes a body, and nothing more besides that."[24] The blows and the abuse demonstrated force him to acknowledge his own corporeality, and the person "becomes flesh." For the torturer, this marks the beginning of his "creation": that is, a body writhing in pain.

> The fellow man is transformed into flesh, and in this transformation he is already brought to the edge of death; if worse comes to worst, he is driven beyond the borders of death into Nothingness. With that the torturer and the murderer realizes his own destructive being, without having to lose himself in it entirely, like his martyred victim. He can, after all, cease the torture when it suits him. He has control of the other's scream of pain and death; he is master over flesh and spirit, life and death.[25]

With great astonishment, Améry was forced to admit that "in this world there can be the other as absolute sovereign, and sovereignty reveals itself as the power to inflict suffering and to destroy."[26] He also comes to realize the "boundless existence of the other, as he boundlessly asserts himself through torture, and astonishment at what one can become oneself: flesh and death."[27] The murderer, for his part, realizes his own sovereignty and "destructive being." In the end, the "torturer has expanded into the body of his fellow man and extinguished what was his spirit."[28]

And similar to Canetti, Améry also highlights the role of the survivor, who savors his absolute power: "the power of the torturer, under which the tortured moans, is nothing other than the triumph of the survivor over the one who is plunged from the world into agony and death."[29] Although "no bridge leads from the tormentor to the martyred," they are nonetheless united in a "horrible and perverted togetherness"—it is impossible for the "delight of tormenting" to exist without the "pain of being tormented."[30]

Humiliation and Desecration: The Semantics of Cruelty

Former Polish prisoner Stanislaw Chwiejczak was arrested and taken from his village in July 1943 as part of the "resettlement campaign" in the Zamość region and remained at Majdanek until March 1944. He later described one of Heinz Villain's "sporting events" as follows:

> Villain carried out various exercises with the prisoners. . . . He didn't like how we did our exercises. He came over and told us "lie down, stand up." The older prisoners among us were soon so weak that they were no longer able to rise. Villain kicked them on the back of the head and pushed them into the sand until all signs of life had been extinguished. . . . That happened more than once. . . . The second exercise was in March 1944, a penalty exercise for the entire Field [Field IV]. Villain issued the commands: "Form a detachment" and "Report and return, by block." . . . The ground was very muddy, so we kept getting stuck. The weaker ones fell, the stronger ones walked right over them. The order was repeated in that sequence, with the SS men and Kapos driving us forward with whips and sticks. Many prisoners who got stuck in the muddy clay soil died.[31]

This specific form of violence—forcing weakened prisoners to carry out pseudo-military drills—was a form of mistreatment employed throughout the men's concentration camps. As survivor Anise Postel-Vinay pointed out in a recent article, this form of violence did not occur at Ravensbrück.[32] Most likely, it had its origins in the early years of the concentration camps. For example, former Dachau prisoners reported that, as early as 1933 and 1934, the mainly Communist and Socialist prisoners were forced to carry out penal exercises as a form of humiliation.[33] According to

Stanislav Zámečnik, this soon resulted in unintended consequences, as noted with annoyance by a higher SS officer: the Communists, who were well-schooled in such maneuvers, often performed the drills with greater precision than the SS. As a result, according to Zámečnik, the penal exercises were suspended and, eventually, altered or replaced with new forms of abuse.

Paul Martin Neurath was also subjected to this form of punishment during his captivity at Dachau and Buchenwald in 1938 and 1939:

> "Penal exercises" were a form of intensified drill, and a true Hell. Generally, entire groups were punished that way, entire blocks, for example. One of the SS officers issued the commands, sometimes assisted by others. . . . The officers shouted the orders, and the masses carried them out. "Drop down! Stand up! On the double, march! On your belly! Caterpillar! (This entailed crawling forward on ones' elbows and stomach.) Roll left! Roll right! Stand up! Knee bends! Frog hops! (This involved hopping forward with knees bent.) Hop forward! Right! Left! Forward! Up! Down! Up! Down! Line up in the right corner! Approach the gate! Fan out! On your belly! Up! Down!"[34]

As Veronika Springmann has noted, such "calisthenics," as they were dubiously referred to by the SS, were an idiosyncratic and radical mix or adaptation of physical exercise and military drill: "While drills were aimed directly *at* the bodies of the recruits, these exercises [*Körpertechnik*] were directed *against* the bodies of the prisoners."[35] However, these exercises were not directed solely against the body as a material entity, but also—and above all—were directed against the body as a symbol representing the racial and/or political enemy.

As Paul Martin Neurath wrote in his 1951 sociological investigation of the Buchenwald concentration camp:

> It's hard to explain what was so Hellish about it, and why it was so different from a standard military drill. . . . Sometimes it was the cruelty of the exercises, like the frog jumps, the rolls, the caterpillar. Sometimes it was the condition of the ground: deep mud, puddles, sand, and gravel. The most terrible aspect was the tempo. Up—Down—Up—Down—Up—Down. Sometimes running at this tempo was all it took to extinguish a man's last spark of life. And to top it all off, there was the utter arbitrariness and senselessness of it all.[36]

The penal drills, therefore, were an experience of absolute power. For the SS, the fact that a relatively small group of men could exhort a much larger group of prisoners to their deaths served as an affirmation of their overwhelming dominance (*Über-Macht*). The prisoners, in turn, were forced to experience their subjugation "in the flesh." In the concentration camps, moreover, these "calisthenic exercises" were very much conceived as a form of mockery. As Veronika Springmann notes, in Nazi Germany, calisthenics had otherwise been employed as a means of strengthening the "Aryan body" of the *Volksgemeinschaft*. In the concentration camps, they were nothing more than a vehicle used by the SS to make a public mockery of the weakened and debilitated bodies of the prisoners: "The humiliation was twofold, involving both a demonstration of physical weakness and the loss of self-determination over one's own body."[37] That the prisoners were often forced to line up naked in front of the SS men, as is documented in photographs from the Mauthausen concentration camp, further testifies to the humiliatory intent behind that particular form of violence.[38]

In the scene described by Chwiejczak, the Majdanek prisoners were forced to run until many of them, already weakened, ended up stuck in the mud, where they were beaten to death by Kapos. The remaining prisoners were then compelled to run over the bodies of their fellow inmates—an act of degradation and cruelty that was central to this form of violence. The prisoners were forced to ignore their fallen comrades, and even to trample them underfoot. In so doing, the prisoners became an unwilling party to degradation of their fellow inmates.

Such descriptions of "calisthenics" or "drills" as a form of domination and humiliation figure mainly in the postwar testimony of male concentration camp survivors. This does not mean, however, that this particular form of violence did not exist in the women's camps. [39] However, as Anise Postel-Vinay has argued for Ravensbrück, no accounts of such "drills" exist for the Majdanek camp, which makes it unlikely that this particular form of cruelty was commonly employed at the Majdanek women's camp.

Looking at the testimony of survivors, it appears the female guards at Majdanek employed two main forms of cruelty. The first was violence in the form of punching, hitting, and kicking; the second involved the use of dogs against prisoners. In survivors' later testimony, the cruelty of two *Aufseherinnen*, Hermine Braunsteiner and Hildegard Lächert, was remembered as particularly notorious:

> The worst *Aufseherin* was "Brigida." She was young and not unattractive, with dark and somewhat frizzy hair. She never stood still and her hands were always covered in blood. . . . I seem to recall that some prisoners also called her "Bloody Brigida." I believe I remember the Polish word for "bloody" was "kreviczna."[40]

This description by Nechama Frenkel coincides with that of countless former prisoners, all of whom described Lächert as exceptionally cruel and always looking for a pretext to beat prisoners.[41] "I will never forget her. We called her Bloody Brigida. She always wanted to see the blood flow,"[42] recalled Lola Givner. Lächert was greatly feared in the camp and widely viewed by the prisoners as a sadist.[43]

According to the testimony of survivors, Lächert was the only female guard who also regularly mistreated male prisoners.[44] "With great pleasure and great frequency, she used to kick the so-called *Muselmänner*[45] in the genitals and then, when they fell, stomp on them. It must have been a source of great satisfaction for her,"[46] recalled Maryla Reich. In this episode, the *Aufseherin* attacked a prisoner who, suffering from starvation and utter exhaustion, had abandoned the struggle for survival. Maria Kaufmann-Krasowska also recounted witnessing Lächert in a similar incident:

> She had little iron balls on her whip and metal spikes on her boots. . . . I once saw her tear apart a male prisoner near the bathing facility with her whip and her shoes. Afterward, there was nothing of him left but a few shreds. . . . She went up to him and ordered him to bend over. Then she hit and kicked the man, on his entire body.[47]

Whether Lächert indeed had affixed pieces of metal to her shoes and her whip, as some prisoners claimed, or whether this memory has more to do with an attempt on the part of the prisoners to explain her enormous and even deadly brutality and violence, remains unknown.[48] What is clear, however, is that Lächert became completely caught up in her orgy of violence, a state that Wolfgang Sofsky has described as a form of frenzy.[49]

However, Lächert's strikes of the whip and her boot-clad kicks did more than cause pain; they disfigured the prisoners, often turning their bodies into little more than a gaping wound. She disfigured, debased, and exposed, nearly tearing to shreds the body of the male prisoner. By targeting the face and the genitals, Lächert focused on two especially vulnerable and sexually coded parts of the body. According to Véronique Nahoum-Grappe, a body that is disfigured beyond recognition represents an attempt by the perpetrator to "eradicate" or extinguish the "social and moral being" of the individual even prior to his or her death.[50] In this sense, Lächert's cruelty not only was intended to inflict the greatest possible degree of pain, but also was meant to disfigure, desecrate, emasculate, and dehumanize the body of her victim.

The dogs that some of the *Aufseherinnen* kept with them also figured prominently in the testimony of survivors. According to their testimony, the dogs were trained to be aggressive and to attack prisoners on command. Here, too, Hildegard Lächert received frequent mention.[51] During an interrogation, Charlotte Wöllert recalled that the female guards transferred from Ravensbrück to Majdanek in October 1942 brought two or three dogs with them, which they were later ordered to turn over to the SS men.[52] However, there were some female dog handlers at Majdanek,[53] as Hermine Braunsteiner recalled: "There were also dogs in Majdanek, but only trained *Aufseherinnen* got to be dog handlers, and I wasn't one of them. Dogs were used for the external detachments, to help prevent escape attempts."[54] In her testimony, Rosa Reischl also recalled that Lächert, whose assignments included watch over a gardening detachment, often had a dog at her side.[55]

In his autobiography, Auschwitz commandant Rudolf Höss recalled that Heinrich Himmler believed dogs were particularly useful in the women's concentration camps. Women, he believed, were more intimidated by dogs than were men; the use of dogs also helped reduce the number of guards needed in the camp.[56] In a February

1943 letter to Oswald Pohl and Richard Glücks, Himmler explained in greater detail his rationale for the use of dogs:

> Dogs used to patrol the perimeter of a camp must be trained to become slavering beasts, similar to the attack-dogs of Africa. They must be trained in such a way that they will tear a person to shreds at the command of their handler. For this reason, the dogs must be handled to ensure that no accidents take place. They should only be let out after dark, when the camp is locked down for the night, and must be captured again in the morning.[57]

In an interrogation, former dog handler Otto Z. confirmed that his dog, named "Treu Edgar von Schütting" after the popular brewery in Görtlitz from which he had been acquired, was extremely vicious: "It's true that I had to keep control over my dog; he was very aggressive and would otherwise bite."[58]

In general, specially trained SS dog handlers brought the animals to the outer cordon of guard posts, and accompanied the dogs on external labor detachments and night patrols. In an interrogation, Otto Z. recalled taking part in "searches for escaped prisoners" and being ordered to bring his dog to "pursuits" following "attacks by partisans" in the surrounding area.[59]

Although the dogs were intended to assist the female guards in their work, Rudolf Höss, for his part, was critical of the canine units at Auschwitz. As we have already seen in chapter 6, the Auschwitz commandant held the *Aufseherinnen* (and, to some extent, also the lower-ranking SS men) in very low esteem:

> Out of boredom, or just for fun, they would order the dogs to attack prisoners. When they were caught, they would claim the prisoner was behaving strangely and the dog attacked on its own; that they had dropped the lead, and so forth. They always had an excuse. The regulations required them to spend time training their dogs on a daily basis. And because training new dog handlers was so time consuming, the handlers could only be dismissed in the case of very serious infractions, after a punishment ordered by an SS court, or if they had mistreated or severely neglected the dog. . . . I had all sorts of trouble with the canine unit.[60]

Höss's comment that such vicious acts were furthered by the boredom and tedium of long, monotonous hours on duty is collaborated in a statement made by Lächert: "We had to stand there and stay on duty, whether it was raining, snowing, cold, or hot. Just imagine, standing around there like a mule, twelve hours at a time. At that point, you don't care about anything, anymore."[61]

Extreme cruelty toward prisoners using dogs was commonplace across the Nazi concentration camp system, and was also employed by the Majdanek *Aufseherinnen*. Several survivors recalled how Hildegard Lächert used to command her dog to attack female inmates:

> Once, in the summer, when we were cleaning the barracks . . . I heard a woman start to scream. It was Wladka, a Polish woman. . . . I looked over and saw that "Brigida" had set her large German shepherd on the girl. The dog bit her hands, which the girl was holding in front of her face to protect herself. Then the dog began tearing her clothes; at that point, rhubarb the girl had hidden under her clothes started to show. The dog grew more and more agitated, and "Brigida" kept spurring him on. He tore off all her clothing. Then "Brigida" assembled us for a kind of roll call; we were forced to stand in a triangle-formation, with the girl in the middle, and watch her punishment. I found out later that the girl had become pregnant by an SS soldier, a man "Brigida" also liked. That was the first time in my life I saw what an umbilical cord looked like, and a fetus. Two girls had to carry Wladka away on a stretcher. . . . After the dog had torn the clothing from her body, she was covered in blood. You could see shredded bits of flesh hanging down, and the long umbilical cord.[62]

Another witness statement confirms that Lächert commanded her dog during the attack, "Human, go get that dog"[63] ("dog," in this case, being used as a demeaning reference to the young woman). Here, the *Aufseherin* was using her dog to attack a pregnant woman, targeting the most vulnerable parts of her body in an act of cruel desecration and killing her unborn child.

For the agents of this violence, their acts might also be described as a "pleasurable discovery of the self" (*lustvolle Selbst-Erfindung*).[64] In any event, incidents such as these demonstrate the extent to which some female guards and SS men reveled in their power and dominance over the prisoners, and the "inventiveness" with which they carried out these acts of humiliation and defilement.

The Social Context of Violence in the Camps

After the clearing of the Warsaw Ghetto in spring 1943, several hundred Jewish women and young children were brought to Majdanek. They were initially spared from selections, and were housed in the women's camp (Field V), separately from the other female prisoners.[65] In late May 1943, however, the entire group was taken to the gas chambers and killed. During the operation, the *Aufseherinnen* were ordered to gather the children together under supervision of the SS physicians. Survivors report that they shoved and whipped the women and children.[66] Nechama Frenkel recalled the events as follows:

> They grabbed the children by the hair and legs and threw them on the wagon. All the children were driven to the gas chambers and murdered. . . . I would like to specify that the incident I describe above, with the children, took place in full view. There were many mothers among us who were not permitted to say goodbye to their children.[67]

A second such gassing of children took place in late summer 1943. In mid-August, a second group of several hundred women and young children had arrived from the Białystok ghetto. Like the first group, they were initially housed in a separate barracks on the women's field, which was then "cleared" in late August or early September.[68] According to Maryla Reich, an attempt was first made to lure the children out of the barracks with apples and candies. When this didn't work, the children were beaten and thrown on the wagon.[69] This time, only the children were killed; the mothers, instead, were to be put to work at the Ostindustrie company facilities.[70] The mothers, of course, tried to resist the removal of their children. "The *Aufseherinnen* tore the children out of the arms of some of the mothers, and brutally threw the children on the wagon to take them to the gas chamber,"[71] Teresa-Maria Slizewicz recalled. Danuta Medryk also witnessed the removal of the children, which was supervised by SS physician Max Blanke:

> Near the tractor, with two trailers attached to the back, there was a barrack, surrounded by barbed wire, where Jewish children were housed. There were also some mothers there with the children. Suddenly, the gate opened and a group of SS men entered. I didn't recognize any of them. Next to Ehrich [the chief guard], though, there was a group of *Aufseherinnen*, among whom I recognized the following individuals: Braunsteiner, Anna M., Orlowsky, and I believe also Ehlert. Konietzny, Mussfeldt and Dr. Rindfleisch were also nearby. The SS men forced the children out of the block; they ripped down the barbed wire fence that surrounded the block and chased the children. . . . The children scattered in every direction throughout the entire field. At that moment, I noticed Dr. Blanke approaching the trailers on a motorbike. Once Dr. Blanke arrived, he started yelling at the female guards and the SS men, and with hand motions urged them to hurry up. The Polish prisoners refused to help and just stood there. I mean the female prisoners, the Polish prisoner-functionaries. Ehrich and Braunsteiner then struck them; Braunsteiner hit them in the face, and Ehrich kicked them. But I also saw Braunsteiner kick the Jewish children.[72]

In an interrogation, *Aufseherin* Luzie H. described rounding up children during one of these internal transports, presumably the later of the two, that August:

> On that day, everyone had to remain after the count at roll call. The children were taken away from them. All the detachments were standing in the square. Every *Aufseherin* was standing by her detachment. A detachment of SS men went through the barracks. . . . I don't remember who gave the orders. We might have been ordered to remain standing after roll call. The prisoners must have heard something was up, because a number of children had been hidden. . . . The SS men threw the children out of the barracks and onto the wagons.[73]

Luzie H. was the only female guard to testify about the murder of these children;

all of the other *Aufseherinnen* refused to answer questions on the topic.[74] In her recollection, the female guards were ordered to "keep everyone quiet."[75] "I also remember how the SS detachments searched the barracks for infants. The mothers made a terrible fuss. . . . When the chief guard arrived, I started yelling at one of the women. The chief guard told me to be humane."[76] In the interrogation, Luzie H. acknowledged this gesture by the chief guard, saying, "The chief guard was a clever woman."[77] Luzie H. also described the incident in Eberhard Fechner's documentary:

> I wanted quiet. I saw the chief guard approach, so I started screaming at them to be quiet. But only because the chief guard was there, you see. I wanted to do my duty. She passed by me and whispered to me, "Frau *Aufseherin*, have some sympathy for the women." You see, I had assumed that she would demand that I keep them quiet.[78]

As this incident demonstrates, the actions of the *Aufseherinnen* cannot be solely explained as a consequence of the military structure of command. At times, their actions were even carried out in anticipation of orders by their superiors. In her harsh response, Luzie H. believed she was complying with Ehrich's expectations; in an unexpected twist, however, the chief guard instead showed a measure of empathy for the frantic mothers. As Luzie H.'s account also makes clear, interaction with the mothers and children intensified a situation that, even for the most jaded of the *Aufseherinnen*, was already highly charged. The female guards' unease, in turn, caused them to step up their level of brutality. The SS units that carried out mass shootings also behaved with exceptional brutality when babies and children were among the victims.[79] The ethical and social transgression of violence toward children appears to have itself contributed to a further escalation of violence.

Testimony by survivor Antonia Kurcz demonstrates how the actions of the various *Aufseherinnen* meshed with one another:

> Suddenly I noticed, or actually I heard the terrible screams of a child; I saw that a child, a girl four or five years' of age, had her hand caught in the door of a wagon. By that, I mean the platform. Braunsteiner was in the wagon; I recognized her. She did not respond to the child's screams. She wouldn't allow anyone to remove the child's hand from the door, and ordered the driver to proceed. I myself heard her say that the child's hand didn't need to be removed.[80]

While it is true that Hildegard Braunsteiner was remarkable for her exceptional cruelty,[81] it must also be said that—even as they distanced themselves from her actions—the inaction and silence of her colleagues helped create an aura of social acceptance and impunity. In this sense, then, inaction is very much a form of silent assent, communicating to all involved that the basic tenets of humanity no longer apply, and that no aid is forthcoming.

According to anthropologist Véronique Nahoum-Grappe, the context of impunity and social acceptance, in which some individuals (but not necessarily all) feel themselves empowered to be extremely violent, is a basic prerequisite for (though not the cause of) cruel behavior.[82] This context is established by all participants and must be constantly reaffirmed, even by those individuals who hold themselves out as passive observers. This "active dimension of watching," Harald Welzer has argued, is an oft-underestimated aspect of violence. According to Welzer, "Simply by virtue of their presence and their lack of intervention, observers ensure that the framework in which the participants operate remains in force, unquestioned.[83] The brutal colleagues thus serve as "negative figures of reference" (*negative Referenzfiguren*),[84] who allow the "normal" colleagues to view themselves as humane and compassionate. This microsocial context helps to hasten what Nahoum-Grappe refers to as an "escalation of transgression."[85] It is the act of toleration that enables cruelty; the more that is tolerated, the greater the cruelty that becomes possible.

The Gendered Dimension of Violence and Cruelty

In closing, we again turn to the example of Deputy Guard Binz and the scene in the Ravensbrück bunker. In considering the cultural and anthropological context, it is clear that Binz's further abuse of the unconscious, perhaps even lifeless, prisoner is not simply "gratuitous." Rather, it allowed the *Aufseherin* to revel in her position of overwhelming power, even though—or perhaps especially because—the victim was lying motionless on the ground. Since acts of cruelty do not require a counterpart who is capable of action, there was no need for an "echo" that might reverberate from the victim in the form of moans or screams of pain. In rocking back and forth on the calves of her helpless victim, Binz "inscribed" herself on her victim's body; even in the unlikely event the woman somehow survived, the *Aufseherin* made certain she had left her mark. Binz's mistreatment of an unconscious woman, perhaps even a corpse, represented an intensification of an already desecratory confrontation. In this way, we see that cruelty surpasses and exceeds the basic acts of violence and murder. Unlike cruelty, violence and killing are self-limiting in their capacity for escalation, as sociologist Heinrich Popitz has argued—if only because death establishes a definitive and final boundary.[86]

Moreover, such acts of cruelty have an effect that extends beyond the direct participants. Indeed, their reach extends much further. Germane Tillion, for example, did not personally witness the acts of punishment and desecration in the bunker. She related an account that was told to her by a friend, and never personally saw Binz "in action." This fact, however, does not cast doubt on the cruelty of the female guard. Rather, it shows that the effect of physical violence, and especially of cruelty, extends well beyond its immediate audience. Accounts of this particularly sadistic scene later circulated around the camp, helping *Aufseherin* Binz to secure her reputation and status. According to Tillion, Binz was immensely feared by the prisoners:

> The chief guard was completely overshadowed by her deputy, Dorothea Binz. She was the true star of the camp. Wherever she appeared, a whiff of terror would pass over us. She used to walk slowly through the prisoner ranks [during roll call], her riding crop behind her back, and through her narrowed eyes kept a watch for the weakest or most fearful women, whom she would then shower with lashes and blows. (As was often seen, she crushed any show of courage.)[87]

While Tillion's use of the word "star" here is, of course, sarcastic, it is also suggestive of the aura that surrounded the guard. This irony is echoed in a description of Hildegard Lächert offered by Towa Lederman: "I can't remember any *Aufseherinnen* other than 'Brigida,' because no one else was as 'popular' as she was."[88] Most of the Jewish and Polish survivors recalled Lächert as an "attractive" or "good-looking" woman.[89] As Riwka Landau told the court, "You might say 'Bloody Brigida' was the leading lady in the camp. She seemed so attractive to us; in part because next to her we were barely human. She was straight, slim, tall, dark blond, and about 25 years old."[90] In the Majdanek trial, Lola Givner told the court, "I will never forget her. We called her Bloody Brigida. She always wanted to see the blood flow. I recognize her eyes and her nose. Today, she's fat and ugly, but she was quite attractive back then."[91]

How is it possible, then, that the *Aufseherin* referred to by her colleagues as a "poor little rabbit" in an ill-fitting uniform left such a powerful impression on survivors, who later recalled her as an imposing figure? Lächert's position of power, her robust health and well-nourished figure, and even her uniform, which contrasted with the shabby clothing of the prisoners, may have contributed to this perception of attractiveness. In any case, such attributions of attractiveness also signified Lächert's position of absolute domination. Moreover, Lächert's reputation for exceptional cruelty also lent her an additional aura of notoriety. Female violence is subject to a stereotyped reception.[92] As Véronique Nahoum-Grappe has argued, cruelty is often figured as female in the popular imagination, while violence is often connoted as masculine. In this sense, a violent woman, such as Hermine Braunsteiner, suffers a loss of "femininity." By contrast, a woman who perpetrates acts of cruelty appears to gain in feminine attributes.[93]

At the same time, the gendered descriptions that survivors later gave of the *Aufseherinnen* often had a distinctly negative cast and connotation. This is particularly the case in descriptions of former Ravensbrück guards offered by German and Austrian survivors, who echoed Isa Vermehren's description of the Ravensbrück warders as "dumb girls" with "fat, clumsy fingers":[94]

> It was hard to tell one apart from the next. They all had the same figure, which mainly followed the diagonal: they were amply endowed up top and in front, and even more so down below, from the back.[95] . . . From my window, I could observe the entire flock of *Aufseherinnen* twice a day, about seventy of them, when they gathered for roll call in front of their office. I never thought such ugliness could

> be possible! It was hard to tell one from the other. . . . And the way they swayed, waddled, dragged, pushed, pulled, maneuvered, and balanced their way through the landscape—truly, it was a parade of outrageousness. Each and every one of them had permed hair like wild seaweed, which sat on top of their fat faces like a badly fitting wig—fat faces? Red faces, spongy faces, formless faces, "visages" in the worst sense of the word, in which all evil, stupidity, insolence, brutality—in short, the worst of human nature—made its mark. You might think I am exaggerating, but what use is it to point out an exception here or there, when it would only serve to make the general rule all the more apparent? Hands, legs, feet—they were all of the same cloddish nature, which didn't dare to claim attractiveness. And yet, they all seemed to believe they cut a jaunty figure. There is no other way to account for the shameless display of their own ugliness.[96]

This description again points to the class distinctions that shaped Isa Vermehren's perceptions of the female guards; as a member of the *Bildungsbürgertum* or educated middle class, the young women seemed to her crude and unsophisticated, even fatuous. For their part, the *Aufseherinnen* were annoyed by the air of superiority affected by the political prisoners, with whom they shared both national background and gender.

In both Ravensbrück and Majdanek, female violence was regarded as something exceptional. In their autobiographical accounts and in the witness stand before the court, survivors tended to remember violence committed by women more vividly and with greater precision than that committed by men. For this reason, it was easier to document the criminal acts committed by Hermine Braunsteiner and Hildegard Lächert at the Majdanek trial in Düsseldorf than it was to document the abuses of the male defendants. As an accessory to murder, Lächert was sentenced to a prison term of twelve years, while Braunsteiner received a sentence of life in prison.[97] Of the seven male defendants, including Hermann Hackmann, Emil Laurich, and Heinz Villain, each was sentenced to between three and ten years as accessories to murder, while one defendant was acquitted.[98] This same tendency might also help to explain why, in press accounts of the trial, the former female guards were generally identified by the nicknames they had been given in the camp, while the former SS men were generally identified by their "civilian" names.[99]

Masculinity and violence share a long tradition; indeed, the two are often seen as "inseparable" in the popular imagination.[100] The cruel *Aufseherin*, by contrast, was always recalled by survivors as a "woman" and as such was defined by her gender. This observation is lent further credence in the work of Constanze Jaiser, who examined representations of violence in the accounts of Jewish and non-Jewish women who survived Auschwitz and Ravensbrück. According to Jaiser, the violence of the *Aufseherinnen* staff was largely attributed to personal motivations, and particularly to "abnormal" sexuality or sexual perversion.[101] Moving beyond such psychologizing and essentializing explanations is, indeed, one of the central aims of my study, which endeavors to examine the violence and cruelty of the female guards as a response to their day-to-day work and as a social practice. This, in turn, requires an examination of the women's background and experiences, their specific practices of violence, and finally, the variety of meanings attributed to their violence within the "universe" of the concentration camp.

In closing this study, and especially in this last chapter, it is important to emphasize, yet again, that cruelty is by no means a uniquely "feminine" quality. As exemplified by the actions of Heinz Villain, the violence inflicted by SS men at Majdanek was no less notorious in terms of the depth of its cruelty. However, the atrocities committed by SS men appear to have made a less indelible impression on the memories of survivors. This apparent double standard was also largely ignored in the press accounts of the Majdanek trial. By contrast, the female guards who took part in selections, beatings, and murders violated accepted social norms for female behavior, and the crimes they committed attracted substantially more attention than did those of their male counterparts. The ongoing influence of this gendered conception of violence is again demonstrated in the abuses committed in 2004 during the Iraq War, in which the face of a female soldier, Lynndie England,[102] has become lodged in the collective memory, even as the names and faces of the male soldiers who also took part have largely faded from our recollection.

Conclusion

The twenty-eight SS *Aufseherinnen* who worked at Majdanek between fall 1942 and spring 1944 were not, to use Karin Orth's words, "born experts of terror."[1] Rather, they became violent within the context of a very specific institutional and sociocultural setting. As a social setting, however, the Majdanek camp was by no means a static entity. Instead, following arguments set forth by Alf Lüdtke, it is best understood as a dynamic arena involving a variety of actors. For this reason, a historical investigation of the everyday actions and experiences of the SS staff offers a lens through which to view the daily operations of the camp. Analyzing the social and cultural dynamics of violence within the workaday setting of the camp allows us to scrutinize the precise actions and concrete experiences of the *Aufseherinnen* and, in so doing, gain a better understanding of the complex meanings and ambiguities inherent in the practices of violence within the camp.

The Concentration Camp as Disciplinary Space and Site of Empowerment

For many new recruits, their initial "concentration camp experience," in the words of Michael Pollak, was at the Ravensbrück central women's camp. Many of the female guards who did their initial training at Ravensbrück later went on to work at Majdanek. As many Ravensbrück survivors later recalled, when the new recruits arrived at the camp, they were unsure of themselves, timid and insecure. Within a matter of just a few weeks, though, they were transformed into "SS *Aufseherinnen*." The living arrangements at the concentration camp as well as its paramilitary structure played a central role in this transformation. The young recruits lived in barracks housing, wore a uniform, and were assigned a firearm, all of which—taken together—served a disciplinary purpose and helped to foster a new sense of empowerment. This was particularly heightened by their uniforms and firearms. At the same time, the female guards' status as members of a supposedly homogeneous group afforded them a strong and appealing sense of corporate identity. Their training in the concentration camp also presented an opportunity to obtain new professional qualifications, a secure standard of living, and, unofficially, numerous opportunities for personal enrichment.

Although the *Aufseherinnen* were low-level staff members and subject to supposedly strict regulations, their daily duties afforded them many opportunities for autonomy and even for bending the rules. Living and working in a concentration camp entailed more than following regulations, carrying out orders, living in barracks housing, and demonstrating obedience to a military hierarchy. Rather, the uniforms and weapons, camp regulations, and administrative duties combined to foster a sense of professional identity and group belonging among the women; at the same time, they lent a sense of legitimacy to their work. In testing the opportunities for power and violence available to them in their everyday work at Ravensbrück, the recruits began to internalize the disciplinary techniques to which they were subjected, while also embracing their newfound sense of authority.

As my analysis has shown, the gap between official guidelines and everyday practices was crucial in this respect. Even though the *Aufseherinnen* were constrained by the institutional, political, and ideological context in which they operated, they had substantial room to maneuver and a broad scope for interpretation when it came to the official guidelines—and they made ample use of those opportunities. Under official guidelines, female guards were permitted to use violence only to prevent escapes and to punish prisoners who had committed "infractions." Though in theory these punishments were highly regulated, in everyday practice the prisoners at Ravensbrück were subjected to a constant rain of slaps, blows, and even kicks. Even the ostensibly highly regulated floggings carried out in the bunkers often far exceeded the prescribed form and number of lashes, as the example of Chief Guard Dorothea Binz demonstrates.

The Spiral of Violence at Majdanek

As was also the case at other concentration camps in the "East," Majdanek underwent a quantitative and qualitative escalation of violence, as Michael Wildt has noted. The female guards played an important role in the dynamics of this violence, which was directed not only at Jewish inmates, but also at Polish and Soviet prisoners. How else can we account for the fact that even *Aufseherinnen* who had little reputation for violence at Ravensbrück went on to behave with exceptional brutality and cruelty once at Majdanek?

One important explanation can be found in Majdanek's dual function as both concentration and extermination camp. The arrival of the first female guards, in October 1942, coincided with the inception of Hitler's Final Solution and the beginnings of large-scale killing in the gas chambers. As a result, the women were confronted with an entirely different camp environment than they had known at Ravensbrück. At Majdanek, as we have seen, even the less-violent female guards (and SS men) were in daily contact—whether directly or indirectly—with killing. Even though they did not take part in the exterminations, the *Aufseherinnen* participated in the selection of prisoners. Violence, death, and mass annihilation were all around them, a presence felt even during leisure hours. The odor of burning bodies, the sound of gunfire, and the sight of corpses being taken for disposal were inescapable realities, both during work hours and while off-duty.

A second factor contributing to the escalation of violence was the resentment many female guards felt at being transferred to Majdanek. Extremely primitive sanitation conditions and the constant threat of epidemics were a source of distress for the newly arrived *Aufseherinnen* (and SS men). What we can describe as a form of structural violence, following Johan Galtung, was, of course, a problem created by the SS staff's own mismanagement of the camp. The extremely poor living conditions and epidemics resulted in the death of many thousands of inmates. For the SS staff, by contrast, such conditions generally resulted in hospitalization, at most. Despite this privileged position, most of the *Aufseherinnen* were repulsed at the mere thought of contact with the largely Eastern European prisoners who were weakened, sick, and in extremely poor physical condition. At the same time, though, the guards appear to have enjoyed the benefits that their status as occupiers accorded them, not least the many opportunities they had to help themselves to the personal belongings of incoming Jewish prisoners. Some of the hardships of the Majdanek posting were real—that is, the threat of epidemics, the distance from home and family, unfamiliar geographical and weather conditions, and spartan housing arrangements. Others were mere figments of their imagination: the supposed inferiority of Polish culture, the fear of attack by partisans, and the belief that Jewish and Slavic prisoners were "subhuman." Whether real or imagined, however, these hardships and the sense of frustration, revulsion, and fear they elicited contributed to the escalation of brutality and violence.

The massive and daily exercise of violence at Majdanek also raises the question of the social dynamics of violence. Most existing research on the camps has argued that the daily exercise of violence toward prisoners was intended as a tool to dominate, break, and destroy them. By contrast, my study has shown that the female guards' brutality also represented an attempt to assert status among their fellow staff. Following Michel Foucault, for the SS staff, violence was also a means of communicating power and authority within the group. In many instances, this served to further escalate the violence. This social context and its group dynamics are key to understanding the women's propensity for violence.

Finally, my study also considered practices of violence that were primarily intended to humiliate, defile, and cause pain. In carrying out acts of cruelty, Elias Canetti has argued, aggressors experience, even revel in, their own overwhelming power. Indeed, for cruelty to exist, an imbalance of power must necessarily exist. As Véronique Nahoum-Grappe has also emphasized, this power imbalance is made ever more extreme when aggressors operate with absolute impunity. The context of impunity also serves to escalate the spiral of cruelty and contribute to the transgression of ordinary boundaries. As Nahoum-Grappe has described, the cruel gesture is "clear-sighted" and precise. As such, it must be understood as a "subtle" form of communication between the aggressor, the victim, and the audience. As is true for practices of violence, the microsocial context is essential to understanding cruelty. Although the cruelest *Aufseherinnen* and SS men were feared even by their colleagues, and their cruelty was implicitly tolerated, such fear did not always bring with it added respect. Nonetheless, this passivity created the conditions that allowed cruelty to occur and to escalate. In a context of collective violence, not acting, or refusing to see, not only amounts to tacit approval; acquiescence also has an active aspect.

Group and Gender Dynamics

The social climate among the female guards can at best be described as ambivalent. Although there were tensions among the women, and cliques soon formed, postwar interrogations show the women frequently referring to themselves as "we *Aufseherinnen*," which suggests they also shared a strong sense of group identity. Despite the friction and rivalries, even after the war the women continued to identify as members of a group, as former colleagues, and to a certain extent also as "partners in crime." For the female guards, conditions at Majdanek required at least some level of cohesion. At Majdanek, the *Aufseherinnen* found themselves "on foreign soil," in an environment of unaccustomed violence. They also had to assert themselves against their male colleagues, by whom they were vastly outnumbered. While there were never more than twenty or so female guards stationed at Majdanek at any given time, there were about 1,200 SS men at the camp. The female SS staff was thus a tiny minority in what was a male-dominated, paramilitary society.

The *Aufseherinnen* occupied the lowest rung on the SS hierarchy. However, this does not mean the women were entirely "subjugated" to SS authority. Rather, the female staff found ways to assert themselves within this male-dominated society. As in other women's concentration camps, a great deal of the friction between the female guards and the senior SS leaders derived from the fact that the male officers had trained and risen through the ranks within an all-male system organized along Eicke's paramilitary model. Yet none of the administrators at Majdanek had any experience running a women's camp. Many of the SS men, particularly in the higher ranks, regarded the *Aufseherinnen* as intruders in a military and male-dominated sphere—not least because of the women's propensity for violence.

Among the Majdanek guard staff, the dynamics of violence also had a gendered dimension. For example, both the female guards and the SS men were likely to escalate their violence when an observer of the opposite sex was in the vicinity. The means of violence was also divided along gender lines. Both male and female guards often wielded their leather boots to inflict brutal, even deadly, kicks on helpless prisoners. In contrast to the men, however, the *Aufseherinnen* rarely made use of the firearms. Thus, although the women were officially authorized to carry a firearm, in practice the use of firearms by the female guards was taboo in the camp. This taboo was encouraged by the SS men who, confronted with the unaccustomed presence of uniformed and armed women, sought to reclaim an exclusively "male" sphere by ascribing a "feminine ineptness" to their female colleagues when it came to the handling of guns. Overall, the relationships between the *Aufseherinnen* and SS men were complex and varied, a mixture of flirting and teasing, competitiveness and condescension, personal and professional disagreements, and even friendships, romances, and marriages.

The only place in which a strict separation between the male and female spheres appears to have been maintained, then, was in the actual "work" of killing. *Aufseherinnen* at Auschwitz and Majdanek carried out selections among the female prisoners, in part as a result of the camps' dual function as both concentration and extermination camps. However, they never took an active part in mass shootings or in killing operations in the gas chambers, nor did they assist in disposing of the dead bodies.

Work Ethic and Work Identities

In many postwar interrogations, the former Majdanek *Aufseherinnen* emphasized their lack of power vis-à-vis their daily duties. These protestations, however, contrast sharply with other statements and descriptions that suggest the women identified strongly with their work and the sense of power and authority they enjoyed. Some of the women's self-representations in their postwar testimony also display hints of professional ambition. For example, Hermine Braunsteiner always emphasized that she entered service as an "ordinary" guard, and depicted herself as an insignificant cog in a massive machine. Immediately after the war, though, Braunsteiner enjoyed recounting, with a barely hidden sense of pride, that she had received a war service medal in "acknowledgment" for her work at Ravensbrück.

Upon closer examination, the perpetrators' day-to-day definition of "work" helped shape both the form of violence and the specific acts of violence that they carried out. In the selections and in the gas chambers, the staff had to meet their daily quotas. In the supervision of forced labor in the prisoner detachments, the female guards had to maintain the proper work rhythm among prisoners and ensure that the daily output was met. Here we see the benefits of viewing camp violence through the lens of everyday life. In both the forced-labor details and the extermination process, various stages of work needed to be coordinated and monitored. Carrying out these duties required a dedicated staff who displayed the necessary "work ethic." To the *Aufseherinnen* at Majdanek, performing their jobs well was a matter of personal pride. The appreciation and respect they received for their work, such as ideological support in the form of pronouncements from Heinrich Himmler, shaped the women's everyday work experience. The everyday quality of their work also conferred on the women a sense of purpose and legitimacy.

Even after they had acclimated to their new environment, however, the women remained aware of the horrors of the camp and the violence that took place there. This aspect of their work was an ever-present feature, both on the job and during their leisure hours. It was demonstrated in the women's fear of the crematorium, the jokes made by their colleagues, and their references to the unpleasant odor of burning bodies, the sound of gunfire, and so forth. Even though the staff grew at least somewhat accustomed to these aspects, it must certainly have remained discomfiting on some level. Hertha Ehlert's postwar testimony is particularly illuminating in this respect. Ehlert was sometimes assigned to work in the prisoner's bath, which was part of the gas chamber complex at Majdanek. In the bath, she was confronted with the realities of the killing process, and she recalled this work as extremely disturbing. In one interrogation, she described how anxious she became after listening to the "screams and wails" of the Polish women and children sent there to shower and dress before being registered as prisoners. By contrast, Ehlert claimed that she rather enjoyed her work in the laundry, situated such that she could see and hear little of the killing. For camp staff, then, looking away and averting their eyes was a form of accommodation. Yet even as the day-to-day horrors of the camp could not be banished entirely, in other respects they could experience work at Majdanek as quite "pleasant."

The actions of Erich Muhsfeldt, the head of the crematorium, demonstrate that such scruples about mass murder could be overcome. At the Auschwitz Trial in Krakow, Muhsfeldt testified that he was initially reluctant to take on command of the burial detachment at Majdanek. In time, though, he came to take pride in his work. He particularly appreciated the skill and expertise that the work required, which appealed to his work ethic and, for him, lent meaning to his work. The "corporal punishments" carried out at Ravensbrück and Majdanek, and the response to escape attempts at Majdanek both demonstrate that the camp staff took advantage of opportunities to exercise initiative and display their commitment to their work—for example, when a female guard administered the 25 prescribed lashes of the whip, and then added another one for good measure. In carrying out their daily duties, each and every *Aufseherin* and SS man contributed to the violence and extermination that was central to Majdanek. While Nazi ideology offered a supposed rationale, the concentration camp as an institutional setting created the framework for this violence. Moreover, it was the implementers on the ground who adapted this framework in various ways as they carried out their daily duties. The result was a range of violent practices not originally envisioned and, in fact, not always welcomed by policymakers.

Patriotism or Nazi ideology played a far less direct role in the workaday violence and killing than has generally been assumed in scholarly research. The abstract ideals of the Nazi regime were not in themselves sufficient motivation for the *Aufseherinnen* to spend years working in a concentration camp. It would be more accurate to say that, as the *Aufseherinnen* carried out their daily duties, racial ideology and Social Darwinism came to serve as a justification for their work in the concentration camp. This was true both at Ravensbrück and, especially, at Majdanek. In occupied Poland and at Majdanek, predisposed racial prejudices were not only affirmed in day-to-day work, they were embraced, appropriated, and radicalized. For the SS staff, the workaday context was at once motivating and transformative—the daily quotas that had to be filled, finding solutions to problems large and small, the gratification of a job well done, and the pleasure taken in productivity. An analysis that foregrounds these everyday dynamics shows that the violence exercised at Majdanek was not so much carried out in response to orders "from above"—meaning from Heinrich Himmler and the central camp administration, or the Inspectorate of Concentration Camps (IKL), or the Chief Economic and Administrative Office (WVHA). Rather, this violence was far more the product of the complex interactions and power relations among the staff on the ground.

For this reason, this study focused less on the ideology of violence, and more on the concrete actions and accommodations undertaken by the men and women who carried that violence out. This does not mean that ideology has no explanatory value when it comes to considering the practices of violence and cruelty. That said, however, the available source material and the microsocial perspective have led me to a rather different insight: even though the Nazi concentration camps were products of exterminatory racism, the female guards and SS men who worked in the camps were motivated mainly by personal needs and benefits. For the young, mostly unmarried women, born in the early 1920s, and from relatively modest backgrounds, work as a camp guard offered, above all, a good salary, a secure job, and the status of a civil service employee. For the former factory workers and housemaids, such employment afforded, first and foremost, an opportunity for social advancement rather than the fulfillment of a political calling. In addition, the women were also motivated by opportunities for personal enrichment, the thrill of adventure, recognition for their service, and the opportunity to satisfy their ambitions.

In sum, both the *Aufseherinnen* and the SS men experienced the concentration camp primarily as a workplace, and their duties primarily as work that needed to be carried out according to a high standard. Their violent acts were part of a complex and by no means linear process, which emerged through a complex interplay of normative, institutional, social, and situational dynamics. In analyzing their work experiences and practices of violence in their everyday context, it becomes clear that, in spite of the totalitarian framework and the institutional setting that existed at the camp, the staff at Majdanek at all times had options available to them and room to maneuver when it came time to act. Only rarely, however, did they refuse to take part in violence. More to the point: the violence they exercised on the prisoners often exceeded their assigned responsibilities and duties, and they undertook this escalation of violence on their own initiative.

Notes

INTRODUCTION

1. In compliance with German data protection laws, this work uses the full last names only for individuals who were tried in court after 1945, or who can be considered public or historical figures.
2. Statement by Hermine Ryan Braunsteiner on 22 August 1973 in Düsseldorf, Hauptstaatsarchiv [HstA] Düsseldorf, Gerichte Republik [Ger. Rep.] 432 No. 193, p. 62ff.
3. The camp, bordering the Lublin district of Majdan Tatarski, was officially referred to as "Prisoner of War Camp of the Armed-SS Lublin" and later as "Concentration Camp Lublin." In this study I adopt the name Majdanek, which the inmates used during their incarceration.
4. See telex from Headquarters Lublin to the Chief Economic and Administration Main Office (WVHA), HStA Düsseldorf, Ger. Rep. No. 429, p. 72.
5. See telex from Prisoner of War Camp (KGL) Lublin to the WVHA on 29 January 1943, HStA Düsseldorf, Ger. Rep. 432 No. 429 p. 15; letter from the WVHA on 17 March 1943 to the Ravensbrück Concentration Camp and KL Lublin, HStA Düsseldorf, Ger. Rep. 432 No. 430, p. 189; letters from the WVHA on 1 March 1943 and 22 March 1943 to KL Ravensbrück and KL Lublin, HStA Düsseldorf, Ger. Rep. 432 No. 430, pp.

210 and 190; telex by Commandant Florstedt to the WHVA on 21 July 1943, HStA Düsseldorf, Ger. Rep. 432 No. 429, p. 27.

6. Christopher R. Browning, *Ordinary Men: Reserve Police Battalion 101 and the Final Solution* (New York: HarperCollins, 1992).
7. See Ulrich Herbert, Karin Orth, and Christoph Dieckmann, eds., *Die nationalsozialistischen Konzentrationslager: Entwicklung und Struktur*, 2 vols. (Göttingen: Wallstein, 1998); Wolfgang Benz and Barbara Distel, eds., *Terror ohne System. Die ersten Konzentrationslager im Nationalsozialismus 1933–1935*, vol. 1, *Geschichte der Konzentrationslager 1933–1945* (Berlin: Metropol, 2001);Benz and Distel, eds., *Herrschaft und Gewalt. Frühe Konzentrationslager 1933–1939*, vol. 2 (Berlin: Metropol, 2002); Benz and Distel, eds., *Instrumentarium der Macht. Frühe Konzentrationslager 1933–1937*, vol. 3, *Geschichte der Konzentrationslager 1933–1945* (Berlin: Metropol, 2003). See also the series edited by Benz and Distel, *Der Ort des Terrors. Geschichte der nationalsozialistischen Konzentrationslager. Organisation des Terrors*, vols. 1–7 (Munich: C.H. Beck, 2005–2008). An excellent overview of recent scholarship on concentration camps is provided in Jane Caplan and Nikolaus Wachsmann, eds., *Concentration Camps in Nazi Germany: The New Histories* (London: Routledge, 2010).
8. Wolfgang Kirstein, *Das Konzentrationslager als Institution totalen Terrors. Das Beispiel des KZ Natzweiler* (Pfaffenweiler: Centaurus-Verlagsgesellschaft, 1992).
9. Wolfgang Sofsky, *The Order of Terror: The Concentration Camp* (Princeton, NJ: Princeton University Press, 1997).
10. On the definition of absolute power, see Sofsky, *The Order of Terror*, 16–27.
11. See Gerhard Armanski, *Maschinen des Terrors: das Lager (KZ und GULAG) in der Moderne* (Münster: Westfalisches Dampfboot, 1993); Armanski, "Der GULag—Zwangsjacke des Fortschritts," in *Strategien des Überlebens: Häftlingsgesellschaften in KZ und Gulag*, ed. Hans Schafranek and Robert Streibel (Vienna: Picus Verlag, 1996), 16–43. A comparable approach, not explicitly applied to concentration camps but to the Holocaust, was used by Zygmunt Bauman in *Modernity and the Holocaust* (Ithaca, NY: Cornell University Press, 1989).
12. See Sofsky, *The Order of Terror*.
13. See Alf Lüdtke, "Der Bann der Worte: 'Todesfabriken.' Vom Reden über den NS-Völkermord—das auch ein Verschweigen ist," *WerkstattGeschichte* 13 (1996): 5–18; see also Lüdtke, "Die Fiktion der Institution. Herrschaftspraxis und Vernichtung der europäischen Juden im 20. Jahrhundert," in *Institutionen und Ereignis. Über historische Praktiken und Vorstellungen gesellschaftlichen Ordnens*, ed. Reinhard Blänkner and Bernhard Jussen (Göttingen: Vandenhoeck & Ruprecht, 1998), 355–79.
14. Heinrich Himmler (1900–1945) was the *Reichsführer-SS* from 1929 until 1945. For more information, see Richard Breitman, *The Architect of Genocide: Himmler and the Final Solution* (Hanover, NH: University Press of New England, 1992); Johannes Tuchel, "Heinrich Himmler—Der Reichsführer SS," in *Die SS. Elite unter dem Totenkopf. 30 Lebensläufe*, ed. Ronald Smelser and Enrico Syring (Paderborn:

Schöningh, 2000), 234–53; see also Peter Longerich, *Heinrich Himmler*, trans. Jeremy Noakes and Lesley Sharpe (Oxford: Oxford University Press, 2012).

15. See Jacques Revel, *Jeux d'échelles. La microanalyse à l'expérience* (Paris: Gallimard, 1996).
16. Jacques Sémelin, "Introduction: Violences extrêmes: peut-on comprendre?," *Revue internationale des sciences sociales* 147 (2002): 479–81, 481.
17. Daniel Goldhagen made an initial attempt to do so for the police battalions in the East, the "work" camps and the death marches. Since then, other historians have presented some research See Daniel J. Goldhagen's *Hitler's Willing Executioners: Ordinary Germans and the Holocaust* (New York: Knopf, 1996); Daniel Blatman, *Les marches de la mort. La dernière étape du génocide nazi, été 1944–printemps 1945* (Paris: Fayard, 2009); Stefan Hördler, *Ordnung und Inferno. Das KZ-System im letzten Kriegsjahr* (Göttingen: Wallstein, 2014).
18. Marc Buggeln, *Slave Labor in Nazi Concentration Camps* (Oxford: Oxford University Press, 2014); see also Nikolaus Wachsmann, *KL: A History of the Nazi Concentration Camps* (New York: Farrar, Straus & Giroux, 2015).
19. Institut für Zeitgeschichte [hereafter IfZ] München, Schumacher Collection 1329, Fa-183.
20. Gudrun Schwarz, *Eine Frau an seiner Seite. Ehefrauen in der "SS-Sippengemeinschaft"* (Hamburg: Hamburger Edition, 1997).
21. Alf Lüdtke, "Introduction: What Is the History of Everyday Life and Who Are Its Practitioners?," in *The History of Everyday Life: Reconstructing Historical Experiences and Ways of Life* (Princeton, NJ: Princeton University Press, 1995), 3–40. See Geoff Eley, *Nazism as Fascism: Violence, Ideology, and the Ground of Consent in Germany, 1930–1945* (New York: Routledge, 2013).
22. See A. S. Bergerson, E. Mailänder Koslov, G. Reuveni, P. Steege, and D. Sweeney, "Forum: Everyday Life in Nazi Germany," *German History* 27, no. 4 (2009): 560–79.
23. Michael Pollak, *Die Grenzen des Sagbaren. Lebensgeschichten von KZ-Überlebenden als Augenzeugenberichte und als Identitätsarbeit* (New York: Campus Verlag, 1988). See also Michael Pollak, *L'Expérience concentrationnaire. Essai sur le maintien de l'identité sociale* (Paris: Éditions Métaillé 2000).
24. David Rousset, *L'Univers concentrationnaire* (Paris: Editions du Pavois, 1946).

Chapter One. Methodological and Theoretical Considerations

1. Karin Orth, *Die Konzentrationslager-SS. Sozialstrukturelle Analysen und biographische Studien* (Göttingen: Wallstein Verlag 2000); Karin Orth, "Egon Zill—ein typischer Vertreter der Konzentrationslager-SS," in *Karrieren der Gewalt. Nationalsozialistische Täterbiographien*, ed. Klaus-Michael Mallmann and Gerhard Paul (Darmstadt, 2004), 264–73.
2. See, for example, the excellent synthesis by Nikolaus Wachsmann, *KL: A History of the*

Nazi Concentration Camps (New York: Farrar, Straus & Giroux, 2015).

3. Marc Buggeln, *Slave Labor in Nazi Concentration Camps* (Oxford: Oxford University Press, 2014).
4. Dirk Riedel, *Ordnungshüter und Massenmörder im Dienst der Volksgemeinschaft. Der KZ-Kommandant Hans Loritz* (Berlin: Metropol, 2010); Stefan Hördler, *Ordnung und Inferno. Das KZ-System im letzten Kriegsjahr* (Göttingen: Wallstein, 2014).
5. Simone Erpel, ed., *Im Gefolge der SS: Aufseherinnen des Frauen-KZ Ravensbrück. Begleitband zur Ausstellung* (Berlin: Metropol, 2007); see also the publications of Insa Eschebach, Irmtraud Heike, Johannes Schwartz, and Gudrun Schwarz.
6. Anette Kretzer, *NS-Täterschaft und Geschlecht. Der erste britische Ravensbrück-Prozess 1946/47 in Hamburg* (Berlin: Metropol, 2009); Ljiljana Heise, *KZ-Aufseherinnen vor Gericht. Greta Bösel—"Another of Those Brutal Types of Women"?* (Frankfurt am Main: Peter Lang, 2009); John Cramer, *Belsen Trial 1945. Der Lüneburger Prozess gegen Wachpersonal der Konzentrationslager Auschwitz und Bergen-Belsen* (Bergen-Belsen - Dokumente und Forschungen 1). (Göttingen: Wallstein Verlag, 2011).
7. See, for example, Wendy Lower, *Hitler's Furies: German Women in the Nazi Killing Fields* (New York: Houghton Mifflin Harcourt, 2013).
8. Bernhard Strebel, *Das KZ Ravensbrück. Geschichte eines Lagerkomplexes* (Paderborn: F. Schöningh, 2003), 39ff. On the development of the Nazi concentration camps, see Johannes Tuchel, *Konzentrationslager. Organisationsgeschichte und Funktion der "Inspektion der Konzentrationslager" 1934–1938* (Boppard am Rhein: Boldt, 1991); Klaus Drobisch and Günther Wieland, *System der NS-Konzentrationslager, 1933–1939* (Berlin: Akademie Verlag, 1993); Jan Erik Schulte, *Zwangsarbeit und Vernichtung: das Wirtschaftsimperium der SS: Oswald Pohl und das SS-Wirtschafts-Verwaltungshauptamt 1933–1945* (Paderborn: Schöningh, 2001).
9. On the same day as the Reichstag Fire, 27 February 1933, Paul von Hindenburg issued a "Decree of the Reich President for the Protection of the People and the State." The term "protective custody" was not mentioned in this decree. See Ulrich Herbert, "Von der Gegnerbekämpfung zur 'rassischen Generalprävention.' 'Schutzhaft' und Konzentrationslager in der Konzeption der Gestapo-Führung 1933–1939," in *Die nationalsozialistischen Konzentrationslager*, ed. Ulrich Herbert, Karin Orth, and Christoph Dieckmann (Göttingen: Wallstein, 1998), 1:60–86.
10. Strebel, *Das KZ Ravensbrück*, 31ff.
11. Johannes Tuchel, "Organisationsgeschichte der 'frühen' Konzentrationslager," in *Instrumentarium der Macht. Frühe Konzentrationslager 1933–1937*, ed. Wolfgang Benz and Barbara Distel (Berlin: Metropol, 2003), 9–26, 12.
12. Ibid.
13. These included Gotteszell (Schwäbisch Gmünd), Stadelheim (Munich), Barnimstrasse (Berlin), Fuhlsbüttel (Hamburg), Brauweiler (Westphalia), Bergkamen-Schönhausen (Westphalia), Lübeck-Lauerhof, and Moringen. Hanna Elling, *Frauen im Widerstand 1933–1945* (Frankfurt: Röderberg-Verlag, 1978), 25–28; Sibyl Milton, "Deutsche und deutsch-jüdische Frauen als Verfolgte des NS-Staates," *Dachauer Hefte* 3 (1987): 3–20,

6ff.; Renate Riebe, "Frauenkonzentrationslager 1933–1939," *Dachauer Hefte* 14 (1998): 125–40, 125ff.; Strebel, *Das KZ Ravensbrück*, 37.

14. Gabriele Herz, *The Women's Camp in Moringen: A Memoir of Imprisonment in Germany, 1936–1937* (New York: Berghahn 2006).
15. Riebe, "Frauenkonzentrationslager," 127ff.
16. Klaus Drobisch, "Frauenkonzentrationslager im Schloss Lichtenburg," *Dachauer Hefte* 3 (1987): 101–15, 103.
17. Strebel, *Das KZ Ravensbrück*, 39.
18. From this point on, the number of incarcerated women grew rapidly. Before then, women prisoners constituted a tiny minority. Status reports from Ravensbrück in the course of 1939 indicate persecution of women that was increasingly racially and politically motivated. The roll call on 21 May 1939 records female prisoners; by the end of the year their number had increased to 1,170. Strebel, *Das KZ Ravensbrück*, 104.
19. Gudrun Schwarz, "SS-Aufseherinnen in nationalsozialistischen Konzentrationslagern (1933–1945)," *Dachauer Hefte* 10 (1994): 32–49, 37.
20. See Gudrun Schwarz, *Eine Frau an seiner Seite. Ehefrauen in der "SS-Sippengemeinschaft"* (Hamburg: Hamburger Edition, 1997).
21. With regard to the Armed SS and, particularly, the Concentration Camp SS (Karin Orth), the issue of whether it should be called a paramilitary or military organization remains controversial. The SS was divided into various suborganizations, some of which had paramilitary structures, such as the General SS ("Allgemeine-SS"), while others were military in organization, such as the Armed SS, which, from 1935, was built up to rival the Wehrmacht. As Bernd Wegner notes in the introduction to his study, the Armed SS cannot, despite its military structure, be called "military" in a "traditional" sense, as military functions were only part of the Armed SS's list of tasks. The Dispositional Troop and the Death's Head units were used in concentration camps. Although both also provided troops for the combat Armed SS, guarding concentration camps cannot be considered a military deployment. Bernd Wegner, *Hitlers Politische Soldaten. Die Waffen-SS, 1933–1945* (Paderborn: Schöningh, 2006), 17.
22. Undated form by Ravensbrück Concentration Camp concerning applications for female guards (application form), NS/4/Ra 1, Bundesarchiv [hereafter BA].
23. Each concentration camp was organized in different sections. The *Schutzhaftlager* was the camp compound or "protective custody camp" and was a separate section of the camp complex. The prisoners were held in this section. For a more detailed description see "The Inner Organization of Majdanek" in chapter 2.
24. See Strebel, *Das KZ Ravensbrück*, 274–88. See also chapter 2 of this work.
25. See Wachsmann, *KL: A History of the Nazi Concentration Camps.*
26. I thank Johannes Schwartz for this information.
27. Strebel, *Das KZ Ravensbrück*, 73ff.
28. On Ravensbrück as a training camp, see chapter 4 of this work.
29. Institut für Zeitgeschichte Munich, Collection Schumacher 329, Fa-183.

30. See "Frauen im Konzentrationslager," *Deutsche Freiheit*, 5 October 1934.
31. Joan W. Scott, "Gender: A Useful Category of Historical Analysis," *American Historical Review* 91, no. 5 (1986): 1053–75.
32. Geoff Eley, *Nazism as Fascism: Violence, Ideology, and the Ground of Consent in Germany, 1930–1945* (New York: Routledge, 2013), 13–58; see also Geoff Eley, *A Crooked Line: From Cultural History to the History of Society* (Ann Arbor: University of Michigan Press, 2005).
33. Adam Tooze, *The Wages of Destruction: The Making and Breaking of the Nazi Economy* (London: Penguin, 2006).
34. See Andrew Stuart Bergerson, *Ordinary Germans in Extraordinary Times: The Nazi Revolution in Hildesheim* (Bloomington: Indiana University Press, 2004); Paul Steege, *Black Market, Cold War: Everyday Life in Berlin, 1946–1949* (Cambridge: Cambridge University Press, 2007); Monica Black, *Death in Berlin: From Weimar to Divided Germany* (Cambridge: Cambridge University Press, 2010).
35. See Elizabeth Heineman, "The Hour of the Woman: Memories of Germany's "Crisis Years" and West German National Identity," *American Historical Review* 101, no. 2 (1996): 354–95; Elizabeth Harvey, *Women and the Nazi East: Agents and Witnesses of Germanization* (New Haven: Yale University Press, 2003); Michael Wildt, *Hitler's Volksgemeinschaft and the Dynamics of Racial Exclusion: Violence against Jews in Provincial Germany, 1919–1939* (New York: Berghahn Books, 2011).
36. D. Sweeney, in A. S. Bergerson, E. Mailänder Koslov, G. Reuveni, P. Steege, and D. Sweeney, "Forum: Everyday Life in Nazi Germany," *German History* 27, no. 4 (2009): 560–79, 561.
37. Eley, *Nazism as Fascism*, 15.
38. Alf Lüdtke, *Eigen-Sinn: Fabrikalltag, Arbeitererfahrung und Politik vom Kaiserreich bis in den Faschismus* (Hamburg: Ergebnisse-Verlag, 1993), 9–21, 15.
39. Alf Lüdtke, "War as Work: Aspects of Soldering in the Twentieth-Century Wars," in *No Man's Land of Violence: Extreme Wars in the 20th Century*, ed. Alf Lüdtke and Bernd Weisbrod (Göttingen: Wallstein 2006), 127–51, 151.
40. Geoff Eley, "Labor History, Social History, *Alltagsgeschichte*: Experience, Culture, and the Politics of the Everyday—A New Direction for German History?," *Journal for Modern History* 61, no. 2 (1989): 297–343.
41. Eley, *Nazism as Fascism*, 48.
42. Alf Lüdtke, "Alltag: Der blinde Fleck?," *Deutschland Archiv. Zeitschrift für das vereinigte Deutschland* 5 (2006): 900.
43. Dan Stone, "The Decision Making Process in Context," in *Histories of the Holocaust* (Oxford: Oxford University Press, 2010), 64–112; Donald Bloxham and Dirk A. Moses, *The Oxford Handbook of Genocide Studies* (Oxford: Oxford University Press, 2010); Donald Bloxham, *The Final Solution: A Genocide* (Oxford: Oxford University Press, 2009).
44. A further dissertation has been completed. See Johannes Schwartz, "Handlungsräume und Verhaltensweisen von KZ-Aufseherinnen. Das 'weibliche Gefolge der Waffen-SS'

im Frauen-Konzentrationslager Ravensbrück und in den KZ-Außenlagern in und bei Neubrandenburg" (Erfurt University, 2010).

45. D. Sweeney, in A. S. Bergerson, E. Mailänder Koslov, G. Reuveni, P. Steege, and D. Sweeney, "Forum: Everyday Life in Nazi Germany," *German History* 27, no. 4 (2009): 560–79, 561.
46. Jie-Hyun Lim, "Mapping Mass Dictatorship: Towards a Transnational History of Twentieth-Century Dictatorship," in *Gender Politics and Mass Dictatorship: Global Perspectives*, ed. Jie-Hyun Lim and Karen Petrone (New York: Palgrave Macmillan, 2011), 1–22.
47. P. Steege, in: A. S. Bergerson, E. Mailänder Koslov, G. Reuveni, P. Steege, and D. Sweeney, "Forum: Everyday Life in Nazi Germany," *German History* 27, no. 4 (2009): 560–79, 562.
48. Klaus Bergmann and Susanne Thun, "Didaktik der Alltagsgeschichte," in *Handbuch der Geschichtsdidaktik*, ed. Klaus Bergmann et al. (Düsseldorf: Schwann, 1985), 315–20, 315; see also Hubert C. Ehalt, "Geschichte von unten," in *Geschichte von unten. Fragestellungen, Methoden und Projekte einer Geschichte des Alltags*, ed. Bergmann et al. (Vienna, 1984), 11–39, 24.
49. Definition by Alf Lüdtke, cited in Helmut Konrad, "Zur Theorie und Methodik der Alltagsgeschichtsschreibung," in *Geschichte und ihre Quellen. Festschrift für Friedrich Hausmann* (Graz, 1987), 591–99, 592.
50. Lüdtke, *Eigen-Sinn*, 120–60, 144.
51. See Alf Lüdtke, "Introduction," in *Herrschaft als soziale Praxis, Historische und sozialanthropologische Studien*, ed. Alf Lüdtke (Göttingen: Vandenhoeck & Ruprecht, 1991), 9–62; see also Michel Foucault, *The History of Sexuality*, vol. 1, translated from the French by Robert Hurley (New York, 1988).
52. P. Steege, in A. S. Bergerson, E. Mailänder Koslov, G. Reuveni, P. Steege, and D. Sweeney, "Forum: Everyday Life in Nazi Germany," *German History* 27, no. 4 (2009): 560–79, 562.
53. Lüdtke, "Alltag: Der blinde Fleck?," 894–901, 897.
54. This point is further addressed in the forthcoming collaborative monograph authored by the team that calls itself ATG26 and is tentatively titled *Ruptures of the Everyday: Views of Modern Germany from the Ground*. Focusing on the microsocial interactions of ordinary Germans, this book weaves together the fragments of experience into an integrative and coherent story of German self-authorization during a century of unprecedented violence.
55. Lüdtke, *Eigen-Sinn*, 144. Lüdtke refers to a "peculiar and unmediated concurrence of the politicization of the private and the privatization of politics" (18).
56. Alf Lüdtke, "Was ist und wer treibt Alltagsgeschichte?," in *Zur Rekonstruktion historischer Erfahrungen und Lebensweisen* (New York: Campus, 1989), 9–47, 39; see also Karl Marx, "Nationalökonomie," in *Die Frühschriften*, ed. S. Landshut (Stuttgart, 1955), 225–316.
57. Alf Lüdtke, "Stofflichkeit, Macht-Lust und Reiz der Oberfläche," in *Sozialgeschichte,*

Alltagsgeschichte, Mikrogeschichte, ed. Winfried Schulze (Göttingen, 1994), 65–80, 72.

58. Erving Goffman, *Asylums: Essays on the Social Situation of Mental Patients and Other Inmates* (New Brunswick, NJ: Aldine Transaction, 2007); Michel Foucault, *Discipline and Punish*, trans. Alan Sheridan (London: Penguin Books, 1991).
59. Wolfgang Kirstein, *Das Konzentrationslager als Institution totalen Terrors. Das Beispiel des KZ Natzweiler* (Pfaffenweiler, 1992); Wolfgang Sofsky, *The Order of Terror: The Concentration Camp* (Princeton, NJ: Princeton University Press, 1997).
60. Zygmunt Bauman, *Modernity and the Holocaust* (Oxford: Oxford University Press, 1992).
61. See the chapter on institutions I co-authored in ATG26, *Ruptures of the Everyday*; see also Alf Lüdtke, "Die Fiktion der Institution. Herrschaftspraxis und Vernichtung der europäischen Juden im 20. Jahrhundert." In *Institutionen und Ereignis*, ed. Reinhard Blänkner and Bernhard Jussen (Göttingen: V & R, 1998), 355–79; Alf Lüdtke and Michael Wildt, "Staats-Gewalt: Ausnahmezustand und Sicherheitsregimes," in *Staats-Gewalt: Ausnahmezustand und Sicherheitsregimes. Historische Perspektiven*, ed. Alf Lüdtke and Michael Wildt (Göttingen: Wallstein, 2008), 7–38.
62. In the printed English version the discussion that followed Foucault's lecture was not translated. That is why the author and translator refer occasionally to an online translation that is more complete in this regard. Michel Foucault, "The Meshes of Power," in *Space, Knowledge and Power: Foucault and Geography*, ed. J. W. Crampton and S. Eldon (Burlington, VT: Ashgate, 2007), 153–62, esp. 155.
63. See Michel Foucault, *Discipline and Punish*, trans. Alan Sheridan (London: Penguin Books, 1991); Michel Foucault, *The History of Sexuality*, vol. 1, translated from the French by Robert Hurley (New York, 1988).
64. Michel Foucault, "The Subject and Power," in *Essential Works of Foucault*, vol. 3, *Power*, ed. James D. Faubion (New York: New Press, 2000), 337.
65. Ibid., 220.
66. "'Die Sachen komplizierter machen.' Ein Gespräch mit Ulrich Johannes Schneider," *Phase* 2, vol. 17 (2005): 2ff.
67. Philipp Sarasin, *Wie weiter mit ... Michel Foucault* (Hamburg: Hamburger Edition, 2008), 37.
68. Lüdtke, "Introduction" to *Herrschaft als soziale Praxis*, 9–62. On the concept of "fields of force," see E. P. Thompson, "Eighteenth-Century English Society: Class Struggle without Class?," in *Social History* 3 (1978): 133–65. See also chapter 10 of this work.
69. Elias Canetti, *Crowds and Power*, trans. Carol Stewart (New York: Continuum, 1962).
70. Alf Lüdtke, "War as Work: Aspects of Soldiering in Twentieth-Century Wars," in *No Man's Land of Violence: Extreme Wars in the Twentieth Century*, ed. Alf Lüdtke and Bernd Weisbrod (Göttingen: Wallstein, 2006), 127–51. See also Alf Lüdtke, "Gewalt und Alltag im 20. Jahrhundert," in *Gewalt und Terror. 11 Vorlesungen*, ed. Wolfgang Bergsdorf, Dietmar Herz, and Hans Hoffmeister (Weimar, 2003), 35–52, 35; Joanna Bourke, *An Intimate History of Killing: Face-to-Face Killing in Twentieth Century Warfare* (New York: Basic Books, 1999); Elaine Scarry, *The Body in Pain: The Making*

and Unmaking of the World (New York: Oxford University Press, 1985).

71. Jan Philipp Reemtsma, *Trust and Violence: An Essay on a Modern Relationship*, trans. Dominic Bonfiglio (Princeton, NJ: Princeton University Press, 2012), 55.
72. Reemtsma, *Trust and Violence*, 66.
73. Michel Foucault, "The Subject and Power," *Critical Inquiry* 8, no. 4 (Summer 1982): 789.
74. In fall 2001, a conference on the subject of "Violences extrêmes" was held in Paris, providing an opportunity for historians, political scientists, anthropologists, sociologists, and psychologists to consider the phenomenon of extreme violence.
75. Jacques Sémelin, "Introduction: Extreme Violence: Can We Understand It?," *International Social Science Journal* 54, no. 174 (2002): 429–31, 430.
76. Friedrich Kluge, *Etymologisches Wörterbuch der deutschen Sprache* (New York: de Gruyter, 2002), 371.
77. Véronique Nahoum-Grappe, "The Anthropology of Extreme Violence: The Crime of Desecration," *International Social Science Journal* 54, no. 174 (2002): 549–57.
78. Véronique Nahoum-Grappe, "L'usage politique de la cruauté: l'épuration ethnique (ex-Yougoslavie, 1991–1995)," in *De la violence*, ed. Françoise Héritier (Paris, 1996), 273–323, 293ff.
79. Ibid., 288.
80. See Jacques Sémelin, "From Massacre to the Genocidal Process," *International Social Science Journal* 54, no. 174 (2002): 433–42; see also Jacques Sémelin, *Purify and Destroy: The Political Uses of Massacre and Genocide* (New York: Columbia University Press, 2009).
81. See William A. Schabas, *Genocide in International Law: The Crime of Crimes* (New York: Cambridge University Press, 2000); see also William A. Schabas, "What's in a Word? Atrocity Crimes and the 'Genocide' Label," lecture given at Uppsala University, Hugo Valentin Centre, Uppsala, Sweden, 2013, http://www.valentin.uu.se.
82. For a discussion of issues associated with the term "genocide," see Birthe Kundrus, "Entscheidungen für den Völkermord? Einleitende Überlegungen zu einem historiographischen Problem," *Mittelweg 36*, vol. 6 (2006): 4–17; Michael Wildt, "Biopolitik, ethnische Säuberungen und Volkssouveränität," *Mittelweg 36*, vol. 6 (2006): 87–106.
83. Sémelin, "From Massacre to the Genocidal Process," 433–42.
84. Ibid., 486ff.
85. In this regard, the work of ethnologist Jeanette Toussaint, who collects oral history testimonies of children of former female camp guards in Austria and Germany, is remarkable; see, for example, Jeanette Toussaint, "Meine Mutter war Aufseherin," *Tel Aviver Jahrbuch für deutsche Geschichte* 36 (2008): 78–92.
86. Insa Eschebach, "Das Aufseherinnenhaus. Überlegungen zu einer Ausstellung über SS-Aufseherinnen in der Gedenkstätte Ravensbrück," *GedenkstättenRundbrief* 75 (1997): 1–11, 7ff.
87. For a detailed overview, see Volker Zimmermann, *NS-Täter vor Gericht. Düsseldorf*

und die Strafprozesse wegen nationalsozialistischer Gewaltverbrechen, vol. 12 of *Juristische Zeitgeschichte* (Düsseldorf, 2001), 169–93; Elissa Mailänder Koslov, "Der Düsseldorfer Majdanek-Prozess (1975–1981): Ein Wettlauf mit der Zeit?," in *Beiträge zur nationalsozialistischen Verfolgung in Norddeutschland* (ed. Neuengamme Concentration Camp Memorial), vol. 9 (2005): 74–88.

88. Transcriptions of the content of witness statements were abolished in cases before regional courts and superior state courts by the First Act to Reform Criminal Proceedings Law (1. StVRG § 273 Abs. 2 StPO) of 9 December 1974 (BGBl. I, S. 3393). I thank Dr. Holger Schlüter for this information.
89. Dieter Ambach and Thomas Köhler, *Lublin-Majdanek. Das Konzentrations- und Vernichtungslager im Spiegel von Zeugenaussagen*, vol. 12 of *Juristische Zeitgeschichte* (Düsseldorf, 2003).
90. Unlike Germany, at this time Austria had an independent judiciary. Between 1945 and 1955 the "People's Courts" constituted an exceptional type of court with its own definitions of criminal offenses. Elissa Mailänder Koslov, "'Weil es einer Wienerin gar nicht liegt, so brutal zu sein . . .' Frauenbilder im Wiener Volksgerichtsverfahren gegen eine österreichische KZ-Aufseherin (1946–1949)," *Zeitgeschichte* 3 (2005): 128–50.
91. See Alexandra-Eileen Wenck, "Verbrechen als 'Pflichterfüllung'? Die Strafverfolgung nationalsozialistischer Gewaltverbrechen am Beispiel des Konzentrationslagers Bergen-Belsen," *Beiträge zur Geschichte der nationalsozialistischen Verfolgung in Norddeutschland* 3 (1997): 38–55; John Cramer, "Farce oder Vorbild? Der erste Belsen-Prozess in Lüneburg 1945," in *Tatort KZ. Neue Beiträge zur Geschichte der Konzentrationslager*, ed. Ulrich Fritz, Silvija Kavcic, and Nicole Warmbold (Ulm, 2003), 201–19; Cramer, "'Tapfer, unbescholten und mit reinem Gewissen.' KZ-Aufseherinnen im ersten Belsen-Prozess eines britischen Militärgerichts 1945," in *Im Gefolge der SS: Aufseherinnen des Frauen-KZ Ravensbrück. Begleitband zur Ausstellung*, ed. Simone Erpel (Berlin, 2007), 103–13. I thank John Cramer for his help in making testimony transcripts available, and for valuable information.
92. The court ruled against further prosecution of Alois K. as the accusations could not be proven. There was also insufficient evidence to prosecute other former guard company members. See Landesgericht (LG, regional court) Graz 13 Vr3329/63, vol. 3, Dokumentationsarchiv des österreichischen Widerstandes (DÖW), p. 83.
93. I thank Winfried R. Garscha for his help and support.
94. Pierre Bourdieu, "L'illusion biographique," *Actes de la Recherche en Sciences Sociales* 62–63 (June 1986): 69–72, 71.
95. Michael Pollak, *Die Grenzen des Sagbaren* (Frankfurt: Campus Verlag, 1995), 96.
96. See Denis Laborde, "Glauben und Wissen. Die Pariser Prozesse gegen politische Aktivisten aus dem Baskenland," *Historische Anthropologie. Kultur, Gesellschaft, Alltag* 2 (2001): 254–69.
97. See Christopher Browning, "German Memory, Juridical Interrogation, and Historical Reconstruction: Writing Perpetrator History from Postwar Testimony," in *Probing the Limits of Representation: Nazism and the "Final Solution,"* ed. Saul Friedländer

(Cambridge, MA: Harvard University Press 1992), 22–36; see also Christopher Browning, *Remembering Survival: Inside a Nazi Slave Labor Camp* (New York: Norton 2010).

98. See Harald Welzer, *Das kommunikative Gedächtnis. Eine Theorie der Erinnerung* (Munich, 2002); see also Hans J. Markowitsch and Harald Welzer, *The Development of Autobiographical Memory*, trans. David Emmans (New York: Psychology Press, 2010).
99. Harald Welzer, *Täter. Wie aus ganz normalen Menschen Massenmörder werden* (Frankfurt, 2005), 304–7, 305.
100. Olaf Jensen and Harald Welzer, "Ein Wort gibt das andere, oder: Selbstreflexivität als Methode," *Forum Qualitative Sozialforschung/Forum: Qualitative Social Research* 4, no. 2, available at http://www.qualitative-research.net.
101. Eschebach, "Das Aufseherinnenhaus," 8.
102. See Christopher Browning, *Ordinary Men: Reserve Police Battalion 101 and the Final Solution in Poland* (New York: HarperCollins, 1992); Welzer, *Täter*.
103. Statement by Maria Kaufmann-Krasowska on 24 February 1978, main hearing, HStA Düsseldorf, Ger. Rep. 432 No. 284, p. 10 (see Maria Kaufmann-Krasowska, in Ambach and Köhler, *Lublin-Majdanek*, 117).
104. Statement by Julian Gregorowicz on 19 April 1977, main hearing, HStA Düsseldorf, Ger. Rep. 432 No. 283, p. 4 (Ambach and Köhler, *Lublin-Majdanek*, 149).
105. Mordekhai Strigler, *Maidanek. Lumières consommées*, translated from Yiddish into French by Maurice Pfeffer (Paris, 1998); Zacheusz Pawalk, *"Ich habe überlebt . . ." Ein Häftling berichtet* (Hamburg, 1979); Danuta Brzosko-Medryk, "Niebo bez ptaków" (Warsaw, 1968), German: "Der Himmel ohne Vögel" (1975), Hauptstaatsarchiv Düsseldorf Ger. Rep. 432 No. 416.
106. Dionys Lenard, "Flucht aus Majdanek," *Dachauer Hefte* 7 (1991): 144–73. Lenard originally gave his report to Ferdinand Hoffmann, the representative of the Jewish Center, as the Slovak Jewish council was known. One copy reached Rabbi Armin Frieder, who copied an abbreviated version into his own diary, which is kept today in the Yad Vashem memorial in Jerusalem. In 1961, this version was translated into Hebrew and published in Livia Rothkirchen's book *The Destruction of Slovak Jewry* (Jerusalem: Yad Vashem Press, 1961). Ferdinand Hoffmann, who held the complete manuscript and had sole knowledge of the author's identity, sent the original testimony to Lenard's sister in 1968. Tomasz Kranz of the Majdanek Memorial translated the report into German in 1991.
107. There are numerous English translations of these texts, but the author decided to remain with the German original version. These quoted passages have been translated for these volume. Isa Vermehren, *Reise durch den letzten Akt. Ravensbrück, Buchenwald, Dachau: eine Frau berichtet* (1946; Reinbek, 1979); Nanda Herbermann, *Der gesegnete Abgrund. Schutzhäftling Nr. 6582 im Frauenkonzentrationslager Ravensbrück* (1948; Annweiler: 2002); Margarete Buber-Neumann, *Als Gefangene bei Stalin und Hitler. Eine Welt im Dunkel* (1949; Berlin, 1997); Charlotte Müller, *Die Klempnerkolonne in Ravensbrück. Erinnerungen des Häftlings Nr. 10787* (1981;

Berlin, 1990); Lucia Schmidt-Fels, *Deportiert nach Ravensbrück—Bericht einer Zeugin 1943–1945* (Düsseldorf, 1981); Antonia Bruha, *Ich war keine Heldin* (Vienna, 1984).

108. Germaine Tillion, *Ravensbrück* (Paris, 1988).
109. See Pollak, *Grenzen des Sagbaren.*
110. Women were labeled as eugenically or socially inferior mainly due to behavior that was deemed sexually promiscuous, or due to a "genetic disposition" that made their reproduction undesirable in the eyes of the Nazi authorities. Men were generally classified as "asocial" on the basis of criminality, chronic unemployment, alcoholism and the like. See Christa Schikorra, *Kontinuitäten der Ausgrenzung. "Asoziale" Häftlinge im Konzentrationslager Ravensbrück* (Berlin, 2001); Burkhard Jellonnek, *Homosexuelle unterm Hakenkreuz—Die Verfolgung von Homosexuellen im Dritten Reich* (Paderborn, 1990); Claudia Schoppmann, *Nationalsozialistische Sexualpolitik und weibliche Homosexualität* (Pfaffenweiler, 1991); Günter Grau, *Homosexualität in der NS-Zeit* (Frankfurt am Main, 1993); Neuengamme Concentration Camp Memorial, ed., *Verfolgung Homosexueller im Nationalsozialismus—Beiträge zur Geschichte der nationalsozialistischen Verfolgung in Norddeutschland* (Bremen, 1999); Andreas Pretzel and Gabriele Rossbach/Kulturring in Berlin e.V., eds., "Wegen der zu erwartenden hohen Strafe," *Homosexuellenverfolgung in Berlin 1933–1945* (Berlin, 2000); Conference: "Homosexuelle in Konzentrationslagern," edited by Olaf Mussmann, Bad Münstereifel, 2000.
111. Martin Broszat, ed., *Kommandant in Auschwitz. Autobiographische Aufzeichnungen des Rudolf Höss* (Munich, 2000); see also *Commandant of Auschwitz: The Autobiography of Rudolf Hoess,* translated from the German by Constantine FitzGibbon (London: Weidenfeld and Nicolson, 1959); Rudolf Höss, Pery Broad, and Johann Paul Kremer, *KL Auschwitz Seen by the SS* (New York: Howard Fertig, 2007).
112. These documents have been made available by the families. See Katrin Stoll, "Walter Sonntag—ein SS-Arzt vor Gericht," *Zeitschrift für Geschichtswissenschaft* 5 (2002): 918–39; Christine Wolters, *Tuberkulose und Menschenversuche im Nationalsozialismus: das Netzwerk hinter den Tbc-Experimenten im Konzentrationslager Sachsenhausen* (Stuttgart: F. Steiner, 2011); Christine Wolters, "'Zur 'Belohnung' wurde ich der Malaria-Versuchsstation zugeteilt . . .' Die Karriere des Dr. Rudolf Brachtel," in *Lagersystem und Repräsentation. Interdisziplinäre Studien zur Geschichte der Konzentrationslager,* ed. Ralph Gabriel et al. (Tübingen, 2004), 29–45; Marco Pukrop, "Dr. med. Heinrich Rindfleisch. Eine Lagerarztkarriere im KZ Majdanek," in *KZ-Verbrechen. Beiträge zur Geschichte der nationalsozialistischen Konzentrationslager und ihrer Erinnerung,* ed. Wojcech Lenarczyk et al. (Berlin, 2007), 34–51.
113. Eberhard Fechner, *Norddeutscher Rundfunk: Der Prozess: Eine Darstellung des Majdanek-Verfahrens in Düsseldorf* (1984), three parts, video cassettes, 270 mins.
114. I thank retired prosecutor Dieter Ambach for this information.
115. Simone Emmelius, *Fechners Methode. Studien zu seinen Gesprächsfilmen* (Mainz, 1996), 14. See also Sabine Horn, "'... ich fühlte mich damals als Soldat und nicht

als Nazi'. Der Majdanek-Prozess im Fernsehen—aus geschlechtergeschichtlicher Perspektive betrachtet," in *"Bestien" und "Befehlsempfänger." Frauen und Männer in NS-Prozessen nach 1945*, ed. Ulricke Weckel and Edgar Wolfrum (Göttingen: Vandenhoeck & Ruprech, 2003), 222–49, 237–45; Julie Maeck, *Montrer la Shoah à la télévision* De 1960 à nos jours (Paris: Nouveau monde, 2009).

116. Eberhard Fechner, transcription of interview with Erna Wallisch, 15 June 1980, manuscript (private archive). Partial transcript of the interview published in *Falter* 7 (2008): 14–15.
117. See Elissa Mailänder, "Der Fall Hermine Braunsteiner—Eine geschlechtergeschichtliche Studie," in *Das KZ Lublin-Majdanek und die Justiz. Strafverfolgung und verweigerte Gerechtigkeit: Polen, Deutschland und Österreich im Vergleich*, ed. Claudia Kurestidis-Haider et al. (Graz: Clio, 2011), 223–37.
118. Ute Wrocklage, "Neu entdeckte Fotografien aus dem KZ Neuengamme aus den Beständen des Public Record Office," *Beiträge zur Geschichte der nationalsozialistischen Verfolgung in Norddeutschland* 4 (1998): 146–59; Wrocklage, "The Photograph Album of the Career of Karl Otto Koch," in *From Sachsenburg to Sachsenhausen: Pictures from the Photograph Album of a Concentration Camp Commandant*, ed. Günter Morsch, catalog (Berlin, 2007), 19–42; Wrocklage, "Das SS-Fotoalbum des Frauen-Konzentrationslagers Ravensbrück," in Erpel, *Im Gefolge der SS*, 233–51.
119. See arrival of Soviet POWs in Mauthausen in October 1941, in *Das sichtbare Unfassbare. Fotografien vom Konzentrationslager Mauthausen*, catalog of an exhibition of the same name, Amicales de Mauthausen, déportés et amis Paris, Amical de Mauthausen y otros campos Barcelona, Bundesministerium für Inneres (Vienna, 2005), 72–81; Photos of actual and alleged shootings during "escape attempts," ibid., 100–107.
120. Ibid., 27. See also *Mémoire des camps. Photographies des camps de concentration et d'extermination (1933–1999)*, ed. Clément Chéroux, exhibition catalog (Paris, 2001); Georges Didi-Huberman, *Images malgré tout* (Paris, 2003); Didi-Huberman, "Das Öffnen der Lager und das Schliessen der Augen," in *Auszug aus dem Lager. Zur Überwindung des modernen Raumparadigmas in der politischen Philosophie*, ed. Ludger Schwarte (Berlin, 2007): 11–41.
121. *Das sichtbare Unfassbare*, 108–13.
122. Ibid., 122–27.
123. In the case of private photographs, copyright in Germany covers not only the creators of images but also the persons represented in them. Photographic images are open to public access only ten years after the death of the subject(s), or, in the case where death cannot be established, one hundred years after their birth. This protects not only the individual's rights but also those of any legal heirs. *Strictly speaking*, a historian can only reproduce photographs for which he or she has obtained permission from all the pictured individuals. I could not provide this information for all the depicted guards and was thus initially denied permission to use the images.

Chapter Two. The Majdanek Concentration and Death Camp: An Overview

1. Danzig and the area ceded to Poland in 1918 became the independent Reichsgau Wartheland and Gau Danzig-West Prussia, while the district of Kattowitz (Katowice) and the Olsa region (Cieszyn Silesia) became part of the German province of Silesia, and the districts of Sudauen (Suwałki) and Zichenau (Ciechanów) were incorporated into the province of East Prussia.
2. Bogdan Musial, "Die Verfolgung und Vernichtung der Juden im Generalgouvernement. Die Zivilverwaltung und die Shoah," in *Die Täter der Shoah. Fanatische Nationalsozialisten oder ganz normale Deutsche?*, ed. Gerhard Paul (Göttingen, 2002), 187–203, 187ff.
3. See Bogdan Musial, *Deutsche Zivilverwaltung und Judenverfolgung im Generalgouvernement. Eine Fallstudie zum Distrikt Lublin 1939–1944* (Wiesbaden, 1999), 23–79.
4. Dieter Schenk, *Hans Frank. Hitlers Kronjurist und Generalgouverneur* (Frankfurt am Main, 2008).
5. Mayor Ernst Zörner was governor of the Lublin district from 1939 to 1943, and SS Gruppenführer and Obergruppenführer of the Police Dr. Richard Wendler was district governor from 1943 to 1944.
6. See Larry V. Thompson, "Friedrich-Wilhelm Krüger. Höherer SS- und Polizeiführer Ost," in *Die SS: Elite unter dem Totenkopf. 30 Lebensläufe*, ed. Roland Smelser and Enrico Syring (Paderborn, 2000), 320–31.
7. By 1941 Himmler occupied a powerful position, wielding control over the entire German executive staff, with one exception: the military. Ruth Bettina Birn, *Die Höheren SS- und Polizeiführer, Himmlers Vertreter im Reich und in den besetzten Gebieten* (Düsseldorf, 1986); see also Peter Longerich, *Heinrich Himmler. Biographie* (Berlin, 2008).
8. See Martin Broszat, *Nationalsozialistische Polenpolitik 1939–1945* (Stuttgart, 1961); Czesław Madajczyk, *Die Okkupationspolitik Nazideutschlands in Polen 1939–1945* (Cologne, 1988).
9. See Musial, *Deutsche Zivilverwaltung*, 181ff.
10. For a discussion of the deportations within the Generalgouvernement and the Madagascar Plan, see Michael Wildt, *Generationen des Unbedingten. Das Führungskorps des Reichssicherheitshauptamtes* (Hamburg, 2003), 486–506; Michael Wildt, *An Uncompromising Generation: The Nazi Leadership of the Reich Security Main Office*, trans. Tom Lampert (Madison: University of Wisconsin Press, 2009), 242–67.
11. Tomasz Kranz, "Das KL Lublin—zwischen Planung und Realisierung," in *Die nationalsozialistischen Konzentrationslager—Entwicklung und Struktur*, ed. Ulrich Herbert, Karin Orth, and Christoph Dieckmann (Göttingen, 1997), 1:363. See also

Tomasz Kranz, Extermination of Jews at the Majdanek Concentration Camp, Lublin: Państwowe Muzeum na Majdanku, 2007. Regarding the planned Jewish reservation, see Dieter Pohl, *Von der "Judenpolitik" zum Judenmord. Der Distrikt Lublin des Generalgouvernements 1939–1944* (Frankfurt am Main, 1993), 47–51.

12. Ibid., 177.
13. Ibid., 26–33, 47–50, 178; see also Raul Hilberg, *The Destruction of the European Jews* (Chicago: Quadrangle Books, 1961); Christopher Browning, *The Path to Genocide: Essays on Launching the Final Solution* (New York: Cambridge University Press, 1992); Christopher Browning, with contributions by Jürgen Matthäus, *The Origins of the Final Solution: The Evolution of Nazi Jewish Policy, September 1939–March 1942* (Lincoln: University of Nebraska Press, 2004).
14. Dieter Pohl, "Die Stellung des Distrikts Lublin in der 'Endlösung der Judenfrage,'" in *"Aktion Reinhardt." Der Völkermord an den Juden im Generalgouvernement 1941–1944*, ed. Bogdan Musial (Osnabrück, 2004), 87–107, 88.
15. Musial, *Deutsche Zivilverwaltung*, 30ff.
16. See Czesław Madajczyk, ed., *Vom Generalplan Ost zum Generalsiedlungsplan* (Munich, 1994); Mechtild Rössler and Sabine Schleiermacher, eds., *Der "Generalplan Ost." Hauptlinien der nationalsozialistischen Planungs- und Vernichtungspolitik* (Berlin, 1993).
17. Although this plan was implemented only on a small scale, about 100,000 Poles were forcibly resettled, compelled into forced labor, or killed. Pohl, *Von der "Judenpolitik" zum Judenmord*, 95–97.
18. Wolfgang Scheffler, "Historisches Gutachten 'Zur Judenverfolgung des nationalsozialistischen Staats—unter besonderer Berücksichtigung der Verhältnisse im Generalgouvernement—und zur Geschichte des Lagers Majdanek im System nationalsozialistischer Vernichtungs- und Konzentrationslager,'" 1976, HStA Düsseldorf, Ger. Rep. 432 No. 278, p. 112; see also Broszat, *Nationalsozialistische Polenpolitik*, 85–102; Czesław Madajczyk, *Die Okkupationspolitik Nazideutschlands in Polen 1939–1945* (Cologne, 1988), 389–539.
19. Götz Aly, *"Final Solution": Nazi Population Policy and the Murder of the European Jews*, trans. Belinda Cooper and Allison Brown (New York: Oxford University Press, 1999); see also Pohl, *Von der "Judenpolitik" zum Judenmord*, 89–112. On settlement policies in occupied Poland, see Elizabeth Harvey, *Women in the Nazi East: Agents and Witnesses of Germanization* (New Haven: Yale University Press, 2003).
20. Pohl, *Von der "Judenpolitik" zum Judenmord*, 181.
21. Ibid, 178.
22. The SS and Police Leader of Lublin nominally answered to his superior, the Head SS and Police Leader Friedrich Wilhelm Krüger. In practice, however, he was largely responsible for settlement policies in the Lublin district. Globocnik held his office from late 1939 to autumn 1943, and then was succeeded by SS Group Leader Jakob Sporrenberg. As Schwindt emphasizes in her work, Globocnik played a key role in Majdanek's development, as well as during the phase in which it functioned as

a death camp. See Barbara Schwindt, *Das Konzentrations- und Vernichtungslager Majdanek. Funktionswandel im Kontext der "Endlösung"* (Würzburg, 2005), 74–76. On Globocnik, see Peter Black, "Odilo Globocnik, Himmlers Vorposten im Osten," in *Die SS: Elite unter dem Totenkopf*, ed. Smelser and Syring, 103–15.

23. Memorandum Heinrich Himmler, 20 July 1941, in Bundesarchiv Berlin [BA] Document Center [BDC], personnel file Globocnik, cited in Jan Schulte, *Zwangsarbeit und Vernichtung: das Wirtschaftsimperium der SS: Oswald Pohl und das SS-Wirtschafts-Verwaltungshauptamt 1933–1945* (Paderborn, 2001), 263; see also Kranz, "KL Lublin," 366.
24. See chapter 5 of this work.
25. See also Christopher R. Browning, *Nazi Policy, Jewish Workers, German Killers* (New York: Cambridge University Press, 2000).
26. Scheffler, "Historisches Gutachten," 116.
27. Karin Orth, *Das System der nationalsozialistischen Konzentrationslager. Eine politische Ordnungsgeschichte* (Munich, 2002), 205–13; Scheffler, "Historisches Gutachten," 117ff.; Kranz, "Das KL Lublin," 367; Schwindt, *Konzentrations- und Vernichtungslager Majdanek*, 69. Regarding the IKL, see chapter 2 of this work.
28. In 1940, Hans Frank refused permission for the construction of four concentration camps in the Generalgouvernement on financial grounds. See Schwindt, *Konzentrations- und Vernichtungslager Majdanek*, 69.
29. Wilhelm Krüger, the Higher SS and Police Leader East (HSSPF Ost), officially reported to Governor-General Frank. However, as the main representative of the Reichsführer SS in the region, Krüger reported directly to Himmler. As a result, there were frequent disagreements and jurisdictional disputes between Krüger and Frank on security issues and questions of "racial policy." On the rivalry between occupation authorities in the Lublin district, Governor Ernst Zörner and the SS and Police Leader Odilo Globocnik, as well as higher-level administrative disputes between Governor-General Frank and Reichsführer SS Heinrich Himmler, see Pohl, *Von der "Judenpolitik" zum Judenmord*, 47–55, 95–97; Schwindt, *Konzentrations- und Vernichtungslager Majdanek*, 76ff.
30. Kranz, "KL Lublin," 369ff. Karin Orth largely follows Kranz's time frame, but does not regard the final months between April and July 1994 as an independent phase. Orth, *Das System der nationalsozialistischen Konzentrationslager*, 205–13. Barbara Schwindt, whose study focuses on the history of the camp within the extermination of the Jews, identifies three phases of the camp. The first phase (fall 1941 to summer 1942) was the phase of "extermination through work." The second phase, from summer 1942 to spring 1943, encompassed the transition from a labor camp to a death camp. The third phase, which extended from spring to fall 1943, was the phase of mass extermination. Schwindt, *Konzentrations- und Vernichtungslager Majdanek*, 73–286.
31. Tomasz Kranz, "Zeittafel," in *Unser Schicksal—eine Mahnung für Euch. Berichte und Erinnerungen der Häftlinge von Majdanek*, ed. Tomasz Kranz (Lublin, 1994), 209–14, 205.

32. Ibid., 206ff.
33. See the interrogation of Hermann Hackmann of 26 September 1973 in Düsseldorf, HStA Düsseldorf, Ger. Rep. 432 No. 248, p. 726ff.; see also the interrogation of Robert Seitz of 5 December 1961 in Karlsruhe, HStA Düsseldorf, Ger. Rep. 432 No. 266, p. 83.
34. Majdanek was not the only place where Soviet prisoners of war were subjected to inhuman treatment and callous disregard for human life. Of the 3.35 million Soviet troops captured by the Germans in 1941, nearly 60 percent had died of hunger and systematic neglect by February 1, 1942. Between late June 1941 and April 15, 1942, some 290,560 Soviet POWs died in the Wehrmacht and SS camps in the Generalgouvernement, which represents 85.7 percent of the Soviet POWs who were held in the Generalgouvernement during that time. For this reason, historians generally speak of the mass murder of Soviet POWs. See Christian Streit, *Keine Kameraden. Die Wehrmacht und die sowjetischen Kriegsgefangenen 1941–1945* (Stuttgart, 1978), 134; Christian Gerlach, *Krieg, Ernährung, Völkermord. Deutsche Vernichtungspolitik im Zweiten Weltkrieg* (Zürich, 2001), 11–78, 13, 29–53; Hamburger Institut für Sozialforschung, ed., *Verbrechen der Wehrmacht. Dimensionen des Vernichtungskrieges 1941–1944. Ausstellungskatalog* (Hamburg, 2002), 187–286.
35. Schwindt, *Konzentrations- und Vernichtungslager Majdanek*, 82ff. This often led to conflicts between the SS and the civilian administration, since many Jews who did not have a work card had already been assigned to a work detail by the civilian administration.
36. Ibid., 76–112, 291.
37. Ibid., 65–67, 70. By contrast, Dieter Pohl proceeds from the assumption that Majdanek was originally conceived as a camp for non-Jewish prisoners, meaning Soviet prisoners of war and Poles. Dieter Pohl, *Die nationalsozialistische Judenverfolgung in Ostgalizien 1941–1944, Organisation und Durchführung eines staatlichen Massenverbrechens* (Munich, 1997), 338.
38. At this time, Jews were mainly incarcerated in forced-labor camps and ghettos. Orth, *System der nationalsozialistischen Konzentrationslager*, 112.
39. Schwindt, *Konzentrations- und Vernichtungslager Majdanek*, 67. The concentration camps for Jews in the Baltic, Kaunas, Riga-Kaiserwald, and Vaivara were not established until 1943.
40. Schwindt, *Konzentrations- und Vernichtungslager Majdanek*, 116.
41. Between March and June 1942, an estimated 12,000 Jews from Slovakia were sent to Majdanek. In April 1942, 1,200 Jews from the Lublin ghetto of Majdan Tatarski arrived at the camp. From March to June, 4,000 Czech Jews arrived from Theresienstadt. In October 1942, a further 3,000 Jews arrived at Majdanek after the dissolution of Majdan Tatarski. See Kranz, "Zeittafel," 209–14, and Kranz, "Die Belegstärke des Konzentrationslagers Majdanek," in *Zur Erfassung der Häftlingssterblichkeit im Konzentrationslager Lublin* (Lublin, 2007), 12–20.
42. See chapter 5, "The Shock of Arrival."
43. Orth, *System der nationalsozialistischen Konzentrationslager*, 113–21. See also Walter

Grode, *Die "Sonderbehandlung 14f13" in den Konzentrationslagern des Dritten Reiches. Ein Beitrag zur Dynamik faschistischer Vernichtungspolitik* (Frankfurt am Main, 1987). On Ravensbrück, the "14f13" killing program, and the gassings in the Uckermark, see Bernhard Strebel, *Geschichte eines Lagerkomplexes* (Paderborn, 2003), 320–39, 459–86. See also Bernhard Strebel, "Ravensbrück—das zentrale Frauenkonzentrationslager," in *Die nationalsozialistischen Konzentrationslager: Entwicklung und Struktur*, ed. U. Herbert, K. Orth, and C. Dieckmann (Göttingen: Wallstein, 1998), 1:215–58; and Orth, *System der nationalsozialistischen Konzentrationslager*, 191.

44. The overall building plan for Majdanek was scaled back, and the plan to build a central SS base in Lublin was abandoned. Schwindt, *Konzentrations- und Vernichtungslager Majdanek*, 112ff.
45. See Dieter Pohl, "Die Stellung des Distrikts Lublin in der 'Endlösung der Judenfrage,'" in *"Aktion Reinhardt." Der Völkermord an den Juden im Generalgouvernement 1941–1944*, ed. Bogdan Musial (Osnabrück, 2004), 87–107.
46. Schwindt, *Konzentrations- und Vernichtungslager Majdanek*, 125. According to a letter by Globocnik to the SS Chief Economic and Administration Office (SS Wirtschafts-Verwaltungshauptamt; WVHA), Himmler issued this order verbally to the SS Police Leader of Lublin. Globocnik passed on this order to Oswald Pohl in a letter of 15 July 1942. Telex by the SS Brigade Leader Globocnik to the Chief of the SS-WVHA, 15 July 1942; reprinted in Josef Marszalek, *Majdanek. Konzentrationslager Lublin* (Warsaw, 1984), 138–43.
47. Kranz, "Zeittafel," 213.
48. Schwindt, *Konzentrations- und Vernichtungslager Majdanek*, 153–55.
49. Ibid., 116, 154.
50. Statement by Hermine Böttcher née Brückner, 27 June 1979, main hearing, HStA Düsseldorf, Ger. Rep. 432 No. 282, p. 1.
51. See letter by Globocnik to Himmler, 1 October 1941, Bundesarchiv [BA] BDC (Globocnik). Musial reconstructs the planning as follows: in a letter to Himmler dated 1 October 1941, Globocnik suggested that, in view of the catastrophic food shortage, the Jews in occupied Poland should be killed. Himmler apparently presented this plan to Hitler. Only a short time later, on 17 October 1941, Hitler presented his vision for the occupied "East" to a small circle of confederates as follows: "There is only one task: Germanization through the introduction of Germans [to the area], and treating the original inhabitants like Indians. . . . In this matter, I am as cold as ice. I am nothing but the executor of the will of history." Musial, *Deutsche Zivilverwaltung*, 204.
52. Dieter Pohl and Christian Gerlach argue that Globocnik's order initially applied only to the Lublin district, and then was gradually expanded in scope. By contrast, Bogdan Musial argues that the heads of the civilian administration in the Generalgouvernement believed as early as October 1941 that the annihilation of Jews would soon encompass the entire Generalgouvernement. See Pohl, *Von der "Judenpolitik" zum Judenmord*, 101; Gerlach, "Wannsee-Konferenz," 9; Musial, *Deutsche Zivilverwaltung*, 207ff.

53. Kurt Pätzold and Erika Schwarz, *Tagesordnung: Judenmord. Die Wannsee-Konferenz am 20. Januar 1942. Eine Dokumentation zur Organisation der "Endlösung"* (Berlin, 1992); see also Christopher R. Browning, "Nazi Resettlement Policy and the Search for a Solution for the Jewish Question, 1939–1941," in *The Path to Genocide: Essays on Launching the Final Solution*, ed. Christoper R. Browning (New York: Cambridge University Press, 1992), 3–26; Browning, "From 'Ethnic Cleansing' to Genocide to the 'Final Solution:' The Evolution of Nazi Jewish Policy, 1939–1941," in Browning, *Nazi Policy, Jewish Workers, German Killers* (Cambridge, 2000), 1–25; Browning, "Nazi Policy: Decisions for the Final Solution," in ibid., 26–57.
54. Christian Gerlach dates the decision to murder all the Jews of Europe to early December 1941. See Gerlach, "Die Wannsee-Konferenz, das Schicksal der deutschen Juden und Hitlers politische Grundsatzentscheidung, alle Juden Europas zu ermorden," in Gerlach, *Krieg, Ernährung, Völkermord. Deutsche Vernichtungspolitik im Zweiten Weltkrieg* (Zürich, 2001), 79–152.
55. See Pohl, *Von der "Judenpolitik" zum Judenmord*, 113–17; Musial, *Deutsche Zivilverwaltung*, 229–35, Schwindt, *Konzentrations- und Vernichtungslager Majdanek*, 90–94. See also Ayse Sila Cehreli, "Chełmno, Bełzec, Sobibór, Treblinka. Politique génocidaire nazie et résistance juive dans les centres de mise à mort (novembre 1941–janvier 1945) (thèse d'histoire présentéé à l'université Paris I–Panthéon Sorbonne, 2007) and Cehreli, Ayse Sila, *Témoignage du Khurbn. La résistance juive dans les centres de mise à mort—Chełmno, Bełzec, Sobibór, Treblinka* (Paris: Éditions Kimé 2013).
56. Pohl, *Nationalsozialistische Judenverfolgung in Ostgalizien*, 186–88; Thomas Sandkühler, *"Endlösung" in Galizien. Der Judenmord in Ostpolen und die Rettungsinitiative von Berthold Beitz 1941–1944* (Bonn, 1996), 208–12.
57. The SS built a total of seven gas chambers at Majdanek. See chapter 7 of this work.
58. As Karin Orth notes, Bełzec and Sobibor were not ordinary concentration camps, since everything that characterized the IKL concentration camps (the camp compound, the barracks, the roll calls, the work details, the multilayered system of surveillance, and the multilayered system of prisoner-functionaries) was all absent in these camps. For this reason, Orth suggests the term "site of annihilation" is more accurate. Orth, *System der nationalsozialistischen Konzentrationslager*, 198ff.
59. Operation Reinhardt was named after Reinhard Heydrich, who was assassinated in May 1942. The contemporary spelling varied, and is still disputed by scholars today. Surviving Nazi documents refer both to Operation Reinhardt and Operation Reinhard, and Globocnik also used both variants. For a detailed discussion, see Peter Black, "Die Trawniki-Männer und die 'Aktion Reinhardt,'" in *"Aktion Reinhardt." Der Völkermord an den Juden im Generalgouvernement 1941–1944*, ed. Bogdan Musial (Osnabrück, 2004), 309–52, 309, 319 (fn. 3). See also Dieter Pohl, "Die Stellung des Distrikts Lublin in der 'Endlösung der Judenfrage,'" in ibid., 87–107, 102; and Pohl, *Von der "Judenpolitik" zum Judenmord*, 102–4, 143–48.
60. Orth, *System der nationalsozialistischen Konzentrationslager*, 206ff.; Schwindt, *Konzentrations- und Vernichtungslager Majdanek*, 239–54.

61. Schwindt, *Konzentrations- und Vernichtungslager Majdanek*, 134–200, 203–68.
62. See also chapter 7 of this work.
63. On December 12, 1943, there were only 4,410 male prisoners in the camp as well as 2,259 Soviet POWs and 2,155 prisoners in the women's camp. See Kranz, "Zeittafel," 217–19.
64. See Pohl, "Die Stellung des Distrikts Lublin," 91, 103.
65. Kranz, "KL Lublin," 378–79; Josef Marszalek, *Majdanek. Konzentrationslager Lublin* (Warsaw, 1984), 138–43; Dieter Pohl, "Die Ermordung der Juden im Generalgouvernement," in *"Nationalsozialistische Vernichtungspolitik 1939–1945." Neue Forschungen und Kontroversen*, ed. Ulrich Herbert (Frankfurt am Main, 1998), 98–121, esp. 118.
66. Schwindt, *Konzentrations- und Vernichtungslager Majdanek*, 90–286.
67. Pohl, "Die Stellung des Distrikts Lublin," 91, 103.
68. Kranz, "Zeittafel," 215.
69. Kranz, "KL Lublin," 376.
70. Orth, *System der nationalsozialistischen Konzentrationslager*, 212.
71. Kranz, "Zeittafel," 220.
72. Marszalek, *Majdanek*, 184–91.
73. Letter to the Commandant of the Lublin concentration camp and Auschwitz concentration camp SS-WVHA Office Group D—Concentration Camps, 13 April 1944, HStA Düsseldorf, Ger. Rep. 432 No. 430, p. 279.
74. Orth, *System der nationalsozialistischen Konzentrationslager*, 213.
75. Kranz, "Zeittafel," 221.
76. See Johannes Tuchel, "Organisationsgeschichte der 'frühen' Konzentrationslager," in *Instrumentarium der Macht. Frühe Konzentrationslager 1933–1937*, ed. Wolfgang Benz and Barbara Distel (Berlin, 2003), 9–26.
77. It consisted of a "disciplinary and penal code for the prison camp" as well as "service regulations for accompanying and overseeing prisoners." See chapter 9 of this work.
78. Martin Broszat, "Nationalsozialistische Konzentrationslager 1933–1945," in *Anatomie des SS-Staates*, ed. Hans Buchheim et al. (Freiburg, 1965), 2:53.
79. Tuchel, "Organisationsgeschichte," 21.
80. Theodor Eicke was replaced in September 1939 by Richard Glücks, who would remain Inspector of Concentration Camps until the end of the war. The administrative chief of the SS, Obergruppenführer (General) Oswald Pohl, was assigned to head the newly founded SS-WVHA, based in Oranienburg.
81. See Schulte, *Zwangsarbeit und Vernichtung*.
82. Kranz, "KL Lublin," 371; see Kranz, "Zeittafel," 203–21.
83. See Karin Orth, *Die Konzentrationslager-SS. Sozialstrukturelle Analysen und biographische Studien* (Göttingen, 2000), 189–91.
84. Orth, *System der nationalsozialistischen Konzentrationslager*, 207; see also chapters 7 and 9 of this work.
85. See Orth, *Konzentrationslager-SS*, 85–98, 181–89, 233–40.

86. Ibid., 242–46.
87. "Aufgabengebiete in einem Konzentrationslager" (Spring 1942), BA, NS3/391, p. 4; quoted in Strebel, "Das KZ Ravensbrück," 52.
88. Günter Morsch, "Organisations- und Verwaltungsstruktur der Konzentrationslager," in *Der Ort des Terrors*, ed. Benz and Distel, 58–75, 61.
89. See chapter 9, "License to Kill?"
90. Morsch, "Organisations- und Verwaltungsstruktur," 65ff.
91. Regarding the RSHA, see Wildt, *An Uncompromising Generation*.
92. See Josef Marszałek, *Majdanek, The Concentration Camp in Lublin*, trans. Lech Petrowicz (Warsaw: Interpress, 1986).
93. Morsch, "Organisations- und Verwaltungsstruktur," 68ff.
94. For a brief time in October 1942, the women's camp was located on Field V; then it was moved to the clothing works at the "Old Airfield." As the number of prisoners continued to rise, the women's camp was reestablished on Field V in January 1943. From that point until summer 1943, there were two women's camps in operation. On September 1, 1943, the women's camp was moved from Field V to Field I. See Marszałek, *Majdanek*, 47. See interrogation of Hermine Böttcher on 11 December 1974 in Hannover, HStA Düsseldorf, Ger. Rep. 432 No. 290, p. 2.
95. Interrogation of Alice Orlowski of 17 October 1946 in Hildesheim, HStA Düsseldorf, Ger. Rep. 432 No. 213, p. 768. See also interrogation of Alice Orlowski of 25 June 1947 in Cracow, HStA Düsseldorf, Ger. Rep. 432 No. 296, pp. 2–3.
96. Service Regulations for the Ravensbrück Women's Concentration Camp [hereafter Ravensbrück Service Regulations], National Archives and Records Administration [NARA], RG 549, 000-50-11, Box 522, Folder no. 3, p. 21a. These Ravensbrück regulations served as the model for all other concentration camps with female inmates.
97. In Field V, the office was located in the first barracks on the right. In Field I, the office was in the first barracks on the left. See interrogation of Hermine Böttcher on 11 December 1974 in Hannover, HStA Düsseldorf, Ger. Rep. 432 No. 290, p. 2; interrogation of Hermine Böttcher née Brückner on 27 June 1979, main hearing, HStA Düsseldorf, Ger. Rep. 432 No. 282, p. 2. See also interrogation of Alice Orlowski of 17 October 1946 in Hildesheim, HStA Düsseldorf, Ger. Rep. 432 No. 213, p. 768, and interrogation of Alice Orlowski of 25 June 1947 in Cracow, HStA Düsseldorf, Ger. Rep. 432 No. 296, p. 2ff.
98. Throughout this study, I employ the term "prisoner-functionary" rather than "kapo," the term originally used to describe the inmates who acted as foremen of labor detachments, since "kapo" has a negative connotation within the commemorative and other literature in the field. See Eugen Kogon, *Der SS-Staat. Das System der deutschen Konzentrationslager (1945)* (Cologne, 2000), 89; see also Aleksandar Tišma, *Kapo*, trans. Barbara Antkowiak (Munich, 1999).
99. Interrogation of Charlotte W. of 7 July 1972 in Düsseldorf, HStA Düsseldorf, Ger. 432 No. 235, p. 76ff.

100. H[ans] G[ünther] Adler, "Selbstverwaltung und Widerstand in den Konzentrationslagern der SS," *Vierteljahrshefte für Zeitgeschichte* 8 (1960): 221–36. More recent studies replace the Nazi term "self-administration" with the phrase "system of prisoner-functionaries"; Karin Orth, "Gab es eine Lagergesellschaft? 'Kriminelle' und politische Häftlinge im Konzentrationslager," in *Ausbeutung, Vernichtung, Öffentlichkeit. Neue Studien zur nationalsozialistischen Lagerpolitik*, vol. 4, *Darstellungen und Quellen zur Geschichte von Auschwitz*, ed. Norbert Frei, Sybille Steinbacher, Bernd C. Wagner (Munich: Institut für Zeitgeschichte, 2000), 109–33.
101. Bernhard Strebel, "Unterschiede in der Grauzone? Über die Lagerältesten im Frauen- und Männerlager des KZ Ravensbrück," *Beiträge zur Geschichte der nationalsozialistischen Verfolgung in Norddeutschland* 4 (1998): 57–68, esp. 59. See also Orth, "Gab es eine Lagergesellschaft?," 120ff., 132.
102. Klaus Drobisch and Günther Wieland, *System der NS-Konzentrationslager 1933–1939* (Berlin, 1993), 315ff.
103. Kogon, *Der SS-Staat*, 389.
104. H[ans] G[ünther] Adler, *Theresienstadt 1941–1945. Das Antlitz einer Zwangsgemeinschaft. Geschichte, Soziologie, Psychologie* (Tübingen, 1960).
105. Falk Pingel, *Häftlingeunter SS-Herrschaft. Widerstand, Selbstbehauptung und Vernichtung im Konzentrationslager* (Hamburg, 1978), 56.
106. Werner Röhr, "Absolute Macht oder abgeleitete Macht? Funktionshäftlinge im Konzentrationslager zwischen Kollaboration und Widerstand," in *Tod oder Überleben? Neue Forschungen zur Geschichte des Konzentrationslagers Ravensbrück*, ed. Werner Röhr and Brigitte Berlekamp (Berlin, 2001), 239. See also the work of sociologist Michael Pollak, *L'expérience concentrationnaire. Essai sur le maintien de l'identité sociale* (Paris, 2000); and Wolfgang Sofsky, *The Order of Terror: The Concentration Camp* (Princeton, NJ: Princeton University Press, 1997), 117–29.
107. For a sociological discussion, see Maja Suderland, *Inside Concentration Camps: Social Life at the Extremes*, trans. Jessica Spengler (Cambridge: Polity Press, 2013).
108. Grzegorz Plewik, Johannes Schwartz, and Lavern Wolfram, "Zur Zukunft der Gedenkstätte Majdanek," in *KZ-Verbrechen. Beiträge zur Geschichte der nationalsozialistischen Konzentrationslager und ihrer Erinnerung*, ed. Wojcech Lenarczyk et al.(Berlin, 2007), 245–63, 249.
109. On Rindfleisch's career, see Marco Pukrop, "Dr. med. Heinrich Rindfleisch. Eine Lagerarztkarriere im KZ Majdanek," in *KZ-Verbrechen*, ed. Lenarczyk et al., 34–51.
110. See Christoph Kopke, "Das KZ als Experimentierfeld: Ernst Günther Schenck und die Plantage in Dachau," in *Lagersystem und Repräsentation. Interdisziplinäre Studien zur Geschichte der Konzentrationslager*, ed. Ralph Gabriel et al. (Tübingen, 2004), 13–28; Christine Wolters, "Zur 'Belohnung' wurde ich der Malaria-Versuchsstationzugeteilt . . . Die Karriere des Dr. Rudolf Brachtel," in *Lagersystem und Repräsentation*, ed. Gabriel et al., 29–45; Marion Hulverscheidt, "Menschen, Mücken und Malaria—Das wissenschaftliche Umfeld des KZ-Malariaforschers Claus Schilling," in *Medizin im Nationalsozialismus und das System der Konzentrationslager*, ed. Judith Hahn, Silvija

Kavčič, and Christoph Kopke (Frankfurt am Main, 2005), 108–26; on Mengele, see also Sven Keller, *Günzburg und der Fall Mengele. Die Heimatstadt und die Jagd nach dem NS-Verbrecher* (Munich, 2003).

111. Mirroring the expansion, the concentration camp network grew steadily, and the guard units also began to expand beginning in 1936. Beginning on April 1, 1937, these guard troops, called the SS Death's Head Regiment (Totenkopfstandarte), were distributed among three camps. The first SS Death's Head Regiment was stationed at Dachau, the second in Sachsenhausen, and the third at Buchenwald. In fall 1938, a fourth regiment was established at the Mauthausen camp. After the start of the war, the regiments were increasingly also used for combat duty. The commander of the SS Death's Head Units (*Totenkopfverbände*) was Theodor Eicke, the former Inspector of Concentration Camps. See Morsch, "Organisations- und Verwaltungsstruktur," 58–75, 59ff.; Charles W. Sydnor, *Soldiers of Destruction: The SS Death's Head Division, 1933–1945* (Princeton, NJ: Princeton University Press, 1990).
112. See Tomasz Kranz, *Das Konzentrationslager Majdanek. Einleitung zum Ausstellungskatalog: Mitten in Europa. Konzentrationslager Majdanek* (Münster: Stadtmuseum, 2001).
113. Morsch, "Organisations- und Verwaltungsstruktur," 59.
114. Kranz, "Zeittafel," 210.
115. Testimonies specifically use the term field and therefore I decided to remain true to the original source language instead of using the arguably more accurate translation of area or section.
116. Anonymous female Jewish survivor, in Eberhard Fechner, *Norddeutscher Rundfunk: Der Prozess: Eine Darstellung des Majdanek-Verfahrens in Düsseldorf* (video cassettes; 1984), part 1.
117. Wolfgang Scheffler, in Fechner, *Der Prozess*, part 1.
118. Testimony by Rywka Awronska from 15 February 1978, main hearing, HStA Düsseldorf, Ger. Rep. 432 No. 282, p. 10 (Dieter Ambach and Thomas Köhler, eds. *Lublin-Majdanek. Das Konzentrations- und Vernichtungslager im Spiegel von Zeugenaussagen*, vol. 12, *Juristische Zeitgeschichte* [Dusseldorf, 2003], 104).
119. On the barracks, see Axel Dossmann, Jan Wenzel, and Kai Wenzel, *Architektur auf Zeit. Baracken, Pavillons, Container* (Berlin, 2006).
120. See Hermann Kaienburg, "Vernichtung durch Arbeit." *Der Fall Neuengamme. Die Wirtschaftsbestrebungen der SS und ihre Auswirkungen auf die Existenzbedingungen der KZ-Gefangenen* (Bonn: Dietz, 1990).
121. Pohl, *Von der "Judenpolitik" zum Judenmord*, 181.
122. See chapter 5 of this work.
123. According to testimony by a Majdanek survivor, in Fechner, *Der Prozess*, part 1.
124. See Bernhard Strebel, "Verlängerter Arm der SS oder schützende Hand? Drei Fallbeispiele von weiblichen Funktionshäftlingen im KZ Ravensbrück," *WerkstattGeschichte* 12 (1995): 35–49.
125. See Czesław Rajca and Anna Wiśniewska, *Majdanek: The Concentration Camp of*

Lublin, trans. Anna Zagórska (Lublin: State Museum Majdanek, 1983).

126. Kranz, "KL Lublin," 369.
127. In 1981, the Düsseldorf Regional Court concluded that at least 250,000 people died at Majdanek. Wolfgang Scheffler places that total at 200,000. In 1992, the Lublin historian Czesław Rajca calculated a total of 235,000 victims. See Jósef Marszałek, *Majdanek. Konzentrationslager Lublin* (Warsaw, 1984), 70–73; Scheffler, "Historisches Gutachten," 185; Winiewska and Rajca, *Majdanek*, 23; Kranz, "KL Lublin," 381, 388.
128. Schwindt, *Das Konzentrations- und Vernichtungslager Majdanek*, 291.
129. The Jews came from Lublin District (26,000); the Warsaw ghetto (20,000); Białystok ghetto (6,500); the forced-labor camps of the Lublin district (4,000); Slovakia (8,500); the Protectorate (3,000); Germany and Austria (3,000); France, the Netherlands, and Greece (2,000); and various other forced-labor camps.
130. Tomasz Kranz, "Ewidencja Zgonowi Smiertelnosc Wiezow KL Lublin," *Zeszyty Majdanka* 23 (2005): 7–53.
131. Kranz, "KL Lublin," 381.

Chapter Three. Women Looking for Work: Paths to Careers in the Concentration Camps

1. Until September 1944 the training usually took three months. The recruitment procedure was then speeded up: the guards were for the most part recruited in factories or in the immediate vicinity of a camp and then trained in the closest main camp. See Bernhard Strebel, *Das KZ Ravensbrück. Geschichte eines Lagerkomplexes* (Paderborn: Schöningh, 2003), 81.
2. Gudrun Schwarz, "SS-Aufseherinnen in nationalsozialistischen Konzentrationslagern (1933–1945)," *Dachauer Hefte* 10 (1994): 32–49, 39.
3. Erika Buchmann, *Die Frauen von Ravensbrück* (Berlin: Kongress-Verlag, 1959), 6.
4. See testimony of Jane B., Zentrale Stelle der Landesjustizverwaltungen zur Aufklärung von NS-Verbrechen in Ludwigsburg (ZSL), 409 AR-Z 77/72, vol. 2, pp. 154–60, and testimony of Margarete Mewes, ZSL, 409 AR-Z 77/72, vol. 3, pp. 510–23, cited in Irmtraud Heike, "Johanna Langefeld—Die Biographie einer KZ-Oberaufseherin," *WerkstattGeschichte* 12 (1995): 7–19, 9. See also Ino Arndt, "Das Frauenkonzentrationslager Ravensbrück," *Dachauer Hefte* 3 (1987), 125–57, 134; see also Irmtraud Heike, "'. . . da es sich ja lediglich um die Bewachung der Häftlinge handelt . . .' Lagerverwaltung und Bewachungspersonal," in *Frauen in Konzentrationslagern. Bergen-Belsen, Ravensbrück*, ed. Claus Füllberg-Stolberg et al. (Bremen: Edition Temmen, 1994), 221–40, 232.
5. Janet Anschütz and Irmtraud Heike, *Feinde im eigenen Land. Zwangsarbeit in Hannover im Zweiten Weltkrieg* (Bielefeld: Verlag für Regionalgeschichte, 2000), 187.
6. Undated form from Ravensbrück Concentration Camp concerning applications of female guards (application form), BA NS/4/Ra 1.

7. Strebel, *Das KZ Ravensbrück*, 67.
8. Michel Foucault, "Die Maschen der Macht," in *Michel Foucault, Analytik der Macht*, ed. Daniel Defert and François Ewald, with assistance from Jacques Lagrange (Frankfurt, 2005), 220–39, esp. 226.
9. Statement by Hildegard, Lublin Concentration Camp Headquarters, 24 Feb. 1943, HStA Düsseldorf, Ger. Rep. 432 No. 430, p. 218.
10. Ibid., 219.
11. Letter from WVHA Office Group D—Concentration Camps of 8 June 1943 to the Camp Commandants of Au., Bu., Da., Flo., Gro.Ro., Hi., Lu., Mau., Na., Neu., Rav., Sh., Stu., Herz., Riga, Heidelager, Z.I.L. Bergen-Belsen, re: Employment of female guards, HStA Düsseldorf, Ger. Rep. 432 No. 429, p. 37.
12. On the activity fields of women during wartime, see Adelheid von Saldern, "Opfer oder (Mit-)Täterinnen? Kontroversen über die Rolle der Frauen im NS-Staat," *Sozialwissenschaftliche Informationen (SOWI)* 20 (1991): 97–193; Karin Hausen, ed., *Geschlechterhierarchie und Arbeitsteilung. Zur Geschichte ungleicher Erwerbschancen von Männern und Frauen* (Göttingen: Vandenhoeck und Ruprecht, 1993); Birthe Kundrus, *"Kriegerfrauen." Sozialpolitik und Geschlechterverhältnisse im Ersten und Zweiten Weltkrieg in Deutschland* (Hamburg: Christians, 1995); Elizabeth Harvey, "Erinnern und Verdrängen. Deutsche Frauen und der 'Volkstumskampf' im besetzten Polen," in *Heimat-Front. Militär und Geschlechterverhältnisse im Zeitalter der Weltkriege*, ed. Karen Hagemann and Stefanie Schüler-Springorum (New York: Campus Verlag, 2002), 291–310.
13. The term "Waffen-SS" (or Armed SS) was introduced informally into the language of the SS administration in early November 1939, and was officially adopted within a year. According to Bernd Wegner, the term represented both the aim of developing an SS army that was independent of the Wehrmacht and the assertion of the equal value of all units and divisions of the SS. Bernd Wegner, *Hitlers Politische Soldaten. Die Waffen-SS. 1933–1945*, 7th ed. (Paderborn, 2006), 124–32, 128.
14. See Letter from the WVHA Office Group D—Concentration Camps of 29 February 1944 to the Camp Commandants of Auschwitz, Herzogenbusch, Lublin, Ravensbrück, Stutthof, Re: deployment books for employees of the Armed-SS (Female Concentration Camp Guards), HStA Düsseldorf, Ger. Rep. 432 No. 429, p. 60.
15. See Heike, "Bewachung," 237.
16. By comparison, an unmarried female factory worker in the textile industry earned RM 76 a month gross in 1944. See Dörte Winkler, *Frauenarbeit im "Dritten Reich"* (Hamburg: Hoffmann und Campe, 1977), 202; Heike, "Bewachung," 224.
17. Letter from Ravensbrück Concentration Camp to Lublin Concentration Camp Headquarters on 25 February 1944, re: Service ranks for female camp guards, HStA Düsseldorf, Ger. Rep. 432 No. 429, p. 105.
18. The working-hours regulations of 30 April 1938 (RGBl. I, p. 447) set the standard working week at 48 hours. During the war, that figure was raised several times. The 60-hour week was introduced on 31 August 1944 (RGBl. I, p. 191). See Ulrich Herbert,

Fremdarbeiter. Politik und Praxis des "Ausländer Einsatzes" in der Kriegswirtschaft in Deutschland 1938–1945 (Berlin, 1985); Rüdiger Hachtmann, *Industriearbeit im Dritten Reich* (Göttingen: Vandenhoeck & Ruprecht, 1989).

19. Götz Aly, *Hitlers Volksstaat. Raub, Rassenkrieg und nationaler Sozialismus* (Frankfurt am Main: S. Fischer, 2005), 48. See Jonathan Steinberg, *Die Deutsche Bank und ihre Goldtransaktionen während des Zweiten Weltkrieges* (Munich: Beck, 1999), 16.
20. Statement by Hermine Ryan (née Braunsteiner) on 11 May 1946 in Vienna, Dokumentationsarchiv des österreichischen Widerstandes (DÖW), Regional Court Vienna (LG Vienna) Vg 1 Vr 5670/48, p. 1.
21. Statement by Hermine Ryan (née Braunsteiner) on 20 August 1973 in Düsseldorf, HStA Düsseldorf, Ger. Rep. 432 No. 193, pp. 46ff.
22. Ibid., 46ff.
23. Ibid., 47ff.
24. See Ursula Nienhaus, *Berufsstand weiblich. Die ersten weiblichen Angestellten* (Berlin: Transit, 1982); Karin Walser, *Dienstmädchen. Frauenarbeit und Weiblichkeitsbilder um 1900* (Frankfurt: Extrabuch, 1985); Carola Lipp, *Schimpfende Weiber und patriotische Jungfrauen* (Moos/Baden-Baden: Elster, 1986); Dorothee Wierling, *Mädchen für alles. Arbeitsalltag und Lebensgeschichte städtischer Dienstmädchen um die Jahrhundertwende* (Bonn, 1987).
25. See Ernst Bruckmüller, *Sozialgeschichte Österreichs* (Vienna, 2001), 373–417.
26. Statement by Hermine Ryan (née Braunsteiner) on 20 August 1973 in Düsseldorf, HStA Düsseldorf, Ger. Rep. 432 No. 193, pp. 49ff.
27. Ibid., 48.
28. Ibid., 48ff.
29. Ibid., 49.
30. Ibid., 50ff.
31. Until 1942 the "Der Reichsbund freier Schwestern und Pflegerinnen," also known as the "Blaue Schwesternschaft," was distinct from the "Braune Schwestern," affiliated with the Nazi Party. See Ilsemarie Walter, "Auswirkungen des 'Anschlusses' auf die österreichische Krankenpflege," in *Medizin und Nationalsozialismus. Wege der Aufarbeitung, Wiener Gespräche zur Sozialgeschichte der Medizin*, ed. Sonia Horn et al. (Vienna, 2001), 143–59.
32. Statement by Hermine Ryan (née Braunsteiner) on 20 August 1973 in Düsseldorf, HStA Düsseldorf, Ger. Rep. 432 No. 193, p. 51.
33. Ibid., 50ff. It is interesting to note that along with Braunsteiner, Hermann Hackmann (and almost certainly others among the SS staff at Majdanek) had been involved in a *Turnverein*. The role of these gymnastics associations as a political crossroad for young people and as a job market in fascist Germany and Austria should be explored in more detail.
34. In the repressive atmosphere of the crisis years of 1929 and 1930, many working women were forced out of their jobs to make way for men. After the Nazi seizure of power, unemployment remained a problem of undiminished proportions and

was addressed with measures that included gender-specific discrimination against working women. See Lore Kleiber, "'Wo ihr seid, da soll die Sonne scheinen!'—Der Frauenarbeitsdienst am Ende der Weimarer Republik und im Nationalsozialismus," in *Mutterkreuz und Arbeitsbuch. Zur Geschichte der Frauen in der Weimarer Republik und im Nationalsozialismus*, ed. Frauengruppe Faschismusforschung (Frankfurt am Main: Fischer, 1981), 188–214, esp. 189.

35. Statement by Hermine Ryan (née Braunsteiner) on 20 August 1973 in Düsseldorf, HStA Düsseldorf, Ger. Rep. 432 No. 193, pp. 51ff.
36. Ibid.
37. Ibid., 52ff.
38. Ibid., 53.
39. For a discussion of postwar memories, see Annette Leo, *"Das ist so'n zweischneidiges Schwert hier unser KZ . . ." Der Fürstenberger Alltag und das Frauenkonzentrationslager Ravenbrück* (Berlin: Metropol 2007).
40. Statement by Hermine Ryan (née Braunsteiner) on 20 August 1973 in Düsseldorf, HStA Düsseldorf, Ger. Rep. 432 No. 193, p. 56.
41. See Kleiber, "Wo ihr seid."
42. Statement by Erna Wallisch (née Pfannstiel) on 14 January 1965 in Vienna, DÖW, Regional Court (LG) Graz 13/Vr 3329/63, vol. 1, p. 461.
43. See Angela Vogel, *Das Pflichtjahr für Mädchen. Nationalsozialistische Arbeitseinsatzpolitik im Zeichen der Kriegswirtschaft* (New York: Peter Lang, 1997).
44. For further information, see Stefan Bajohr, "Weiblicher Arbeitsdienst im 'Dritten Reich.' Ein Konflikt zwischen Ideologie und Ökonomie," *VfZG* 28 (1980): 331–57; Franka Maubach, *Die Stellung halten. Kriegserfahrungen und Lebensgeschichten von Wehrmachthelferinnen* (Göttingen: Vandenhoeck & Ruprecht 2009); and Christina Altenstrasser, "Zwischen Ideologie und ökonomischer Notwendigkeit. Der 'Reichsarbeitsdienst für die weibliche Jugend,'" in *Frauen im Reichsgau Oberdonau. Geschlechtsspezifische Bruchlinien im Nationalsozialismus*, ed. Gabriella Hauch (Linz: Oberösterreichisches Landesarchiv, 2006), 107–29, 61–69.
45. On the Hadamar euthanasia facility, see Patricia L. Heberer, "'Exitus heute in Hadamar': The Hadamar Facility and 'Euthanasia' in Nazi Germany" (PhD diss., University of Maryland, 2001).
46. Eberhard Fechner, transcription of interview with Erna Wallisch, 15 June 1980, manuscript (private collection), 2ff. Parts of interview transcript published in *Falter* 7 (2008): 14–15.
47. The German term *Volksschule* generally referred to the years of compulsory education every citizen and resident was required to attend. In Germany and Switzerland, it was equivalent to mandatory eight to nine years of primary and secondary school, whereas in Austria the term only refers to four years of primary school.
48. Fechner, transcription of interview with Erna Wallisch, 15 June 1980, manuscript (private collection), 4ff.
49. Ibid., 5ff.

50. See Stefanie Oppel, *Die Rolle der Arbeitsämter bei der Rekrutierung von SS-Aufseherinnen* (Freiburg, 2006); Winkler, *Frauenarbeit.*
51. Margarete Buber-Neumann, *Als Gefangene bei Stalin und Hitler. Eine Welt im Dunkel* (Berlin: Ullstein, 1997), 320ff., 322.
52. Statement by Rosa Süss (née Reischl) on 29 August 1973 in Düsseldorf, HStA Düsseldorf, Ger. Rep. 432 No. 252, p. 68.
53. Statement by Charlotte W. on 21 May 1970 in Lübeck, HStA Düsseldorf, Ger. Rep. 432 No. 234, p. 31.
54. See Stefanie Oppel and Marianne Essmann, "Von der Kontoristin zur SS-Aufseherin. Dienstverpflichtung als Zwangsmassnahme?," in *Im Gefolge der SS. Aufseherinnen des Frauen-KZ Ravensbrück. Begleitband zur Ausstellung*, ed. Simone Erpel (Berlin: Metropol, 2007), 81–88; Oppel, *Die Rolle der Arbeitsämter.*
55. Statement by Charlotte Mayer (née Wöllert) on 28 August 1973 in Düsseldorf, HStA Düsseldorf, Ger. Rep. 432 No. 234, p. 46.
56. Here Wöllert is referring to the Berlin Document Center (BDC), which after the war collected the personal data of SS employees. The BDC is now located at the National Archives (Bundesarchiv) in Berlin.
57. Statement by Charlotte Mayer (née Wöllert) on 19 August 1970 in Cologne, HStA Düsseldorf, Ger. Rep. 432 No. 234, p. 35.
58. "Domjüch" originally denoted simply the location of the new building of the "Mecklenburg-Strelitzsche Landesirrenanstalt," erected in 1902 beside Domjüch Lake in the northern part of the town of Neustrelitz. It soon came to be a synonym for the complex of buildings and the psychiatric institution itself. See Christiane Witzke, *Domjüch: Erinnerungen an eine Heil- und Pflegeanstalt in Mecklenburg-Strelitz* (Neubrandenburg, 2001). See also Brigitte Kepplinger, "Frauen in der Tötungsanstalt: Der weibliche Anteil an den Euthanasiemorden in Hartheim," in *Frauen in Oberdonau. Geschlechterspezifische Bruchlinien im Nationalsozialismus*, ed. Gabriella Hauch (Linz, 2006), 381–98.
59. I thank Christiane Witzke for this information.
60. Statement by Hildegard Lächert on 27 June 1947 in Krakow, HStA Düsseldorf, Ger. Rep. 432 No. 295, p. 1.
61. Ibid.
62. Hildegard Lächert in Eberhard Fechner, *Norddeutscher Rundfunk: Der Prozess: Eine Darstellung des Majdanek-Verfahrens in Düsseldorf*, videotape (1984), part 1.
63. Statement by Hildegard Lächert on 27 June 1947 in Krakow, HStA Düsseldorf, Ger. Rep. 432 No. 295, p. 2.
64. Reinhard Plewe and Jan Thomas Köhler, *Baugeschichte Frauen-Konzentrationslager Ravensbrück, Schriftenreihe der Stiftung Brandenburgische Gedenkstätte Ravensbrück* (Berlin, 2001), 10:20; see Jeanette Toussaint, "Nach Dienstschluss," in Erpel, *"Im Gefolge der SS,"* 89–100. See also chapter 4 of this work.
65. Hildegard Lächert, in Fechner, *Der Prozess*, part 1.
66. Letter by Chief Guard Ehrich to Lublin Concentration Camp Headquarters on 22

July 1943, Re: Good-conduct certificate for *Aufseherin* Lächert Hildegard, HStA Düsseldorf, Ger. Rep. 432 No. 429, p. 23.

67. Roll call by name of civilian employees on 29 September 1943 to the Senior SS and Police Leaders in the Generalgouvernement, Krakow, DÖW, LG Graz 13/Vr 3329/63, vol. 4, p. 129.
68. Statement by Luzie H. on 8 November 1972 in Düsseldorf, HStA Düsseldorf, Ger. Rep. 432 No. 292, p. 66.
69. Luzie H., in Fechner, *Der Prozess*, part 1.
70. Statement by Anna M. on 2 August 1961 in Stuttgart, HStA Düsseldorf, Ger. Rep. 432 No. 234, p. 16.
71. All girls and young women between the ages of ten and twenty-one were supposed to join the BDM. Its main function was to indoctrinate them in the spirit of Nazism and to prepare them for their future roles as women in the Nazi national community. BDM members were also deployed in various functions in Labor Service and even in War-Help Service. See Dagmar Reese, *"Straff, aber nicht stramm—herb, aber nicht derb." Zur Vergesellschaftung von Mädchen durch den Bund Deutscher Mädel im sozialkulturellen Vergleich zweier Milieus* (Weinheim, 1989).
72. Statement by Anna M. on 2 August 1961 in Stuttgart, HStA Düsseldorf, Ger. Rep. 432 No. 234, p. 13.
73. See Marc Buggeln, *Slave Labor in Nazi Concentration Camps* (Oxford: Oxford University Press, 2014).
74. On Ravensbrück, see Strebel, *Das KZ Ravensbrück*, 211–28.
75. See ibid., 73 and 79.
76. See Karin Berger, "'Hut ab Frau Sedlmayer!' Zur Militarisierung und Ausbeutung von Frauen im nationalsozialistischen Österreich," in *NS-Herrschaft in Österreich 1938–1945*, ed. Emmerich Talos, Ernst Hanisch, and Wolfgang Neugebauer (Vienna, 1988), 141–59; Ingrid Bauer, "Eine frauen- und geschlechterspezifische Perspektivierung des Nationalsozialismus," in *NS-Herrschaft in Österreich 1938–1945*, ed. Emmerich Talos, Ernst Hanisch, and Wolfgang Neugebauer, rev. ed. (Vienna, 2000), 407–43, 426ff.
77. Oppel, *Die Rolle der Arbeitsämter*, 80–91.
78. See also the section of chapter 4 titled "The Concentration Camp as Residence: Architecture and Its Effects".
79. Buber-Neumann, *Als Gefangene bei Stalin und Hitler*, 320ff.
80. See Strebel, *Das KZ Ravensbrück*, 81.
81. Martin Broszat, ed., *Kommandant in Auschwitz. Autobiographische Aufzeichnungen des Rudolf Höss*, 17th ed. (Munich, 2000), 178.
82. Deposition of Gertrud Elli Heise, Investigation Team, 20 January 1946, Neumünster, Public Record Office (PRO) War Office (WO) 309/429, no page number.
83. Handwritten activity report of Gertrud Heise, Neumünster, 21 August 1945, PRO WO 309/429, no page number. See also statement by Edith W. on 27 September 1977 in Düsseldorf, HStA Düsseldorf, Ger. Rep. 432 No. 286, p. 315.
84. Statement by Hermine Böttcher (née Brückner) on 11 December 1974 in Hannover,

HStA Düsseldorf, Ger. Rep. 432 No. 290, p. 1.

85. Statement by Herta B. on 30 October 1974 in Waldshut, HStA Düsseldorf, Ger. Rep. 432 No. 203, p. 23.
86. Telex by Commandant Florstedt to the WVHA on 21 July 1943, HStA Düsseldorf, Ger. Rep. 432 No. 429, p. 27.
87. Statement by Elisabeth H. on 27 August 1975 in Cologne, HStA Düsseldorf, Ger. Rep. 432 No. 252, p. 132.
88. Statement by Luise Danz on 30 June 1947 in Krakow, HStA Düsseldorf, Ger. Rep. 432 No. 57, p. 11127.
89. Statement by Alice Orlowski on 27 August 1973 in Düsseldorf, HStA Düsseldorf, Ger. Rep. 432 No. 262, p. 320.
90. Statement by Alice Orlowski on 18 April 1961 in Eitorf/Sieg, HStA Düsseldorf, Ger. Rep. 432 No. 5, p. 812.
91. Statement by Alice Orlowski on 17 October 1946 in Hildesheim, HStA Düsseldorf, Ger. Rep. 432 No. 213, p. 768.
92. Statement by Alice Orlowski on 27 August 1973 in Düsseldorf, HStA Düsseldorf, Ger. Rep. 432 No. 262, p. 321.
93. Ibid., 320.
94. Statement by Alice Orlowski on 25 June 1947 in Krakow, HStA Düsseldorf, Ger. Rep. 432 No. 296, p. 1.
95. Statement by Hermann Hackmann on 27 November 1967 in Göttingen, HStA Düsseldorf, Ger. Rep. 432 No. 247, p. 568.
96. Hermann Hackmann, in Fechner, *Der Prozess*, part 1.
97. The Allgemeine SS ("General SS") was the largest branch of the Schutzstaffel (SS) paramilitary force. It was officially established in fall 1934 to distinguish its members from the SS-Verfügungstruppe, which later became the Waffen-SS, and the SS-Totenkopfverbände (SS employed in the concentration camps).
98. An *Anwärter* is literally a "candidate," which is the lowest paramilitary rank in the Nazi party and SS.
99. *Aktive SS* or "Active SS" was the lowest rank in the Allgemeine SS for a young candidate.
100. Statement by Hermann Hackmann on 27 November 1967 in Göttingen, HStA Düsseldorf, Ger. Rep. 432 No. 247, p. 569.
101. The Nazis incarcerated German opponents to the regime and prominent European politicians as "special" or "honorary prisoners" (*Sonder- und Ehrenhäftlinge*) in order to use them as a bargaining chip with the Allies for exchanges of hostages and prisoners of war. Volker Koop, *In Hitlers Hand: "Sonder- und Ehrenhäftlinge" der SS* (Cologne: Böhlau Verlag, 2010).
102. Statement by Hermann Hackmann on 27 November 1967 in Göttingen, HStA Düsseldorf, Ger. Rep. 432 No. 247, p. 570.
103. Hermann Hackmann, in Fechner, *Der Prozess*, part 1.
104. Heinz Villain, in Fechner, *Der Prozess*, part 1.

105. Ibid.
106. Ibid.
107. Statement by Wilhelm Reinartz on 11 March 1965 in Langenfeld, HStA Düsseldorf, Ger. Rep. 432 No. 240, pp. 164 and 164a.
108. Statement by Eduard R. on 12 January 1965 in Vienna, DÖW, LG Graz 13/Vr 3329/63, vol. 1, p. 435.
109. Ibid., 435–37.
110. Statement by Eduard R. on 13 January 1965 in Vienna, DÖW, LG Graz 13/Vr 3329/63, vol. 1, p. 451.
111. Otto Z., in Fechner, *Der Prozess*, part 1.
112. Statement by Otto Z. on 20 February 1970 in Munich, HStA Düsseldorf, Ger. Rep. 432 No. 204, p. 26.
113. See Karin Orth, "Bewachung," in *Der Ort des Terrors. Geschichte der nationalsozialistischen Konzentrationslager*, ed. Wolfgang Benz and Barbara Distel (Munich: C.H. Beck, 2005), 1:126–40.
114. See Jeanette Toussaint, "'Unter Ausnützung ihrer dienstlichen Gewalt.' Österreichische Volksgerichtsverfahren gegen ehemalige SS-Aufseherinnen aus Oberdonau: 1945–1950," in *Frauen in Oberdonau. Geschlechterspezifische Bruchlinienim Nationalsozialismus*, ed. Gabriella Hauch (Linz, 2006), 399–423.
115. Ibid.
116. See Heike, "Bewachung"; Strebel, *Das KZ Ravensbrück*, 84.
117. Bernhard Strebel has estimated that 10 percent of the female guards employed in Ravensbrück had applied of their own volition, 20 percent had been assigned jobs there by the Labor Department, and 70 percent had been sent there from the companies where they worked. Strebel, *Das KZ Ravensbrück*, 84.
118. See Insa Eschebach, "Das Aufseherinnenhaus. Überlegungen zu einer Ausstellung über SS-Aufseherinnen in der Gedenkstätte Ravensbrück," *Gedenkstätten Rundbrief*, no. 75 (March 1997), 10.
119. Schwarz, "SS-Aufseherinnen," 41.
120. See Notice of commitment from the Burgstädt Labor Office to Marianne Essmann on 18 August 1944, BstU Chem 3 Stks 15/48, p. 24, in Oppel, *Die Rolle der Arbeitsämter*, 91.
121. Ibid., 90ff.
122. Heike, "Bewachung," 235; Strebel, *Das KZ Ravensbrück*, 83.
123. See application form.
124. On living conditions in Berlin, see Eva Brücker, "'Und ich bin heil da 'rausgekommen.' Gewalt und Sexualität in einer Berliner Arbeiternachbarschaft zwischen 1916/17 und 1958," in *Physische Gewalt. Studien zur Geschichte der Neuzeit*, ed. Thomas Lindenberger and Alf Lüdtke (Frankfurt, 1995), 337–65.

Chapter 4. Ravensbrück Training Camp: The Concentration Camp as Disciplinary Space

1. Statement by Alice Orlowski on 27 August 1973 in Düsseldorf, HStA Düsseldorf, Ger. Rep. 432 No. 262, p. 320.
2. See Rousset, *L'Univers concentrationnaire* (Paris: Editions du Pavois, 1946).
3. Undated form from Ravensbrück Concentration Camp, concerning the application of female camp guards (application form), BA, NS/4/Ra 1.
4. The French word is "débauche," which denotes excessive, generally erotic, misconduct.
5. Emphasis in original.
6. Tillion, *Ravensbrück* (Paris, 1988), 140. Tillion's account has also been published in English translation as Germaine Tillion, *Ravensbrück*, trans. Gerald Satterwhite (Garden City, NY: Anchor Press, 1975). However, the details that are of particular interest for this work, such as violence and female guards, are not always accurately translated. For purposes of this study I use my own translations based on the 1988 French version, which I have prepared together with the translator of my German manuscript. All later references to Tillion's book are based on this 1988 edition and my own translations.
7. On Hitler's order, in December 1941 the chief of the Wehrmacht Supreme Command (OKW), Wilhelm Keitel, formulated the "Night and Fog Decree," which mandated combatting resistance movements in the occupied West European countries with the death penalty or incarceration in a concentration camp. See Bernhard Strebel, *Das KZ Ravensbrück. Geschichte eines Lagerkomplexes* (Berlin, 2003), 166–68; Christel Trouvé, "Die 'Nacht und Nebel'-Häftlinge 1942–1945," *Dachauer Hefte* 21 (2005): 50–65.
8. The study was originally published as Germaine Tillion, "A la recherche de la vérité," in *Ravensbrück* (Neuchâtel, 1946), 11–88. Tillion extensively revised this Ravensbrück study twice, in 1973 and 1988. In the present work, I refer to the 1988 edition (Germaine Tillion, *Ravensbrück* [Paris, 1988]), which is also the basis for the German translation: Germaine Tillion, *Frauenkonzentrationslager Ravensbrück* (Lüneburg, 1998).
9. Margarete Buber-Neumann, *Als Gefangene bei Stalin und Hitler. Eine Welt im Dunkel (1949)* (Berlin, 1997), 321ff.
10. In 1943, e.g., four *Aufseherinnen* were discharged from Majdanek for pregnancy, another for disability/sickness. See letter by Lublin Concentration Camp on 10 December 1943 to the WVHA in Oranienburg, HStA Düsseldorf, Ger. Rep. 432 No. 429, p. 140.
11. Michel Foucault, "The Meshes of Power," in *Space, Knowledge and Power: Foucault and Geography*, ed J. W. Crampton and S. Eldon (Aldershot: Ashgate, 2007), 160.
12. Ibid., 154.
13. Michel Foucault, "The Mesh of Power," *Viewpoint Magazine*, 12 September 2012, http://viewpointmag.com/2012/09/12/the-mesh-of-power/.
14. Work by Insa Eschebach has been an exception. See also Christian Dürr's study of

prisoner society "disciplinary techniques"; Christian Dürr, *Jenseits der Disziplin. Eine Analyse der Machtordnung in nationalsozialistischen Konzentrationslagern* (Vienna, 2004).

15. Foucault, "The Meshes of Power," 156.
16. On the problematics of "orders and obedience," see chapter 9 of this work.
17. Statement by Herta B. on 30 October 1974 in Waldshut, HStA Düsseldorf, Ger. Rep. 432 No. 203, p. 24.
18. Form, service contract, HStA Düsseldorf, Ger. Rep. 432 No. 429, p. 106.
19. Statement by Hildegard R., Lublin Concentration Camp Headquarters, 24 February 1943, HStA Düsseldorf, Ger. Rep. 432 No. 430, p. 214.
20. Statement by Hildegard R., Lublin Concentration Camp Headquarters, 24 February 1943, HStA Düsseldorf, Ger. Rep. 432 No. 430, p. 216.
21. Statement by Hildegard R., Lublin Concentration Camp Headquarters, 24 February 1943, HStA Düsseldorf, Ger. Rep. 432 No. 430, p. 215.
22. Statement by Rosa Süss (née Reischl) on 29 August 1973 in Düsseldorf, HStA Düsseldorf, Ger. Rep. 432 No. 252, p. 68; see also statement by Rosa Süss (née Reischl) on 26 June 1979, main hearing, HStA Düsseldorf, Ger. Rep. 432 No. 286, p. 5.
23. See statement by Elisabeth H. on 27 August 1975 in Cologne, HStA Düsseldorf, Ger. Rep. 432 No. 252, p. 132v; statement by Elisabeth H. on 15 June 1976, main hearing, HStA Düsseldorf, Ger. Rep. 432 No. 286, p. 200.
24. Statement by Herta B. (née P.), on 15 June 1976, main hearing, HStA Düsseldorf, Ger. Rep. 432 No. 285, no page number.
25. Declaration of honor by SS-Oberscharführer Herbert A., Lublin Concentration Camp Headquarters, 24 April 1942, HStA Düsseldorf, Ger. Rep. 432 No. 429, p. 32. See also declaration of honor by Hermine Brückner, 6 January 1945, Prague State Archive.
26. Oath by Hildegard R., Lublin Concentration Camp Headquarters, 24 February 1943, HStA Düsseldorf, Ger. Rep. 432 No. 430, p. 217.
27. Johannes Schwartz, *Die SS-Aufseherinnen von Ravensbrück. Individuelle Handlungsspielräume und ideologische Vorstellungen* (Magisterarbeit, Humboldt-Universität zu Berlin, 2002), 26ff.
28. Buber-Neumann, *Gefangene*, 322.
29. See Annette F. Timm, *The Politics of Fertility in Twentieth Century Berlin* (New York: Cambridge University Press, 2010).
30. See Julia Roos, "Backlash against Prostitutes' Rights: Origins and Dynamics of Nazi Prostitution Policies," *Journal of the History of Sexuality* 11, nos. 1/2 (January/April 2002): 67–94. Reprinted in Dagmar Herzog, ed., *Sexuality and German Fascism* (New York: Berghahn Books, 2005).
31. See training plan of 2nd SS-Totenkopf-Sturmbann, Lublin, 6 November 1942, Archiwum Panstwowego Muzeum na Majdanku (APMM), I.f.3, p. 21; see also training plan of the 5th SS-Totenkopf-Sturmbann, Lublin, undated (probably after February 1943), ibid., 25–27.
32. Statement by Anna David, 8 January 1946, Ravensbrück Memorial/Brandenburg

Memorials Foundation (MGR/StBG), transl. transcript 251; cited in Strebel, *Das KZ Ravensbrück*, 94.

33. See statement by Hermine Braunsteiner on 11 May 1946 in Vienna, DÖW, State Criminal Court (LG) Vienna Vg 1 Vr 5670/48, p. 2.
34. Internal camp letter by the Commandant to the Chief Guard, Lublin Concentration Camp, on 8 April 1943, re pistol shooting by female guards, HStA Düsseldorf, Ger. Rep. 432 No. 430, p. 195.
35. See Strebel, *Das KZ Ravensbrück*, 96.
36. Statement by Hermine Ryan Braunsteiner on 20 August 1973 in Düsseldorf, HStA Düsseldorf, Ger. Rep. 432 No. 193, p. 54. See also statement by Charlotte W. on 21 May 1970 in Lübeck, HStA Düsseldorf, Ger. Rep. 432 No. 234, p. 31; statement by Hermine Böttcher on 11 December 1974 in Hannover, HStA Düsseldorf, Ger. Rep. 432 No. 290, pp. 1ff.; statement by Luise Danz on 30 June 1947 in Krakow, HStA Düsseldorf, Ger. Rep. 432 No. 57, p. 11128.
37. On Braunsteiner's activities in Ravensbrück, see Elissa Mailänder Koslov, "'Weil es einer Wienerin gar nicht liegt.' so brutal zu sein . . . Frauenbilder im Wiener Volksgerichtsverfahren gegen eine österreichische KZ-Aufseherin (1946–1949)," *Zeitgeschichte* 3 (2005): 128–50.
38. Statement by Rosa Süss (née Reischl) on 29 August 1973 in Düsseldorf, HStA Düsseldorf, Ger. Rep. 432 No. 252, p. 68. See also statement by Rosa Süss (née Reischl) on 26 June 1979, main hearing, HStA Düsseldorf, Ger. Rep. 432 No. 286, p. 5; and statement by witness Erika Bergmann on 9 July 1965, MGR/StBG, no file number, p. 3, cited in Insa Eschebach, "'Ich bin unschuldig.' Aussageprotokolle als historische Quellen. Der Rostocker Ravensbrück-Prozeß 1966," *WerkstattGeschichte* 12 (1995): 65–70, esp. 68ff.
39. Statement by Charlotte Mayer (née Wöllert), 31 March 1976, transcript of main hearing, HStA Düsseldorf, Ger. Rep. 432 No. 288, p. 64.
40. Statement by Erika W. on 26 February 1975 in Düsseldorf, HStA Düsseldorf, Ger. Rep. 432 No. 215, p. 1144.
41. See telex of Commandant Florstedt to the WVHA on 21 July 1943, HStA Düsseldorf, Ger. Rep. 432 No. 429, p. 27.
42. See statement by Alice Orlowski on 18 April 1961 in Eitorf/Sieg, HStA Düsseldorf, Ger. Rep. 432 No. 5, p. 812.
43. Strebel, *Das KZ Ravensbrück*, 25. This order was certainly preceded by two others, and most probably there were others as well; unfortunately, the incomplete documentation does not permit any investigation of changes and/or developments, as the orders cannot be compared to one another.
44. Headquarters Order No. 3, Ravensbrück Concentration Camp, 24 July 1942, BA NS 4 Ra, p. 3. See also Ino Arndt, "Das Frauenkonzentrationslager Ravensbrück," *Dachauer Hefte* 3 (1987): 125–57, 135; Gudrun Schwarz, "SS-Aufseherinnen in nationalsozialistischen Konzentrationslagern (1933–1945)," *Dachauer Hefte* 10 (1994): 32–49, 41f.; Strebel, *Das KZ Ravensbrück*, 96.

45. Ibid.
46. Letter from SS-WVHA, Office Group D on 27 July 1941 to the camp commandants of all concentration camps, ZStL, Ordner 311e, p. 113; cited in Schwarz, "SS-Aufseherinnen," 43.
47. Letter of the detail leader of "SS-Kommando Freia" in Freiberg/Saxony to the Headquarters of the Flossenbürg Concentration Camp on 29 November 1944, BAK, NS 4 FL/10; cited in Schwarz, "SS-Aufseherinnen," 43.
48. Ibid.
49. Günter Morsch, "Organisations- und Verwaltungsstruktur der Konzentrationslager," in *Der Ort des Terrors. Geschichte der nationalsozialistischen Konzentrationslager*, ed. Wolfgang Benz and Barbara Distel (Munich: C.H. Beck, 2005), 1:58–75, 70; see also Jens-Christian Wagner, *Produktion des Todes. Das KZ Mittelbau-Dora* (Göttingen, 2001), 296ff.
50. See Julia Timpe, "Hitler's Happy People: *Kraft durch Freude*'s Everyday Production of Joy in the Third Reich" (diss., Brown University, 2013).
51. See Timpe, "Hitler's Happy People." Timpe's new project, "Happiness and Destruction in the Third Reich," is focusing specifically on events put on by KdF in concentration camps for the entertainment of SS guards.
52. Isabell Sprenger, *Groß-Rosen. Ein Konzentrationslager in Schlesien* (Cologne, 1996), 99.
53. Letter of the Chief Guard on 26 August 1943 to the Commandant of Lublin Concentration Camp, Re: Report on female guards, HStA Düsseldorf, Ger. Rep. 432 No. 429, p. 14.
54. 1st SS-Totenkopf Mounted Regiment, "Service Regulation for Ideological Training," undated (Militärarchiv des Bundesarchivs: RS 4/859), cited in Bernd Wegner, *Hitlers Politische Soldaten. Die Waffen-SS. 1933–1945*, 7th ed. (Paderborn, 2006), 191.
55. Service regulation for Ravensbrück Concentration Camp (Lagerordnung Ravensbrück), in National Archives and Records Administration [hereafter NARA], RG 549, 000-50-11, Box 522, Folder no. 3, 5–6. The first two pages of the otherwise complete original are missing. The original pages were found by Bernhard Strebel in the Bundesarchiv in Berlin and are titled "Purpose and Organization of the Concentration Camp," BA, NS 3/391, p. 1. Therefore, Bernhard Strebel dates the Ravensbrück Camp Order to 1939, because the sentence "Special regulations are issued in case of war" is found on the second page. This service regulation was modified several times until 1945, yet the incomplete documentation means the changes can no longer be traced. Strebel, *Das KZ Ravensbrück*, 25.
56. Letter of Detail Leader of the Willischthal subcamp of 1 January 1945, BAK, NS 4 FL/10; see also letter of the Detail Leader of the Oederan subcamp to the Headquarters Flossenbürg Concentration Camps on 12 January 1945, ibid.; cited in Schwarz, "SS-Aufseherinnen," 43.
57. Reinhard Plewe and Jan Thomas Köhler, *Baugeschichte Frauen-Konzentrationslager Ravensbrück, Schriftenreihe der Stiftung Brandenburgische Gedenkstätte Ravensbrück* (Berlin, 2001), 10:58.

58. Jeanette Toussaint, "Nach Dienstschluss," in *Im Gefolge der SS: Aufseherinnen des Frauen-KZ Ravensbrück. Begleitband zur Ausstellung*, ed. Simone Erpel (Berlin, 2007), 89–100, 92.
59. Wegner, *Hitlers Politische Soldaten*, 190ff.
60. "Erfahrungen in der Schulung," lecture of the "Schulungsamt" chief on 25 January 1939 on the occasion of the Gruppenführer conference in "Haus der Flieger," p. 6 (BA, NS 19/neu 1969), cited in Wegner, *Hitlers Politische Soldaten*, 190.
61. These forms were intended for SS personnel that were transferred or on leave and registered all items turned in upon leaving the camp, such as weapons and uniforms.
62. Gottfried Köwel, *Die heitere Welt von Spiegelberg* (Vienna: Gallus Verlag, 1940); Rolf Lennar, *Der ungefährliche Dritte* (Budweis: Verlagsanstalt Moldavia, 1941); Else Marquardsen-Kamphövener, *Tapfere kleine Lore. Ein Liebesroman* (Berlin: Zeitschriftenverlag, 1936); Walter Kabel, *Die Bajadere Mola Pur* (Berlin: Verlag für moderne Lektüre, 1926).
63. See Elissa Mailänder Koslov, "'Die heitere Welt von Spiegelberg'—eine Freizeitlektüre von SS-Aufseherinnen," in *Tagungsband des Sechsten österreichischen Zeitgeschichtetages "Macht, Kunst, Kommunikation" 2003* (Innsbruck, 2004), 238–42.
64. See Jürgen Matthäus, "Die 'Judenfrage' als Schulungsthema von SS und Polizei. 'Inneres Erlebnis' und Handlungslegitimation," in *Ausbildungsziel Judenmord? "Weltanschauliche Erziehung" von SS, Polizei und Waffen-SS im Rahmen der "Endlösung,"* ed. Jürgen Matthäus et al. (Frankfurt am Main, 2003), 35–86; Jürgen Förster, "Die weltanschauliche Erziehung in der Waffen-SS. 'Kein totes Wissen, sondern lebendiger Nationalsozialismus,'" ibid., 87–113.
65. Wegner, *Hitlers Politische Soldaten*, 193.
66. See Strebel, *Das KZ Ravensbrück*, 281ff.
67. Isa Vermehren, *Reise durch den letzten Akt. Ravensbrück, Buchenwald, Dachau: eine Frau berichtet (1946)* (Reinbek, 1979), 18ff.
68. Plewe and Köhler, *Baugeschichte Ravensbrück*, 18.
69. Ralph Gabriel, "Nationalsozialistische Biopolitik und die Architektur der Konzentrationslager," in *Auszug aus dem Lager. Zur Überwindung des modernen Raumparadigmas in der politischen Philosophie*, ed. Ludger Schwarte (Berlin, 2007), 207.
70. Plewe and Köhler, *Baugeschichte Ravensbrück*, 29.
71. Michel Foucault, *Discipline and Punish: The Birth of the Prison*, trans. Alan Sheridan (New York: Random House, 1979); see especially his discussion of "docile bodies" in part 3, "Discipline."
72. Gabriel, "Nationalsozialistische Biopolitik und die Architektur der Konzentrationslager," 207.
73. Strebel, *Das KZ Ravensbrück*, 92.
74. Plewe and Köhler, *Baugeschichte Ravensbrück*, 27.
75. Irmtraud Heike, " . . . da es sich ja lediglich um die Bewachung der Häftlinge handelt . . ." Lagerverwaltung und Bewachungspersonal, in *Frauen in Konzentrationslagern.*

Bergen-Belsen, Ravensbrück, ed. Claus Füllberg-Stolberg et al. (Bremen, 1994), 32–49, 225.

76. Bernhard Strebel has pointed out that Ravensbrück was not exclusively a women's camp and included a small men's camp. See Bernhard Strebel, "Das Männerlager im KZ Ravensbrück 1941–1945," *Dachauer Hefte* 14 (1998): 141–74.
77. Strebel, *Das KZ Ravensbrück*, 94.
78. Plewe and Köhler, *Baugeschichte Ravensbrück*, 62.
79. Ibid., p. 27.
80. Foucault, *Discipline and Punish*.
81. Ibid., 147.
82. See Strebel, *Das KZ Ravensbrück*, 51ff.
83. Insa Eschebach, "Das Aufseherinnenhaus. Überlegungen zu einer Ausstellung über SS-Aufseherinnen in der Gedenkstätte Ravensbrück," *Gedenkstätten Rundbrief*, no. 75 (March 1997): 1.
84. It is uncertain where the male headquarters personnel were located. Citing the account of a former *Aufseherin*, Strebel believes that they lived in nearby Fürstenberg. Strebel, *Das KZ Ravensbrück*, 91ff.; Plewe and Köhler, *Baugeschichte Ravensbrück*, 17.
85. Plewe and Köhler, *Baugeschichte Ravensbrück*, 68.
86. Ute Wrocklage, "Das SS-Fotoalbum des Frauen-Konzentrationslager Ravensbrück," in *Im Gefolge der SS*, ed. Simone Erpel, 233–51.
87. In June 1994, not long after the withdrawal of Soviet forces, the Brandenburg Memorials Foundation decided to incorporate three buildings of the former SS lodgings in the memorial's concept. One of the former *Aufseherinnen* houses would be devoted to illustrating the history of the female guards of Ravensbrück. The permanent exhibition "Im Gefolge der Waffen-SS . . ." opened there in fall 2004.
88. Strebel, *Das KZ Ravensbrück*, 73–78. Prisoner numbers also grew here in 1943 and especially 1944; ibid., 104–11.
89. Ibid., 92.
90. Guided tour through the SS lodgings by Reinhard Plewe, November 2003.
91. Eschebach, "Das Aufseherinnenhaus," 2.
92. Rudolf Höss, in Martin Broszat, ed., *Kommandant in Auschwitz. Autobiographische Aufzeichnungen des Höss*, 17th ed. (Munich, 2000), 176ff.
93. Eschebach, "Das Aufseherinnenhaus," 4.
94. Ibid., 2ff.
95. Elisabeth Portmann, "Schutz und Betreuung der werktätigen Frau im Kriege" (diss., Rechts- und staatswissenschaftliche Fakultät der Philipps-Universität Marburg, 1943), manuscript, 51ff; cited in Eschebach, "Das Aufseherinnenhaus," 2ff.
96. Ibid.
97. Eschebach, "Das Aufseherinnenhaus," 3.
98. Toussaint, "Nach Dienstschluss," 91ff.
99. Ibid.
100. Guided tour through the SS lodgings by Reinhard Plewe, November 2003.

101. Ibid.
102. Headquarters Order No. 3 from Ravensbrück Women's Concentration Camp on 24 July 1942, BA, NS/4/Ra 1, p. 3.
103. Plewe and Köhler, *Baugeschichte Ravensbrück*, p. 20.
104. Eschebach, "Das Aufseherinnenhaus," 4.
105. Alf Lüdtke, "Was ist und wer treibt Alltagsgeschichte?," in *Zur Rekonstruktion historischer Erfahrungen und Lebensweisen* (New York, 1989), 9–47, 13.
106. Ibid.
107. Alf Lüdtke, "Die Kaserne," in *Orte des Alltages*, ed. Hans Gerhard Haupt (Munich, 1994), 227–37, 233.
108. Foucault, *Discipline and Punish.*
109. Ibid.
110. Herta Ehlert, cross-examination by Colonel Backhouse, 15 October 1945, PRO WO 235/15, p. 84.
111. Statement by Hermine Braunsteiner on 22 November 1949, main hearing, DÖW, LG Vienna Vg 1 Vr 5670/48, p. 202. See also statement by Hermine Ryan Braunsteiner on 20 August 1973 in Düsseldorf, HStA Düsseldorf, Ger. Rep. 432 No. 193, p. 54.
112. Statement by Hermine Ryan Braunsteiner on 20 August 1973 in Düsseldorf, HStA Düsseldorf, Ger. Rep. 432 No. 193, p. 55.
113. Statement by Erika W. on 26 February 1975 in Düsseldorf, HStA Düsseldorf, Ger. Rep. 432 No. 215, p. 1146.
114. Statement by Charlotte Mayer (née Wöllert) on 31 March 1976, main hearing, HStA Düsseldorf, Ger. Rep. 432 No. 288, pp. 68–69; see also statement by Luzie H. on 8 November 1972 in Düsseldorf, HStA Düsseldorf, Ger. Rep. 432 No. 292, p. 66.
115. Heike, "Bewachung," 224.
116. Ravensbrück Concentration Camp pamphlet concerning employment of female guards, June 1944, Commissioner for the Documents of the State Security Service of the Former GDR ("Gauck Authority" or BStU), AV 8/74, vol. 20, p. 76; cited in Strebel, *Das KZ Ravensbrück*, 94.
117. Service regulation for Ravensbrück Concentration Camp (Lagerordnung Ravensbrück), 22. The meaning of the abbreviation *(t) m 24* in this document is unknown.
118. Gundula Wolter, *Hosen, weiblich. Kulturgeschichte der Frauenhose* (Marburg, 1994), 220.
119. A special brochure of the periodical *Neue Frauenkleidung und Frauenkultur* in 1917 says: "The functionality must lead to a style that, in a certain sense, is always synonymous with beauty. However, a working woman's clothing should never be meant to enhance that woman's beauty in a way that would make her more attractive and appealing as a feminine being. This applies especially to areas of work in which men and women interact where, unavoidably in such times of war as these, the most diverse elements encounter one other." Cited in Wolter, *Hosen, weiblich*, 214ff.
120. Eschebach, "SS-Aufseherinnen," 39–48, esp. 46.
121. Leokadia W., interviewed by Insa Eschebach on 1 May 1995.

122. Paula Diehl, *Macht–Mythos–Utopie. Die Körperbilder der SS-Männer* (Berlin, 2005), 166ff.
123. Service regulation for Ravensbrück Concentration Camp (Lagerordnung Ravensbrück), 22.
124. "Comp." stands for *Vergütungsgruppe*, which refers to the guards' wage category.
125. Letter of the SS-WVHA on 8 March 1944, Re: Changes in service insignia for *Aufseherinnen* in the camps, HStA Düsseldorf, Ger. Rep. 432 No. 429, p. 100.
126. Statement by Luzie H. on 8 November 1972 in Düsseldorf, HStA Düsseldorf, Ger. Rep. 432 No. 292, p. 66.
127. Strebel, *Das KZ Ravensbrück*, 97. On the decoration of female guards in the Gross-Rosen Concentration Camp complex see Isabell Sprenger, *Gross-Rosen: Ein Konzerntrationslager in Schlesien* (Vienna: Böhlau Verlag, 1997), 273.
128. Statement by Hermine Braunsteiner Ryan on 26 November 1979, main hearing, HStA Düsseldorf, Ger. Rep. 432 No. 288, no page number. See also statement by Hermine Braunsteiner on 9 April 1946 in Vienna, DÖW, LG Vienna Vg 1 Vr 5670/48, p. 3; statement by Hermine Braunsteiner on 11 May 1946 in Vienna, ibid., 2.
129. Statement by Hermine Braunsteiner on 22 November 1949, main hearing, DÖW, LG Vienna Vg 1 Vr 5670/48, p. 207. In a recorded list of suggestions in Ravensbrück from March 1944, seven *Aufseherinnen* and an NS nurse were recommended as recipients of this citation. List of suggestions, 1 March 1944, NARA, RG-338-000-50-11; cited in Strebel, *Das KZ Ravensbrück*, 97.
130. I thank retired prosecutor Dieter Ambach for this information.
131. SA especially and, most of all, those in SS uniforms emphasized this separation and marked it additionally with symbols of violence visualized through their uniforms and paramilitary display. Diehl, *Macht–Mythos–Utopie*, 168.
132. According to Paula Diehl, the death's head of the SS was more than a purely symbolic reference to death. In her discussion of Nazi symbolism, Diehl describes an adroit "recycling of symbols." By adopting the Prussian Hussar tradition, the SS carried on a martial symbolism in which the wearer both represented and embodied death. Ibid., 181–91.
133. Statement by Erika W. on 26 February 1975 in Düsseldorf, HStA Düsseldorf, Ger. Rep. 432 No. 215, p. 1146.
134. See also Toussaint, "Nach Dienstschluss," 93.
135. See chapter 3 of this work.
136. Buber-Neumann, *Gefangene*, 321.
137. Statement by Alice Orlowski on 25 June 1947 in Krakow, HStA Düsseldorf, Ger. Rep. 432 No. 296, p. 7.
138. Statement by Hermine Böttcher on 11 December 1974 in Hannover, HStA Düsseldorf, Ger. Rep. 432 No. 290, p. 7.
139. Friedrich Kluge, *Etymologisches Wörterbuch der deutschen Sprache* (Berlin, 2002), 504.
140. Statement by Rosa Süss (née Reischl) on 26 June 1979, main hearing, HStA Düsseldorf, Ger. Rep. 432 No. 286, p. 2.

141. According to Diehl, black leather boots put a twofold symbolism of domination on display: On the one hand they connoted a feudal hegemonic relationship of lord and serf, which was expressed through ownership of a horse and informed the later tradition of officerhood. On the other hand the boots signified the unity of rider and steed, thereby expressing movement, speed, and power. Diehl, *Macht–Mythos–Utopie*, 196.
142. Hildegard Lächert, in Eberhard Fechner, *Norddeutscher Rundfunk: Der Prozess: Eine Darstellung des Majdanek-Verfahrens in Düsseldorf*, videotape (1984), part 2.
143. On the problematics of power, see chapters 9 and 10.
144. Vermehren, *Reise*, 76ff.
145. Alf Lüdtke, "Einleitung," in *Herrschaft als soziale Praxis, Historische und sozialanthropologische Studien* (Göttingen: 1991), 16ff.
146. Diehl, *Macht—Mythos—Utopie*, 172.
147. Foucault, *Discipline and Punish*.
148. Jan Novak, in Fechner, *Der Prozess*, part 2.
149. Headquarters Order No. 3 from the Ravensbrück Women's Concentration Camp on 24 July 1942, BA, NS/4/Ra 1, pp. 3–5.
150. Eschebach, "Das Aufseherinnenhaus," 3.
151. See statement by Rosa Süss (née Reischl) on 26 June 1979, main hearing, HStA Düsseldorf, Ger. Rep. 432 No. 286, p. 2.
152. Alf Lüdtke, *Eigen-Sinn: Fabrikalltag, Arbeitererfahrung und Politik vom Kaiserreich bis in den Faschismus* (Hamburg, 1993), 9.
153. Ibid.
154. Ibid.
155. Ibid., 120–61, 140.
156. Eric D. Weitz and Geoff Eley, "Romantisierung des Eigen-Sinns? Eine Kontroverse aus Übersee," *Werkstatt Geschichte* 10 (1995): 57–64, esp. 63.
157. On the problematics of norms and practice, see chapter 9 of this work.
158. Letter by Hildegard B. to the Commandant of Lublin Concentration Camp, Max Koegel, 10 October 1942, HStA Düsseldorf, Ger. Rep. 432 No. 429, p. 77.

Chapter 5. Going East: Transfer to the Majdanek Concentration and Extermination Camp, 1942–1944

1. Eberhard Fechner, transcription of interview with Erna Wallisch, 15 June 1980, manuscript (private collection), 10ff.
2. Statement by Luise Danz on 30 June 1947 in Krakow, HStA Düsseldorf, Ger. Rep. 432 No. 57, 11128.
3. Statement by Rosa Süss (née Reischl) on 29 August 1973 in Düsseldorf, HstA Düsseldorf, Ger. Rep. 432 No. 252, p. 69.
4. Deposition Gertrud Heise, Investigation Team, 29 January 1946, Neumünster, Public

Record Office (PRO) War Office (WO) 309/429, no page number.

5. Statement by Alice Orlowski on 21 October 1946 in Hildesheim, HStA Düsseldorf, Ger. Rep. 432 No. 213, p. 769; see also statement by Alice Orlowski on 18 April 1961 in Eitorf/Sieg, HStA Düsseldorf, Ger. Rep. 432 No. 5, pp. 812ff.
6. Statement by Alice Orlowski on 27 August 1973 in Düsseldorf, HStA Düsseldorf, Ger. Rep. 432 No. 262, p. 320; see also statement by Alice Orlowski on 25 June 1947 in Krakow, HStA Düsseldorf, Ger. Rep. 432 No. 296, p. 2. Herta B., Elisabeth H., and Elfriede Z. were transferred together with Orlowski.
7. This was probably the administrative director SS-Hauptsturmführer Kurt Seitz, whom Margarete Buber-Neumann also mentions in her report. See Margarete Buber-Neumann, *Als Gefangene bei Stalin und Hitler. Eine Welt im Dunkel* (Berlin, 1997), 211 and 315.
8. Statement by Hermine Braunsteiner on 22 November 1949 in Vienna, DÖW, LG Vienna Vg 1 Vr 5670/48, p. 9; see also statement by Hermine Ryan Braunsteiner on 22 August 1973 in Düsseldorf, HStA Düsseldorf, Ger. Rep. 432 No. 193, p. 62.
9. Statement by Herta Ehlert on 9 June 1970 in Bad Homburg, HStA Düsseldorf, Ger. Rep. 432 No. 292, p. 42; see also statement by Herta Ehlert on 13 October 1945 in Lüneburg, Transcript of the Official Shorthand Notes, Trial against Josef Kramer and 44 Others, PRO WO 235/15, pp. 61ff.
10. As described above, "asocials" were a particular group of inmates who had been incarcerated for socio-hygienic reasons. See esp. Christa Schikorra, *Kontinuitäten der Ausgrenzung. "Asoziale" Häftlinge im Konzentrationslager Ravensbrück* (Berlin, 2001).
11. Statement by Hertha Nauman (married name: Ehlert) on 18 April 1972 in Bad Homburg, HStA Düsseldorf, Ger. Rep. 432 No. 296, p. 7461.
12. Buber-Neumann, *Gefangene*, 305.
13. Nanda Herbermann, *Der gesegnete Abgrund. Schutzhäftling No. 6582 im Frauenkonzentrationslager Ravensbrück* (Annweiler, 2002), 88.
14. Ibid., 129.
15. See Karin Orth, "Experten des Terrors. Die Konzentrationslager-SS und die Shoah," in *Die Täter der Shoah. Fanatische Nationalsozialisten oder ganz normale Deutsche?*, ed. Gerhard Paul (Göttingen: Wallstein, 2002), 189–91.
16. See ibid., 242–46.
17. Ibid., 243.
18. Bogdan Musial, *Deutsche Zivilverwaltung und Judenverfolgung im Generalgouvernement. Eine Fallstudie zum Distrikt Lublin 1939–1944* (Wiesbaden, 1999), 81.
19. Kurt Ludwig von Burgsdorff, *Bericht über meine Tätigkeit als Leiter des Distrikts Krakow im Jahre 1944*, part 1, Archiwum Głownej Komisji Badania Zbrodni preciwko Narodowi Polskiemu—Instytut Pamięci Narodowej (AGK) (Archive of the Main Commission for Investigations of Crimes against the Polish Nation), Sąd Okręgowy w Krakowie (SOK) (Krakow District Court) 705, p. 9. Cited in Musial, *Deutsche Zivilverwaltung*, 86.

20. Gazette of the Main Department of Propaganda, 1942, No. 2: Archiwum Głownej Komisji Badania Zbrodni preciwko Narodowi Polskiemu—Instytut Pamięci Narodowej (AGK) (Archive of the Main Commission for Investigations of Crimes against the Polish Nation), Najwyższy Trybunał Narodowy (NTN) (The Supreme National Tribunal) 292, pp. 21ff. Cited in Musial, *Deutsche Zivilverwaltung*, 81.
21. While inspecting Auschwitz on 1 March 1941, Himmler ordered the establishment of a "Prisoner of War Camp Auschwitz" in Birkenau, 3 km. from the main camp. It was intended to become the biggest Nazi concentration camp with a capacity of 200,000 prisoners. The plan was realized only in part. See Höss, in Martin Broszat, ed., *Kommandant in Auschwitz. Autobiographische Aufzeichnungen des Rudolf Höss*, 17th ed. (Munich, 2000), 147ff., 270ff.
22. Wolfgang Scheffler, "Historisches Gutachten zur Judenverfolgung des nationalsozialistischen Staats—unter besonderer Berücksichtigung der Verhältnisse im Generalgouvernement—und zur Geschichte des Lagers Majdanek im System nationalsozialistischer Vernichtungs- und Konzentrationslager," manuscript (1976), 112, 120.
23. Ralph Gabriel, "Nationalsozialistische Biopolitik und die Architektur der Konzentrationslager," in *Auszug aus dem Lager. Zur Überwindung des modernen Raumparadigmas in der politischen Philosophie*, ed. Ludger Schwarte (Berlin, 2007).
24. Letter from the WVHA to the Construction Inspection Office of the Armed SS and police in Krakow, Archiwum Panstwowe Muzeum na Majdanku (APMM), No. 164, p. 14; see also Tomasz Kranz, "Das KL Lublin—zwischen Planung und Realisierung," in *Die nationalsozialistischen Konzentrationslager—Entwicklung und Struktur*, ed. Ulrich Herbert, Karin Orth, and Christoph Dieckmann (Göttingen, 1997), 1:363–89, 368.
25. Broszat, ed., *Kommandant in Auschwitz*, 148.
26. Scheffler, "Historisches Gutachten," 112, 114.
27. See chapter 2 of this work.
28. Kranz, "KL Lublin," 369.
29. The colleagues were Hermine Brückner, Anna David, Herta Ehlert, and Irmgard K. See telegram of KGL Lublin to the WVHA on 29 January 1943, HStA Düsseldorf, Ger. Rep. 432 No. 429, p. 15.
30. Statement by Rosa Süss (née Reischl) on 29 August 1973 in Düsseldorf, HStA Düsseldorf, Ger. Rep. 432 No. 252, pp. 72–74.
31. On the crematorium, see chapter 7 of this work.
32. The SS men mentioned here could have included Deputy Crematorium Director Robert Seitz, who, by his own account, lived in a room directly adjacent to the crematorium. It is also possible that German prisoner-functionaries from the crematorium detail slept in another room next to the crematorium. Crematorium chief Erich Muhsfeldt lived away off the camp grounds with his family. See statement by Robert Seitz on 17 March 1965 in Liedolsheim, HStA Düsseldorf, Ger. Rep. 432 No. 266, p. 143.
33. Statement by Charlotte Mayer (née Wöllert) on 19 August 1970 in Cologne, HStA Düsseldorf, Ger. Rep. 432 No. 234, p. 36.

34. Statement by Charlotte Mayer (née Wöllert) on 31 March 1976, main hearing, HStA Düsseldorf, Ger. Rep. 432 No. 288, p. 65; see also statement by Erna Wallisch (née Pfannstiel) on 14 January 1965 in Vienna, DÖW, LG Graz 13/Vr 3329/63, vol. 1, p. 461.
35. See telegram of SS-Brigadeführer Globocnik to the chief of the SS-WVHA, 15 July 1942, Facsimile in Josef Marszalek, *Majdanek. Konzentrationslager Lublin* (Warsaw, 1984), no page number.
36. These were Braunsteiner, Brückner, David, Ehlert, Ehrich, Elisabeth E., Ruth E., Lächert, Anna M., Pfannstiel, Reischl, Charlotte W., Edith W., and Wöllert; see letter to Headquarters of the Lublin Concentration Camp on 17 December 1943, HStA Düsseldorf, Ger. Rep. 432 No. 430, p. 278.
37. Statement by Charlotte Mayer (née Wöllert) on 19 August 1970 in Cologne, HStA Düsseldorf, Ger. Rep. 432 No. 234, p. 36.
38. Statement by Hermine Ryan Braunsteiner on 22 August 1973 in Düsseldorf, HStA Düsseldorf, Ger. Rep. 432 No. 193, p. 64; see also 67.
39. See statement by Ruth E. on 14 June 1978, main hearing, HStA Düsseldorf, Ger. Rep. 432 No. 287, p. 3; see also statement by Erna Wallisch (née Pfannstiel) on 30 November 1972 in Vienna, HStA Düsseldorf, Ger. Rep. 432 No. 235, p. 166.
40. Statement by Charlotte W. on 7 August 1972 in Düsseldorf, HStA Düsseldorf, Ger. Rep. 432 No. 235, p. 73.
41. Statement by Hertha Nauman (divorced name: Ehlert) on 18 April 1972 in Bad Homburg, HStA Düsseldorf, Ger. Rep. 432 No. 296, p. 7461. See also statement by Herta Ehlert on 9 June 1970 in Bad Homburg, HStA Düsseldorf, Ger. Rep. 432 No. 292, p. 43; and statement by Erna Wallisch (née Pfannstiel) on 29 March 1965 in Vienna, DÖW, LG Graz 13/Vr 3329/63, vol. 4, p. 383r.
42. Statement by Charlotte Mayer (née Wöllert) on 28 August 1973 in Düsseldorf, HStA Düsseldorf, Ger. Rep. 432 No. 234, p. 46.
43. Statement by Charlotte W. to the investigating magistrate (*Untersuchungsrichter*) on 7 August 1972 in Düsseldorf, HStA Düsseldorf, Ger. Rep. 432 No. 235, p. 73.
44. Statement by Hermann Hackmann on 26 September 1973 in Düsseldorf, HStA Düsseldorf, Ger. Rep. 432 No. 248, p. 729.
45. Statement by Charlotte Mayer (née Wöllert) on 31 March 1976, main hearing, HStA Düsseldorf, Ger. Rep. 432 No. 288, p. 66.
46. See statement by Heinz Petrick on 23 October 1973, StA Cologne/U-Richter, Düsseldorf, HStA Düsseldorf, Ger. Rep. 432 No. 233, pp. 463–64.
47. Statement by Charlotte Mayer (née Wöllert) on 31 March 1976, main hearing, HStA Düsseldorf, Ger. Rep. 432 No. 288, p. 70.
48. Statement by Anna M. on 2 August 1961 in Stuttgart, HStA Düsseldorf, Ger. Rep. 432 No. 234, p. 17.
49. Statement by Rosa Süss (née Reischl) on 29 August 1973 in Düsseldorf, HStA Düsseldorf, Ger. Rep. 432 No. 252, p. 72.
50. Statement by Hermine Böttcher on 11 December 1974 in Hannover, HStA Düsseldorf, Ger. Rep. 432 No. 290, p. 2. See also statement by Hertha Nauman (married name:

Ehlert) on 18 April 1972 in Bad Homburg, HStA Düsseldorf, Ger. Rep. 432 No. 296, p. 7461; statement by Herta B. on 30 October 1974 in Waldhut, HStA Düsseldorf, Ger. Rep. 432 No. 203, p. 24; statement by Luzie H. on 21 December 1976, main hearing, HStA Düsseldorf, Ger. Rep. 432 No. 285, p. 172.

51. Fechner, transcription of interview with Erna Wallisch, 15 June 1980, manuscript (private collection), 15.
52. See chapter 2 of this work.
53. Fechner, transcription of interview with Erna Wallisch, 15 June 1980, manuscript (private collection), 23.
54. Statement by Luzie H. on 8 November 1972 in Düsseldorf, HStA Düsseldorf, Ger. Rep. 432 No. 292, p. 68.
55. See statement by Otto Z. on 8 March 1972 in Munich, HStA Düsseldorf, Ger. Rep. 432 No. 204, p. 69.
56. Statement by Charlotte Mayer (née Wöllert) on 28 August 1973 in Düsseldorf, HStA Düsseldorf, Ger. Rep. 432 No. 234, p. 47; statement by Alice Orlowski on 25 June 1947 in Krakow, HStA Düsseldorf, Ger. Rep. 432 No. 296, p. 2; statement by Erna Wallisch (née Pfannstiel) on 30 November 1972 in Vienna, HStA Düsseldorf, Ger. Rep. 432 No. 235, p. 166.
57. Statement by Charlotte W. on 7 August 1972 in Düsseldorf, HStA Düsseldorf, Ger. Rep. 432 No. 235, p. 73.
58. Statement by Alice Orlowski on 27 August 1973 in Düsseldorf, HStA Düsseldorf, Ger. Rep. 432 No. 262, p. 324.
59. Elisabeth R. (after her divorce, Elisabeth H.) in Eberhard Fechner, *Norddeutscher Rundfunk: Der Prozess: Eine Darstellung des Majdanek-Verfahrens in Düsseldorf*, videotape (1984), part 1.
60. Statement by Hertha Nauman (née Ehlert) on 18 April 1972 in Bad Homburg, HStA Düsseldorf, Ger. Rep. 432 No. 296, p. 7461.
61. Report on the activities of the research institute in Bad Homburg in the first five quarters of the war (1 September 1939–30 November 1940), National Archives and Records Administration [NARA], Microfilm T84, roll 490, mooG373ta.
62. Emphasis in original.
63. *Das Generalgouvernement.* Reisehandbuch von Karl Baedeker (Leipzig, 1943), xxv–xxvi.
64. "Abriss über Klima und Wetter von Europäisch-Russland, Reichsamt für Wetterdienst," brochure (Berlin, 1941), 3, NARA, Microfilm T84, roll 490, m/47 G373 cop. I.
65. "Die Verschlammung im Europäischen Russland, Reichsamt für Wetterdienst (Luftwaffe). Nur für den Dienstgebrauch!," Berlin, September 1943, p. 1, NARA, Microfilm T84, roll 490, 551.46 G 373v; see also the brochure "Abriss über Klima," 3.
66. Statement by Erika W. on 9 June 1976, main hearing, HStA Düsseldorf, Ger. Rep. 432 No. 283, p. 181.
67. Fechner, transcription of interview with Erna Wallisch, 15 June 1980, manuscript (private collection), 15.

68. Statement by Anna M. on 2 August 1961 in Stuttgart, HStA Düsseldorf, Ger. Rep. 432 No. 234, p. 19, see also 18; statement by Erna Wallisch (née Pfannstiel) on 14 January 1965 in Vienna, DÖW, LG Graz 13/Vr 3329/63, vol. 1, p. 463; statement by Hermine Böttcher on 11 December 1974 in Hannover, HStA Düsseldorf, Ger. Rep. 432 No. 290, p. 2.
69. Statement by Alice Orlowski on 18 April 1961 in Eitorf/Sieg, HStA Düsseldorf, Ger. Rep. 432 No. 5, p. 814.
70. Deposition Gertrud Heise, Investigation Team, 29 January 1946, Neumünster, PRO, WO 309/429, not numbered.
71. Ibid.
72. See chapters 9 and 10 of this work.
73. Barbara Schwindt, *Das Konzentrations- und Vernichtungslager Majdanek. Funktionswandel im Kontext der "Endlösung"* (Würzburg, 2005), 165ff.
74. See chapter 2 of this work.
75. Schwindt, *Das Konzentrations- und Vernichtungslager Majdanek*, 164, 171. On the practice of killing, see chapter 7 of this work.
76. Scheffler, "Historisches Gutachten," 160.
77. Statement by Hermine Ryan Braunsteiner on 22 August 1973 in Düsseldorf, HStA Düsseldorf, Ger. Rep. 432 No. 193, pp. 64ff.
78. Statement by Hildegard Lächert on 30 August 1973 in Düsseldorf, HstA Düsseldorf, Ger. Rep. 432 No. 252, pp. 102ff.
79. See statement by Ruth E. on 14 June 1978, main hearing, HStA Düsseldorf, Ger. Rep. 432 No. 287, p. 1.
80. Statement by Herta B. on 15 June 1976, main hearing, HStA Düsseldorf, Ger. Rep. 432 No. 285, not numbered; see also statement by Herta B. on 30 October 1974 in Waldhut, HStA Düsseldorf, Ger. Rep. 432 No. 203, pp. 24 and 28.
81. Statement by Elisabeth H. on 27 August 1975 in Cologne, HStA Düsseldorf, Ger. Rep. 432 No. 252, p. 134. See also statement by Elisabeth H. on 15 June 1976, main hearing, HStA Düsseldorf, Ger. Rep. 432 No. 286, p. 211.
82. Statement by Rosa Süss (née Reischl) on 29 August 1973 in Düsseldorf, HStA Düsseldorf, Ger. Rep. 432 No. 252, p. 75.
83. Statement by M. R. of the StA Cologne on 4 June 1975 in Waldkirchen, HstA Düsseldorf, Ger. Rep. 432 No. 252, pp. 129ff.
84. Statement by Hermann Hackmann on 26 September 1973 in Düsseldorf, HStA Düsseldorf, Ger. Rep. 432 No. 248, p. 728.
85. Statement by Wilhelm Reinartz on 11 March 1965 in Langenfeld, HstA Düsseldorf, Ger. Rep. 432 No. 240, p. 164a.
86. Statement by Robert Seitz on 5 December 1961 in Karlsruhe, HStA Düsseldorf, Ger. Rep. 432 No. 266, p. 83.
87. Reserve Infirmary Lublin, ID Rosa Reischl, HStA Düsseldorf, Ger. Rep. 432 No. 430, p. 253.
88. Telegram of the Commandant Lublin Concentration Camp to M. R. on 3 November

1943, HStA Düsseldorf, Ger. Rep. 432 No. 430, p. 153.

89. Telegram of the WVHA Office Group D—Concentration Camps to the Lublin Concentration Camp on 3 April 1943, HStA Düsseldorf, Ger. Rep. 432 No. 429, p. 30.
90. See related insults such as "mangy Jewesses" in chapter 10 of this work.
91. Elias Canetti, *Crowds and Power*, trans. Carol Stewart (New York: Continuum, 1962), 275.
92. On the practice of violence, see chapters 10 and 11 of this work.
93. See letter of SS-Totenkopfsturmbann to Headquarters on 22 February 1943, Betreff: Zuteilung von Waschmittel, Archiwum Panstwowego Muzeum a Majdaneku (APMM) If5, p. 193.
94. See letter of the Commandant to the Chief Guard of the Women's Camp Lublin on 19 March 1943, Betreff: Reinigung von Leibwäsche für Aufseherinnen, Archiwum Panstwowego Muzeum a Majdaneku (APMM) I.d.32, p. 15.
95. See *Das Generalgouvernement*, ix, xiii.
96. Personal file of Dr. Fritz Cuhorst, Lubliner Impressionen No. 2, Stadtarchiv Stuttgart, Bestand 212/2 Bü 99. See also Klaus-Michael Mallmann, Volker Riess, and Wolfram Pyta, eds., *Deutscher Osten 1939–1945. Der Weltanschauungskrieg in Photos und Texten* (Darmstadt, 2003), 14.
97. *Das Generalgouvernement*, iv.
98. Entry "Trient, den 1. September früh" (last two sentences), Johann Wolfgang von Goethe, *Italienische Reise I*, ed. Christoph Ditzel and Hans Georg Dewitz, in *Sämtliche Werke*, vol. 15:1 (Frankfurt am Main, 1993), 29.
99. On the image of Italy, see Martin Luchsinger, *Mythos Italien. Denkbilder des Fremden in der deutschsprachigen Gegenwartsliteratur* (Cologne, 1996).
100. Werner Präg, Wolfgang Jacobmeyer, and Hans Frank, *Das Diensttagebuch des deutschen Generalgouverneurs in Polen 1939–1945* (Stuttgart, 1975), 48.
101. Ibid., 18.
102. *Das Generalgouvernement*, lii.
103. Musial, *Deutsche Zivilverwaltung*, 23ff. See also Dietmut Majer, *"Fremdvölkische" im Dritten Reich. Ein Beitrag zur nationalsozialistischen Rechtssetzung und Rechtspraxis in Verwaltung und Justiz unter besonderer Berücksichtigung der eingegliederten Ostgebiete und des Generalgouvernements* (Boppard, 1981), 483–86.
104. Höss, in Broszat, ed., *Kommandant in Auschwitz*, 134.
105. See Edward Said, *Orientalism* (New York: Pantheon, 1978).
106. Vejas Gabriel Liulevicius, *War Land on the Eastern Front: Culture, National Identity, and German Occupation in World War I* (Cambridge: Cambridge University Press, 2000); also *Kriegsland Osten. Eroberung, Kolonisierung und Militärherrschaft im Ersten Weltkrieg* (Hamburg, 2002). Other studies mention the topic without analyzing it: Eduard Mühle, ed., *Germany and the European East in the Twentieth Century* (Oxford: Berg, 2003); Klaus-Michael Mallmann, Volker Reiss, and Wolfgang Pyta, *Deutscher Osten 1939–1945. Der Weltanschauungskrieg in Photos und Texten* (Darmstadt: Wissenschaftliche, Buchgesellschaft, 2003).

107. See Jürgen Zimmerer, "Die Geburt des 'Ostlandes' aus dem Geiste des Kolonialismus. Die nationalsozialistische Eroberungs- und Beherrschungspolitik in postkolonialer Perspektive," *Sozial-Geschichte* 1 (2004): 10–43; David Furber, "Going East: Colonialism and German Life in Nazi-Occupied Poland" (PhD diss., SUNY Buffalo, 2003).
108. Michael Wildt, "Biopolitik, ethnische Säuberungen und Volkssouveränität. Eine Skizze," *Mittelweg 36*, vol. 6 (2006): 87–106, 94.
109. See Liulevicius, *War Land.*
110. Statement by Jan Novak on 20 April 1977, Düsseldorf, main hearing, HStA Düsseldorf, Ger. Rep. 432 No. 285, pp. 16ff.; see Jan Novak, in Dieter Ambach, and Thomas Köhler, eds., *Lublin-Majdanek. Das Konzentrations- und Vernichtungslager im Spiegel von Zeugenaussagen*, vol. 12 of *Juristische Zeitgeschichte* (Düsseldorf, 2003), 173ff.
111. Hermann Hackmann, in Fechner, *Der Prozess*, part 1.
112. "They came from the Wehrmacht POW camp Lamsdorf in a completely decrepit condition. They had been brought there in marches lasting weeks. On the way there was hardly any food, during marching breaks they were simply led to the nearest fields and, like animals, ate whatever was edible. . . . I was supposed to build the Birkenau POW camp with these prisoners, who could hardly stand up anymore. . . . I still remember exactly how we were constantly giving them more food. But it was no use. Their emaciated bodies could not digest anything anymore. . . . They died like flies. . . . They had no more regard for one another anymore. The sheer instinct for self-preservation no longer permitted the slightest gestures of humanity. Cases of cannibalism were hardly the exception at Auschwitz. I found a Russian among piles of bricks whose body had been torn open. His liver was missing. . . . These were no longer humans, they had become animals, solely on the lookout for food." Höss, in Broszat, ed., *Kommandant in Auschwitz*, 157–59.
113. Statement by Hermann Hackmann on 11 October 1973 in Düsseldorf, HStA Düsseldorf, Ger. Rep. 432 No. 248, p. 782.
114. Hermann Hackmann, in Fechner, *Der Prozess*, part 1.
115. See Wolfram Wette, *Die Wehrmacht. Feindbilder, Vernichtungskrieg, Legenden* (Frankfurt am Main, 2002), 25–28, esp. 25. See also Hamburger Institut für Sozialforschung, ed., *Verbrechen der Wehrmacht. Dimensionen des Vernichtungskrieges 1941–1944*. Exhibition catalog (Hamburg, 2002); Hans-Erich Volkmann, ed., *Das Russlandbild im Dritten Reich* (Cologne: 1994); Ernst Klee and Willi Dressen, *"Gott mit uns." Der deutsche Vernichtungskrieg im Osten 1939–1945* (Frankfurt am Main, 1989).
116. Jacques Sémelin, "Analyser le massacre. Réflexions comparatives," *Questions de Recherches/Research in Question* 7 (2002): 2–42, http:/www.ceri-sciences-po.org/publica/qdr.htm, p. 15.
117. Statement by Hertha Nauman (divorced name: Ehlert) on 18 April 1972 in Bad Homburg, HStA Düsseldorf, Ger. Rep. 432 No. 296, p. 7467.
118. See Christian Ingrao, "Violence de guerre, violence génocide: Les Einsatzgruppen," in *La Violence de guerre, 1914–1945. Approches comparées des deux conflits mondiaux*, ed. Stéphane Audoin-Rouzeau et al. (Bruxelles, 2002), 219–41, 222–24.

119. Elisabeth H., in Fechner, *Der Prozess*, part 1.
120. Dieter Pohl, *Von der "Judenpolitik" zum Judenmord: der Distrikt Lublin des Generalgouvernements 1939–1944* (Berlin, 1993), 177.
121. See, e.g., Brigitte Hamann, *Hitlers Vienna. Lehrjahre eines Diktators* (Munich, 1996); Beatrix Hoffmann-Holter, "'Ostjuden hinaus!' Jüdische Kriegsflüchtlinge in Wien 1914–1924," in *Die Stadt ohne Juden*, ed. Gutram Geser and Armin Loacker, Edition Film und Text 3 (Vienna: Film Archiv Austria, 2000), 311–46.
122. Michael Wildt, "'Wir wollen in unserer Stadt keine Juden sehen,' Antisemitismus und Volksgemeinschaft in der deutschen Provinz," *Mittelweg 36*, no. 5 (2004): 83–102.
123. Musial, *Deutsche Zivilverwaltung*, 187.
124. Ibid., 184.
125. This contempt did not prevent the German occupiers from employing Jewish maids, contractors, cooks, seamstresses, dentists, unpaid workers, and so-called "house Jews." They exploited the labor and skills of these people until the last minute, enjoying a level of luxury they could never have afforded in the Reich. See Musial, *Deutsche Zivilverwaltung*, 189; see also Götz Aly and Susanne Heim, *Vordenker der Vernichtung. Auschwitz und die deutschen Pläne für eine neue europäische Ordnung* (Frankfurt am Main, 2004), 188–90.
126. See Elisabeth Harvey, *Women in the Nazi East: Agents and Witnesses of Germanization* (New Haven: Yale University Press, 2003), 128–37; Walter Manoschek, ed., *"Es gibt nur eines für das Judentum: Vernichtung." Das Judenbild in deutschen Soldatenbriefen 1939–1944* (Hamburg, 1996); Musial, *Deutsche Zivilverwaltung*, 183–88.
127. Statement by Charlotte Mayer (née Wöllert), StA Hamburg, Cologne August 19, 1970, HStA Düsseldorf, Ger. Rep. 432 No. 234, p. 37.
128. Baedeker, *Das Generalgouvernement*, ix.
129. Ibid., xiii.
130. See Johanna Gehmacher, Elizabeth Harvey, and Sophia Kemlein, eds., *Zwischen Kriegen: Nationen, Nationalismen und Geschlechterverhältnisse in Mittel- und Osteuropa 1918–1939* (Osnabrück, 2004).
131. See Musial, *Deutsche Zivilverwaltung*, 189; see also Aly and Heim, *Vordenker*, 188.
132. Baedeker, *Das Generalgouvernement*, xix–xx; italics in original.
133. Harvey, *Women in the Nazi East*, 145–90. See also Lora Wildenthal, *German Women for Empire, 1884–1945* (Durham, NC: Duke University Press, 2001); also "Koloniale Frauenorganisationen in der deutschen Kolonialbewegung des Kaiserreichs," in *Phantasiereiche. Zur Kulturgeschichte des deutschen Kolonialismus*, ed. Birthe Kundrus (Frankfurt am Main, 2003), 202–13.
134. Harvey, *Women in the Nazi East*, 167.
135. Fechner, transcription of interview with Erna Wallisch, 15 June 1980, manuscript (private collection), 28.
136. *Das Generalgouvernement*, 127.
137. I thank the research director of the Majdanek Memorial Site, Tomasz Kranz, for this source.

138. Luzie H., in Fechner, *Der Prozess*, part 2.
139. Alf Lüdtke, "Die Fiktion der Institution: Herrschaftspraxis und Vernichtung der europäischen Juden im 20. Jahrhundert," in *Institutionen und Ereignis. Über historische Praktiken und Vorstellungen gesellschaftlichen Ordnens*, ed. Reinhard Blänkner and Bernhard Jussen (Göttingen: Vandenhoeck & Ruprecht, 1998), 355–79, 356.
140. A letter from the Lublin camp commandant confirms on 17 November 1943 the sending back of seventeen signed mandates to the RuSHA. Forms for two sick *Aufseherinnen* were supposed to be handed in later. See HStA Düsseldorf, Ger. Rep. 432 No. 430, p. 148.
141. Nazi Germanization policies were extended to the "Protectorate of Bohemia and Moravia" and later to occupied Poland and the occupied Soviet regions. Expulsions and forced resettlement of "racially inferior" peoples, and settlement of "Volk" Germans were directed by the SS racial experts in the RuSHA. See Isabel Heinemann, *"Rasse, Siedlung, deutsches Blut." Das Rasse- und Siedlungshauptamt der SS und die rassenpolitische Neuordnung Europas* (Göttingen, 2003).
142. See Gudrun Schwarz, *Eine Frau an seiner Seite. Ehefrauen in der "SS-Sippengemeinschaft"* (Hamburg: Hamburger Edition, 1997).
143. As recorded in a letter from the SS and Police Leader Lublin to the Headquarters of the Lublin Concentration Camp on 10 October 1943, HStA Düsseldorf, Ger. Rep. 432 No. 430, p. 156.
144. To comply with the "Engagement and Marriage Order" that Himmler issued in 1931 and repeatedly tightened, as future members of the "SS clan," future SS wives had to meet strict ideological, racial, and hereditary criteria and submit relevant documentation. See Schwarz, *Eine Frau an seiner Seite*, 24–51, 45.
145. See File Ferdinand K., BA, BDC, Microfilm C5553, picture no. 910, 912; File Robert M., BA, BDC, Microfilm D5310, picture no. 430, 432; File Georg W., BA, BDC, Microfilm G0560, picture no. 1812, 1814, 1816.
146. See File Ferdinand K., BA, BDC, Microfilm C5553, Picture no. 856; File Robert M., BA, BDC, Microfilm D5310, picture no. 382.
147. See File Ferdinand K., BA, BDC, Microfilm C5553, pictures 844–920.
148. R.u.S. questionnaire, Bundesarchiv, ibid., picture no. 910.
149. File Robert M., BA, BDC, Microfilm D5310, picture nos. 348–470; see also statement by Charlotte Mayer (née Wöllert), StA Hamburg, Cologne 19 August 1970, HStA Düsseldorf, Ger. Rep. 432 No. 234, p. 35.
150. The letter actually reads: "a) whether it is a substantial inner-ear defect, b) whether otosclerosis can be ruled out with certainty, c) whether exogenous reasons for the hearing defect can be assumed, d) at what age the condition appeared." Letter from the Chief of the RuSHA-SS on 8 March 1943, File Robert M., BA, BDC, Microfilm D5310, picture no. 386.
151. Ibid.
152. Letter by the Chief of the RuSHA-SS on 8 March 1943, ibid., picture no. 385.
153. Letter by the Chief of the RuSHA-SS on 18 March 1943, ibid., picture no. 378.

154. Statement by Charlotte Mayer (née Wöllert) on 18 January 1979 in Düsseldorf, HStA Düsseldorf, Ger. Rep. 432 No. 288, not numbered. See also statement by Charlotte W. on 21 May 1970 in Lübeck, HStA Düsseldorf, Ger. Rep. 432 No. 234, p. 31.
155. See File Georg W., BA, RS, BDC, Microfilm G0560, picture nos. 1720–1822.
156. Application for approval of emergency aid, ibid., picture no. 1780.
157. Statement by Erna Wallisch (née Pfannstiel) on 14 January 1965 in Vienna, DÖW, LG Graz 13/Vr 3329/63, vol. 1, p. 471.
158. Certification by headquarters in Lublin on 2 June 1944, HStA Düsseldorf, Ger. Rep. 432 No. 429, p. 52. See also entry certification, issued by headquarters in Lublin on 22 June 1944, HStA Düsseldorf, Ger. Rep. 432 No. 429, p. 94.
159. See telegram Erna Pfannstiel from Fürstenberg/Mecklenburg to headquarters in Lublin on 1 and 9 February 1944, HStA Düsseldorf, Ger. Rep. 432 No. 429, pp. 121 and 119.
160. Telegram of headquarters in Lublin to Erna Pfannstiel in Fürstenberg/Mecklenburg on 9 February 1944, HStA Düsseldorf, Ger. Rep. 432 No. 429, p. 118.
161. Telegram Erna Pfannstiel in Fürstenberg/Mecklenburg to headquarters in Lublin on 2 March 1944, HStA Düsseldorf, Ger. Rep. 432 No. 429, p. 102.
162. Letter from headquarters in Lublin to Erna Pfannstiel in Fürstenberg/Mecklenburg on 2 March 1944, HStA Düsseldorf, Ger. Rep. 432 No. 429, p. 101.
163. Telegram from headquarters in Lublin to Erna Pfannstiel in Fürstenberg/Mecklenburg on 8 March 1944, HStA Düsseldorf, Ger. Rep. 432 No. 429, p. 97.
164. Statement by Erna Wallisch (née Pfannstiel) on 14 January 1965 in Vienna, DÖW, LG Graz 13/Vr 3329/63, vol. 1, p. 471. See also statement by Georg W. on 13 January 1965, ibid., 451–59; Certification by Lublin Registry Office, File Georg W., BA, BDC, Microfilm G0560, picture no. 1740.
165. Statement by Ruth E. on 14 June 1978 in Düsseldorf, HStA Düsseldorf, Ger. Rep. 432 No. 287, p. 1.
166. Letter of the WVHA Office Group D—Concentration Camps on 12 November 1942 to the camp commandants of Auschwitz and Lublin, HStA Düsseldorf, Ger. Rep. 432 No. 430, p. 222. In compliance with the Auschwitz order, Ruth E. was sent to Majdanek on 19 November 1942; ibid., 226.
167. File Anton W., BA, BDC, Microfilm G5269, picture no. 1806 (clan file, dated 26 March 1943).
168. See questionnaire, dated 26 March 1943, Ravensbrück, ibid., picture nos. 1802 and 1806.
169. Ibid., picture no. 1804.
170. Ibid., picture no. 1810.
171. Quoted in Paula Diehl, "'Opfer der Vergangenheit': Konstruktion eines Feindbildes," in *Abgeschlossene Kapitel? Zur Geschichte der Konzentrationslager und NS-Prozesse*, ed. Sabine Moller, Miriam Rürup, and Christel Trouvé (Tübingen, 2002), 134–44, 144.
172. Ibid., 144.
173. Gudrun Brockhaus, *Schauder und Idylle. Faschismus als Erlebnisangebot* (Munich,

1997), 41, see also 266–310.

174. See chapters 10 and 11 of this work.
175. Heinz Villain, in Fechner, *Der Prozess*, part 1.
176. Fechner, transcription of interview with Erna Wallisch, 15 June 1980, manuscript (private collection), 15.
177. The German word for such goods, "Marketender," comes from the Italian *mercatante*, which in the sixteenth century meant traders who followed the troops out on their campaigns and supplied them with food. Friedrich Kluge, *Etymologisches Wörterbuch der deutschen Sprache* (Berlin, 2002), 599.
178. Hildegard Lächert, in Fechner, *Der Prozess*, part 2.
179. Statement by Otto Z. on 6 April 1977, main hearing, HStA Düsseldorf, Ger. Rep. 432 No. 287, p. 284 (in Ambach and Köhler, *Lublin-Majdanek*, 98).
180. Otto Z., in Fechner, *Der Prozess*, part 2.
181. Statement by Georg W. on 13 January 1965 in Vienna, DÖW, LG Graz 13/Vr 3329/63, vol. 1, p. 457.
182. See also chapters 6, 7, and 9 of this work.
183. Statement by Georg W. on 13 January 1965 in Vienna, DÖW, LG Graz 13/Vr 3329/63, vol. 1, pp. 455ff.
184. Statement by Herta Ehlert on 15 October 1945 in Lüneburg, Transcript of the Official Shorthand Notes, Trial against Josef Kramer and 44 Others, PRO WO 235/15, pp. 99–100.

Chapter 6. Work Conditions at Majdanek

1. See statement by Hermine Braunsteiner on 22 November 1949, main hearing, LG Vienna Vg 1 Vr 5670/48, pp. 204–5.
2. Statement by Charlotte Mayer (née Wöllert) on 28 August 1973 in Düsseldorf, HStA Düsseldorf, Ger. Rep. 432 No. 234, pp. 47–48.
3. Statement by Luzie H. on 21 December 1976, main hearing, HStA Düsseldorf, Ger. Rep. 432 No. 285, p. 171.
4. Eberhard Fechner, transcription of interview with Erna Wallisch, 15 June 1980, manuscript (private collection), 19; see also statement by Luise Danz on 30 June 1947 in Krakow, HStA Düsseldorf, Ger. Rep. 432 No. 57, p. 11128.
5. Telex from headquarters in Lublin to the WVHA, HStA Düsseldorf, Ger. Rep. 432 No. 429, p. 72.
6. Hildegard Lächert and Charlotte Wöllert came as "replacements" for the originally planned female guards Margarete G. and Walpurga K.; see letter of the WVHA Office Group D–Concentration Camps on 15 October 1942, HStA Düsseldorf, Ger. Rep. 432 No. 429, p. 78.
7. See letter of the WVHA Office Group D–Concentration Camps on 12 November 1942 to the camp commandants of Auschwitz and Lublin, HStA Düsseldorf, Ger. Rep. 432

No. 430, p. 222. According to the Auschwitz order, Ruth E. was sent to Majdanek on 19 November 1942; see HStA Düsseldorf, Ger. Rep. 432 No. 429, p. 226.

8. Statement by Erika W. on 26 February 1975 in Wolfsburg, HStA Düsseldorf, Ger. Rep. 432 No. 215, p. 1144. On the status of minors, see letter of the WVHA Office Group D–Concentration Camps on 15 December 1943 to the concentration camps Auschwitz, Herzogenbusch, Lublin, Ravensbrück, Stutthof, and the SS-Stewards in the Ostland Area for the concentration camps Riga, Kauen, and Vaivara, HStA Düsseldorf, Ger. Rep. 432 No. 430, p. 137.
9. Letter of the Chief Guard to the Commandant of the Lublin Concentration Camp, Re: Enlargement of supervision personnel over female prisoners in the clothing works of the Armed SS, 1 December 1942, HStA Düsseldorf, Ger. Rep. 432 No. 430, p. 254.
10. Letter of the Commandant of the Lublin POW camp, Re: Female guards for the POW camp Lublin, on 11 December 1942, HStA Düsseldorf, Ger. Rep. 432 No. 430, p. 258.
11. See telex of SS-Brigadeführer and Generalmajor of the Armed SS Glücks to the SS- and Police Leader Lublin, SS-Obergruppenführer Globocnik, HStA Düsseldorf, Ger. Rep. 432 No. 429, p. 16.
12. Supplementary notes to statement by Charlotte Mayer (née Wöllert) on 31 March 1976, main hearing, HStA Düsseldorf, Ger. Rep. 432 No. 288, no page number.
13. See chapter 5 of this work.
14. Statement by Hildegard Lächert on 27 June 1947 in Krakow, HStA Düsseldorf, Ger. Rep. 432 No. 295, p. 5.
15. Statement by Anna M. on 2 August 1961 in Stuttgart, HStA Düsseldorf, Ger. Rep. 432 No. 234, p. 28.
16. Letter of the troop physician of Lublin Concentration Camp to Headquarters of Lublin Concentration Camp on 7 June 1943, HStA Ger. Rep. 432 No. 429, p. 36. See also letter of Headquarters of Lublin Concentration Camp to Charlotte W. on 1 July 1943, HStA Düsseldorf, Ger. Rep. 432 No. 429, p. 33; statement by Charlotte W., Untersuchungsrichter, Düsseldorf, 7 August 1972, HStA Düsseldorf, Ger. Rep. 432 No. 235, p. 79.
17. Letter to the WVHA on 10 December 1943, re: filing of departed female guards, HStA Düsseldorf, Ger. Rep. 432 No. 430, p. 140. See also statement by Ruth E., transcript of main hearing, Düsseldorf, 14 June 1978, HStA Düsseldorf, Ger. Rep. 432 No. 287, p. 1; statement by Edith W., transcript of main hearing, Düsseldorf, 27 September 1977, HStA Düsseldorf, Ger. Rep. 432 No. 286, p. 315.
18. See letter of the WHVA to the Lublin POW Camp and the Auschwitz Concentration Camp, HStA Düsseldorf, Ger. Rep. 432 No. 430, p. 202; orders of Ravensbrück Women's Concentration Camp on 27 January 1943, HStA Düsseldorf, Ger. Rep. 432 No. 429, p. 17.
19. See letter of the WVHA on 1 March 1943 to the Ravensbrück and Lublin Concentration Camps, HStA Düsseldorf, Ger. Rep. 432 No. 430, p. 210.
20. See letter of the WVHA on 17 March 1943 to the Ravensbrück and Lublin Concentration Camps, HStA Düsseldorf, Ger. Rep. 432 No. 430, p. 189.

21. See letter of the WVHA on 22 March 1943 to the Ravensbrück and Lublin Concentration Camps, HStA Düsseldorf, Ger. Rep. 432 No. 430, p. 190; see also internal letter of the Lublin Concentration Camp, 27 March 1943, HStA Düsseldorf, Ger. Rep. 158 No. 292, pp. 62ff.
22. On Suhren's biography, see Bernhard Strebel, *Das KZ Ravensbrück. Geschichte eines Lagerkomplexes* (Berlin, 2003), 58–60.
23. Letter of the Commandant of the Ravensbrück Women's Concentration Camp to the WVHA Office Group D–Concentration Camps on 13 March 1943, Re: transfer of female guards, HStA Düsseldorf, Ger. Rep. 432 No. 430, p. 192.
24. See also chapter 5 of this work.
25. Letter of the Commandant of the Lublin Concentration Camp to the WVHA Office Group D–Concentration Camps on 28 June 1943, Re: Female guards, HStA Düsseldorf, Ger. Rep. 432 No. 429, p. 28.
26. Letter of the SS-WVHA Office Group D–Concentration Camps on 5 July 1943 to the Commandant of Lublin Concentration Camp, Re: Transfer of female guards, HStA Düsseldorf, Ger. Rep. 432 No. 429, p. 29.
27. See Strebel, *Das KZ Ravensbrück*, 419–58.
28. See letter of the SS-WVHA Office Group D–Concentration Camps on 9 July 1943 to the Commandants of Ravensbrück and Lublin Concentration Camps, Re: Transfer of female guards, HStA Düsseldorf, Ger. Rep. 432 No. 429, p. 30.
29. Telex of Commandant Florstedt to the SS-WVHA on 21 July 1943, HStA Düsseldorf, Ger. Rep. 432 No. 429, p. 27.
30. Telex of the SS-WVHA Office Group D–Concentration Camps on 21 July 1943 to the Commandant of Lublin Concentration Camp, HStA Düsseldorf, Ger. Rep. 432 No. 429, p. 26.
31. These were Herta B., Braunsteiner, Brückner, Danz, David, Ehlert, Ehrich, Luzie H., Elisabeth H., Heise, Macha, Anna M., Orlowski, Pfannstiel, Reischl, Anna S., Charlotte W., Wöllert, and Elfriede Z. See List of Female Guards at the Lublin Concentration Camp on 6 November 1943, and letter of the Chief Guard to Headquarters of the Lublin Concentration Camp on 15 December 1943, HStA Düsseldorf, Ger. Rep. 432 No. 430, pp. 251 and 255.
32. Letter of the Commandant of Lublin Concentration Camp to the SS-WVHA Office Group D–Concentration Camps on 15 December 1943, HStA Düsseldorf, Ger. Rep. 432 No. 430, p. 186.
33. A request by her husband on this matter exists. In it he argues that his wife must take care of the "household" on the property of her in-laws and her parents' farm and should therefore be given a position nearby by the Leipzig Labor Office. Letter by Arno H., Obergefreiter to the Lublin Concentration Camp on 7 November 1943, HStA Düsseldorf, Ger. Rep. 432 No. 430, p. 139.
34. See letter from the Commandant of the Lublin Concentration Camp to the WVHA on 16 December 1943, Re: Discharge of *Aufseherin* Elisabeth H., HStA Düsseldorf, Ger. Rep. 432 No. 430, p. 184; see also letter of the WVHA to the Commandant of

the Lublin Concentration Camp on 23 December 1943, Re: Discharge of *Aufseherin* Elisabeth H., HStA Düsseldorf, Ger. Rep. 432 No. 430, p. 138.

35. See letter of the Commandant of Lublin Concentration Camp to the SS-WVHA Office Group D–Concentration Camps on 22 December 1943, Re: Exchange transfer of *Aufseherin* Hermine Braunsteiner, HStA Düsseldorf, Ger. Rep. 432 No. 430, p. 188; see also letter of the Chief Guard to the Headquarters of Lublin Concentration Camp on 17 January 1944, HStA Düsseldorf, Ger. Rep. 432 No. 429, p. 131.
36. See letter of the SS-WVHA Office Group D–Concentration Camps on 30 December 1943 to the Lagerkommandanten Ravensbrück Concentration Camp and Lublin Concentration Camp, HStA Düsseldorf, Ger. Rep. 432 No. 429, p. 128; see also letter of Chief Guard Ehrich to the Headquarters of Lublin Concentration Camp on 17 January 1944, HStA Düsseldorf, Ger. Rep. 432 No. 429, p. 132.
37. See letter of Chief Guard Ehrich to the Headquarters of Lublin Concentration Camp on 8 February 1944, HStA Düsseldorf, Ger. Rep. 432 No. 429, p. 114.
38. See letter of the Chief Guard to the Headquarters of Lublin Concentration Camp on 17 January 1944, HStA Düsseldorf, Ger. Rep. 432 No. 429, p. 133.
39. See letter of the SS-WVHA Office Group D–Concentration Camps on 31 January 1944, HStA Düsseldorf, Ger. Rep. 432 No. 429, p. 130; see also letter of the Chief Guard to Headquarters of Lublin Concentration Camp on 20 February 1944, HStA Düsseldorf, Ger. Rep. 432 No. 429, p. 113.
40. This affected Herta B., Ehrich, Danz, Ehlert, Heise, Anna M., Orlowski, Charlotte W., Bodem, Brückner, David, Luzie H., Elisabeth H., Macha, Mayer, Reischl, Anna S., and Elfriede Z.; see letter of the Commandant of Lublin Concentration Camp to the SS-WVHA Office Group D–Concentration Camps on 24 April 1944, Re: Notification of change, HStA Düsseldorf, Ger. Rep. 432 No. 430, p. 245.
41. See Alf Lüdtke, "Die Kaserne," in *Orte des Alltags*, ed. Hans Gerhard Haupt (Munich, 1994), 227–37, 231.
42. Statement by Hertha Nauman (divorced name: Ehlert) on 18 April 1972 in Bad Homburg, HStA Düsseldorf, Ger. Rep. 432 No. 296, p. 7469. Besides Braunsteiner, the clique surrounding the Chief Guard included Anna M., Ruth E., and Edith W. See also chapters 10 and 11 of this work.
43. See statement by Elisabeth H. on 27 August 1975 in Cologne, HStA Düsseldorf, Ger. Rep. 432 No. 252, p. 133v; statement by Elisabeth H. on 15 December 1976, main hearing, HStA Düsseldorf, Ger. Rep. 432 No. 286, p. 209; statement by Rosa Süss (née Reischl) on 29 August 1973 in Düsseldorf, HStA Düsseldorf, Ger. Rep. 432 No. 252, p. 71; statement by Charlotte Mayer (née Wöllert) on 27 June 1979, main hearing, HStA Düsseldorf, Ger. Rep. 432 No. 285, p. 4; statement by Charlotte Mayer (née Wöllert) on 31 March 1976, main hearing, HStA Düsseldorf, Ger. Rep. 432 No. 288 (no page number).
44. Fechner, transcription of interview with Erna Wallisch, 15 June 1980, manuscript (private collection), 24.
45. Ibid., 39.
46. See statement by Charlotte Mayer (née Wöllert) on 28 August 1973 in Düsseldorf,

HStA Düsseldorf, Ger. Rep. 432 No. 234, p. 48.

47. Statement by Charlotte Mayer (née Wöllert) on 27 June 1979, main hearing, HStA Düsseldorf, Ger. Rep. 432 No. 285, p. 4.
48. See statement by Herta B. on 30 October 1974 in Waldshut, HStA Düsseldorf, Ger. Rep. 432 No. 203, p. 28.
49. Statement by Hermine Böttcher (née Brückner) on 27 June 1979, main hearing, HStA Düsseldorf, Ger. Rep. 432 No. 282, p. 4.
50. Statement by Luzie H. on 21 December 1976, main hearing, HStA Düsseldorf, Ger. Rep. 432 No. 285, p. 178.
51. Statement by Rosa Süss (née Reischl) on 26 June 1979, main hearing, HStA Düsseldorf, Ger. Rep. 432 No. 286, p. 3.
52. Statement by Herta B. on 30 October 1974 in Waldshut, HStA Düsseldorf, Ger. Rep. 432 No. 203, p. 28.
53. Statement by Hertha Nauman gesch. Ehlert on 18 April 1972, Bad Homburg, HStA Düsseldorf, Ger. Rep. 432 No. 296, p. 7462.
54. See statement by Erika W. on 9 June 1976, main hearing, HStA Düsseldorf, Ger. Rep. 432 No. 283, p. 183.
55. See Alexa Stiller, "On the Margins of Volksgemeinschaft: Criteria for Belonging to the Volk within the Nazi Germanization Policy in the Annexed Territories, 1939–1945," in *Heimat, Region and Empire: New Approaches to Spatial Identities in National Socialist Germany*, ed. Claus-Christian W. Szejnmann and Maiken Umbach (Basingstoke: Palgrave Macmillan, 2012), 235–51.
56. For example, Eduard R. and Georg W. See chapter 3 of this work.
57. Arnold Brendler, in Dieter Ambach and Thomas Köhler, eds., *Lublin-Majdanek. Das Konzentrations- und Vernichtungslager im Spiegel von Zeugenaussagen*, vol. 12 of *Juristische Zeitgeschichte* (Düsseldorf, 2003), 67.
58. Otto Z., in Eberhard Fechner, *Norddeutscher Rundfunk: Der Prozess: Eine Darstellung des Majdanek-Verfahrens in Düsseldorf*, videotape (1984).
59. Statement by Eduard R. on 12 January 1965 in Vienna, DÖW, Landesgericht (LG) Graz 13/Vr 3329/63, vol. 1, pp. 437–39.
60. Letter of an SS-Führer of the SS-Totenkopfsturmbann to the Commandant of Lublin POW Camp, 24 January 1943, Archiwum Panstwowego Muzeum na Majdaneku Panstwowe (APMM), I.f.5, p. 35.
61. Anton K., in Ambach and Köhler, *Lublin-Majdanek*, 86.
62. Headquarters Order No. 1/44 on 31 January 1944, HStA Düsseldorf, Ger. Rep. 432 No. 231, pp. 8–10, here 9.
63. Statement by Otto Z. on 6 April 1977, main hearing, HStA Düsseldorf, Ger. Rep. 432 No. 287, p. 283 (Ambach and Köhler, *Lublin-Majdanek*, 98).
64. Letter of Commandant Florstedt on 1 March 1943 to SS-T-Sturmbann Lublin Concentration Camp, Re: Deploying wives of SS members without children for work, Archiwum Panstwowego Muzeum na Majdanku Panstwowe (APMM), I.f.5, p. 211.
65. Letter of the Führer of the SS-T-Sturmbann Lublin Concentration Camp on 3 March

1943 to Commandant Florstedt, Re: Deploying wives of SS members without children for work, APMM, I.f.5, p. 227.

66. Letter of Commandant Florstedt on 31 March 1943 to the SS-T-Sturmbann Lublin Concentration Camp, Re: Deploying wives of SS members without children for work, APMM, I.f.5, p. 239.
67. Statement by Luzie H. on 21 December 1976, main hearing, HStA Düsseldorf, Ger. Rep. 432 No. 285, p. 179.
68. Statement by Hermine Böttcher (née Brückner) on 27 June 1979, main hearing, HStA Düsseldorf, Ger. Rep. 432 No. 282, p. 2. On cooperation, see chapters 5, 8, and 10 of this work.
69. Statement by Charlotte Mayer (née Wöllert) on 19 August 1970 in Cologne, HStA Düsseldorf, Ger. Rep. 432 No. 234, p. 36; see also statement by Charlotte Mayer (née Wöllert) on 31 March 1976, main hearing, HStA Düsseldorf, Ger. Rep. 432 No. 288, p. 70.
70. Statement by Alice Orlowski on 25 June 1947 in Krakow, HStA Düsseldorf, Ger. Rep. 432 No. 296, p. 2.
71. See Karin Orth, "Experten des Terrors. Die Konzentrationslager-SS und die Shoah," in *Die Täter der Shoah. Fanatische Nationalsozialisten oder ganz normale Deutsche?*, ed. Gerhard Paul (Göttingen: Wallstein, 2002). On Höss, see 105–24, 176–81, 282ff.
72. Höss, in Martin Broszat, ed., *Kommandant in Auschwitz. Autobiographische Aufzeichnungen des Rudolf Höss*, 17th ed. (Munich, 2000), 177–79.
73. Ibid., 179.
74. Ibid., 136.
75. Ibid., 176ff.
76. Ibid., 180.
77. Ibid., 177.
78. As a trained prison official, Langefeld spoke out against corporal punishment for female prisoners, which had been ordered by Himmler and introduced in 1940, because she saw the concentration camps as juridically and educationally "legitimated" institutions whose main purpose was "improvement" and "education." See Strebel, *Das KZ Ravensbrück*, 68ff., 443–46; Irmtraud Heike, "Johanna Langefeld—Die Biographie einer Oberaufseherin," *WerkstattGeschichte* 12 (1995): 7–19. See also Johannes Schwartz, "Das Selbstverständnis Johanna Langefelds als SS-Oberaufseherin," in *Tatort KZ. Neue Beiträge zur Geschichte der Konzentrationslager*, ed. Ulrich Fritz, Silvija Kavcic, and Nicole Warmbold (Ulm, 2003), 71–95.
79. Johannes Schwartz, "Geschlechterspezifischer Eigensinn von NS-Täterinnen am Beispiel der KZ-Oberaufseherin Johanna Langefeld," in *Frauen als Täterinnen im Nationalsozialismus, Protokollband der Fachtagung vom 17.–18. September in Bernburg*, ed. Viola Schubert-Lehnhardt (Gerbstadt, 2005), 56–82, 73–75; see also Strebel, *Das KZ Ravensbrück*, 70.
80. Letter from Richard Glücks (WVHA) on 24 October 1942 to the Commandants of the Ravensbrück, Auschwitz and Lublin Women's Concentration Camps. Re: Camp

compound service in the women's camps, HStA Düsseldorf, Ger. Rep. 432 No. 430, p. 251; see also letter from Richard Glücks to the Commandants of the Concentration Camps, 24 October 1942, Bundesarchiv Zwischenarchiv Dahlwitz-Hoppegarten, ZM 1491, p. 251, cited in Heike, "Johanna Langefeld," 13.

81. Höss, in Broszat, ed., *Kommandant in Auschwitz*, 177ff.
82. Strebel, *Das KZ Ravensbrück*, 70. Irmtraud Heike attributes this to resistance by the male headquarters staff; Heike, "Johanna Langefeld," 14.
83. Schwartz, "Geschlechterspezifischer Eigensinn," 76ff.; see also Strebel, *Das KZ Ravensbrück*, 71.
84. Report of 17 April 1943, HStA Düsseldorf, Ger. Rep. 432 No. 429, p. 47.
85. Report on 19 April 1943, HStA Düsseldorf, Ger. Rep. 432 No. 429, p. 46.
86. See chapter 10 of this work.
87. See statement by Rosa Süss (née Reischl) on 9 May 1974 in Neureichenau, HStA Düsseldorf, Ger. Rep. 432 No. 252, p. 120; statement by Elisabeth H. on 27 August 1975 in Cologne, HStA Düsseldorf, Ger. Rep. 432 No. 252, pp. 133r–134v.
88. Statement by Rosa Süss (née Reischl) on 26 June 197, main hearing, HStA Düsseldorf, Ger. Rep. 432 No. 286, p. 6.
89. Statement by Charlotte W. on 7 August 1972 in Düsseldorf, HStA Düsseldorf, Ger. Rep. 432 No. 235, pp. 78ff.
90. Statement by Jan Ude M. on 27 September 1972 in Düsseldorf, HStA Düsseldorf, Ger. Rep. 432 No. 228, pp. 150–51.
91. Statement by Georg Gröner on 28 November 1963 in Ansbach, HStA Düsseldorf, Ger. Rep. 432 No. 240, p. 223.
92. Statement by Hildegard Lächert on 28 August 1973 in Düsseldorf, HStA Düsseldorf, Ger. Rep. 432 No. 238, p. 578.
93. Statement by Rosa Süss (née Reischl) on 26 June 1979, main hearing, HStA Düsseldorf, Ger. Rep. 432 No. 286, p. 3.
94. Statement by Otto Z. on 20 February 1970 in Munich, HStA Düsseldorf, Ger. Rep. 432 No. 204, p. 28.
95. KOL probably stands for "Konzentrationslager" or concentration camp; what the abbreviation "W. u. G." stands for is unknown.
96. Sonderbefehl, Lublin, 22 February 1943, HStA Düsseldorf, Ger. Rep. 158 No. 292, p. 5.
97. See statement by Alice Orlowski on 30 August 1973 in Düsseldorf, HStA Düsseldorf, Ger. Rep. 432 No. 252, p. 88. See also Statement by Rosa Süss (née Reischl) on 26 June 1979, main hearing, HStA Düsseldorf, Ger. Rep. 432 No. 286, pp. 5ff.
98. Headquarters Order No. 1/44 on 31 January 1944, HStA Düsseldorf, Ger. Rep. 432 No. 231, pp. 8–10, here 9.
99. Ibid.
100. See Birthe Kundrus, "'Die Unmoral deutscher Soldatenfrauen.' Diskurs, Alltagsverhalten und Ahndungspraxis 1939–1945," in *Zwischen Karriere und Verfolgung. Handlungsräume von Frauen im nationalsozialistischen Deutschland*, ed. Kirsten Heinsohn, Barbara Vogel, and Ulrike Weckel (Frankfurt am Main, 1997), 96–110.

Chapter 7. Annihilation as Work: The Daily Work of Killing in the Camp

1. For Auschwitz, Andreas Kilian, Eric Friedler, and Barbara Siebert have investigated this process of annihilation in detail. The extent to which conditions differed in Majdanek must remain an open question, as an investigation of the *Sonderkommandos* has yet to be undertaken. Regardless, the division of labor between the SS and prisoner details as well as the division of the work into stages were broadly comparable. Eric Friedler, Barbara Siebert, and Andreas Kilian, *Zeugen aus der Todeszone. Das jüdische Sonderkommando in Auschwitz* (Munich, 2005). See also the Hamburg Institut für Sozialgeschichte, ed., *Die Auschwitz-Hefte. Texte der polnischen Zeitschrift "Przeglad Lekarski" über historische, psychische und medizinische Aspekte des Lebens und Sterbens in Auschwitz*, 2 vols. (Weinheim, 1987); Richard Glazar, *Die Falle mit dem grünen Zaun: Überleben in Treblinka* (Frankfurt am Main, 1992); Gideon Greif, *"Wir weinten tränenlos." Augenzeugenberichte des jüdischen "Sonderkommandos" in Auschwitz* (Frankfurt am Main, 2001). See also Ayse Sila Cehreli, *Témoignage du Khurbn: la résistance juive dans les centres de mise à mort: Chełmno, Bełzec, Sobibór, Treblinka* (Paris: Éditions Kimé, 2013).
2. Statement by Hermann Hackmann on 26 September 1973, Düsseldorf, HStA Düsseldorf, Ger. Rep. 432 No. 248, p. 730; see also Statement by Jan Novak on 20 April 1977, main hearing, HStA Düsseldorf, Ger. Rep. 432 No. 285, p. 10. See also Jan Novak, in Dieter Ambach and Thomas Köhler, *Lublin-Majdanek. Das Konzentrations- und Vernichtungslager im Spiegel von Zeugenaussagen*, vol. 12 of *Juristische Zeitgeschichte* (Düsseldorf, 2003), S. 171; Statement by Wilhelm Reinartz, undated, main hearing, HStA Düsseldorf, Ger. Rep. 432 No. 288, p. 38.
3. Statement by Jan Novak on 20 April 1977, main hearing, HStA Düsseldorf, Ger. Rep. 432 No. 285, p. 12 (Ambach and Köhler, *Lublin-Majdanek*, 172).
4. Ibid., 14 (173).
5. Ibid., 27ff. (176).
6. Statement by Jan Novak on 20 April 1977, Düsseldorf, main hearing, HStA Düsseldorf, Ger. Rep. 432 No. 285, pp. 27ff. (Ambach and Köhler, *Lublin-Majdanek*, 176ff.).
7. Statement by Wilhelm Reinartz on 23 March 1976 in the main hearing, HStA Düsseldorf, Ger. Rep. 432 No. 288, p. 39.
8. Statement by Jan Novak on 20 April 1977, Düsseldorf, main hearing, HStA Düsseldorf, Ger. Rep. 432 No. 285, p. 26 (Ambach and Köhler, *Lublin-Majdanek*, 176).
9. Statement by Jan Novak on 17 May 1972 in Warsaw, HStA Düsseldorf, Ger. Rep. 432, No. 250, p. 271.
10. Statement by Josef Ochlewski on 18 January 1973 in Warsaw, HStA Düsseldorf, Ger. Rep. 432, No. 296, pp. 5ff.
11. Ibid.
12. Statement by Henryk Wieliczanski on 16 May 1972 in Lodz, HStA Düsseldorf, Ger.

Rep. 432, No. 300, p. 2.

13. Statement by Jan Novak on 20 April 1977, main hearing, HStA Düsseldorf, Ger. Rep. 432 No. 285, p. 15 (Ambach and Köhler, *Lublin-Majdanek*, 174).
14. See ibid., 37 (179).
15. Ibid., 30 (177).
16. Ibid., 31 (178).
17. Statement by Hermann Hackmann on 4 October 1973 in Düsseldorf, HStA Düsseldorf, Ger. Rep. 432 No. 248, pp. 762ff.
18. Survivor, in Eberhard Fechner, *Norddeutscher Rundfunk: Der Prozess: Eine Darstellung des Majdanek-Verfahrens in Düsseldorf*, videotape (1984), part 1; see also statement by Teresa-Maria Slizewicz on 23 May 1972 in Warsaw, HStA Düsseldorf, Rep. 432 No. 235, pp. 80ff.
19. Statement by Dora Abend on 30 October 1978, main hearing, HStA Düsseldorf, Ger. Rep. 432 No. 282, pp. 3ff. (Ambach and Köhler, *Lublin-Majdanek*, 99).
20. Statement by Erna Wallisch (née Pfannstiel) on 30 November 1972 in Vienna, HStA Düsseldorf, Ger. Rep. 432 No. 235, pp. 168ff.
21. On the striking of prisoners, see chapter 10 of this work.
22. Statement by Chela Apelbaum on 16 January 1979, main hearing, HStA Düsseldorf, Ger. Rep. 432 No. 282, p. 2 (Ambach and Köhler, *Lublin-Majdanek*, 100ff.).
23. Ibid., 5–6 (101).
24. See chapter 11 of this work.
25. See statement by Hildegard Lächert on 30 August 1973 in Düsseldorf, HStA Düsseldorf, Ger. Rep. 432 No. 252, pp. 100ff.; statement by Luzie H. on 21 December 1976, main hearing, HStA Düsseldorf, Ger. Rep. 432 No. 285, p. 178; statement by Alice Orlowski on 30 August 1973 in Düsseldorf, HStA Düsseldorf, Ger. Rep. 432 No. 252, p. 91; statement by Erna Wallisch on 14 January 1965 in Vienna, DÖW, LG Graz 13/Vr 3329/63, vol. 1, pp. 465–67; statement by Hermine Böttcher on 11 December 1974 in Hannover, HStA Düsseldorf, Ger. Rep. 432 No. 290, p. 5.
26. See Barbara Schwindt, *Das Konzentrations- und Vernichtungslager Majdanek. Funktionswandel im Kontext der "Endlösung"* (Würzburg, 2005), 122–204.
27. See ibid., 205–86.
28. Statement by Luzie H. on 9 August 1972 in Düsseldorf, HStA Düsseldorf, Ger. Rep. 432 No. 43, p. 8126.
29. Statement by Georg Gröner on 5 May 1965, HStA Düsseldorf, Ger. Rep. 432 No. 240, p. 222.
30. See Tomasz Kranz, "Das Konzentrationslager Majdanek und die 'Aktion Reinhardt,'" in *"Aktion Reinhardt." Der Völkermord an den Juden im Generalgouvernement 1941–1944*, ed. Bogdan Musial (Osnabrück, 2004), 233–55.
31. Statement by Hermann Hackmann on 27 September 1973 in Düsseldorf, HStA Düsseldorf, Ger. Rep. 432 No. 248, p. 741.
32. Statement by Erich Muhsfeldt on 14 August 1947 in Krakow, HStA Düsseldorf, Ger. Rep. 432 No. 204, p. 96.

33. Emil Laurich, in Fechner, *Der Prozess*, part 3.
34. Statement by Jan Novak on 20 April 1977, main hearing, HStA Düsseldorf, Ger. Rep. 432 No. 285, p. 21 (Ambach and Köhler, *Lublin-Majdanek*, 175).
35. Statement by Hermann Hackmann, undated, main hearing, HStA Düsseldorf, Ger. Rep. 432 No. 288, pp. 21–23.
36. Statement by Heinz Petrick on 5 August 1974 in Düsseldorf, HStA Düsseldorf, Ger. Rep. 432, No. 233, pp. 631ff.
37. See statement by Jan Novak on 20 April 1977, main hearing, HStA Düsseldorf, Ger. Rep. 432 No. 285, p. 22 (Ambach and Köhler, *Lublin-Majdanek*, 175).
38. Statement by Otto Z. on 6 April 1977, main hearing, HStA Düsseldorf, Ger. Rep. 432 No. 287, p. 280 (Ambach and Köhler, *Lublin-Majdanek*, 97).
39. Ibid., 278ff. (96ff.).
40. Ibid., 280 (97).
41. Statement by Otto Z. on 8 March 1972 in Munich, HStA Düsseldorf, Ger. Rep. 432 No. 204, p. 64.
42. Statement by Otto Z. on 6 April 1977, main hearing, HStA Düsseldorf, Ger. Rep. 432 No. 287, p. 284 (Zakis, in Ambach and Köhler, *Lublin-Majdanek*, 98).
43. See Peter Black, "Die Trawniki-Männer und die 'Aktion Reinhard,'" in *"Aktion Reinhardt." Der Völkermord an den Juden im Generalgouvernement 1941–1944*, ed. Bogdan Musial (Osnabrück, 2004), 309–52.
44. See statement by Josef Anton B. on 18 April 1973 in Düsseldorf, HStA Düsseldorf, Ger. Rep. 432 No. 248, p. 955.
45. See statement by Adam C. on 9 August 1944 through the Russian-Polish Commission, HStA Düsseldorf, Ger. Rep. 432 No. 274, pp. 114–18; statement by Kazimierz G. on 9 August 1944 through the Russian-Polish Commission, HStA Düsseldorf, Ger. Rep. 432 No. 274, pp. 119ff.
46. Statement by Hermann Hackmann, undated, main hearing, HStA Düsseldorf, Ger. Rep. 432 No. 288, p. 20.
47. See chapter 5.
48. See Karin Orth, *Das System der nationalsozialistischen Konzentrationslager. Eine politische Ordnungsgeschichte* (Munich, 2002), 208.
49. See Wolfgang Scheffler, "Historisches Gutachten Zur Judenverfolgung des nationalsozialistischen Staats—unter besonderer Berücksichtigung der Verhältnisse im Generalgouvernement—und zur Geschichte des Lagers Majdanek im System nationalsozialistischer Vernichtungs- und Konzentrationslager," manuscript (1976), 181–84; Josef Marszalek, *Majdanek. Konzentrationslager Lublin* (Warsaw, 1984), 131–32; Dieter Pohl, *Von der "Judenpolitik" zum Judenmord: der Distrikt Lublin des Generalgouvernements 1939–1944* (Frankfurt, 1993), 170–74; Schwindt, *Majdanek*, 268–86.
50. Henryka Ostrowska, in Fechner, *Der Prozess*, part 3.
51. Statement by Danuta Medryk on 13 May 1977, main hearing, HStA Düsseldorf, Ger. Rep. 432 No. 285, p. 125 (Ambach and Köhler, *Lublin-Majdanek*, 167).

52. Statement by Erich Muhsfeldt on 16 August 1947 in Krakow, HStA Düsseldorf, Ger. Rep. 432 No. 204, p. 104.
53. See Fechner, *Der Prozess*, part 3.
54. Statement by Maryla Reich on 17 May 1978, main hearing, HStA Düsseldorf, Ger. Rep. 432 No. 286, p. 20 (Ambach and Köhler, *Lublin-Majdanek*, 133).
55. See statement by Robert Seitz on 5 December 1961 in Karlsruhe, HStA Düsseldorf, Ger. Rep. 432 No. 266, pp. 87–88.
56. Statement by Erich Muhsfeldt on 16 August 1947 in Krakow, HStA Düsseldorf, Ger. Rep. 432 No. 204, p. 106. See also Christopher Browning, *Ordinary Men: Reserve Police Battalion 101 and the Final Solution in Poland* (New York: HarperCollins, 1992), ch. 15.
57. Johann B., in Fechner, *Der Prozess*, part 3.
58. Statement by Otto Z. on 8 March 1972 in Munich, HStA Düsseldorf, Ger. Rep. 432 No. 204, p. 68.
59. See statement by Alice Orlowski on 30 August 1973 in Düsseldorf, HStA Düsseldorf, Ger. Rep. 432 No. 252, pp. 87ff.
60. Statement by Alice Orlowski on 18 April 1961 in Eitorf/Sieg, HStA Düsseldorf, Ger. Rep. 432 No. 5, pp. 816ff.
61. Statement by Erna Wallisch on 14 January 1965 in Vienna, DÖW, LG Graz 13/Vr 3329/63, vol. 1, p. 467ff.
62. Statement by Erna Wallisch (née Pfannstiel) on 30 November 1972 in Vienna, HStA Düsseldorf, Ger. Rep. 432 No. 235, p. 171.
63. Statement by Luzie H. on 8 November 1972 in Düsseldorf, HStA Düsseldorf, Ger. Rep. 432 No. 292, p. 71.
64. Statement by Luzie H., transcript of the main hearing, 21 December 1976, prosecutors' notes, HStA Düsseldorf, Ger. Rep. 432 No. 285, pp. 171ff.
65. Luzie H., in Fechner, *Der Prozess*, part 3.
66. Statement by Maryla Reich on 17 May 1978, main hearing, HStA Düsseldorf, Ger. Rep. 432 No. 286, p. 20 (Ambach and Köhler, *Lublin-Majdanek*, 130–33, 133).
67. Statement by Hertha Ehlert (married name Nauman) on 9 June 1970 in Bad Homburg, HStA Düsseldorf, Ger. Rep. 432 No. 292, p. 44.
68. See statement by Herta B. on 30 October 1974 in Waldshut, HStA Düsseldorf, Ger. Rep. 432 No. 203, pp. 24ff.; statement by Herta Bienek (married name Pakozdi) on 15 June 1976, main hearing, HStA Düsseldorf, Ger. Rep. 432 No. 285, no page number; statement by Rosa Süss (née Reischl) on 29 August 1973 in Düsseldorf, HStA Düsseldorf, Ger. Rep. 432 No. 252, p. 81, see also 75ff. and 79; statement by Elisabeth H. on 15 June 1976, main hearing, HStA Düsseldorf, Ger. Rep. 432 No. 286, p. 207.
69. Statement by Otto Z. on 8 March 1972 in Munich, HStA Düsseldorf, Ger. Rep. 432 No. 204, p. 69.
70. Statement by Otto Z. on 20 February 1970 in Munich, HStA Düsseldorf, Ger. Rep. 432 No. 204, p. 29.
71. Statement by Josef M. on 24 February 1972 in Bad Reichenhall, HStA Düsseldorf, Ger. Rep. 432 No. 247, p. 354.

72. Statement by Robert Seitz on 17 March 1965 in Liedolsheim, HStA Düsseldorf, Ger. Rep. 432 No. 266, pp. 141–43.
73. Luzie H., in Fechner, *Der Prozess*, part 2.
74. Historian Barbara Schwindt has produced a detailed study of the construction process and operation of the gas chambers. I have based my brief rendering on Schwindt, *Majdanek*, 158–61, 166ff.
75. Letter by Karl Naumann to the SS Economist Krakow, 22 October 1942, Archiwum Panstwowe w Lubline (APL), Central Department 8, p. 22. Until July 1942 only Barracks 42 was intended as a delousing facility; cited in Schwindt, *Majdanek*, 156.
76. See Schwindt, *Majdanek*, 156–71.
77. The camp acquired Zyklon B from the Hamburg company Tesch und Stabenow, Internationale Gesellschaft zur Schädlingsbekämpfung (TeSta). The first order took place on 25 July 1942; see Schwindt, *Majdanek*, 163.
78. See ibid., 156–61 (report by the Polish-Soviet Commission on August 1944, Gosudarstvenni Archiv Rossiiskoi Federatsii, Moscow [GARF], 7021–107–9, pp. 229–43).
79. Even if Chamber IV was used primarily to disinfect clothing, it cannot be ruled out that people were gassed there. Schwindt, *Majdanek*, 166ff.
80. Jean-Claude Pressac, "The Deficiencies and Inconsistencies of the 'Leuchter Report,'" in *Demolishing Holocaust Denial: The End of the "Leuchter Report,"* ed. Shelly Shapiro (New York: Beate Klarsfeld Foundation, 1990), 31–58, 52.
81. See statement by Otto Z. on 20 February 1970 in Munich, HStA Düsseldorf, Ger. Rep. 432, No. 204, p. 28; statement by Otto Z. on 8 March 1972 in Munich, HStA Düsseldorf, Ger. Rep. 432 No. 204, pp. 67ff.
82. Statement by Georg W. on 13 January 1965 in Vienna, DÖW, LG Graz 13/Vr 3329/63, vol. 1, p. 455.
83. Statement by Georg W. on 29 March 1965 in Vienna, DÖW, LG Graz 13/Vr 3329/63, vol. 4, p. 380.
84. See statement by Robert Seitz on 5 December 1961 in Karlsruhe, HStA Düsseldorf, Ger. Rep. 432 No. 266, p. 85.
85. See statement by Luzie H. on 9 August 1972 in Düsseldorf, HStA Düsseldorf, Ger. Rep. 432 No. 43, p. 8125.
86. These statements were translated from German into Russian, and then rendered back into German by the Düsseldorf Regional Court in 1974. Statement by Wilhelm Reinartz on 22 and 23 October 1945 through the NKVD, HStA Düsseldorf, Ger. Rep. 432 No. 297, no page number; statement by Wilhelm Reinartz on 2 November 1945 through the NKVD, HStA Düsseldorf, Ger. Rep. 432 No. 242, pp. 972–1573; statement by Wilhelm Reinartz on 30 January 1946 through the NKVD, HStA Düsseldorf, Ger. Rep. 432 No. 297, no page number; statement by Wilhelm Reinartz on 3 May 1946 through the NKVD, HStA Düsseldorf, Ger. Rep. 432 No. 242, pp. 986ff.
87. Statement by Ernst Fischer on 1 April 1965 in Sitterswald/Saar, HStA Düsseldorf, Ger. Rep. 432 No. 266, p. 187.

88. Ibid.
89. Statement by Georg Gröner on 28 November 1963, HStA Düsseldorf, Ger. Rep. 432 No. 240, pp. 220ff.
90. On Rindfleisch's career, see Marco Pukrop, "Dr. med. Heinrich Rindfleisch. Eine Lagerarztkarriere im KZ Majdanek," in *KZ-Verbrechen. Beiträge zur Geschichte der nationalsozialistischen Konzentrationslager und ihrer Erinnerung*, ed. Wojcech Lenarczyk, Andreas Mix, Johannes Schwartz, and Veronika Springmann (Berlin, 2007), 34–51.
91. Statement by Georg Gröner on 5 May 1965, HStA Düsseldorf, Ger. Rep. 432 No. 240, p. 225.
92. Statement by Georg Gröner on 28 November 1963, HStA Düsseldorf, Ger. Rep. 432 No. 240, pp. 220ff.
93. Statement by Erna Wallisch (née Pfannstiel) on 30 November 1972 in Vienna, HStA Düsseldorf, Ger. Rep. 432 No. 235, p. 170.
94. Statement by Hertha Nauman (divorced name: Ehlert) on 18 April 1972 in Bad Homburg, HStA Düsseldorf, Ger. Rep. 432 No. 296, p. 7466.
95. Luzie H., in Fechner, *Der Prozess*, part 2; see also statement by Luzie H. on 21 December 1976, main hearing, HStA Düsseldorf, Ger. Rep. 432 No. 285, p. 174.
96. Statement by Luzie H. on 8 November 1972 in Düsseldorf, HStA Düsseldorf, Ger. Rep. 432 No. 292, pp. 68ff.
97. See statement by Erich Muhsfeldt on 16 August 1947 in Krakow, HStA Düsseldorf, Ger. Rep. 432 No. 204, pp. 95, 97, 101, 103; statement by Erich Muhsfeldt on 14 August 1947 in Krakow, ibid., 112–13.
98. Statement by Ernst Fischer on 1 April 1965 in Sitterswald/Saar, HStA Düsseldorf, Ger. Rep. 432 No. 266, p. 187.
99. See statement by Erich Muhsfeldt on 14 August 1947 in Krakow, HStA Düsseldorf, Ger. Rep. 432 No. 204, p. 96.
100. Ibid.
101. Statement by Robert Seitz on 17 March 1965 in Liedolsheim, HStA Düsseldorf, Ger. Rep. 432 No. 266, p. 140.
102. Statement Erich Muhsfeldt on 14 August 1947 in Krakow, HStA Düsseldorf, Ger. Rep. 432 No. 204, p. 95.
103. Statement by Robert Seitz on 17 March 1965 in Liedolsheim, HStA Düsseldorf, Ger. Rep. 432 No. 266, p. 140.
104. Ibid., 143.
105. Statement by Wanda Bialas on 30 October 1979, main hearing, HStA Düsseldorf, Ger. Rep. 282, p. 2 (Ambach and Köhler, *Lublin-Majdanek*, 140).
106. Statement by Robert Seitz on 5 December 1961 in Karlsruhe, HStA Düsseldorf, Ger. Rep. 432 No. 266, p. 84.
107. Statement by Erich Muhsfeldt on 14 August 1947 in Krakow, HStA Düsseldorf, Ger. Rep. 432 No. 204, pp. 99–100.
108. See advertising and information material, HStA Düsseldorf, Ger. Rep. 432 No. 420, pp.

539–50. Detailed research has since been conducted on the company Topf & Söhne: see Eckard Schwarzenberger, *Topf & Söhne. Arbeiten an einem Täterort* (Erfurt, 2001); Aleida Assmann, Frank Hiddemann, and Eckhard Schwarzenberger, eds., *Firma Topf & Söhne: Hersteller der Öfen für Auschwitz. Ein Fabrikgelände als Erinnerungsort?* (New York: Campus Verlag, 2002).

109. See Robert Jan van Pelt, *The Case for Auschwitz: Evidence from the Irving Trial* (Bloomington: Indiana University Press, 2002).

110. Statement by Julian Gregorowicz on 19 April 1977, main hearing, HStA Düsseldorf, Ger. Rep. 432 No. 283, p. 4 (Ambach and Köhler, *Lublin-Majdanek*, 149).

111. Statement by Erich Muhsfeldt on 14 August 1947 in Krakow, HStA Düsseldorf, Ger. Rep. 432 No. 204, p. 100. According to Muhsfeldt, both ovens were disassembled in early 1943 and moved to Płaszów.

112. The guard Otto Z. also recalled that prisoners dug mass graves, because the death rate in the camp was allegedly so high that the corpses could not all be incinerated in the crematorium. See statement by Otto Z. on 20 February 1970, LKA-NW, Munich, HStA Düsseldorf, Ger. Rep. 432 No. 204, p. 30.

113. Statement by Erich Muhsfeldt on 14 August 1947 in Krakow, HStA Düsseldorf, Ger. Rep. 432 No. 204, p. 101. According to Muhsfeldt, the German prisoner-functionary was a Reich German prisoner. One of his successors was a Jewish prisoner from Vienna; see 101 and 125.

114. See statement by Adam Czuprin on 9 August 1944 for the Russian-Polish Commission, HStA Düsseldorf, Ger. Rep. 432, No. 274, pp. 114–18; statement by Kazimierz Gagol on 9 August 1944 through the Russian-Polish Commission, HStA Düsseldorf, Ger. Rep. 432 No. 274, pp. 119ff.

115. Statement by Robert Seitz on 5 December 1961 in Karlsruhe, HStA Düsseldorf, Ger. Rep. 432 No. 266, pp. 85ff.

116. Statement by Erich Muhsfeldt on 14 August 1947 in Krakow, HStA Düsseldorf, Ger. Rep. 432 No. 204, pp. 101ff.; see also statement by Robert Seitz on 17 March 1965 in Liedolsheim, HStA Düsseldorf, Ger. Rep. 432 No. 266, p. 141.

117. Statement by Erich Muhsfeldt on 16 August 1947 in Krakow, HStA Düsseldorf, Ger. Rep. 432 No. 204, p. 108.

118. Ibid., 110.

119. Luzie H., in Fechner, *Der Prozess*, part 3.

120. Statement by Anna M., Zentrale Stelle, Stuttgart, 2 August 1961, HStA Düsseldorf, Ger. Rep. 432 No. 234, pp. 23ff.

121. Coke is derived from a bituminous coal that is low in ash and sulfur. It burns with a very faint blue flame and, ideally, produces little soot or visible smoke.

122. Statement by Erich Muhsfeldt on 16 August 1947 in Krakow, HStA Düsseldorf, Ger. Rep. 432 No. 204, p. 110.

123. Ibid., 111.

124. Statement by Luzie H. on 21 December 1976, main hearing, HStA Düsseldorf, Ger. Rep. 432 No. 285, pp. 171ff. See also statement by Anna M. on 2 August 1961 in

Stuttgart, HStA Düsseldorf, Ger. Rep. 432 No. 234, pp. 22ff.

125. Statement by Charlotte Mayer (née Wöllert) on 28 August 1973 in Düsseldorf, HStA Düsseldorf, Ger. Rep. 432 No. 234, pp. 47ff.
126. Luzie H., in Fechner, *Der Prozess*, part 2.
127. Hildegard Lächert, in Fechner, *Der Prozess*, part 2.
128. See statement by Herta B. on 30 October 1974 in Waldshut, HStA Düsseldorf, Ger. Rep. 432 No. 203, p. 28; statement by Rosa Süss (née Reischl) on 29 August 1973 in Düsseldorf, HStA Düsseldorf, Ger. Rep. 432 No. 252, p. 82; statement by Charlotte Mayer (née Wöllert) on 27 June 1979, main hearing, HStA Düsseldorf, Ger. Rep. 432 No. 285, p. 3.
129. Hildegard Lächert, in Fechner, *Der Prozess*, part 2.
130. Eberhard Fechner, transcription of interview with Erna Wallisch, 15 June 1980, manuscript (private collection), 29.
131. Heinz Villain, in Fechner, *Der Prozess*, part 1.
132. Statement by Lilli Laurich, main hearing, 22 April 1980, HStA Düsseldorf, Ger. Rep. 432 No. 284, no page number, pp. 1ff.
133. Lilli Laurich, in Fechner, *Der Prozess*, part 2.
134. Luzie H., in Fechner, *Der Prozess*, part 2.
135. Statement by Otto Z. on 20 February 1970 in Munich, HStA Düsseldorf, Ger. Rep. 432 No. 204, p. 29.
136. Christian Ingrao, "Violence de guerre, violence génocide: les Einsatzgruppen," in *La Violence de guerre 1914–1945. Approches comparées des deux conflits mondiaux*, ed. Stéphane Audoin-Rouzeau et al. (Brussels, 2002), 219–41, 236ff; Christian Ingrao, *Croire et détruire: les intellectuels dans la machine de guerre SS* (Paris: Fayard 2010).
137. Statement by Hertha Nauman (divorced name: Ehlert) on 18 April 1972 in Bad Homburg, HStA Düsseldorf, Ger. Rep. 432 No. 296, p. 7466.
138. Ibid., 7465.
139. Ibid., 7467.
140. On images of the enemy, see chapter 5 of this work.
141. See also chapters 10 and 11 of this work.
142. See Friedler, Siebert, and Kilian, *Zeugen aus der Todeszone*, 8.
143. Dieter Pohl, *Die nationalsozialistische Judenverfolgung in Ostgalizien 1941–1944. Organisation und Durchführung eines staatlichen Massenverbrechens* (Munich, 1997), 405.
144. Friedler, Siebert, and Kilian, *Zeugen aus der Todeszone*, 19. See Rudolf Höss, "Die Endlösung der Judenfrage im KL Auschwitz," in *Kommandant in Auschwitz. Autobiographische Aufzeichnungen des Rudolf Höss*, ed. Martin Broszat, 17th ed. (Munich, 2000), 237–59.
145. Hans Buchheim, "Befehl und Gehorsam," in *Anatomie des SS-Staates*, ed. Hans Buchheim et al. (Munich, 1999), 215–320, 242.
146. Alf Lüdtke, "Die Fiktion der Institution. Herrschaftspraxis und Vernichtung der europäischen Juden im 20. Jahrhundert," in *Institutionen und Ereignis. Über historische*

Praktiken und Vorstellungen gesellschaftlichen Ordnens, ed. Reinhard Blänkner and Bernhard Jussen (Göttingen: Vandenhoeck & Ruprecht, 1998), 369.

147. Alf Lüdtke, *Eigen-Sinn. Fabrikalltag, Arbeitererfahrungen und Politik vom Kaiserreich bis in den Faschismus* (Hamburg, 1993), 9–22, 19.
148. Alf Lüdtke, "'Fehlgreifen in der Wahl der Mittel.' Optionen im Alltag militärischen Handelns," *Mittelweg 36*, no. 1 (2003): 61–75, 68.
149. English translation, http://www.nizkor.org/hweb/people/h/himmler-heinrich/posen/oct-04-43/ausrottung-transl-nizkor.html.
150. See Karin Orth, "Die 'Anständigkeit' der Täter. Texte und Bemerkungen," *SOWI* 25, no. 2 (1996): 112–15.
151. Harald Welzer, *Täter. Wie aus ganz normalen Menschen Massenmörder werden, unter Mitarbeit von Manuela Christ* (Frankfurt, 2005), 165.
152. Harald Welzer, "Härte und Rollendistanz. Zur Sozialpsychologie des Verwaltungsmassenmords," *Leviathan* 21 (1993): 358–73.
153. Gudrun Brockhaus, *Schauder und Idylle. Faschismus als Erlebnisangebot* (Munich, 1997), 235.
154. Ibid., 236.
155. Suggestion List No. 6 for awarding of the War Merit Cross 2nd Class with Swords on 30 December 1943, HStA Düsseldorf, Ger. Rep. 432 No. 419, p. 331.
156. Ibid., 330.
157. Female guards also received this citation. On Hermine Braunsteiner, see chapter 4 of this work.
158. Otto Z., in Fechner, *Der Prozess*, part 2.
159. Rosa Reischl, in Fechner, *Der Prozess*, part 2.

Chapter 8. Escapes and Their Meaning within the Structure of Power and Violence in the Camp

1. See the essays in Ludger Schwarte, ed., *Auszug aus dem Lager. Zur Überwindung des modernen Raumparadigmas in der politischen Philosophie* (Berlin, 2007).
2. Höss, in Martin Broszat, ed., *Kommandant in Auschwitz. Autobiographische Aufzeichnungen des Rudolf Höss*, 17th ed. (Munich, 2000), 277.
3. Ibid., 127ff.
4. An example from Mauthausen Concentration Camp: On 2 February 1945, 495 Soviet Russians succeeded in escaping from the camp. It was the biggest escape in the history of the Nazi camps. By the next day, with the ready assistance of the local population, Volkssturm militia, and Hitler Youth, 300 of the fugitives had been recaptured. Of these, only 57 were brought back to the camp alive. This murderous hunt for the fugitives went down in local parlance as the "Mühlviertel Hare Chase." See Gordon J. Horwitz, *In the Shadow of Death: Living outside the Gates of Mauthausen* (New York: Free Press, 1990), 124–43.

5. Höss, in Broszat, ed., *Kommandant in Auschwitz*, 128.
6. Ibid., 128.
7. Dionys Lenard, "Flucht aus Majdanek," *Dachauer Hefte* 7 (1991): 144–73, 147.
8. On escape attempts at Ravensbrück, see Eugenia Kocwa, *Flucht aus Ravensbrück* (East Berlin, 1973), 82; Odette Fabius, *Sonnenaufgang über der Hölle* (Berlin, 1997); Bernhard Strebel, *Das KZ Ravensbrück. Geschichte eines Lagerkomplexes* (Berlin, 2003), 279ff., 537ff.
9. Michel Foucault, "The Subject and Power," *Critical Inquiry* 8, no. 4 (Summer 1982): 777–95.
10. Lenard, "Flucht aus Majdanek," 147.
11. Statement by Hermann Hackmann on 4 October 1973 in Düsseldorf, HStA Düsseldorf, Ger. Rep. 432 No. 248, p. 767.
12. Witness Anton K., in Dieter Ambach and Thomas Köhler, eds., *Lublin-Majdanek. Das Konzentrations- und Vernichtungslager im Spiegel von Zeugenaussagen*, vol. 12 of *Juristische Zeitgeschichte* (Düsseldorf, 2003), 85ff.; see also statement by Hermann Hackmann on 27 September 1973 in Düsseldorf, HStA Düsseldorf, Ger. Rep. 432 No. 248, pp. 744ff.
13. Statement by Hermann Hackmann on 27 September 1973 in Düsseldorf, HStA Düsseldorf, Ger. Rep. 432 No. 248, p. 743.
14. Statement by Hermann Hackmann on 4 October 1973 in Düsseldorf, HStA Düsseldorf, Ger. Rep. 432 No. 248, p. 769.
15. Statement by Fritz Petrick on 8 October 1964 in Munich, HStA Düsseldorf, Ger. Rep. 432 No. 232, p. 116.
16. Heinz Villain, in Eberhard Fechner, *Norddeutscher Rundfunk: Der Prozess: Eine Darstellung des Majdanek-Verfahrens in Düsseldorf*, videotape (1984), part 3.
17. Statement by Hermann Hackmann on 4 October 1973 in Düsseldorf, HStA Düsseldorf, Ger. Rep. 432 No. 248, p. 765.
18. Hermann Hackmann, in Fechner, *Der Prozess*, part 3.
19. Accounts vary regarding the number of individuals shot. It was estimated to be between 40 and 60 people.
20. Statement by Fritz Petrick on 8 October 1964 in Munich, HStA Düsseldorf, Ger. Rep. 432 No. 232, pp. 116ff.
21. Statement by Otto Peer on 28 November 1972 in Linz, HStA Düsseldorf, Ger. Rep. 432 No. 250, pp. 390–92.
22. Hermann Hackmann, in Fechner, *Der Prozess*, part 3.
23. Statement by Hermann Hackmann on 27 September 1973 in Düsseldorf, HStA Düsseldorf, Ger. Rep. 432 No. 248, pp. 751ff.
24. Statement by Hermann Hackmann on 4 October 1973 in Düsseldorf, HStA Düsseldorf, Ger. Rep. 432 No. 248, p. 771.
25. See Wolfgang Sofsky, *The Order of Terror: The Concentration Camp* (Princeton, NJ: Princeton University Press, 1997), 214–23.
26. Ibid., 221.

27. In the late 1950s, the American ethnologist Milton Singer coined the term "cultural performance" to describe "particular instances of cultural organization" through which a society presents itself for both its own members and outsiders. According to Erika Fischer-Lichte, "cultural performance" refers to "every kind of performance," encompassing theater and concert performances as well as rituals, ceremonies, and festivals. Erika Fischer-Lichte, "Performance, Inszenierung, Ritual. Zur Klärung kulturwissenschaftlicher Schlüsselbegriffe," in *Geschichtswissenschaft und "Performative Turn." Ritual, Inszenierung und Performanz vom Mittelalter bis zur Neuzeit*, ed. Jürgen Martschukat and Steffen Patzold (Cologne, 2003), 33–54, 38. See also Erika Fischer-Lichte, *Ästhetik des Performativen* (Frankfurt am Main, 2004); Milton Singer, ed., *Traditional India: Structure and Changes* (Philadelphia: American Folklore Society, 1959).
28. In other camps the slogans included "Hurray, I've come back!" "A bird flew past," etc. See Hans Marsalek, *Die Geschichte des Konzentrationslagers Mauthausen* (Vienna, 1980), 250.
29. Höss, in Broszat, ed., *Kommandant in Auschwitz*, 128.
30. See Lagerordnung Ravensbrück, National Archives and Records Administration [NARA], RG 549, 000–50–11, Box 522, Folder no. 3, pp. 39–43.
31. On penal codes and practice, see chapter 9 of this work.
32. This verbatim text is also found in the Disciplinary and Penal Code for the Esterwegen Concentration Camp from 1 August 1934. See Johannes Tuchel, *Die Inspektion der Konzentrationslager, 1938–1945. Das System des Terrors. Eine Dokumentation* (Berlin, 1994), 37–39; see also Stanislav Zámečnik, "Das frühe Konzentrationslager Dachau," in *Terror ohne System. Die ersten Konzentrationslager im Nationalsozialismus 1933–1935. Geschichte der Konzentrationslager 1933–1945*, ed. Wolfgang Benz and Barbara Distel (Berlin, 2001), 13–39, 23.
33. See Stanislaw Gorondowski, "Bericht über Mauthausen," *Dachauer Hefte* 2 (1986): 123–32, 132. One can assume that as the war continued and the system of concentration camps rapidly expanded, the practice of punishment intensified in the camps.
34. Statement by Hermann Hackmann on 27 September 1973 in Düsseldorf, HStA Düsseldorf, Ger. Rep. 432 No. 248, pp. 737–39.
35. Statement by Fritz Petrick on 8 October 1964 in Munich, HStA Düsseldorf, Ger. Rep. 432 No. 232, p. 119.
36. Statement by Hermann Hackmann on 27 September 1973 in Düsseldorf, HStA Düsseldorf, Ger. Rep. 432 No. 248, p. 737; see also statement by Hermann Hackmann, undated, main hearing, HStA Düsseldorf, Ger. Rep. 432 No. 288, p. 30.
37. See letter of the RSHA IV D 2, 6 January 1943, signed Heinrich Himmler, Bundesarchiv [BA], R–58/3568, pp. 15–20.
38. Statement by Andrzej Stanislawski on 2 June 1972 in Gdansk, Ger. Rep. 432 No. 299, pp. 2ff.
39. Richard van Dülmen, *Theater des Schreckens. Gerichtspraxis und Strafrituale der*

frühen Neuzeit (Munich, 1985), 65ff.

40. Death by hanging, which was especially widespread in the Middle Ages, was abolished in the seventeenth century "in favor of" decapitation. Death by the sword, previously the exclusive privilege of the nobility, was from then on practiced on all classes. Richard J. Evans, *Rituals of Retribution: Capital Punishment in Germany, 1600–1987* (New York: Oxford University Press, 1996), 47ff.
41. See ibid., 622.
42. See ibid., 621.
43. See Bernd-A. Rusinek, *Gesellschaft in der Katastrophe. Terror, Illegalität, Widerstand (1944/1945)* (Essen, 1989).
44. Evans, *Rituals*, 717.
45. Sofsky, *The Order of Terror*, 221.
46. Statement by Jerzy Kwiatowski on 9 September 1967 in Warsaw, HStA Düsseldorf, Ger. Rep. 432 No. 227, pp. 43ff. To date no such photographic documents have been found. They were probably systematically destroyed during evacuation.
47. Luzie H., in Fechner, *Der Prozess*, part 2.
48. Statement by Maryla Reich on 17 May 1978, main hearing, HStA Düsseldorf, Ger. Rep. 432 No. 286, p. 10 (Ambach and Köhler, *Lublin-Majdanek*, 131ff.).
49. Statement by Chela Apelbaum on 16 January 1979, main hearing, HStA Düsseldorf, Ger. Rep. 432 No. 282, pp. 4–5 (Ambach and Köhler, *Lublin-Majdanek*, 100ff.). See statement by Dora Abend on 30 October 1978, main hearing, HStA Düsseldorf, Ger. Rep. 432 No. 282, p. 4 (Ambach and Köhler, *Lublin-Majdanek*, 99); statement by Riwka Landau on 14 December 1978, main hearing, HStA Düsseldorf, Ger. Rep. 432 No. 282, p. 4 (Ambach and Köhler, *Lublin-Majdanek*, 118); statement by Henrika Mitron on 7 February 1979, main hearing, HStA Düsseldorf, Ger. Rep. 432 No. 285, p. 9 (Ambach and Köhler, *Lublin-Majdanek*, 125); statement by Rachel Nurman on 24 April 1979, main hearing, HStA Düsseldorf, Ger. Rep. 432 No. 285, p. 6 (Ambach and Köhler, *Lublin-Majdanek*, 128); statement by Hela Rosenbaum on 9 May 1978, main hearing, HStA Düsseldorf, Ger. Rep. 432 No. 286, p. 6 (Ambach and Köhler, *Lublin-Majdanek*, 135); statement by Barbara Steiner on 25 October 1978, HStA Düsseldorf, Ger. Rep. 432 No. 286, p. 8 (Ambach and Köhler, *Lublin-Majdanek*, 138).
50. See statement by Luzie H., transcript of the main hearing, 21 December 1976, Prosecution's notes, HStA Düsseldorf, Ger. Rep. 432 No. 285, p. 177.
51. This practice recalls the *theatrum poenarum* of the seventeenth century, in which it was commonplace to leave the corpse hanging from the gallows for several days as a deterrent. On deterrence and the death penalty, see Jürgen Martschukat, *Inszeniertes Töten. Eine Geschichte der Todesstrafe vom 17. bis zum 18. Jahrhundert* (Cologne, 2000), 26ff., 74–83. Martschukat cites two examples, in which the executed was brought down from the gallows only after several months, and in the other case after five years.
52. Michel Foucault, *Discipline and Punish: The Birth of the Prison* (New York: Vintage, 1997), 57.

53. Statement by Anna Biel on 10 June 1970 in Opole, HStA Düsseldorf, Ger. Rep. 432 No. 245, pp. 66–67.
54. Martschukat, *Inszeniertes Töten*, 244.
55. The former *Aufseherinnen* confirmed this in the interrogations. They noted unanimously that hanging was intended as a deterrent. See statement by Hildegard Lächert, 30 August 1973, HStA Düsseldorf, Ger. Rep. 432 No. 252, p. 100; statement by Hermine B. through the StA Cologne on 11 December 1974, HStA Düsseldorf, Ger. Rep. 432 No. 290, p. 6.
56. Jürgen Martschukat, "'The Duty of Society.' Todesstrafe als Performance der Modernität in den USA um 1900," in *Geschichtswissenschaft und "Performative Turn,"* ed. Martschukat and Patzold, 229–53, 240.
57. As Sven Reinhardt's study on fascist groups in Italy and Germany has shown, violence was one of the key moments in which fascist society constituted itself. See Sven Reichardt, *Faschistische Kampfbünde. Gewalt und Gemeinschaft im italienischen Faschismus und in der deutschen SA* (Cologne, 2002).
58. Statement by Henrika Mitron on 7 February 1979, main hearing, HStA Düsseldorf, Ger. Rep. 432 No. 285, p. 9 (Ambach and Köhler, *Lublin-Majdanek*, 125).
59. See Point 79 of the indictment, HStA Düsseldorf, Ger. Rep. 432 No. 76, pp. 279–280; see also Ger. Rep. 432 No. 377.
60. Statement by Nechama Frenkel on 12 September 1979, main hearing, HStA Düsseldorf, Ger. Rep. 432 No. 283, p. 6 (Ambach and Köhler, *Lublin-Majdanek*, 109).
61. Statement by Maryla Reich on 17 May 1978, main hearing, HStA Düsseldorf, Ger. Rep. 432 No. 286, p. 10 (Ambach and Köhler, *Lublin-Majdanek*, 131ff.).
62. Statement by Hela Rosenbaum on 9 May 1978, main hearing, HStA Düsseldorf, Ger. Rep. 432 No. 286, p. 6 (Ambach and Köhler, *Lublin-Majdanek*, p. 135); see also statement by Maria Kaufmann-Krasowska on 24 February 1978, main hearing, HStA Düsseldorf, Ger. Rep. 432 No. 284, pp. 6ff. (Ambach and Köhler, *Lublin-Majdanek*, 114ff.).
63. Statement by Janina Rawska-Bot on 5 February 1979, main hearing, HStA Düsseldorf, Ger. Rep. 432 No. 286, p. 7 (Ambach and Köhler, *Lublin-Majdanek*, 193).
64. Statement by Riwka Landau on 14 December 1978, main hearing, HStA Düsseldorf, Ger. Rep. 432 No. 284, p. 4 (Ambach and Köhler, *Lublin-Majdanek*, 118).
65. Interview with prosecutor Dieter Ambach, in Ambach and Köhler, *Lublin-Majdanek*, xvii.
66. Christopher Browning, *Ordinary Men: Reserve Police Battalion 101 and the Final Solution in Poland* (New York: HarperCollins, 1992), xviii.
67. Ibid.
68. See Harald Welzer, *Das kommunikative Gedächtnis. Eine Theorie der Erinnerung* (Munich, 2002).
69. See Thomas Köhler, "Historische Realität versus subjektive Erinnerungstradierung? Überlegungen anhand von Zeugenaussagen des 'Majdanek-Prozesses,'" in *Lagersystem und Repräsentation. Interdisziplinäre Studien zur Geschichte der Konzentrationslager,*

ed. Ralph Gabriel et al. (Tübingen, 2003), 140–55.

70. Martschukat, "The Duty of Society," 246.
71. Interview by the author with Dieter Ambach on 9 May 2003.
72. See Fischer-Lichte, "Performance, Inszenierung, Ritual," 39.
73. Statement by Krystina Tarasiewicz on 5 June 1979, main hearing, HStA Düsseldorf, Ger. Rep. 432 No. 286, p. 6 (Ambach and Köhler, *Lublin-Majdanek*, 210).
74. Statement by Barbara Steiner on 25 October 1978, main hearing, HStA Düsseldorf, Ger. Rep. 432 No. 286, p. 8 (Ambach and Köhler, *Lublin-Majdanek*, 138).
75. Statement by Mira Awronski on 13 December 1978, main hearing, HStA Düsseldorf, Ger. Rep. 432 No. 282, p. 4.
76. Statement by Wanda Bialas on 30 October 1979, main hearing, HStA Düsseldorf, Ger. Rep. 432 No. 282, p. 6 (Ambach and Köhler, *Lublin-Majdanek*, 142).
77. Statement by Maryla Reich on 17 May 1978, main hearing, HStA Düsseldorf, Ger. Rep. 432 No. 286, p. 10 (Ambach and Köhler, *Lublin-Majdanek*, 131ff.).
78. Statement by Dora Abend on 30 October 1978, main hearing, HStA Düsseldorf, Ger. Rep. 432 No. 282, p. 4 (Ambach and Köhler, *Lublin-Majdanek*, 99).
79. Statement by Maria Kaufmann-Krasowska on 24 February 1978, main hearing, HStA Düsseldorf, Ger. Rep. 432 No. 284, pp. 6ff. (Ambach and Köhler, *Lublin-Majdanek*, 115).
80. Statement by Rachel Nurman on 24 April 1979, main hearing, HStA, Düsseldorf, Ger. Rep. 432 No. 285, pp. 5ff. (Ambach and Köhler, *Lublin-Majdanek*, 128).
81. Lenard, "Flucht aus Majdanek," 166.
82. Ibid., 168ff.

Chapter 9. License to Kill? Unauthorized Actions by the Camp Guards

1. Statement by Erna Wallisch née Pfannstiel on 30 November 1972 in Vienna, HStA Düsseldorf, Ger. Rep. 432 No. 235, p. 169.
2. Hildegard Lächert, in Eberhard Fechner, *Norddeutscher Rundfunk: Der Prozess: Eine Darstellung des Majdanek-Verfahrens in Düsseldorf*, videotape (1984), part 2.
3. Statement by Robert Seitz on 17 March 1965 in Liedolsheim, HStA Düsseldorf, Ger. Rep. 432 No. 266, p. 142.
4. See Alf Lüdtke, "Einleitung," in *Herrschaft als soziale Praxis: Historische und sozialanthropologische Studien*, ed. Alf Lüdtke (Göttingen, 1991), 9–62; Marian Füssel, "Die Kunst der Schwachen. Zum Begriff der 'Aneignung' in der Geschichtswissenschaft," *Sozial.Geschichte* 3 (2006): 7–28.
5. Letter of the WVHA on 2 December 1942 to the Commandants of Concentration Camps Dachau, Sachsenhausen, Buchenwald, Mauthausen, Flossenbürg, Neuengamme, Auschwitz, Gross-Rosen, Natzweiler, Niederhagen-Wewelsburg, Stutthof, Ravensbrück, and Prisoner of War Camp Lublin, Institut für Zeitgeschichte (IfZ) Munich, Fa 183/1, pp. 345ff.

6. Letter of the WVHA on 20 January 1943 to the Commandants of the Concentration Camps Dachau, Sachsenhausen, Buchenwald, Mauthausen, Flossenbürg, Neuengamme, Auschwitz, Gross-Rosen, Natzweiler, Niederhagen-Wewelsburg, Stutthof, Ravensbrück, Herzogenbusch and Prisoner of War Camp Lublin, IfZ, Fa 506/12, p. 62.
7. See Bernhard Strebel, *Das KZ Ravensbrück. Geschichte eines Lagerkomplexes* (Berlin, 2003), 274–88.
8. On the "Dachau model" and disciplinary and penal regulations issued by Theodor Eicke, see chapter 2 of this work.
9. This term was originated by Theodor Eicke. See Stanislav Zámečnik, "Das frühe Konzentrationslager Dachau," in *Terror ohne System. Die ersten Konzentrationslager im Nationalsozialismus 1933–1935*, vol. 1, *Geschichte der Konzentrationslager 1933–1945*, ed. Wolfgang Benz and Barbara Distel (Berlin, 2001), 13–39, 23.
10. Lagerordnung Ravensbrück, in National Archives and Records Administration [hereafter NARA], RG 549, 000-50-11 Box 522, Folder no. 3, pp. 39–41.
11. Dionys Lenard, "Flucht aus Majdanek," *Dachauer Hefte* 7 (1991): 144–73, 157.
12. Paul Martin Neurath, *Die Gesellschaft des Terrors. Innenansicht der Konzentrationslager Dachau und Buchenwald* (Frankfurt am Main, 2004), 135. After his release and escape to the United States, Neurath completed a sociological dissertation on the "Society of Terror," with which he earned his PhD from Columbia University in 1943. See Paul Martin Neurath, "Social Life in the German Concentration Camps Dachau and Buchenwald" (PhD diss., Faculty of Political Science, Columbia University, 1951).
13. Lucia Schmidt-Fels, *Deportiert nach Ravensbrück: Bericht einer Zeugin (1943–1945)* (Annweiler, 2004), 91; see also Charlotte Müller, *Die Klempnerkolonne in Ravensbrück. Erinnerungen des Häftlings No. 10787* (Berlin, 1990), 76.
14. Wolfgang Sofsky, *The Order of Terror: The Concentration Camp* (Princeton, NJ: Princeton University Press, 1997), 113.
15. Ibid., 217.
16. Statement by Maurice Nègre, in *Camps de Concentration. Crimes contre la personne humaine. Documents pour servir à l'histoire de la guerre* (Fontenay-aux-Roses, 1945), 48 (translation into German by EM; into English by translator); see also Eugen Kogon, *Der SS-Staat. Das System der deutschen Konzentrationslager* (Munich, 2000), 124–55, 127.
17. Statement by Madame Lajeunesse, in *Camps de Concentration*, 48 (translation into German by EM; into English by translator).
18. Lagerordnung Ravensbrück, 39.
19. Ibid., 21a–33.
20. Ibid., 34, see also 22–23.
21. Declaration of honor, undated, in Archiv Mahn- und Gedenkstätte Ravensbrück/Stiftung Brandenburgische Gedenkstätten (MGR/StBG) II/3–4-15. See also chapter 4 of this work.

22. See Günter Morsch, "Organisations- und Verwaltungsstruktur der Konzentrationslager," in *Der Ort des Terrors*, vol. 1, *Geschichte der nationalsozialistischen Konzentrationslager*, ed. Wolfgang Benz and Barbara Distel (Munich: C.H. Beck, 2005), 58–75; Karin Orth, "Bewachung," in ibid., 126–40.
23. Lagerordnung Ravensbrück, 6.
24. Margarete Buber-Neumann, *Als Gefangene bei Stalin und Hitler. Eine Welt im Dunkel* (Berlin, 1997), 313.
25. On Chief Guard Johanna Langefeld, see Irmtraud Heike, "Johanna Langefeld—Die Biographie einer Oberaufseherin," *WerkstattGeschichte* 12 (1995); Johannes Schwartz, "Das Selbstverständnis Johanna Langefelds," in *Tatort KZ. Neue Beiträge zur Geschichte der Konzentrationslager*, ed. Ulrich Fritz, Silvija Kavčič, and Nicole Warmbold (Ulm, 2003).
26. See Johannes Schwartz, "Handlungsoptionen von KZ-Aufseherinnen. Drei alltags- und geschlechtergeschichtliche biographische Studien," in *NS-Täter aus interdisziplinärer Perspektive*, ed. Helgard Kramer (Munich, 2006), 349–74; Schwartz, "Geschlechterspezifischer Eigensinn von NS-Täterinnen am Beispiel der KZ-Oberaufseherin Johanna Langefeld," in *Frauen als Täterinnen im Nationalsozialismus, Protokollband der Fachtagung vom 17.–18. September in Bernburg*, ed. Viola Schubert-Lehnhardt (Gerbstadt, 2005), 61ff.
27. Lagerordnung Ravensbrück, 42.
28. Penal order form from Women's Concentration Camp Ravensbrück, MGR/StBG, II/3-3-4. A copy of a comparable form from Auschwitz can be found in Johannes Tuchel, *Die Inspektion der Konzentrationslager, 1938–1945. Das System des Terrors. Eine Dokumentation* (Berlin, 1994), 102ff.
29. Letter of the WVHA on 4 April 1942 to the Commandants of the Concentration Camps Dachau, Sachsenhausen, Buchenwald, Mauthausen, Flossenbürg, Neuengamme, Auschwitz, Gross-Rosen, Natzweiler, Niederhagen-Wewelsburg, Stutthof, Arbeitsdorf, Ravensbrück, Prisoner of War Camp Lublin, BA, NS 3/425, p. 65.
30. Letter of the WVHA on 14 July 1943 to the commandants of the concentration camps Auschwitz, Ravensbrück, Herzogenbusch, Lublin and Stutthof, BA, NS 3/426, p. 107; see also letter of the WVHA on 11 August 1942 to the commandants of the concentration camps Dachau, Sachsenhausen, Buchenwald, Mauthausen, Flossenbürg, Neuengamme, Auschwitz, Gross-Rosen, Natzweiler, Niederhagen-Wewelsburg, Stutthof, Ravensbrück and Prisoner of War Camp Lublin, BA, NS 3/426, p. 100. This must have been a very special privilege, as the *Lagerordnung* cited above explicitly forbade prisoners from smoking. Furthermore, cigarettes could be used as barter; see Sofsky, *The Order of Terror*, 153–63.
31. Lagerordnung Ravensbrück, 43.
32. Statement by Dorothea Binz on 24 August 1946, TNA, WO 235/310, p. 10. I thank Johannes Schwartz for this information. From September 1940, Dorothea Binz was deputy director of the penal block and became director of the cell block in the

summer of 1942. Unofficially Binz assumed the post of deputy chief guard in July 1943 and was officially confirmed in this function in February 1944. See Johannes Schwartz, "Handlungsräume einer KZ-Aufseherin. Dorothea Binz—Leiterin of the Zellenbaus und Oberaufseherin," in *"Im Gefolge der SS": Aufseherinnen des Frauen-Konzentrationslagers Ravensbrück*, ed. Simone Erpel, exhibition catalog (Berlin, 2007), 59–71.

33. Müller, *Die Klempnerkolonne*, 77ff.
34. Martschukat, "The Duty of Society," in *Geschichtswissenschaft und "Performative Turn." Ritual, Inszenierung und Performanz vom Mittelalter bis zur Neuzeit*, ed. Jürgen Martschukat and Stefan Patzold (Cologne, 2003), 242.
35. Germaine Tillion, *Ravensbrück* (Paris, 1988), 139.
36. Statement by Hermann Hackmann, undated, main hearing, HStA Düsseldorf, Ger. Rep. 432 No. 288, p. 18.
37. Statement by Hermann Hackmann on 27 September 1973 in Düsseldorf, HStA Düsseldorf, Ger. Rep. 432 No. 248, p. 736.
38. Luzie H., in Fechner, *Der Prozess*, part 2.
39. Statement by Eugenia Lipinska on 17 January 1978, main hearing, HStA Düsseldorf, Ger. Rep. 432 No. 284, p. 5; see also Dieter Ambach and Thomas Köhler, eds., *Lublin-Majdanek. Das Konzentrations- und Vernichtungslager im Spiegel von Zeugenaussagen*, vol. 12 of *Juristische Zeitgeschichte* (Düsseldorf, 2003), 160.
40. Statement by Danuta Medryk on 13 May 1977, main hearing, HStA Düsseldorf, Ger. Rep. 432 No. 285, p. 125 (Ambach and Köhler, *Lublin-Majdanek*, 167).
41. Statement by Herta Ehlert on 15 October 1945, Transcript of the Official Shorthand Notes, Trial against Josef Kramer and 44 Others, Public Record Office [PRO] WO 235/15, p. 85.
42. See Insa Eschebach, ed., *Ravensbrück. Der Zellenbau: Geschichte und Gedenken, Schriftenreihe der Stiftung Brandenburgischer Gedenkstätten*, vol. 18 (Berlin, 2008). Regarding the slaps meted out by staff at Madjanek, see chapter 10 of this work. On the cruelty of the head of the Ravensbrück jail, see chapter 11 of this work.
43. Sentry Regulations for the Concentration- and Extermination Camp Lublin-Majdanek [hereafter Sentry Regulations Majdanek], Lublin, 25 August 1943, BA, NS/4/Lu1, pp. 13-20 and pp. 78–87.
44. The Ravensbrück Camp Regulations state: "Anyone who makes preparations to escape or tries to tempt fellow prisoners, or fails to immediately report such individuals. A person suspected of trying to escape is anyone who leaves the place of work without an *Aufseherin*, enters the neutral zone, or tampers with the fence." Ravensbrück Camp Regulations, p. 41.
45. Sentry Regulations Majdanek, 19 (emphasis in original).
46. Ibid., 15.
47. Instruction on tasks and duties of sentries [hereafter Instruction sentries], undated, IfZ Munich, 183/1, pp. 117–22, esp. 119ff.
48. Instruction sentries, 118.

49. Ibid., 120.
50. Statement by Otto Z. on 6 April 1977, main hearing, HStA Düsseldorf, Ger. Rep. 432 No. 287, p. 284.
51. Ibid., 279ff. (Ambach and Köhler, *Lublin-Majdanek*, 97); see also statement by Otto Z. on 8 March 1972 in Munich, HStA Düsseldorf, Ger. Rep. 432 No. 204, p. 65.
52. Statement by Otto Z. on 6 April 1977, main hearing, Düsseldorf, HStA Düsseldorf, Ger. Rep. 432 No. 287, p. 284 (Ambach and Köhler, *Lublin-Majdanek*, 98).
53. See also chapter 7 of this work.
54. Statement by Otto Z. on 8 March 1972 in Munich, HStA Düsseldorf, Ger. Rep. 432 No. 204, p. 64.
55. Statement by Hermann Hackmann on 6 August 1974 in Düsseldorf, HStA Düsseldorf, Ger. Rep. 432 No. 248, p. 941.
56. Statement by Otto Z. on 6 April 1977, main hearing, Düsseldorf, HStA Düsseldorf, Ger. Rep. 432 No. 287, p. 279 (Ambach and Köhler, *Lublin-Majdanek*, 96–98, 97).
57. Statement by Jerzy Kwiatowski on 13 September 1967 in Warsaw, HStA Düsseldorf, Ger. Rep. 432 No. 227, pp. 47–48.
58. Luzie H., in Fechner, *Der Prozess*, part 2.
59. Morsch, "Organisations- und Verwaltungsstruktur," 64.
60. Statement by Ernst F. on 22 May 1973 in Kirchheimbolanden, HStA Düsseldorf, Ger. Rep. 432 No. 252, p. 63.
61. Ibid., pp. 63ff.
62. Statement by Ernst F., investigating magistrate at Düsseldorf Regional Court, Kirchheimbolanden, 22 May 1973, HStA Düsseldorf, Ger. Rep. 432 No. 252, p. 64.
63. Telex from Oranienburg on 28 December 1943 to the Camp Commandants of Ravensbrück Concentration Camp, Auschwitz II, Flossenbürg, Stutthof, Riga, Lublin, Mauthausen, Herzogenbusch, Buchenwald, Dachau, and the SS economists in Riga, HStA Düsseldorf, Ger. Rep. 432 No. 429, p. 136.
64. List of previously punished female guards at the Lublin Women's Concentration Camp on 28 December 1943, HStA Düsseldorf, Ger. Rep. 432 No. 430, p. 240.
65. Gertrud Heise told the British investigative authorities in 1945 that she had been sentenced to 14 days' detention in Majdanek in 1943 because of a "sentry offense." CI Questionnaire, Arrest Report, Gertrud Heise, 28 June 1945, PRO WO 309/429, no page number.
66. In January 1944 Himmler also introduced more lenient conditions for the female guards; they were no longer to be placed in detention, but instead punished with fines or a reprimand. Letter of the WVHA Amtsgruppe–D on 17 January 1944 to the Camp Commandants of the Concentration Camps Da., Sah., Bu., Mau., Flo., Au. I–III., Gr. R., Natz., Stu., Lubl., Rav., Herz., War., Group Leader D, Detention Camp Bergen-Belsen and Hinzert, Re: Imposition of disciplinary punishments on female guards, IfZ Munich, Fa 506/12, p. 149.
67. Statement by Fritz Petrick on 23 October 1973 in StA Düsseldorf, HStA Düsseldorf, Ger. Rep. 432 No. 233, p. 462.

68. Statement by Fritz Petrick on 8 October 1964, StA Cologne, Munich, HStA Düsseldorf, Ger. Rep. 432 No. 232, p. 114.
69. See chapter 7 of this work. See also Hans Buchheim, "Die Sondergerichtsbarkeit der SS und Polizei," in *Anatomie des SS-Staates*, ed. Hans Buchheim, Martin Broszat, Hans-Adolf Jacobsen, and Helmut Krausnick (Munich, 1999), 153–60; Wolfgang Scheffler, "Zur Gerichtspraxis der SS- und Polizeigerichte im Dritten Reich," in *Klassenjustiz und Pluralismus. Festschrift für Ernst Frankel zum 75. Geburtstag am 26 Dec. 1973*, ed. Günther Doecker and Winfried Steffani (Hamburg, 1974), 224–35; Bernd Wegner, "Die Sondergerichtsbarkeit von SS- und Polizei. Militärjustiz oder Grundlegung einer SS-gemäßen Rechtsordnung?" in *Das Unrechtsregime. Internationale Forschung über den Nationalsozialismus*, vol. 1, *Ideologie–Herrschaftssystem–Wirkung in Europa. Festschrift für Werner Joachim zum 65 Geburtstag*, ed. Ursula Büttner et al. (Geburtstag, 1986), 243–59.
70. See investigations by the prosecution, HStA Düsseldorf, Ger. Rep. 432 No. 233, p. 461.
71. See chapter 5 of this book.
72. Statement by Erna Wallisch (née Pfannstiel) on 14 January 1965 in Vienna, DÖW, LG Graz 13/Vr 3329/63, vol. 1, p. 471. See also the statement by Georg W. on 13 January 1965 in Vienna, DÖW, LG Graz 13/Vr 3329/63, vol. 1, pp. 451–59.
73. Unfortunately there is no information as to how and why the attempt at deception was discovered.
74. See chapter 8 in this work.
75. See Final Report of the SS-Police Court Berlin III on 17 February 1943 of an investigative hearing against SS-Standartenführer Karl Koch, HStA Düsseldorf, Ger. Rep. 432 No. 224, pp. 20–23, 21.
76. Ibid., 20.
77. Ibid. The two sentries on duty had already been cleared of negligent prisoner liberation by the prosecution through field judgments of the SS- and Police Court Krakow.
78. The "Prince Eugen" Division was an Armed SS unit composed almost exclusively of ethnic Germans. Ninety percent of the division's members came from the Banat, Serbia, Romania, Croatia, Slovakia, and Hungary. The unit was deployed in 1943 and 1944 mainly in Yugoslavia to "combat partisans." See Thomas Casagrande, *Die Volksdeutsche SS-Division "Prinz Eugen." Die Banater Schwaben und die nationalsozialistischen Kriegsverbrechen* (Frankfurt am Main, 2003).
79. As early as fall 1942, investigations against Koch were already being conducted by Josias Erbprinz zu Waldeck and Pyrmont in his function as Senior SS- and Police Leader Fulda Werra and Lord of the Courts for Buchenwald. Although probes of the bookkeeping revealed that Koch had embezzled funds, the case was abandoned through the intervention of Glücks and Pohl, and Koch was transferred to Majdanek on probation. See Karin Orth, *Die Konzentrationslager-SS. Sozialstrukturelle Analysen und biographische Studien* (Göttingen, 2000), 189ff.
80. Ibid., 206–10.

81. Statement by Hermann Hackmann on 26 September 1973 in Düsseldorf, HStA Düsseldorf, Ger. Rep. 432 No. 248, p. 719.
82. Orth, *Die Konzentrationslager-SS*, 208.
83. See Sofsky, *The Order of Terror*, 217.
84. Hans Buchheim, "Befehl und Gehorsam," in *Anatomie des SS-Staates*, ed. Hans Buchheim, Martin Broszat, Hans-Adolf Jacobsen, and Helmut Krausnick (Munich, 1999), 215–320, 246.
85. See Lüdtke, "Einleitung," in *Herrschaft als soziale Praxis*, 11.
86. One of the few researchers who, instead of referring summarily to "punishments," distinguishes instead between "comparatively regulated punishment procedures" and "arbitrary acts of excess" is Wolfgang Sofsky. See Sofsky, *The Order of Terror*, 331; see also Wolfgang Kirstein, *Das Konzentrationslager als Institution totalen Terrors. Das Beispiel des KL Natzweiler* (Pfaffenweiler: Centaurus-Verlagsgesellschaft, 1992), 85–93; Strebel, *Das KZ Ravensbrück*, 269–88.
87. Under Theodor Eicke's leadership, the personnel in the early concentration camp Dachau (1933 and 1934) were indoctrinated to use "ruthless harshness and severity" toward the prisoners. This was where a broad consensus for violence became prevalent among the first SS men, who would later make careers in concentration camps occupying senior positions. Many future concentration camp commandants were influenced by this early "school of terror." The constant fluctuation of camp personnel spread this consensus and practice "concentrically" in the camps. See Orth, *Die Konzentrationslager-SS*, 127–52.
88. Statement by Otto Z. on 6 April 1977, main hearing, HStA Düsseldorf, Ger. Rep. 432 No. 287, p. 283 (Ambach and Köhler, *Lublin-Majdanek*, 98).
89. See chapter 8 in this work.
90. Buchheim, "Befehl und Gehorsam," 216.
91. Ibid., 216ff.
92. "Handlungsspielräume," prepared by Alf Lüdtke with the collaboration of Marcus Gryglewski and Magnus Koch, in *Verbrechen der Wehrmacht*, ed. Hamburger Institut für Sozialforschung (Hamburg: Hamburger Edition, 1999), 579.
93. Alf Lüdtke, "Die Fiktion der Institution. Herrschaftspraxis und Vernichtung der europäischen Juden im 20. Jahrhundert." In *Institutionen und Ereignis*, ed. Reinhard Blänkner and Bernhard Jussen (Göttingen: V & R, 1998), 355–79, 368.
94. Statement by Hertha Nauman (divorced name: Ehlert) on 9 June 1970 in Bad Homburg, HStA Düsseldorf, Ger. Rep. 432 No. 292, p. 43.
95. Statement by Hertha Nauman (divorced name: Ehlert), undated, main hearing, HStA Düsseldorf, Ger. Rep. 432 No. 285, p. 191.

Chapter 10. Violence as Social Practice

1. Albert Scherr, "Körperlichkeit, Gewalt und soziale Ausgrenzung in der 'postindustriellen' Wissensgesellschaft," in *Gewalt*, ed. Wilhelm Heitmeyer and Hans-Georg Soeffner (Frankfurt am Main, 2004), 202–26, 208.
2. Alf Lüdtke, "Einleitung," in *Herrschaft als soziale Praxis, Historische und sozialanthropologische Studien* (Göttingen, 1991). On the concept of "fields of force," see the earlier discussion of E. P. Thompson, "Eighteenth-Century English Society: Class Struggle Without Class?," *Social History* 3 (1978).
3. Ibid., 12–18, 18.
4. Statement by Irene Kohn on 22 November 1949, main hearing, LG Vienna Vg 1Vr 5670/48, DÖW, pp. 11ff.
5. Viktoria Filler, ibid., 9.
6. See statement by Hermine Braunsteiner on 8 April 1948, main hearing, LG Vienna Vg 1Vr 5670/48, DÖW, p. 112; statement by Hermine Braunsteiner on 24 August 1948, ibid., 113.
7. Statement by Hermine Braunsteiner on 22 November 1949, main hearing, ibid., 2.
8. Thomas Lindenberger and Alf Lüdtke, "Einleitung," in *Physische Gewalt. Studien zur Geschichte der Neuzeit*, ed. Alf Lüdtke (Frankfurt, 1995), 24; see also Lüdtke, "Gewalt und Alltag im 20. Jahrhundert," in *Gewalt und Terror, 11 Vorlesungen*, ed. Wolfgang Bergsdorf, Dietmar Herz, and Hans Hoffmeister (Weimar, 2003), 35–52.
9. Statement by Edith W., 27 September 1977, main hearing, HStA Düsseldorf, Ger. Rep. 432 No. 286, pp. 315–16.
10. See Wolfgang Sofsky, *The Order of Terror: The Concentration Camp* (Princeton, NJ: Princeton University Press, 1997).
11. See Insa Eschebach, "SS-Aufseherinnen des Frauenkonzentrationslagers Ravensbrück. Erinnerungen ehemaliger Häftlinge," *WerkstattGeschichte* 13 (1996): 42.
12. Charlotte Müller, *Die Klempnerkolonne in Ravensbrück. Erinnerungen des Häftlings Nr. 10787* (Berlin, 1990), 67.
13. Elissa Mailänder Koslov, "Weil es einer Wienerin gar nicht liegt, so brutal zu sein . . ." Frauenbilder im Wiener Volksgerichtsverfahren gegen eine österreichische KZ-Aufseherin (1946–1949)," *Zeitgeschichte* 3 (2005): 128–50.
14. Jean Améry, "Torture," in *At the Mind's Limits: Contemplations by a Survivor on Auschwitz and Its Realities* (Bloomington: Indiana University Press, 1980), 21–40; here 29.
15. Lucia Schmidt-Fels, *Deportiert nach Ravensbrück—Bericht einer Zeugin 1943–1945* (Düsseldorf, 1981), 90ff.
16. Unidentified witness, in Eberhard Fechner, *Norddeutscher Rundfunk: Der Prozess: Eine Darstellung des Majdanek-Verfahrens in Düsseldorf*, videotape (1984), part 2.
17. Statement by Janina Rawska-Bot on 5 February 1979, main hearing, HStA Düsseldorf, Ger. Rep. 432 No. 286, p. 4, published in Dieter Ambach and Thomas Köhler, eds.,

Lublin-Majdanek. Das Konzentrations- und Vernichtungslager im Spiegel von Zeugenaussagen, vol. 12 of *Juristische Zeitgeschichte* (Düsseldorf, 2003), 192.

18. Statement by Eugenia Lipinska on 17 January 1978, main hearing, HStA Düsseldorf, Ger. Rep. 432 No. 284, p. 3 (Ambach and Köhler, *Lublin-Majdanek*, 160).
19. See Alf Lüdtke, *Eigen-Sinn: Fabrikalltag, Arbeitererfahrung und Politik vom Kaiserreich bis in den Faschismus* (Hamburg, 1993), 120–61, 141ff.
20. Statement by Anna Warmser on 22 November 1949, main hearing, LG Vienna, pp. 7–8; see also Auguste Schaffler, ibid., 10.
21. See statement by Charlotte W. on 21 May 1970 in Lübeck, HStA Düsseldorf, Ger. 432 No. 234, p. 31.
22. See chapter 5 in this work.
23. Statement by Rywka Aweonska on 15 February 1978, HStA Düsseldorf, Ger. Rep. 432 No. 282, p. 7 (Ambach and Köhler, *Lublin-Majdanek*, 103).
24. Statement by Stanislaw Chwiejczak on 17 September 1980, main hearing, HStA Düsseldorf, Ger. Rep. 432 No. 282, pp. 8ff.
25. Statement by Lola Givner on 14 December 1978, main hearing, HStA Düsseldorf, Ger. Rep. 432 No. 283, pp. 2ff. (Ambach and Köhler, *Lublin-Majdanek*, 111).
26. See chapter 4 in this work.
27. Statement by Jadwiga Landowska on 24 January 1973 in Warsaw, HStA Düsseldorf, Ger. Rep. 432 No. 213, p. 566. See also statement by Nechama Frenkel on 12 September 1979, HStA Düsseldorf, Ger. Rep. 432 No. 283, p. 4 (Ambach and Köhler, *Lublin-Majdanek*, 108); statement by Natalia Grzybek on 18 January 1978, main hearing, HStA Düsseldorf, Ger. Rep. 432 No. 283, p. 3 (Ambach and Köhler, *Lublin-Majdanek*, 152); statement by Hanna Narkiewicz-Jodko on 26 April 1977, main hearing, HStA Düsseldorf, Ger. Rep. 432 No. 285, p. 52 (Ambach and Köhler, *Lublin-Majdanek*, 169); statement by Maria Kaufmann-Krasowska on 24 February 1978, main hearing, HStA Düsseldorf, Ger. Rep. 432 No. 284, pp. 2–3 (Ambach and Köhler, *Lublin-Majdanek*, 113ff.); statement by Henrika Mitron on 7 February 1979, main hearing, HStA Düsseldorf, Ger. Rep. 432 No. 285, p. 4 (Ambach and Köhler, *Lublin-Majdanek*, 124).
28. Statement by Bronislawa Ulasowa on 18 August 1947 in Katowice, HStA Düsseldorf, Ger. Rep. 432 No. 213, p. 608. See also statement by Henryka Ostrowska on 1 June 1977, main hearing, HStA Düsseldorf, Ger. Rep. 432 No. 283, p. 142 (Ambach and Köhler, *Lublin-Majdanek*, 184); statement by Luzie H. on 21 December 1976, main hearing, HStA Düsseldorf, Ger. Rep. 432 No. 285, p. 178.
29. Statement by Nechama Frenkel on 12 September 1979, main hearing, HStA Düsseldorf, Ger. Rep. 432 No. 283, p. 48 (Ambach and Köhler, *Lublin-Majdanek*, 109); see also statement by Lola Givner on 14 December 1978, main hearing, HStA Düsseldorf, Ger. Rep. 432 No. 283, p. 6 (Ambach and Köhler, *Lublin-Majdanek*, 111).
30. Statement by Maria Kaufmann-Krasowska on 24 February 1978, main hearing, HStA Düsseldorf, Ger. Rep. 432 No. 284, p. 2 (Ambach and Köhler, *Lublin-Majdanek*, 113–17, 113).
31. Statement by Barbara Steiner on 25 October 1978, main hearing, HStA Düsseldorf,

Ger. Rep. 432 No. 286, p. 4 (Ambach and Köhler, *Lublin-Majdanek*, 137).

32. Statement by Henryka Ostrowska on 1 June 1977, main hearing, HStA Düsseldorf, Ger. Rep. 432 No. 283, p. 145 (Ambach and Köhler, *Lublin-Majdanek*, 185).
33. Statement by Danuta Medryk on 13 May 1977, main hearing, HStA Düsseldorf, Ger. Rep. 432 No. 285, p. 125 (Ambach and Köhler, *Lublin-Majdanek*, 167).
34. Statement by Hertha Nauman (divorced name: Ehlert) on 18 April 1972 in Bad Homburg, HStA Düsseldorf, Ger. Rep. 432 No. 296, p. 7464.
35. Statement by Hertha Nauman (divorced name: Ehlert) on 9 June 1976, main hearing, HStA Düsseldorf, Ger. Rep. 432 No. 285, pp. 186ff.
36. Statement by Alice Orlowski on 30 August 1973 in Düsseldorf, HStA Düsseldorf, Ger. Rep. 432 No. 252, pp. 84ff.
37. Statement by Alice Orlowski on 27 August 1973 in Düsseldorf, HStA Düsseldorf, Ger. Rep. 432 No. 262, p. 325.
38. Statement by Hertha Nauman (divorced name: Ehlert) on 18 April 1972 in Bad Homburg, HStA Düsseldorf, Ger. Rep. 432 No. 296, p. 7467.
39. Moschko, in Fechner, *Der Prozess*, part 2.
40. Ibid.
41. Unidentified survivor, ibid.
42. Statement by Henrika Mitron on 7 February 1979, main hearing, HStA Düsseldorf, Ger. Rep. 432 No. 285, p. 11 (Ambach and Köhler, *Lublin-Majdanek*, 125).
43. Eschebach, "SS-Aufseherinnen," 46.
44. Statement by Jan Novak on 17 May 1972 in Warsaw, HStA Düsseldorf, Ger. Rep. 432 No. 250, pp. 277ff.
45. See Erika Fischer-Lichte, "Performance, Inszenierung, Ritual. Zur Klärung kulturwissenschaftlicher Schlüsselbegriffe," in *Geschichtswissenschaft und "Performative Turn." Ritual, Inszenierung und Performanz vom Mittelalter bis zur Neuzeit*, ed. Jürgen Martschukat and Stefan Patzold (Cologne, 2003), 39.
46. Michel Foucault, "The Subject and Power," *Critical Inquiry* 8, no. 4 (Summer 1982): 340.
47. Elias Canetti also underscores the structural connection between power and force, entities that are inextricably intertwined: "When force gives itself time to operate it becomes power, but when the moment of crisis arrives, the moment of irrevocable decision, it reverts to being pure force. Power is more general and operates over a wider space than force, it includes much more, but is less dynamic. It is more ceremonious and even has a certain measure of patience." Elias Canetti, *Crowds and Power*, trans. Carol Stewart (New York: Continuum, 1973), 281. Canetti's concept of power is defined as a power to issue orders and only indirectly connected with the exercise of physical force. For Canetti, power in the moment of crisis is "pure force."
48. Foucault, "The Subject and Power," 340.
49. See also chapter 5 of this work.
50. Statement by Jan Novak on 20 April 1977, main hearing, HStA Düsseldorf, Ger. Rep. 432 No. 285, p. 17 (Ambach and Köhler, *Lublin-Majdanek*, 173ff.).

51. Statement by Hermann Hackmann, undated, main hearing, HStA Düsseldorf, Ger. Rep. 432 No. 288, p. 1.
52. Ibid., 18ff.
53. Erika Thiel, *Geschichte des Kostüms. Die europäische Mode von den Anfängen bis zur Gegenwart* (Berlin, 2004), 112ff.
54. Statement by Henryka Ostrowska on 1 June 1977, main hearing, HStA Düsseldorf, Ger. Rep. 432 No. 285, p. 149 (Ambach and Köhler, *Lublin-Majdanek*, 186).
55. Statement by Hanna Narkiewicz-Jodko on 26 April 1977, main hearing, HStA Düsseldorf, Ger. Rep. 432 No. 285, p. 51 (Ambach and Köhler, *Lublin-Majdanek*, 169).
56. Statement by Charlotte W. on 21 May 1970 in Lübeck, HStA Düsseldorf, Ger. Rep. 432 No. 234, p. 32.
57. Statement by Maryla Reich on 17 May 1978, main hearing, HStA Düsseldorf, Ger. Rep. 432 No. 286, p. 19 (Ambach and Köhler, *Lublin-Majdanek*, 133).
58. Statement by Hanna Narkiewicz-Jodko on 26 April 1977, main hearing, HStA Düsseldorf, Ger. Rep. 432 No. 285, p. 58 (Ambach and Köhler, *Lublin-Majdanek*, 170).
59. On the Trawnikis, see Peter Black, "Die Trawniki-Männer und die 'Aktion Reinhard,'" in *"Aktion Reinhardt." Der Völkermord an den Juden im Generalgouvernement 1941–1944*, ed. Bogdan Musial (Osnabrück, 2004), 309–52.
60. Letter by Chief Guard Else Ehrich to the Headquarters of Lublin Concentration Camp on 22 July 1943, Re: Letter of Conduct for *Aufseherin* Lächert Hildegard, HStA Düsseldorf, Ger. Rep. 432 No. 429, p. 23.
61. Statement by Charlotte Mayer née Wöllert on 27 June 1979, main hearing, HStA Düsseldorf, Ger. Rep. 432 No. 285, p. 4. See also chapter 6 in this work.
62. Ibid.
63. See chapter 11 in this work.
64. See Annette F. Timm, *The Politics of Fertility in Twentieth-Century Berlin* (Cambridge: Cambridge University Press, 2010), 118–86; Elizabeth Heineman, *What Difference Does a Husband Make? Women and Marital Status in Nazi and Postwar Germany* (Berkeley: University of California Press, 1999), 17–43.
65. Statement by Charlotte Mayer (née Wöllert) on 27 June 1979, main hearing, HStA Düsseldorf, Ger. Rep. 432 No. 285, p. 1.
66. Statement by Elisabeth H. on 27 August 1975 in Cologne, HStA Düsseldorf, Ger. 432 No. 252, p. 134.
67. Statement by Erika W. on 26 February 1975 in Düsseldorf, HStA Düsseldorf, Ger. Rep. 432, No. 215, p. 1146; see also statement by Edith W. on 27 September 1977, main hearing, HStA Düsseldorf, Ger. Rep. 432 No. 286, p. 315.
68. Eberhard Fechner, transcription of interview with Erna Wallisch, 15 June 1980, manuscript (private collection), 24ff.
69. Statement by Erna Wallisch (née Pfannstiel) on 30 November 1972 in Vienna, HStA Düsseldorf, Ger. Rep. 432 No. 235, p. 167.
70. Statement by Erna Wallisch (née Pfannstiel) on 14 January 1965 in Vienna, DÖW, Graz Regional Court 13/Vr 3329/63, vol. 1, p. 467.

71. Statement by Elisabeth H. on 27 August 1975 in Cologne, HStA Düsseldorf, Ger. Rep. 432 No. 252, p. 133; see also statement by Elisabeth H. on 15 June 1976, main hearing, HStA Düsseldorf, Ger. Rep. 432 No. 286, p. 204.
72. Statement by Hertha Nauman (divorced name: Ehlert) on 9 June 1970 in Bad Homburg, HStA Düsseldorf, Ger. Rep. 432 No. 292, p. 42.
73. Statement by Hertha Nauman (divorced name: Ehlert) on 9 June 1976, main hearing, HStA Düsseldorf, Ger. Rep. 432 No. 285, p. 187.
74. Statement by Hertha Nauman (divorced name: Ehlert) on 18 April 1972 in Bad Homburg, HStA Düsseldorf, Ger. Rep. 432 No. 296, p. 7462.
75. Statement by Hertha Nauman (divorced name: Ehlert) on 9 June 1970 in Bad Homburg, HStA Düsseldorf, Ger. Rep. 432 No. 292, p. 43.
76. See statement by Elisabeth H. on 27 August 1975 in Cologne, HStA Düsseldorf, Ger. 432 No. 252, p. 133; statement by Elisabeth H. on 15 June 1976, main hearing, HStA Düsseldorf, Ger. Rep. 432 No. 286, p. 203. See also statement by Charlotte Mayer (née Wöllert) on 28 August 1973 in Düsseldorf, HStA Düsseldorf, Ger. Rep. 432 No. 234, p. 48.
77. Statement by Ruth E. on 14 June 1978, main hearing, HStA Düsseldorf, Ger. Rep. 432 No. 287, p. 2; see also statement by Edith W. on 27 September 1977, main hearing, HStA Düsseldorf, Ger. Rep. 432 No. 286, p. 315.
78. Statement by Charlotte W. on 21 May 1970 in Lübeck, HStA Düsseldorf, Ger. Rep. 432 No. 234, p. 34.
79. Hilde Zimmermann, in *"Ich geb Dir einen Mantel, dass Du ihn noch in Freiheit tragen kannst." Widerstehen im KZ. Österreichische Frauen erzählen*, ed. Karin Berger, Elisabeth Holzinger, Lotte Podgornik, and Lisbeth N. Trallori (Vienna, 1987), 15–22, 19.
80. Müller, *Die Klempnerkolonne*, 67.
81. Margarete Buber-Neumann, *Als Gefangene bei Stalin und Hitler. Eine Welt im Dunkel* (Berlin, 1997), 322.
82. Statement by Judith Gelbard on 15 August 1978, main hearing, HStA Düsseldorf, Ger. Rep. 432 No. 283, p. 2 (Ambach and Köhler, *Lublin-Majdanek*, 109).
83. Statement by Hanna Narkiewicz-Jodko on 26 April 1977, main hearing, HStA Düsseldorf, Ger. Rep. 432 No. 285, pp. 51ff. (Ambach and Köhler, *Lublin-Majdanek*, 169).
84. Statement by Irena Marszalek on 17 December 1980, main hearing, HStA Düsseldorf, Ger. Rep. 432 No. 285, p. 3.
85. Ibid., 6.
86. Statement by Barbara Steiner on 25 October 1978, main hearing, HStA Düsseldorf, Ger. Rep. 432 No. 286, p. 4 (Ambach and Köhler, *Lublin-Majdanek*, 137).
87. See R. W. Connell, "Swots and Wimps: The Interplay of Masculinity and Education," *Oxford Review of Education* 15, no. 3 (1989): 291–303; R. W. Connell, *Masculinities*, 2nd ed. (Berkeley: University of California Press, 2005).
88. Germaine Tillion, *Ravensbrück* (Paris, 1988), 141.
89. Statement by Anna M. on 2 August 1961 in Stuttgart, HStA Düsseldorf, Ger. Rep. 432

No. 234, pp. 20ff.

90. Statement by Hertha Nauman (divorced name: Ehlert) on 9 June 1970 in Bad Homburg, HStA Düsseldorf, Ger. Rep. 432 No. 292, p. 43.
91. Statement by Hertha Nauman (divorced name: Ehlert) on 18 April 1972 in Bad Homburg, HStA Düsseldorf, Ger. Rep. 432 No. 296, p. 7463.
92. Lüdtke, "Einleitung," in *Herrschaft als soziale Praxis*, 14ff.
93. Lüdtke, *Eigen-Sinn*, 138.
94. See statement by Edward Maszonski on 9 August 1977, main hearing, HStA Düsseldorf, Ger. Rep. 432 No. 285, p. 6.
95. Statement by Natalia Grzybek on 18 January 1978, main hearing, HStA Düsseldorf, Ger. Rep. 432 No. 283, p. 3 (Ambach and Köhler, *Lublin-Majdanek*, 152).
96. See statement by Rosa Süss (née Reischl) on 29 August 1973 in Düsseldorf, HStA Düsseldorf, Ger. Rep. 432 No. 252, pp. 68, 71, 79, 81; statement by Luise Danz on 30 June 1947 in Krakow, HStA Düsseldorf, Ger. Rep. 432 No. 57, p. 11128; statement by Alice Orlowski on 25 June 1947 in Krakow, HStA Düsseldorf, Ger. Rep. 432 No. 296, p. 7; statement by Herta B. on 30 October 1974 in Waldshut, HStA Düsseldorf, Ger. Rep. 432 No. 203, p. 27; statement by Herta Bienek (married name Pakozdi) on 15 June 1976, main hearing, HStA Düsseldorf, Ger. Rep. 432 No. 285, no page number; statement by Erna Wallisch (née Pfannstiel) on 30 November 1972 in Vienna, HStA Düsseldorf, Ger. Rep. 432 No. 235, p. 167.
97. Statement by Hildegard Lächert on 28 August 1973 in Düsseldorf, HStA Düsseldorf, Ger. Rep. 432 No. 238, pp. 576–/577; see also statement by Lächert on 27 June 1947 in Krakow, HStA Düsseldorf, Ger. Rep. 432 No. 295, p. 4.
98. Statement by Hermine Böttcher (née Brückner) on 27 June 1979, main hearing, HStA Düsseldorf, Ger. Rep. 432 No. 282, pp. 5ff.; see also statement by Böttcher on 11 December 1974 in Hannover, HStA Düsseldorf, Ger. Rep. 432 No. 290, p. 7.
99. See chapter 8 in this work.
100. Statement by Elisabeth H. on 27 August 1975 in Cologne, HStA Düsseldorf, Ger. 432 No. 252, p. 134r. In court Elisabeth H. testified that the *Aufseherinnen* did not carry pistols in an official capacity. She herself had occasionally held one in her hand, she said, adding that female guards did not have to carry pistols when on leave in the city of Lublin. She said she no longer knew which *Aufseherinnen* carried pistols; it was possible, she said, that she "may have carried" pistols of her "friends." Statement by Elisabeth H. on 15 June 1976, main hearing, HStA Düsseldorf, Ger. Rep. 432 No. 286, p. 207.
101. Statement by Luzie H., transcript of the main hearing, 21 December 1976, prosecution's notes, HStA Düsseldorf, Ger. Rep. 432 No. 285, pp. 173 and 179.
102. See statement by Hertha Nauman (divorced name: Ehlert), StA Cologne, Bad Homburg, 18 April 1972, HStA Düsseldorf, Ger. Rep. 432 No. 296, p. 7462.
103. Statement by Hertha Nauman (divorced name: Ehlert) on 9 June 1976, main hearing, HStA Düsseldorf, Ger. Rep. 432 No. 285, p. 187.
104. Ibid., 191.

105. See statement by Hermine Braunsteiner on 11 May 1946 in Vienna, DÖW, LG Vienna Vg 1 Vr 5670/48, p. 2.
106. See Letter of the Commandant to the Chief Guard Ehrich, SS Recreational Facility "Stadelberghaus," 10 April 1943, HStA Düsseldorf, Ger. Rep. 432 No. 430, p. 196.
107. See dockets Herta B., Braunsteiner, David, Ehlert, Ehrich, Elisabeth H., Lächert, Pfannstiel, Orlowski, HStA Düsseldorf, Ger. Rep. 432 No. 429, pp. 2, 4, 6, 7, 21, 127, 129, Ger. Rep. 432 No. 430, pp. 117, 220, 262.
108. Statement by Leo Miller on 29 March 1977, main hearing, HStA Düsseldorf, Ger. Rep. 432 No. 285, p. 2 (Ambach and Köhler, *Lublin-Majdanek*, 120).
109. Statement by Boleslawa Janiszek on 29 January 1973 in Warsaw, HStA Düsseldorf, Ger. Rep. 432 No. 225, p. 19.
110. Statement by Krystyna Suchanska on 3 June 1972 in Gdansk, HStA Düsseldorf, Ger. Rep. 432 No. 254, p. 61.
111. Statement by Charlotte W. on 7 August 1972 in Düsseldorf, HStA Düsseldorf, Ger. 432 No. 235, p. 76.
112. Statement by Luzie H. on 8 November 1972 in Düsseldorf, HStA Düsseldorf, Ger. Rep. 432 No. 292, p. 70.
113. Statement by Hermine Böttcher on 11 December 1974 in Hannover, HStA Düsseldorf, Ger. Rep. 432 No. 290, p. 6.
114. Statement by Elisabeth H. on 27 August 1975 in Cologne, HStA Düsseldorf, Ger. 432 No. 252, p. 133r.
115. Statement by Rosa Süss (née Reischl) on 29 August 1973 in Düsseldorf, HStA Düsseldorf, Ger. Rep. 432 No. 252, p. 78.
116. The term hysteria (from the Greek *hystera*: uterus) was commonplace in the nineteenth century as a psychological diagnosis for a neurotic derangement among women; it is now obsolete. See Georges Didi-Huberman, *Die Erfindung der Hysterie. Die photographische Klinik von Jean-Martin Charcot* (Paderborn, 1997); Christina von Braun, *Nichtich: (Logik, Lüge, Libido)* (Frankfurt am Main, 1990).
117. List of previously disciplined Aufseherinnen, Lublin Women's Concentration Camp, 28 December 1943, HStA Düsseldorf, Ger. Rep. 432 No. 430, p. 240. See chapter 9 of this work.
118. See chapter 8 in this work.
119. In this interrogation, Lächert claimed that she was arrested in early August 1943 on the accusation of having given her pistol to partisans, spent several weeks in custody in Majdanek, and, early in July 1943, was discharged from concentration camp service. The personnel list from 29 September 1943 indicates that she had been discharged from Majdanek on 30 September because of pregnancy. By her own account, Lächert did not yet know at the time of her discharge that she was pregnant. The matter with the service pistol was confirmed by Wöllert. See statement by Hildegard Lächert on 30 August 1973 in Düsseldorf, HStA Düsseldorf, Ger. Rep. 432 No. 252, p. 98. See also personnel list, 29 November 1943, HStA Düsseldorf, Ger. Rep. 432 No. 430, p. 140; statement by Hildegard Lächert on 28 August 1973 in Düsseldorf, HStA Düsseldorf,

Ger. Rep. 432 No. 238, pp. 576ff.; statement by Charlotte Mayer (née Wöllert) on 27 June 1979, main hearing, HStA Düsseldorf, Ger. Rep. 432 No. 285, p. 2.

120. Statement by Hildegard Lächert on 27 June 1947 in Krakow, HStA Düsseldorf, Ger. Rep. 432 No. 295, pp. 2ff.
121. Statement by Alice Orlowski on 30 August 1973 in Düsseldorf, HStA Düsseldorf, Ger. Rep. 432 No. 252, p. 89.
122. See Alain Testard, *Essai sur les fondements de la division sexuelle du travail chez les chasseurs-cueilleurs* (Paris, 1986).
123. Ruth Seifert, "Identität, Militär und Geschlecht. Zur identitätspolitischen Bedeutung einer kulturellen Konstruktion," in *Landsknechte, Soldatenfrauen und Nationalkrieger. Militär, Krieg und Geschlechterordnung im historischen Wandel*, ed. Karin Hagemann and Stefanie Schüler-Springorum (Frankfurt am Main, 1998), 53–66, 57.
124. Insa Eschebach, "NS-Prozesse in der sowjetischen Besatzungszone und der DDR. Einige Überlegungen zu den Strafverfahrensakten ehemaliger SS-Aufseherinnen des Frauenkonzentrationslagers Ravensbrück," in Die frühen Nachkriegsprozesse, *Beiträge zur Geschichte der nationalsozialistischen Verfolgung in Norddeutschland* 3 (1997): 65–74, 69.
125. Insa Eschebach, "Das Aufseherinnenhaus. Überlegungen zu einer Ausstellung über SS-Aufseherinnen in der Gedenkstätte Ravensbrück," *Gedenkstätten Rundbrief* 75 (March 1997): 6; see also Jens Ebert and Insa Eschebach, *"Die Kommandeuse." Erna Dorn—zwischen Nationalsozialismus und Kaltem Krieg* (Berlin, 1994), 98ff.

Chapter 11. Cruelty: An Anthropological Perspective

1. On Dorothea Binz, see chapter 9, fn. 1118.
2. Germaine Tillion, *Ravensbrück* (Paris, 1988), 139.
3. Ibid., 139.
4. Primo Levi, *The Drowned and the Saved*, trans. Raymond Rosenthal (New York: Summit Books, 1988), 105–26.
5. Wolfgang Sofsky, *The Order of Terror: The Concentration Camp* (Princeton, NJ: Princeton University Press, 1997), 224.
6. Ibid., 224.
7. See Herbert Jäger, *Verbrechen unter totalitärer Herrschaft. Studien zur nationalsozialistischen Gewaltkriminalität* (Frankfurt am Main, 1982), 22–43.
8. Véronique Nahoum-Grappe, "Anthropologie de la violence extrême: le crime de profanation," *Revue internationale des sciences sociales* 147 (2002): 604.
9. Statement by Jan Novak on 17 May 1972 in Warsaw, HStA Düsseldorf, Ger. Rep. 432 No. 296, pp. 7ff.
10. Véronique Nahoum-Grappe, "L'usage politique de la cruauté: l'épuration ethnique (ex-Yougoslavie, 1991–1995)," in *De la violence*, ed. Françoise Héritier (Paris, 1996), 296.
11. Ibid., 297.

12. "There is nothing that man fears more than the touch of the unknown," Canetti writes in his introduction. "Man always tends to avoid physical contact with anything strange. . . . All the distances which men create around themselves are dictated by this fear." Elias Canetti, *Crowds and Power*, trans. Carol Stewart (New York: Continuum, 1962), 15.
13. Ibid., 251.
14. Canetti distinguishes among various forms of survival. One fundamental form of survival is *killing*, which borders on watching others die—for example, in the aftermath of a survived battle or epidemic. Biologically surviving one's contemporaries and previous generations is a "natural" form of survival. All these forms share a "satisfaction in survival." See Canetti, *Crowds and Power*, 227.
15. Ibid., 249.
16. Nahoum-Grappe, "L'usage politique de la cruauté," 296.
17. Jean Améry, *At the Mind's Limits* (Bloomington: Indiana University Press, 2009), 27 (emphasis in original).
18. Ibid., 29.
19. Ibid., 28.
20. Christine Künzel, *Vergewaltigungslektüren. Zur Codierung sexueller Gewalt in Literatur und Recht* (Frankfurt am Main, 2003), 259ff.
21. Améry, *At the Mind's Limits*, 28.
22. In her study of the body in pain, Elaine Scarry has likewise demonstrated that there is no vocabulary for experiencing pain. See Elaine Scarry, *The Body in Pain: The Making and Unmaking of the World* (New York: Oxford University Press, 1985).
23. Améry, *At the Mind's Limits*, 33 (emphasis in original).
24. Ibid.
25. Ibid., 35.
26. Ibid., 38ff.
27. Ibid.
28. Ibid., 35.
29. Ibid., 38ff.
30. Ibid., 34.
31. Statement by Stanislaw Chwiejczak on 17 September 1980, main hearing, HStA Düsseldorf, Ger. Rep. 432 No. 282, pp. 7–8.
32. Anise Postel-Vinay, "Camps d'hommes, camps de femmes: Premières approches. Etude d'une ancienne déportée de Ravensbrück," *Histoire@Politique. Politique, culture, société*, no. 5 (May-August 2008): 8.
33. Stanislav Zámečnik, "Das frühe Konzentrationslager Dachau," in *Terror ohne System. Die ersten Konzentrationslager im Nationalsozialismus 1933–1935*, vol. 1, *Geschichte der Konzentrationslager 1933–1945*, ed. Wolfgang Benz and Barbara Distel (Berlin, 2001), 13–39.
34. Paul Martin Neurath, *Die Gesellschaft des Terrors. Innenansicht der Konzentrationslager Dachau und Buchenwald* (Frankfurt am Main, 2004), 142.

35. Veronika Springmann, *Rennen auf Leben und Tod: "Sport machen" als Praxis der Gewalt im Konzentrationslager*, in *KZ-Verbrechen. Beiträge zur Geschichte der Konzentrationslager und ihrer Erinnerung*, ed. Wojciech Lenarczyk, Andreas Mix, Johannes Schwartz, and Veronika Springmann (Berlin, 2007), 96.
36. Neurath, *Die Gesellschaft des Terrors*, 142.
37. Springmann, *Rennen auf Leben und Tod: "Sport machen,"* 101.
38. *Das sichtbare Unfassbare. Fotografien vom Konzentrationslager Mauthausen*. Amicales de Mauthausen, déportés et amis Paris, Amical de Mauthausen y otros campos Barcelona, Federal Interior Ministry, Austria (Vienna, 2005), 92–95.
39. Springmann, *Rennen auf Leben und Tod: "Sport machen,"* 99.
40. Statement by Nechama Frenkel on 12 September 1979, HStA Düsseldorf, Ger. Rep. 432 No. 283, p. 4 (Dieter Ambach and Thomas Köhler, eds., *Lublin-Majdanek. Das Konzentrations- und Vernichtungslager im Spiegel von Zeugenaussagen*, vol. 12 of *Juristische Zeitgeschichte* (Düsseldorf, 2003), 113.
41. See statement by Rywka Awronska on 15 February 1978, main hearing, HStA Düsseldorf, Ger. Rep. 432 No. 282, p. 6 (Ambach and Köhler, *Lublin-Majdanek*, 103); statement by Hanna Narkiewicz-Jodko on 26 April 1977, main hearing, HStA Düsseldorf, Ger. Rep. 432 No. 285, p. 52 (Ambach and Köhler, *Lublin-Majdanek*, 169). See also statement by Natalia Grzybek on 18 January 1978, main hearing, HStA Düsseldorf, Ger. Rep. 432 No. 283, p. 3 (Ambach and Köhler, *Lublin-Majdanek*, 152).
42. Statement by Lola Givner on 14 December 1978, main hearing, HStA Düsseldorf, Ger. Rep. 432 No. 283, p. 3.
43. See statement by Paula Joskowitz on 8 February 1979, HStA Düsseldorf, Ger. Rep. 432 No. 284, pp. 2ff. (Ambach and Köhler, *Lublin-Majdanek*, 112); statement by Janina Rowska-Bot on 5 February 1979, main hearing, HStA Düsseldorf, Ger. Rep. 432 No. 286, p. 3 (Ambach and Köhler, *Lublin-Majdanek*, 191ff.).
44. See chapter 10 in this work.
45. The "Muselmänner" were those inmates at Auschwitz who, in Primo Levi's description, were the "weak, the inept, those doomed to selection." Primo Levi, *Survival in Auschwitz* (New York: Simon & Schuster, 1996), 88. At Majdanek, such prisoners were refered as "Gammel," derived from the German word *gammeln*, meaning "rotting." See Sofsky, *The Order of Terror*, 25, 199–205; and Nicole Warmbold, *Lagersprache. Zur Sprache der Opfer in den Konzentrationslagern Sachsenhausen, Dachau, Buchenwald* (Bremen: Hempen, 2008).
46. Statement by Maryla Reich on 17 May 1978, main hearing, HStA Düsseldorf, Ger. Rep. 432 No. 286, p. 18 (Ambach and Köhler, *Lublin-Majdanek*, 132ff.). See also statement by Rachel Nurman on 24 April 1979, main hearing, HStA Düsseldorf, Ger. Rep. 432 No. 285, p. 5 (Ambach and Köhler, *Lublin-Majdanek*, 127ff.); statement by Nechama Frenkel on 12 September 1979, HStA Düsseldorf, Ger. Rep. 432 No. 283, p. 4 (Ambach and Köhler, *Lublin-Majdanek*, 108).
47. Statement by Maria Kaufmann-Krasowska on 24 February 1978, main hearing, HStA Düsseldorf, Ger. Rep. 432 No. 284, p. 4 (Ambach and Köhler, *Lublin-Majdanek*, 114).

48. Her colleague Rosa Reischl was the only one to confirm that the guards' jackboots were equipped with iron plates in front and back. See statement by Rosa Süss (née Reischl) on 26 June 1979, main hearing, HStA Düsseldorf, Ger. Rep. 432 No. 286, p. 2.
49. See Wolfgang Sofsky, "Gewaltformen—Taten und Bilder. Wolfgang Sofsky im Gespräch mit Fritz W. Kramer und Alf Lüdtke," *Historische Anthropologie* 12 (2004): 164.
50. Nahoum-Grappe, "Anthropologie de la violence extrême," 606.
51. See statement by Rywka Awronska on 15 February 1978, HStA Düsseldorf, Ger. Rep. 432 No. 282, p. 6 (Ambach and Köhler, *Lublin-Majdanek*, 103); statement by Judith Gelbard on 15 August 1978, main hearing, HStA Düsseldorf, Ger. Rep. 432 No. 283, p. 2 (Ambach and Köhler, *Lublin-Majdanek*, 109); statement by Riwka Landau on 13 December 1978, main hearing, HStA Düsseldorf, Ger. Rep. 432 No. 284, p. 2 (Ambach and Köhler, *Lublin-Majdanek*, 117); statement by Towa Ledermann on 15 August 1978, main hearing, HStA Düsseldorf, Ger. Rep. 432 No. 284, p. 3 (Ambach and Köhler, *Lublin-Majdanek*, 119); statement by Henrika Mitron on 7 February 1979, main hearing, HStA Düsseldorf, Ger. Rep. 432 No. 285, p. 10 (Ambach and Köhler, *Lublin-Majdanek*, 125); statement by Dora Abend on 30 October 1978, main hearing, HStA Düsseldorf, Ger. Rep. 432 No. 282, p. 4 (Ambach and Köhler, *Lublin-Majdanek*, p. 99).
52. Statement by Charlotte Mayer (née Wöllert) on 28 August 1973 in Düsseldorf, HStA Düsseldorf, Ger. Rep. 432 No. 234, p. 46.
53. See figure 10.
54. Statement by Hermine Braunsteiner on 22 November 1949, main hearing, DÖW, LG Vienna Vg 1 Vr 5670/48, p. 205.
55. See statement by Rosa Süss (née Reischl) on 29 August 1973 in Düsseldorf, HStA Düsseldorf, Ger. Rep. 432 No. 252, p. 82.
56. Höss, in Martin Broszat, ed., *Kommandant in Auschwitz. Autobiographische Aufzeichnungen des Rudolf Höss*, 17th ed. (Munich, 2000), 180ff.
57. Letter of the Reichsführer-SS to Pohl and Glücks on 8 February 1943, Ravensbrück Memorial/Foundation of Brandenburg Memorials (MGR/StBG), II/1–1-2.
58. Statement by Otto Z. on 28 May 1977 in Düsseldorf, HStA Düsseldorf, Ger. Rep. 432 No. 204, p. 140.
59. Statement by Otto Z. on 6 April 1977, main hearing, HStA Düsseldorf, Ger. Rep. 432 No. 287, p. 278.
60. Höss, in Broszat, ed., *Kommandant in Auschwitz*, 181ff.
61. Hildegard Lächert, in Eberhard Fechner, *Norddeutscher Rundfunk: Der Prozess: Eine Darstellung des Majdanek-Verfahrens in Düsseldorf*, videotape (1984), part 2.
62. Statement by Janina Rowska-Bot on 5 February 1979, main hearing, HStA Düsseldorf, Ger. Rep. 432 No. 286, pp. 6ff. (Ambach and Köhler, *Lublin-Majdanek*, 192ff.); see also statement by Barbara Briks on 8 December 1980, main hearing, HStA Düsseldorf, Ger. Rep. 432 No. 282, p. 5 (Ambach and Köhler, *Lublin-Majdanek*, 105).
63. Statement by Lola Givner on 14 December 1978, main hearing, HStA Düsseldorf, Ger. Rep. 432 No. 283, p. 3 (Ambach and Köhler, *Lublin-Majdanek*, 111); see also statement

by Paula Joskowitz on 8 February 1979, HStA Düsseldorf, Ger. Rep. 432 No. 284, pp. 3ff. (Ambach and Köhler, *Lublin-Majdanek*, 112ff.).

64. Thomas Lindenberger and Alf Lüdtke, eds., "Einleitung," in *Physische Gewalt. Studien zur Geschichte der Neuzeit* (Frankfurt am Main, 1995), 7–38, 7.
65. Barbara Schwindt, *Das Konzentrations- und Vernichtungslager Majdanek. Funktionswandel im Kontext der "Endlösung"* (Würzburg, 2005), 238.
66. See statement by Henrika Mitron on 14 March 1973 in New York, HStA Düsseldorf, Ger. Rep. 432 No. 227, p. 167.
67. Statement by Nechama Frenkel on 13 March 1962 in Ashkelon, HstA Düsseldorf, Ger. Rep. 432 No. 203, p. 11.
68. See Schwindt, *Das Konzentrations- und Vernichtungslager Majdanek*, 254–60.
69. See statement by Maryla Reich on 3 April 1962 in Tel Aviv, HStA Düsseldorf, Ger. Rep. 432 No. 225, p. 32.
70. See Schwindt, *Das Konzentrations- und Vernichtungslager Majdanek*, 261ff.
71. Statement by Teresa-Maria Slizewicz on 23 May 1972 in Warsaw, HStA Düsseldorf, Ger. Rep. 432 No. 235, pp. 80–81.
72. Statement by Danuta Czaykowska-Medryk on 22 January 1973 in Warsaw, HStA Düsseldorf, Ger. Rep. 432 No. 213, pp. 539–41; see also statement by Danuta Czaykowska-Medryk on 13 May 1977, main hearing, HStA Düsseldorf, Ger. Rep. 432 No. 285, p. 123 (Ambach and Köhler, *Lublin-Majdanek*, 166).
73. Statement by Luzie H., 21 December 1976, main hearing, notes of the prosecution, HStA Düsseldorf, Ger. Rep. 432 No. 285, pp. 175–77.
74. Another guard, Charlotte Wöllert, stated that she had heard in stories "that children were held in a special barracks on the women's field. What happened to the children I do not know. I never heard anything about that." See statement by Charlotte Mayer (née Wöllert) on 28 August 1973 in Düsseldorf, HStA Düsseldorf, Ger. Rep. 432 No. 234, p. 51.
75. Statement by Luzie H. on 21 December 1976, main hearing, HStA Düsseldorf, Ger. Rep. 432 No. 285, p. 178. See also statement by Alice Orlowski on 30 August 1973 in Düsseldorf, HStA Düsseldorf, Ger. Rep. 432 No. 252, pp. 89ff.
76. Statement by Luzie H., transcript of the main hearing, 21 December 1976, notes of the prosecution, HStA Düsseldorf, Ger. Rep. 432 No. 285, p. 176; see statement by Luzie H., Investigating Magistrate, Düsseldorf Regional Court, 8 November 1972, HStA Düsseldorf, Ger. Rep. 432 No. 292, p. 72.
77. Statement by Luzie H. on 8 November 1972 in Düsseldorf, HStA Düsseldorf, Ger. Rep. 432 No. 292, p. 72.
78. Luzie H., in Fechner, *Der Prozess*, part 2.
79. See Harald Welzer, *Täter. Wie aus ganz normalen Menschen Massenmörder werden, unter Mitarbeit von Manuela Christ* (Frankfurt am Main, 2005), 304–7, 173–88.
80. Statement by Antonia Kurcz on 29 November 1972 in Warsaw, HStA Düsseldorf Ger. Rep. 432 No. 237, pp. 495ff.; see also statement by Nechama Frenkel on 13 March 1962 in Ashkelon, HStA Düsseldorf Ger. Rep. 432 No. 203, p. 11.

81. See statement by Henrika Mitron on 7 February 1979, main hearing, HStA Düsseldorf, Ger. Rep. 432 No. 285, p. 8 (Ambach and Köhler, *Lublin-Majdanek*, 125); statement by Chela Apelbaum on 16 January 1979, main hearing, HStA Düsseldorf, Ger. Rep. 432 No. 282, p. 4 (Ambach and Köhler, *Lublin-Majdanek*, 100).
82. See Nahoum-Grappe, "L'usage politique de la cruauté," 311.
83. Welzer, *Täter*, 148.
84. Ibid., 161.
85. Nahoum-Grappe, "L'usage politique de la cruauté," 301, see also 308.
86. It conversely affects the relationship of violence and the transgression of boundaries. See Heinrich Popitz, *Phänomene der Macht* (Tübingen, 2004), 52ff.
87. Tillion, *Ravensbrück*, 139.
88. Statement by Towa Ledermann on 15 August 1978, main hearing, HStA Düsseldorf, Ger. Rep. 432 No. 284, pp. 3–4 (Ambach and Köhler, *Lublin-Majdanek*, 119).
89. See statement by Chela Apelbaum on 16 January 1979, main hearing, HStA Düsseldorf, Ger. Rep. 432 No. 282, p. 4 (Ambach and Köhler, *Lublin-Majdanek*, 100); statement by Barbara Briks on 8 December 1980, main hearing, HStA Düsseldorf, Ger. Rep. 432 No. 282, p. 2 (Ambach and Köhler, *Lublin-Majdanek*, 104); statement by Henrika Mitron on 7 February 1979, main hearing, HStA Düsseldorf Ger. Rep. 432 No. 285, p. 4 (Ambach and Köhler, *Lublin-Majdanek*, 124); statement by Rachel Nurman on 24 April 1979, main hearing, HStA Düsseldorf, Ger. Rep. 432 No. 285, p. 3 (Ambach and Köhler, *Lublin-Majdanek*, 127).
90. Statement by Riwka Landau on 13 December 1978, main hearing, HStA Düsseldorf, Ger. Rep. 432 No. 284, p. 2 (Ambach and Köhler, *Lublin-Majdanek*, 117).
91. Statement by Lola Givner on 14 December 1978, main hearing, HStA Düsseldorf, Ger. Rep. 432 No. 283, p. 3.
92. Laura Sjoberg and Caron E. Gentry, *Mothers, Monsters, Whores: Women's Violence in Global Politics* (New York: Zed Books, 2007).
93. Nahoum-Grappe, "L'usage politique de la cruauté," 298ff.
94. Isa Vermehren, *Reise durch den letzten Akt. Ravensbrück, Buchenwald, Dachau: eine Frau berichtet* (Reinbek, 1979), 84. See also Charlotte Müller, *Die Klempnerkolonne in Ravensbrück. Erinnerungen des Häftlings Nr. 10787* (Berlin, 1990); Lucia Schmidt-Fels, *Deportiert nach Ravensbrück—Bericht einer Zeugin 1943–1945* (Düsseldorf, 1981); Nanda Herbermann, *Der gesegnete Abgrund. Schutzhäftling Nr. 6582 im Frauenkonzentrationslager Ravensbrück*, 4th ed. (Annweiler, 2002); Margarete Buber-Neumann, *Als Gefangene bei Stalin und Hitler. Eine Welt im Dunkel* (Berlin, 1997).
95. Vermehren, *Reise durch den letzten Akt*, 75ff.
96. Ibid., 75ff.
97. On 30 June 1981, Hildegard Lächert was sentenced to twelve years' imprisonment for "joint accessory to murder in two cases of 100 people in total"; Hermine Ryan-Braunsteiner was the only one of the defendants to be given a life sentence for "joint murder in two cases of 100 people in total." On the verdict, see Falko Kruse, "Das

Majdanek-Urteil. Von den Grenzen deutscher Rechtsprechung," *Kritische Justiz* 2 (1985): 140–58.

98. Hermann Hackmann, ten years' imprisonment for joint accessory to murder in two cases of 141 people in total; Emil Laurich, eight years' imprisonment for joint accessory to murder in five cases of 195 people in total; Heinz Villain, six years' imprisonment for joint accessory to murder of 41 people; Thomas Ellwanger, three years' imprisonment for joint accessory to murder of at least 41 people; Arnold Strippel, three and a half years' imprisonment for joint accessory to murder of 41 people. Heinrich Groffmann was cleared of all charges for lack of evidence. See HStA Düsseldorf, Ger. Rep. 432 No. 101ff.
99. See *Die Zeit*, 1 September 1978. The trial observer and journalist Ingrid Müller-Münch uses the guards' nicknames almost exclusively in her book on the "women of Majdanek"; Ingrid Müller-Münch, *Die Frauen von Majdanek. Vom zerstörten Leben der Opfer und der Mörderinnen* (Reinbek, 1982); see also the article by Thorsten Schmitz, "Die Stute von Majdanek," *Süddeutsche Zeitung Magazin*, 13 December 1996.
100. See Miranda Alison, "Wartime Sexual Violence: Women's Human Rights and Questions on Masculinity," *Review of International Studies* 33 (2007): 75–90; Sjoberg and Gentry, *Mothers, Monsters, Whores*.
101. Constanze Jaiser, "Repräsentation von Sexualität und Gewalt in Zeugnissen jüdischer und nichtjüdischer Überlebender," in *Genozid und Geschlecht. Jüdische Frauen im nationalsozialistischen Lagersystem*, ed. Gisela Bock (Frankfurt am Main, 2005), 123–48, 138.
102. Juliet Rogers, "The Pure Subject of Torture: Or, Lynndie England Does Not Exist," *Australian Feminist Law Journal* 35 (2011): 75–87.

Conclusion

1. Karin Orth, "Experten des Terrors. Die Konzentrationslager-SS und die Shoah," in *Die Täter der Shoah. Fanatische Nationalsozialisten oder ganz normale Deutsche?*, ed. Gerhard Paul (Göttingen: Wallstein, 2002), 93–108.

Bibliography

Archives

Archiwum Panstwowe Muzeum na Majdanku (APMM), Lublin

I.d.32 Dokumentensammlung

I.f.3 Dokumentensammlung

No. 164 Kopiensammlung

Bundesarchiv Berlin Lichterfelde (BA), Berlin

NS/3 SS-Wirtschaftsverwaltungshauptamt

NS/4 Konzentrationslager

R 58 Reichssicherheitshauptamt

BDC (former Berlin Document Center)

Dokumentationsarchiv des österreichischen Widerstandes (DÖW), Vienna

Landesgericht LG Graz 13/Vr 3329/63 (Investigation of Graz Regional Criminal Court in the matter of Alois K. and other SS members at the Lublin Concentration Camp)

Landesgericht LG Vienna Vg 1 Vr 5670/48 (Investigation and trial before the Vienna People's Court of Hermine Braunsteiner for war crimes and crimes against humanity at the Ravensbrück and Majdanek concentration camps)

Institut für Zeitgeschichte (IfZ), Munich

Fa 183/1 (Dokumentensammlung Konzentrationslager, Bundesarchiv Sammlung Schumacher 329)
Fa 506/12 (Dokumentensammlung Konzentrationslager)

Landesarchiv Nordrhein-Westfalen Hauptstaatsarchiv Düsseldorf (LAV NRW HStA Düsseldorf), Düsseldorf

Gerichte Republik 432 Konzentrationslager Lublin-Majdanek (ehemaliges Verfahren der Kölner Staatsanwaltschaft Az.: 8 KS 1/75)

No. 1-138 Hauptakten
No. 176-201 Vollstreckungs-, Bewährungs-, Gnaden- und Hafthefte
No. 202-261 Beschuldigtenhefte
No. 406-412 Beschuldigtenhefte
No. 283-302 Vernehmungsprotokolle
No. 355 Vernehmungsprotokolle der Verhörspersonen
No. 429/430 Polnische Dokumente über SS-Aufseherinnen
No. 278 (Historical expert opinion by Prof. Wolfgang Scheffler)

Mahn- und Gedenkstätte Ravensbrück/Stiftung Brandenburgische Gedenkstätten (MGR/StBG), Ravensbrück

FoII Fotomaterial
II/3-3-4 Dokumentensammlung

National Archives and Records Administration (NARA), Washington, DC

RG 338-000-50-011 Konzentrationslager Ravensbrück
Microfilm T84, roll 490 (Weather reports of the Wehrmacht for Eastern Europe)

Public Record Office (PRO) Kew, London

WO 235/15: KZ Bergen-Belsen: Belsen-Trial (First Bergen-Belsen Trial)
WO 309/429: KZ Bergen-Belsen: No 1 War Crimes Investigation Team, Depositions

Other Primary Sources

Films and Exhibitions

Cheroux, Clément, ed. Mémoire des camps. *Photographies des camps de concentration et d'extermination (1933–1999).* Exhibition catalog. Paris, 2001.

Das sichtbare Unfassbare. Fotografien vom Konzentrationslager Mauthausen. Katalog zur gleichnamigen Ausstellung. Amicales de Mauthausen, déportés et amis Paris, Amical de Mauthausen y otros campos Barcelona, Bundesministerium für Inneres. Vienna: Mandelbaum, 2005.

Fechner, Eberhard. *Norddeutscher Rundfunk: Der Prozess: Eine Darstellung des Majdanek-Verfahrens in Düsseldorf.* 1984. 3 parts (videotape), 270 min.

Hamburger Institut für Sozialforschung, ed. *Verbrechen der Wehrmacht. Dimensionen des Vernichtungskrieges 1941–1944.* Exhibition catalog. Hamburg, 2002.

Published Memoirs and Testimonies

Améry, Jean. "Die Tortur." In *Jenseits von Schuld und Sühne. Bewältigungsversuche eines Überwältigten,* 41–70. 2nd ed. Munich: Klett, 1966.

Berger, Karin, Elisabeth Holzinger, Lotte Podgornik, and Lisbeth N. Trallori, eds. *"Ich geb Dir einen Mantel, dass Du ihn noch in Freiheit tragen kannst." Widerstehen im KZ. Österreichische Frauen erzählen.* Vienna, 1987.

Brosko-Medryk, Danuta. "Niebo bez ptaków." Warsaw, 1968. *Der Himmler ohne Vögel* (1975), German translation at the Hauptstaatsarchiv Düsseldorf, Gerichte Republik 432 No. 416.

Broszat, Martin, ed. *Kommandant in Auschwitz. Autobiographische Aufzeichnungen des Rudolf Höss.* 17th ed. Munich, 2000.

Buber-Neumann, Margarete. *Als Gefangene bei Stalin und Hitler. Eine Welt im Dunkel.* 1949; Berlin, 1997.

Camps de Concentration. Crimes contre la personne humaine. Documents pour servir à l'histoire de la guerre. Office Française d'édition. Fontenay-aux-Roses, November 1945.

Fabius, Odette. *Sonnenaufgang über der Hölle.* Berlin, 1997.

Fechner, Eberhard. Transcription of interview with Erna Wallisch, 15 June 1980, manuscript (private collection), 41 pages. Portions have been reprinted in *Falter* 7 (2008): 14–15.

Glazar, Richard. *Die Falle mit dem grünen Zaun: Überleben in Treblika.* Frankfurt am Main, 1992.

Gorondowski, Stanislaw. "Bericht über Mauthausen." *Dachauer Hefte* 2 (1986): 123–32.

Greif, Gideon. *"Wir weinten tränenlos." Augenzeugenberichte des jüdischen "Sonderkommandos" in Auschwitz.* 1995; Frankfurt am Main, 2001.

Hamburger Institut für Sozialforschung, ed. *Die Auschwitz-Hefte. Texte der polnischen Zeitschrift "Przeglad Lekarski" über historische, psychische und medizinische Aspekte des Lebens und Sterbens in Auschwitz.* 2 vols. Weinheim, 1987.

Herbermann, Nanda. *Der gesegnete Abgrund. Schutzhäftling Nr. 6582 im Frauenkonzentrationslager Ravensbrück.* 4th expanded edition. Annweiler, 2002.

Kocwa, Eugenia. *Flucht aus Ravensbrück.* Berlin/Ost, 1973.

Kogon, Eugen. *Der SS-Staat. Das System der deutschen Konzentrationslager.* 1945; Munich, 2000.

Lenard, Dionys. "Flucht aus Majdanek." *Dachauer Hefte* 7 (1991): 144–73.

Levi, Primo. *I sommersi e i salvati.* 1986; Torino, 2003.

———. *The Drowned and the Saved.* Translated by Raymond Rosenthal. New York: Summit Books, 1988.

Müller, Charlotte. *Die Klempnerkolonne in Ravensbrück. Erinnerungen des Häftlings Nr. 10787.* Berlin, 1990.

Neurath, Paul Martin, *Die Gesellschaft des Terrors. Innenansicht der Konzentrationslager Dachau und Buchenwald.* 1951; Frankfurt am Main, 2004.

Pawalk, Zacheusz. *"Ich habe überlebt . . ." Ein Häftling berichtet.* Hamburg, 1979.

Präg, Werner, Wolfgang Jacobmeyer, and Hans Frank. *Das Diensttagebuch des deutschen Generalgouverneurs in Polen 1939–1945.* Stuttgart, 1975.

Rousset, David. *L'Univers concentrationnaire.* Paris: Editions du Pavois, 1946.

Schmidt-Fels, Lucia. *Deportiert nach Ravensbrück—Bericht einer Zeugin 1943–1945.* Düsseldorf, 1981.

Strigler, Mordekhai. *Maidanek. Lumières consommées.* Texte traduit du yiddish par Maurice Pfeffer. Paris, 1998.

Tillion, Germaine. *Ravensbrück.* Paris, 1988.

Vermehren, Isa. *Reise durch den letzten Akt. Ravensbrück, Buchenwald, Dachau: eine Frau berichtet.* 1946; Reinbek, 1979.

Secondary Literature

Adler, H[ans] G[ünther]. "Selbstverwaltung und Widerstand in den Konzentrationslagern der SS." *Vierteljahrshefte für Zeitgeschichte* 8 (1960): 221–36.

———. *Theresienstadt 1941–1945. Das Antlitz einer Zwangsgemeinschaft. Geschichte, Soziologie, Psychologie.* Tübingen, 1960.

Alison, Miranda. "Wartime Sexual Violence: Women's Human Rights and Questions on Masculinity." *Review of International Studies* 33 (2007): 75–90.

Aly, Götz. *"Endlösung." Völkerverschiebung und der Mord an den europäischen Juden.* Frankfurt am Main, 1995.

———. *"Final Solution": Nazi Population Policy and the Murder of the European Jews.* Translated by Belinda Cooper and Allison Brown. New York: Oxford University Press, 1999.

———. *Hitlers Volksstaat. Raub, Rassenkrieg und nationaler Sozialismus.* Frankfurt am Main: S. Fischer, 2005.

Aly, Götz, and Susanne Heim. *Vordenker der Vernichtung. Auschwitz und die deutschen Pläne für eine neue europäische Ordnung.* Frankfurt am Main, 2004.

Améry, Jean. *At the Mind's Limits.* Bloomington: Indiana University Press, 2009.

Anschütz, Janet, and Irmtraud Heike. *Feinde im eigenen Land. Zwangsarbeit in Hannover im Zweiten Weltkrieg.* Bielefeld, 2000.

Ambach, Dieter, and Thomas Köhler, eds. *Lublin-Majdanek. Das Konzentrations- und Vernichtungslager im Spiegel von Zeugenaussagen.* Vol. 12 of *Juristische Zeitgeschichte.* Düsseldorf, 2003.

Armanski, Gerhard. "Der GULag—Zwangsjacke des Fortschritts." In *Strategien des Überlebens: Häftlingsgesellschaften in KZ und Gulag*, ed. Hans Schafranek and Robert Streibel, 16–43. Vienna: Picus Verlag, 1996.

———. Maschinen des Terrors: das Lager (KZ und GULAG) in der Moderne. Münster:

Westfalisches Dampfboot, 1993.

Arndt, Ino. Das Frauenkonzentrationslager Ravensbrück. *Dachauer Hefte* 3 (1987): 125–57.

Assmann, Aleida, Frank Hiddemann, and Eckard Schwarzenberger, eds. *Firma Topf & Söhne: Hersteller der Öfen für Auschwitz. Ein Fabrikgelände als Erinnerungsort?* New York, 2002.

ATG26. *Ruptures of the Everyday: Views of Modern Germany from the Ground.* New York: Berghahn Books, forthcoming.

Bauer, Ingrid. "Eine frauen- und geschlechterspezifische Perspektivierung des Nationalsozialismus." In *NS-Herrschaft in Österreich 1938–1945*, ed. Emmerich Talos, Ernst Hanisch, and Wolfgang Neugebauer, 407–43. Rev. ed. Vienna, 2000.

Bauman, Zygmunt. *Modernity and the Holocaust.* Ithaca, NY: Cornell University Press, 1989.

Benz, Wolfgang, and Barbara Distel, eds. *Herrschaft und Gewalt. Frühe Konzentrationslager 1933–1939.* Berlin, 2002.

———, eds. *Terror ohne System. Die ersten Konzentrationslager 1933–1945.* Vol. 1. Berlin, 2001.

Berger, Karin. "Hut ab Frau Sedlmayer! Zur Militarisierung und Ausbeutung von Frauen im nationalsozialistischen Österreich." In *NS-Herrschaft in Österreich 1838–1945*, ed. Emmerich Talos, Ernst Hanisch, and Wolfgang Neugebauer, 141–59. Vienna, 1988.

Bergerson, Andrew Stuart. *Ordinary Germans in Extraordinary Times: The Nazi Revolution in Hildesheim.* Bloomington: Indiana University Press, 2004.

Bergerson, A. S., E. Mailänder Koslov, G. Reuveni, P. Steege, and D. Sweeney. "Forum: Everyday Life in Nazi Germany." *German History* 27, no. 4 (2009): 560–79.

Bergmann, Klaus, and Susanne Thun. "Didaktik der Alltagsgeschichte." In *Handbuch der Geschichtsdidaktik*, ed. Klaus Bergmann et al., 315–20. 3rd rev. and expanded edition. Düsseldorf: Schwann, 1985.

Bezwinska, Jadwiga, and Danuta Czech. *KL Auschwitz Seen by the SS: Hoess, Broad, Kremer.* Selection, elaboration, and notes. New York: Howard Fertig, 2007.

Birn, Ruth Bettina. *Die Höheren SS- und Polizeiführer, Himmlers Vertreter im Reich und in den besetzten Gebieten.* Düsseldorf, 1986.

Black, Monica. *Death in Berlin: From Weimar to Divided Germany.* Cambridge: Cambridge University Press, 2010.

Black, Peter. "Die Trawniki-Männer und die 'Aktion Reinhard.'" In *"Aktion Reinhardt." Der Völkermord an den Juden im Generalgouvernement 1941–1944*, ed. Bogdan Musial, 309–52. Osnabrück, 2004.

———. "Odilo Globocnik, Himmlers Vorposten im Osten." In *Die SS: Elite unter dem Totenkopf. 30 Lebensläufe*, ed. Roland Smelser and Enrico Syring, 103–15. Paderborn, 2000.

Blatman, Daniel. *Les marches de la mort. La dernière étape du génocide nazi, été 1944–printemps 1945.* Paris: Fayard, 2009.

Bock, Gisela, ed. *Genozid und Geschlecht. Jüdische Frauen im nationalsozialistischen Lagersystem.* Frankfurt am Main, 2005.

Bourdieu, Pierre. "Die biographische Illusion." *BIOS, Zeitschrift für Biographieforschung und Oral-History* 1 (1990): 75–82.

———. "L'illusion biographique." *Actes de la Recherche en Sciences Sociales* 62–63 (June 1986): 69–72, 71.

Braun, Christina von. *Nichtich: (Logik, Lüge, Libido)*. Frankfurt am Main, 1990.

Brayard, Florent. *La "solution finale de la question juive." La technique, le temps et les catégories de la décision*. Paris, 2004.

Breitman, Richard. *The Architect of Genocide: Himmler and the Final Solution*. Hanover, NH: University Press of New England, 1992.

Brockhaus, Gudrun. *Schauder und Idylle. Faschismus als Erlebnisangebot*. Munich, 1997.

Broszat, Martin. "Nationalsozialistische Konzentrationslager 1933–1945." In *Anatomie des SS-Staates*, ed. Hans Buchheim, Martin Broszat, Hans-Adolf Jacobsen, and Helmut Krausnick, 2:323–477. Munich, 1999.

———. *Nationalsozialistische Polenpolitik 1939–1945* (Schriftenreihe der Vierteljahrshefte für Zeitgeschichte, No. 2). Stuttgart, 1961.

Browning, Christopher R. "Die nationalsozialistische Ghettoisierungspolitik in Polen 1939–1941." In *Der Weg zur "Endlösung." Entscheidungen und Täter*, 37–65. Berlin, 1998.

———. "Die nationalsozialistische Umsiedlungspolitik und die Suche nach einer 'Lösung der Judenfrage' 1939–1941." In Christopher R. Browning, *Der Weg zur "Endlösung." Entscheidungen und Täter*, 13–36. Berlin, 1998.

———. "From 'Ethnic Cleansing' to Genocide to the 'Final Solution': The Evolution of Nazi Jewish Policy, 1939–1941." In Christopher R. Browning, *Nazi Policy, Jewish Workers, German Killers*, 1–25. New York: Cambridge University Press, 2000.

———. *Ganz normale Männer. Das Reserve-Polizeibataillon 101 und die "Endlösung" in Polen*. Reinbek, 1999.

———. "German Memory, Juridical Interrogation, and Historical Reconstruction: Writing Perpetrator History from Postwar Testimony." In *Probing the Limits of Representation: Nazism and the "Final Solution,"* ed. Saul Friedländer, 22–36. Cambridge, MA: Harvard University Press, 1992.

———. "Nazi Policy: Decisions for the Final Solution." In Christopher R. Browning, *Nazi Policy, Jewish Workers, German Killers*, pp. 26–57. New York: Cambridge University Press, 2000.

———. *Nazi Policy, Jewish Workers, German Killers*. New York: Cambridge University Press, 2000.

———. "Nazi Resettlement Policy and the Search for a Solution for the Jewish Question, 1939–1941." In *The Path to Genocide: Essays on Launching the Final Solution*. New York: Cambridge University Press, 1992.

———. *Ordinary Men: Reserve Police Battalion 101 and the Final Solution in Poland*. New York: HarperCollins, 1992.

———. *The Path to Genocide: Essays on Launching the Final Solution*. New York: Cambridge University Press, 1992.

———. *Remembering Survival: Inside a Nazi Slave Labor Camp*. New York: Norton 2010.

Brücker, Eva. "'Und ich bin heil da 'rausgekommen.' Gewalt und Sexualität in einer Berliner Arbeiternachbarschaft zwischen 1916/17 und 1958." In *Physische Gewalt. Studien zur Geschichte der Neuzeit*, ed. Thomas Lindenberger and Alf Lüdtke. Frankfurt am Main, 1995.

Bruckmüller, Ernst. *Sozialgeschichte Österreichs*. Vienna, 2001.

Buchheim, Hans. "Befehl und Gehorsam." In *Anatomie des SS-Staates*, ed. Hans Buchheim, Martin Broszat, Hans-Adolf Jacobsen, and Helmut Krausnick, 215–320. Munich, 1999.

———. "Die Sondergerichtsbarkeit der SS und Polizei." In *Anatomie des SS-Staates*, ed. Hans Buchheim, Martin Broszat, Hans-Adolf Jacobsen, and Helmut Krausnick, 153–60. Munich, 1999.

Buggeln, Marc. *Slave Labor in Nazi Concentration Camps*. Oxford: Oxford University Press, 2014.

Burin, Philippe. *Hitler et les juifs. Génèse d'un génocide*. Paris, 1989.

Canetti, Elias. *Crowds and Power*. Translated by Carol Stewart. New York: Continuum, 1962.

Caplan, Jane, and Nikolaus Wachsmann, eds. *Concentration Camps in Nazi Germany: The New Histories*. London: Routledge, 2010.

Casagrande, Thomas. *Die Volksdeutsche SS-Division "Prinz Eugen." Die Banater Schwaben und die nationalsozialistischen Kriegsverbrechen*. Frankfurt am Main, 2003.

Cehreli, Ayse Sila. "Chełmno, Bełzec, Sobibór, Treblinka: Politique génocidaire nazie et résistance juive dans les centres de mise à mort (novembre 1941–janvier 1945)." Thèse d'histoire présentée à l'université Paris I–Panthéon Sorbonne, 2007.

———. *Témoignage du Khurbn. La résistance juive dans les centres de mise à mort—Chełmno, Bełzec, Sobibór, Treblinka*. Paris: Éditions Kimé, 2013.

Cramer, John. *Belsen Trial 1945. Der Lüneburger Prozess gegen Wachpersonal der Konzentrationslager Auschwitz und Bergen-Belsen* (Bergen-Belsen—Dokumente und Forschungen 1). Göttingen: Wallstein Verlag, 2011.

Cramer, John. "Farce oder Vorbild? Der erste Belsen-Prozess in Lüneburg 1945." In *Tatort KZ. Neue Beiträge zur Geschichte der Konzentrationslager*, ed. Ulrich Fritz, Silvija Kavčič, and Nicole Warmbold, 201–19. Ulm, 2003.

———. "'Tapfer, unbescholten und mit reinem Gewissen.' KZ-Aufseherinnen im ersten Belsen-Prozess eines britischen Militärgerichts 1945." In *"Im Gefolge der SS": Aufseherinnen des Frauen-KZ Ravensbrück. Begleitband zur Ausstellung*, ed. Simone Erpel, 103–13. Berlin, 2007.

Das Generalgouvernement. Reisehandbuch von Karl Baedeker. Leipzig, 1943.

Didi-Huberman, Georges. "Das Öffnen der Lager und das Schließen der Augen." In *Auszug aus dem Lager. Zur Überwindung des modernen Raumparadigmas in der politischen Philosophie*, ed. Ludger Schwarte, 11–41. Berlin, 2007.

———. *Die Erfindung der Hysterie. Die photographische Klinik von Jean-Martin Charcot*. Paderborn, 1997.

———. *Images malgré tout*. Paris, 2003.

Diehl, Paula. *Macht—Mythos—Utopie. Die Körperbilder der SS-Männer*. Berlin, 2005.

———. "'Opfer der Vergangenheit': Konstruktion eines Feindbildes." In *Abgeschlossene Kapitel? Zur Geschichte der Konzentrationslager und NS-Prozesse*, ed. Sabine Moller, Miriam Rürup, and Christel Trouvé, 134–44. Tübingen, 2002.

Dossmann, Axel, Jan Wenzel, and Kai Wenzel. *Architektur auf Zeit. Baracken, Pavillons, Container*. Berlin, 2006.

Drobisch, Klaus. "Frauenkonzentrationslager im Schloß Lichtenburg." *Dachauer Hefte* 3 (1987): 101–15.

Drobisch, Klaus, and Günther Wieland. *System der Konzentrationslager 1933–1939*. Berlin, 1993.

Dülmen, Richard van. *Theater des Schreckens. Gerichtspraxis und Strafrituale der frühen Neuzeit*. Munich, 1985.

Ebert, Jens, and Insa Eschebach. *"Die Kommandeuse." Erna Dorn—zwischen Nationalsozialismus und Kaltem Krieg*. Berlin, 1994.

Ehalt, Hubert C. "Geschichte von unten." In *Geschichte von unten. Fragestellungen, Methoden und Projekte einer Geschichte des Alltags*, ed. Hubert C. Ehalt, 11–39. Vienna, 1984.

Eley, Geoff. *A Crooked Line: From Cultural History to the History of Society*. Ann Arbor: University of Michigan Press, 2005.

———. *Nazism as Fascism: Violence, Ideology, and the Ground of Consent in Germany, 1930–1945*. New York: Routledge, 2013.

Elling, Hanna. *Frauen im Widerstand 1933–1945*. Frankfurt am Main, 1978.

Emmelius, Simone. *Fechners Methode. Studien zu seinen Gesprächsfilmen*. Mainz, 1996.

Erpel, Simone, ed. *"Im Gefolge der SS": Aufseherinnen des Frauen-KZ Ravensbrück. Begleitband zur Ausstellung*. Berlin, 2007.

Eschebach, Insa, ed. "Das Aufseherinnenhaus. Überlegungen zu einer Ausstellung über SS-Aufseherinnen in der Gedenkstätte Ravensbrück." *Gedenkstätten Rundbrief*, no. 75 (March 1997): 1–11.

———. "'Ich bin unschuldig.' Vernehmungsprotokolle als historische Quellen. Der Rostocker Ravensbrück-Prozeß 1966." *Werkstatt Geschichte* 12 (1995): 65–70.

———. "NS-Prozesse in der sowjetischen Besatzungszone und der DDR. Einige Überlegungen zu den Strafverfahrensakten ehemaliger SS- Aufseherinnen des Frauenkonzentrationslagers Ravensbrück." In *Die frühen Nachkriegsprozesse. Beiträge zur Geschichte der nationalsozialistischen Verfolgung in Norddeutschland*, ed. Kurt Buck (Bremen: Edition Temmen, 1997), 3:65–74.

———. *Ravensbrück. Der Zellenbau. Geschichte und Gedenken*. Vol. 18, *Schriftenreihe der Stiftung Brandenburgischer Gedenkstätten*. Berlin, 2008.

———. "SS-Aufseherinnen des Frauenkonzentrationslagers Ravensbrück. Erinnerungen ehemaliger Häftlinge." *WerkstattGeschichte* 13 (1996): 39–48.

Evans, Richard J. *Rituals of Retribution: Capital Punishment in Germany, 1600–1987*. New York: Oxford University Press, 1996.

Fischer-Lichte, Erika. *Ästhetik des Performativen*. Frankfurt am Main, 2004.

———. "Performance, Inszenierung, Ritual. Zur Klärung kulturwissenschaftlicher

Schlüsselbegriffe." In *Geschichtswissenschaft und "Performative Turn." Ritual, Inszenierung und Performanz vom Mittelalter bis zur Neuzeit*, ed. Jürgen Martschukat and Stefan Patzold, 33–54. Cologne, 2003.

Foucault, Michel. "Die Maschen der Macht." In Michel Foucault, *Analytik der Macht*, ed. Daniel Defert and François Ewald, with assistance from Jacques Lagrange, 220–39. Frankfurt am Main, 2005.

———. *The History of Sexuality*. Vol. 1. Translated from the French by Robert Hurley. New York, 1988.

———. "Les mailles du pouvoir." In Michel Foucault, *Dits et écrits II, 1976–1988*, ed. Daniel Defert and François Ewald, with assistance from Jacques Lagrange, 1001–23. Paris, 2001.

———. "The Meshes of Power." In *Space, Knowledge and Power: Foucault and Geography*, ed J. W. Crampton and S. Eldon. Aldershot: Ashgate, 2007.

———. *Sexualität und Wahrheit. Erster Band. Der Wille zum Wissen*. Frankfurt am Main, 1977.

———. "The Subject and Power." *Critical Inquiry* 8, no. 4 (Summer 1982): 777–95.

———. "Subjekt und Macht." In Michel Foucault, *Analytik der Macht*, ed. Daniel Defert and François Ewald, with assistance from Jacques Lagrange, 240–63. Frankfurt am Main, 2005.

———. "Le sujet et le pouvoir." In Michel Foucault, *Dits et écrits II, 1976–1988*, ed. Daniel Defert and François Ewald, with assistance from Jacques Lagrange, 1041–69. Paris, 2001.

———. *Surveiller et punir: Naissance de la prison*. Paris, 2002.

———. *Überwachen und Strafen. Die Geburt des Gefängnisses*. Frankfurt am Main, 1994.

Friedler, Eric, Barbara Siebert, and Andreas Kilian. *Zeugen aus der Todeszone. Das jüdische Sonderkommando in Auschwitz*. Munich, 2005.

Füllberg-Stolberg, Claus, et al., eds. *Frauen in Konzentrationslagern. Bergen-Belsen, Ravensbrück*. Bremen: Edition Temmen, 1994.

Furber, David. "Going East: Colonialism and German Life in Nazi-Occupied Poland." PhD diss., SUNY Buffalo, 2003.

Füssel, Marian. "Die Kunst der Schwachen. Zum Begriff der 'Aneignung' in der Geschichtswissenschaft." *Sozial.Geschichte* 21, no. 3 (2006): 7–28.

Gabriel, Ralph. "Nationalsozialistische Biopolitik und die Architektur der Konzentrationslager." In *Auszug aus dem Lager. Zur Überwindung des modernen Raumparadigmas in der politischen Philosophie*, ed. Ludger Schwarte, 201–19. Berlin, 2007.

Gehmacher, Johanna, Elizabeth Harvey, and Sophia Kemlein, eds. *Zwischen Kriegen: Nationen, Nationalismen und Geschlechterverhältnisse in Mittel- und Osteuropa 1918–1939*. Osnabrück, 2004.

Gerlach, Christian. "Die Ausweitung der deutschen Massenmorde in den besetzten sowjetischen Gebieten im Herbst 1941. Überlegungen zur Vernichtungspolitik gegen Juden und sowjetische Kriegsgefangene." In Christian Gerlach, *Krieg, Ernährung,*

Völkermord. Deutsche Vernichtungspolitik im Zweiten Weltkrieg. Zürich, 2001.

———. "Die Wannsee-Konferenz, das Schicksal der deutschen Juden und Hitlers politische Grundsatzentscheidung, alle Juden Europas zu ermorden." In Christian Gerlach, *Krieg, Ernährung, Völkermord. Deutsche Vernichtungspolitik im Zweiten Weltkrieg*, 79–152. Zürich, 2001.

Goethe, Johann Wolfgang von. *Italienische Reise I*. In *Sämtliche Werke*, vol. 15:1, ed. Christoph Ditzel and Hans Georg Dewitz. Frankfurt am Main, 1993.

Goldhagen, Daniel J. *Hitler's Willing Executioners: Ordinary Germans and the Holocaust*. New York: Knopf, 1996.

Grau, Günter. *Homosexualität in der NS-Zeit*. Frankfurt am Main, 1993.

Grode, Walter. *Die "Sonderbehandlung 14f13" in den Konzentrationslagern des Dritten Reiches. Ein Beitrag zur Dynamik faschistischer Vernichtungspolitik*. Frankfurt am Main, 1987.

Gryn, Edward, and Zofia Murawska. *Das Konzentrationslager Majdanek*. Translated by Rita Jusiak. Lublin, 1966.

Hachtmann, Rüdiger. *Industriearbeit im Dritten Reich*. Göttingen, 1989.

Hamann, Brigitte. *Hitlers Vienna. Lehrjahre eines Diktators*. Munich, 1996.

Harvey, Elizabeth. "Erinnern und Verdrängen. Deutsche Frauen und der 'Volkstumskampf' im besetzten Polen." In *Heimat-Front. Militär und Geschlechterverhältnisse im Zeitalter der Weltkriege*, ed. Karen Hagemann and Stefanie Schüler-Springorum, 291–310. New York: Campus Verlag, 2002.

———. *Women and the Nazi East: Agents and Witnesses of Germanization*. New Haven: Yale University Press, 2003.

Hauch, Gabriella, ed. *Frauen in Oberdonau. Geschlechterspezifische Bruchlinien im Nationalsozialismus*. Linz, 2006.

Hausen, Karin, ed. *Geschlechterhierarchie und Arbeitsteilung. Zur Geschichte ungleicher Erwerbschancen von Männern und Frauen*. Göttingen, 1993.

Heberer, Patricia L. "'Exitus heute in Hadamar': The Hadamar Facility and 'Euthanasia' in Nazi Germany." PhD diss., University of Maryland, 2001.

Heike, Irmtraud, "'... da es sich ja lediglich um die Bewachung der Häftlinge handelt ...' Lagerverwaltung und Bewachungspersonal." In *Frauen in Konzentrationslagern. Bergen-Belsen, Ravensbrück*, ed. Claus Füllberg-Stolberg et al., 221–40. Bremen, 1994.

———. "Johanna Langefeld—Die Biographie einer Oberaufseherin." *WerkstattGeschichte* 12 (1995): 7–19.

Heineman, Elizabeth. "The Hour of the Woman: Memories of Germany's 'Crisis Years' and West German National Identity." *American Historical Review* 101, no. 2 (1996): 354–95.

Heise, Ljiljana. *KZ-Aufseherinnen vor Gericht. Greta Bösel—"Another of Those Brutal Types of Women?"* Frankfurt am Main: Peter Lang, 2009.

Herbert, Ulrich. *Fremdarbeiter. Politik und Praxis des "Ausländer Einsatzes" in der Kriegswirtschaft in Deutschland 1938–1945*. Berlin, 1985.

———. "Von der Gegnerbekämpfung zur 'rassischen Generalprävention.' 'Schutzhaft' und Konzentrationslager in der Konzeption der Gestapo-Führung 1933–1939." In *Die nationalsozialistischen Konzentrationslager: Entwicklung und Struktur*, ed. Christoph Dieckmann, Ulrich Herbert, and Karin Orth, 1:60–86. Göttingen: Wallstein, 1998.

Hilberg, Raul. *Die Vernichtung der europäischen Juden*. Frankfurt am Main, 1990.

Herz, Gabriele. *The Women's Camp in Moringen: A Memoir of Imprisonment in Germany, 1936–1937*. New York: Berghahn, 2006.

Hoffmann-Holter, Beatrix. "'Ostjuden hinaus!' Jüdische Kriegsflüchtlinge in Vienna 1914–1924." In *Die Stadt ohne Juden*, ed. Gutram Geser and Armin Loacker. Edition Film und Text 3. Vienna: Film Archiv Austria, 2000.

Hördler, Stefan. *Ordnung und Inferno. Das KZ-System im letzten Kriegsjahr*. Göttingen: Wallstein, 2014.

Horn, Sabine, "'. . . ich fühlte mich damals als Soldat und nicht als Nazi.' Der Majdanek-Prozess im Fernsehen—aus geschlechtergeschichtlicher Perspektive betrachtet." In *"Bestien" und "Befehlsempfänger." Frauen und Männer in NS-Prozessen nach 1945*, ed. Ulricke Weckel and Edgar Wolfrum, 222–49. Göttingen, 2003.

Horwitz, Gordon J. *In the Shadow of Death: Living outside the Gates of Mauthausen*. New York: Free Press, 1990.

Hulverscheidt, Marion. "Menschen, Mücken und Malaria—Das wissenschaftliche Umfeld des KZ-Malariaforschers Claus Schilling." In *Medizin im Nationalsozialismus und das System der Konzentrationslager*, ed. Judith Hahn, Silvija Kavčič, and Christoph Kopke, 108–26. Frankfurt am Main, 2005.

Ingrao, Christian. *Les chasseurs noirs. La brigade Dirlewanger*. Paris, 2006.

———. "Conquérir, aménager, exterminer. Recherches récentes sur la Shoah." *Annales* 2 (2003): 417–38.

———. "Culture de guerre, imaginaire nazi, violence génocide. Le cas des cadres du S.D." *Revue d'histoire moderne et contemporaine* 2 (2000): 265–89.

———. "Violence de guerre, violence génocide: les Einsatzgruppen." In *La Violence de guerre 1914–1945. Approches comparées des deux conflits mondiaux*, ed. Stéphane Audoin-Rouzeau, Annette Becker, Christian Ingrao, and Henry Rousso, 219–41. Brussels, 2002.

Jäger, Herbert. *Verbrechen unter totalitärer Herrschaft. Studien zur nationalsozialistischen Gewaltkriminalität*. Frankfurt am Main, 1982.

Jaiser, Constanze. "Repräsentation von Sexualität und Gewalt in Zeugnissen jüdischer und nichtjüdischer Überlebender." In *Genozid und Geschlecht. Jüdische Frauen im nationalsozialistischen Lagersystem*, ed. Gisela Bock, 123–48. Frankfurt am Main, 2005.

Jellonnek, Burkhard. *Homosexuelle unterm Hakenkreuz. Die Verfolgung von Homosexuellen im Dritten Reich*. Paderborn, 1990.

Jensen, Olaf, and Harald Welzer. "Ein Wort gibt das andere, oder: Selbstreflexivität als Methode." *Forum: Qualitative Sozialforschung/Forum: Qualitative Social Research* 4, no. 2, art. 32 (May 2003). http://www.qualitative-research.net/index.php/fqs/article/view/705/1528.

Kabel, Walter. *Die Bajadere Mola Pur*. Berlin, 1926.

Kaienburg, Hermann. *"Vernichtung durch Arbeit." Der Fall Neuengamme. Die Wirtschaftsbestrebungen der SS und ihre Auswirkungen auf die Existenzbedingungen der KZ-Gefangenen*. Bonn, 1990.

Keller, Sven. *Günzburg und der Fall Mengele. Die Heimatstadt und die Jagd nach dem NS-Verbrecher*. Munich, 2003.

Kepplinger, Brigitte. "Frauen in der Tötungsanstalt: Der weibliche Anteil an den Euthanasiemorden in Hartheim." In *Frauen in Oberdonau. Geschlechterspezifische Bruchlinien im Nationalsozialismus*, ed. Gabriella Hauch, 381–98. Linz, 2006.

Kirstein, Wolfgang. *Das Konzentrationslager als Institution totalen Terrors. Das Beispiel des KL Natzweiler*. Pfaffenweiler: Centaurus-Verlagsgesellschaft, 1992.

Klee, Ernst, and Willi Dressen. "Gott mit uns." *Der deutsche Vernichtungskrieg im Osten 1939–1945*. Frankfurt am Main, 1989.

Kleiber, Lore. "'Wo ihr seid, da soll die Sonne scheinen!' Der Frauenarbeitsdienst am Ende der Weimarer Republik und im Nationalsozialismus." In *Mutterkreuz und Arbeitsbuch. Zur Geschichte der Frauen in der Weimarer Republik und im Nationalsozialismus*, ed. Frauengruppe Faschismusforschung, 188–214. Frankfurt am Main, 1981.

Köhler, Thomas. "Historische Realität versus subjektive Erinnerungstradierung? Überlegungen anhand von Zeugenaussagen des 'Majdanek-Prozesses.'" In *Lagersystem und Repräsentation. Interdisziplinäre Studien zur Geschichte der Konzentrationslager*, ed. Ralph Gabriel, Elissa Mailänder Koslov, Monika Neuhofer, and Else Rieger, 140–55. Tübingen, 2003.

Konrad, Helmut. "Zur Theorie und Methodik der Alltagsgeschichtsschreibung." In *Geschichte und ihre Quellen. Festschrift für Friedrich Hausmann*, 591–99. Graz, 1987.

Kopke, Christoph. "Das KZ als Experimentierfeld: Ernst Günther Schenck und die Plantage in Dachau." In *Lagersystem und Repräsentation. Interdisziplinäre Studien zur Geschichte der Konzentrationslager*, ed. Ralph Gabriel, Elissa Mailänder Koslov, Monika Neuhofer, and Else Rieger, 13–28. Tübingen, 2004.

Kotek, Joël, and Pierre Rigoulot. *Le siècle des camps. Détention, concentration, extermination. Cent ans de mal radical*. Paris, 2000.

Köwel, Gottfried. *Die heitere Welt von Spiegelberg*. Vienna, 1940.

Kranz, Tomasz. "Das KL Lublin—zwischen Planung und Realisierung." In *Die nationalsozialistischen Konzentrationslager—Entwicklung und Struktur*, ed. Ulrich Herbert, Karin Orth, and Christoph Dieckmann, 1:363–89. Göttingen, 1997.

———. "Das Konzentrationslager Majdanek und die 'Aktion Reinhardt.'" In *"Aktion Reinhardt." Der Völkermord an den Juden im Generalgouvernement 1941–1944*, ed. Bogdan Musial, 233–55. Osnabrück, 2004.

———. "Ewidencja Zgonow i Smiertelnose Wiezow KL Lublin." *Zeszyty Majdanka* 23 (2005): 7–53.

———. "Zeittafel." In *Unser Schicksal—eine Mahnung für Euch: Berichte und Erinnerungen der Häftlinge von Majdanek*, ed. Tomasz Kranz, 209–14. Lublin, 1994.

———. *Zur Erfassung der Häftlingssterblichkeit im Konzentrationslager Lublin*. Lublin, 2007.

Kruse, Falko. "Das Majdanek-Urteil. Von den Grenzen deutscher Rechtsprechung." *Kritische Justiz* (1985): 140–58.

Kundrus, Birthe. "Die Kolonien—'Kinder des Gefühls und der Phantasie.'" In *Phantasiereiche. Zur Kulturgeschichte des deutschen Kolonialismus*, ed. Birthe Kundrus. Frankfurt am Main, 2003.

———. "'Die Unmoral deutscher Soldatenfrauen.' Diskurs, Alltagsverhalten und Ahndungspraxis 1939–1945." In *Zwischen Karriere und Verfolgung. Handlungsräume von Frauen im nationalsozialistischen Deutschland*, ed. Kirsten Heinsohn, Barbara Vogel, and Ulrike Weckel. Frankfurt am Main, 1997.

———. "Entscheidungen für den Völkermord? Einleitende Überlegungen zu einem historiographischen Problem." *Mittelweg 36*, no. 6 (2006): 4–17.

———. "Handlungsräume. Zur Geschlechtergeschichte des Nationalsozialismus." In *Frauen und Widerstand. Schriftenreihe der Forschungsgemeinschaft 20. Juli*, ed. Jana Leichsenring, 1:14–35. Münster, 2003.

———. *"Kriegerfrauen." Sozialpolitik und Geschlechterverhältnisse im Ersten und Zweiten Weltkrieg in Deutschland.* Hamburg: Christians, 1995.

———. *Moderne Imperialisten. Das Kaiserreich im Spiegel seiner Kolonien.* Cologne, 2003.

Künzel, Christine. *Vergewaltigungslektüren. Zur Codierung sexueller Gewalt in Literatur und Recht.* Frankfurt am Main, 2003.

KZ-Gedenkstätte Neuengamme, ed. *Verfolgung Homosexueller im Nationalsozialismus—Beiträge zur Geschichte der nationalsozialistischen Verfolgung in Norddeutschland.* Bremen, 1999.

Koop, Volker. *In Hitlers Hand: "Sonder- und Ehrenhäftlinge" der SS.* Cologne: Böhlau Verlag, 2010.

Laborde, Denis. "Glauben und Wissen. Die Pariser Prozesse gegen politische Aktivisten aus dem Baskenland." *Historische Anthropologie. Kultur, Gesellschaft, Alltag* 9, no. 2 (2001): 254–69.

Lenarczyk, Wojcech, Andreas Mix, Johannes Schwartz, and Veronika Springmann, eds. *KZ-Verbrechen. Beiträge zur Geschichte der nationalsozialistischen Konzentrationslager und ihrer Erinnerung.* Berlin, 2007.

Lennar, Rolf. *Der ungefährliche Dritte.* Budweis, 1941.

Lim, Jie-Hyun. "Mapping Mass Dictatorship: Towards a Transnational History of Twentieth-Century Dictatorship." In *Gender Politics and Mass Dictatorship: Global Perspectives*, ed. Jie-Hyun Lim and Karen Petrone. New York: Palgrave Macmillan, 2011.

Lindenberger, Thomas, and Alf Lüdtke, eds. *Physische Gewalt. Studien zur Geschichte der Neuzeit.* Frankfurt am Main, 1995.

Lipp, Carola. *Schimpfende Weiber und patriotische Jungfrauen.* Moos/Baden-Baden: Elster, 1986.

Liulevicius, Vejas Gabriel. *Kriegsland Osten. Eroberung, Kolonisierung und Militärherrschaft im Ersten Weltkrieg.* Hamburg, 2002.

———. *War Land on the Eastern Front: Culture, National Identity, and German*

Occupation in World War I. Cambridge: Cambridge University Press, 2000.

Longerich, Peter. *Heinrich Himmler. Biographie.* Berlin, 2008.

——. *Heinrich Himmler: A Life.* Translated by Jeremy Noakes and Lesley Sharpe. New York: Oxford University Press, 2012.

Lower, Wendy. *Hitler's Furies: German Women in the Nazi Killing Fields.* New York: Houghton Mifflin Harcourt, 2013.

Luchsinger, Martin. *Mythos Italien. Denkbilder des Fremden in der deutschsprachigen Gegenwartsliteratur.* Cologne, 1996.

Lüdtke, Alf. "Alltag: Der blinde Fleck?" *Deutschland Archiv. Zeitschrift für das vereinigte Deutschland* 5 (2006): 894–901.

——. "Der Bann der Worte: 'Todesfabriken.' Vom Reden über den NS-Völkermord—das auch ein Verschweigen ist." *WerkstattGeschichte* 13 (1996): 5–18.

——. "Die Fiktion der Institution. Herrschaftspraxis und Vernichtung der europäischen Juden im 20. Jahrhundert." In *Institutionen und Ereignis. Über historische Praktiken und Vorstellungen gesellschaftlichen Ordnens*, ed. Reinhard Blänkner and Bernhard Jussen, 355–79. Göttingen: V & R, 1998.

——. "Die Kaserne." In *Orte des Alltags*, ed. Hans Gerhard Haupt. Munich, 1994.

——. "Einleitung." In Alf Lüdtke, *Eigen-Sinn: Fabrikalltag, Arbeitererfahrung und Politik vom Kaiserreich bis in den Faschismus*, 9–22. Hamburg, 1993.

——. "Einleitung." In *Herrschaft als soziale Praxis: Historische und sozialanthropologische Studien*, ed. Alf Lüdtke, 9–62. Göttingen, 1991.

——. "'Fehlgreifen in der Wahl der Mittel.' Optionen im Alltag militärischen Handelns." *Mittelweg 36*, no. 1 (2003): 61–75.

——. "Gewalt und Alltag im 20. Jahrhundert." In *Gewalt und Terror, 11 Vorlesungen*, ed. Wolfgang Bergsdorf, Dietmar Herz, and Hans Hoffmeister, 35–52. Weimar, 2003.

——. "Introduction: What Is the History of Everyday Life and Who Are Its Practitioners?" In *The History of Everyday Life: Reconstructing Historical Experiences and Ways of Life*, 3–40. Princeton, NJ: Princeton University Press, 1995.

——. "Stofflichkeit, Macht-Lust und Reiz der Oberfläche." In *Sozialgeschichte, Alltagsgeschichte, Mikrogeschichte*, ed. Winfried Schulze, 65–80. Göttingen, 1994.

——. "Thesen zur Wiederholbarkeit. 'Normalität' und Massenhaftigkeit von Tötungsgewalt im 20. Jahrhundert." In *Kulturen der Gewalt. Ritualisierung und Symbolisierung von Gewalt in der Geschichte*, ed. Rolf Peter Sieferle and Helga Breuninger, 280–89. New York: Campus Verlag, 1998.

——. "War as Work: Aspects of Soldering in the Twentieth-Century Wars." In *No Man's Land of Violence: Extreme Wars in the 20th Century*, ed. Alf Lüdtke and Bernd Weisbrod, 127–51. Göttingen: Wallstein, 2006.

——. "Was ist und wer treibt Alltagsgeschichte?" In *Zur Rekonstruktion historischer Erfahrungen und Lebensweisen*, ed. Alf Lüdtke. Frankfurt am Main, 1989.

Lüdtke, Alf, and Pausen Lohn. "Neckereien: Eigensinn und Politik bei Fabrikarbeitern in Deutschland um 1900." In Alf Lüdtke, *Eigen-Sinn. Fabrikalltag, Arbeitererfahrungen und Politik vom Kaiserreich bis in den Faschismus*, 120–61. Hamburg: Ergebnisse

Verlag, 1993.
Lüdtke, Alf, and Michael Wildt. "Staats-Gewalt: Ausnahmezustand und Sicherheitsregimes." In *Staats-Gewalt: Ausnahmezustand und Sicherheitsregimes. Historische Perspektiven*, ed. Alf Lüdtke and Michael Wildt, 7–38. Göttingen: Wallstein 2008.
Madajczyk, Czesław. *Die Okkupationspolitik Nazideutschlands in Polen 1939–1945*. Cologne, 1988.
———, ed. *Vom Generalplan Ost zum Generalsiedlungsplan*. Munich, 1994.
Maeck, Julie. *Montrer la Shoah à la télévision. De 1960 à nos jours*. Paris: Nouveau monde, 2009.
Mailänder, Elissa. "Der Fall Hermine Braunsteiner—Eine geschlechtergeschichtliche Studie." In *Das KZ Lublin-Majdanek und die Justiz. Strafverfolgung und verweigerte Gerechtigkeit: Polen, Deutschland und Österreich im Vergleich*, ed. Claudia Kurestidis-Haider et al., 223–37. Graz: Clio, 2011.
Mailänder Koslov, Elissa. "'Die heitere Welt von Spiegelberg'—eine Freizeitlektüre von SS-Aufseherinnen." In *Tagungsband des Sechsten österreichischen Zeitgeschichtetages "Macht, Kunst, Kommunikation" 2003*, 238–42. Innsbruck, 2004.
———. "'Weil es einer Wienerin gar nicht liegt, so brutal zu sein . . .' Frauenbilder im Wiener Volksgerichtsverfahren gegen eine österreichische KZ-Aufseherin (1946–1949)." *Zeitgeschichte* 3 (2005): 128–50.
———. "Der Düsseldorfer Majdanek-Prozess (1975–1981): Ein Wettlauf mit der Zeit?" In *Beiträge zur nationalsozialistischen Verfolgung in Norddeutschland*, ed. KZ-Gedenkstätte Neuengamme, no. 9, 74–88. Bremen, 2005.
———. "Lebenslauf einer SS-Aufseherin." In *Tatort KZ. Neue Beiträge zur Geschichte der Konzentrationslager*, ed. Uli Fritz, Silvija Kavčič, and Nicole Warmbold, 96–116. Ulm, 2003.
———. "Alles Theater? Dekodierung einer Hinrichtung im Frauenlager von Majdanek." In *Auszug aus dem Lager. Zur Überwindung des modernen Raumparadigmas in der politischen Philosophie*, ed. Ludger Schwarte, 246–67. Berlin, 2007.
———. "Täterinnenbilder im Düsseldorfer Majdanek-Prozess (1975–1981)." In *"Im Gefolge der SS": Aufseherinnen des Frauen-Konzentrationslagers Ravensbrück*, ed. Simone Erpel, 211–20. Exhibition catalog. Berlin, 2007.
Majer, Dietmut. *"Fremdvölkische" im Dritten Reich. Ein Beitrag zur nationalsozialistischen Rechtssetzung und Rechtspraxis in Verwaltung und Justiz unter besonderer Berücksichtigung der eingegliederten Ostgebiete und des Generalgouvernements*. Boppard am Rhein, 1981.
Mallmann, Klaus-Michael, and Gerhard Paul, eds. *Karrieren der Gewalt. Nationalsozialistische Täterbiographien*. Darmstadt, 2004.
Mallmann, Klaus-Michael, Volker Reiss, and Wolfgang Pyta. *Deutscher Osten 1939–1945. Der Weltanschauungskrieg in Photos und Texten*. Darmstadt, 2003.
Manoschek, Walter, ed. *"Es gibt nur eines für das Judentum: Vernichtung." Das Judenbild in deutschen Soldatenbriefen 1939–1944*. Hamburg, 1996.

Markowitsch, Hans J., and Harald Welzer. *The Development of Autobiographical Memory.* Translated by David Emmans. New York: Psychology Press, 2010.

Marquardsen-Kamphövener, Else. *Tapfere kleine Lore. Ein Liebesroman.* Berlin, 1936.

Marsalek, Hans. *Die Geschichte des Konzentrationslagers Mauthausen.* Vienna, 1980.

Marszalek, Josef. *Majdanek. Konzentrationslager Lublin.* Warsaw, 1984.

Martschukat, Jürgen. "'The Duty of Society.' Todesstrafe als Performance der Modernität in den USA um 1900." In *Geschichtswissenschaft und "Performative Turn." Ritual, Inszenierung und Performanz vom Mittelalter bis zur Neuzeit,* ed. Jürgen Martschukat and Stefan Patzold, 229–53. Cologne, 2003.

———. *Inszeniertes Töten. Eine Geschichte der Todesstrafe vom 17. bis zum 18. Jahrhundert.* Cologne, 2000.

Matthäus, Jürgen, et al. *Ausbildungsziel Judenmord? "Weltanschauliche Erziehung" von SS, Polizei und Waffen-SS im Rahmen der "Endlösung."* Frankfurt am Main, 2003.

Milton, Sibyl. "Deutsche und deutsch-jüdische Frauen als Verfolgte des NS-Staates." *Dachauer Hefte* 3 (1987): 3–20.

Morsch, Günter. "Organisations- und Verwaltungsstruktur der Konzentrationslager." In *Der Ort des Terrors. Geschichte der nationalsozialistischen Konzentrationslager,* vol. 1, ed. Wolfgang Benz and Barbara Distel, 58–75. Munich: C.H. Beck, 2005.

Mühle, Eduard, ed. *Germany and the European East in the Twentieth Century.* Oxford: Berg, 2003.

Müller-Münch, Ingrid. *Die Frauen von Majdanek. Vom zerstörten Leben der Opfer und der Mörderinnen.* Reinbek, 1982.

Musial, Bogdan. *Deutsche Zivilverwaltung und Judenverfolgung im Generalgouvernement. Eine Fallstudie zum Distrikt Lublin 1939–1944.* Wiesbaden, 1999.

Mussmann, Olaf, ed. *Wissenschaftliche Tagung: Homosexuelle in Konzentrationslagern.* Bad Münstereifel, 2000.

Nahoum-Grappe, Véronique. "Anthropologie de la violence extrême: le crime de profanation." *Revue internationale des sciences sociales* 147 (2002): 601–9.

———. "The Anthropology of Extreme Violence: The Crime of Desecration." *International Social Science Journal* 54, no. 174 (2002): 549–57.

———. "L'usage politique de la cruauté: l'épuration ethnique (ex-Yougoslavie, 1991–1995)." In *De la violence,* ed. Françoise Héritier, 273–23. Paris, 1996.

Neugebauer, Wolfgang. "Der erste Österreichertransport in das KZ Dachau 1938." *Dachauer Hefte* 14 (1998): 17–30.

Neurath, Paul Martin. "Social Life in the German Concentration Camps Dachau and Buchenwald." PhD diss., Columbia University, 1951.

Nienhaus, Ursula. *Berufsstand weiblich. Die ersten weiblichen Angestellten.* Berlin: Transit 1982.

Oppel, Stefanie. *Die Rolle der Arbeitsämter bei der Rekrutierung von SS-Aufseherinnen.* Freiburg, 2006.

———. "Marianne Essmann: Von der Kontoristin zur SS-Aufseherin. Dienstverpflichtung als Zwangsmaßnahme?" In *"Im Gefolge der SS": Aufseherinnen des Frauen-KZ*

Ravensbrück. Begleitband zur Ausstellung, ed. Simone Erpel, 81–88. Berlin: Metropol, 2007.

Orth, Karin. "Bewachung." In *Der Ort des Terrors*, vol. 1, *Geschichte der nationalsozialistischen Konzentrationslager*, ed. Wolfgang Benz and Barbara Distel, 126–40. Munich: C.H. Beck, 2005.

———. *Das System der nationalsozialistischen Konzentrationslager. Eine politische Ordnungsgeschichte*. Munich, 2002.

———. "Die 'Anständigkeit' der Täter. Texte und Bemerkungen." *SOWI* 25, no. 2 (1996): 12–15.

———. *Die Konzentrationslager-SS. Sozialstrukturelle Analysen und biographische Studien*. Göttingen, 2000.

———. "Egon Zill—ein typischer Vertreter der Konzentrationslager-SS." In *Karrieren der Gewalt. Nationalsozialistische Täterbiographien*, ed. Klaus-Michael Mallmann and Gerhard Paul, 264–73. Darmstadt, 2004.

———. "Experten des Terrors. Die Konzentrationslager-SS und die Shoah." In *Die Täter der Shoah. Fanatische Nationalsozialisten oder ganz normale Deutsche?*, ed. Gerhard Paul, 93–108. Göttingen: Wallstein 2002.

———. "Gab es eine Lagergesellschaft? 'Kriminelle' und politische Häftlinge im Konzentrationslager." In *Ausbeutung, Vernichtung, Öffentlichkeit. Neue Studien zur nationalsozialistischen Lagerpolitik. Darstellungen und Quellen zur Geschichte von Auschwitz*, ed. Norbert Frei, Sybille Steinbacher, and Bernd C. Wagner, 109–33. Munich: Institut für Zeitgeschichte, 2000.

Pawalk, Zacheusz. *"Ich habe überlebt . . ." Ein Häftling berichtet*. Hamburg, 1979.

Pingel, Falk. *Häftlinge unter SS-Herrschaft. Widerstand, Selbstbehauptung und Vernichtung im Konzentrationslager*. Hamburg, 1978.

Plewe, Reinhard, and Jan Thomas Köhler. *Baugeschichte Frauen-Konzentrationslager Ravensbrück, Schriftenreihe der Stiftung Brandenburgische Gedenkstätte Ravensbrück*. Vol. 10. Berlin, 2001.

Pohl, Dieter. "Die Ermordung der Juden im Generalgouvernement." In *"Nationalsozialistische Vernichtungspolitik 1939–1945." Neue Forschungen und Kontroversen*, ed. Ulrich Herbert, 98–121. Frankfurt am Main, 1998.

———. *Die nationalsozialistische Judenverfolgung in Ostgalizien 1941–1944. Organisation und Durchführung eines staatlichen Massenverbrechens*. Munich, 1997.

———. "Die Stellung des Distrikts Lublin in der 'Endlösung der Judenfrage.'" In *"Aktion Reinhardt." Der Völkermord an den Juden im Generalgouvernement 1941–1944*, ed. Bogdan Musial, 87–107. Osnabrück, 2004.

———. *Von der "Judenpolitik" zum Judenmord: der Distrikt Lublin des Generalgouvernements 1939–1944*. Frankfurt am Main, 1993.

Pollak, Michael. *Die Grenzen des Sagbaren. Lebensgeschichten von KZ-Überlebenden als Augenzeugenberichte und als Identitätsarbeit*. Frankfurt am Main: Campus Verlag, 1988.

———. *L'expérience concentrationnaire: Essai dur le maintien de l'identité sociale*. Paris:

Métailié, 2000.

Popitz, Heinrich. *Phänomene der Macht.* Tübingen, 2004.

Portmann, Elisabeth. "Schutz und Betreuung der werktätigen Frau im Kriege." Diss., Rechts- und staatswissenschaftliche Fakultät der Philipps-Universität Marburg, 1943 (manuscript).

Pressac, Jean-Claude. "The Deficiencies and Inconsistencies of the 'Leuchter Report.'" In *Demolishing Holocaust Denial: The End of the "Leuchter Report,"* ed. Shelly Shapiro, 31–58. New York: Beate Klarsfeld Foundation, 1990.

Pretzel, Andreas, and Gabriele Rossbach, eds. *"Wegen der zu erwartenden hohen Strafe." Homosexuellenverfolgung in Berlin 1933–1945.* Berlin, 2000; Conference: "Homosexuelle in Konzentrationslagern," edited by Olaf Mussmann, Bad Münstereifelm, 2000.

Pukrop, Marco. "Dr. med. Heinrich Rindfleisch. Eine Lagerarztkarriere im KZ Majdanek." In *KZ-Verbrechen. Beiträge zur Geschichte der nationalsozialistischen Konzentrationslager und ihrer Erinnerung,* ed. Wojcech Lenarczyk, Andreas Mix, Johannes Schwartz, and Veronika Springmann, 34–51. Berlin, 2007.

Raithel, Thomas, and Irene Strenge. "Die Reichstagsbrandverordnung vom 28. Februar 1933." *Vierteljahrshefte für Zeitgeschichte* 48 (2000): 413–60.

Reemtsma, Jan Philipp. *Vertrauen und Gewalt. Versuch über eine besondere Konstellation der Moderne.* Hamburg, 2008.

Reese, Dagmar. *"Straff, aber nicht stramm—herb, aber nicht derb." Zur Vergesellschaftung von Mädchen durch den Bund Deutscher Mädel im sozialkulturellen Vergleich zweier Milieus.* Weinheim, 1989.

Riebe, Renate. "Frauenkonzentrationslager 1933–1939." *Dachauer Hefte* 14 (1998): 125–40.

Reichardt, Sven. *Faschistische Kampfbünde. Gewalt und Gemeinschaft im italienischen Faschismus und in der deutschen SA.* Cologne, 2002.

Revel, Jacques. *Jeux d'échelles. La micro-analyse à l'expérience.* Paris: Gallimard, 1996.

Riedel, Dirk. *Ordnungshüter und Massenmörder im Dienst der Volksgemeinschaft. Der KZ-Kommandant Hans Loritz.* Berlin: Metropol, 2010.

Roos, Julia. "Backlash against Prostitutes' Rights: Origins and Dynamics of Nazi Prostitution Policies." *Journal of the History of Sexuality* 11, nos. 1/2 (January/April 2002): 67–94. Reprinted in Dagmar Herzog, ed., *Sexuality and German Fascism.* New York: Berghahn Books, 2005.

Rössler, Mechtild, and Sabine Schleiermacher, eds. *Der "Generalplan Ost." Hauptlinien der nationalsozialistischen Planungs- und Vernichtungspolitik.* Berlin, 1993.

Rusinek, Bernd-A. *Gesellschaft in der Katastrophe. Terror, Illegalität, Widerstand: Köln 1944–1945.* Essen, 1989.

Said, Edward. *Orientalism.* New York: Pantheon, 1978.

Saldern, Adelheid von. "Opfer oder (Mit-)Täterinnen? Kontroversen über die Rolle der Frauen im NS-Staat." *Sozialwissenschaftliche Informationen (SOWI)* 20 (1991): 97–193.

Sandkühler, Thomas. "Endlösung." *In Galizien. Der Judenmord in Ost- polen und die Rettungsaktionen von Berthold Beitz, 1941–1944.* Bonn, 1996.

Sarasin, Philipp. "Wie weiter mit Michel Foucault?" In *Wie weiter mit . . . ?*, ed. Hamburger Institut für Sozialforschung. Hamburg, 2008.

Scarry, Elaine. *The Body in Pain: The Making and Unmaking of the World*. New York: Oxford University Press, 1985.

Schabas, William A. *Genocide in International Law: The Crime of Crimes*. New York: Cambridge University Press, 2000.

———. *What's in a Word? Atrocity Crimes and the "Genocide" Label.* Adler lecture, with *Communism's "Bright Past": Narratives of Loyalty to the Party before, during and after the Gulag*. Uppsala: Uppsala University, Hugo Valentin Centre, 2013.

Scheffler, Wolfgang. "Historisches Gutachten zur Judenverfolgung des nationalsozialistischen Staats—unter besonderer Berücksichtigung der Verhältnisse im Generalgouvernement—und zur Geschichte des Lagers Majdanek im System nationalsozialistischer Vernichtungs- und Konzentrationslager." Manuscript. 1976.

———. "Zur Gerichtspraxis der SS- und Polizeigerichte im Dritten Reich." In *Klassenjustiz und Pluralismus. Festschrift für Ernst Frankel zum 75. Geburtstag am 26. Dezember 1973*, ed. Günther Doecker and Winfried Steffani, 224–35. Hamburg, 1974.

Schenk, Dieter. *Hans Frank. Hitlers Kronjurist und Generalgouverneur*. Frankfurt am Main, 2008.

Scherr, Albert. "Körperlichkeit, Gewalt und soziale Ausgrenzung in der "postindustriellen" Wissensgesellschaft." In *Gewalt*, ed. Wilhelm Heitmeyer and Hans-Georg Soeffner, 202–26. Frankfurt am Main, 2004.

Schikorra, Christa. *Kontinuitäten der Ausgrenzung. "Asoziale" Häftlinge im Konzentrationslager Ravensbrück*. Berlin, 2001.

Schoppmann, Claudia. *Nationalsozialistische Sexualpolitik und weibliche Homosexualität*. Pfaffenweiler, 1991.

Schubert-Lehnhardt, Viola, ed. *Frauen als Täterinnen im National sozialismus, Protokollband der Fachtagung vom 17.–18. September in Bernburg*. Gerbstadt, 2005.

Schulte, Jan Erik. *Zwangsarbeit und Vernichtung: das Wirtschaftsimperium der SS: Oswald Pohl und das SS-Wirtschafts-Verwaltungshauptamt 1933–1945*. Paderborn, 2001.

Schultz, Hans-Dietrich. "Räume sind nicht, Räume werden gemacht. Zur Genese 'Mitteleuropas' in der deutschen Geographie." *Europa regional* 5, no. 1 (1997): 2–14.

Schwartz, Johannes. "Das Selbstverständnis Johanna Langefelds als SS- Oberaufseherin." In *Tatort KZ. Neue Beiträge zur Geschichte der Konzentrationslager*, ed. Ulrich Fritz, Silvija Kavčič, and Nicole Warmbold, 71–95. Ulm, 2003.

———. "Die SS-Aufseherinnen von Ravensbrück. Individuelle Handlungsspielräume und ideologische Vorstellungen." Master's thesis, Humboldt-Universität zu Berlin, 2002.

———. "Geschlechterspezifischer Eigensinn von NS-Täterinnen am Beispiel der KZ-Oberaufseherin Johanna Langefeld." In *Frauen als Täterinnen im Nationalsozialismus, Protokollband der Fachtagung vom 17.–18. September in Bernburg*, ed. Viola Schubert-Lehnhardt, 56–82. Gerbstadt, 2005.

———. "Handlungsoptionen von KZ-Aufseherinnen. Drei alltags- und geschlechtergeschichtliche biographische Studien." In *NS-Täter aus interdisziplinärer*

Perspektive, ed. Helgard Kramer, 59–71. Munich, 2006.

———. "Handlungsräume einer KZ-Aufseherin. Dorothea Binz—Leiterin des Zellenbaus und Oberaufseherin." In *"Im Gefolge der SS": Aufseherinnen des Frauen-Konzentrationslagers Ravensbrück*, ed. Simone Erpel, 59–71. Exhibition catalog. Berlin, 2007.

Schwarz, Gudrun. *Die nationalsozialistischen Lager*. Frankfurt am Main, 1990.

———. *Eine Frau an seiner Seite. Ehefrauen in der "SS-Sippengemeinschaft."* Hamburg: Hamburger Edition, 1997.

———. "SS-Aufseherinnen in nationalsozialistischen Konzentrationslagern (1933–1945)." *Dachauer Hefte* 10 (1994): 32–49.

Schwarzenberger, Eckard. *Topf & Söhne. Arbeiten an einem Täterort*. Erfurt, 2001.

Schwindt, Barbara. *Das Konzentrations- und Vernichtungslager Majdanek. Funktionswandel im Kontext der "Endlösung."* Würzburg, 2005.

Scott, Joan W. "Feministische Echos und Nachbeben." *WerkstattGeschichte* 33 (2002): 59–77.

Seifert, Ruth. "Identität, Militär und Geschlecht. Zur identitätspolitischen Bedeutung einer kulturellen Konstruktion." In *Landsknechte, Soldatenfrauen und Nationalkrieger. Militär, Krieg und Geschlechterordnung im historischen Wandel*, ed. Karin Hagemann and Stefanie Schüler-Springorum, 53–66. Frankfurt am Main, 1998.

Semelin, Jacques. "Du massacre au processus génocidaire." *Revue internationale des sciences sociales* 147 (2002): 483–92.

———. "Introduction: Extreme Violence: Can We Understand It?" *International Social Science Journal* 54, no. 174 (2002): 429–31.

———. "Introduction: Violences extrêmes: peut-on comprendre?" *Revue internationale des sciences sociales* 147 (2002): 479–81.

———. *Purify and Destroy: The Political Uses of Massacre and Genocide*. New York: Columbia University Press, 2009.

———. *Säubern und Vernichten. Die politische Dimension von Massakern und Völkermorden*. Hamburg, 2007.

Singer, Milton, ed. *Traditional India: Structure and Changes*. Philadelphia: American Folklore Society, 1959.

Sjoberg, Laura, and Caron E. Gentry. *Mothers, Monsters, Whores: Women's Violence in Global Politics*. New York: Zed Books, 2007.

Sofsky, Wolfgang, *Die Ordnung des Terrors. Das Konzentrationslager*. Frankfurt am Main: Fischer, 1999.

———. "Gewaltformen—Taten und Bilder. Wolfgang Sofsky im Gespräch mit Fritz W. Kramer und Alf Lüdtke." *Historische Anthropologie* 12 (2004): 157–78.

———. *The Order of Terror: The Concentration Camp*. Princeton, NJ: Princeton University Press, 1997.

Sprenger, Isabell. *Gross-Rosen: Ein Konzerntrationslager in Schlesien*. Vienna: Böhlau Verlag, 1997.

Steege, Paul. *Black Market, Cold War: Everyday Life in Berlin, 1946–1949*. Cambridge:

Cambridge University Press, 2007.

Stoll, Katrin. "Walter Sonntag—ein SS-Arzt vor Gericht." *Zeitschrift für Geschichtswissenschaft* 5 (2002): 918–39.

Strebel, Bernhard. *Das KZ Ravensbrück. Geschichte eines Lagerkomplexes.* With an introduction by Germaine Tillion. Berlin, 2003.

———. "Das Männerlager im KZ Ravensbrück 1941–1945." *Dachauer Hefte* 14 (1998): 141–74.

———. "Ravensbrück—das zentrale Frauenkonzentrationslager." In *Die nationalsozialistischen Konzentrationslager: Entwicklung und Struktur*, ed. Christoph Dieckmann, Ulrich Herbert, and Karin Orth, 1:215–58. Göttingen, 1998.

———. "Unterschiede in der Grauzone? Über die Lagerältesten im Frauen- und Männerlager des KZ Ravensbrück." *Beiträge zur Geschichte der nationalsozialistischen Verfolgung in Norddeutschland* 4 (1998): 57–68.

———. "Verlängerter Arm der SS oder schützende Hand? Drei Fallbeispiele von weiblichen Funktionshäftlingen im KZ Ravensbrück." *WerkstattGeschichte* 12 (1995): 35–49.

Streit, Christian. *Keine Kameraden. Die Wehrmacht und die sowjetischen Kriegsgefangenen 1941–1945.* Stuttgart, 1978.

Suderland, Maja. *Inside Concentration Camps: Social Life at the Extremes.* Translated by Jessica Spengler. Cambridge: Polity Press, 2013.

Sydnor, Charles W. *Soldiers of Destruction: The SS Death's Head Division, 1933–1945.* Princeton, NJ: Princeton University Press, 1990.

Thiel, Erika. *Geschichte des Kostüms. Die europäische Mode von den Anfängen bis zur Gegenwart.* 8th ed. Berlin, 2004.

Thompson, E. P. "Eighteenth-Century English Society: Class Struggle without Class?" *Social History* 3 (1978): 133–65.

Thompson, Larry V. "Friedrich-Wilhelm Krüger. Höherer SS- und Polizeiführer Ost." In *Die SS: Elite unter dem Totenkopf. 30 Lebensläufe*, ed. Roland Smelser and Enrico Syring, 320–31. Paderborn: Schöningh, 2000.

Timm, Annette F. *The Politics of Fertility in Twentieth Century Berlin.* New York: Cambridge University Press, 2010.

Timpe, Julia. "Hitler's Happy People: *Kraft durch Freude*'s Everyday Production of Joy in the Third Reich." PhD diss., Brown University, 2013.

Tooze, Adam. *The Wages of Destruction: The Making and Breaking of the Nazi Economy.* London: Penguin, 2006.

Toussaint, Jeanette. "Nach Dienstschluss." In *"Im Gefolge der SS": Aufseherinnen des Frauen-KZ Ravensbrück*, ed. Simone Erpel, 89–100. Exhibition catalog. Berlin, 2007.

———. "'Unter Ausnützung ihrer dienstlichen Gewalt.' Österreichische Volksgerichtsverfahren gegen ehemalige SS-Aufseherinnen aus Oberdonau: 1945–1950." In *Frauen in Oberdonau. Geschlechterspezifische Bruchlinien im Nationalsozialismus*, ed. Gabriella Hauch, 399–423. Linz, 2006.

Tröger, Annemarie. "Frauen im wesensgemässen Einsatz." In *Mutterkreuz und Arbeitsbuch. Zur Geschichte der Frauen in der Weimarer Republik und im Nationalsozialismus*, ed.

Frauengruppe Faschismusforschung, 246–72. Frankfurt am Main: Fischer, 1981.

Tuchel, Johannes. *Die Inspektion der Konzentrationslager, 1938–1945. Das System des Terrors. Eine Dokumentation.* Berlin, 1994.

———. "Heinrich Himmler—Der Reichsführer SS." In *Die SS. Elite unter dem Totenkopf*, ed. Ronald Smelser and Enrico Syring, 234–53. Paderborn, 2000.

———. *Konzentrationslager. Organisationsgeschichte und Funktion der "Inspektion der Konzentrationslager" 1934–1938.* Boppard am Rhein, 1991.

———. "Organisationsgeschichte der 'frühen' Konzentrationslager." In *Der Ort des Terrors. Geschichte der nationalsozialistischen Konzentrationslager*, vol. 1, *Die Organisation des Terrors*, ed. Wolfgang Benz and Barbara Distel, 43–57. Munich, 2005.

———. "Organisationsgeschichte der 'frühen ' Konzentrationslager." In *Instrumentarium der Macht. Frühe Konzentrationslager 1933–1937*, ed. Wolfgang Benz and Barbara Distel, 9–26. Berlin, 2003.

Vogel, Angela. *Das Pflichtjahr für Mädchen. Nationalsozialistische Arbeitseinsatzpolitik im Zeichen der Kriegswirtschaft.* New York: Peter Lang, 1997.

Volkmann, Hans-Erich, ed. *Das Russlandbild im Dritten Reich.* Cologne, 1994.

Wachsmann, Nikolaus. *KL: A History of the Nazi Concentration Camps.* New York: Farrar, Straus & Giroux, 2015.

Wagner, Jens-Christian. *Produktion des Todes. Das KZ Mittelbau-Dora.* Göttingen, 2001.

Walser, Karin. *Dienstmädchen. Frauenarbeit und Weiblichkeitsbilder um 1900.* Frankfurt am Main: Extrabuch, 1985.

Walter, Ilsemarie. "Auswirkungen des 'Anschlusses' auf die österreichische Krankenpflege." In *Medizin und Nationalsozialismus. Wege der Aufarbeitung, Wiener Gespräche zur Sozialgeschichte der Medizin*, ed. Sonia Horn et al., 143–59. Vienna, 2001.

Wegner, Bernd. "Die Sondergerichtsbarkeit von SS- und Polizei. Militärjustiz oder Grundlegung einer SS-gemäßen Rechtsordnung?" In *Das Unrechtsregime. Internationale Forschung über den Nationalsozialismus*, vol. 1, *Ideologie—Herrschaftssystem—Wirkung in Europa. Festschrift für Werner Joachim zum 65*, ed. Ursula Büttner et al., 243–59. Geburtstag, 1986.

———. *Hitlers Politische Soldaten. Die Waffen-SS. 1933–1945.* 7th ed. (Paderborn: Schöningh, 2006).

Weitz, Eric D., and Geoff Eley. "Romantisierung des Eigen-Sinns? Eine Kontroverse aus Übersee." *WerkstattGeschichte* 10 (1995): 57–64.

Welzer, Harald. *Das kommunikative Gedächtnis. Eine Theorie der Erinnerung.* Munich, 2002.

———. Härte und Rollendistanz. "Zur Sozialpsychologie des Verwaltungsmassenmords." *Leviathan* 21 (1993): 358–73.

———. *Täter. Wie aus ganz normalen Menschen Massenmörder werden, unter Mitarbeit von Manuela Christ.* Frankfurt am Main, 2005.

Wenck, Alexandra-Eileen. "Verbrechen als 'Pflichterfüllung?' Die Strafverfolgung nationalsozialistischer Gewaltverbrechen am Beispiel des Konzentrationslagers

Bergen-Belsen." *Beiträge zur Geschichte der nationalsozialistischen Verfolgung in Norddeutschland* 3 (1997): 38–55.

Wieling, Dorothea. *Mädchen für alles. Arbeitsalltag und Lebensgeschichte städtischer Dienstmädchen um die Jahrhundertwende*. Bonn, 1987.

Wildenthal, Lora. *German Women for Empire, 1884–1945*. Durham, NC: Duke University Press, 2001.

———. "Koloniale Frauenorganisationen in der deutschen Kolonialbewegung des Kaiserreichs." In *Phantasiereiche. Zur Kulturgeschichte des deutschen Kolonialismus*, ed. Birthe Kundrus, 202–13. Frankfurt am Main, 2003.

Wildt, Michael. "Biopolitik, ethnische Säuberungen und Volkssouveränität. Eine Skizze." *Mittelweg 36*, no. 6 (2006): 87–106.

———. *Hitler's Volksgemeinschaft and the Dynamics of Racial Exclusion: Violence against Jews in Provincial Germany, 1919–1939*. New York: Berghahn Books, 2011.

———. "'Wir wollen in unserer Stadt keine Juden sehen': Anti-semitismus und Volksgemeinschaft in der deutschen Provinz." *Mittelweg 36*, no. 5 (2004): 83–102.

Winkler, Dörte. *Frauenarbeit im "Dritten Reich."* Hamburg: Hoffmann und Campe, 1977.

Wisniewska, Anna, and Czeslaw Raica. *Majdanek. Das Lubliner Konzentrationslager*. Translated into German by Tomasz Kranz. Lublin, 1997.

Witzke, Christiane. *Domjüch: Erinnerungen an eine Heil- und Pflege anstalt in Mecklenburg-Strelitz*. Neubrandenburg, 2001.

Wolter, Gundula. *Hosen, weiblich. Kulturgeschichte der Frauenhose*. Marburg, 1994.

Wolters, Christine. "Tuberkulose und Menschenversuche im Nationalsozialismus. Das Netzwerk hinter den Tuberkulose-Experimenten im Konzentrationslager Sachsenhausen." Diss. rer. biol. hum., Hannover, 2008.

———. *Tuberkulose und Menschenversuche im Nationalsozialismus: das Netzwerk hinter den Tbc-Experimenten im Konzentrationslager Sachsenhausen*. Stuttgart: F. Steiner, 2011.

——— "'Zur "Belohnung" wurde ich der Malaria-Versuchsstation zugeteilt . . .' Die Karriere des Dr. Rudolf Brachtel." In *Lagersystem und Repräsentation. Interdisziplinäre Studien zur Geschichte der Konzentrationslager*, ed. Ralph Gabriel, Elissa Mailänder Koslov, Monika Neuhofer, and Else Rieger. Tübingen, 2004.

Wrocklage, Ute. "Das SS-Fotoalbum des Frauen-Konzentrationslagers Ravensbrück." In *"Im Gefolge der SS": Aufseherinnen des Frauen-KZ Ravensbrück*, ed. Simone Erpel, 233–51. Exhibition catalog. Berlin, 2007.

———. "Neu entdeckte Fotografien aus dem KZ Neuengamme aus den Beständen des Public Record Office." *Beiträge zur Geschichte der nationalsozialistischen Verfolgung in Norddeutschland* 4 (1998): 146–59.

———. "The Photograph Album of the Career of Karl Otto Koch." In *From Sachsenburg to Sachsenhausen. Pictures from the Photograph Album of a Concentration Camp Commandant*, ed. Günter Morsch, 19–42. Catalog. Berlin, 2007.

Zámečnik, Stanislav. "Das frühe Konzentrationslager Dachau." In *Terror ohne System. Die ersten Konzentrationslager im Nationalsozialismus 1933–1935*, vol. 1, *Geschichte der Konzentrationslager 1933–1945*, ed. Wolfgang Benz and Barbara Distel, 13–39. Berlin, 2001.

Zimmerer, Jürgen. "Die Geburt des 'Ostlandes' aus dem Geiste des Kolonialismus. Die nationalsozialistische Eroberungs- und Beherrschungspolitik in post-kolonialer Perspektive." *Sozial.Geschichte* 19 (2004): 10–43.

Zimmermann, Volker. *NS-Täter vor Gericht. Düsseldorf und die Strafprozesse wegen nationalsozialistischer Gewaltverbrechen*. Vol. 12 of *Juristische Zeitgeschichte*, 169–93. Düsseldorf, 2001.

Index

Page numbers in **boldface** refer to illustrations

Z